The Cambridge Companion to International Arbitration

This Cambridge Companion explores the main senses of the term 'international arbitration', including the arbitration of private commercial disputes, disputes between a State and a foreign investor, between States, and also between a State and its parts. It treats these various forms as being inter-related, if not always conceptually, then as a matter of history, rather than as collective victims of imprecise language. The book touches on not only current debates but also more foundational aspects, such as the tension between party autonomy and State authority, and the pacifist roots of modern international arbitration. Thus, it aims to offer a concise survey of the history, the main issues as well as the latest developments in a single, handy volume. It will be an invaluable introduction to the subject for students studying international arbitration, commercial law and international law, and also lawyers and the general reader.

Chin Leng Lim is Choh-Ming Li Professor of Law at The Chinese University of Hong Kong, Honorary Senior Fellow at the British Institute of International and Comparative Law, and Visiting Professor at King's College, London. He is a barrister at Keating Chambers, London.

Cambridge Companions to Law

Cambridge Companions to Law offers thought-provoking introductions to different legal disciplines, invaluable to both the student and the scholar. Edited by world- leading academics, each offers a collection of essays which both map out the subject and allow the reader to delve deeper. Critical and enlightening, the Companions library represents legal scholarship at its best.

The Cambridge Companion to European Union Private Law
Edited by Christian Twigg-Flesner

The Cambridge Companion to International Law
Edited by James Crawford and Martti Koskenniemi

The Cambridge Companion to Comparative Law
Edited by Mauro Bussani and Ugo Mattei

The Cambridge Companion to Human Rights Law
Edited by Conor Gearty and Costas Douzinas

The Cambridge Companion to Public Law
Edited by Mark Elliott and David Feldman

The Cambridge Companion to International Criminal Law
Edited by William A. Schabas

The Cambridge Companion to Natural Law Jurisprudence
Edited by George Duke and Robert P. George

The Cambridge Companion to Comparative Family Law
Edited by Shazia Choudhry and Jonathan Herring

The Cambridge Companion to Comparative Constitutional Law
Edited by Roger Masterman and Robert Schütze

The Cambridge Companion to the First Amendment and Religious Liberty
Edited by Michael D. Breidenbach and Owen Anderson

The Cambridge Companion to the Philosophy of Law
Edited by John Tasioulas

The Cambridge Companion to Legal Positivism
Edited by Torben Spaak and Patricia Mindus

The Cambridge Companion to Hugo Grotius
Edited by Randall Lesaffer and Janne E. Nijman

The Cambridge Companion to International Arbitration
Edited by Chin Leng Lim

The Cambridge Companion to Business & Human Rights Law
Edited by Ilias Bantekas and Michael Stein

The Cambridge Companion to International Arbitration

Edited by

C. L. Lim
The Chinese University of Hong Kong
Barrister, Middle Temple

CAMBRIDGE
UNIVERSITY PRESS

CAMBRIDGE
UNIVERSITY PRESS

University Printing House, Cambridge CB2 8BS, United Kingdom

One Liberty Plaza, 20th Floor, New York, NY 10006, USA

477 Williamstown Road, Port Melbourne, VIC 3207, Australia

314–321, 3rd Floor, Plot 3, Splendor Forum, Jasola District Centre, New Delhi – 110025, India

103 Penang Road, #05–06/07, Visioncrest Commercial, Singapore 238467

Cambridge University Press is part of the University of Cambridge.

It furthers the University's mission by disseminating knowledge in the pursuit of education, learning, and research at the highest international levels of excellence.

www.cambridge.org
Information on this title: www.cambridge.org/9781108480598
DOI: 10.1017/9781108635752

First published 2021

A catalogue record for this publication is available from the British Library.

Library of Congress Cataloging-in-Publication Data
Names: Lim, C. L. (Chin L.), editor.
Title: The Cambridge companion to international arbitration / edited by C.L Lim, the Chinese University of Hong Kong Barrister, Middle Temple.
Other titles: International arbitration
Description: Cambridge, United Kingdom ; New York, NY : Cambridge University Press, 2021. | Series: Cclw cambridge companions to law | Includes bibliographical references and index.
Identifiers: LCCN 2021024728 (print) | LCCN 2021024729 (ebook) | ISBN 9781108480598 (hardback) | ISBN 9781108727785 (paperback) | ISBN 9781108635752 (epub)
Subjects: LCSH: International commercial arbitration. | Arbitration and award. | Investments, Foreign (International law) | BISAC: LAW / Arbitration, Negotiation, Mediation
Classification: LCC K2400 .C36 2021 (print) | LCC K2400 (ebook) | DDC 341.5/22–dc23
LC record available at https://lccn.loc.gov/2021024728
LC ebook record available at https://lccn.loc.gov/2021024729

ISBN 978-1-108-48059-8 Hardback
ISBN 978-1-108-72778-5 Paperback

To Lyn

Contents

Contributors

Daniela Argüello, Legal Counsel, ICSID, Washington, DC, USA

Gary F. Bell, Associate Professor, Faculty of Law, National University of Singapore, Singapore

George A. Bermann, Jean Monnet Professor of EU Law, Walter Gellhorn Professor of Law, Columbia Law School, New York City, NY, USA

Andrea K. Bjorklund, L. Yves Fortier Chair in International Arbitration and International Commercial Law, McGill University, Montreal, QC, Canada

Adrian Briggs, QC (honoris causa), Professor of Private International Law, University of Oxford and Sir Richard Gozney Fellow and Tutor at St. Edmund Hall, Oxford; Barrister, Blackstone Chambers, London, England

Giuditta Cordero-Moss, Professor, Department of Private Law, University of Oslo, Norway

Olufemi Elias, UN Assistant Secretary-General and Registrar of the United Nations International Residual Mechanism for Criminal Tribunals, The Hague, Netherlands; formerly Executive Secretary of the World Bank Administrative Tribunal, Washington, DC, USA

Bryant G. Garth, Distinguished Professor of Law, University of California, Irvine, CA, USA

Sir Christopher Greenwood, GBE, CMG, QC, Judge, Iran-US Claims Tribunal, The Hague, Netherlands; 24 Lincoln's Inn Fields, London; and Master, Magdalene College, Cambridge, England; formerly Judge at the International Court of Justice

Florian Haugeneder, Partner, KNOETZL, Vienna, Austria

Matthew Hodgson, Partner, Allen & Overy, Hong Kong

Meg Kinnear, Secretary-General, ICSID, Washington, DC, USA

Chin Leng Lim, Choh-Ming Li Professor of Law, The Chinese University of Hong Kong; Visiting Professor, King's College London; Hon Senior Fellow, British Institute of International & Comparative Law; Barrister, Keating Chambers, London, England

Siobhán McInerney-Lankford, Senior Counsel, World Bank, Washington, DC, USA

Maurice Mendelson, QC, Professor Emeritus of International Law, University College London; Barrister, Blackstone Chambers, London, England

Ralf Michaels, Director, Max Planck Institute for Comparative & International Private Law, Hamburg, Germany; Chair in Global Law, Queen Mary University of London, England

David Neuberger, The Right Honourable the Lord Neuberger of Abbotsbury, GBS, One Essex Court, London, England; Non-Permanent Judge of the Hong Kong Court of Final Appeal; formerly President of the Supreme Court of the United Kingdom

Jan Paulsson, Founding Partner, Three Crowns, Bahrain, London, Paris and Washington, DC; Michael Klein Distinguished Scholar Chair Emeritus, University of Miami Law School, FL, USA

Natalie L. Reid, Partner, Debevoise & Plimpton, New York City, NY, USA

Michael Reisman, Myres S. McDougal Professor of International Law, Yale Law School, New Haven, CT, USA

Garth Schofield, Senior Legal Counsel at the Permanent Court of Arbitration, The Hague, Netherlands

Muthucumaraswamy Sornarajah, Emeritus Professor, Faculty of Law, National University of Singapore, Singapore

Jae Hee Suh, Senior Associate, Allen & Overy, Singapore

Christopher K. Tahbaz, Partner, Debevoise & Plimpton, New York City, NY, USA

Lukas Vanhonnaeker, McGill University, Montreal, QC, Canada

Foreword

The Cambridge Companion to International Arbitration is an admirably ambitious and valuable book. Within the space of a single (if substantial) volume, it aims to cover and to discuss all aspects of the different forms of international arbitration, an expression which includes international commercial arbitration, foreign investor-State arbitration, inter-State arbitration and intra-State arbitration.

While the high quality of this book will be appreciated by anyone who has cause to consult the text, a quicker way to gauge its worth is to go through the contents page with names of the authors of the various chapters. It would be invidious to single out only some of those authors, and it would be rather tedious if I were to discuss every one of them. Suffice it to say that the list of the authors is almost a rollcall of honour of the academics and practitioners in the world of twenty-first-century international arbitration.

Between them, the authors not only cover the present practices and problems but also explain the historical background, which is not only interesting in itself but also helps in understanding the present state of play. All lawyers know that contractual interpretation requires words to be interpreted in their context and not *in abstracto*. Similarly, if one wants to understand and appreciate the current state of international arbitration, it is important to understand its origins and how and why it developed in the way that it did. Thus, most readers would be surprised to be told that international commercial arbitration grew out of American businessmen allying themselves with European and other public international lawyers. So, too, many readers will be unfamiliar with the French dream of delocalised international commercial arbitration, and they might regard the absence in public international law of a mechanism to supervise and set aside inter-State awards as a grave weakness.

The *Companion* also looks to the future, which is not only very stimulating but also very important. Anyone involved or interested in any enterprise should be interested in its future, and anyone with a stake in international arbitration should be preparing for some very significant changes in what is, in so many respects, a very fast-changing world. Technology has already made an enormous difference in so many different areas to the way arbitration can be conducted, but so far, its effect has been largely procedural; it appears likely that the next phase of development, particularly with artificial intelligence, will not only be more revolutionary and more challenging but also be to more substantive aspects. Having said that, I think that at times we are at risk of being almost hypnotised by technological change. There are many other types of change, and it is impressive that the editor has ensured that there is more than one chapter on what the future may hold for the various different types of international arbitration.

The *Companion* casts its net both deeply and widely. Thus, there is a chapter on the important and interesting topic of arbitration and world peace – a very high-level topic. At the same time, the book quite rightly faces up to highly practical issues which more academic treatises avoid. I have in mind issues such as corruption, which anyone, whether or not involved with international arbitration, knows is a very serious and endemic problem in some parts of the world and is potentially present anywhere. Clearly, corruption can, at worst, undermine the reputation of arbitration at least in some parts of the world, and, less dramatically, it can pervert the course of an individual arbitration, just as it can pervert the course of justice in a particular case. The full treatment of the topic in this book is therefore to be particularly welcomed. Similarly, but on a much less sinister level, the great changes which have happened with two of the most significant financial aspects of arbitration, funding and costs, receive a very welcome treatment. Those issues, like so many issues which relate to arbitration, strike a strong chord with me, as a relatively recently retired judge, because they apply equally to litigation.

As a former judge who now practices as an international arbitrator, the differences and similarities between the role of a judge and the role of an arbitrator have intrigued me since I embarked on my arbitral career. Indeed, they had already been of some interest to me, not least because I had sat as an arbitrator a few times before I started out even as a deputy judge. The differences are perhaps more interesting than the similarities, but let me start with the similarities.

On the face of it, at least, the similarities are plain and anodyne. Both an arbitrator and a judge are obliged to conduct a fair, impartial and honest procedure, which must accord with the rules of the tribunal in which they are acting. Slightly more controversially, each must give a decision which accords with the applicable law. I believe that that proposition may be potentially controversial in relation to arbitrators, because there is a view that arbitrators can – indeed, should – be more flexible than judges when it comes to legal issues. In my opinion, however, if a contract says that a case is to be decided according to the law of X, then an arbitrator would not be complying with his duty if he did not apply the law of X to the facts of the case, even if it produced a result which he did not like or did not consider reflected the moral or commercial merits of the case. So, in a common law context, if the case law of X indicates a certain result, an arbitrator must follow that case law in the same way as a judge in X would have to do.

Again, at least from my perspective as a common lawyer, neither a judge nor an arbitrator should get involved in trying to mediate or settle the dispute which she has been appointed to resolve. This statement, which would have appeared self-evident to a common lawyer forty years ago, now needs to be qualified even in respect of a judge. There is much to be said, at least in an appropriate case, for a judge encouraging settlement, even (at least sometimes) with herself as mediator, at an early stage in a case, in order to save the parties from the stress, time and expense of litigation, provided that she will not be the judge trying the case if it does not settle. The proviso is appropriate because a judge cannot try a case if she has already expressed views about the merits and because the parties are unlikely to be candid in settlement/mediation discussions with someone who may well be judging the dispute if it does not settle. An arbitrator would not be expected to be so ready to bow out of an appointment, and, at the risk of being seen to be reactionary, I can see real problems in an arbitrator also acting as mediator. However, there is no reason in principle why the terms of an arbitrator's appointment should not include the possibility of his also acting as mediator, and the notions of med-arb, arb-med, med-arb-med or even arb-med-arb are gaining traction in some quarters, if not in others.

Turning to differences between the two roles, after twenty-one years as a judge, the first thing that struck me as I started out as an arbitrator was that I had to be selected: this was the precise opposite of my experience as a judge, which was that neither of the parties should have the right to 'judge pick'. Even if the parties agreed that they did or did not want a particular judge, it was highly questionable whether they should have their way. The difference highlights a fundamental distinction. At least in a traditional arbitration, an arbitrator is simply one party to what is a multi-party private law contractual dispute-resolution system which involves a hearing which requires him to observe certain rules including impartiality and applying the law. By contrast, while a judge also has to observe certain rules and to be impartial, the origin of that duty is exclusively in public law and indeed one of the two most fundamental aspects of constitutional principle, namely the rule of law. This private law/public law distinction is manifest in another way. A judge must, save in those exceptional cases where justice requires otherwise, carry out her role in public: open justice is a fundamental requirement of virtually all civilized legal systems. But one of the traditional attractions of arbitration is privacy.

The private law/public law distinction follows through into the conduct of proceedings. Because she is carrying out a public function, a judge has the right – indeed, the duty – to form her own judgment on all issues which come before her, even where the issues have been agreed between the parties. That is because she is carrying out a public function and has to take into account the public interest. An arbitrator is in a very different position: subject, of course, to the terms of his appointment (including the rules of any relevant institution), he cannot normally go behind what the parties agree. So, a judge, conscious of the need not to waste court time, to ensure there is no abuse of process and to avoid the law falling into disrepute, should not agree to time being taken up with what she believes to be pointless and time-consuming evidence or argument. By contrast, it is very hard for an arbitrator to take such a line against the parties' wishes, unless of course the contract under which he has been appointed permits it.

Another big difference arises in relation to rights of appeal. In many countries, a right of appeal against a judge's decision is automatic, and in virtually all countries where it is not, there is a right of appeal where there is an arguable point of law. By contrast, in the overwhelming majority of cases, an arbitrator's decision is either appealable only in very limited circumstances or simply unappealable. The fact that her decision is susceptible to an appeal can serve to reinforce a judge's consciousness that her duty is to apply the law, however unattractive the consequences in a particular case. By contrast, the temptation for an arbitrator to 'cheat' on the law in a case when he considers that its proper application would lead to an unjust result can be reinforced by the knowledge that his decision is unlikely to be appealed. As I have said, in my opinion, this is a temptation which should be resisted, but this is not only as a matter of principle. If arbitrators start to get a reputation for not applying the law, then confidence in arbitration will wither.

A more indirect and unanticipated consequence of severely curtailing appeals against arbitration awards is that there has been a significant increase in challenges to awards on grounds of procedural unfairness. As a result, arbitrators have become very concerned with procedural issues, leading to so-called due process paranoia. While concern about this development may be overstated, it does appear to me that since I first became involved in arbitration as a junior barrister in the 1970s, there has been a real switch. Arbitration in the 1970s was considered to be quicker, cheaper and more informal than litigation; forty-five years on, arbitration has become more procedurally fixated than litigation, and I very much doubt that it is much quicker and would be surprised if it was cheaper.

Arbitration is moving more and more into public consciousness as it plays a more and more important part in the field of international affairs and increasingly resolves disputes which have international and domestic implications of both a political and an economic nature. That means that there is an increasing awareness of the need for higher and consistent standards and also for the need for greater openness. So long as awards are not published, there can be little hope of improving predictability and consistency, which are so important in all areas of life. Already many investor-state arbitration awards are published, and some hearings are even held in public, and even some commercial arbitration awards are published, on an appropriately redacted basis. There are moves afoot to ensure that arbitrators are made subject to greater regulation and to reconsider the professional responsibility of those involved – possibly on a more international basis than heretofore. The rules of the various arbitral institutions are also, at least as I see it, being amended in some respects to give arbitrators powers which more closely align them with judges in terms of flexibility.

So, international arbitration is an area of work which is interesting and increasingly important, but it is also continually changing in many of its practices and rules and continues to throw up many difficult new issues. The *Companion* will be an invaluable book for anyone seeking to navigate the treacherous seas of international arbitration, whether she is a practising lawyer, arbitrator, legal academic or anyone with an interest in the topic.

David Neuberger
Temple, London
10 November 2019

Preface

This book explores three principal senses of the term 'international arbitration' involving the arbitration, first, of private commercial disputes; secondly, of disputes between host countries and foreign investors; and thirdly, of disputes between – or even within – States. More than being victims of imprecise language use, these seemingly distinct forms are in various ways interrelated conceptually or as a matter of their history. The book's chapters address current debates and foundational aspects, such as the tension between party autonomy and State authority. They also touch on the modern history of the subject, from the pacifist roots of much of modern international arbitration to the contribution of twentieth-century transnational lawyers.

There are a number of major organising themes. A first involves debate over the 'delocalisation' of 'international' arbitration. Is that, however, not solely of interest in the limited sphere of commercial arbitration? Such scepticism may be too quick. Take, for example, the fact that delocalised arbitration was assumed in the Permanent Court of Arbitration's rules on inter-State disputes. Yet even in inter-State disputes, curial supervision may be highly relevant to arbitration's sovereign users. It could be that two States cannot agree on arbitration precisely because they cannot agree on having national curial supervision, where one considers the arbitration to be wholly domestic in nature while the other denies that. The delocalisation question may be to intra-State arbitration just as essential, and likewise in foreign investor-to-State disputes, delocalisation is a chief difference in choosing between ICSID and non-ICSID arbitration.

Yet other readers may say that a second theme, 'arbitrating for peace', is similarly only of special concern, namely only to public international lawyers. This is not so. Peace was an original aim both in the development of international commercial arbitration and to the architects of modern international investment arbitration. Arbitrating international commercial and investment disputes became, in the modern age, an extension of the nineteenth-century public international lawyer's preoccupation with pacifism. There can be debate about whether this was not simply a case of merchantmen coveting the prestige enjoyed by Statesmen-lawyers. Yet, if we were to argue over this, then the book would have prompted reflection while, at the same time, offering those who embark upon the subject for the first time a joined-up perspective.

Finally, it may be important to appreciate the professional and intellectual contribution of a transnational legal sensibility – one which does not always draw a bright line between international law and domestic legal ideas. Our reader might say that 'commercial disputes are about contract whereas inter-State arbitration involves public international law disputes'. Yet States quarrel over contract while general contractual principles are themselves, potentially, a source of international law. Lord Asquith resorted to general contractual principles in reasoning that indigenous Abu Dhabi law could not have been up to the task of construing a modern deed of concession. He has been criticised by postcolonial scholars who, at the same time, accept René Dupuy's 'order of the international law of contracts', what Professor Gaillard calls a 'transnational justice system' or, to use a term popularised by Professor Daniel Cohen, 'the arbitral legal order'. Might it be that there is a sphere where contracts and treaties operate in conjunction? After all, the New York Convention's particular genius was to turn contractual promises to arbitrate into a treaty obligation of States to enforce such promises. In international investment treaties, umbrella clauses seek to convert a State's contractual breach into a treaty breach. There is a place where transnational lawyers live where the waters of treaty and contract may not intermingle but stream alongside each other.

There is, admittedly, in this book what is a resurrection of a rather old Anglo-French debate. F. A. Mann once wrote that 'England rejects the delocalisation of contracts and arbitration'. Gaillard called this view 'ridiculous'. Yet the delocalisation debate matters to what we do. Is it to be the choice of law rule of the seat, a free selection of choice of law approaches or something else? If an award has been set aside, is one bound by the courts of the seat in future enforcement proceedings elsewhere? A difference in theoretical assumptions cuts deep in the field, as Gaillard himself tried to show – even if, in practice at least, a tribunal is likely to be very mindful of the laws of the place of the seat. Still, the seat may be more important in one place and less so in another, to one arbitration community rather than to another.

If this *Companion* should stimulate a newcomer's appetite while finding a small place on the arbitrator's bed table, it will already have exceeded its aim. No book would have been possible, however, without the commitment of an exceptional cast of distinguished contributors. All have more pressing demands. I am deeply grateful to each and every one, not least to Lord Neuberger for his most kind, generous foreword. I would like also to thank Ms. Finola O'Sullivan at Cambridge University Press for giving such full-hearted encouragement and the very professional Ms. Marianne Nield, also of Cambridge. Professor Emmanuel Gaillard generously read an early draft while 'arbitromania' emerged in conversation with Mr. Arshad Ghaffar of the London Bar, whose wit is always appreciated. Ms. Alice Giovane was my early assistant, and upon her return to Paris, two others became indispensable, Ms. Yuanyuan Zhang and Ms. Xueji Su. I am grateful to one and all. My wife, Lyn, bore once again the usual, many sacrifices, and so I dedicate this book to her.

Treaties, National Legislation, Cases and Awards

Arbitral Awards

Arbitration Rules

International Cases

Barcelona Traction, Light and Power Company, Limited (Belgium v. Spain) [1970] ICJ Rep 3, 375n87, 377n94
Brazilian Loans (France v. Brazil)(1929) PCIJ Series A no 21, 375n87
Case Concerning the Delimitation of the Continental Shelf (UK v. France) [1978-78] 18 RIAA 3, 365
Case Concerning the Delimitation of the Maritime Boundary in the Gulf of Maine Area (Canada/United States of America) [1984] ICJ Rep 246., 338
Certain Norwegian Loans (France v. Norway) [1957] ICJ Rep 9, 375n87
City of Tokyo 5 Per Cent Loan of 1912-Plan for Resumption of Payment of Principal and Interest on the French Tranche of the Loan (1960) 29 ILR 11, 250, 250n38, 276
Corfu Channel (United Kingdom of Great Britain and Northern Ireland v. Albania) Judgment on Preliminary Objection, ICJ Reports 1948, 328
Dogger Bank Case (Great Britain v. Russia), (1908) 2 Am. J. Int'l L. 931, 386, 386n125
Electricité de Beyrouth Company (France v. Lebanon), 375n87
Electricity Company of Sofia and Bulgaria (Belgium v. Bulgaria), 375n87
Elettronica Sicula S.p.A. (ELSI) (U.S. v. Italy) [1989] ICJ Rep 15, 332n18
Factory at Chorzow (Germany v. Poland), 1928 PCIJ (ser. A, No. 17), 231n22, 375n87
Fisheries Jurisdiction (United Kingdom v. Iceland) Judgment, [1974] ICJ Rep 3, 340
Interhandel (Switzerland v. United States of America) Land and Maritime Boundary between Cameroon and Nigeria (Cameroon v. Nigeria: Equatorial Guinea intervening) (Judgment) [2002] ICJ Rep 2002, 375n87
Land, Island and Maritime Frontier Dispute (El Salvador/Honduras: Nicaragua Intervening) (Judgment) ICJ Rep 1992, 336
Losinger & Co. (Switzerland v. Yugoslavia), 375n87
Maritime Delimitation and Territorial Questions between Qatar and Bahrain (Qatar v. Bahrain) 91 ILR 543, 341
Oscar Chinn (United Kingdom v. Belgium), 375n87
Pajzs, Csaky and Esterhazy (Hungary v. Yugoslavia), 375n87
Panevezys-Saldutiskis Railway (Estonia v. Lithuania), 375n87
S. S. "Wimbledon," UK v. Germany, (1923) PCIJ Series A01, 191–2
Serbian Loans (France v. Serbia), 1929 PCIJ (ser. A, No. 20), 375n87
Société Commerciale de Belgique (Belgium v. Greece), 375n87
Southern Bluefin Tuna (New Zealand v. Japan, Australia v. Japan) International Tribunal for the Law of the Sea, Cases Nos. 3&4, 30, 30n161, 372n77
Temple of Preah Vihear (Cambodia v. Thailand), (2011) ICJ Reports 537, 324n63
Timor Sea Conciliation (Timor-Leste v. Australia), Report and Recommendations of the Compulsory Conciliation Commission, 9 May 2018, 387–8, 388n132

National Cases by Country

Australia

European Union

France

Holland

Hong Kong

Mauritius

Netherlands

The Russian Federation v. Veteran Petroleum Limited, Yukos Universal Limited and Hulley Enterprises Limited (C/09/477160 / HA ZA 15-1, 15-2 and 15-112), District Court of The Hague, 32n170

Singapore

AQZ v. ARA [2015] 2 SLR 972, 140
BCY v. BCZ [2016] SGHC 249, 17n79, 18n82, 69n30
BNA v. BNB and Anor [2019] SGCA 84, 17n74, 17n79, 18n82, 18n83
HSBC Institutional Trust Services (Singapore) Ltd v. Toshin Development Singapore Pte Ltd [2012] 4 SLR 738, 144n18
JVL Agro Industries Ltd v. Agritrade International Pte Ltd [2016] SGHC 126, [2016] 4 SLR 768, 74
PT First Media TBK v. Astro Nusantara International and Others [2013] SGCA 57, 473n26

Sweden

State of Ukraine v. Norsk Hydro ASA, Svea Hovrätt, T 3108-06, 17 December 2007; T 339-08, 2 June 2008, 101n8

Switzerland

Beverly Overseas SA v. Privnedna Bank Zagreb, Federal Supreme Court of Switzerland, 28 March 2001, 421n53
National Power Corporation (Philippines) v. Westinghouse (USA), Federal Supreme Court of Switzerland, 2 September 1993, 419n44, 419n47
Omnium de Traitement et de Valorisation - OTV (France) v. Hilmarton (UK), Court of Appeal of the Canton of Geneva, 17 November 1989; Federal Supreme Court of Switzerland, 17 April 1990, 413n16, 416n34, 421n56

United Kingdom

Bank Mellat v. Helliniki Techniki SA [1984] 1 QB 291, 301, [1983] 3 All ER 428 (CA), 12n40, 15n62
Dallah Real Estate and Tourism Holding Co v. Ministry of Religious Affairs, Government of Pakistan [2010] UKSC 46, [2011] 1 AC 763, 19n90, 92n35, 96n43, 101n9
Diag Human SE v. Czech Republic [2014] EWHC 1639 (Comm), 96n44
Emirates Trading Agency LLC v. Prime Mineral Exports Private Limited [2014] EWHC 2104 (Comm), 144n18
Essar Oilfield Services Ltd v. Norscot Rig Management Pvt Ltd [2016] EWHC 2361 (Comm), 456, 456n61, 458, 458n69
E.T.I. Eurotelecom and Anor. v. Bolivia [2008] EWCA Civ. 880, 24n120

Evergreen Marine v. Fast Shipping [2014] EWHC 4893 (QB), 457, 457n65
Excalibur Ventures LLC v. Texas Keystone Inc. and others [2011] EWHC 1624 (Comm), 129n48, 461n76
Fiona Trust & Holdings Corp v. Privalov [2007] EWCA Civ 20; [2008] 1 Lloyds Rep 254, 16n72, 419n47
Gazprom OAO EU:C:2015:316, [2015] 1 WLR 4937, 80n4, 86n17
Halliburton Company v. Chubb Bermuda Insurance Limited, UKSC 2018/0100, 400n46
Harbour Assurance Co. (UK). Ltd. v. Kansa General Insurance Co., Ltd. [1993] 1 Lloyd's Rep 455, 16n72, 21n101
Konkola Copper Mines v. U&M Mining Zambia Ltd [2014] EWHC 2374 (Comm), 458, 458n68
Merchant International Co Ltd v. NAK Naftogaz [2012] EWCA Civ 196, [2012] 1 WLR 3036, 94n38
National Iranian Oil Company v. Crescent Petroleum Company International Ltd, Crescent Gas Corporation Ltd [2016] EWHC 510 (Comm) (Burton J.), 16n72
Occidental v. Ecuador [2005] EWCA Civ. 1116, 23, 23n109, 32, 32n171
Pattni v. Ali [2006] UKPC 51, [2007] 2 AC 85, 91n31
Pena Copper Mines Ltd v. Rio Tinto Co. [1911] 105 LT 846, 130n51
Premium Nafta Products Limited v. Fili Shipping Company Limited [2007] UKHL 40, 419n47
Roger Shashoua v. Mukesh Sharma [2009] EWHC 957, 449n36
Rubin v. Eurofinance SA [2012] UKSC 46, [2013] 1 AC 236, 90n29
Sabbagh v. Khoury & Ors [2018] EWHC 1330 (Comm), 129n48
Soleimany v. Soleimany, England and Wales Court of Appeal (Civil Division), 30 January 1998, 420n48
Stati v. Republic of Kazakhstan (No 2) [2018] EWCA Civ 1896 [2019] 1 WLR 897, 90n28, 95n40
Sulamérica Cia Nacional de Seguros S.A. v. Enesa Engenharia S.A. [2012] EWCA Civ 638; [2013] 1 WLR 102, 17n79, 18n82, 69n30
Ust-Kamenogorsk Hydropower Plant JSC v. AES [2013] UKSC 35, 130n54
Weissfisch v. Julius [2006] EWCA Civ 218, 129n48
Wight v. Eckhardt Marine GmbH [2003] UKPC 37, [2004] 1 AC 147, 93n36
Yukos Capital Sarl v. OJSC Oil Co Rosneft [2012] EWCA Civ 855, [2014] QB 458, 96n45, 127n38

United States

British Ins. Co. v. Water St. Ins. Co. , 93 F. Supp. 2d 506 (S.D.N.Y. 2000), 142n10
Campbell v. American Family Life Assur. Co. of Columbus, 613 F. Supp. 2d 1114 (D. Minn. 2009), 142n10
Chromalloy Aeroservices v. Arab Republic of Egypt, 939 F. Supp. 907 (D.D. C. 1996), 109n21, 127n38
Commonwealth Coatings Corp. v. Continental Casualty Co. , 393 U.S. 145 (1968), 159, 159n112

National Legislation by Country

Albania

Austria

Egypt

France

Germany

Hong Kong

Italy

Norway

Singapore

South Korea

Sweden

Switzerland

United Kingdom

United States

Venezuela

Treaties and Other International Instruments

United Nations General Assembly Resolutions

Part I

The History, Doctrines and Sociology of the Growth of Transnational Justice

1 Development of the Principal Forms from Antiquity to Arbitromania

C. L. Lim

1.1 From Antiquity to Arbitromania

International arbitration differs from domestic arbitration. As Jan Paulsson puts it, 'international arbitration is no more a "type" of arbitration than a sea elephant is a type of elephant'.[1] Yet as with sea elephants there are different species of international arbitration. This book is about how the lines by which international arbitration's principal forms – in the contexts of commercial disputes, disputes between a foreign investor and a State, disputes purely between States, and even between the State and its constituent part – grew separately but whose growth joined and overlapped.[2] One misconception should perhaps be dispelled at the outset; that the classifications just mentioned depend upon the identity or status of the parties. For States too, and not just private parties, may become involved in an international commercial dispute. Not just with non-State, private actors but also between themselves. The distinction that matters lies instead in the precise legal relationship giving rise to the dispute submitted to arbitration. Less rare is a dispute under a foreign investment contract between a State and a private party which is submitted to arbitration seated in a neutral place or to 'delocalised' International Centre for the Settlement of Investment Disputes (ICSID) arbitration. Thus, for the purposes of this *Companion*, an inter-State arbitration, properly called, is one whose applicable law is public international law. In the case of intra-

[1] Jan Paulsson, 'International Arbitration Is Not Arbitration', (2008) *Stockholm International Arbitration Review* 1.

[2] While sports arbitration or tourism arbitration, construction arbitration or energy arbitration may also be 'international' these are classifications by industry. They may be considered on the whole to be types of international commercial arbitration, or international investment (meaning foreign investor-State) arbitration. However, WTO dispute settlement or the United Nations Compensation Commission are considered, in this *Companion*, to be distinct from arbitration even if, in the case of WTO panels, parties are free to choose their panellists together.

State arbitration the precise nature of the parties' legal relationship – whether that is a matter of domestic law, even domestic private law, or public international law – may form a large part of the issue.

As to the development of these forms, they are not as I have mentioned entirely separate. The term *international arbitration* evokes still some recollection of nineteenth-century peace societies, but it is even more often used today in a different sense altogether, as a short-hand for a lucrative form of commercial lawyering. Still, there are surprising connections and commonalities between the two senses. American business crossed the Atlantic, with men calling themselves 'merchants of peace'[3] to make common cause with the Grand Old Men of Europe – those in the European international law professoriate well known as promoters of inter-State arbitration ('international adjudication', they called it) and who viewed themselves as a part of the Peace Movement of a previous century:[4]

> In the wake of the savagery of World War I, people of good will sought urgently for ways to avert its recurrence. Peace, it was reasonably thought would be buttressed if peoples and their governments had mutually reinforcing stakes in systems of cooperation. Trade was an obvious thing. … Of course, commercial transactions lead to disputes. … It is, therefore, essential that such disputes be resolved fairly and efficiently lest the unreliability of bargains become an impediment to trade. Thus, the idea of international arbitration as a tool of peace emerged.

In this manner international arbitration, spanning both diplomacy and international commerce since medieval times, witnessed the shrewd co-optation of the idealism of the public international law professoriate who were well versed in (1) inter-State arbitration in the early years of the twentieth century.[5] This was how (2) modern international commercial arbitration was established, resurrected – as we shall see – from a medieval past. In turn, (3) foreign investor-State arbitration grew also out of these

[3] The title of George Ridgeway's work, cited also in Paulsson, 'Not Arbitration', *op. cit.*, 5.

[4] Paulsson, 'Not Arbitration', *op. cit.*, 4.

[5] Yves Dezalay and Bryant G. Garth, 'Constructing a Transatlantic Marketplace of Disputes on the Symbolic Foundations of International Justice', in Gregoire Mallaard and Jerome Sgard (eds.), *Contractual Knowledge: One Hundred Years of Legal Experimentation in Global Markets* (Cambridge: Cambridge University Press, 2016), 185, and *see* Chapter 2 in this volume.

pacifist roots, not least through the efforts of Aaron Broches at the World Bank.[6] As did (4) intra-State arbitration – arbitration between a State and a part thereof[7] – which has developed out of the Permanent Court of Arbitration having addressed itself to mixed arbitration between State and non-State entities.[8]

In a similar vein, contemporary 'international arbitration', occupying the worlds of scholarship and legal practice, remains known to and is practised by diplomats, merchantmen – and women – alike. These women and men come from every corner, including the post-colonial world.

Still, as a matter of history, it is arbitration in ancient European antiquity which commentators have invoked, assuring their readers of a prestige gained through longevity.[9] In Ancient Greece:[10]

> The city states employed arbitration to solve a wide range of cooperation problems, from the treatment of foreigners to the specification and regulation of borders. . . . Like their modern counterparts the city-states concluded many bilateral treaties. . . . The city-states inserted arbitration clauses in many of their treaties. . . . Arbitration spanned the entire system of city-states.

[6] *See* Chapter 11 in this volume.

[7] *See* Garth Schofield's discussion of the *Abyei* arbitration in Chapter 16 in this volume.

[8] It is largely in this sort of sense that arbitration between a State and a part thereof is 'international' in the first place, for it could well be a purely domestic arbitration, in other words a true elephant rather than a sea elephant. *See further* Freya Bartens, 'The Abyei Arbitration: A Model Procedure for intra-State Dispute Settlement in Resource Rich Areas?', (2011) 1 *Goettingen Int'l L Jo* 417, 428 for a discussion of intra-State arbitration's procedural roots in Radio Corporation of America v. the National Government of the Republic of China, Award of the Tribunal, 13 April 1935. On the adoption in the *Abyei* arbitration of the 1993 PCA Optional Rules for Arbitrating Disputes between Two Parties of Which Only One is a State, *see* Brooks Daly, 'The Abyei Arbitration: Procedural Aspects of an Intra-State Border Arbitration' (2010) 23 *Leiden Jo Int'l L* 801, 807–808. *See further* Brooks W. Daly et al., *A Guide to the PCA Arbitration Rules* (Oxford: Oxford University Press, 2014) for a discussion of what is now the 2012 PCA Arbitration Rules. *See also* Vaughan Lowe and Antonios Tzanakopoulos, 'Introduction: The Abyei Arbitration', in Heather Clark and Lise Bosman (eds), *The Abyei Arbitration (The Government of Sudan/The Sudan People's Liberation Movement/Army) Final Award of 2009*, PCA Award Series, (2012) Volume 9, p. 1; Wendy J. Miles and Daisy Mallett, 'The Abyei Arbitration and the Use of Arbitration to Resolve Inter-State and Intra-State Conflicts', (2010) 1 *Jo Int'l Disp Settl'mnt* 313.

[9] *See e.g.* D. W. Rivkin, 'The Impact of International Arbitration on the Rule of Law' (2013) 29 *Arb Int'l* 327, Christian Reus-Smit, *The Moral Purpose of the State: Culture, Social Identity and Institutional Rationality in International Relations* (Princeton, NJ: Princeton, 2009), 44.

[10] Reus-Smit, *op. cit.*, 44–45.

Therein lies the analogue to modern inter-State arbitration although, despite such well-established roots, the form owes more to British and American state practice in the nineteenth century. Most notably, to the Jay Treaty commissions and the *Alabama Claims* arbitration,[11] to European practice and to that century's societal peace movements. It culminated in the 1899 Convention on the Pacific Settlement of International Disputes and the Permanent Court of Arbitration.[12] Inter-State arbitration remains today the domain of eminent jurists even with the encroachment of the international law firms which seek to transform it into a technocratic form.

In ancient times there was private arbitration too, the *Iliad* is authority for that proposition.[13] But it was to be commercial arbitration during the medieval period, which in England pre-dated the common law,[14] which now governs the lawyers' historical imagination.[15] They speak of a system of arbitration so powerful that it has become the dominant mode of cross-border commercial dispute resolution – 'arbitromania'.[16] As with Homer there is Shakespeare's reference to Roman arbitration in the *Rape of Lucrece*.[17] This medieval merchant habit – in the English trade fairs, and in Germany, Switzerland, Northern Italy and France[18] – was to inspire Lord Mustill and others to speak of a 'New Lex Mercatoria'.[19] Today, it

[11] United States of America v. Great Britain (Alabama Claims), Award, 14 September 1872. *See* Chapter 14 of this volume.

[12] For a concise overview of the Anglo-European history, *see* Gary Born, *International Arbitration: Cases and Materials* (Alphen aan den Rijn, NL: Kluwer, 2011), 2–31.

[13] N. G. L. Hammond, 'Arbitration in Ancient Greece' (1985) 1 *Arb Int'l* 188 is often cited in this regard.

[14] Rivkin, *op. cit.*, 331.

[15] For criticism, *see* Chapter 6 in this volume.

[16] Such that iconic judgments, such as Mitsubishi v. Soler 473 US 614 (1985), now seem quaint – 'as international trade has expanded in recent decades, so too has the use of international arbitration'.

[17] Rivkin, *op. cit.*, 330. The relevant Western literature includes Hammond, *op. cit.*; Derek Roebuck, *Ancient Greek Arbitration* (Oxford: Holo Books, 2001); Rivkin, *op, cit.*, and the woks cited therein; Thomas Kuehn, 'Arbitration and Law in Renaissance Florence' (1987) 11 *Renaissance and Reformation* 289; Lauro Martines, *Lawyers and Statecraft in Renaissance Florence* (Princeton, 2015), 348 *et seq.* This is not to say that arbitration was not known or equally well-established in other cultures, such as in Arab culture and Islam. The nineteenth century image on the cover of this book depicts the Battle of Siffin (657 CE) in connection with which arbitration was famously unsuccessful.

[18] Born, *Cases and Materials, op. cit.*, 13–15.

[19] Michael Mustill, 'The New Lex Mercatoria: The First Twenty-Five Years' (1988) *Arb Int'l* 86. For the 'old', *see e.g.* the Introduction in Mary Elisabeth Basile et al. (eds.), *Lex Mercatoria and Legal Pluralism: A Late Thirteenth-Century Treatise and Its Afterlife* (Cambridge,

forms the basis not only of so much of modern international commercial arbitration but also (3) foreign investor-State (or 'international investment') arbitration.

As with any field of writing however there are competing narratives, such as in the post-colonial and Far Eastern literature. Sornarajah argues that international arbitration was for much of the developing world but a mere twentieth-century Anglo-European construct which had supplanted earlier gunboat diplomacy.[20] Shalakany, writing in the same vein, contends that international arbitration is to be more accurately perceived as an extension of the techniques of European and American extraterritoriality during the eighteenth and nineteenth centuries; in which it took the form of the European Mixed Courts in the Middle East and the Far East. These were, after all, 'mixed' – i.e. cosmopolitan – tribunals. Admittedly, the Third World resisted arbitration in the post-war twentieth-century period,[21] but it was also the Asian-African Legal Consultative Organisation (AALCO) which eventually proposed the 1985 UNCITRAL Model Law.[22] And thus, according to Shalakany, did the Asian and African nations end up embracing that which earlier had been rehearsed in their own territories.

This book addresses modern international arbitration, broadly speaking in three or three-and-a-half principal forms:

1. international commercial arbitration;
2. international investment (foreign investor-State) arbitration;
3. arbitration between States ('inter-State arbitration'); and by extension thereof
4. between the State and a sub-component of it which may be seeking autonomy, secession or independence (so-called intra- or sub-State arbitration).

Mass.: Ames Foundation, 1998); W. A. Bewes, *The Romance of the Law Merchant* (London: Sweet & Maxwell, 1923).

20 M. Sornarajah, 'The Climate of International Commercial Arbitration' (1991) 8 *J Int'l Arb* 47, 51.

21 Amr Shalakany, 'Arbitration in the Third World: A Plea for Reassessing Bias under the Spectre of Neoliberalism' (2000) *Harvard ILJ* 419, 431.

22 UNCITRAL Model Law on International Commercial Arbitration (ML), adopted 21 June 1985, revised in 2006. AALCO also created the Cairo and Kuala Lumpur regional centres for arbitration.

The first is most commonplace, the most widespread, although no less intriguing. It was international commercial arbitration which instigated a lasting and rich debate over the reach of public authority over private disputes. That issue, as this chapter will endeavour to show, continues to occupy our legal imagination. But because international commercial arbitration is imagined to have grown from its medieval merchant form, it also carries within it – in terms of a professional sensibility – the same long-standing prejudice against State authority. Its ambition – it is said – is, wisely or not, to free itself entirely of the State. Julian Lew, quoting F. A. Mann, had once asked,[23]

> Do you dream? When do you dream? What do you dream about? Do you dream about international arbitration? Is there a dream for international arbitration? Is the concept of delocalised arbitration, or arbitration not controlled by national law, a dream or a nightmare? Is autonomous arbitration a reality, or is 'every arbitration necessarily . . . a national arbitration, that is to say, subject to a specific system of national law'?

Here Mann becomes a foil – the sceptic who believed every arbitration ultimately to be governed by some national law, the *lex fori*, more accurately the *lex arbitri* or *la lois de l'arbitrage*, whether that law should be the law of the seat or the national law chosen by the parties to govern their contract.[24] Mann after all was a high representative of an English sensibility:[25]

> the statement: 'arbitrations are subject to the law chosen by the parties as the *lex fori*' cannot have any validity in the absence of a legal rule to this effect. On the other hand, arbitrators are inevitably subject to the legislative jurisdiction of the country in which the tribunal functions. Whatever the intentions of the parties may be, the legislative and judicial authorities of the seat control the tribunal's existence, composition and activities. It is primarily the law of the seat that decides whether and on what conditions arbitration is permitted at all. No country other than that of the seat has such complete and effective control over the arbitration tribunal.

It was precisely this truth however which the New York Convention on the Recognition and Enforcement of Foreign Arbitral Awards[26] has subverted;

[23] Julian Lew, 'Achieving the Dream: Autonomous Arbitration' (2006) 22 *Arb Int'l* 179; F. A. Mann, 'Lex Facit Arbitrum' (1986) 2 *Arb Int'l* 241, 244.

[24] Mann 'Lex Facit', *op. cit.*, 245.

[25] *Ibid.*, 246.

[26] 10 June 1958.

doing so by remitting control to a plurality of Contracting States whose courts are generally speaking expected to enforce arbitration agreements and awards from any other New York Convention country. But that is to rush the story.

1.2 Chapter Outline

Section 1.3, on international commercial arbitration, discusses where national authority ends and arbitration's 'autonomy' begins. What is the place, if any, of national legal policies and national conflict of laws rules? By arbitration's autonomy we mean the parties' autonomy to choose the procedure and substantive laws of the arbitration, the authority of the tribunal to decide its own competence, and even the application of transnational principles rather than national rules in some of these aspects.

As for international investment arbitration between a foreign investor and its host State,[27] discussed in Section 1.4, that has an overlapping but now distinctive history. Although the pacific settlement of public debt and foreign investment disputes in modern times goes as far back as the Drago-Porter Convention of 1907,[28] modern international investment arbitration only emerged in the late 1950s with internationalised contracts, the first bilateral investment treaty, and in the 1960s with the creation of the International Centre for the Settlement of Investment Disputes (ICSID). All of this culminated in the 1990s with the sudden burst of investment treaty arbitrations.

Finally, there is inter-State arbitration – that between sovereigns, apparently beyond the reach of national legal authority. Its history diverges somewhat from that discernible shared history between the first two forms mentioned above although attributes of inter-sovereign dispute settlement continue to be seen, sitting alongside the influence of international commercial arbitration, in modern investor-State arbitration.[29] This, together

[27] Rather than arbitration between two States concerning the enforcement of a debt or an investment; *see e.g. Arbitral Opinion Relative to the Gold of the National Bank of Albania*, Brussels, 20 February 1953, (1953) 10 *Annuaire Suisse de Droit International* 11; Oliver J. Lissitzyn, (1955) 49 *Am J Int'l L* 403.

[28] *See* Chapter 13 in this volume.

[29] These include the peculiarities and sensitivities which are involved when it is a sovereign party which is before a tribunal.

with arbitration between a sovereign State and one of its components – intra-State arbitration – will be discussed in Section 1.5. As I have mentioned, inter-State arbitration owes much to British and American state practice in the nineteenth century, most notably to the Jay Treaty commissions and the *Alabama Claims* arbitration,[30] to European practice as well and to the peace movements of that century which culminated in the 1899 Convention on the Pacific Settlement of International Disputes and the Permanent Court of Arbitration.[31]

1.3 International Commercial Arbitration

The modern impetus for international commercial arbitration was to come from the establishment in Paris of the International Chamber of Commerce (ICC) in 1919. One whose International Court of Arbitration was, thereafter, created in 1923. The contribution of the ICC and of French arbitration scholars has been enormous. In the English literature a classic comparison drawn is that between the English and French approaches to arbitration, together with comparisons drawn with the other famous continental forms.[32] The following discussion introduces a complex interaction between[33]

1. the proper law of the agreement to arbitrate;
2. the *lex fori, lex arbitri, la lois de l'arbitrage* or the procedural law of the arbitration as it is variously called, including the doctrines of separability and *kompetenz-kompetenz*;
3. the *lex causae*, that is the law applicable to the substance of the dispute; and
4. the law governing the recognition and enforcement of foreign arbitral awards, most significantly the influence of the New York Convention.

[30] United States of America v. Great Britain (Alabama Claims), Award, 14 September 1872.

[31] For a concise overview of the Anglo-European history, *see* Born, *Cases and Materials, op. cit.*, 2–31.

[32] Not least of which is arbitration under Swiss Rules of International Arbitration. For the classic telling of the tale of the entry of American disputes lawyers into the international commercial arbitration field, *see* Yves Dezalay and Bryan Garth, *Dealing in Virtue* (Chicago: University of Chicago, 1996).

[33] Redfern and Hunter, *op. cit.*, para. 3. 07. *See further* Chapter 3 of this volume.

Together they illustrate an important tension between two perspectives – (1) the first which emphasises the role of national law and national courts, sometimes called the 'territorial' approach and (2) a second perspective which emphasises instead the operation of 'transnational' legal rules and principles, as well as the functioning of an autonomous or 'delocalised' arbitral legal order free from any singular national legal or curial supervision.[34]

1.3.1 Seat versus Delocalisation

Paulsson characterises the debate between State authority and party autonomy as:[35]

> a domain to which erudite and disputatious scholars, as generations come and go, have devoted pages as countless as the stars, destined to be read, it seems, chiefly by others intending to add to the production.

Yet anyone approaching the subject for the first time will find it useful to organise her thoughts around a tension between the two ideas. This is a subject where the answers to practical legal questions still depend upon the view taken of the scope of State authority when viewed against the freedom of contract – that freedom upon which international commercial arbitration in particular is based. Some call this a tension between the 'jurisdictional' and 'contractualist' views.[36]

Today, the delocalisation debate often revolves around whether there is any need left for State authority in that sphere where the parties have exercised their freedom of contract – i.e. whether contracts (and therefore arbitration agreements and awards) can exist apart from State authority.[37] The traditional view, some might just refer to it as the 'English view', is that

[34] For an introduction, *see e.g.* Wang Shengchang and Cao Lijun, 'The Role of National Courts and Lex Fori in International Commercial Arbitration' in Loukas A. Mistelis and Julian D. M. Lew (eds.), *Pervasive Problems in International Arbitration* (The Hague: Kluwer, 2006), 155.

[35] Jan Paulsson, *The Idea of Arbitration* (Oxford: Oxford University Press, 2014), 33.

[36] Lew, 'Dream', *op. cit.*, 186.

[37] *See further*, however, Emmanuel Gaillard, 'International Arbitration as a Transnational System of Justice' in Albert Jan van den Berg (ed.), *Arbitration – The Next Fifty Years* (Alphen aan den Rijn: Kluwer, 2012), 66, 66–73, who argues that delocalisation does not necessarily entail the absence of all State authority but merely that of the authority of the place of the seat.

much as contracts are given force by national contract laws arbitration too must have its curial law.[38] In the absence of contractual provision to the contrary,[39] the usual answer is that the curial law is the law of the seat.[40] There are important practical dimensions to the debate. For example, any attempt by the courts of a State to interfere with the initiation, process or outcome of an arbitration could be, if not improper, futile. Delocalisation is ultimately an argument about the functional absence of international commercial arbitration's need for curial support by, or indeed the approval of, the courts of the seat. Delocalisation is persuasive where the argument is that even an award set aside by the courts of the place of the seat may be recognised and enforced elsewhere.[41]

As a scholarly artefact however – since the arbitration field is both practical and scholarly – delocalisation is given credence by late

38 Redfern and Hunter, *op. cit.*, para. 3. 84.

39 Described as 'almost unknown' by Mustill and Boyd; *see further* Sir Michael J. Mustill and Stewart C. Boyd, *Commercial Arbitration*, 2nd ed. (London: Sweet & Maxwell, 1989), 64 *et seq.*

40 Redfern and Hunter, *op. cit.*, 3.53. Mustill and Boyd, *op. cit.*, 64 *et seq. See* Bank Mellat v. Helliniki Techniki SA [1984] 1 QB 291, 301, [1983] 3 All ER 428 (CA). Even though, as Fouchard, Gaillard and Goldman have pointed out, the UNCITRAL Model Law does not speak of 'the seat of the arbitration' as such; E. Gaillard and J. Savage (eds.), *Fouchard, Gaillard and Goldman on International Commercial Arbitration* (The Hague: Kluwer, 1999), paras. 1179–1180. It may be said that this is only true in a literal sense. For its part, the New York Convention speaks in art. V(1)(a) of the 'law of the country where the award was made'.

41 Gaillard, 'International Arbitration as a Transnational System of Justice', *op. cit.*, 66–73; also Jan Paulsson, 'Arbitration Unbound: Award Detached from the Law of Its Country of Origin', (1981) 30 *ICLQ* 358; William W. Park, 'The *Lex Loci Arbitri* and International Commercial Arbitration', (1983) 32 *ICLQ* 21. *See further* Chapter 6 in this volume, where Michaels argues that as such international commercial arbitration still needs the support of national authority but Gaillard's point is that such support comes from the New York Convention, and international treaty. There is no necessary inconsistency – of arbitration wanting to be apart from but at the same time deriving from State authority. Professor Michaels addresses the term *delocalisation* in a much broader sense in which it is sometimes used, which is that arbitration does not rely upon State authority at all but that proposition has always been untenable, at least when put in these broad terms. An award would ultimately need to be enforced – or enforceable – somewhere, by some national authority. Gaillard attributed this broad proposition to Professor Michael Reisman; Gaillard, 'International Arbitration as a Transnational System of Justice', *op. cit.*, 68–69. While Paulsson seems also to have been criticised (Park, '*Lex Loci Arbitri*', *op. cit.*, 25) for being a dangerous heretic in maintaining what appears to be this broad sense of delocalisation, he does not in fact put it in such wide terms but confines himself to the enforceability of the award regardless of its validity in the place in which the award was made; 'Delocalisation of International Commercial Arbitration: When and Why It Matters', (1983) 32 *ICLQ* 53, 54.

twentieth-century globalisation and, prior to that, the growth in the 1970s and 1980s of a transnational commercial private law.[42] A 'new *lex mercatoria*' in the parlance of Lord Mustill,[43] or 'transnational law' as Emmanuel Gaillard calls it,[44] exists supposedly without a need for State law. According to Berthold Goldman, that law consists of[45]

> A set of general principles, and customary rules spontaneously referred to or elaborated in the framework of international trade, without reference to a particular national system of laws.

While according to Gaillard transnational law is derived from multiple legal sources.[46] In contrast, in England, F. A. Mann had complained that[47]

> For many years there has been a school of thought which advocated the conception of a 'transnational contract' (a word unfortunately, but harmlessly, used also by Lord Diplock in one particular context), which is not subject to any law, which is a *contrat anational*, which is governed only by some *lex mercatoria* or general principles of law, is *rechtsordnungslos* or simply 'transnational'.

Gaillard has cautioned, more recently, however that not all talk of the 'new' *lex mercatoria* or, when used interchangeably, 'transnational law' treats the thing described as something which is independent necessarily of national or sovereign lawmaking.[48]

In the arbitration context the term *delocalisation* has its own distinct nuances. As a theory about arbitration it seeks to unmoor international commercial arbitration from the national legal authority of the place of the

[42] Dezalay and Garth, *op. cit.*, 11.

[43] Mustill, 'New Lex Mercatoria', *op. cit.* For a survey of modern opinions, *see e.g.* Abu F. M. Maniruzzaman, 'The Lex Mercatoria and International Contracts: A Challenge for International Commercial Arbitration?' (1999) 14 *Am U Intl L Rev* 657, 660–670.

[44] Emmanuel Gaillard, 'Transnational Law: A Legal System or a Method of Decision-Making?' (2001) 17 *Arb Int'l* 1; Fouchard, Gaillard and Goldman, *op. cit.*, para. 1443 *et seq.*; Mustill, 'New Lex Mercatoria', *op. cit.*

[45] Berthold Goldman, 'The Applicable Law: General Principles of Law: The Lex Mercatoria' in Julian D. M. Lew (ed.), *Contemporary Problems in International Arbitration* (Berlin: Springer, 1986), 113, 116.

[46] Gaillard, 'Transnational Law', *op. cit.*, 61.

[47] F. A. Mann, 'England Rejects 'Delocalised' Contracts and Arbitration' (1984) 33 *ICLQ* 193, 196.

[48] *See* C. Schmitthoff, 'International Business Law: A New Law Merchant' in Chia-jui Cheng (ed.), *Clive Schmitthoff's Select Essays on International Trade Law* (Dordrecht: Nijhoff. 1988), 20; discussed in Maniruzzaman, *op. cit.*, 661.

seat.[49] In this way arbitration becomes an autonomous legal order,[50] rather than being territorial; what Gaillard calls a 'transnational justice system'.[51] Delocalisation's proponents reject the notion that every arbitration and award must have its basis in some specific national law. They suggest that arbitrations and awards can be supported by multiple national legal systems at once,[52] and do not therefore need the acknowledgement of the national law of the place of the seat – which Paulsson in turn dubs a 'pluralistic', as opposed to a 'territorial', approach.[53] According to the pluralistic theory, 'international' arbitration becomes delocalised – rather than being territorial – because it is given legal force not just by the law of the seat. 'The arbitrator "has no forum"',[54] because an arbitration whose seat is in country A can still be assisted by a freezing order or a search order made by the courts in country B.[55] Such international judicial support matters more in practical, functional terms when as is often the case the seat is but no more than a neutral place and the respondent's assets typically are not even located there.

Against such views, proponents of the territorial approach point out the need for a safeguard against denials of justice and violations of due process. The procedure adopted by the parties typically is also subject to mandatory forum rules. There are also national public policies which often feature when a dispute is said to be 'non-arbitrable'.[56] In this way the *lex fori* – or 'it would be more exact . . . to speak of the *lex arbitri* or . . . *la loi de l'arbitrage*'[57] – seeks to limit party autonomy from the outset.[58]

49 Redfern and Hunter, *op. cit.*, para. 3.53 onwards, esp. para. 3.76 *et seq.*

50 Gaillard cites Daniel Cohen who uses the term *arbitral legal order. See* Emmanuel Gaillard, *Legal Theory of International Arbitration* (Boston: Nijhoff, 2010), 39. *See further* Gaillard, 'International Arbitration as a Transnational System of Justice', *op. cit.*, 66. According to Professor Gaillard 'the expression was [already] used loosely at the time'; correspondence with Gaillard, 7 October 2019.

51 *See further* Lew, *op. cit.*, 179.

52 Gaillard, 'International Arbitration as a Transnational System of Justice' *op. cit.*, 67–70.

53 Paulsson, *Idea*, *op. cit.*, 29 *et seq.*

54 Fouchard, Gaillard and Goldman, *op. cit.*, para. 1181, quoting Berthold Goldman.

55 *See e.g.* the English Arbitration Act 1996, s. 44; Hong Kong Arbitration Ordinance (Cap. 609), ss. 45(2), 60(1).

56 Alastair Henderson, 'Lex Arbitri, Procedural Law and the Seat of the Arbitration' (2014) 26 *SAcLJ* 886.

57 To quote Mann, 'Lex Facit Arbitrum' *op. cit.*, 245.

58 In some jurisdictions matters may be more complex, such as the rule in Singapore that if a tribunal does not enforce the agreement to arbitrate then the Singapore courts may yet compel it.

It involves more than an inquiry into the procedure 'within' the arbitration. Rather, the questions involved include those which are 'external' to the arbitration and includes the application of national laws by national courts.[59] This is not to mention that the assistance of State courts is often also welcomed. From assistance with the tribunal's constitution to the need to support tribunal orders of interlocutory relief as well as the application of default procedures.

Currently, as debate over transnational law shifts to its substantive content rather than its sources or functional need,[60] its existence is no longer in real doubt. Mann's own reservations had less to do with 'a-national contracts' than the risk of arbitrators who are left unsupervised by any proper legal authority deciding disputes *ex aequo et bono*. Mann had at least supported a limited class of transnational or 'a-national' contracts; those governed by general principles of law which are also a source of public international law.[61] However, he rejected delocalised or 'floating' arbitrations premised upon the idea of an 'a-national' agreement to arbitrate.[62] According to Mann, there is no 'international' commercial arbitration as such.[63] There is private law and there are national conflict of laws rules which point to national contract law, there are agreements under public international law on which commercial arbitrations can also be based, but there is no such thing as international commercial arbitration without curial supervision. Today the practitioner find traces of seat thinking in our most basic instruments. The next section will mention the idea in the New York Convention that an award may be refused recognition if the arbitration agreement is not valid 'under the law of the country where the award was made'.[64] Similarly, that same article, Article V, speaks of such refusal where the composition of the tribunal or the arbitral procedure was, in the absence of party agreement, not 'in

[59] Also, the *lex arbitri* is not strictly just 'procedural'. *See* Redfern and Hunter, *op. cit.*, para. 3.62; Jan Paulsson, 'Arbitration in Three Dimensions', (2011) 60 *ICLQ* 291.

[60] Gaillard, 'Transnational Law' *op. cit.*, 60.

[61] Mann, 'England Rejects' *op. cit.*, 196; F. A. Mann, *Studies in International Law* (Oxford: Oxford University Press, 1973), 191 *et seq* and 222 *et seq*.

[62] 'Floating in the transnational firmament'; Bank Mellat v. Helliniki Techniki SA, *op. cit.* (per Kerr LJ). *See* Mann, 'England Rejects' *op. cit.*, 197 *et seq*. The reader will wish to turn to Professor Cordero-Moss' treatment of the issue, in Chapter 5 in this volume.

[63] Mann, 'England Rejects' *op. cit.*, 197; Mann, 'Lex Facit Arbitrum' *op. cit.*, 244,

[64] Art. V(1)(a).

accordance with the law of the country where the arbitration took place',[65] and where the award has been set aside or suspended by 'a competent authority of the country in which, or under the law of which, that award was made'.[66] There are similar references in the Model Law to itself as *lex arbitri*.[67]

In contrast, the 'Dijon School' – or perhaps the 'French School' might be a better term[68] – comprising such august figures as Berthold Goldman and Philippe Fouchard, advocated both the idea of transnational law and that of delocalised arbitration.[69]

1.3.2 Delocalisation and the Arbitration Agreement

To begin at the beginning, what law governs the arbitral agreement?[70] We might say that whatever that law an arbitration agreement is separable and the French School considers that 'separability' doctrine at least to be a transnational rule. Mr Justice Steyn (as he then was) sought to sway the law in England and Wales towards this continental learning.[71] Today, the separability doctrine applies by virtue of English law under Section 7 of the Arbitration Act in England, even if by way of the recognition of a transnational principle.[72] So while transnational principles have been received

[65] Art. V(1)(d).

[66] Art. V(1)(e).

[67] Regarding the annulment of awards where the Model Law refers to the following grounds – invalidity of the arbitration agreement under 'the law of this State', and where the composition of the tribunal or the arbitral procedure was, absent party agreement, not in accordance with 'this Law'. *See* art. 34(2)(a)(i) and (iv), respectively.

[68] I am grateful to the late Emmanuel Gaillard for this point where he had explained to me that the agenda of the so-called Dijon School was perhaps not detailed and coherent enough; that there were French scholars, members of a broader 'French School', who fell outside of it; correspondence with Gaillard, 7 October 2019.

[69] Klaus Peter Berger, 'Berthold Goldman and the Dijon School: The Rebirth of the Lex Mercatoria', www.trans-lex.org; Thomas Schultz, 'The Concept of Law in Transnational Arbitral Legal Orders and Some of its Consequences' (2011) 2 *Jo Int'l Disp Res* 59. The French School is Mann's target, *see* Mann, 'Lex Facit Arbitrum' *op. cit.*, 244, together with the views of Clive Schmitthoff in England among others, 'England Rejects'; *op. cit.*, 196.

[70] Putting aside dispute about the scope of the arbitration agreement as an issue of 'arbitrability'.

[71] Dezalay and Garth, *op. cit.*, 139.

[72] Following the 1985 UNCITRAL Model Law (hereinafter ML), discussed further below, art. 16(1); Mustill and Boyd, *op. cit.*, 2001 Companion, 266. *See* Harbour Assurance Co. (UK). Ltd. v. Kansa General Insurance Co., Ltd. [1993] 1 Lloyd's Rep 455; Fiona Trust &

into English law there is at the same time nothing unusual about comparative learning.[73] The doctrine separates the arbitration agreement from questions about the validity of the main contract in which it is to be found or contained, such that avoidance, rescission or termination of the main or underlying contract does not affect the validity of the arbitration agreement itself. However, the separability doctrine also points to a potential difference between the law governing the main contract and that governing the arbitration clause or agreement.[74]

The arbitration agreement itself could be invalid according to the law which governs it,[75] which leads to the question – what law governs the arbitration agreement? The law governing the arbitration agreement affects such questions as the capacity of the parties, or whether the requirement that the agreement must be in writing has been met.[76] Under English law, the traditional view was that what law governs the arbitration agreement is a procedural question and thus becomes a matter for the law of the seat.[77] As we have seen, under the New York Convention, in the absence of the parties' choice of the governing law, if the arbitration agreement is invalid under the law of the place where the award was made that becomes a ground for refusal of recognition and enforcement of the award.[78]

Absent party choice, traditional choice of law analysis searches out the law with which the arbitration agreement is most closely connected.[79]

Holdings Corp v. Privalov [2008] 1 Lloyds Rep 254 and more recently, National Iranian Oil Company v. Crescent Petroleum Company International Ltd, Crescent Gas Corporation Ltd [2016] EWHC 510 (Comm) (Burton J.).

73 *See* Chapter 3 in this volume.

74 *See* the recent Singapore case in BNA v. BNB and Anor [2019] SGCA 84, para. 27, discussing the decision below.

75 In this *Companion*, Professor Cordero-Moss discusses the implications of the law governing the arbitration agreement for electronic and oral agreements to arbitrate, as well as for questions concerning the capacity of the parties and the scope of the arbitration agreement. *See* Chapter 5 in this volume.

76 New York Convention of 1958 (NYC), arts. II, IV; ML, art. 7(1) and (2). Following the 2006 revisions, art. 7 under 'Option 2' of the 2006 revised ML now omits the writing requirement altogether.

77 Fouchard, Gaillard and Goldman, *op. cit.*, para, 424. Although the English courts have applied both the law which governs the main contract and the law of the seat, as discussed below.

78 *Ibid.*, paras. 429–431.

79 Sulamerica CIA Nacional De Seguros SA v. Enesa Engenharia SA [2012] EWCA Civ 638; [2013] 1 WLR 102, para. 9. For a comparison, *see*, in Singapore, BCY v. BCZ [2016] SGHC 249; aff'd in BNA v. BNB and Anor [2019] SGCA 84 (this was common ground between the

The weight to be accorded to various connecting factors may be different however from when determining the law governing the main contract – for example, the seat of the arbitration might feature strongly in relation to the law governing the arbitration agreement, but not in respect of the law governing the main contract. Tribunals have also been known to look to an express choice of arbitration rules as evidence of a choice of the law of the seat, or to the parties' choice of the language of the arbitration.[80] Under traditional common law principles,[81] in the absence of an express choice the inquiry moves to whether there has been an implied choice of the law governing the agreement to arbitrate and failing that one seeks the law having the closest connection with the arbitration agreement. In England, following *Sulamerica*, a rebuttable presumption now exists – at least where the parties have chosen the law governing the main or container contract – in favour of that same law.[82] So in England, and to the extent that still sways our understanding under Anglo-Commonwealth laws elsewhere,[83] the authorities are now split between a rebuttable presumption that the law governing the main contract also governs the arbitration agreement and the law of the seat.

As a practical matter, at least from the tribunal's perspective, any tribunal is at least likely to consider that a risk of the award being set aside may be too great to bear.[84] But compare now delocalisation's

parties). See further now, Enka Insaat ve Sanayi AS v. OOO Insurance Company Chubb [2020] UKSC 38.

80 *Ibid.*, paras. 425, 426–434.

81 Rome I, as we have seen, does not apply to the arbitration agreement, and thus the agreement is governed as a matter of common law by the proper law of the contract. One asks if there has been an express choice by the parties or an implied choice, but if the answer to both questions is no, then one asks which law has the closest and most real connection to the agreement. *See* Dicey and Morris, *Conflict of Laws*, 11th ed., by Lawrence Collins et al. (London: Sweet & Maxwell, 1987), Chapter 32.

82 Sulamerica CIA Nacional De Seguros SA v. Enesa Engenharia SA [2012] EWCA Civ 638; [2013] 1 WLR 102, para. 26 (Moore-Bick LJ with whom Hallett LJ agreed). For an excellent discussion, *see* Renato Nazzini, 'The Law Governing the Arbitration Agreement: A Transnational Solution?' in Renato Nazzini (ed.), *Transnational Construction Arbitration* (London: Informa, 2018), 5. For a comparison, *see*, in Singapore, BCY v. BCZ [2016] SGHC 249; aff'd in BNA v. BNB [2019] SGHC 142; *see further* BNA v. BNB and Anor [2019] SGCA 84, reversing the learned High Court judge albeit not on this point.

83 BNA v. BNB and Anor [2019] SGCA 84.

84 For a Chinese example, *see* C. L. Lim, 'The Function of the Transnational Chinese Contract' (2019) 20 *JWIT* 313, 333; Weidong Zhu, 'The Recognition and Enforcement of the Arbitral Awards "With No Foreign Element"' (2015) 32 *J Intl Arb* 351.

proponents who say that the agreement to arbitrate is governed by transnational law.[85] They point out that the European Union's Rome I Regulation, which applies to contractual choice of law, expressly states that it does not apply to arbitration agreements.[86] Thus, they say, private international law analysis has no application whatsoever to arbitration agreements.[87]

As Redfern and Hunter see it, however, delocalisation in this *first* limited sense, in the sense of an absence of effective supervision,[88] is achieved only if the law of the seat sanctions it or if the tribunal were to ignore successfully the courts of the seat.[89] There was the famous Belgian initiative to deny curial intervention with parties having no connection with Belgium. This was done in the belief that it would appeal to such parties. However, rather than having become more attractive, because presumably Belgium had become more 'friendly' towards international arbitration, parties shied from Belgian arbitration. Similarly, as the UK Supreme Court observed in *Dallah*, under French law arbitration agreements derive their existence, validity and effect from 'supra-national' rather than national law.[90] Yet that is so only because French law says so.

There is, however, a *second* and more limited sense to what the French School intends. Under the New York Convention, even an award set aside by the courts of the place of the seat of the arbitration could derive its validity from elsewhere, namely in its recognition and enforcement by the courts of another Contracting State to the New York Convention.[91]

[85] *See* Fouchard, Gaillard and Goldman, *op. cit.*, paras. 435 onwards; Gary Born, 'The Law Governing International Arbitral Agreements: An International Perspective' (2014) 26 *SAcLJ* 814; Nazzini, *op. cit.*; also, Renato Nazzini, 'The Law Applicable to the Arbitration Agreement: Towards Transnational Principles' (2016) 65 *ICLQ* 68.

[86] *See* now Article 1(2)(e) of the Rome Regulation on the Law Applicable to Contractual Obligations [Council Reg. (EC) No. 593/2008, 17 June 2008]. In this volume, Professor Briggs (Chapter 4) agrees that private international law has no application but he does not accept the French view.

[87] *See further* Chapter 4 of this volume.

[88] Supervision, rather than recognition and enforcement; *cf.* Gaillard, 'International Arbitration as a Transnational System of Justice', *op. cit.*, 66–73.

[89] Redfern and Hunter, *op. cit.*, paras. 3.73–3.90.

[90] *See ibid.*, para. 3.77; Dallah Real Estate and Tourism Holding Co. v. Ministry of Religious Affairs, Government of Pakistan [2010] UKSC 4, 15.

[91] This is also discussed further in Chapter 20 of this volume.

1.3.3 Delocalisation, Plural Enforcement and the New York Convention

The French School's second sense of delocalisation, as just mentioned, is sustained by a framework of powerful global legal instruments. Three international instruments had laid the foundations for the growth of international commercial arbitration – the New York Convention, the UNCITRAL Arbitration Rules and the UNCITRAL Model Law.

The New York Convention mandates that national courts should if the necessary conditions are fulfilled, namely if there is an arbitration agreement in writing, enforce an agreement to arbitrate (art. 2). Importantly, as with the UNCITRAL Model Law,[92] the Convention stipulates the recognition and enforcement of foreign arbitral awards. Limited grounds only are provided for the discretionary refusal to accord such recognition and enforcement.[93] The difference between the Convention and the Model Law is that the former imposes an international treaty obligation. It is the New York Convention's facilitation of the enforcement of awards which, arguably, makes arbitration 'delocalised' in the sense that an arbitration agreement or an award need not depend upon the enforcement of the courts of the seat of the arbitration.[94] It is also what makes international commercial arbitration attractive in comparison with international litigation since an award has greater reach in terms of its enforceability under the New York Convention. It is this imbalance between international litigation and international arbitration which the Hague Choice of Court Convention seeks in turn to redress.[95] The courts in the place of the seat of the award may set the award aside, but the New York Convention does not compel the courts of another Contracting State to abide by such an annulment. The Convention in avoiding the need for a 'double exequatur' had taken a critical step in the direction of delocalisation by detaching recognition and enforcement from the judicial supervision of the courts of the seat of the arbitration.[96]

Turning to the 1985 UNCITRAL Model Law, it contains provisions which draw the line – in several places – between where national authority ends

[92] ML, arts. 35 and 36.

[93] Art. V of the NY Convention is comparable to the grounds for set aside in ML, art. 34.

[94] Which was the case if only we were to imagine a time when all arbitration was domestic.

[95] *See* Hague Convention of 30 June 2005 on Choice of Court Agreements.

[96] A requirement, in other words, that leave shall first be obtained for enforcement from the courts of the place of the seat of the arbitration. *See* Emmanuel Gaillard and George A. Bermann (eds.), *Guide on the Convention on the Recognition and Enforcement of Foreign Arbitral Awards* (Leiden: Brill, 2017), 132–133, 221–222.

and party autonomy reigns. Its importance lies however as model legislation which delineates the scope of the authority of national courts vis-à-vis that of the tribunal. Thus the Model Law goes by many names in more than 60 different jurisdictions. It also demonstrated developing world acceptance of international commercial arbitration,[97] and was intended to augment the New York Convention. The Model Law would aim towards uniform arbitral procedures internationally, as proposed by AALCO, and to clarify the rules on the authority of the national courts of the place of the seat including their authority to annul an award.[98]

Article 1 stipulates that it applies only to 'commercial' – as opposed, for example, to 'investment' – arbitration whose popularity was to grow only subsequently. However, national authorities need not adopt this limitation (dubbed the 'commercial exception') and in certain instances they have not, such as in Hong Kong in contrast to Mainland China. Importantly, the Model Law upholds the doctrine of *kompetenz-kompetenz* – in other words, that it is the tribunal's determination of its own authority which should generally prevail. However this excludes the jurisdiction of the courts only to a degree. The Model Law contemplates an element of judicial supervision.[99] A party to an arbitration may thus apply to the competent national court – e.g. the Commercial Court in England and Wales – to review the tribunal's determination of its own jurisdiction.[100] The Model Law also seeks to uphold a second doctrine; that of separability, discussed earlier above.[101] While the *kompetenz-kompetenz* doctrine reinforces arbitration's relative insulation from judicial supervision, the separability doctrine elevates the arbitration agreement relative to the other contractual

[97] UNGA res. 40/72, 40 GAOR Supp. No. 53, A/40/53, 308 (adopted 11 December 1985). *See further* Howard M. Holtzmann and Joseph E. Neuhaus, *A Guide to the UNCITRAL Model Law on International Commercial Arbitration: Legislative History and Commentary* (Deventer: Kluwer, 1989); M. Sornarajah, 'The UNCITRAL Model Law: A Third World Viewpoint' (1989) 6 *J Int'l Arb* 7.

[98] Holtzmann and Neuhaus, *op. cit.*, 9 *et seq.*

[99] ML, Art. 5.

[100] ML, Art. 16(3). *See further* Redfern and Hunter, *op. cit.*, especially paras. 10.41 *et seq.* Perhaps the Commercial Court is an imperfect example since in England the Model Law has not been adopted entirely. See the English Arbitration Act, 1996, s. 32.

[101] ML, Art. 16(1). For separability and the kompetenz-kompetenz rule, respectively, in the United Kingdom, *see e.g.* Arbitration Act 1996, ss. 7 and 30. For the doctrine of separability *see* Harbour Assurance Co (UK) Ltd v. Kansa General International Insurance Co Ltd [1993] QB 701 in the United Kingdom, and in the United States *see* Prima Paint v. Flood & Conklin, 388 US 395, 404–405 (1967).

provisions and national contract law.[102] Both doctrines where there is State involvement, in foreign investor-State arbitration discussed below for example, also serve to 'disempower national laws', such as where Libya sought to annul oil concession contracts using its sovereign, public authority and asserted unsuccessfully that the arbitration agreements contained therein were likewise to be considered null and void.[103]

Subject only to the Model Law's mandatory requirements, proponents of delocalisation have suggested that absent party choice the Model Law leaves it to the arbitrators to decide the procedural law.[104] Which, finally, brings us to the UNCITRAL Arbitration Rules which were first adopted in 1976[105] and have since been revised in 2010. These were intended to provide a ready-made procedural framework for un-administered arbitrations. They have been adopted widely by tribunals such as the Iran–United States Claims Tribunal (IUCT) in addition to arbitration institutions; especially institutions in Africa, Asia and the Far East. These include AALCO's Cairo and Kuala Lumpur Regional Arbitration Centres, the latter of which recently was renamed, as well as the Singapore International Arbitration Centre (SIAC) and the Hong Kong International Arbitration Centre (HKIAC). While the UNCITRAL Rules were intended originally to be used in international commercial arbitration, they are also used widely in international investment arbitration. Choice of arbitration under the UNCITRAL Rules is commonly found as an option in bilateral investment treaties (BITs).[106]

1.4 Foreign Investor-State Arbitration of International Investment Disputes

International investment arbitration or investor-State arbitration need not be based on treaty even if this narrower definition is familiar. A broader

[102] Fouchard, Gaillard and Goldman, citing French rulings, consider separability to be a substantive principle of transnational law; *op. cit.*, paras. 435 *et seq.*

[103] Shalakany. *op. cit.*, 440.

[104] ML, Art. 19(2); Fouchard, Gaillard and Goldman, *op. cit.*, para. 1180; *cf.* ICSID Convention, Art. 42(1) which states that both the host State law and international law will apply.

[105] UNGA res. 31/98, 15 December 1976.

[106] For an introduction to the Rules, *see* the introduction in David D. Caron and Lee M. Caplan, *The UNCITRAL Arbitration Rules, A Commentary*, 2nd ed. (Oxford: Oxford University Press, 2013).

definition is used in this *Companion* which refers to arbitration between an investor and State where the subject matter concerns an investment. It would include contractually based (investment contract arbitration) rather than being confined to treaty-based investor-State arbitration. The reader might think of ICSID arbitration which accounts certainly for the majority of known investor-State arbitrations, but just as common is investor-State arbitration brought on the basis of the UNCITRAL Rules or which is administered by another arbitration institution.[107] Such 'non-ICSID' arbitration is also facilitated by the existence of the New York Convention and the Model Law. An investment award may therefore still be sought to be set aside by a national court in the case of a non-ICSID arbitration.[108] Of course, there could arise, as was the case in *Occidental v. Ecuador*, questions of non-justiciability.[109] We can put that aside. In this section, the reader's attention is drawn to the delocalisation of investor-State arbitration, particularly in respect of the law governing the arbitration agreement, the *lex arbitri* and the regime for the enforcement of awards.

Mention has been made of the Drago-Porter Convention and inter-State arbitration involving questions of public debt, as well as mixed commissions and the international judicial settlement of investment disputes. These had all pre-existed investor-State arbitration in its modern form.[110] Chronologically, investor-State arbitration had begun with investment contract arbitration which emerged during the 1950s. The growth of investment contract arbitration coincided with the internationalisation of State contracts, most famously in the Libyan oil arbitrations. In *BP v. Libya*,[111] *Texaco v. Libya*,[112] and *LIAMCO v. Libya*,[113] a common clause in the three oil concessions had stipulated that 'principles of law of Libya common to the principles of international law' and failing that 'the general

107 ICC, LCIA, Stockholm Centre, SIAC, the HKIAC or AIAC, to name a few.

108 But not exclusively. For an unsuccessful attempt to set aside an ICSID Award in England. *see* Viorel Micula and ors. v. Romania [2017] EWHC 31 (Comm) (Blair J.), para. 53.

109 Occidental v. Ecuador [2005]EWCA Civ. 1116. In *Occidental*, the irony was that it was the investor which had argued that the matter was non-justiciable (i.e. that arbitration based upon a BIT or other treaty right is 'delocalised').

110 *See* C. L. Lim, Jean Ho and Martins Paparinskis, *International Investment Law and Arbitration: Commentary, Awards and Other Materials* (Cambridge: Cambridge University Press, 2018), Chapter 1.

111 BP v. Libya (1997) 53 I.L.R. 297.

112 Texaco v. Libya, 19 January 1977, 17 I.L.M. 1.

113 LIAMCO v. Libya (1977) 20 I.L.M. 1.

principles of law' shall be applied. The Libyan arbitrations had been preceded by the *Abu Dhabi* arbitration,[114] in which Lord Asquith – observing that Abu Dhabi law lacked principles for the construction of modern commercial instruments – considered that 'principles rooted in the good sense and common practice of the generality of civilised nations'[115] ought to be applied. The Libyan arbitrations were to develop the idea of the transnational contract despite varying analyses.[116] Moreover, of the three original Libyan arbitrations, only the arbitrator in *BP* considered the *lex arbitri* to be the law of the seat of the arbitration,[117] while in the earlier 1955 *Aramco* arbitration the tribunal had reasoned that since one of the parties was a State the procedural law of the arbitration should therefore be international law. Were it otherwise, a sovereign State will become subject to the indignity of a procedural law rooted in another sovereign State's municipal law.[118] This indeed was also the reasoning in *Texaco*.[119]

It is worth mentioning that it was perhaps in *Texaco v. Libya* that one of the most notable early expositions of the delocalisation theory was to be found in arbitral practice. In *Texaco*, the arbitrator Dupuy had considered that the choice of international arbitration placed the contract itself within a specific legal order, one which he termed 'the order of the international law of contracts'. This is a tantalising statement for while the statement occurs in the context of a discussion of the governing law of the contract – suggesting, perhaps controversially, that an arbitration clause can point towards international law as the governing law – it placed international arbitration itself within a legal order that is to be differentiated from the international legal order as well, at the same time, as any domestic legal system.

In ICSID arbitration, delocalisation is given by ICSID's 1965 Convention ('Washington Convention').[120] Its full title is the Convention on the

[114] (1951) 18 I.L.R. 144.

[115] Including the English common law.

[116] Shalakany, *op. cit.*, 448–452.

[117] *Ibid.*, 449; BP v. Libya, op. cit., Part III of the Award.

[118] Aramco Arbitration, 27 I.L.R. (1963), 117, at 155–156.

[119] *See* Texaco v. Libya, *op. cit.*, paras. 11–13.

[120] What remains to be fully tested are the words 'unless otherwise stated', on which *see further* Christoph H. Schreuer et al., *The ICSID Convention: A Commentary*, 2nd ed. (Cambridge University Press, 2009), 351; C. L. Lim, 'The Function of the Transnational Chinese Contract' (2019) 20 *JWIT* 313, 324, discussing the Mauritanian example; also dicta, in Occidental Petroleum v. Ecuador, *op. cit.*, para. 38 (Mance LJ), and albeit

Settlement of Investment Disputes between States and Nationals of Other States.[121] ICSID arbitration does not usually have a seat but rather the procedural law is supplied by the Convention itself and the ICSID Rules.[122] The ICSID Convention contains provisions on whether the parties have consented to arbitration, the jurisdiction and powers of the tribunal, interim relief and the recognition and enforcement of ICSID awards. Unlike non-ICSID arbitration which would rely on the architecture described in connection with international commercial arbitration – principally the Model Law and the New York Convention, and in the case especially of ad hoc arbitration possibly the adoption of the UNCITRAL Rules as well – there is no regime under the ICSID Convention for the setting aside of an award by a national court.[123]

The ICSID regime is thus generally different from that under the Model Law and the New York Convention. There is – at least typically – no 'seat', and rather than annulment by national courts there is a special treaty annulment procedure according to which an award may be challenged before an annulment committee whose character is international rather than being national and judicial.[124]

That the respondent is a sovereign State also means that foreign sovereign immunity and the Act of State doctrine could feature as obstacles to judicial supervision. Indeed, the chief benefit of the delocalised nature of

concerning an application to the English courts for a freezing order in E.T.I. Eurotelecom and Anor. v. Bolivia [2008] EWCA Civ. 880, paras. 102–109 (Collins LJ).

121 18 March 1965, 4 ILM 524 (1965). Currently it has 154 parties.

122 'Usually' for even in the case of ICSID arbitration, the issue may not be wholly free from doubt. Take, for example, the case of two 2004 production sharing agreements between the Chinese oil company, CNPC, and the Islamic Republic of Mauritania. There, ICSID arbitration was selected but the agreement stipulates Paris as the 'seat'. It also states as *lex arbitri* 'that of the Islamic Republic of Mauritania as well as the rules and customs of the international law applicable to the matter'. *See* Lim, 'Function', *op. cit.* We could be looking at a pathological clause, but Article 26 of the ICSID Convention, stating that consent to ICSID arbitration shall in the absence of express party choice be deemed to exclude 'any other remedy', could suggest that party autonomy forms an exception to the delocalisation of ICSID arbitration. *See* Schreuer, *op. cit.*, 351.

123 Article 53 of the ICSID Convention; Schreuer, *op. cit.*, 1096–1098. *Cf.* Nils Eliasson, 'Investment Treaty Arbitration and Hong Kong' in *Arbitration in Hong Kong: A Practical Guide*, 2nd ed. (HK: Sweet & Maxwell, 2012), 735, 757–760 for a discussion of attempts to set aside investment arbitration awards before national courts on the ground that the tribunal had exceeded its jurisdiction.

124 Markus Burgstaller and Charles B. Rosenberg, 'Challenging International Arbitral Awards: To ICSID or Not to ICSID', (2011) 27 *Arb Int'l* 91.

ICSID arbitration is that it circumvents the immunity problem. So far as recognition and enforcement are concerned, the ICSID Convention operates in a broadly similar way to the New York Convention.[125] Simply, the Convention parties are obliged to honour an ICSID Award where, unlike ad hoc or other institutional arbitration, compliance is also backed by the imprimatur of the World Bank.[126]

ICSID 'delocalisation' has been tested in national courts. In the courts of England and Wales, Collins LJ as he then was took a robust view of the self-contained nature of ICSID arbitration whose curial law lies in treaty.[127] However, the case had turned on legislative construction. His Lordship had simply considered that UK legislation made no exception to the delocalisation of ICSID arbitration.[128] Thus it may be said that, even here, 'delocalisation' was again a matter of national law.[129]

In time, contractual protection of investments – including contractual agreements to arbitrate – which ICSID's framers assumed would become the mainstay of ICSID's work[130] began to yield to treaty protection instead. What treaty-based arbitration introduced, though by no means singularly,[131] was the idea of a unilateral offer to arbitrate where the parties' consent to arbitration is perfected when, for example, the investor submits a notice of arbitration.[132] It was Jan Paulsson who coined the term *arbitration without privity*.[133]

125 ICSID Convention, art. 54.

126 *See* Chapter 12 in this volume.

127 ETI Euro Telecom International NV v. Republic of Bolivia [2008] EWCA Civ 880, paras. 102–109; Robert Merkin and Louis Flannery, *Arbitration Act 1996*, 5th ed. (London: Routledge, 2014), 174. Also discussed in Lim, Ho and Paparinskis, International Investment Law and Arbitration, *op. cit.*, 186–192.

128 Finding that neither s.44 of the Arbitration Act 1996 nor the Civil Jurisdiction and Judgments Act 1982, s. 25 (as extended by the Civil Jurisdiction and Judgments Act 1982 (Interim Relief) Order 1997) had decided otherwise; *ETI Euro Telecom, op. cit.*, paras. 92–98.

129 What if one were to seek to subject ICSID arbitration to some national law as the *lex arbitri*? A clause stipulating such an arrangement could be considered pathological. However, it may not be, *see further e.g.* Lim, 'Function' *op. cit.*, 323–324 for an example, *cf.* article 26 of the ICSID Convention. It states that consent to ICSID arbitration be deemed consent to exclude 'any other remedy' *in the absence of party choice.*

130 *See* Chapter 12 in this volume.

131 For unilateral offers to arbitrate in national laws, *see* Michele Potesta, 'The Interpretation of Consent to ICSID Arbitration Contained in Domestic Investment Laws' (2011) 27 *Arb Int'l* 149. *See also* Jan Paulsson, 'The Pyramids Case' in *Collected Courses of the International Academy for Arbitration Law, Year 2012*, vol. 1, 1 (2014).

132 A. M. Steingruber, *Consent in International Arbitration* (Oxford: Oxford University Press, 2012) 11–12, 25 *et seq.*

133 Jan Paulsson, 'Arbitration without Privity' (1995) 10 *ICSID Rev – FILJ* 232.

So long as a State has in writing offered to submit investment disputes to arbitration that would suffice. Such writing could appear in legislation, an investment licence or authorisation or typically in a treaty – most commonly today in a BIT or investment chapter contained within a free trade agreement. So far as ICSID itself is concerned, the idea that ICSID will accept such a form of consent was established by Aaron Broches.[134] The key idea however was to remove the investor's home State from the dispute, thereby defusing it politically and diplomatically. Some readers will recall the *Don Pacifico Affair* where Lord Palmerston had despatched a naval squadron to institute a blockade of Piraeus and an embargo on Greek shipping.[135] In Parliament he declared,[136]

> whether, as the Roman, in days of old, held himself free from indignity, when he could say civis Romanus sum; so also a British subject, in whatever land he may be, shall feel confident that the watchful eye and the strong arm of England, will protect him against injustice and wrong.

Mr Broches had sought to avoid the need to answer such questions,[137] and this brings us finally to the subject of inter-sovereign disputes.

1.5 Arbitration between States and Intra-State Arbitration

The modern growth of inter-State arbitration governed by and/or applying public international law, putting aside its antecedents in Greek antiquity, is attributed to a revival through the eighteenth-century mixed commissions – the Jay Treaty commissions are commonly cited[138] – but more importantly in the later, nineteenth-century *Alabama Claims* arbitration.[139] There followed the work of the International Law Institute in examining arbitral procedure, then the Hague Peace Conferences of 1899 and 1907 which sought to 'consolidate or codify the international

[134] Paulsson. 'Pyramids Case' *op. cit.*, 20.

[135] Lord McNair, *The Law of Treaties*, Vol. 2 (Oxford: Oxford University Press, 1956), 238–241; O. Thomas Johnson and Jonathan Gimblett, 'From Gunboats to BITs', *2012 YIILP* (Oxford: Oxford University Press, 2012), 649, 652.

[136] Palmerston, 25 June 1850, *Hansard* CXII [3rd Ser.], 380–444.

[137] *See further* Chapter 11 in this volume.

[138] George Schwarzenberger, 'Present Day Relevance of the Jay Treaty Arbitrations', (1978) 53 *Notre Dame L Rev* 715.

[139] Alabama Claims, *op. cit.*

law governing inter-State litigation'.[140] Inter-State arbitration's origins are therefore distinct from those of international commercial arbitration.[141] We might say that, together, they constitute the two most basic forms of international arbitration with investor-State arbitration occupying an intermediate place and adaptation therefrom.

However, despite its ancient roots inter-State arbitration fell into disuse by the time the European State system was formed,[142] and there it lay dormant until the mid nineteenth century through the efforts most notably of the United States and the United Kingdom.[143] But this Anglo-American effort did not mean that arbitration was not in use elsewhere too, such as for example in the 1874 case of the *Italian-Swiss Frontier.*[144] The great landmark event may have been the 1794 US–UK Jay Treaty which, occurring in part in the wake of the 1783 Treaty of Paris which ended the American War of Independence, had spawned three mixed commissions addressing inter-State and mixed (individual vs. sovereign) disputes concerning war debts, British action against American ships and property in the former's war with France, and a demarcation (by the St. Croix Commission) of the United States–Canada border.[145] Another key event was the emergence of the doctrine of *kompetenz-kompetenz* – that the tribunal is the judge of its own jurisdictional competence.[146] However, it was the *Alabama Claims* arbitration, concerning the American claim that Great Britain had violated neutrality in the context of the American Civil War, which gave form to present-day inter-State arbitration as well as great impetus to the idea of international law as an instrument of peace. A hundred cases followed

[140] Shabtai Rosenne, *Interpretation, Revision and Other Recourse from International Judgments and Awards* (The Hague: Brill, 2007), 9; *see further* Shabtai Rosenne, *The Hague Peace Conferences of 1899 and 1907 and International Arbitration: Reports and Documents* (The Hague: Asser, 2001). *See further* Chapter 16 in this volume.

[141] Although there is the argument that the mixed courts of the colonial era were a precursor; Shalakany, *op. cit.*, 431.

[142] Rivkin, *op. cit.*, 334.

[143] Jan Paulsson, 'The Alabama Claims Arbitration: Statecraft and Stagecraft' in Joel Dahlquist et al. (eds.), *Arbitrating for Peace: How Arbitration Made a Difference* (Hague: Kluwer, 2016), 7, 8.

[144] 23 September 1874, XXVIII *RIAA* 141.

[145] 19 November 1794, UK–US, Bevans 13. This history to mixed disputes shows that the latest innovations are often no more than examples of adaptation and learning.

[146] Stephen Schwebel, 'Introduction' in Dahlquist, *op. cit.*, 1, 1; Rivkin, *op. cit.*, 334.

in the next 30 years.[147] Arbitration's apparent success in assuring peace where hostilities had once loomed[148] had, as previously mentioned, stirred the nineteenth-century peace movement with the support of Italy, France, Germany (despite its stance at the Hague Peace Conference) and most famously the Russian Tsar, Nicholas II, together with the United States and the United Kingdom. It led to the creation in 1899 of the Permanent Court of Arbitration (PCA).

The PCA is an arbitral institution and inter-governmental organisation established in 1900 with 121 States Members at present.[149] The British idea of a tribunal of arbitrators from which panels could be formed was adopted with, as Schofield explains in this volume, the additional flexibility of allowing parties to form as well special tribunals which nonetheless would have access to the facilities and staff of the PCA's International Bureau.[150] To this day, there is no 'compulsory arbitration', putting aside treaty compromissory clauses, although it had been proposed when the Permanent Court of Arbitration was formed. It was a militarily powerful Germany which had resisted the notion.[151]

What distinguished inter-State arbitration during the nineteenth century was the application of law and legal reasoning to inter-State disputes, which would then lead to a binding decision.[152] The American jurist, John Bassett Moore, considered international arbitration to be international adjudication in the proper sense.[153] It was distinct from conciliation and mediation. However, following the World War I and the creation of the Permanent Court of International Justice (PCIJ) one might have supposed that inter-State arbitration would surely decline. Tobias Asser's view had been that the PCA was but 'the phantom of a

[147] *Alabama Claims*, *op. cit.*; *see further* Paulsson, 'Alabama Claims' *op. cit.*, 8; citing Manley O. Hudson, *International Tribunals: Past and Future* (Washington, DC: Carnegie, 1944), 5.

[148] However, *see* Chapter 14 in this volume.

[149] Chapter 16 in this volume.

[150] *Ibid.*

[151] Schwebel, *op. cit.*, 2. The ICJ has no jurisdiction unless and to the extent that a State consents to the Court's jurisdiction, for example under Article 36(2) of the Court's Statute or jurisdiction under a treaty compromissory clause. *Ibid.*, 3. And even with optional clause jurisdiction under art. 36(2), in such cases 'states merely accept' the Court's jurisdiction 'in anticipation of their being involved in a dispute'; J. L. Brierly, *The Law of Nations* (Oxford: Clarendon, 1963), 355. *See further* Chapter 15 of this volume.

[152] John Bassett Moore, *International Adjudications: Ancient and Modern* (Oxford: Oxford University Press, 1929), xxxvi–xci.

[153] *Ibid.*

Court'.[154] It certainly was the case that there formed 'a strong sentiment that the newly created court should be preferred'.[155] This was despite notable arbitrations involving both inter-State disputes and the first 'mixed' dispute between an individual and a State.[156] The notable arbitrations included the *Norwegian Shipowners' Claims* arbitration which continued to apply the classical principles governing the protection of foreign-owned property despite early doubt which had been cast on those classical principles following the Mexican and Russian revolutions.[157] Mention could be made too of the *de Sabla Claim*,[158] as well also of the *Island of Palmas* case in which Max Huber's Award contributed not only to our understanding of the principles governing territorial acquisition but also of the doctrine of inter-temporal law.[159]

Mr Schofield points out, in this volume, that following the World War II there was however a revival and that there were some 40 inter-State arbitrations which took place between 1945 and 1990.[160] Today, we can count, amongst the most famous arbitrations in recent years, the *Southern Bluefin Tuna* arbitration,[161] and the deeply controversial *South China Sea* arbitration.[162] At the same time, the PCA continued to be involved in modern investor-State disputes, not least in the *Channel Tunnel* arbitration,[163] *Yukos Universal* v. *Russia*,[164] and *Chevron*

[154] Garth Schofield, Chapter 16 in this volume, quoting Asser.

[155] *Ibid.*

[156] For the latter, *see* Radio Corporation of America v. China, Award, ICGJ 389 (PCA 1935), 13 April 1935. For a brief survey of these disputes, *see* Schwebel, *op. cit.*

[157] Award, 13 October 1922 (PCA).

[158] Marguerite de Joly de Sabla (United States) v. Panama, 29 June 1933, VI RIAA 358.

[159] The Island of Palmas Case (or Miangas) (US v. The Netherlands), Award, 4 April 1928 (PCA); R. Y. Jennings, *The Acquisition of Territory in International Law* (Manchester: MUP, 1963).

[160] *See* Chapter 16 in this volume.

[161] Southern Bluefin Tuna (NZ v. Japan, Australia v. Japan), Award on Jurisdiction and Admissibility, 4 August 2000, XXIII RIAA 1, in which the tribunal found notably that both it and ITLOS lacked jurisdiction since the dispute fell outside the scope of UNCLOS, an argument which was to be revived by Chinese scholars in the aftermath of the more recent *South China Sea* arbitration.

[162] South China Sea Arbitration (Republic of Philippines v. The People's Republic of China), Award, 12 July 2016; Award on Jurisdiction and Admissibility,

[163] Channel Tunnel Group and Another v. UK Secretary for Transport and Another, Partial Award, 30 January 2007, PCA.

[164] Yukos Universal Limited (Isle of Man) v. The Russian Federation, Final Award, 18 July 2014 (UNCITRAL Arbitration Rules).

v. Ecuador.[165] During the latter part of the twentieth century and early twenty-first century, resort to inter-State arbitration has extended to the new developing nations of Africa and Asia. Think of the *Rann of Kutch,*[166] *Kishenganga,*[167] and the earlier-mentioned *South China Sea* arbitrations.

Moore had viewed inter-State arbitration as the central example of 'international adjudication' but its chief characteristics today, with the emergence first of the PCIJ and subsequently of the International Court of Justice, are that as with all arbitrations there is party autonomy, not least in choosing the arbitrators, while at the same time the *lex arbitri* is international law and so too the *lex causae.* Typically, the agreement to arbitrate is treaty based, or contained in an internationalised contract.[168] Ordinarily, there is no procedure to set aside an inter-State award – for the reason that such arbitration is beyond national judicial reach. This is because arbitration in the pursuit of peace relies – rightly or not – on the finality of awards. That is if not the whole point nearly all of it.

Closer inquiry should at least prompt some doubt however about whether inter-State arbitral awards should always be immune from challenge even if any standing remedy for that defect may be harder to discern. If two sovereign States were to arbitrate a commercial dispute – for example, before an ad hoc tribunal – why should there be no room for judicial oversight if there has been fraud? True, the practical hurdles flow from the fact that the dispute has a 'public international' character, unlike how in England arbitration is viewed contractually and is dominated – notwithstanding the enormous contribution of statute – by the law of contract.[169] In inter-State arbitration the agreement to arbitrate is often governed by treaty, or as has been mentioned by public international law

[165] Chevron Corporation and Texaco Petroleum Corporation v. Republic of Ecuador, PCA Case No. 2009-23, pending (UNCITRAL Arbitration Rules).

[166] The Indo-Pakistan Western Boundary (Rann of Kutch) between India and Pakistan (India, Pakistan), 19 February 1968, XVII RIAA 1.

[167] In the Matter of the Indus Waters Kishenganga Arbitration (Pakistan v. India), Final Award, 20 December 2013 (PCA).

[168] Or at least a contract which one side asserts has become internationalised, and that therefore the dispute should be referred to arbitration administered by the Permanent Court of Arbitration. *See e.g.* the 'Water Dispute' between Malaysia and Singapore, Singapore Ministry of Foreign Affairs Press Release. 'Water Issue Is about Sanctity Of Agreements, Not about Price Alone, Says Singapore Foreign Minister Prof S Jayakumar', 25 January 2003.

[169] Mustill and Boyd, *op. cit.*, 32 *et seq* (history), and also 36 (compared to judicial review).

principles even where the dispute centres around contract. In any case, these hurdles express themselves in public law terms; in the doctrine of foreign State immunity under international law and the possible existence of a non-justiciability doctrine under national constitutional laws.

We may be permitted a small detour in order to compare the hybrid case of investment arbitration. This is only to bring the issues into sharper focus. *Occidental v. Ecuador* and *Russia* v. *Yukos Universal et al.* despite having been concerned with investor-State arbitration offer useful illustrations of the potential limits of the public law constraints just mentioned. As with the Hague District Court's 2016 annulment in *Yukos*,[170] it was the respondent State itself in *Occidental* which had initiated annulment proceedings before a national court.[171] In *Occidental*, strangely perhaps it was the private claimant which pleaded non-justiciability. The parties had failed to agree on the place of arbitration and the arbitrators chose London. Occidental won in the arbitration proceedings but it was Ecuador as the sovereign party which sought to have the award set aside in England.

In the case of inter-State arbitration there is however no asymmetry of rights and immunities. The State which seeks to have an award set aside may waive its own immunity but unlike in investor-State arbitration the sovereign party on the other side may and in nearly all cases probably should and will strive to object on grounds of immunity or, as with the claimant in *Occidental*, on the ground of non-justiciability. If immunity is waived the courts of the place of the seat possess jurisdiction on the basis of the usual principles of civil jurisdiction.[172] Thus, the seemingly delocalised nature of arbitration between States arises only by virtue of the fact that the arbitration takes place between two or more co-equal sovereigns whose relationship is often governed by public international law. We should be careful to note that this is not a question of the *lex arbitri* as such. In the example of *BP v. Libya*, discussed earlier, the fact that a

[170] The Russian Federation v. Veteran Petroleum Limited, Yukos Universal Limited and Hulley Enterprises Limited (C/09/477160/HA ZA 15–1, 15–2 and 15–112), District Court of the Hague.

[171] Occidental v. Ecuador, *op. cit.*

[172] For English law, *see* Mustill and Boyd, *op. cit.*, 86 et seq., esp. 87–89. The position for service out now being governed by Part 6, Section IV of the Civil Procedure Rules, *see* Adrian Briggs, *Civil Jurisdiction and Judgments*, 6th ed. (London: Informa, 2015), para. 4.59.

sovereign State is involved in arbitration did not mean that the procedural law of the arbitration was international law. Similarly, there is no reason to suppose that in the case of an arbitration between two States the *lex arbitri* should always be international law rather than some domestic law.[173]

It might be said that in inter-sovereign disputes high matters of State are implicated. That is probably an exaggeration. It may be so but only in degree not type. Imagine a disagreement leading to a dispute between a sovereign State and some part of it which it is decided should be submitted to international arbitration. Will the stakes be less high? In the *Abyei* arbitration two decades of civil war had led to a peace agreement and the creation of a boundary commission which had produced a report.[174] This led to further hostilities and ultimately to an agreement to submit a dispute over whether the commission exceeded its mandate to arbitration.[175] One can imagine that typically a sovereign State in an 'intra-sovereign' matter would if it only could prefer the seat of the arbitration to be located within it. But even if that were to prove impossible, can it then turn around and claim that the form of arbitration which it would have preferred would not only be 'international arbitration' but also of the 'delocalised' variety in the sense of being beyond the reach of any national judicial supervision? Whether the courts of the place of the arbitration would review the award is a separate question altogether. If anything, it would be the non-sovereign party which would wish for 'international' arbitration, but not necessarily in the delocalised sense just mentioned.

The problem is real. In the *Croatia–Slovenia* arbitration which had concerned the maritime border along the Bay of Savudrija/Piran, improper communications between Slovenia and its party-appointed arbitrator led Croatia to seek to terminate the proceedings. Croatia argued that the arbitration agreement was invalid and sought its rescission under Article 60 of the Vienna Convention on the Law of Treaties. The tribunal responded by citing the *kompetenz-kompetenz* rule under the PCA's Optional Rules. Rejecting the Croatian challenge, the tribunal reasoned that if accepted such challenges would undermine treaty compromissory

[173] Under which immunity may not apply. For example, under a restrictive theory of sovereign immunity. *See further e.g.* C. L. Lim, 'Worldwide Litigation over Foreign Sovereign Assets', (2016) 10 *Disp Res'n Int'l* 145 for a discussion of comparative regimes.

[174] *See* Chapter 14 in this volume.

[175] *See further* Vaughan Lowe and Antonios Tzanakopoulos, 'Introduction: The Abyei Arbitration', in *The Abyei Arbitration (The Government of Sudan/The Sudan People's Liberation Movement/Army) Final Award of 2009* (The Hague: PCA, 2012), 1.

clauses.[176] Rather than invalidate the arbitration agreement, the proceedings in *Croatia–Slovenia* were commenced afresh instead with a replacement arbitrator.[177] Croatia rejected the award and, recently, the People's Republic of China reacted in a similar way in the *South China Sea* arbitration for different reasons. Admittedly, in such situations there is minority State practice of resort to auto-interpretation in rejecting awards, but is there not a better way?

The general unavailability of a review on the merits often is viewed as part of the quest for finality. However, Brierly considered this to have been a gap in the law.[178] Such a view of the importance of award finality under the PCA's Optional Rules – as the late Shabtai Rosenne once explained – had been inspired by the UNCITRAL Model Law. Yet practical solutions need not lead to judicial oversight of inter-State arbitration. They include an altogether new arbitration in the sort of situation we find in the *Croatia–Slovenia* and *South China Sea* arbitrations. In the *South China Sea* arbitration one can at least imagine a further arbitration on the question of whether the tribunal had exceeded its jurisdiction. This in many ways was what happened in *Abyei* when a dispute over the boundary commission's report led subsequently to arbitration.[179] There is also the possibility of having recourse to the International Court of Justice, should consent to the Court's jurisdiction be established.[180] The analogies above may be inexact but international lawyers have too long prized finality while in recent times the rejection of awards has become commonplace and a minority practice of auto-interpretation by disenchanted parties continues to grow.

1.6 The Cambridge Companion to International Arbitration

During the twentieth century, the great arbitration instruments – the New York Convention of 1958, the UNCITRAL Rules of 1976, the UNCITRAL

[176] Croatia v. Slovenia, PCA Case Repository 2012-04, Partial Award, P 16 (Perm. Ct. Arb. 30 June 2016), 37–41.

[177] *See* Matko Ilic, 'Croatia v. Slovenia: The Defiled Proceedings' (2017) 9 *Arb L Rev* 347.

[178] 'Or rather in the machinery for applying the law'; Brierly, *op. cit.*, 351. *See however e.g.* Arbitral Award of 31 July 1989 (Guinea-Bissau v. Senegal) 1991 I.C.J. 53 (12 November).

[179] See Lowe and Tzanakopoulos, 'Introduction', *op. cit.*

[180] *See e.g.* Arbitral Award of 31 July 1989 (Guinea-Bissau v. Senegal) 1991 I.C.J. 53 (12 November). *See further* J. G. Merrills, *International Dispute Settlement*, 5th ed, (Cambridge, Cambridge University Press, 2011), 100–106; also Chapter 15 of this volume.

Model Law of 1985 (and subsequent iterations) which grew out of the context of international commercial arbitration – as well as the 1965 ICSID Convention, NAFTA Chapter 11, the Energy Charter treaty and the explosion in BITs when viewed together with the persistence of Moore's international adjudication by arbitral tribunals secured the system which we have. It is a system of arbitration between individuals, between individuals and States and between as well as within sovereign States.

The present *Cambridge Companion* volume aims to bring these diverse forms together in a single discussion, paying particular attention to their separate histories, their essential framework and key concepts, and the similarities as well as the differences between the different forms.

Three sections follow, containing chapters which introduce and discuss key aspects of international commercial arbitration (Part II), international investment arbitration (Part III), and sovereign inter-State as well as intra-State arbitration (Part IV), before concluding (in Part V) with a discussion of current issues which often are cross-cutting. Before that, however, this part (Part I) continues with Professor Garth's chapter, giving the reader a sense of how the arbitration profession locates itself in legal practice and the sociological factors which have shaped commercial arbitration as a transnational legal practice.

It is followed by the opening chapter in Part II by Singapore's Professor Bell of international commercial arbitration's close proximity with the practice and academic field of comparative law. There follows a chapter by Professor Adrian Briggs QC of international commercial arbitration's connections with private international law reasoning and techniques. This chapter raises fundamental questions about choice of law and the submission of arbitration to national jurisdictional authority, topics which also receive treatment in Professor Cordero-Moss' chapter on the *lex arbitri* and the procedural law of the seat of the arbitration, not least its role and the place of its conflict of laws rules. Her aim is to explore the part played by national jurisdictional authority from the determination of the formal validity of the arbitration agreement to the law governing matters of procedural irregularity, the composition of the tribunal and the rules on the annulment of awards. Two subsequent chapters offer a wider lens – Professor Michaels revisits the conceptual debate over delocalisation and as with all three sections there is a chapter at the end of this section, by Professor George Bermann, who looks to the future.

In Part III, Professor Jan Paulsson introduces international investment arbitration in light of current developments. Professor M. Sornarajah then addresses a significant aspect of practice, namely the routine – near-automatic – challenge to the jurisdiction of the tribunal in investment treaty arbitration. Professor Bjorklund deals with the very complex issue of the applicable law in investment arbitration. The overall function of that chapter in this book mirrors the treatment of the place of private international law rules and the role of the *lex arbitri* (which includes the supply of choice of law rules) in the previous section on international commercial arbitration. This area is only deceptively simple as one might often hear, in investment treaty arbitration, that a bilateral investment treaty (BIT) supplies the substantive law. But imagine a treaty umbrella clause in the BIT. Non-payment under the underlying contract may amount to a treaty breach but are damages to be assessed under treaty law too?[181] Two further chapters ensue. The chapter by Drs Elias and McInerney on the historic role of the World Bank, followed by a chapter by Ms. Kinnear whom everyone in practice in the field knows, and Ms Arguello, on ICSID arbitration today. A contribution by Professor Reisman brings up the rear by reproducing his well-known speech on the future of investment arbitration.

In Part IV's opening chapter, Judge Sir Christopher Greenwood QC offers a thoughtful introduction to inter-State arbitration, arguing that we sometimes read its contribution too narrowly perhaps by confining ourselves only to the prevention of war. There follows Mr Garth Schofield's chapter on the history and work of the Permanent Court of Arbitration. That work is not limited to the settlement of inter-State disputes and investor-State disputes but includes, as he shows in his discussion of the *Abyei* arbitration, intra-State arbitration. This last is a variant which does not always, as

[181] Under the principles of English law, for example, questions pertaining to heads of damages are considered substantive and therefore governed by the *lex causae* or the proper law of the contract while the quantification or assessment of damages is procedural and therefore to be governed by the *lex fori*; Boys v. Chaplin [1971] AC 356 (HL). In SGS v. Philippines, ICSID Case No. ARB/02/6, Decision on Jurisdiction, 29 January 2004, para. 127, the tribunal considered the question of damages assessment to be governed by contract, while a treaty breach would be governed by the treaty. In El Paso Energy International Co. v. Argentina, ICSID Case No. ARB/03/15, Decision on Objection to Jurisdiction, 27 April 2006, the tribunal referred to the governance of damages assessment by the 'national law' of the contract, para. 76. For these awards, *see* Lim, Ho and Paparinskis, *International Investment Law and Arbitration, op. cit.*, 357, 363.

I have said, fit neatly into our usual categories. In some instances it may not even amount to international arbitration at all. Professor Maurice Mendelson QC concludes the section with his discussion of the advantages and disadvantages of inter-State arbitration at the present time, accompanied by a discussion of the problem of consent and procedural issues.

Finally, Part V addresses a range of current issues which cut across the different forms of international arbitration just mentioned. Mr Christopher Tahbaz and Ms Natalie Reid discuss professional responsibilities and arbitrator conflicts, Mr Florian Haugeneder addresses how tribunals handle and should handle corruption. Both topics are at the forefront of contemporary discussion. Criticism of the small pool of arbitrators, repeat appointments and double-hatting are part and parcel of the backlash against investment arbitration while there are grumblings that States may furnish a defence of corruption too easily, or worse tolerate corruption with a view to having a ready defence to a future claim. Mr Matthew Hodgson, writing with Ms Jae Hee Suh, then discuss the methods and growing regulation in respect of the financing of arbitration claims today, and the comparative rules and current practice regarding the award of costs. Just as importantly, they address as well related issues, including the tribunal's role in modern costs management.

The editor's final chapter explores the current trend towards greater judicialisation. Where is international arbitration amidst new ideas? Where today we have a proposal for a Multilateral Investment Court[182] and the proliferation of new international commercial courts from Europe to Dubai, Singapore and China?[183] This is a question to which the following chapters in this *Cambridge Companion* seek also to answer.

[182] If there should be any need to declare any potential scholarly conflict it is so declared (on account of the editor's participation in these discussions at UNCITRAL WG III as the representative of an observer entity).

[183] *See* Chapter 20 of this volume.

2 Dealing in Virtue

A Perspective from Almost 25 Years Later

Bryant G. Garth

2.1 Introduction

Dealing in Virtue, which Yves Dezalay and I published in 1996,[1] was an effort to understand the origins of international commercial arbitration, its rise to become the default dispute resolution process for transnational disputes, how the arbitrators gained their positions and earned the legitimacy to be selected in high-stakes disputes, and how the rise of international commercial arbitration affected dispute resolution within national States. We interviewed some 400 members of the international commercial arbitration community. One of the most noted findings was that there was a tension between what we termed the "grand old men" of international commercial arbitration and a group of arbitration technocrats who both challenged them and preserved and defended their world. The grand old men were senior arbitrators who had made their careers in academia or practice or in the judiciary, arbitrated part-time (at least until the boom in arbitration in the 1980s), and in Weberian terms told to us in an interview of a technocrat, relied on their charisma for legitimacy. The technocrats, many of them trained by the grand old men, grew up in international commercial arbitration, did it full time, saw it as a career, and believed legitimacy depended on the technical quality of the proceeding and the decisions. The large law firms tended to get behind the technocrats, but they recognized that in major disputes they needed the grand old men. There were of course few women and there were few arbitrators from outside of the developed Western world.

The book, perhaps surprisingly, has continued to attract interest from the arbitration community. One reason is the growth and controversial nature of

[1] Yves Dezalay and Bryant G. Garth, *Dealing in Virtue: International Commercial Arbitration and the Construction of a Transnational Legal Order* (Chicago: University of Chicago Press, 1996) (herinafter *Dealing in Virtue*).

international investment arbitration, which was not a major phenomenon at the time that we wrote. Much of the recent interest in the book relates to this sense of crisis in international investment arbitration. Recent examples of current interest include a podcast in May[2] and an edited book dedicated to a leading arbitrator, Charles Brower, published in 2015 entitled *Practicing Virtue,*[3] explicitly taking the title from our book. The book contains an article, drawing on *Dealing in Virtue,* on the "Sociology of International Commercial Arbitration" by a leading arbitrator, Emmanuel Gaillard.[4] Also notable is a scholarly article authored by Florian Grisel, published in 2017 in the *Law and Society Review*, and entitled "Competition and Cooperation In International Commercial Arbitration: The Birth of Transnational Legal Profession."[5] The latter article sought to correct the book's overemphasis, according to the author, on conflict rather than the cooperation at the center of the arbitral community.

This chapter will first revisit the origins of international commercial arbitration on the basis of work we completed in 2016.[6] This work shows how some of the early credibility of international commercial arbitration came from leading public international law scholars who invested in building scholarship around this topic. Second, taking a cue from Grisel's critical Article, I will revisit the "conflict versus cooperation" issue as a key to understanding arbitration and the themes of the book. The simplified reading is that the technocrats took on the grand old men and won. The story is more complicated and charisma is far from eliminated from the field. Third, I will discuss some of the questions of legitimacy that are discussed mainly about investment arbitration – namely, the diversity of the field of arbitrators in terms of race, gender, and national origin on the

[2] On the Arbitration Station, *see* www.thearbitrationstation.com/.

[3] David D. Caron, Stephan W. Schill, Abby Cohen Smutny and Epaminontas E. Triantafilou (eds.), *Practising Virtue: Inside International Arbitration* (Oxford: Oxford University Press, 2015) (herinafter *Practising Virtue).*

[4] Emmanuel Gaillard, "Sociology of International Arbitration" in David D. Caron, Stephan W. Schill, Abby Cohen Smutny and Epaminontas E. Triantafilou (eds.), *Practising Virtue: Inside International Arbitration* (Oxford: Oxford University Press, 2015), 189–201.

[5] Florian Grisel, "Competition and Cooperation in International Commercial Arbitration: The Birth of Transnational Legal Profession" (2017) 51 *Law and Society Review* 790.

[6] Yves Dezalay and Bryant G. Garth, "Constructing a Transatlantic Marketplace of Disputes on the Symbolic Foundations of International Justice" in Gregoire Mallaard and Jerome Sgard (eds.), *Contractual Knowledge: One Hundred Years of Legal experimentation in Global Markets* (Cambridge: Cambridge University Press, 2016) (hereinafter Constructing a Transatlantic Marketplace).

one hand, and a supposed too close connection to business as opposed to States in international investment arbitration.[7] Fourth, I will suggest some movement to refurbish the field in relation to these criticisms. Finally, in view of the political climate around trade and investment today, I will mention some of the speculations of the last chapter of the book, which are rarely mentioned.

2.2 Reexamining the Development of International Commercial Arbitration

First, to revisit the history,[8] the early twentieth-century movement to establish arbitration domestically and internationally was promoted by the leaders of the US Chambers of Commerce, and especially the Chamber of Commerce of New York. It led to the creation in Paris of an International Chamber of Commerce.[9] In order to build credibility, these entrepreneurs sought to draw on the prestige and visibility of projects seeking to promote international arbitration as a means for handling interstate conflicts. Those projects were highly visible and popular at that time. The advocates of commercial arbitration contended that this merchant justice would contribute to international peace in the same manner as the Permanent Court of Arbitration. They called themselves "Merchants of Peace."[10] They were strongly behind the establishment of the International Chamber of Commerce in 1920 in Paris with its aspirations to promote international commercial arbitration.

Even before World War II, there was learned investment in international commercial arbitration from the international law community. We see this investment in a number of lectures at The Hague Academy of International Law. The lectures came mainly from a group of emigrants and Jews

[7] Based in part on Bryant G. Garth, "One Window into the State of Insiders' Arbitration Scholarship: A Review of Practising Virtue: Inside International Arbitration" (2017) 19 *Journal of World Investment and Trade* 155; Bryant G. Garth "Transnational Arbitral Community" in *Max Planck Encyclopedia of International Procedural Law [MPEiPro]* (Oxford: Oxford University Press, 2019).

[8] Drawing on Constructing a Transatlantic Marketplace; Garth, *supra* note 7 (2019).

[9] Imre Szalai, *Outsourcing Justice: The Rise of Modern Arbitration Laws in America* (Carolina Academic Press, 2013); Constructing a Transatlantic Marketplace.

[10] George L. Ridgeway, *Merchants of Peace* (Boston: Little Brown, 1959).

producing scholarly works that opened the way for commercial arbitration to be adopted by the mainstream. The names included Frédéric Eisemann, Charles Carabiber, Bertold Goldman, Martin Domke, Arthur Nussbaum, René David, and Hersch Lauterpacht.[11] They produced much of the work that could then be used to bring international commercial arbitration into the mainstream. Other scholars in the 1950s, also in lectures at the Hague, examined related issues. In 1958, F. Munch, for example, wrote on the effect of foreign nationalizations.[12] The Rt. Honorable Lord Shawcross, a barrister who served as chief prosecutor for the British at Nuremburg, delivered a lecture at the Hague on the problems of foreign investment in international law.[13] There were connections to the ICC as well. Charles Carabiber, who lectured on the evolution of international commercial arbitration in 1950 (1950), was originally from Istanbul, studied there and in Paris, became a professor and an avocat at the Cour d'Appel in Paris, advised the Iranian government, and also became the President of the Court of Arbitration of the ICC.

When the ICC took the lead in seeking to advance international commercial arbitration with a convention on the enforcement of awards, which became the New York Convention of 1958, academics also were strongly present in the negotiations – including Pieter Sanders, a lawyer, diplomat, and professor; Mario Matteucci, a professor and the director of the League of Nations Institute for the Unification of Private Law in Rome; Benjamin Wortley, a Professor of Commercial Law in Manchester, England; Conseiller d'Etat Georges Holleaux, a prominent French academic; René Arnaud, the co-founder of the ICC in 1918; and others, including Martin Domke of the American Arbitration Association.[14]

Domke was the major promoter of international commercial arbitration within the American Arbitration Association (AAA) in the United States until his retirement in 1967. He was a German-trained lawyer who

[11] *See* Jerome Sgard, "A Tale of Three Cities: The Construction of International Commercial Arbitration" in Gregoire Mallaard and Jerome Sgard (eds.), *Contractual Knowledge: One Hundred Years of Legal experimentation in Global Markets* (Cambridge: Cambridge University Press, 2016) for profiles.

[12] F. Münch, F., "Les effets d'une nationalisation à l'étranger" (1959) 98 *Recueil des Cours* 411.

[13] Lord H. W. Shawcross, "The Problems of Foreign Investment in International Law" (1961) 102 *Recueil des Cours* 335.

[14] Ottarndt Glossner, "From New York (1958) to Geneva (1961) – A Veteran's Diary" in *The New York Convention: Experience and Future* (New York, United Nations, 1999).

went to the United States in 1943 and began a long career with the AAA as Vice-President.[15] Domke wrote much on domestic US arbitration, but he also sought to build up the prestige of AAA arbitration by linking arbitration to international law professors and international commercial arbitration associated with the ICC. The US arbitration movement, which had close ties to the business community, built a strong alliance with European law professors to promote international commercial arbitration. The success of the New York Convention in 1958, which considerably enhanced the enforceability of international commercial arbitration, was a product of this alliance.

The transnational arbitration community at that time, as indicated by the preceding paragraphs, included a group of "hobbyists" at the ICC and in other places such as the AAA in New York. They handled a few arbitrations likely of relatively low stakes.[16] The group included notables and prominent professors, but it also included a number of emigres on the margins of national legal professions. Still, the ICC was hardly more than a virtual institution. The workload was very light until the 1980s. There were 3,000 requests for arbitration between 1923 and 1976 and then 7,000 more between 1976 and 1998.[17] The question is what led from this group to the flourishing of international commercial arbitration in the 1980s and beyond.

The take-off period in the late 1970s and 1980s is often described as a globalization of business investment and trade that required means of resolving disputes. The work of the hobbyists at the ICC is thus seen as effectively meeting that demand.[18] The hobbyists, from this perspective, borrowed from different systems to create a hybrid mechanism of transnational private justice that gained a consensus as the best way to resolve transnational business disputes.[19] The demand met an efficient means of supply.

Another way to look at the take-off period, a theme of *Dealing in Virtue*, is that it required a kind of legitimacy that was not taken for

[15] Pieter Sanders (ed.), *International Arbitration: Liber Amicorum for Martin Domke* (The Hague: Martinus Nijhoff, 1967).

[16] Grisel, *supra* note 5.

[17] W. Lawrence Craig, William W. Park and Jan Paulson, *International Chamber of Commerce Arbitration*, 3rd ed. (New York: Oceana, 2000), 2.

[18] Sgard, *supra* note 11; Grisel, *supra* note 5.

[19] *Id.*

granted in the 1970s. The demand requires a belief that what arbitration had to offer was right for large corporations. Thomas Hale in his recent book *Between Interests and Law* supports this perspective.[20] He observes that the success of international commercial arbitration required both an "arbitration epistemic community" – the hobbyists from our point of view – and the recognition that the relevant powerful "interests" would be served by the field. From this perspective, a key was the period of the battles for the control of oil production in the period after World War II.[21] The events included nationalizations of a number of the concessions of the Seven Sisters oil companies. The long-standing concession agreements entered into between the oil companies and the oil-producing States – most of which dated from the time of the League of Nations and its mandates – contained arbitration clauses that could be invoked. The clauses were inserted in the interwar period because of the perceived legitimacy of State-State arbitration and the role of international law experts (including those who lectured at the Hague) who consulted with the large oil companies.[22]

In the 1970s, in particular, the oil companies chose to invoke the arbitration clauses as one additional option to fight the battle over the appropriation of economic profits.[23] The main focus, as any history of the oil industry makes clear, was on diplomatic means.[24] Partly because it was a sideshow, the arbitration lawyers on both sides were able to take control of the proceedings and treat the legal disputes as epic legal battles involving grand legal principles exemplified in the Hague lectures. The result was a series of closely reasoned arbitral opinions by notable authorities that have long been the staple of international law courses. They had virtually no practical impact at the time, but that lack of practical impact allowed the field initially to develop. Those with key positions in the cases gained stature and credibility, and the combination of factors jumpstarted this transnational legal field and put it into a perfect position to take advantage of the disputes that then emerged in the 1970s and 1980s as

[20] Thomas Hale, *Between Interests and Law* (Cambridge: Cambridge University Press, 2015).

[21] *Dealing in Virtue.*

[22] Elihu Lauterpacht, *The Life of Hersch Lauterpacht* (Cambridge: Cambridge University Press, 2012).

[23] *Dealing in Virtue.*

[24] Daniel Yergin, *The Prize: The Epic Quest for Oil, Money, and Power* (New York: Simon and Schuster, 1990).

petrodollars and Eurodollars were invested in major infrastructure projects leading to high-stakes arbitrations.

The oil crises, in short, provided the initial funding and credibility to a group of self-proclaimed amateurs and hobbyists who then became the backbone of the international commercial arbitration industry in the 1980s. It also brought lawyers from leading US and British law firms who participated in the arbitrations into the arbitration world and made them receptive to the expansion of this form of dispute resolution in the interests of their clients.[25] These arbitrations enhanced the credibility of European law and the European law professors linked to the ICC. They made it clear that the *lex mercatoria* – one of their major intellectual products – was not inconsistent with the interests of multinational corporations[26] but that there was also a certain autonomy that could be emphasized by professors in the south and others anxious to participate in this field.

The new prosperity of international commercial arbitration thus came with a group of members of the inner circle of commercial arbitration. First, there were the hobbyists who played the leading role in and around the ICC until that point. Next were notable European academics including especially those who had been involved in the petroleum arbitrations, including individuals such as Pierre Lalive of Geneva. Others connected to the arbitrations, including a few Western-educated academics from developing countries, exemplified by Ahmed El-Kosheri of Egypt,[27] were also prominent. And a group of US law firms, mostly those headquartered in Paris and many of whom were connected to the petroleum arbitrations, became important at the same time.

The alliance between European academics and US corporate lawyers is a key to the success of the field, combining legal theory from Europe and the resources and connections to multinational clients of the law firms.[28] The core of the transnational arbitration community is made up out of these groups. An early expansion – spurred by a combination of US law firms seeking to create a competitor to the ICC and British enthusiasts anxious to

[25] *Dealing in Virtue.*

[26] Hale, *supra* note 20.

[27] *See* A. S. El-Kosheri, "Le régime juridique créé par les accords de participation dans le domaine pétrolier" (1975) 147 *Recueil des Cours* 219.

[28] Constructing a Transatlantic Marketplace.

become part of the growing market as arbitrators and lawyers – came with the reform of the London Court of International Arbitration in 1985–1986. From the position of strength, the transnational arbitration community began to expand out of its initial European–US core.

Through a process involving transnational networks, local conferences introducing international arbitration, and cooptation of local elites, the field of international commercial arbitration gained institutionalization in places where arbitration had been marginal or rejected, including Latin America[29] and China.[30] The key role of local notables in this expansion relates to the need to gain legislation and judicial deference to international arbitration – taking potential disputes from the domestic courts. As Hale points out, elite legal professionals were essential to persuade their governments and legal professions that arbitration is legitimate and in the interests of the country and its lawyers and judges.

One indicator of a self-consciousness of the process is the global movement of the International Council for Commercial Arbitration's (ICCA) major conferences. ICCA, the major international group for commercial arbitration, moved from New Delhi in 2000 to London in 2002, Beijing in 2004, Montreal in 2006, Dublin in 2008, Rio de Janeiro in 2010, Singapore in 2012, Miami in 2014, and Mauritius in 2016.

As discussed below, the local notables in turn invest in the legal capital connected to international commercial arbitration as a condition of entry, reinforcing the core while extending the field to new terrains. Those at the periphery helped therefore to provide the local legitimacy for the inner group of the arbitration community to handle the largest and most important disputes.[31] The local notables gained a place, but the terms of exchange were quite unequal. First, the number of places at the main table for those in the periphery remains relatively small, even if the number has grown for places that are considered central to the future of international commercial arbitration, such as China. Furthermore, those at the periphery seeking entrance into the transnational arbitration community have had to erase much of their local identity to be taken seriously as neutrals, while those at the core benefited by the presumption of neutrality – in the sense, for

[29] Hale, *supra* note 20, at 299–309 (on Argentina networks)

[30] *Id.* at 348–349.

[31] Won Kidane, *The Culture of International Arbitration* (Oxford: Oxford University Press, 2017).

example, of not being deemed to be hostile to multinationals or too sympathetic to developing countries.

2.3 Conflict versus Consensus

One school of thought, recently articulated by Grisel, insists on a story of harmony and consensus as the key to the history of international commercial arbitration. The argument, as noted above, is that the transnational arbitration community, centered in the ICC in Paris and dominated by relatively marginal individuals bridging legal cultures, "cherry picked"[32] from different systems in the 1950s and earlier to create a successful "hybrid" process acceptable to all nationalities, governed by a set of "general principles of law" known as the lex mercatoria. The process then gradually legalized to satisfy the "demand" that came from growing sophistication and higher stakes.[33] The hybrid procedures and legalization led to the acquisition of "legitimacy at the transnational level."[34] People aspiring to be arbitrators necessarily "mimick[ed] features that brought success."[35] This is a story of creating a neutral institution that met an emerging demand.

Grisel contrasts his approach with our work,[36] which, he suggests, promotes a story of conflict. It "emphasized incompatibilities between systems, tensions that they produced what they portray as a zero-sum competition between two types of practitioners, which the common law technocrats won, and the grand old men of the civil law lost, in the 1980s and 1990s."[37] He states also that the our work stresses the result of this victory was the technocrats becoming "the prevailing elite" who drove the "judicialization" of international commercial arbitration.[38] This story is one reading that people have made of our book. Grisel wants instead to emphasize the harmony of the field. The emphasis on harmony, to be sure, is consistent with the self-identity of the elite of the arbitration

[32] Grisel, *supra* note 5, at 810.
[33] *Id.* at 808.
[34] *Id.* at 819.
[35] *Id.* at 812.
[36] *Dealing in Virtue.*
[37] Grisel, *supra* note 5, at 793.
[38] *Id.*

community. His study of the characteristics of a group of 25 leaders of the that community confirms that "all come from or live in the developed world, roughly all are the same age [around 61], and they generally have elite educational backgrounds" – with eight having degrees from Oxford, Cambridge, Harvard, or Yale.[39] The explanation is that all achieved their status by following their predecessors – "combining various professional strands: an affiliation with a bar, a significant display of academic activities, and strong connections to arbitral institutions."[40] It is a matter of getting the right credentials open to all: "They have consciously designed their cosmopolitan journey to build transnational legitimacy."[41] In other words, they did what it takes on the merits to gain entry into the cosmopolitan world. That world is open, legitimate, legalized, and therefore well suited for international commercial arbitration and investment arbitration.

The more sociological perspective that we employ would look more both at the rules of the game of the field of international commercial arbitration and how they relate to the people who occupy the field. First, the rules of the game inevitably reflect global power arrangements. As Hale argued (2015), the rise of international commercial arbitration depended not only on an epistemic community agreeing on the virtues of arbitration but also on the ability of the institution to serve prevailing hierarchies of power – generally, at the outset, favoring multinational corporations from the major industrial world over the interests of developing countries. In Hale's words, "Dispute institutions (be they domestic, intergovernmental, or transnational) have almost never run against the interests of dominant economic groups. When they have, interest groups and States have mobilized to counter them."[42] As with respect to law generally, international commercial arbitration can be both independent in any given case and generally serve the interests of the large corporations.[43] The success of international commercial arbitration in gaining legitimacy relates to both aspects.

In terms of the people who decide, the tilt of the rules of the game toward prevailing power arrangements is reflected in a core and periphery,

[39] *Id.* at 814.
[40] *Id.*
[41] *Id.*
[42] Hale, *supra* note 20, 11.
[43] On being of two minds, *see* Robert Lerner, *Ernst Kantorowicz: A Life* (Princeton: Princeton University Press, 2017).

noted in fact by the makeup of the elite educational backgrounds of the core members of the community. They come disproportionately from the Western industrialized nations and the elite schools of those nations. They have ties with those already in the community through mentorship, old school ties, and links to the ICC, the LCIA, and the corporate law firms who handle the major arbitrations. They publish in the major journals of the field and cite to each other.

They are cosmopolitan, to be sure, but it is a cosmopolitanism that connotes comfort in the world's financial capitals and elite universities. The neutrality essential to gain entry is to be contrasted with too much of an orientation toward developing countries or even states generally within investment arbitration. Those from the elite schools of the Western industrial countries are almost by definition neutral and acceptable, while it takes extra work for an outsider to demonstrate the credentials and the neutrality that is essential to gain stature in the arbitration community. From the perspective of the insiders, there is a consensus and a kind of harmony because all respect the general rules of the game. From a more sociological perspective, however, the forms of capital that are valued in international commercial arbitration are consistent with an elite and a periphery sustaining the basic norms and status of international commercial arbitration.

The rules of the game and the related composition of the transnational arbitration community, however, do not stand still. First, there is geographical spread, led by local legal networks.[44] There is a process of absorption and change as the community gains ground in, for notable examples, China and Latin America. Local elites, typically fortified with relatively cosmopolitan connections, are invited in or seek entry. Successful entry typically leads to more openness to local practices, such as more mediation in Chinese arbitration.[45] But the entry depends on recognizing the core of international commercial arbitration and also the hierarchies of the insiders who embody that core. The process of incorporation is a hierarchical one with a core and periphery. At the same time, the

[44] Hale, *supra* note 20.

[45] Kun Fan, "'Glocalization' of International Arbitration: Transnational Standards Struggling with Local Norms" (2013) 18 *Harvard Negotiation Law Review* 175; Kun Fan, "'Glocalization' of International Arbitration: Rethinking about Tradition-Modernity and East-West Binaries" (2016) 11 *University of Pennsylvania East Asia Law Review* 244.

opening to new groups, even if respecting the core norms of the arbitration community, allows it to evolve slowly to accept practices and perspectives that might have been outside. It provides a way also to recognize changing global power dynamics, such as the rise of the emerging markets especially of China, India and Brazil.

The processes of expanding the domain of international commercial arbitration can be described as a matter of consensus or a matter of conflict. The formula for change can be described relatively simply. Those who want to get into the field or strengthen their position argue that in order for the transnational arbitration community to be more legitimate, it requires more arbitrators aware of the perspective from, for example, China. The criticism might be strong, but it comes with a general acceptance of the basic rules of the game. This process is not just about geographical expansion but also about change and maintenance. I shall provide several examples later in this essay.

Scholarly writing is a key part of the process of change more generally. There is a kind of scholarly formula that reaffirms the field while suggesting moderate change. Such writings defend the core and at the same time argue that expanding the profile of arbitrators will enhance the credibility and legitimacy of the field. The historical success of the field, indeed, comes from this kind of advocacy. It brings in new persons and perspectives without challenging the core of the field – and the leading position of the notable arbitrators found within that core. It is also, however, competition over the rules of the game of the field. More precisely, the scholarship seeks to promote both the individual author, what he or she represents in the field, and the field itself.

One example comes from the book on arbitration entitled *Practicing Virtue.*[46] Sundaresh Menon, the Chief Justice of the Supreme Court of Singapore, provides a detailed examination of problems with the regimes of international private governance, including the fact that "the arbitration industry is dominated by insiders who tend on the whole to be reasonably comfortable with the status quo."[47] It also embraces the core of the field:

[46] *Practising Virtue.*

[47] Sundaresh Menon, "The Transnational Protection of Private Rights: Issues, Challenges, and Possible Solutions" in David D. Caron, Stephan W. Schill, Abby Cohen Smutny and Epaminontas E. Triantafilou (eds.), *Practising Virtue: Inside International Arbitration* (Oxford: Oxford University Press, 2015), 17, 38.

"investor-state arbitration, despite some signs of a backlash, remains the best available method for the protection of private investments from the acts of a foreign host state."[48] The question is then what might be done to make it better. Among other suggestions, the author notes, "there is a perceived lack of representation among arbitrators from developing countries, including from Asia,"[49] and that it "might be time to recognize that courts have a potential significant role to play in the resolution of commercial disputes, alongside arbitration."[50] The author, as noted above, is Chief Justice of the Supreme Court of Singapore, where there is also a new International Commercial Court. Put simply, what the author represents, he suggests, will help promote and legitimize the field. Menon's article can be deemed a story of conflict or consensus, but the main point is to see how the challenges lead to the evolution of the institution.

2.4 Potential Lags in the Evolutionary Process

The evolution is not always smooth. There is a crisis today especially in investment arbitration which relates to how this evolution is taking place. The issue of the representativeness of arbitrators is one issue. It is not new but the focus on gender especially is now more pronounced. The dominance of representation from Europe and North America is almost built into the system, but it has changed slowly. The issue of representation especially of women has become prominent recently.[51] The increase in the number of investment arbitrations has allowed systematic study of who the arbitrators are in investment arbitrations. Sergio Puig pioneered in network analyses of the data from the International Convention for the Settlement of Investment Disputes (ICSID) administered through the World Bank. Puig found "419 different arbitrators sat on ICSID tribunals and ad hoc Committees during the analyzed period. However, more than half of the individuals were appointed only to a single proceeding. More extreme,

48 *Id.* at 35.
49 *Id.* at 31.
50 *Id.* at 35.
51 Catherine Rogers, "The Key to Unlocking the Arbitrator Diversity Paradox?: Arbitrator Intelligence" (2017) 27 *Arbitrator Intelligence*; Lucy Greenwood and C. Mark Baker, "Is the Balance Getting Better? An Update on the Issue of Gender Diversity in International Arbitration" (2015) 31 *Arbitration International* 413.

a total 10% of the total pool accounts for half of the appointments."[52] Looking in more detail at the core of elite arbitrators in the ICSID disputes, Puig further noted:

> The size of the core of the arbitration network is small. What stands out, however, is that around 93% of all the appointments are to male arbitrators, suggesting an extreme gender imbalance. It gets even worse: only two women, Professors Brigitte Stern and Gabrielle Kaufmann-Kohler combined, held three-fourths of all female appointments, pushing the male-female composition of arbitrators in the network to an embarrassing 95%–5% ratio.
>
> In terms of nationality, the imbalance is also clear. While 87 nationalities are represented among the appointees, most arbitrators are from specific developed countries. Individuals of seven nations (New Zealand, Australia, Canada, Switzerland, France, the United Kingdom, and the United States) represent almost half of total appointments.[53]

One point that Puig underscores is that a small number of developed countries produce most of the arbitrators. A second point is confirmation that those who appoint arbitrators have a penchant for playing it safe – going for the tried and true.[54] As a result, the best known arbitrators get a good portion of the new business. Puig finds that there are roughly 25 "power brokers" at the center.

A recent expansion of Puig's work[55] by Langford, Behn, and Lie expands the data set in two directions.[56] First, they have a larger data set that includes more than just the ICSID investment arbitrations. Second, they focus not only on arbitrators, but also on legal counsel, expert witnesses, and secretaries. They also find a top 25 that, while accounting for just 4 percent of all arbitral appointments, is represented in more than a third of the investment arbitrations.[57] There are some differences, but the list is very close to that of Puig.[58] The demographics are the same: predominantly male from developed Western countries. Considering

52 Sergio Puig, "Social Capital in the Arbitration Market" (2014) 25 *European Journal of International Law* 387.

53 *Id.*

54 *Id.*

55 Malcolm Langford, Daniel Behn, and Runar Lie, "The Revolving Door in International Investment Arbitration" (2017) 20 *Journal of International Economic Law* 301.

56 *Id.* at 5.

57 *Id.* at 10.

58 *Id.* at 13.

especially the role of counsel, they find that the power brokers are also very involved in many instances as counsel. And despite criticism within the transnational arbitration community, the revolving door between counsel and arbitrator is an ongoing part of the practice of a core group of the power brokers.

Other indicators of who is within the core of arbitration more generally are various commercial rankings of arbitrators and arbitration law firms. One is "who's who legal," which annually lists the top firms and the top "thought leaders" from North America, Europe, and the rest of the world. Another is Chambers and Partner's list of "most in demand arbitrators" for international arbitration, which lists 30 in its "band one." All these indicators, as noted, point to a concentration of the arbitration business in the hands of a relatively few elite practitioners. One of the top arbitrators, Emmanuel Gaillard, both supports and pushes back on this finding in a recent essay on the sociology of international arbitration.[59] Gaillard argues that the criticisms of the elite corps of arbitration miss both the "hundreds of occasional or less frequent appointments" which take place around the "perceived core players" and the fact that it is the "conservatism of the parties," not the fault of the arbitrators, that accounts for the same names appearing over and over.[60]

The bigger crisis is in the legitimacy of international investment arbitration – charged with being biased toward the corporations at the expense of the states. The debate came with the rise of international investment arbitration in the past two decades, involving high-stakes disputes between investors and host countries. The arbitrators in these disputes, as noted above, tend to come from the elite of international commercial arbitrations. The investment arbitrators are charged by a number of commentators and NGOs with a bias in favor of multinational corporations – the investors – and against host countries.[61] The very public rejection of investment arbitration by the European Community is

[59] Gaillard, *supra* note 4.

[60] *Id.* at 20.

[61] European Commission, Press release, "Commission proposes new Investment Court System for TTIP and other EU trade and investment negotiations" (Brussels, September 16, 2015); Anthea Roberts, "Clash of Paradigms: Actors and Analogies Shaping the Investment Treaty System" (2013) 107 *American Journal of International Law* 45; Cecilia Olivet and Pia Eberhardt, *Profiting from Injustice: Challenging the Investment Arbitration Industry* (Brussels/Amsterdam: Corporate Europe Observatory & the Transnational Institute, 2013).

one example of this narrative. The EC proposes a "new Investment Court System . . . composed of fully qualified judges, [with] proceedings [that]-will be transparent, and cases [that] will be decided on the basis of clear rules. In addition, the Court will be subject to review by a new Appeal Tribunal." As a result, according to the EC statement "we protect the governments right to regulate, and ensure that investment disputes will be adjudicated in full accordance with the rule of law."[62] This could be a real threat to international investment arbitration and perhaps also challenge commercial arbitration.

One way to approach the current notions of crisis and reform is to draw again on history.[63] The first big wave of international commercial arbitrations came in the 1980s and typically involved States on one side and corporations on the other. The States had been persuaded to go along with arbitration clauses and had some faith in the system. This was the era of the *lex mercatoria*. But the developing States tended to lose these arbitrations, and one of the complaints was that the *lex mercatoria* served as a way to discount local laws and State activities.

It appears in retrospect that a "generational battle" at that time in the arbitration community helped to keep the developing world invested in arbitration. This generational battle reflected a shift in power toward the corporate law firms and their approaches, and also toward arbitration centers, including the ICC, which sought to rationalize in the face of increasing caseloads. The younger generation promoted more formal and rational law versus the "grand old men" and the *lex mercatoria* (which itself had helped to legalize commercial arbitration in the first place). What is less noted is that the younger generation also suggested that the transformation would help developing countries and give them more favorable outcomes. Jan Paulsson's articles about ICSID and relegitimation in the 1980s along with his representation in ICSID proceedings make this point.[64] He and others were pushing the older generation, defended notably by Pierre Lalive, and that push might have helped keep the system open enough to survive what might have been a severe crisis. The younger generation and their allies offered a group of arbitrators and counsel to

[62] European Commission, *supra* note 61.

[63] *Dealing in Virtue*.

[64] Jan Paulsson, "Third World Participation in International Commercial Arbitration" (1987) 2 *ICSID Review – Foreign Investment Law Journal* 19.

make the system friendlier to developing States and also more open to the technologies and approaches of large law firms.

It is worth reiterating that this generational warfare can be seen as evidence of division and conflict. Certainly there were strong attacks on the lex mercatoria,[65] and there were counterattacks on the ICC's attempts to rationalize their processes, criticized as the problem of growing "bureaucratization." Younger arbitrators such as Paulsson sharpened the conflict by arguing in a kind of manifesto that the new world of arbitration represented a dramatic change: "The age of innocence has come to an end . . . the subject has inevitably lost some of its charm. Once the delightful discipline of a handful of academic aficionados on the fringe of international law, it has become a matter of serious concern for great numbers of professionals determined to master a process because it is essential to their business. They labor, but not for love."[66]

The rhetoric of conflict, however, is also consistent with the formula of arguing in terms of what is necessary for the legitimacy of arbitration and consistent with its key norms. Indeed, the generational conflict masked the fact that the individuals had more in common than divided them, including a stake in the preservation of the role of the transnational arbitration community presiding over international commercial arbitration. The conflict within the community, however, was central to adjusting it to a new global balance of power and to the legitimation crisis experienced in the developing world.

Today's legitimation crisis identified with investment arbitration raises the question of whether the same kinds of processes of change are taking place today. The situation is similar in the sense that the older generation is perceived by many as out of line with emerging social concerns and a changing relationship between States and investors that provides more space for State regulation. According to one arbitrator,

"[T]he older generation of arbitrators were deeply shaped (or even scarred) by their experience with the NIEO [New International Economic Order] and Charter of Economic Rights and Duties of States and that era's wave of expropriations. This experience, I believe, led many in the old

[65] Michael Mustill, "The New Lex Mercatoria: The First Five Years" in M. Bos and I. Brownlie (eds.), *Liber Amicorum for the Rt. Hon. Lord Wilberforce* (Oxford: Clarendon Press, 1987), 149–181.

[66] Jan Paulsson, "Introduction" (1985) 1 *Arbitration International* 1, 2.

guard to consider the proliferation of BITs as proving that the West prevailed over developing States and their misguided views on investment protection. When sitting as arbitrators, many in the old guard assume that they (not the States parties themselves) know what's in the States' long-term best interests. This is partly why, in my view, you see these arbitrators ignore or circumvent local litigation requirements, cooling-off periods, limitations on subject matters capable of arbitration, and so forth. I think younger arbitrators are more likely to respect treaties as written."[67]

Any such generational division is more muted than in the 1980s and 1990s. One reason is that the most important arbitrators in investor arbitration now are the very same people who led the field 20 years ago, except now the young generation has matured as well.[68] There is not as much space for newcomers in the major investment arbitrations as there was in the past. The crisis might look very different if there was an important and identifiable group or generation that, again, had enough clout to challenge the system while also investing in its overall maintenance and success. Nevertheless, it is certainly possible to see a movement against the perspective of the more conservative investment arbitrators.

The fractures within the arbitration community over investment arbitration are evident in an edited volume on *Practicing Virtue*.[69] It is especially instructive in this respect, since it is dedicated to Charles Brower, one of the leading investment arbitrators. Brower is notable in particular because of his identification especially with the side of the investors. That itself is controversial. Emmanuel Gaillard, another leading arbitrator, notes in his chapter on the sociology of arbitration that the field has moved from a "solidaristic to a polarized arbitration field."[70] Referring to the challenge of NGOs and other attacks on international investment arbitration, Gaillard pushes against a certain group of arbitrators who, he notes, take a consistent role as "defending states or defending the interests of foreign investors."[71] Albert Jan van den Berg, another top arbitrator, uses his chapter in the book to reiterate his recipe contra Brower in particular to have a moratorium on dissenting opinions in investment arbitration as a way to make investment arbitration "function better and

[67] Cited in Garth, *supra* note 7.
[68] Puig, *supra* note 52.
[69] *Practising Virtue*; *see* the more general discussion in Garth, *supra* note 7.
[70] Gaillard, *supra* note 4, at 199.
[71] *Id.* at 200.

be more credible."[72] He seeks to build the legitimacy of investment arbitration as neutral and not merely a reflection of the political views of each arbitrator – selected to match the ideology of their appointing party.

Other chapters in the same book debate technical aspects of international investment arbitration where Brower has been important. A chapter on "most favoured nation" clauses in *Bilateral Investment Treaties*, by Sir Christopher Greenwood, is a good illustration.[73] Greenwood comes from a career as an academic and QC in public international law and is currently a Judge of the International Court of Justice. The very technical analysis within the chapter does not address Brower directly, but it appears to use sophistication in public international law to cast doubt on the enthusiasm for using MFN clauses to extend the rights to investment arbitration. This approach reflects the criticism of the arbitrators who have predominated in investment arbitration that they come from international economic law rather than public law[74] and that therefore they do not give enough credit to the States' position. On the other hand, in the same volume, several chapters expressly defend Brower's international economic law point of view in strong technical detail, for example, with respect to "contemporaneity" and with respect to the use of the Vienna Convention.[75] Anthea Roberts, a leading international law professor who is not an insider in the international arbitration community, refers to this difference as a culture clash while arguing for more influence among the public international law community.[76]

The final chapter is authored by Pierre-Marie Dupuy and Julie Maupin.[77] Dupuy is one of the most accomplished public international lawyers.

[72] Albert Jan van den Berg, "Charles Brower's Problems with 100% – Dissenting Opinions by Party-Appointed Arbitrators in Investment Arbitration" in David D. Caron, Stephan W. Schill, Abby Cohen Smutny and Epaminontas E. Triantafilou (eds.), *Practising Virtue: Inside International Arbitration* (Oxford: Oxford University Press, 2015), 504, 505.

[73] Christopher Greenwood, "Reflections on 'Most Favoured Nation' Clauses" in David D. Caron, Stephan W. Schill, Abby Cohen Smutny and Epaminontas E. Triantafilou (eds.) *Practising Virtue: Inside International Arbitration* (Oxford: Oxford University Press, 2015), 556–564.

[74] Roberts, *supra* note 61.

[75] *Practising Virtue.*

[76] Roberts, *supra* note 61.

[77] Pierre-Marie Dupuy and Julie Maupin, "Of Wit, Wisdom, and Balance in International Law" in David D. Caron, Stephan W. Schill, Abby Cohen Smutny and Epaminontas E. Triantafilou (eds.), *Practising Virtue: Inside International Arbitration* (Oxford: Oxford University Press, 2015), 706.

The chapter starts by praising Brower for his ability to get along with individuals who take very different positions, notably Dupuy himself.[78] The article discusses the Tokyo Resolution, adopted in September 2013, which focused on "the difficult task of envisaging a 'balanced' investor-State arbitration regime that protects both the pecuniary interests of foreign investors and the regulatory interests of sovereign states."[79] The chapter actually gives Brower "much credit" for the enterprise due to his role as one of the "leading voices to respond to investment arbitration's critics by insisting that the system is not unbalanced and needs no revision."[80] The chapter addresses technical issues with respect to the definition of investment, umbrella clauses, MFN clauses, expropriation, and the fair and equitable treatment of investors. It calls for a rebalancing in these areas of concern. The conclusion stated at the beginning of the chapter is that, with respect to Brower's perspective, "We conclude that the latter are without exception wittier in form, while the former [the Tokyo Resolution proposals] ultimately display the superior balance of wisdom in substance."[81] The chapter also opines that the proposals raise "questions as to whether certain active investment arbitrators who have become known as 'pro-claimant' or 'pro-State' will be able to maintain their one-sided repeat appointment streaks."[82] The conclusion of the chapter is again to celebrate Brower's wit while stating, "Yet, there is also wisdom, subtler and stronger, in balance."[83]

The transnational arbitration community has in fact become divided over how best to preserve its position with respect to international investment disputes. Nevertheless, however slowly, there is evidence that the field is shifting to open up more to the perspectives of public international law which, itself, has become much more the domain of transnational corporate law firms than in the past.[84] The question is whether investor-State disputes will continue to employ the institutions of international

[78] *Id.* at 707.
[79] *Id.*
[80] *Id.* at 708.
[81] *Id.* at 709.
[82] *Id.* at 716.
[83] *Id.* at 721.
[84] Sara Dezalay and Yves Dezalay, "Professionals of International Justice. From the Shadow of State Diplomacy to the Pull of the Market of Arbitration" in André Nollkaemper, Jean d'Aspremont, Wouter Werner and Tarcisio Gazzini (eds.), *International Law as a Profession* (Cambridge: Cambridge University Press, 2017).

investment arbitration, with States perhaps mollified by new entrants closer to public international law, or whether the legitimacy crisis will in fact lead to new transnational courts.

2.5 Revisiting the Last Chapter of Dealing in Virtue

Finally, I would like to mention one chapter of the book that has almost completely been neglected – the last chapter. We suggested in this chapter that the growth and success of international commercial arbitration could not be taken for granted. In particular, we suggested that the relative absence of the state from the world of the ICC and international commercial arbitration could change. The stakes are high enough and State battles could resurface. We suggested that "modern trade battles are played in the first place on the terrain of the state."[85] And, "States – and among them supranational entities – and State jurisdictions may intervene increasingly on the scene of economic conflicts."[86] The trade wars and protectionism that we see today may suggest that our speculations were not too far off.

[85] *Dealing in Virtue* 314.
[86] *Dealing in Virtue* 315.

Part II

International Commercial Arbitration as a Transnational Justice System

3 Arbitration and Comparative Law

Gary F. Bell

3.1 Introduction

Comparisons can be theoretical but they become very practical when one has to choose between two or more options. Given the centrality of party autonomy in arbitration, i.e. the centrality of the parties' choices, given the great discretion tribunals have in making choices when the parties have not done so, and given the need to understand often unfamiliar chosen laws, it is not surprising that comparative law plays a central role in international arbitration. The importance of comparative law to arbitration was emphasised in an article by Professor René David, one of the most famous professors of comparative law, which was published only a year after the signature of the New York Convention (translation in the footnote):

> La diffusion actuelle de l'arbitrage et le caractère international que revêt le développement de cette institution donnent un intérêt particulier à l'étude de l'arbitrage en droit comparé. L'intérêt de cette étude est à la fois d'ordre théorique et d'ordre pratique: nous nous proposons dans cette conférence de montrer, à propos de cette matière de l'arbitrage, le caractère vraiment indispensable des études de droit comparé, et de mettre en valeur la variété des applications de ces études.[1]

If comparative law is essential to arbitration, it could also be said that international commercial arbitration has changed the discipline of comparative law:

[1] 'The current diffusion of arbitration and the international character of the development of this institution give particular interest to the study of arbitration in comparative law. The interest of this study is at once theoretical and practical: we propose in this lecture to show, with regard to this subject of arbitration, the truly indispensable nature of comparative law studies, and to highlight the variety of applications of these studies'. R. David, 'Arbitrage et droit comparé' (1959) 11(1) *Revue internationale de droit comparé* 5. This translation by the author of this chapter is an adaptation and modification of a rougher translation by Google Translate.

International commercial arbitration has radically transformed the role of comparative law. Not long ago, comparative law was perceived to be an academic discipline. Its primary function was to provoke reflection on various legal systems and could at its best lead to legislative reform. International commercial arbitration revolutionized the field, transforming comparative law into an eminently practical and often lucrative discipline. Indeed, in many instances important international commercial litigations are won based on the resolution of issues of comparative law.[2]

This chapter will first look at how essential comparative law is in the day-to-day practice of international commercial arbitration and then, at how a theoretical study of comparative law is part of almost all arbitration law reforms and all updates of arbitration rules taking place today. This chapter will use international commercial arbitration as its paradigm, but many remarks will also be relevant in the context of investment arbitrations.

3.2 The Practical Importance of Comparative Law in Arbitration

3.2.1 Prolegomenon: The Variety of Laws

Before looking into the ways in which comparative law is relevant in arbitration practice it is important to recognise the great diversity of rules and laws that the arbitration community will encounter. Each nation has at least one arbitration law or *lex arbitri* and sometimes many (in federations for example). These laws may follow a model (the English Act, the UNCITRAL Model Law) or could be quite different from most other arbitration laws (Indonesian arbitration law for example). There are also arbitration laws that do not have their source in a State such as Islamic arbitration law and treaty-based arbitrations. The contract and the arbitration agreement may be governed by civil law, common law or Islamic law often as adopted or applied in a particular State or tradition, with

[2] Emmanuel Gaillard, 'The Use of Comparative Law in International Commercial Arbitration' in Pieter Sanders (ed.), *Arbitration in Settlement of International Commercial Disputes Involving the Far East and Arbitration in Combined Transportation, ICCA Congress Series*, vol. 4 (Deventer: Kluwer, 1989), 283. *See also* Frédéric Gilles Sourgens, 'Comparative Law as Rhetoric: An Analysis of the Use of Comparative Law in International Arbitration' (2007) 8:1 *Pepperdine Dispute Resolution Law Journal*, Article 1.

their different means of interpretation of the formation and contents of the contract itself. There will be a diversity of rules of conflict of laws in international law, in State law and in arbitration rules. There is an increasingly large number of arbitration rules to choose from, and a large number of so-called best practices, often in the form of soft law, on how to proceed with the arbitration and to gather evidence. And the New York Convention[3] (NYC) is implemented more or less efficiently through national legislation or other legal mechanisms and through national courts. There are a lot of laws and rules, and an ability to compare them all would no doubt be useful.

However, no one has knowledge of all these laws and rules. Although there are comparative law books comparing a few jurisdictions or rules, no book compares them all. When it comes to choosing or applying a law or some rules we are unfamiliar with, counsel and tribunals all rely on what is written about these laws in books and articles or in opinions we get from experts. But we must tread carefully. Sometimes the descriptions of the laws of a given jurisdiction focus too much on the law in books rather than the law in action (are courts efficient and reliable?) and sometimes the writings by local lawyers on their own law tend to be too favourable to that law and not sufficiently aware of its comparative advantages and disadvantages.

For example, the mention that a jurisdiction has adopted the UNCITRAL Model Law[4] is by no means a guarantee that it is a great seat for an arbitration. One must analyse the extent to which the Model Law was adopted,[5] and even, more importantly, whether the courts of that jurisdiction interpret the law according to so-called international

[3] New York Convention on the Recognition and Enforcement of Foreign Arbitral Awards, New York, 10 June 1958, in force 7 June 1959, 330 UNTS 4739 ('NYC').

[4] *UNCITRAL Model Arbitration Law*, UN Document A/40/17, annex 1, www.uncitral.org/pdf/english/texts/arbitration/ml-arb/07-86998_Ebook.pdf ('Model Law').

[5] On its website, the UNCITRAL posts the following disclaimer: 'A model law is created as a suggested pattern for lawmakers to consider adopting as part of their domestic legislation. Since States enacting legislation based upon a model law have the flexibility to depart from the text, the above list is only indicative of the enactments that were made known to the UNCITRAL Secretariat. The legislation of each State should be considered in order to identify the exact nature of any possible deviation from the model in the legislative text that was adopted'. *See* https://uncitral.un.org/en/texts/arbitration/modellaw/commercial_arbitration/status.

standards (which often look more like first world standards than truly international ones)[6] or local ones.

Also, because some local writers have a tendency to view their own law far too positively (this is the case even in the developed world when one wants to attract arbitrations to one's jurisdiction), it is often difficult to get accurate information on the law as it is actually practised in a given jurisdiction. This is especially so when the tribunal has to rely on contradictory statements by legal experts. Some local authors are nonetheless able to give an honest and accurate account of the law of their jurisdiction. Take this passage on enforcement in China by a Chinese author as an example of a useful evaluation for comparative purposes:

> What, then, is the situation in China with respect to the recognition and enforcement of arbitral awards? While foreign investors and reports have often claimed that enforcement in China is equivalent to the survival of the fittest in the jungle, official and semi-official PRC sources present a much more positive view. This section endeavours to present to readers an objective picture of the enforcement of arbitral awards in China, based on existing literature, case studies, field interviews and some empirical information. . . .
>
> Despite the respective limitations and the different results, the two surveys together give a general picture of the enforcement status in China. It is neither as hopeless as some foreign investors and reporters are wont to suggest, nor as trouble-free as official and semi-official sources allege.[7]

The multiplicity of laws and rules and the need to sometime be sceptical about their description make comparative law in the field of arbitration particularly difficult at times. This may explain in part why there is a tendency to choose the same old, familiar and reliable seats, laws and rules. English, French, Swiss, Singapore and Hong Kong arbitration laws and courts are well known as are the ICC, SIAC, LCIA and HKIAC Rules.

[6] I will also not use of the word *modern* as in 'modern arbitration laws'. The word suggests some kind of ineluctable destiny where all will eventually come when they see the light. It was used in the expression 'modern investment arbitration' to describe the very process that the EU is now rejecting for some of the very reasons why many 'pre-modern' countries resisted it all along. *Modern*, like the word *progressive*, is simply used to describe laws and positions one agrees with.

[7] Kun Fan, *Arbitration in China: A Legal and Cultural Analysis* (Oxford and Portland: Hart, 2013), 78, 88.

3.2.2 Choosing Arbitration

The parties must first choose arbitration over litigation in court, and with this choice, comes the first comparison.[8] It is in part a comparison between the rules and laws governing the different courts which are being considered and the different types of arbitration, and rules and laws governing arbitration that are being considered. More importantly this exercise usually also involves a comparison, not of written law, but of socio-legal or extra-legal factors – how long will it take and how much will it cost if one goes to this court in that jurisdiction compared to this type of arbitration seated in that jurisdiction? With the proliferation of international commercial courts[9] which aim at competing more directly with arbitration, accurate comparisons of the advantages and disadvantages of such courts over arbitration become increasingly important to clients. To the extent that, for example, the Singapore International Commercial Court (SICC) allows foreign lawyers to represent clients, choosing such a court would not disqualify a party's usual counsel from acting in the case and counsel may therefore choose to recommend the SICC the way they would recommend arbitration – this is unlike the choice of a regular domestic and foreign court in front of which these counsel cannot appear.

3.2.3 Choosing a Seat and a Lex Arbitri

The choice of a seat usually determines the *lex arbitri*. Choosing a seat therefore requires a comparison of the different arbitration laws one may choose. Therefore, many comparative books and articles have been written with titles such as *Droit comparé de l'arbitrage international*[10] or

[8] 'There is comparison first of all between arbitration as a process and the various national processes of litigation'. H. Patrick Glenn, 'Comparative Law and Legal Practice: On Removing the Borders' (2001) 75:4 *Tul L Rev.* 977, 998. For an economic comparison, *see* Bruce L. Benson, 'To Arbitrate or To Litigate: That Is the Question' (1999) 8 *European Journal of Law and Economics* 91.

[9] *See* Gary F. Bell, 'The New International Commercial Courts – Competing with Arbitration? The Example of the Singapore International Commercial Court' (2018) 11:2 *Contemp. Asia Arb. J.* 193.

[10] Jean-François Poudret et Sébastien Besson, *Droit comparé de l'arbitrage international*, (Paris, Genève: Bruylant, LGDJ, Schulthess, 2002) later translated into English now in its second edition: Jean-François Poudret and Sébastien Besson, *Comparative Law of International Arbitration*, 2nd ed., translated by Stephen V. Berti, Annette Ponti (London: Sweet & Maxwell, 2007).

Comparative International Commercial Arbitration.[11] Such useful books, and many other edited books, usually provide a comparative overview of either a regional selection of arbitration laws[12] or of the most popular arbitration seats.[13] To the extent that such books make comparisons between a few jurisdictions, they are indeed comparative and international. It would however be useful if they specifically gave some indication of their geographical limitation when there is one. For example, the extremely helpful book by Poudret and Besson, *Droit comparé de l'arbitrage international*, and its English version, *Comparative Law of International Arbitration*,[14] are indeed international as they cover international instruments, but when it comes to domestic arbitration laws their coverage is essentially European (Belgium, England, France, Germany, Holland, Italy, Sweden and Switzerland) with some references to the laws of the United States. Poudret and Besson must be admired for the wide scope of their incredibly ambitious book, but when it comes to arbitration laws, this books remains a regional endeavour and it might have been useful to reflect this in the title. Of course, this title can be explained by the fact that a large part of international commercial arbitrations in 2007 were probably still taking place in Europe but this would not be the case anymore as Asia and other parts of the world are now taking their share of the international commercial arbitration pie. Maybe the next edition will reflect this new reality. We are all guilty of this to some extent – in this chapter for example I refer mainly to ICC, SIAC and HKIAC Rules simply because these are the rules with which I am most familiar.

The point to be made here is that no book, no one or two authors, however excellent and ambitious, could possibly cover all the arbitration laws of the world, not even the ones most frequently used – no one has the linguistic and legal abilities to write such a book (or series). In comparative law, it is most important to recognise our limits so that we can learn from

[11] Julian D. M. Lew, Loukas A. Mistelis, and Stefan M. Kröll, *Comparative International Commercial Arbitration* (The Hague: Kluwer, 2003).

[12] Gary F. Bell (ed.), *The UNCITRAL Model Law and Asian Arbitration Laws – Implementation and Comparisons* (Cambridge, Cambridge University Press, 2018); Simon Greenberg, Christopher Kee, and J. Romesh Weeramantry, *International Commercial Arbitration: An Asia-Pacific Perspective* (Cambridge: Cambridge University Press, 2011).

[13] For example, Gary B. Born, *International Commercial Arbitration*, 2nd ed. (Alphen aan den Rijn, the Netherlands: Kluwer, 2014).

[14] *Supra* note 10.

others. We often need to have recourse to a variety of sources in order to get the information we need.

Finally, it should be added that, sometimes, ill-advised parties fail to choose a seat which allows either the institution[15] or the tribunal[16] to choose the seat – again in a comparative exercise.

3.2.4 Choosing the Law Governing the Contract

Choosing the law governing the contract is the exercise that is the closest to classical comparative law. A lot has been written on the differences between the civil law and the common law of contract – one can think of regionally focused books in Europe[17] and in Asia[18] that make such comparisons. Nowadays, a lot of jurisdictions have at least one book, in a language other than the national language, often in English, sometime in French or Spanish, on their law of contract. Arbitration practitioners in large international firms are increasingly familiar with both civil and common law of contract from some of the main jurisdictions,[19] and even sometimes with Islamic law of contract.[20] In the past there were some significant limitations to the parties' choice of governing law,[21] but the freedom to choose a law is now increasingly accepted.[22]

It is also increasingly clear that the parties may choose non-national rules of law, such as the UNIDROIT Principles[23] or more vague rules

[15] For example, Art 18 of the Rules of Arbitration of the International Chamber of Commerce, 1 March 2017 ('ICC Rules').

[16] For example, Rule 21.1 of the Arbitration Rules of the Singapore International Arbitration Centre, 6th ed., 1 August 2016.

[17] For example, Hugh G. Beale, Bénédicte Fauvarque-Cosson, Jacobien Rutgers and Stefan Vogenauer, *Cases, Materials and Text on Contract Law* (Oxford; Portland, Oregon: Hart Publishing, 2019).

[18] *See e.g.* the latest of a series of books on Asian contract law: Mindy Chen-Wishart, Alexander Loke, Stefan Vogenauer (eds.), *Studies in the Contract Laws of Asia. III, Contents of Contracts and Unfair Terms* (Oxford: Oxford University Press, 2020).

[19] One should note that there are many varieties of civil and common laws – these are not monolithic legal traditions.

[20] Mainly for Islamic financing transactions.

[21] M. Blessing, 'Choice of Substantive Law in International Arbitration' (1997) 14 *J. Int'l Arb.* 39, 40.

[22] For a general discussion *see* Gary B. Born, *International Arbitration: Law and Practice*, 2nd ed. (Alphen aan den Rijn, the Netherlands: Kluwer, 2016), 239–266.

[23] International Institute for the Unification of Private Law, UNIDROIT Principles of International Commercial Contracts (2016).

such as the '*lex mercatoria*' or 'general principles of law', or even a cumulation of laws or rules of laws.[24] For example, 'the Eurotunnel construction project was thus submitted to "principles common to English and French law"'.[25] This is not commonly done but in some instances the parties do indeed purposely choose such vague general principles of law. These choices of law call for a comparative law analysis to extract such general principles.

If it is increasingly clear that the parties can choose their own law, how the tribunal is to choose a governing law when the parties have not chosen one is a more complex issue. As is well known the rules of conflict of laws of the seat are usually not considered appropriate. Two main approaches are more commonly accepted. First, the indirect method, in which the tribunal first chooses the rules of conflict (private international law) that it will apply and then decides which law applies according to these rules.[26] This method requires in depth knowledge of comparative conflict of law rules also called comparative private international law. The second method, the direct approach, lets the tribunal decide which law is most appropriate without specific reference to any rules of private international law.[27] This second method requires knowledge of comparative contract law.

Whatever approach is taken, the tribunal often has complete discretion to choose either the appropriate rules of private international law, or the appropriate contract law, but it will still have to provide reasons for its decision. Some tribunals explain their discretionary decisions by using comparative private international law to find common or general principles of private international law. For example, they could say that the private international law or contract law of a given jurisdiction is more appropriate because it corresponds to what is the more common position in

[24] Art 28, Model Law which allows the parties to choose the rules of law, i.e. they do not have to choose a national law. Rule 31.1 SIAC Rules is even clearer mentioning 'the law or rules of law designated by the parties'.

[25] Glenn, *supra* note 8. *See also* Emmanuel Gaillard, 'Use of General Principles of International Law in International Long-Term Contracts' (1999) 27 *Int'l Bus. L.* 214, 215.

[26] Model Law art 28(2): 'Failing any designation by the parties, the arbitral tribunal shall apply the law determined by the conflict of laws rules which it considers applicable'.

[27] SIAC Rules 31.1: 'Failing such designation by the parties, the Tribunal shall apply the law or rules of law which it determines to be appropriate'. *See also* ICC Art 21 and Art 36.1 of the *Administered Arbitration Rules of the Hong Kong International Arbitration Centre, 2018* ('HKIAC Rules').

most legal systems. For example, a tribunal could say that it has chosen the contract law of the seller (direct method) because, having compared most rules of private international law, it came to the conclusion that, in contracts of sale, most traders would expect the law of the seller to be applicable. This justification comes from a comparative law exercise. Many arbitrators, when given a choice of law, will choose the rather vague *lex mercatoria* rather than a more precise national law or a more detailed set of non-national rules such as the UNIDROIT Principles. A theoretical justification for that choice is that the application of *lex mercatoria* is simply the application of the comparative law method, 'deriving the substantive solution to the legal issue at hand not from a particular law selected by a traditional choice of law process, but from a comparative law analysis which will enable the arbitrators to apply the rule which is the most widely accepted'.[28] It may be so, but one wonders sometimes whether some arbitrators are not in fact choosing the *lex mercatoria* because they are longing for the power to decide cases *ex aequo et bono*.

3.2.5 Choosing the Law Governing the Arbitration Clause

Almost all will agree that the formal validity of an arbitration clause (essentially the writing requirement) is governed by the *lex arbitri*[29] but there is often disagreement as to which contract law should govern the substantive validity and the interpretation of an arbitration clause, the main contenders being either the substantive law usually chosen by the parties to govern the contract of which the clause is a part or the substantive law of the seat. This chapter will not address that controversy[30] but will point out

[28] Emmanuel Gaillard, 'Transnational Law: A Legal System or Method of Decision Making?' (2001) 17(1) *Arb. Int'l* 59, 62. For a discussion of this theory and the arbitrators' use of comparative methodology, *see* Joshua Karton, *The Culture of International Arbitration and the Evolution of Contract Law* (Oxford: Oxford University Press, 2013).

[29] Art 2, NYC; *see also* Art. 7, Model Law.

[30] Although elsewhere in this *Companion* there lies some discussion. *See e.g.*, for an English case, Sulamérica Cia Nacional de Seguros S.A. v. Enesa Engenharia S.A. [2012] EWCA Civ 638 and for a Singapore case: BCY v. BCZ [2016] SGHC 249. For an explanation of the different approaches and uncertainty of the laws on this point, *see* Born, *supra* note 13 at 472: 'Different national courts, arbitral tribunals and commentators have developed and applied a multiplicity of choice-of-law rules to the substantive validity of international arbitration agreements, ranging from the law chosen by the parties to govern their underlying contract, to the law of the arbitral seat, to the law of the judicial enforcement

that arbitration practitioners will need to be familiar not only with this debate but also with all the potential choices of arbitration laws and substantive laws, made by the parties, the tribunal or even the courts, which could affect the arbitration clause. This is a fascinating exercise of comparative law which unfortunately takes place all too often only when a dispute arises, long after an arbitration clause has been included into a contract.

3.2.6 Choosing Institutional or Ad Hoc Arbitration and Choosing Rules

The parties' advisers must compare the advantages and disadvantages of institutional versus ad hoc arbitration and must also compare the different rules available (linked or not linked to an institution – for example SIAC-administered arbitration under UNCITRAL Rules[31]). Considerations of the rules will often be overtaken by consideration of costs and length of proceedings. A detailed list of the points to be compared in the rules would include the following:

As to the institution: A. the manner in which it is structured and functions; B. the procedure it adopts for selecting the arbitrators it may be called upon to appoint; C. the degree to which it supervises arbitrators, if at all; and D the scale of fees, and what the requirements are for an advance deposit on fees. As to the rules: E. whether they provide an up-to-date and flexible procedure acceptable to both the common-law and civil-law traditions; F. the extent to which they permit the arbitrators to direct the nature and course of the proceedings; G. what provision is made for the use of independent experts; H. what provisions are made to counter possible delaying tactics by the respondent; I. the extent to which the jurisdiction of

forum, to the law of the state with the "closest connection" or "most significant relationship"'. Also important in this debate is whether there should be the presumption '*in favorem validitatis*' when the tribunal chooses the law, *see* Klaus Peter Berger, 'Reexamining the Arbitration Agreement: Applicable Law – Consensus or Confusion?' in Albert Jan van den Berg (ed.), *International Arbitration 2006: Back to Basics?, ICCA Congress Series*, vol. 13 (Alphen aan den Rijn, the Netherlands: Kluwer, 2007), 301, 312ff. *See also* Renato Nazzini, 'The Law Applicable to the Arbitration Agreement: Towards Transnational Principles' (2016) 65 *I.C.L.Q.* 681. When the parties have not made a choice, the Art 5(1)(a) NYC points to 'the law of the country where the award was made'.

[31] *See* Practice Note PN-02/14 (2 January 2014) on Case Administration, Appointment of Arbitrators & Financial Management for Cases under the UNCITRAL Rules 2010, www.siac.org.sg/images/stories/articles/rules/Practice_Note_for_UNCITRAL_Cases_PN-02-14_2-January-2014_UNCITRAL_RULES_2010.pdf.

the arbitrators is defined in the rules; J. what provision is made for interim measures of protection; and K. whether provision is made for the introduction of additional parties into the arbitration.[32]

3.2.7 Choosing the Arbitrator(s)

Having chosen a seat, some laws and some rules, to the extent that parties have some influence on the appointment of the tribunal, these previous choices should probably influence the choice of arbitrators. It might not be wise to appoint a tribunal exclusively knowledgeable in the common law when French law is the law of the contract and the *lex arbitri.* One can save on legal experts and on translation if the tribunal knows the law and its language. The choice of arbitrators is not an exercise in comparative law but an exercise in comparative qualifications for the comparative law work the tribunal will need to undertake.

3.2.8 Choosing How to Proceed with the Arbitration and How to Gather Evidence

Some of the arbitration rules show their civil or common law origins when it comes to how the arbitration proceeds,[33] but most rules now attempt to strike a compromise between civil and common law procedure.[34] For the most part however, arbitration rules do not detail how the arbitration should proceed and they let the parties in collaboration with the tribunal decide on a procedure, a procedural timetable as well as on the way evidence should be gathered.[35] The parties rarely choose in advance the

[32] Sam Aaron, 'International Arbitration III: Choosing an Arbitration Institution and a Set of Rules' (1991) 108 *South African L.J.* 306, 309. *See also* Sam Aaron, 'International Arbitration IV: Choosing an Arbitration Institution and a Set of Rules' (1991) 108 *South African L.J.* 503.

[33] For example, the ICC Terms of Reference are clearly of civil law origin. ICC Rules art 23.

[34] For a list of the difference in procedure between civil and common law, *see* Urs Martin Laeuchli, 'Civil and Common Law: Contrast and Synthesis in International Arbitration' in *ICDR Handbook on International Arbitration & ADR*, 2nd ed. (Juris Legal Information, 2017).

[35] SIAC Rule 19: '19.1 The Tribunal shall conduct the arbitration in such manner as it considers appropriate, after consulting with the parties, to ensure the fair, expeditious, economical and final resolution of the dispute.

'19.2 The Tribunal shall determine the relevance, materiality and admissibility of all evidence. The Tribunal is not required to apply the rules of evidence of any applicable law in making such determination'.

rules of evidence and the details of how an arbitration should proceed, and when they cannot agree on these matters at the start of the arbitration, the tribunal is given wide discretion.

One set of rules that has been widely used is the *IBA Rules on the Taking of Evidence in International Arbitration, 2010*[36] (IBA Rules), first adopted in 1999. It has shaped the way large international arbitrations have proceeded. The IBA Rules tried to find a compromise between civil law and common law procedure, for example, by allowing the production of documents[37] (discovery) as is the case in common law jurisdictions but with a more limited scope, as a compromise with the civil law which does not usually allow for much document production.[38] It is true that it allows the tribunal to appoint expert witnesses as is the case in the civil law,[39] but in practice, parties usually appoint two sets of expert witnesses.[40] The IBA Rules provide that 'the Arbitral Tribunal may ask questions to a witness at any time'[41] as is certainly the case in civil law jurisdictions where the tribunal often asks its questions first (inquisitorial system), but in the IBA Rules it seems to come as an afterthought, after explaining in detail the way counsel will direct and redirect in examining witnesses,[42] as would be the case in the common law.

Although the IBA Rules were written as a compromise between civil law and common law procedures, they have recently been criticised for being too common law influenced and for greatly increasing costs and duration of proceedings. A new set of rules, the *Rules on the Efficient Conduct of Proceedings in International Arbitration (Prague Rules),*[43] published in 2018, aimed at detailing a procedure that is closer to the civil law which would purportedly increase efficiency by encouraging tribunals 'to take a

[36] *IBA Rules on the Taking of Evidence in International Arbitration, 2010* (London: International Bar Association, 2010), www.ibanet.org/Document/Default.aspx?DocumentUid=68336C49-4106-46BF-A1C6-A8F0880444DC.

[37] IBA Rules, art 3.

[38] IBA Rules, a 3(3)(a) requires the party to provide 'a description of each requested Document sufficient to identify it, or . . . a description in sufficient detail (including subject matter) of a narrow and specific requested category of Documents that are reasonably believed to exist'.

[39] IBA Rules, art 6.

[40] IBA Rules, art 5.

[41] IBA Rules, art 8(3)(h).

[42] IBA Rules, art 8(3)(a)-(g).

[43] *See* www.praguerules.com.

more active role in managing the proceedings (as is traditionally done in many civil law countries)'.[44] The Prague Rules discourage the production of documents,[45] put the tribunal clearly in charge of witness examination,[46] and adopts the civil law principle *iura novit curia* (the tribunal knows the law) which allows the tribunal to 'apply legal provisions not pleaded by the parties if it finds it necessary, including, but not limited to, public policy rules' provided the parties are given an opportunity to express their views. Therefore, even if both parties agree that a certain provision of the law does not apply, the tribunal may apply that provision provided that the parties have had a chance to express their views.

The reason I am detailing the IBA and Prague Rules is because this is a completely new choice between the older rules that are indeed, at least to some extent, expensive and sometimes, especially for smaller cases, inefficient,[47] and new Rules that claim to be more efficient. In a large arbitration where hundreds of millions of euros are at stake, one can understand the parties wishing to adopt an expansive procedure, whatever the expenses, especially since there is no appeal in arbitration. Many, however, have reacted almost aggressively to the view that the IBA Rules were too common law, too expensive and, in some cases, inefficient. It seems to me that asking whether a procedure more inspired by the civil law could be more appropriate in some instances is a valid and important exercise of comparative law and should be encouraged. Those who believe that the IBA Rules are the best thing since sliced bread, can still use them – indeed the IBA Rules have worked extremely well in many instances. However, what is the harm of offering an alternative to the parties? Before the adoption of the Prague Rules, I have presided over a few arbitrations, in which, at the request of the parties, which were both from civil law jurisdictions, we followed what the parties referred to as 'a German procedure' which resembled the Prague Rules. These were

[44] Prague Rules, *Note from the Working Group*, 2.

[45] Prague Rules art 4.2.

[46] Prague Rules art 5.9.

[47] For example, in close to 15 years of arbitration practice as an arbitrator, I have granted orders for the production of documents in numerous cases under the IBA Rules, yet, I cannot remember a single case in which a document so produced made much of a difference – there certainly never was any smoking gun, which begs the question: why do parties wish to go through this long and expensive process in almost every case? Of course, there are cases where document production is ordered, and where the documents so ordered are extremely useful, but is document production necessary in almost every case?

medium-size arbitrations and they proceeded very efficiently and very quickly at much lower costs.

It is important that the procedure and the taking of evidence benefit from the flexibility and party autonomy that arbitration promises. Each case is different and even though the IBA Rules are widely used, one should remember that there is no binding practice when it comes to procedure and evidence – flexibility, parties' autonomy and the tribunal's discretion in the absence of a choice by the parties should prevail. Sometimes arbitration counsel and tribunals get caught in formulaic old habits and can't imagine another way of doing things and assume that there is one default, standard way of conducting an arbitration.

For example, in the Singapore case of *JVL Agro Industries Ltd v. Agritrade International Pte Ltd*[48] the High Court stated, that, at least in Singapore, arbitration must be presumed to have adopted an English-style adversarial system, thus rejecting (without naming it) the civil law principle *iura novit curia* (the tribunal knows the law). At paragraph 169, the Court stated, 'The fundamental nature of arbitration is adversarial. It is true that s 12(3) of the Act specifically empowers a tribunal governed by that Act, unless the parties have agreed otherwise, to adopt inquisitorial processes. But the mere fact that the Act considers it necessary expressly to empower a tribunal to proceed inquisitorially shows that the starting point – at least in Singapore – is that arbitration is adversarial'. In my view there should not be a starting point.[49] It may be that the Court nonetheless reached the right decision – even in the civil law, the parties should be given an opportunity to comment on the law the tribunal is considering applying – but in my view the quoted statement overreaches and gives the impression that there is a default procedure in arbitration in Singapore when in fact there should not be any and the parties and the tribunal should decide on the procedure and

[48] [2016] SGHC 126, [2016] 4 SLR 768.

[49] Model Law art 19, in force in Singapore, has no starting point or presumption on procedure:

'Article 19. Determination of rules of procedure

(1) Subject to the provisions of this Law, the parties are free to agree on the procedure to be followed by the arbitral tribunal in conducting the proceedings.

(2) Failing such agreement, the arbitral tribunal may, subject to the provisions of this Law, conduct the arbitration in such manner as it considers appropriate. The power conferred upon the arbitral tribunal includes the power to determine the admissibility, relevance, materiality and weight of any evidence'.

See also SIAC Rule 19, *supra* note 35.

rules of evidence. This is especially important if Singapore is to attract more parties from civil law jurisdictions to conduct arbitrations in Singapore.[50] What I like about the Prague Rules is that they force everyone to come to the realisation that there are other ways we could proceed. Opening minds is one of the benefits of comparative law.

3.2.9 Choosing Where to Contest Jurisdiction and an Award

A party may seek to review a decision on jurisdiction or to set aside an award at the seat or it may wait until the other side tries to enforce the award to resist this at the place of enforcement.[51] Although such a choice may involve strategic considerations, it is also an exercise in comparative law where one would look at the law and jurisprudence of these jurisdictions. With respect to setting aside and resisting enforcement, it involves two separate domestic laws on arbitrability and public policy.[52]

3.2.10 Choosing Where to Enforce an Award

There is often not much choice as to where to enforce an award – one goes where the assets are. However, when a company has assets in multiple jurisdictions, one may be able to choose the jurisdiction where to enforce the award and again, this is an exercise in comparative law in action (legislation, jurisprudence and other factors, such as costs).

3.3 Interpreting and Applying International Law and Unfamiliar Laws

3.3.1 Interpreting and Applying International Law

Some of the laws that must be interpreted are international in nature: the NYC and the Model Law for example do not have their sources in

[50] On the fact that the SIAC does not attract a lot of cases where the governing law is the civil law, *see* Gary F. Bell, 'Teaching More Civil Law at the National University of Singapore: A Necessity for Singapore as a Legal Hub for Asia' (2019) 14 *Asian Journal of Comparative Law* S173, S176–S177.

[51] For example, Model Law art 16(3), 34–36; NYC art V.

[52] NYC V(2). Model Law 34(2)(b).

domestic law. Unfortunately, there are often limitations on what the courts may look at in interpreting international treaties. In Singapore for example, as is the case in most common law countries, the NYC is implemented by a statute and only the statute, not the NYC creates rights and obligations in Singapore. The law therefore does not take the form of an international instrument but of a statute, although its wording is extremely close to the wording of the NYC. Luckily courts in Singapore are now in the habit of looking at decisions in other jurisdictions when their statutes are worded similarly to international treaties. This, however, is not the case everywhere.

Similarly, with the Model Law – most of the text of the 1985 version of the Law is in force in Singapore but not art 2A(1) of the 2006 version which states, 'In the interpretation of this Law, regard is to be had to its international origin and to the need to promote uniformity in its application and the observance of good faith'. Notwithstanding the absence of this article in Singapore and in many other jurisdictions, the courts often look at decisions in other jurisdictions on the text of the Model Law.

Looking at decisions from other jurisdictions to decide on the interpretation of the Model Law is of course an exercise in comparative law. Counsel are not always well prepared for this exercise. In Singapore for example, counsel often cite English cases in support of their interpretation of the Model Law, when England is not a Model Law jurisdiction, and they fail to look at the *UNCITRAL Digest of Cases on the Model Law.*[53]

3.3.2 Interpreting and Applying Unfamiliar Laws

After the laws have been chosen or determined, counsel must plead them and the tribunal must interpret and apply them. This is when knowledge of comparative law comes handy. A good arbitrator would ideally be familiar with more than one legal tradition or system and more than one language. It is often the case that common law trained arbitrators have to apply the law of a civil law jurisdiction and vice versa. Even if the arbitrator does not know the language of the law that she has to apply, it is hoped that she is sufficiently experienced in comparative law to understand the difficulties

[53] UNCITRAL, 2012 Digest of Case Law on the Model Law on International Commercial Arbitration (Vienna: UNCITRAL, 2012).

that arise from using translations of laws and of cases and from discussing the civil law in English or the common law in French.

There are many instances where the main counsel are common law trained and they hire local counsel from the jurisdiction of the law being applied and also hire legal expert witnesses. There are often difficulties when the main counsel do not fully understand the legal system being explained to the tribunal by the expert. No one can be expected to be intimately familiar with all the laws ever encountered in one's arbitration career, but there is a minimum of familiarity required. I always recommend to students interested in an arbitration career that they learn another language and that they learn the civil law if they are from a common law jurisdiction and vice versa.

3.4 The Theoretical Importance of Comparative Law in Arbitration Law Reform

3.4.1 How States Compete to Have the Best Lex Arbitri: An Exercise in Comparative Law

Some States consciously compete to attract arbitrations – arbitration is good for the local economy. In order to so compete, States emulate the arbitration laws and other laws of other jurisdictions. Singapore and Hong Kong are two seats which, in the last 20 years, have grown exponentially and, as part of that growth, their laws have been often amended to adopt the latest legal innovations.[54] This means that governments in these jurisdictions constantly compare their laws with that of other jurisdictions to make sure they have what they believe are the best arbitration laws.

3.4.2 How Institutions Compete to Have the Best Rules: Also, an Exercise in Comparative Law

Arbitral institutions do the same. When one adopts rules on emergency arbitrators, many soon do the same. The SIAC now has an SIAC Court,

[54] For example, Singapore's *International Arbitration Act*, Statute of Singapore, Chapter 143A, was adopted in 1995 and was amended in 1995, 2001, 2002 (twice!), 2006, 2010, 2012 (twice!) and 2016.

not doubt inspired by the ICC Court.[55] Again this is an example of comparative law in action.

3.5 Conclusion

Is there a future for comparative law if arbitration laws and rules are all standardised or harmonised and become more and more the same? No doubt, some matters should be harmonised – without the NYC, international commercial arbitration would not be what it is today. But should everything be harmonised?

Is it not a good thing that French arbitration law is different and forces us to explain why some parties may not want French law? Is it not a good thing that one can choose between an institution that has expansive vetting of awards and one that does not? To some extent, shouldn't international commercial arbitration be more about legal pluralism than the harmonisation of laws? If we believe in party autonomy, we must give the parties real choices, which means that not everything should be harmonised and that comparative law should continue to play a key role in international arbitration.

In fact, it is likely that the future will bring even more diversity. We all thought that we were moving towards a standardised mode of dispute resolution for investment disputes, but since *Slovakia v. Achmea BV*,[56] it seems that international courts may play an increasing role in the future. International Commercial Courts are being set up around the world to compete with international arbitration and the *Hague Convention on Choice of Court*[57] may support the enforcement of their judgments the way the NYC supports the enforcement of awards. Islamic law and Islamic arbitration, which are quite different from Western law and arbitration, are becoming more important in support of Islamic banking and financing.

Because this diversity not going to go away, comparative law will no doubt continue to play a key role in international arbitration.

[55] The SIAC Court was introduced in 2013 by the 5th edition of the SIAC Rules.

[56] Case C-284/16, Court of Justice of European Union.

[57] Convention of 30 June 2005 on Choice of Court Agreements.

Which Law Applies? 4

A Role for Private International Law?

Adrian Briggs

4.1 Introduction

The question whether private international law has a useful role to play in process of arbitration is framed too broadly to produce a concise and useful answer. It is also complicated by the inveterate tension between the doctrinal view, on the one hand, that *lex facit arbitrum*,[1] the law makes the arbitration, and the pragmatic view on the other, that arbitration is a private matter whose very purpose is to keep the process of dispute resolution as far away from the courts, legal procedure and legal doctrine, as possible. It is further complicated by a perception, held by many if confessed by fewer, that private international lawyers do not really understand arbitration, and are forever trying to force it into a mould created and devised by them for proceedings before courts and judgments given by courts.

The role of the *lex arbitri* is considered elsewhere, and insofar as private international law plays any part in that it will also be considered there. In this chapter, to make practical sense of the proper role of private international law in and around arbitration, one may separate the three areas in which it needs to be considered: that is, before, during and after the arbitration. It will be seen that the first is quickly disposed of; the second is the area in which the debate is most controversial but the answer most obvious; and the third is the area in which private international law has the most important part to play.

4.2 Private International Law prior to an Arbitration

Prior to an arbitration, what must the court do? It must refer the parties to arbitration when its own law requires this to be done. There are limitations,

[1] F. A. Mann, 'Lex Facit Arbitrum in International Arbitration: Liber Amicorum for Martin Domke' (1967) P. Sanders (ed.) *The Hague*.

and some small instability in the jurisprudence where the court is made aware that there is a real and genuine dispute about whether there is an operative agreement to arbitrate, but the dominant view is that it simply refers the parties, and leaves the next step, to the tribunal. Although it is conceivable that there is a role for private international law in this exercise, as when, for example, the court called upon to refer the parties to arbitration is lured into an analysis of the content and legal enforceability of a contract which contains an arbitration clause, and is tempted to look to something other than its own domestic law to test the argument, it is far better if, at this stage, it simply applies its arbitration legislation as though the conflict of laws were not an issue.

If the parties are referred to arbitration, a court may find itself asked to restrain one of them from taking judicial proceedings elsewhere, in apparent defiance of the agreement to arbitrate. In such cases the ordinary rules of private international law on anti-suit injunctions are at the disposal of the court. These are generally well understood and sensibly supportive of the agreement to arbitrate; but in order to apply them the court will need to be satisfied that there is (as distinct from there appearing sufficiently to be to refer the parties to a tribunal) an agreement to arbitrate; and it will need to decide, as English courts have not yet done,[2] whether an injunction can properly be ordered when the arbitration is not one which will take place in England. However, at this point private international law simply acts in aid of the contract which the parties appear to have made, and it rarely causes problems. The objection[3] to such injunctions being directed at infringing proceedings before the courts of Member States of the EU fell away when the United Kingdom ceased to be a Member State; in any event it never applied to such orders made by the tribunal itself, for the relevant European legislation made no claim to apply to arbitration or to arbitrators.[4]

[2] A fair reading of the judgment of the Supreme Court in Enka Insaat ve Sanayi AS v OOO Insurance Company Chubb [2020] UKSC 38, [2020] 1 WLR 4117, is that the point was not considered, notwithstanding its mention by the court below.

[3] Case C-185/07 Allianz SpA v. West Tankers Inc [2009] ECR I-663.

[4] Case C-536/13 Gazprom OAO EU:C:2015:316, [2015] 1 WLR 4937, interpreting Art 1.2(d) of the Brussels I Regulation (44/2001; recast as 1215/2012 without material change).

4.3 Private International Law during an Arbitration

A tribunal may need to decide which laws or rules of law are to be applied by it in coming to its conclusions. In proceedings before a court, if the judge is called upon to decide whether this country's law or that country's law is to be applied, the guiding (or constraining) principles are those of the conflict of laws: rules by which judges to answer questions of this kind. Made for use by courts, their application or replication in arbitration is controversial.

Subject always to the provisions of the rules governing the arbitration, and to the law of the seat of the arbitration, the overriding principle is that arbitration both depends on and gives effect to the consent or agreement of the parties to it. It is natural, and it follows, that the law or rules of law which the tribunal will apply will be those specified by the parties. It is almost universally the case that the parties' choice of law (in the sense of national law) or rules of law (in the sense of an amalgam of national laws, or principles which serve an equivalent function, whether public international law, or a secular or religious code of principles, or something yet more elusive) will bind the tribunal to apply what has been chosen. If that which has been chosen can be shown to provide all the information which the tribunal needs, there will be no further enquiry to make. But where the tribunal finds that it does not – because the choice of law or rules of law is limited in material scope, or because there was no choice at all – the function of the tribunal in this regard will be defined by the rules of the arbitration or by the legislation at the seat. This may direct the tribunal to apply rules of the conflict of laws in order to identify the legal system whose materials provision will apply. Such a procedure is provided for in the UNCITRAL Model Law, Article 28,[5] and by those systems which have legislated to give this provision the force of law, such as, in England, Arbitration Act 1996, s 46;[6] the question which it prompts is which set of conflicts rules is referred to. Alternatively, the rules or legislation may direct the tribunal to select the law or rules of law which it considers to be appropriate, without any indication of how this selection is to be carried

[5] Article 28(2) Failing any designation by the parties, the arbitral tribunal shall apply the law determined by the conflict of laws rules which it considers applicable.

[6] Section 46(3) If or to the extent that there is no such choice or agreement, the tribunal shall apply the law determined by the conflict of laws rules which it considers applicable.

out: the question which this prompts is whether private international law has any part to play in this process. We can take these in turn.

4.3.1 Where the Tribunal Is Directed to Fill a Lacuna by Reference to the Conflict of Laws

Where legislation, or rules, refer to the conflict of laws, the question of what this means is one of construction. In answering it, it seems likely that the default answer will be the conflict of laws rules applied by courts at the seat of arbitration. However, it can be objected that this would tie the arbitral process to a set of rules which, because made and designed for courts and judicial proceedings, have no natural application to tribunals and arbitral proceedings.[7] That leads some to argue that if a tribunal is required to take a detour through the conflict of laws, this should be understood as a delocalised, autonomous, a-national 'system' of the conflict of laws.[8] The content of this system, one supposes, will lay some emphasis on what the parties chose, or would have chosen or expected if they had been directed to give the matter thought, but a comprehensive statement of those rules does not appear to be found anywhere.

What would 'universal' rules of the conflict of laws look like? No doubt they would provide that a contract is governed by the law chosen by the parties, but would they limit the choice to laws with which the contract appears to have an objective connection, or deny the choice where it appeared to have been made for illicit purposes? What law would they consider to govern the capacity of a party to contract, or to govern the consequences of the contractual incapacity[9] of a party ? If no law has been chosen to govern a contract, would these principles refer the tribunal to the place or places where the contract was made, or to the law with which it appears to be most closely connected, or to the country with which it is most closely connected, or to the law of the place of performance or something

[7] This is not as powerful as it may seem: it is well understood that when the conflict of laws identifies a rule of domestic law which should be applied, that rule will have been designed by its maker for domestic, not for international, cases: it is applied malgré lui, despite itself.

[8] An impressive quantity of doctrinal writing on this topic can be found by those who wish to find it. It is far from apparent that any of it contributes a practical solution to an actual problem, and equally far from apparent that this ever really happens.

[9] It does not necessarily follow that a contract made by a party which lacks contractual capacity is wholly void.

further yet? Would a claim for the repayment of money be governed by the law which governs the contract? Would the answer be the same whether the contract was discharged for breach, or rescinded for fault, or found to have been a common mistake and void from the start? What law would be applied to an allegation of tortious or unconscionable wrongdoing? Would it matter whether such a wrong was committed within or associated with a contractual relationship? After these, and many more such, questions, a realistic view would be that consensus on the rules of the conflict of laws, or on the common transnational content of the conflict of laws, can exist only at a level of generality so high that it offers no real help to a tribunal dealing with a complex commercial dispute.

These problems are insoluble or if not, are soluble only by assertion. That limits the utility of the answer to the immediate case, with the further consequence that the gradual accretion by which a system builds up a useful body of reliable knowledge will not easily work in the context of arbitration. The obviously rational solution is for the legislator who makes law, or the competent body which devises the rules which apply to the arbitration, to devise a set of conflicts rules and principles, and promulgate these as the particularised provisions which the tribunal will follow wherever the parties have not identified the applicable law by choice.[10] If appended to the rules of the ICC, LCIA, SIAC and so forth, these might function as rules rather than laws, but drafting them would be the work of days rather than weeks. Even better, perhaps, would be for them to be developed under the aegis of UNCITRAL, so that a legislator, or arbitration rule-maker, may simply adopt them. By such practical means the process of law-finding would be transparent, direct and reviewable.[11] For an institution of the importance of international commercial arbitration, it seems obvious that this must be the best and fairest solution.

4.3.2 Where the Tribunal Is Directed to Apply the Appropriate Law without Mention of the Conflict of Laws

If an arbitration is governed by the current rules of an institutional body but the parties have not chosen the law which is to be applied, the tribunal

[10] Alternatively, the component of the rules which gives effect to the choice made by the parties may be incorporated as a rule or rules within it.

[11] To the extent permitted by relevant law.

will be directed to apply 'the rules of law which it determines to be appropriate', or 'the law or rules of law which it determines to be appropriate'.[12] By what methodology is this identification to take place?

One possibility would be that the instruction contained in the rules can be complied with only by an application of rules of conflict of laws, even though the tribunal is not directed to proceed on this basis. This, after all, is how lawyers in national legal systems have imposed order and predictability on the task of finding the appropriate legal rule. If that is so, the path to the answer (and objections to the answer) will be the same as those just mentioned, but without the written instruction to follow it. Another possibility would be to apply 'transnational' principles of private international law, but the objection to that has also been stated. It is hard to see a robust solution in any of these.

An alternative solution may be found, improbably but never mind, in American conflict of laws scholarship. A strand in that rich tapestry denies the utility of traditional conflict of laws connecting factors, which simply point a court to a legal system and leave the judges to apply the law they find there, whether they like it or not. In place of this it compares, side by side, the potentially applicable rules of domestic law, found in the variously connected legal systems, in order to discover the particular rule which is the best fitted for application to the particular case. Most conflict of laws writers outside the United States are unnerved by the seeming subjectivity and unpredictability of the whole exercise, but in the context of arbitration it could be argued that this, or something analogous, is faithful to the amorphous instruction now contained in arbitral rules of the kind with which we are concerned. If the primary purpose of the tribunal is to settle the issue before it, but not to contribute to or develop a system of laws in parallel to that produced by courts, an approach of this

[12] For example, **ICC Rules Art 21(1)** The parties shall be free to agree upon the rules of law to be applied by the arbitral tribunal to the merits of the dispute. In the absence of any such agreement, the arbitral tribunal shall apply the rules of law which it determines to be appropriate. **LCIA Rules 22(3)** The Arbitral Tribunal shall decide the parties' dispute in accordance with the law(s) or rules of law chosen by the parties as applicable to the merits of their dispute. If and to the extent that the Arbitral Tribunal decides that the parties have made no such choice, the Arbitral Tribunal shall apply the law(s) or rules of law which it considers appropriate. **SIAC Rules Art 31.1** The Tribunal shall apply the law or rules of law designated by the parties as applicable to the substance of the dispute. Failing such designation by the parties, the Tribunal shall apply the law or rules of law which it determines to be appropriate.

kind has its attraction. So long as the parties are afforded the opportunity to address the tribunal on the issue, and so long as the tribunal exposes its reasoning in response, it is hard to see where sustainable ground for complaint might be found to exist.

In the final analysis, though courts and tribunals need to work out which country's laws (or which non-country's laws or rules) to apply, their methods need not be the same. Indeed, as tribunals often have a wider menu of choice, their methods must be to some extent different. A court applying its rules of private international law will usually have to decide whether to apply the domestic laws of country A or country B; having decided that, it will take and apply the relevant rules of the system so identified, looking no further into the content or consequences of those laws being applied. It will not usually have to decide whether to apply a rule of civil law or a rule of (say) religious or other non-national rules of law. Its rule book is, to this extent at least, of questionable utility to a tribunal faced in principle with a wider range of overlapping possibilities.

Though it may be abstractly or even theoretically interesting,[13] there seems to be no practical advantage in asserting the existence of an unwritten transnational (private international) law to guide, liberate, or bewilder the tribunal in answering these important questions. The idea that the rules for identification of the law to be applied are unwritten in a secret book, whose contents may be known to the tribunal, but not to or by anyone else, is not recommendable.[14] A written and transparent statement of the rules which will guide a tribunal in this aspect of its work is the only respectable solution.

4.4 Private International Law after an Arbitration

After a foreign arbitration, what may the court do? There are two substantial points to consider. It may be asked to enforce the award by one means or another according to its own procedural law. The New York Convention,

[13] *See e.g.* Fouchard, Gaillard, Goldman, *On International Commercial Arbitration* (Kluwer, 1999); Poudret & Besson, *Comparative Law of International Arbitration* (trans. Berti and Ponti) (2nd ed., Thomson, London, 2007), Chapter 7.

[14] It will also be immune from effective challenge or review for error, which appears to vest in the arbitrators a power which is in the circumstances unjustifiable.

or legislation made to implement it, forms the principal basis for its doing so, but this convention must allow a court to deny the enforcement order applied for where to make it would contradict mandatory rules of law by which the court is bound *qua* court,[15] and does allow it to refuse where it would require the court to contradict its own public policy.[16] The confirmation that this power lies in the enforcing court answers any contention that the freedom of the parties to choose the law permits them to circumvent important laws by which a court would have found them to be bound; it prevents the intolerable evasion of local public policy; it allows tribunals to decide on the basis of what they find to be the applicable law and to leave it to the courts of enforcement to worry about such supervening concerns. It is also consistent with the view that legislation and other rules of civil law are directed at courts, but not generally at arbitrators:[17] this is simply the logic of, and functional division between, private autonomy and public law duty. And it ensures that these important aspects of private international law are located in their proper place and applied by the body whose function it is to apply them; it means that the vexing question of the circumstances in which a system's (but which system's?) mandatory laws, and public policy, impinge on the dispute resolution is left to be determined by the courts for the place, or places, in which judicial sanction by way of enforcement is sought, and on a country-by-country basis, which is exactly as it should be.

The court may also be called upon to consider the effect of foreign judicial decisions given in relation to an arbitral award:[18] the recognition of foreign judgments is unquestionably a matter of private international law. For example, if a court in another country has refused to enforce the award, or has (purported to) set aside the award, the question whether another court is bound to do likewise or accept that there is no longer an award to enforce must be a matter for the application of rules of private international law. This is because unless it is overridden by some other law, the effect in the

[15] The Convention does not say so in express terms, but Art. V(2)(b) can be so interpreted.

[16] Art V(2)(b). There are other points of objection to enforcement, but these are the principal ones which engage with the conflict of laws. The reference to public policy may include fundamental provisions of European law by which a Member State is bound: Case C-126/97 Eco Swiss China Time Ltd v. Benetton International NV [1999] ECR I-3055.

[17] See *e.g.*, in the context of European legislation in jurisdiction, judgments and applicable law, Case C-536/13 Gazprom OAO EU:C:2015:316, [2015] 1 WLR 4937.

[18] At this point the foreign decision may be made in respect of a local arbitration.

legal order of a State of a judicial judgment from another country can only be a matter for the ordinary rules of private international law, and the result will vary from court to court accordingly. That is not to say that these rules, and their application, have finished the process of their evolution.[19]

4.4.1 Enforcement or Not of Foreign Awards

So far as concerns judicial proceedings to enforce a foreign award to which the New York Convention applies, the basic law will be set out in, or in national legislation made to implement, Articles III-V and VII. No major question of private international law arises for the entire question is liable to framed, and answered, by this legislation. As said, if the enforcement of the award would, for example, involve the court making an order whose effect would manifestly conflict with its own public policy, it is obvious that it cannot be made; if the court is asked to make an order which would conflict with legal rules of its own system which have overriding or mandatory effect, it is equally obvious that it cannot be made. So for example, if a decision to enforce the award would have the effect of tacitly condoning the bribery of an individual or corruption of a public official, the court is free to refuse to make it: it would be ludicrous to think the answer could be otherwise. In principle, a court, in making recourse to its public policy, will need to ask whether there is enough of a connection with its own legal order to justify the superimposition of its own laws on a contract, or an award, which was to it foreign. But if an English court is asked to make an order whose effect will in all likelihood be concentrated on and confined to the territory of the United Kingdom, it is hard to deny that the there is a sufficient English interest to warrant the application of English public policy.

If the tribunal has declined to apply a rule of English law which Parliament has directed the courts to apply to the relationship which falls within the grasp of the statute, the fact that the tribunal did as it did is no reason for the court to treat the relevant rule of its own legal system as somehow not mandatory: there is no such thing as 'mandatory unless an arbitral tribunal decides that it is not'. For example, if the tribunal were to

[19] *See* Poudret & Besson, *Comparative Law of International Arbitration* (trans. Berti & Ponti) (2nd ed., Thomson, London: 2007), Chapter 10.

apply rules of English[20] contract law, but not others (such as regulatory or authorisation provisions or rules on fair dealing) which would have made the contract legally unenforceable in court proceedings, an English court, called upon to enforce the award, must surely apply its law in a way which the tribunal may not have considered itself bound to do. Likewise, a court cannot make an order which would have the effect of contradicting Article 6 of the European Convention on Human Rights, and it is irrelevant that the contradiction would take the form of a judicial order enforcing an award.[21] Overriding and mandatory laws, which are properly identified as such and which are made by the legislator who also appointed the judge to office, are the business of judges, whose duty is to apply them *ex officio*. The matter is, however, not really one of private international law, or even of arbitration, but of organic law.

4.4.2 The Effect of Foreign Judicial Judgments in Relation to an Award

Matters are very different, though, when a foreign court has said or decided something which may be said to affect the reasoning of the court which is now seized. If[22] the material issue is approached as one of foreign judgments, the debate takes place within the ordinary framework of private international law: unless resulting from international agreement, the law on the effect of foreign judgments is national law in its entirety. Even so, where that foreign judgment concerns an arbitral award,[23] the path taken by the law – by any legal system's law – on foreign judgments requires more circumspection; the law may be less developed than may be supposed; and the danger of false analogy is never far away. We will start

[20] The analysis would be similar if the tribunal has applied a foreign contract law or an 'a-national' rule of contract law: if the rule of English law under consideration is one which was applicable as a matter of English law even to a contract not so governed, the law is mandatory as far as the court is concerned, and will be applied by accordingly.

[21] In principle, judgments from a court other than the seat may purport to do this, and if the judgment satisfies the rules on recognition it will, in principle, be liable to recognition (though with what effect is a separate question). It is perhaps more likely that judgments of this kind will be refused recognition on orthodox grounds; *see e.g.* Kahara Bodas Co LLC v. Pertamina 335 F 3d 357 (5th Cir. 2003).

[22] See further below for an alternative analysis.

[23] Because arbitration is a form of *lex specialis*. A similar point can be made in relation to insolvency and to foreign judgments made in the context of that.

with foreign judgments which set aside, or purport to set aside, the award, where the orthodox position certainly is that if the courts at the seat of the arbitration set aside the award, the award is dissolved[24] or ceases to exist as an obligation by which the parties are bound. In the common law, at least, this proposition appears to be more assumed than tested; the discussion which follows is intended to question it.[25]

Suppose that a foreign court, typically[26] at the seat of the arbitration, gives a judgment and makes an order by which it sets aside an award. This will certainly mean that the award will not be enforceable in that State. But what about outside it: how should the rules of private international law treat a foreign judgment setting aside an award? Considered as an issue of foreign judgment law, the answer is most likely to be found by separating two issues: whether the judgment itself qualifies for recognition in the first place, and if it does, whether it should be treated as having the same effect in the recognising State as it had or has in the State of origin.

The New York Convention permits, but does not require, the courts of one Contracting State to treat the setting aside by the courts at the seat as conclusive.[27] Perhaps it was taken for granted that this would be done and that it was actually too obvious to need saying. But it was not said; and it is now apparent that it is not obvious. In principle, the effect of a judgment from one court in the legal order of another depends entirely on the rules applicable to foreign judgments in the State addressed. As to these, if one takes a common law system as example, then subject to minor variations

[24] Enka Insaat ve Sanayi AS v OOO Insurance Company Chubb [2020] UKSC 38, [2020] 1 WLR 4117 certainly states (at [146], [193]) that the courts at the seat have this power; the proposition that the courts of other countries must simply accept such a judgment as destroying the award was not really tested.

[25] If a foreign court has given judgment 'converting the award into a judgment', the question whether that (foreign) judgment can itself be enforced as an original foreign judgment, without specific regard to the New York Convention, may be matter considered to be a matter of foreign judgment law, asking whether the foreign order is sufficiently like an original determination of the underlying merits to count as a judgment to which the law on judgments applies; the answer may vary from case to case. But the New York Convention question will be whether it is permissible assess the position of the parties to the award by anything other than the Convention and the legislation made to enact it; the answer may be that it is not. As usual, the answer will only be found by framing the issue with precision.

[26] In principle, at least, the rules of private international law would not limit the recognition of such foreign judgments to those from the seat of the arbitration.

[27] Art V(1)(e). *See also* Art 36(1)(a)(e) of the UNCITRAL Model Law, which is functionally identical.

in law and procedure, the first question is whether the foreign judgment is one *in rem*. If it is, its effect will depend on whether it is a judgment from the courts of the situs of the thing, which in this case would have to be the award itself, which will presumably be taken to be at the seat. It is not wholly fanciful to say that the arbitration-cum-award has a situs as well as a seat; it would lead to the conclusion that a judgment from the courts at the seat setting aside the award would be recognised as conclusive, subject to the usual defences. But there are serious objections: that the award is not sufficiently analogous to a thing to consider the situs as the having decisive authority it does with, say, issues of title to land, ships, company shares and public registers; and that in any event, the seat of the arbitration is a practical necessity rather than a natural dominance. To put it in more direct terms: the award is not there, and is not theirs.[28]

If one turns instead to the rules on foreign judgments *in personam*, the common law will ask whether the party to whom the judgment was adverse was present within the jurisdiction of the foreign court when the judicial proceedings were begun, or submitted to the jurisdiction of the court before the service of process by contractual agreement or after service by voluntary appearance. Many consequential questions arise, which include whether the arbitration agreement is itself a sufficient submission to the courts at the seat for post-hoc proceedings concerned with the arbitration and whether, if not, submission be found on the basis of a party's voluntary appearance in judicial proceedings to set aside the award.

If it is argued that when parties agree to arbitrate at wherever the seat is they submit, by the same token, to the jurisdiction and controlling power of the courts of that country, the reasoning is open to genuine debate.[29] The first truth appears to be that parties who agree to arbitrate seek, to the extent possible, to avoid all entanglements with courts. They may be aware that if the arbitration were to run into trouble, access to a court might be

[28] At this point the analysis diverges from that in Stati v. Republic of Kazakhstan (No 2) [2018] EWCA Civ 1896, [2019] 1 WLR 897, where the view appears to be that the courts of the seat have a unique power to set aside an award.

[29] Something similar has been said of insolvency: that a creditor who lodges a claim with the administrator submits by virtue of that very act to the entire insolvency jurisdiction of the (supervising) court: Rubin v. Eurofinance SA [2012] UKSC 46, [2013] 1 AC 236. But the administrators are appointed by and answerable to the supervising court; arbitrators are not, and there is no real analogy.

necessary or desirable, but this does not obviously mean that they submitted in advance to the post-hoc setting aside power of the courts at[30] that place: this is the issue, correctly framed, and the answer may involve a question of construction of documents evidencing their agreement. True, there do exist more complex (or less coherent) dispute resolution clauses, by which the parties agree to arbitration and to the jurisdiction of courts, and a determined court may find in these a submission in advance to the setting aside power of the named court. But it often appears that the collision of these clauses is accidental rather than designed; the appearance of accident is stark when the commercial relationship between the parties is created by concurrent contracts with dispute resolution provisions which do not dovetail. There are probably no general principles applicable to the interpretation of clauses of this type. However, if any effect is to be given to its judgment, the court addressed will need to establish that the parties did submit to this aspect of the jurisdiction of the foreign court.

If they did, one may still question the suitability of the default rules of *res judicata* by asking whether factors specific to the law of arbitration should lead a court to a more nuanced application of its normal rules on the effect of foreign judgments to one invalidating an award. No common law rule of private international law requires recognition of a foreign judgment to mean that the judgment must be accorded precisely the same effect as it has under the State of origin;[31] English law, not foreign law, determines the effect of a foreign judgment in England. One may therefore ask whether there is something about an arbitral award which means that the rules are modified when foreign judgments given in relation to it. For example, should a judgment ostensibly setting aside an award be interpreted as though it were (no more than) a judgment refusing to give local effect to the award, having no wider effect? If one accepts the principle

[30] *Not*, be it noted, 'the law in force at that place'.

[31] For example, a foreign judgment which purports to operate *in rem*, on property outside its jurisdiction, and which may not be recognised as such, may still be recognised as imposing obligations *in personam* on the defendant to the foreign proceedings: Pattni v. Ali [2006] UKPC 51, [2007] 2 AC 85. There is a sharp contrast with statutory regimes, such as that established by the Brussels I Regulation, and in bilateral treaties but also those which provide for registration of a foreign judgment in a local court which State that the foreign judgment, when registered, takes effect as though it were an original judgment of the registering court.

that *exequatur sur exequatur ne vaut,*[32] should it not follow that *non exequatur sur non exequatur vaut encore moins?*[33]

The tradition of the common law would focus on a foreign judgment and ask whether it met the requirements laid down for the recognition and enforcement of foreign judgments as they have been described above; insofar as it recognised the judgment it would impose an obligation on the parties to abide by it and that obligation would eclipse the facts and matters which produced it; its instinct would be to treat the obligation as one to abide by the foreign judgment in the terms in which it was given. By contrast, at least some at least systems of the civil law family deduce from the autonomy and internationality of arbitration the conclusion that the award does not 'belong' to a legal system in the same way a judgment does; that there is no necessity to treat the status of the award as being under the exclusive jurisdiction[34] of the seat and no obligation to ascribe international effect to its judgment.[35] There is sense and reason in this. It is easy to understand that a legal system should contain and operate rules which, for a variety of reasons, lead it to the conclusion that the award is not to be treated within its territory as an enforceable obligation. It is easy to understand that when the courts at the seat find a flaw in the award and assess it as fatal, the natural terminology for what they do is to set it aside. But it is less easy to understand why that legal system should have transnational power to impede or pre-empt the enforcement of an award beyond its own judicial space. It would have to be justified on the basis that the parties have institutionally submitted to the courts of the seat, in spite of the fact that the point of arbitration is to sideline the courts to the extent possible; this is especially hard when the seat is identified by rules operating in default of actual choice. If this line is taken, a foreign

[32] A judgment authorising the enforcement of another judgment cannot itself be the foundation for an enforcement claim.

[33] A judgment refusing to authorise the enforcement of another judgment is even less valid as the foundation for a decision to refuse enforcement.

[34] For an alternative question, whether the award should be seen as resting exclusively on the law of the seat, *see* below.

[35] *See* the decisions of the French Supreme Court in Hilmarton Ltd v. Omnium de Traitement et de Valorisation (23 March 1994), (1995) 20 Yb Comm Arb 663; PT Putrabali Adyamulia v. Soc Rena Holding (29 June 1007), (2008) 24 Arb Int 293. *See* for evaluation from an English perspective, Dallah Real Estate and Tourism Holding Co v. Ministry of Religious Affairs, Government of Pakistan [2010] UKSC 46, [2011] 1 AC 763, esp at [128]–[131].

judgment setting aside an award will be understood as a judicial refusal to enforce the award, but no more.

At this point an alternative perspective should be considered. This would focus not on court judgments and their overseas effect, but on foreign law as a source of rights and obligations. Suppose an arbitration, having its seat in France, is (in some sense, which it is not necessary to define) the product of French law; and then suppose a French court pronounces a decree setting the award aside so that as a matter of French law the award no longer exists as a source of legal obligation, or as anything at all. If the question of its validity or enforceability should arise before an English court, should the English court instead look to French law, as *lex arbitri/contractus/causae*, to ask whether there is still an enforceable obligation, rather than to the law on foreign judgments?

Although authority is elusive, and although the point is clearly arguable, it is submitted that the answer is not to found by looking to French law as *law* governing the obligation in question, but to the law of foreign judgments as this has been described. Four reasons may be offered. First, there has been no change in the material content of the *lex arbitri* as such, so there is no need to enquire whether French law considers the obligation to have altered or to have been dissolved. It is not analogous to the case in which a contract is made and governed by a law which is subsequently changed by legislation imposing, for example, a statutory moratorium or a compulsory reduction of interest rates.[36] Second, the case is not analogous to one in which the *lex contractus* gives a party an option to rescind a contract which is voidable, or to discharge a contract for breach, or to argue that the contract has been discharged by supervening event. Rather, a court has swooped on the award, and has made an order in connection with it. Third, if this *lex causae* view were taken, there would be a nice question whether the law to which one might look would be the law governing the arbitration as such, or the law of the underlying contract. And fourth, if a foreign court (as distinct from legislator) varies, annuls, or sets aside a contract otherwise valid by its governing law, the effect of its decree is assessed as a judgment, not treated as new data adding to the *lex contractus*.

As a matter of characterisation (a term of art in private international law), the correct legal question is whether an effect brought into existence by the

[36] *See*, for comparison, Wight v. Eckhardt Marine GmbH [2003] UKPC 37, [2004] 1 AC 147.

judgment of a foreign court has any (and if so, what) effect in England. To put the point another way, when an award is judicially annulled, and the effect of this is examined in another State, the court addressed does not look to and apply the law under which the arbitration was constituted, but to the decree of the court which purported to do something to it. That is why reference to the *lex arbitri* on this issue is, on balance, inappropriate. The answer is to be found in the law on foreign judgments.

Returning to the law on foreign judgments, one must guard against a false analogy with what happens when a court sets aside a judgment from another[37] court within its own system. The judicial system which created the judgment in the first place can dissolve it again so that it ceases to exist, and there is usually[38] little more to be said. But even if one accepts that *lex facit arbitrum*, the law makes the arbitration, it does not follow that the court owns it, *curia possidet arbitrum*. The award is not created by the judicial system, and if a court purports to annul the award, it is intervening to exercise State power over the product of lawful private acts. As awards are not products of the judicial system which may purport to set them aside, any pretended analogy between awards and judgments is inexact; even less exact would be any alleged analogy between an arbitral tribunal and its award and an administrative tribunal and its decision. All this is more than enough reason to question whether the setting aside of awards should be treated as, or as analogous to, the setting aside of judgments. Where the award is concerned, the court which considers itself to be the seat may certainly give a judgment which sets aside the award; it does not follow that another court must see the dissolution of the award as a fait accompli.

Of course, if any court were to be recognised as having jurisdiction to set aside an award with international effect, it could only be the court at the seat;[39] the position which is proposed here is that it should not be so

[37] Or, indeed, from itself.

[38] But not invariably: if the appeal judgment can be refused recognition, for example on the basis that it was procured by fraud or bias, the original judgment *may* be considered, in the recognising court, to remain binding on the parties to it: Merchant International Co Ltd v. NAK Naftogaz [2012] EWCA Civ 196, [2012] 1 WLR 3036.

[39] Though it is possible, in theory at least, that the parties may agree to fight this issue before another court and bind themselves to accept its judgment. For an illustration of the complexity which the law as currently (mis)understood can generate, *see* Astro Nusantara International BV v. PT Ayunda Prima Mitra [2018] HKCFA 12.

recognised. The judgment of a foreign court which declares that an award does not qualify for enforcement within the territory of a court should not be, will not be, enforced outside the territory of that court (*non exequatur sur non exequatur vaut encore moins*). The crucial question is whether the judgment of a foreign court which purports to set aside an award should be treated for the purposes of its recognition or enforcement as being, in substance, a judgment refusing to enforce the award, and its territorial effect as likewise confined within the territory of the foreign court. Although there would be at present little support for this view among common law private international lawyers,[40] legal science is in a state of continuous improvement, and this is, it is submitted, an improvement which merits serious consideration. It would preserve the autonomy of the arbitration and the award, would acknowledge the separation between the setting aside of judgments and the treatment of obligations which are not judgments, and it would reflect the territorial autonomy of judicial decisions to enforce or not enforce awards. If this would involve a measured step beyond what the common law rules of private international law have so far accepted,[41] the taking of it would still be entirely consistent with the developing understanding of the relationship between arbitration and private international law. As said above, there is nothing in the New York Convention to require[42] a court to accept that if an award has been set aside by another court there is nothing to enforce. On this issue, as with injunctions in aid and support of the arbitration agreement, about which the Convention is equally silent, it is left to national law to provide the answers.

For the sake of clarity, it should be added that if the courts at the seat annul an award which is unfavourable to the claimant, the consequences of their decision will depend on the order which they make, and on the steps the parties take in relation to it.

[40] Stati v. Republic of Kazakhstan (No 2) [2018] EWCA Civ 1896, [2019] 1 WLR 897, [35]–[36].

[41] According to Dicey, Morris & Collins, *The Conflict of Laws* (Collins: Sweet & Maxwell, 15th ed, 2012) para. 16–148, English law on this issue has yet to be declared by the courts. For a wide-ranging, penetrating, analysis, *see* Petrochilos, *Procedural Law in International Arbitration* (Oxford: 2004), Chapter 7.

[42] Nor to prevent, obviously.

4.4.3 The Proper Role of Issue Estoppel Arising from Foreign Judgments

If a court, seized with proceedings to determine for itself the enforceability of an award, chooses to align its reasoning with the prior decision of a foreign court, that is a matter for its private international law alone.[43] If the foreign court has adjudicated a particular issue which the court now seized has to decide as part of its own enquiry, the ordinary rules on foreign judgments and issue estoppel[44] should be applied, though for the reasons given above, cause of action estoppel will be less likely to apply. So for example, if a foreign court considers that it will not treat the award as binding because it offends the public policy of its law, the second court will have to decide whether the issue of public policy already decided by the foreign court is the same as the issue the court has to decide. This will mean asking whether the two national versions of public policy are sufficiently congruent to mean that the issue has already been judicially ruled upon; it is obvious that a range of answers is possible.[45] Likewise, if a foreign court has decided that a matter was not arbitrable according to its law, or that there was, according to its law, a fatal irregularity in the procedure adopted by the tribunal, *et cetera*, it will be open to the court addressed to treat this issue as res judicata, and incorporate that in its own decision whether to order enforcement of the award. But the final decision whether to order enforcement will be for the court addressed, not for that of the seat or, indeed, elsewhere. The result is that issue estoppel may follow from the recognition of a foreign judgment given in relation to an award, but that cause of action estoppel should not.

[43] And it plainly does not have to: Dallah Real Estate and Tourism Holding Co v. Ministry of Religious Affairs, Government of Pakistan [2010] UKSC 46, [2011] 1 AC 763.

[44] In summary, (1) the party said to be bound by a foreign court's decision on an issue submitted to the jurisdiction of the foreign court and (2) the foreign court made a final and (for it) necessary determination on an issue which arose before it, (3) in circumstances which conformed to the broad requirements of natural and substantial justice; and (4) that same issue arises again for decision in proceedings before the court addressed such that it would be unjust to allow the party who lost the first time to have a second bite at the cherry. For an illustration of the application, *see* Diag Human SE v. Czech Republic [2014] EWHC 1639 (Comm).

[45] *See e.g.* Yukos Capital Sarl v. OJSC Oil Co Rosneft [2012] EWCA Civ 855, [2014] QB 458.

5 The Role of the *Lex Arbitri*

Giuditta Cordero-Moss

5.1 Introduction

It is often affirmed that international arbitration does not have a *forum*. This statement can be seen as one of the manifestations of the doctrine that considers arbitration as a purely international phenomenon, detached from national laws. I have criticised this doctrine in many writings and will not repeat my arguments here.[1] What this chapter deals with is one specific aspect, namely the significance for international arbitration of the arbitration law of the country in which the arbitral tribunal has its formal seat, the *lex arbitri*. The analysis will show that the statement according to which arbitration has no *forum* cannot de understood to mean that the *lex arbitri* has no significance for arbitration.

Admittedly, arbitration enjoys a considerable autonomy from national laws. To a large extent, this is based on international instruments – primarily, the 1958 New York Convention on the Recognition and Enforcement of Foreign Arbitral Awards. If parties decide to submit a dispute to arbitration, according to Article II, the courts of the 168 States which ratified the Convention[2] must decline jurisdiction on that dispute. If the arbitral tribunal chosen by the parties renders an award based on the instructions given by the parties and applies the law chosen by the parties, according to Article III of the Convention, the courts of all those States have to enforce that award. The only, few exceptions are listed in Article V. Furthermore, in some respects, the Convention gives its own, autonomous regulation and thus makes the *lex arbitri* or other national laws redundant, although, as will be discussed in Section 5.2.1, this is not always necessarily true. In other

[1] *See e.g.* G. Cordero-Moss, *International Commercial Contracts* (Cambridge: Cambridge University Press, 2013), 216.

[2] For an updated overview of the status of ratifications *see* the Convention's official site at www.uncitral.org/uncitral/en/uncitral_texts/arbitration/NYConvention_status.html.

respects, however, the New York Convention makes reference to the *lex arbitri*. This will be discussed below.

At the outset of the analysis, there are two observations to be made, regarding what is meant by *seat* and by *law*.

Regarding the former, the New York Convention speaks of the 'country where the award was made'. This is the formal seat of the arbitral tribunal. It is chosen by the parties in the arbitration agreement or later. More rarely, it is determined by the arbitral institution or by the arbitral tribunal. The seat of the tribunal does not necessarily coincide with the place of the various procedural actions. Hearings may have taken place in a different country, or the award may have been rendered by circulating it among the members of the arbitral tribunal, who may reside in three different countries. This does not have any implications for the seat.[3]

Regarding the latter, it is the national law of the country of the seat that is applicable. Unlike recognition and enforcement that are uniformly regulated by the New York Convention, aspects such as the constitution of the arbitral tribunal, the rules of procedure or court control on the validity of the award do not enjoy such a high degree of uniformity as they are mainly regulated in national law. However, the UNCITRAL Model Law on International Commercial Arbitration has been adopted in 85 countries and is widely used as a reference elsewhere. The Model Law was intended as a source of harmonisation in international arbitration. To this end, it was deliberately aligned with the New York Convention.[4] This contributes greatly to the harmonisation of national arbitration laws, thus enhancing the not entirely correct impression that arbitration law is standardised and that there is no need to pay attention to the peculiarities of national laws.

The *lex arbitri* affects various aspects of arbitral proceedings, as will be discussed below: the validity of the arbitration agreement, the procedure of the arbitration, the validity of the arbitral award, the enforcement of the award and the selection of the law applicable to the merits of the dispute.

[3] G. Born, *International Commercial Arbitration* (Wolters Kluwer, 2021) (3rd ed.).

[4] *See* the Explanatory Note by the UNCITRAL Secretariat on the Model Law on International Commercial Arbitration, available at www.uncitral.org/uncitral/en/uncitral_texts/arbitration/1985Model_arbitration.html.

5.2 Lex Arbitri and the Validity of the Arbitration Agreement

The jurisdiction of an arbitral tribunal on a certain dispute and the consequent exclusion of court jurisdiction on the same dispute rely on the already mentioned New York Convention. Article II provides that 'each Contracting State shall recognize an agreement in writing under which the parties undertake to submit to arbitration all or any differences which have arisen or which may arise between them in respect of a defined legal relationship, whether contractual or not, concerning a subject matter capable of settlement by arbitration'. Article II does not make reference to any national law for the validity of the arbitration agreement and seems, therefore, to contain all applicable criteria for validity.

However, Article V(1)(a), regulating exceptions to the enforcement of awards, States that enforcement may be refused if 'the ... agreement referred to in article II ... is not valid under the law to which the parties have subjected it or, failing any indication thereon, under the law of the country where the award was made'. The latter – the *lex arbitri* – is more commonly used: it is rare to see an arbitration clause specifying which law governs the arbitration, and the general choice of law made by the parties to govern their contractual relationship does not extend to the arbitration agreement, not even if this latter takes the form of a clause in the same contract.[5] Coordination of Article II and Article V of the Convention may create some challenges, as will be seen immediately below.

5.2.1 Formal Validity

A large number of contracts contain arbitration clauses entered into electronically, by reference to other documents or even orally. This raises questions, particularly in relation to the requirement of Article II of the New York Convention that arbitration agreements be 'in writing'.

The UNCITRAL issued a recommendation to interpret this provision broadly so that arbitration agreements entered into by electronic means of communication may be considered to comply with the writing

[5] G. Born, *International Commercial Arbitration*, cit., Vol I, para. 3.03[B]. See, however, for England, Enka Insaat ve Sanayi AS v OOO Insurance Company Chubb [2020] UKSC 38.

requirement.[6] The Model Law was amended in 2006 so as to exclude any doubt regarding the admissibility of arbitration agreements entered into electronically. This provides a certain clarity on the enforceability of agreements entered into electronically, but it does not solve all problems.

Under national laws, the formal requirements for arbitration agreements may vary. Article 807 of the Italian Code of Civil Procedure, Article 178(1) of the Swiss Private International Law Act (PILA), Article 1031 of the German Code of Civil Procedure and Section 5 of the English Arbitration Act, for example, require the arbitration agreement to be in writing, albeit with some differences in the specification of how to meet this requirement. Other countries have abolished the writing requirement: Article 1 of the Swedish Arbitration Act and Article 3-10 of the Norwegian Arbitration Act recognise any arbitration agreement, even oral agreements, provided that the parties have reached a consensus. A similar regime is adopted in one of the two options given by Article 7 of the revised Model Law.

Oral arbitration clauses raise various questions. In particular: is an award enforceable under the New York Convention if it was rendered on the basis of an arbitration agreement that, while valid under the *lex arbitri*, is not in writing as required by Article II? Traditionally, despite the reference to national law contained in Article V, it was widely considered that the formal requirements of Article II prevailed over any requirements laid down by applicable national law. This is because the New York Convention was traditionally thought to embody an approach more favourable to arbitration than is found in national laws. However, after some national laws and the amended Model Law have become more arbitration-friendly than the New York Convention in respect of formal requirements, it may rightly be asked whether that view should change and national arbitration laws be given preference. This would be more in line with the wording of Article V(1)(a) and with the spirit of the Convention.[7]

[6] UNCITRAL '*Recommendation regarding the interpretation of article II (2) and article VII*' paragraph 1, of the Convention on the Recognition and Enforcement of Foreign Arbitral Awards, New York, 10 June 1958, adopted by the United Nations Commission on International Trade Law on 7 July 2006 at its thirty-ninth session, A/RES/61/33, available at www.uncitral.org/pdf/english/texts/arbitration/NY-conv/A2E.pdf.

[7] Article VII of the New York Convention permits applying national laws that are more arbitration-friendly than the Convention itself. For a more extensive analysis *see* G. Cordero-Moss, *International Commercial Contracts*, cit., 226.

The *lex arbitri*, therefore, may have relevance to the formal validity of the arbitration agreement.

5.2.2 The Legal Capacity of the Parties to the Arbitration Agreement

According to Article V(1)(a) of the New York Convention, one of the grounds for refusing recognition or enforcement of an award is that one of the parties to the arbitration agreement was under some incapacity under its own law. The Model Law has used this provision as a basis for its own rule on annulment of awards, Article 34(2)(a)(i). Similar references to the law of each of the parties may be found in the arbitration law of countries that have not adopted the Model Law. Thus, two court decisions rendered in countries that have not adopted the Model Law, one of the Swedish Court of Appeal[8] and one of the English Supreme Court,[9] established the ineffectiveness of awards on the basis that the arbitration agreement was not binding on one of the parties in accordance with the law applicable to that party. These decisions are a reminder that the law chosen by the parties to govern the contract does not cover all aspects of the legal relationship between the parties, and that other laws may become applicable in spite of the parties' choice.

In the case of legal capacity, it is the law of each of the parties. The New York Convention does not specify how to select this law. Rules of private international law may be useful to determine which law applies to each party's legal capacity. As will be discussed in Section 5.6, it may be appropriate to apply private international law rules belonging to the *lex arbitri*.

5.2.3 The Scope of the Arbitration Agreement

Elsewhere,[10] I have explained how contract practice incrementally developed detailed descriptions of the scope of arbitration clauses as

[8] State of Ukraine v. Norsk Hydro ASA, Svea Hovrätt, 17 December 2007, T 3108-06, leave to appeal denied on 2 June 2008, case no T 339-08.

[9] Dallah Real Estate & Tourism Holding Co v. Ministry of Religious Affairs, Government of Pakistan [2010] UKSC 46.

[10] G. Cordero-Moss, 'International Arbitration Is Not Only International' in G. Cordero-Moss, *International Commercial Arbitration. Different Forms and Their Features* (Cambridge: Cambridge University Press, 2013), 7–39.

a reaction to the restrictive interpretation that some English court decisions had made of arbitration clauses. English case law has since changed, so that it is no longer necessary to write 'any disputes arising out of or in relation to', or 'this agreement, its termination or validity'. Arbitration clauses are nevertheless still written so as to meet the requirements of the superseded, restrictive jurisprudence. Furthermore, this style is adopted even for model clauses that are not subject to English law. Arbitration clauses, therefore, are unnecessarily detailed. What a detailed arbitration clause may not achieve, however, no matter how clear and precise it is, is to extend the scope of what the *lex arbitri* considers to be arbitrable. The matter of arbitrability will be analysed in Section 5.4.1.

5.3 Lex Arbitri and the Procedure

Generally, the principle of territoriality applies, and arbitration procedure is governed by the *lex arbitri*. The territoriality principle is affirmed, for example, in Article 46 of the Swedish Arbitration Act, Article 176 of the Swiss PILA, Section 2 of the English Arbitration Act and Article 1(2) of the Model Law. The territoriality principle applies only to the law governing the arbitration procedure and does not extend to the law governing the merits of the dispute.

Some States have opened up for the parties to choose the law governing the arbitration procedure. In these States, the parties may derogate the territoriality principle: for example, Article 182(1) of the Swiss PILA and Article 1494 of the French Civil Procedure Code. That the parties have chosen a certain law to govern their contract, however, is not sufficient to make the chosen law applicable also to the procedure. If the parties wish that the arbitral proceeding be regulated by a law different from the law of the place where the arbitral tribunal is seated, their choice should make specific reference to the arbitration procedure (assuming that the arbitration law of the place of arbitration permits them to make such a choice).

It has been authoritatively commented that 'there are compelling reasons to conclude that it is unwise for parties to make agreements selecting a procedural law other than that of the seat. ... Doing so ordinarily introduces serious complexity, uncertainty and risks into the arbitral proceedings'.[11] Irrespective of whether the parties have chosen to submit their dispute to an ad hoc or an institutional arbitration, the arbitral proceeding will thus generally be subject to the *lex arbitri*. If the parties have provided for procedural rules in the agreement or by reference to arbitration rules, these arbitration rules will apply to their proceeding and will prevail over the rules contained in the *lex arbitri*, if the latter permits to be derogated from by agreement of the parties. In the case of mandatory provisions of the *lex arbitri*, however, the latter will override the arbitration rules chosen by the parties. Examples of mandatory provisions are the rules on arbitrability and on due process, such as the necessity of giving both parties the chance to be heard.

The *lex arbitri* usually contains rules on the constitution of the arbitral tribunal, on the powers of the arbitrators to issue interim measures, to summon witnesses and to request assistance from the local courts in such operations, and on the role of courts in the case of a challenge to an arbitrator, as well in case of challenge to the validity of the award.

Arbitration laws are, usually, quite liberal in their regulation of arbitration. The parties desire to have as much flexibility as possible in the organisation of this mechanism for dispute resolution that is chosen precisely because it leaves ample room for private determination. If State law started to regulate arbitration in detail, this method of dispute resolution would probably lose much of its appeal to commercial parties. However, if there were no regulation at all, the parties might fear that fundamental principles of due process might be neglected. Therefore, a successful arbitration law is an instrument that manages to ensure a high degree of flexibility, though providing certain rules to protect the principle of due process.

5.4 Lex Arbitri and Validity of an Arbitral Award

In most jurisdictions the losing party may challenge, before national courts, the validity of an arbitral award that has been rendered in that State. The judicial control on the arbitral award in the phase of challenge is regulated by the *lex arbitri*.

[11] G. Born, *International Commercial Arbitration*, cit., Vol II, para. 11.05[B](2).

In some States, awards rendered in disputes without any contact with that State enjoy a certain detachment from the system of the *lex arbitri*. For example, in Belgium, France, Sweden and Switzerland, the parties may enter into an agreement excluding, at least in part, court control. In most other States, as well as under the Model Law, the control jurisdiction of the courts cannot be excluded.

The list of grounds upon which a court may declare an award invalid varies from State to State. In some States, as in England, the judge has relatively wide powers. Among others, an English judge may verify the arbitral tribunal's application of law,[12] although the possibility of setting aside an award for error in law has been significantly restricted in the English Arbitration Act of 1996. In most other European States, the list of invalidity grounds can be broadly said to coincide with the list contained in Article 34 of the Model Law which, in turn, coincides with the list of grounds upon which an award may be refused enforcement under the New York Convention. These grounds may be summarised as referring to invalidity or irregularity in the following areas: the arbitration agreement (which is governed primarily by the *lex arbitri*, as seen in Section 5.2); the composition of the arbitral tribunal (which may be considered as part of the arbitral procedure and is therefore governed by the parties' agreement, the chosen arbitration rules as well as by the *lex arbitri*, as seen in Section 5.3); the procedure of the arbitration (also governed by the parties' agreement, the chosen arbitration rules as well as by the *lex arbitri*, as seen in Section 5.3); and the scope of power exercised by the tribunal (which is determined primarily by the parties' agreement, but also by the chosen arbitration rules and by the *lex arbitri*). In addition, the award can be declared invalid by a court if there is a contrast with the rule on arbitrability contained in the *lex arbitri* or with the public policy (*ordre public*) in the legal system to which the *lex arbitri* belongs, as will be seen more in detail in Sections 5.4.1 and 5.4.2.

5.4.1 Arbitrability

There are various rules of State law that restrict the parties' ability to submit disputes to arbitration. Thanks to the New York Convention, choosing

[12] Section 69 of the English Arbitration Act.

arbitration excludes court jurisdiction on the dispute and entitles the winning party to obtain court enforcement of the award in any State where the losing party has assets. Arbitration enjoys such a significant recognition as long as the disputed matters concern areas that national legal systems consider suitable for self-regulation by private parties. As soon as matters of public policy or of special economic or social interest are touched on, however, States are reluctant to waive jurisdiction or to lend their courts' authority to enforce private awards. In such areas with important policy implications, States wish to preserve the jurisdiction of their own courts of law: this preference is based on the assumption that an arbitral tribunal would not be able or willing to apply the law as accurately as a judicial court would.

Some decades ago, with some celebrated US decisions,[13] the scope of arbitrability started expanding. Notwithstanding this trend in favour of arbitrability, however, various areas of law are still deemed to be exclusively in the hands of the courts of law. The areas where arbitrability is excluded vary from State to State: as a general rule, arbitration is usually permitted in all matters that fall within the boundaries of private law. This would exclude from the scope of arbitration matters such as competition law, taxation, import and export regulations, concession of rights by administrative authorities, bankruptcy, the protection of intellectual property or criminal law. These matters affect the public interest and are mostly regulated by mandatory rules. Disputes concerning aspects of commercial transactions falling within the scope of the freedom to contract, however, are usually arbitrable, even if the solution of the dispute assumes that the tribunal takes into consideration these mandatory rules as an incidental question. As long as the tribunal is requested to decide upon the private law-consequences of these rules' existence and is not required to apply or enforce any of these rules, there usually are no obstacles to arbitrability.

Recently, the arbitrability exception started being used more frequently, particularly in disputes involving mandatory regulation protecting the weaker party when this regulation belongs to the system of the court where the dispute would be heard if it had not been for the arbitration clause.[14]

[13] Scherk v. Alberto-Culver, 417 US 506 (1974), Mitsubishi Motors Corp. v. Soler Chrysler-Plymouth, Inc., 473 US 614, 628 (1985).

[14] More extensively, G. Cordero-Moss, 'Balancing Arbitrability and Court Control' in H. Muir Watt, L. Bíziková, A. Brandão de Oliveira and D. Fernández Arroyo (eds.), *Global Private International Law, Adjudication without Frontiers* (Edward Elgar Publishing), 82–91.

Since the arbitrability rule may have a different scope according to the law it belongs to, it is necessary to find out which law determines whether the subject of the dispute is arbitrable or not. The New York Convention and the Model Law refer to the arbitrability rule of the court. Hence, the arbitrability of the dispute will be evaluated under the *lex arbitri* if a court of that country is judging on the validity of the award, and under the law of the place of enforcement if a court of that country is asked to enforce the award.

If the dispute has no connection with the court's legal system apart from it being the place of the tribunal's seat or where the presence of assets permits enforcement, however, it is questionable that the court's arbitrability rule may be applied, and the rule on public seems more appropriate.[15]

5.4.2 Public Policy

The rule of public policy has the purpose of permitting the judge not to give effect to an award that would contradict the fundamental principles of the *lex arbitri*. The rule is, in the context of international arbitration, unanimously interpreted very narrowly.[16]

In particular, it does not have the same function as ensuring full compliance with rules and principles of the *lex arbitri*; public policy is usually defined by reference not to specific provisions, but to basic notions of morality and justice, features essential to the moral, political or economic order of the country or to most fundamental notions of morality and justice. In a similar vein, the Court of Justice of the European Union (CJEU) found, regarding the applicability of the public policy exception contained in the then-applicable Brussels Convention on Jurisdiction and Enforcement of Judgments, that a court cannot refuse enforcement of a judgment 'solely on the ground that it considers that national or Community law was misapplied in that decision'.[17] In particular, the enforcing court cannot review the accuracy of the findings of law made in the judgment. Moreover, the judgment must be at

[15] Cordero-Moss, *International Commercial Contracts,* cit., 263.

[16] See G. Cordero-Moss, 'Article V(2)(b)', in H. Kronke, P. Nacimiento, D. Otto, N. C. Port (ed.), *Recognition and Enforcement of Foreign Arbitral Awards: A Global Commentary on the New York Convention* (Kluwer Law International, 2nd edition, forthcoming.

[17] Régie nationale des usines Renault SA v. Maxicar SpA and Orazio Formento, C.38/98, para. 33.

variance, to an unacceptable degree, with the legal order of the enforcing State in as much as it infringes a fundamental principle, and the infringement must constitute a manifest breach of a rule of law regarded as essential or of a right recognised as being fundamental. This CJEU decision is not rendered under the New York Convention, but there is no reason why the reasoning made in respect of public policy as a ground for refusing recognition and enforcement of judgments under the Brussels Convention (or its successor, the Brussels I Regulation) should not also apply to public policy as a ground for refusing recognition and enforcement of awards under the New York Convention or as a ground to set aside an award under the *lex arbitri*.

The foregoing shows that the public policy clause is meant not to ensure application of specific provisions, but to safeguard their inspiring principles. It remains to attempt to define what inspiring principles can be deemed to be of public policy. Not every principle underlying a mandatory rule can be considered a public policy principle. Not even every principle underlying an overriding mandatory rule (i.e. a mandatory rule that is deemed to be so important that it requires to be applied even in international situations and without taking into consideration the general choice of law rules, also known as *lois de police*) can be considered of public policy.[18] It is only the fundamental principles – those that constitute the basis of the society – that can be deemed as public policy. There is no absolute rule to determine public policy: what is fundamental may vary from State to State, and, even within the same State, the conceptions develop, and what was deemed public policy a decade earlier, may not be so any more.

Court decisions in the various States annulling awards or refusing to enforce them on the ground of contrast with the court's public policy are not numerous. A decision that originated a wide debate in legal literature was rendered by the CJEU in the Eco Swiss case:[19] here the Court affirmed that European rules of competition law must be considered to belong to public policy. The wide debate that followed this decision related, among

[18] G. Born, *International Commercial Arbitration*, cit., paras. 26.05[C] ff.; G. Cordero-Moss, *International Commercial Contracts*, cit., 246; L. Radicati di Brozolo, 'Arbitration and Competition Law: The Position of the Courts and of Arbitrators', *Arbitration International*, 2011, 1, 6.

[19] Eco Swiss China Time Ltd. v. Benetton International N.V. C-126/97.

other things, to the scope and effects of the Court's findings.[20] At least two approaches have been taken: the maximalist and minimalist. According to the former, the court has, irrespective of the evaluation made by the arbitral tribunal, the power to independently evaluate whether the award infringes fundamental principles. According to the latter, the court owes deference to the evaluation made by the tribunal. Whether the court applies one or the other approach, depends on the *lex arbitri* in the phase of challenge of the award, and on the law of the place of enforcement, in case the court is called upon to enforce the award.

5.5 Lex Arbitri and Enforcement of an Arbitral Award

The *lex arbitri* is also relevant in the context of the enforcement of an award, in more than one respect.

As was explained in section 5.2, the *lex arbitri* determines the validity of the arbitration agreement, and an invalid arbitration agreement renders the award unenforceable under article V(1)(a) of the New York Convention.

Moreover, as was explained in section 5.3, the *lex arbitri* determines the regularity of the arbitral procedure and the criteria for the composition of the arbitral tribunal, which are also criteria for the enforceability of an award under article V(1)(d) of the New York Convention.

In addition, in article V(1)(e), the New York Convention considers it as a sufficient ground to refuse enforcement of an award that the award was set aside by a competent authority in the State where the award was made. The New York Convention, however, does not specify on what grounds an award may be set aside; this is for the *lex arbitri* to determine. Therefore, even if enforcement is uniformly regulated by the New York Convention, article V(1)(e) opens a channel between the enforcement of an award and the non-harmonised grounds for annulment of the *lex arbitri*. Usually, article V(1)(e) is applied so that an award that has been annulled in its State of origin is considered without any legal effect for the purpose of enforcement in all other countries; however, French and US courts enforce awards

[20] For an overview and a summary of the debate so far, *see* R. di Brozolo, 'Arbitration and Competition Law', *cit. See also* G. Cordero-Moss, 'Inherent Powers and Competition Law', *European International Arbitration Review*, 2017, Vol 6.2, 69–94.

that have been set aside.[21] Recently, a Dutch court[22] decided to enforce an award despite its annulment in the country of origin. This decision, however, cannot directly be compared to an enforcement decision in a usual commercial case, based as it was on considerations of impartiality and independence of the Russian courts is a case involving the interests of the Russian State.

Disregarding an annulment made in the award's country of origin is the exception rather than the rule, and it is certainly not uncontroversial.[23] Hence, the *lex arbitri* may have a considerable impact in the phase of enforcement.

5.6 Lex Arbitri and the Law Applicable to the Substance of the Dispute

The principle of territoriality does not extend to the merits of the dispute. The *lex arbitri* may be applicable to the merits if the parties have chosen it to govern their legal relationship, or if it is selected as applicable by the tribunal on the basis of independent factors. However, the simple circumstance that the arbitral tribunal has its seat in a certain country, is not sufficient basis to apply that country's law to the merits of the dispute. The *lex arbitri*, however, may have significance to the selection of this law. This will be discussed below in two contexts: if the parties have chosen the applicable law, and if the parties have not made a choice.

5.6.1 If the Parties Have Chosen the Law

The law applicable to the substance of the dispute is often chosen by the parties. This choice shall be understood as instructions to the tribunal, and thus as a delimitation of the tribunal's authority.

[21] The most well-known example in France is *Hilmarton*, reported in *Yearbook Commercial Arbitration*, Vol XX, 663–665 and Vol XXII, 696–698. For the USA, *see* the *Chromalloy* decision, reported in *Yearbook Commercial Arbitration*, Vol XXXI, 629ff. and, more recently, Corporación Mexicana de Matenimiento Integral, S De RL De CV v. Pemex-Exploración y Producción, No 13-4022 (2d Cir 2 August 2016).

[22] Decision of the Amsterdam Court of Appeal of 28 April 2009.

[23] For an overview of literature on this matter *see* G. Born, *International Commercial Arbitration*, cit., Vol III, para. 26.05.

Most arbitration rules and most arbitration laws contain provisions relating to the law applicable to the merits of the dispute. They generally state that the arbitral tribunal shall apply the rules of law chosen by the parties to the merits of the dispute.

The New York Convention does not contain any rules directly regulating the choice of law applicable to the substance of the dispute. However, it contains a provision that indirectly affects this matter. According to article V(1)(c), one of the defences that may be brought against enforcement of an award is the eventuality that the tribunal has exceeded its power: 'The award deals with a difference not contemplated by or not falling within the terms of the submission to arbitration, or it contains decisions on matters beyond the scope of the submission to arbitration'.

The provision on excess of power expressly covers the object of the dispute. It does not contain an express rule for the eventuality that the award, despite deciding on an issue submitted by the parties to arbitration, applies a law different from the law chosen by the parties. Therefore, application by the arbitral tribunal of a law that should not have been applied could seem not to constitute a ground for invalidity or unenforceability of the award.

In confirmation of this first impression, enforcement of an arbitral award may not be used as a basis for the courts to review the arbitral tribunal's decision, including its application of the law. This applies both to errors in the application of the substantive law and to errors in the choice of which law to apply.

Whether the tribunal had the authority to apply a certain law, however, is a matter that may be considered as relating to the power of the tribunal and thus the scope of the dispute. The tribunal's power is conferred by the parties, and under article V(1)(c) of the New York Convention an award exceeding this power may be refused enforcement. Admittedly, the defence of excess of power is seldom invoked for the purpose of sanctioning the arbitral tribunals' choice of law.[24] To the extent that the question has been given attention, it seems that it has mainly been answered negatively, both in practice and in theory.[25] However, the matters submitted to arbitration

[24] *See* N. C. Port, S. Ethan Bowers, 'Article V(1)(c)', in H. Kronke, P. Nacimiento, D. Otto, N. C. Port (ed.), *Recognition and Enforcement of Foreign Arbitral Awards: A Global Commentary on the New York Convention* (Kluwer Law International, 2010), 271f.

[25] In theory *see e.g.* Fouchard, Gaillard, Goldman, *On International Commercial Arbitration* (Kluwer Law International Law, 1999), para. 1700. In practice, *see* US District Court, Southern District of California, 7.12.1998 Civ. No. 98-1165-B, 29 Federal Supplement,

depend closely on the criteria that they have to be measured against. A contract does not have legal effects only on the basis of its terms, but it receives its legal force from the applicable law and will be interpreted and construed in light of that law.[26] If the tribunal applies a different law, and assuming that the two laws regulate the question in different ways, it could be considered as if the tribunal had applied a different contract: the assumptions for resolving the dispute would not be the same as those agreed upon by the parties. Therefore, the decision would be on matters different from those submitted by the parties and this would fall within the scope of article V(1)(c).[27] Thus, it is possible to affirm that a court may refuse enforcement of an arbitral award under article V(1)(c) of the New York Convention if the arbitral tribunal manifestly and expressly disregards the parties' choice of law. Indirectly, article V(1)(c) of the New York Convention may thus be deemed to confirm that the arbitral tribunal shall apply the law chosen by the parties.

However, the primacy of the parties' agreement needs to be coordinated with applicable rules on validity and enforceability of the arbitral award. Assume that the parties to a licence agreement chose a non-EU law because they wanted to escape EU competition law, under which the licence agreement would be null. If one party breached the contract and invoked EU competition law as a defence, and if the arbitral tribunal nevertheless applied the law chosen by the parties in the contract, the result would be that the award affirmed a contract that violated EU competition law. However, as Section 5.4.2 showed, the CJEU determined that awards that violate EU competition law are invalid and unenforceable because they infringe public policy. Consequently, the arbitral tribunal

Second Series (S.D.Cal. 1998) 1168–1174, excluding that a decision rendered *ex bono et aequo* exceeded the arbitral tribunal's power. From the reasons of the decision, however, it appears that the court based its reasoning on the conclusion that the parties had actually empowered the tribunal to decide *ex bono et aequo* (therefore it is not surprising that the court did not see any excess of power). Also, a German decision decided similarly, even mentioning, in an *obiter dictum*, that the arbitral tribunal's choice of law may not be reviewed by the court. However, also in this case the court based its conclusion on the fact that the parties had empowered the tribunal to decide *ex bono et aequo* (Landesgericht Hamburg, 18.9.1997, available at *ICCA Yearbook Commercial Arbitration*, Vol XXV, 512).

26 More extensively, *see* G. Cordero-Moss, *International Commercial Contracts*, cit., 80–133.

27 For a similar reasoning *see* the International Law Association (ILA) International Commercial Arbitration Committee, 'International Law Association Report Ascertaining the contents of the applicable law in international commercial arbitration', 19.

might be inclined to restrict the choice of law made by the parties, thus avoiding rendering an invalid or unenforceable award. Does the arbitral tribunal in this case run the risk of exceeding its power? In other words: is the arbitral tribunal forced to choose between two grounds for invalidity or unenforceability of the award, i.e. conflict with public policy article pursuant to article V(2)(b) or excess of power pursuant to article V(1)(c)? This arbitral tribunal's dilemma may be solved applying the rules of private international law (conflict of laws rules). These rules generally recognise the primacy of party autonomy, but they also restrict the scope of the parties' choice in areas such as property, company or competition law. Furthermore, they permit to override the parties' choice to implement particularly important policies (overriding mandatory rules or *lois de police*), and they restrict its effects if it infringes public policy. By considering the parties' choice under the applicable private international law, therefore, the arbitral tribunal may ensure that the award does not violate public policy, and at the same time avoid the risk of exceeding its power. Which role the *lex arbitri* plays in respect of private international law will be discussed in section 5.6.3.

5.6.2 If the Parties Have Not Made a Choice

If the parties have not chosen the law applicable to the merits, the *lex arbitri* has a significant role in two respects: it determines which sources the arbitral tribunal may apply to the merits of the dispute, and it may determine how these sources shall be selected. This latter issue will be discussed in Section 5.6.3.

Regarding the former, it must be pointed out that some arbitration laws, including the Model Law, make a distinction between choosing a 'law' and choosing 'rules of law'. Choosing a law is interpreted as choosing a national law, whereas the phrase *rules of law* is interpreted as permitting to choose from a wider range of sources including also transnational sources and soft law.[28] Arbitration law and arbitration rules often give the parties the possibility of choosing 'rules of law' to govern the dispute. However, the law in some States, including the Model Law, reserves this choice to the parties. If the law has to be selected by the arbitral tribunal

[28] More extensively, *see* G. Cordero-Moss, *International Commercial Contracts*, cit., 300ff.

because the parties did not make a choice, the only sources that may be chosen are 'laws'. Whether the tribunal may choose rules of law or is confined to applying a law, therefore, depends on the *lex arbitri*.

5.6.3 Lex Arbitri and Private International Law

Private international law is that branch of each country's own law that permits to select the law applicable to the merits of a dispute. The applicable law is determined by applying rules of private international law, also known as conflict of laws rules. For disputes before courts of law, it is generally recognised that judges always apply the private international law of their own country. The same approach used to be followed in international commercial arbitration. Nowadays, however, there is no automatic and absolute reference to the private international law of the *lex arbitri*. The international character of arbitration has led various legislatures and arbitral institutions to loosen the link between the place of arbitration and the applicable private international law, or even with conflict rules at all.

Arbitration laws present a variety of solutions to the question of how the arbitral tribunal shall select the applicable law. These range from the application of the private international law of the *lex arbitri*,[29] to the application of the private international law that the arbitral tribunal deems most appropriate,[30] the application of conflict rules specifically designed for arbitration[31] and the *voie directe*.[32] The *voie directe*, introduced by the ICC Rules of Arbitration and followed by other arbitration rules and some arbitration laws, does away with the private international law and is deemed to reflect the most modern approach. Under article 21 of the 2021 ICC Rules of Arbitration, if the parties have not made a choice, the arbitral tribunal may freely choose the applicable rules of law directly and without applying any conflict rules. When they choose to submit a dispute to arbitration under the ICC Rules, thus, the parties agree that the arbitral tribunal is not bound to apply any private international law.

[29] Article 31 of the Norwegian Arbitration Act.
[30] Model Law (article 28(2)) and the English Arbitration Act (article 46(3)).
[31] Article 187 of the Swiss PILA.
[32] Article 1496 of the French Civil Procedure Code.

It is not advisable, however, to abandon in full the guidance that private international law gives.[33] This guidance ensures predictability. In addition, as was discussed in Section 5.6.1, it gives a legal basis for the arbitral tribunal's power in respect of party autonomy. It also contributes to safeguarding the trust in the institution of arbitration, that is necessary to prevent the expansion of the area of what is not arbitrable that was mentioned in Section 5.4.1. Eliminating private international law from arbitration seems thus to be less arbitration-friendly than the intention underlying the reform.

Likewise, eliminating the link between the *lex arbitri* and the applicable conflict rules was meant to enhancing arbitration by increasing its flexibility, but it actually resulted in increased unpredictability. Conflict rules vary from country to country, and not knowing which private international law will be applied does not seem to be a very arbitration-friendly move.

Admittedly, the Hague Conference recently published a soft law instrument with principles on choice of law.[34] Those who believe arbitration to be delocalised may consider a transnational instrument to be more compatible with arbitration than a national system of private international law. However, the Hague Principles do not necessarily provide an answer to all questions, particularly to the dilemmas described in Section 5.6.1. Hence, it may be useful to look for a full system of conflict rules. Given the importance of the *lex arbitri* in a number of important procedural matters, it seems logical to look at the *lex arbitri* also in respect of conflict rules.

It is not unusual that arbitral tribunals exercise their discretion by applying the private international law of the *lex arbitri*, even though they are not bound to do so.

5.7 Conclusion

This chapter has shown that, while international arbitration undoubtedly is based on the will of the parties and international sources to a large extent provide a uniform legal framework, national laws still have a significant relevance. In particular, parties and arbitral tribunals may not disregard the peculiarities of the law of the place of arbitration, the *lex arbitri*.

[33] *See*, more extensively, G. Cordero-Moss 'Conflict of Laws as a Basis to Determine the Arbitral Tribunal's Power' in F. Ferrari, S. Kröll (eds.), *Conflict of Laws in International Commercial Arbitration*, Juris, 2019, 163–185.

[34] 2015 Hague Principles on Choice of Law in International Commercial Contracts, www.hcch.net/en/instruments/conventions/full-text/?cid=135

6 Is Arbitration Autonomous?

Ralf Michaels

6.1 Introduction

Arbitration is often called autonomous – either as a description of reality, or as a desirable situation. This is not at all an uncomplicated claim. What do such claims for autonomous arbitration mean? How does it fit with the history of law and state? Does autonomy exist in practice? Is it conceivable or desirable in theory? And if not, how should we understand the idea of autonomous arbitration instead? These are questions that this chapter addresses, on the basis of well-known debates and topics. The result is that autonomy of arbitration does not exist and probably could not exist. What proponents of autonomy really defend is a particular position for international arbitration.

6.2 The Idea of Autonomy

The notion of autonomy – literally the condition to make one's own laws – has a long and varied history in law. As for arbitration, three different ideas of autonomy can be distinguished:[1] substantive autonomy, procedural autonomy, total autonomy. Historically, they were developed roughly in this order.

6.2.1 Substantive Autonomy

The idea of substantive autonomy – an autonomy from substantive state law – is the oldest. It emerged in the 1960s with theories about a new lex

[1] Different aspects (applicable law, procedure, awards) are distinguished in Markus A. Petsche, '*The Growing Autonomy of International Commercial Arbitration*' (Munich: Sellier European Law Publishers, 2005).

mercatoria as the law that effectively governed trade relationships and ought therefore to be applied. The theory made an empirical and a normative claim. The empirical claim was that there was a law outside or beyond the state. The normative claim was that arbitrators should be allowed to apply this new lex mercatoria when parties had selected it (and perhaps even if they had not); courts should be required to enforce arbitral awards rendered on the basis of lex mercatoria).

The first version, supported mainly in France, was the most radical one.[2] In the most well-known version, lex mercatoria emerges not from states but instead out of private transaction – either from international trade itself as a generator of laws, or from the contract itself as the generator of the entire set of the rules and norms applicable to the parties' dispute resolution (the 'contrat sans loi').[3] Alternative sources are seen in natural law[4] or in the collectivity of all state laws.[5]

That radical version has been quite widely rejected, and for good reason. As for the idea that trade creates the applicable law, the theory invokes traditional ideas of customary law, but the laws governing trades are simply not all of customary nature. As for the idea that the contract itself generates all applicable law, this theory overburdens what the contract itself can perform.

Such considerations led to a slightly different version of autonomy, according to which lex mercatoria is autonomous from both state and commerce and instead emerges from practice, as a result of an autopoietic process.[6] The underlying idea here is that law is a system that is separate from other systems like the political system and the economic system, that it emerges from itself (in autopoietic fashion). But this theory proves too

[2] Berthold Goldman, 'Frontières du droit et lex mercatoria' (1964) 9 *Archives de philosophie du droit* 177.

[3] Jean-Paul Beraudo, 'Faut-il avoir peur du contrat sans loi?' in *Le droit international privé: Esprit et méthodes: Mélanges en l'honneur de Paul Lagarde* (Paris: Dalloz, 2005), 93–112; Lena Gannagé, 'Le contrat sans loi en droit international privé' (2007) 11 *Electronic Journal of Comparative Law*, www.ejc1.org/113/article113-10.pdf.

[4] Bruno Oppetit, *Philosophie du droit* (Paris: Dalloz, 1999).

[5] Emmanuel Gaillard, *Legal Theory of International Arbitration* (Leiden: Martinus Nijhoff Publishers, 2010), 45ff.

[6] Gunther Teubner, 'Global Bukowina: Legal Pluralism in the World Society' in Gunther Teubner, (ed.), *Global Law without a State* (Dartmouth: Aldershot, 1997), 3–28; Peter J. Mazzacano, The Autonomous Nature of the Lex Mercatoria, (2012) 16 *Vindobona Journal of International Commercial Law and Arbitration* 71.

much. According to the theory of autopoiesis, all law exists in autonomy from other subsystems of society; lex mercatoria, in this sense, has no special role to play. Even in an autopoietic concept of law, both state and commerce can play a role, just not as creators of law themselves.

This makes a third, older, version of lex mercatoria more attractive.[7] That third version sees the new lex mercatoria, descriptively, as an amalgam of rules, state and non-state, that together make up the effectively governing law of international trade. In this interpretation, lex mercatoria is not autonomous from the state and its laws. Lex mercatoria is defined not as a separate body of law, but instead as a functional concept of rules relevant for trade, regardless of their source.[8] In this approach, the non-state part of lex mercatoria is thus incomplete; it is supplemented by state law.

The biggest challenge to the theory of an autonomous lex mercatoria never concerned the default rules of contract laws. Parties have always been able to deviate from them in favour of rules they preferred. If lex mercatoria was long criticised for lack of clarity, that problem has been minimised with the codification of non-state contract law in the UNIDROIT Principles and similar private codification.[9] The problem is, instead, the continued role for public policy rules. By now, there is widespread consensus that arbitrators can, even must, apply such rules. For arbitration to be autonomous, it would need to bring about its own public policy rules – either in the form of a truly transnational public policy,[10] or in the form of what is sometimes called constitutionalisation of arbitration.[11] But attempts to substitute a truly transnational public policy, perhaps derived from the collectivity of existing laws, for domestic public policy have not

[7] Clive S. Schmitthoff, 'International Business Law: A New Law Merchant' (1961) 2 *Current Law and Social Problems* 12.

[8] *See also* Ralf Michaels, 'The True Lex Mercatoria: Law beyond the State' (2007) 14 *Indiana Journal of Global Legal Studies* 447.

[9] UNIDROIT Principles of International Commercial Contracts (2016 ed.).

[10] Pierre Lalive, 'Transnational (or Truly International) Public Policy and International Arbitration' in P. Sanders (ed.), *Comparative Arbitration Practice and Public Policy in Arbitration* (Deventer: Kluwer, 1987), 257–318; Gaillard (n 5) 126–134; Gary Born, *International Commercial Arbitration* (Alphen aan den Rijn, NL: Kluwer Law International, 2014) vol III, 3655 ff.

[11] Moritz Renner, 'Private Justice, Public Policy: The Constitutionalization of International Commercial Arbitration' in Walter Mattli/Thomas Dietz (eds.), *International Arbitration & Global Governance* (Oxford: Oxford University Press, 2014), 117–139.

been successful – although some such principles are now occasionally recognised, they have not replaced domestic policies altogether.

6.2.2 Procedural Autonomy

Even then, autonomy in this idea is limited to substantive law and leaves matters of procedural law intact. States are stripped of their role in providing the substantive rules to be applied to a litigation, but their institutions, courts in particular, retain an important role for enforcement – either of arbitral awards based on lex mercatoria, or of lex mercatoria itself. Some of that last limitation is abolished in a second idea, that of procedural autonomy. This idea focuses less on the substantive law to be applied and more on the procedural and institutional context within which disputes are settled. In his 2005 Freshfields Bruckhaus Deringer Lecture, Julian Lew invoked what he called the 'dream' of autonomous arbitration:

> The ideal and expectation is for international arbitration to be established and conducted according to internationally accepted practices, free from the controls of parochial national laws, and without the interference or review of national courts. Arbitration agreements and awards should be recognized and given effect, with little or no complication or review, by national court.
>
> ... International arbitration is, and should be recognised to be, an autonomous process for the determination of all types of international business disputes. It exists in its own space – a non-national or transnational or, if you prefer, and international domain. It has its own space independent of all national jurisdictions.[12]

This idea goes further than that of lex mercatoria in two ways. First, it expands the idea of autonomy to matters of procedure. Arbitrators should not only apply an autonomous non-state law, they should also, perhaps primarily, use procedures that are autonomous. Second, although this is not explicitly spelled out in the quote, the idea is linked to the rise of international arbitration as an institution. Enough expertise and enough institutionalisation now exist to provide for a fully fledged arbitral process

[12] Julian DM Lew, 'Achieving the Dream: Autonomous Arbitration', (2006) 22 *Arbitration International* 179, at 179, 180. For other claims as to the autonomy of international arbitration, *see e.g.* Born (n 10) vol 1 at 217; L. Ali Khan, Arbitral Autonomy, (2013) 74 *Louisiana Law Review* 14.

that need not be grounded in either state laws or an extensive reading of the arbitration agreement.

Nonetheless, this procedural autonomy is not complete either and a close reading of the quote reveals remaining frictions. On the one hand, arbitration should be free from the interference of national courts, but on the other hand courts should be involved in its enforcement. On the one hand, arbitration exists in its own space independent of all national jurisdictions, on the other hand there are links: 'tentacles that float down from the international arbitration domain to the national jurisdiction, to assure recognition of the agreement to arbitrate, to give effect to awards of international tribunals and to obtain assistance for the international arbitration process when needed'.[13] What is meant then is not really full autonomy but rather the ability of arbitration to bind national courts.

6.2.3 Total Autonomy

What would total autonomy of arbitration mean? It would mean an arbitration that would not have to rely on states at all – not only their substantive and procedural laws, but also their institutions. Arbitration, to be totally autonomous, would need to also establish its own enforcement mechanisms.

One way to achieve this would be for arbitration itself to develop its own enforcement mechanism analogous to that of the state. We find such enforcement mechanisms in some religious arbitrations, but they are usually illegal under state law. The state's ability to enforce judgments (and arbitral awards) emerges from its monopoly of violence. As long as this monopoly remains intact, arbitral enforcement mechanisms are problematic.

To avoid collision with the state's monopoly of violence, alternative enforcement mechanisms must be found for a truly autonomous arbitration. Some such mechanisms exist. Parties sometimes agree on escrow payments, into which the winning party can enforce without the need of state court. Some arbitrators (for example in the context of ICANN) may have access to the relevant technologies to enforce their verdicts. Such mechanisms are attractive especially for situations in which access to the courts would either be too cumbersome or time-consuming or altogether

[13] *Ibid.*, at 182.

impossible. In most cases, however access to state enforcement mechanisms is attractive enough. The relatively high level of compliance with arbitral awards is, in all likelihood, a consequence not of parties' implausible levels of good will, and more of the shadow of the law, at least for commercial arbitration. Total autonomy is thus possible, but it is attractive mainly for those groups of society for whom avoidance of state institutions is of particularly high value.

6.3 The History of Autonomy

Arbitration is – by definition, one may think – dispute resolution that is private and hence occurs without the state. It has a long history.[14] It has, however, also a historiography, in which the history is often presented with clear strategic aims in mind.[15] In this historiography, arbitration existed earlier than the modern state, which may suggest that it is a somehow more natural, less contingent, mode of dispute resolution. It existed parallel to the rise of the state, though in somewhat problematic coexistence. And it will exist after the end of the nation state and thus offers itself as a natural successor to litigation. Each of these three points is, while not wrong, considerably more complex.

6.3.1 Arbitration before the State

There has not always been a state. But there have always been disputes, and there have always been dispute resolution mechanisms. This means that non-state dispute resolution pre-exists the state. However, if contemporary arbitration scholarship draws on this significant pedigree to claim its non-state character and therefore its autonomy, that argument rests on a considerable degree of simplification.

A first example emerges from Roman law.[16] Roman law, it is true, recognised the existence of private arbitration in addition to civil

[14] For summary with references, *see* Born n 10) vol 1, 6ff.

[15] Cf. Nikitas Hatzimihail, 'Genealogies of Lex Mercatoria' in Studies in Memoriam of Professor Antonios M. Antapasis (2013) 411; Ralf Michaels, 'Legal Medievalism in Lex Mercatoria Scholarship' (2012) 90 *Texas Law Review*. *See also* 259.

[16] Derek Roebuck & Bruno de Loynes de Fumichon, *Roman Arbitration* (Oxford: Holo Books, 2004).

litigation.[17] However, the idea of autonomous arbitration separate from the Roman State appears somewhat exaggerated. On the one hand, civil litigation in ancient Rome resembled in many ways what we would now call arbitration: the adjudicator, the iudex, was a lay person selected by the parties and often not expected to have specific legal knowledge.[18] On the other hand, although arbitral awards were indeed not open to appeal in ordinary litigation, arbitration was by no means autonomous in any meaningful sense. Arbitration and litigation were not strict competitors but instead mutually supportive mechanisms.[19]

A second example concerns dispute resolution in the Middle Ages, a popular topic in arbitration scholarship. Merchants, so the story goes, could not rely neither on state courts nor on state laws to resolve disputes amongst themselves. Two reasons are given for this. First, state courts and their laws were local and therefore inadequate for the transnational character of markets. Second state courts and laws would instil state interests into dispute resolution and therefore not provide the freedom and efficiency that merchants and their markets required.

There is a significant degree of fiction in this story.[20] As to the first argument, most medieval trade was not transnational, at least in a meaningful sense. Although merchants did travel across the continent, their transactions were concluded at actual places, frequently at fairs. As a consequence, dispute resolution institutions were likewise local: fairs had their own institutions, the modern idea of delocalised arbitration would have seemed fanciful.[21] And these local institutions would not

[17] Reinhard Zimmermann, *The Law of Obligations: Roman Foundations of the Civilian Tradition* (Oxford/New York: Oxford University Press, 1990), 526ff.

[18] *See* Leanne Bablitz, Roman Courts and Private Arbitration, in Paul J. du Plessis, Clifford Ando, and Kaius Tuori (eds.) *The Oxford Handbook of Roman Law and Society* (Oxford/New York: Oxford University Press, 2016), 234ff.

[19] *See* Ivan Milotić, An outline of the arbitral procedure in roman law, forum historiae iuris 2013, https://forhistiur.de/media/zeitschrift/1301milotic.pdf; Milotić, 'Access to Justice by Means of Arbitration in Roman Law' in Alan Uzelac/C. H. van Rhee (eds), *Revisiting Procedural Human Rights* (Cambridge: Intersentia 2017), 243–262.

[20] Emily Kadens, 'The Myth of the Lex Mercatoria' (2012) 90 *Texas Law Review* 1153.

[21] *See also* Albrecht Cordes and Philipp Höhn, 'Extra-Legal and Legal Conflict Management among Long-Distance Traders (1250–1650)' in *The Oxford Handbook of European Legal History* (New York: Oxford University Press 2018), 509–527.

apply, by and large, some mythical transnational lex mercatoria detached from state laws.

As to the second claim concerning the inadequacy of state laws and policies for merchant disputes, the argument has some value, but it only goes so far. Before the eighteenth century, governments rarely regulated matters of contract law in a general and comprehensive fashion. There was then no, or very little, state law from which arbitration could be autonomous. Whether specific local statutes were deemed applicable or not was more a matter of case-by-case decision. On the other hand, the dispute resolution institutions cannot really be called autonomous – they were public institutions, set up within the privileges of the fair and in this sense at least with a link to the government.[22]

These results are not surprising. To speak of autonomy from the state for a period that predates the modern state is anachronistic and misleading. Dispute resolution at all time stood in complex relations to the governments and political institutions of its time. But to the extent that those institutions differed from the modern state, these relations teach us little for today.

6.3.2 Arbitration during the State

If we can learn little about autonomous arbitration from the period prior to the modern state, what can we learn from later periods? The emergence of the modern state between the sixteenth century (when Bodin formulated his ideas on sovereignty) and the late eighteenth century (when enlightened kings and other leaders on the Continent began to regulate law and litigation comprehensively) represents a period of decline of arbitration, in parallel with the rise of state litigation. That decline was not complete of course – England passed the 1698 Arbitration Act;[23] in the United States, arbitration seemed attractive from early on.[24] But such arbitration was

[22] Stephen E. Sachs, 'From St. Ives to Cyberspace: The Modern Distortion of the Medieval "Law Merchant"' (2006) 21 *American University International Law Review* 685; Jeremy Edwards and Sheilagh Ogilvie, What Lessons for Economic Development Can We Draw from the Champagne Fairs?, (2012) 49 *Explorations in Economic History* 131–148.

[23] *See* Henry Horwitz and James Oldham, 'John Locke, Lord Mansfield, and Arbitration During the Eighteenth Century' (1993) 36 *The Historical Journal* 137.

[24] James Oldham and Su Jin Kim, 'Arbitration in America: The Early Years' (2013) 31 *Law and History Review* 241.

never truly autonomous; it always existed in close connection with the state. In civil law systems, arbitration was sometimes viewed with more suspicion as a threat to the state (thus in post-revolutionary France), sometimes subjected to state legislation (thus in Germany). In neither situation was it autonomous.

A special focus could be laid on the role of arbitration in totalitarian regimes. As one leading scholar and practitioner suggests, 'acceptance of arbitration is a distinctive feature of free societies. It is rejected by totalitarian states'.[25] There is some truth to this story, but again, reality is somewhat more complex. On the one hand, totalitarian regimes are not always completely hostile to arbitration. The Nazis rejected, unsurprisingly, the idea of private courts, but gave them a continued role especially for international transactions.[26] Somewhat similarly, the Soviet Union discouraged arbitration for domestic affairs but encouraged it for international transactions.[27] Indeed, arbitration seems more in tune with the Marxist-Leninist disdain for legal fetishism than with the national socialist idea of the total state. China went further: The country has long relied on arbitral institutions, especially (but not only) in order to provide institutions for transnational trade. This has a variety of reasons, among them the limited role of courts as dispute resolution institutions, a traditional Chinese preference for informal dispute resolutions, but also the desire to attract trade. All in all, nondemocratic regimes find it rational to resort to arbitration where that seems advisable. And that arbitration, far from being autonomous from the state, became instrumental.

If therefore totalitarian states are not uniformly opposed to arbitration, arbitration on the other hand is not uniformly opposed to totalitarian states, either. Like any other party, such states or their state-owned entities, can often appoint arbitrators. Such arbitrators are frequently not independent, contrary to the requirement of most arbitration

[25] Jan Paulsson, *The Idea of Arbitration* (New York: Oxford University Press, 2013), 1. *See also ibid.* 105: 'Authoritarian states are jealous of all power, and so resist any dilution of the monopoly of their courts'.

[26] Heinrich Peyerimhoff, *Die grundsätzliche Einstellung des Liberalismus und des Nationalsozialismus zur privaten Schiedsgerichtsbarkeit* (Diss. Tübingen 1943) 39ff; E. J. Cohn, 'Commercial Arbitration and the Rules of Law a Comparative Study' (1941) 4 *University of Toronto Law Journal* 1, at 27, 28, both with contemporaneous references; Born (n 10) vol 1, 52–53.

[27] Paul Fisher, 'The Soviet Union's Approach to Arbitration and Its Enduring Influence upon Arbitration in the Former Soviet Space' (2017) 5 *Russian Law Journal* 129.

regimes.[28] Compromises are made here in order not to prevent such parties from arbitration altogether. As a consequence, the regime of international arbitration tolerates totalitarian regimes.

6.3.3 Arbitration after the State

Does this dependency of arbitration on the state change after the decline of the state? In other words, will arbitration become more autonomous once globalisation has done away with, or at least greatly reduced, the power of the state? This promise is sometimes heard. Under conditions of globalisation, states are considered both unable and inappropriate to adjudicate private disputes, especially in the commercial realm. Indeed, the rise of arbitration in the twentieth and twenty-first centuries can be linked to a multifaceted limitation of the state. First, since at least the early twentieth century, states have found themselves increasingly incapable of managing the numerous disputes that arise. Arbitration has therefore provided a welcome relief for the state and its courts. Second, states and their courts remain (with some exceptions) insufficiently well equipped for transnational litigation. Third, state courts appear particularly inadequate for investment disputes. Fourth, a general neo-liberal ideology has powerfully supported private over public solutions for many issues, including dispute resolution. For these and other reasons, arbitration has seen a tremendous growth in the twentieth century, as have claims for its eventual autonomy.

However, this development does not seem irreversible. Lew's lecture came at the height of globalisation discourse, when the decline of communism had seemingly revealed the promise, and the attacks of 9/11 had demonstrated the threats, of a deterritorialised world. At that point, the argument for a world without states seemed strong. Much has happened since to the idea of an autonomous arbitration – the financial crash of 2008 and the ensuing criticism of non-state market relations,[29] the

[28] Jacques Werner, 'The Independence of Arbitrators in Totalitarian States – Tackling the Tough Issues' (1997) 14 *J. Int'l Arb.* 141.

[29] The financial crash has, however, not surprisingly, led to an increase in the number of arbitration proceedings. *See e.g.* Klaus Peter Berger, 'The Aftermath of the Financial Crisis: Why Arbitration Makes Sense for Banks and Financial Institutions' (2009) 3 *Law and Financial Markets Review* 54; Stephan Wilske, 'The Impact of the Financial Crisis on International Arbitration' (2010) 65 *Dispute Resolution Journal* 82.

backlash against a TTIP arbitration court,[30] the current rise of populist nationalism combined with a criticism of 'cosmopolitanism'.[31] We can see, this suggests, a backlash to the idea of autonomy.

6.4 The Practice of Autonomy

The analysis so far has demonstrated that arbitration has never been truly autonomous from the state, as long as we lived in a world of states. This is perhaps not surprising. Where states exist, arbitration (like any other regime) must arrange itself with them in one way or the other. Indeed, analysis of the practice of autonomy demonstrates that arbitration and the state (and its law) are always intertwined in relevant ways. In fact, Lew himself admits as much: 'just as no man or woman is an island, so no system of dispute resolution can exist in a vacuum. Without prejudice to autonomy, international arbitration does regularly interact with national jurisdictions for its existence to be legitimate and for support, help, and effectiveness'.[32] Such interaction takes place prior to, during and after arbitration proceedings.[33]

6.4.1 Creating Autonomy

If we say that arbitration is autonomous, a first question is from where this autonomy derives. As a theoretical issue, this has long been a matter of

[30] Michael Waibel, Asha Kaushal, Kyo-Hwa Liz Chung and Claire Balchin (eds.), *The Backlash against Investment Arbitration: Perceptions and Reality* (Alphen aan den Rijn, NL: Wolters Kluwer Law & Business, 2010); David D. Caron and Esme Shirlow, 'Dissecting Backlash: The Unarticulated Causes of Backlash and Its Unintended Consequences' in Geir Ulfstein and Andreas Føllesdal (eds.), *The Judicialization of International Law – A Mixed Blessing?* (New York: Oxford University Press, 2018); *see also* Jan Kleinheisterkamp, Is there a Need for Investor-State Arbitration in the Transatlantic Trade and Investment Partnership (TTIP)? (14 February 2014). Available at SSRN: https://ssrn.com/abstract=2410188.

[31] Erik Voeten, 'Populism and Backlashes against International Courts' (2020) 18 *Perspectives on Politics* 407–422.

[32] Julian DM Lew, 'Does National Court Involvement Undermine the International Arbitration Process?' (2009) 24 *American University International Law Review* 489, at 492. *See also ibid.* at 493: 'One might therefore speak of the international arbitration process as stretching its tentacles down from the domain of international arbitration to the national legal systems to forage for legitimacy, support, recognition, and effectiveness.'

[33] *Ibid.* at 496–498.

intense debate, with some arguing for the contract as the source of autonomy, others for the legal system of states, and others finally for international arbitration as an institution. I will come back to this theoretical debate in the next section. As a matter of practice the question is clear, at least in principle: arbitration receives its role, and thus its autonomy, from the law, more specifically the law of the seat.

This result is put into question in various ways. First, although the law of the seat governs the parties' agreement, it is in turn the parties' agreement that determines the law of the seat. In this sense, parties can effectively determine the law that grants them autonomy.[34] Sometimes, this is used to ground autonomy, ultimately, in party determination. This seems erroneous for at least two reasons: First, if the parties' freedom to choose the law of the seat is itself a consequence of the laws of states, then it is not fully free. Second, the freedom to choose the law of the seat is still the freedom to choose a (state) legal regime; it is in this sense not total freedom.

Second, international arbitration as an institution, or as a regime, is so well established by now that it is effectively grounded neither in the state nor in the parties' autonomy. States do legitimate this institution, but they do not bring it about. Nor, however, does the agreement of the parties, which constitutes, in most cases, an opt-in into an existing regime. That regime consists of institutions (like the many existing arbitral institutions), people (the practitioners of arbitration, or the 'guild' as one of them once called them), sets of procedural rules (like the UNCITRAL model law and the UNCITRAL rules as well as the procedural rules of various institutions),[35] substantive law (the ephemeral lex mercatoria, private codifications like the UNIDROIT Principles). Nonetheless, a truly autonomous regime remains what Lew called it: a dream.[36] Existing arbitral institutions are founded under the law of states and are subject to that law: The London Court of International Arbitration is a company set up under English law, the ICC Court of International arbitration is a creature of French law. The UNCITRAL model law is binding only if and insofar it is implemented into the law of domestic state laws; procedural rules are

[34] *See* Horatia Muir Watt, 'Party Autonomy "Party Autonomy" in International Contracts: from the Makings of a Myth to the Requirements of Global Governance' (2010) 6 *European Review of Contract Law* 250.

[35] Hans-Patrick Schroeder, *Die lex mercatoria arbitralis* (Frankfurt am Main and Munich: QUADIS and Sellier, 2007).

[36] Lew, *supra* n 12, at 186–187.

applicable only insofar as they are compatible with the respective state regime. The lex mercatoria maintains connections to state law; the UNIDROIT Principles explicitly defer to mandatory state law.[37]

Third, for one specific legal question it seems arguable that arbitration is indeed independent from the law of the seat. Courts in several jurisdictions have held that arbitral awards can be enforced even if they have been annulled in the seat country.[38] In this sense, the arbitral award at least becomes independent from the law of the seat – though not, of course, of the law of all states, in particular the recognition state.

6.4.2 Defining Autonomy

In practice, therefore, it can safely be said that the autonomy of arbitration emerges from a mix of party discretion, institutional setup and state law. Is arbitration fully autonomous at least in laying down its own scope? The answer is, again mixed.

On the one hand, at least at first, the scope of arbitration is determined within arbitration itself. This is a consequence of the principle of competence-competence: It is in principle up to the arbitrator to determine whether he has jurisdiction and if so, how broad this jurisdiction is.[39] Review by courts is only ex post and is limited.

On the other hand, however, state law does set limits to the scope of arbitration insofar as it determines what matters are in fact arbitrable at all.[40] The twentieth century has seen a trend to expand the scope of arbitrable matters, beyond purely private matters to those of public

[37] *See* Ralf Michaels, 'The UNIDROIT Principles as Global Background Law' (2014) 19 *Uniform Law Review* 643, 660.

[38] *E.g.* Hilmarton v. Omnium de Traitement et de Valorisation (OTV), Cour de cassation, 23 March 1994, (1995) Com. Arb. 66; Chromalloy Aeroservices v. Arab Republic of Egypt, 939 F. Supp. 907 (D.D.C. 1996); Corporación Mexicana de Mantenimiento Integral v. Pemex-Exploración Y Producción, No. 13-4022 (2d Cir. 2 August 2016) ('Pemex'); Yukos Capital S.A.R.L. v. Oao Rosneft, Amsterdam Court of Appeal 28 April 2009, in International Arbitration Court Decisions – 3rd Ed. (2011). For comprehensive analysis, *see* Dennis Solomon, *Die Verbindlichkeit von Schiedssprüchen in der internationalen privaten Schiedsgerichtsbarkeit* (Munich: Sellier 2007); Felix Boor, *Der aufgehobene ausländische Schiedsspruch als 'rechtliches nullum'?* (Berlin: Duncker & Humblot, 2016).

[39] Born (n 10) vol 1, 1399–1401; A.S. Rau, The Allocation of Power between Arbitral Tribunals and State Courts, 390 Recueil Des Cours 9.

[40] Art. V(1)(a), V(2)(a) New York Convention; 1(5) UNCITRAL Model Law.

concern like securities regulation,[41] or antitrust law.[42] Scholars have proposed even further expansion.[43] Nonetheless, as long as there remain limits to arbitrability that are defined by states and not within the arbitration regime itself, that regime cannot be called fully autonomous with regard to the definition of its own scope.

6.4.3 Respecting Autonomy

Once autonomy is granted and defined, courts continue to play a role. Autonomy, even as proclaimed by its staunchest proponents, does not mean absence of courts altogether. Rather, courts are supposed to have several roles. One of those is to respect the existing autonomy of arbitration. Such respect comes in various forms. Before arbitral proceedings, courts are required to dismiss claims that are required to court in breach of an arbitration clause, or at least stay litigation.[44] During the arbitral proceedings, courts are expected to refrain from interfering with the arbitration. After the arbitral proceedings, finally, courts are required to refrain from reviewing the substance of the arbitral award; they are also expected to treat it as res judicata.

Again, this respect is not without limits. Before arbitration, courts maintain an, albeit limited, competence to review whether a valid arbitration agreement exists; they may therefore assert jurisdiction even in the presence of an arbitration agreement. After proceedings, courts maintain two powers. Courts in the seat country maintain the power to annul awards. Courts in other countries can review arbitral awards in enforcement proceedings, albeit in limited ways. Demands to abolish this power of review have remained ineffective.

Two mechanisms deserve special attention. The first concerns annulment proceedings. Although no regular appeals process from an arbitration to the state's courts exists, national arbitration regimes maintain the power to annul arbitral awards rendered under their own law. In this sense, the law of the seat retains control over the arbitration. This is in tension

[41] Scherk v. Alberto-Culver Co., 417 US 506 (1974).

[42] Mitsubishi Motors Corp. v. Soler Chrysler Plymouth Inc., 473 US 614 (1985).

[43] Paulsson (n 25) 115ff.

[44] Article II(1), II(3) NYC; Art. 8(1) UNCITRAL Model Law.

with the idea of autonomy.[45] Consequently, many institutional rules provide the parties with the ability to waive the right to seek annulment.[46] But that right concerns access to court, and whether that can be waived is a matter of state law, not arbitration. Most existing state laws allow for such waivers only under limited circumstances, for example when the parties are foreign. More radically perhaps, scholars have proposed abolishing annulment by state courts altogether, in favour of an independent international review institution.[47]

The second, more controversial, mechanism, is the anti-arbitration injunction.[48] In analogy to anti-suit injunctions, courts occasionally render injunctions to enjoin arbitral proceedings going on. Unlike anti-suit injunctions, which can only be directed against parties, anti-arbitration injunctions can also be directed against the arbitrator (provided the court has personal jurisdiction over him) because the arbitrator, unlike a foreign judge, is not an organ of a sovereign state. Indeed, anti-arbitration injunctions are the clearest rejection of the idea of arbitral autonomy. It is therefore unsurprising that arbitration law scholars are mostly very critical of the device.[49]

6.4.4 Enforcing Autonomy

So far, the discussion concerned autonomy of arbitration as freedom from state intervention. The idea of arbitral autonomy does not only constrain courts, however, it also requires them to become active. It is not enough for courts to respect autonomy, they are also asked to enforce it.

[45] Menalco J. Solis, 'Removing Awards to the Autonomous Arbitral System by Waiving the Annulment Recourse' (2018) 29 *American Review of International Arbitration* 121.

[46] ICC Rules 34(6); LCIA Rules Art. 26(9); SIAC Rules Art. 28(9).

[47] *See* Albert Jan van den Berg, 'Should the Setting Aside of the Arbitral Award be Abolished?' (2014) 29 *ICSID Review* 263, at 287; *see also* Meng Chen and Chengzi Wang, 'Vanishing Set-Aside Authority in International Commercial Arbitration' (2018) 18 *International & Comparative Law Review* 127.

[48] S. R. Subramanian, 'Anti-arbitration injunctions and their compatibility with the New York convention and the Indian law of arbitration: future directions for Indian law and policy' (2018) 34 *Arbitration International* 185. *See e.g.* Weissfisch v. Julius (2006) EWCA Civ 218; Excalibur Ventures LLC v. Texas Keystone Inc. and others (2011) EWHC 1624 (Comm); Sabbagh v. Khoury (2018).

[49] Lew, *supra* n 32, 509–514; Born (n 10) vol 1, 1312–1315.

One way for courts to do this is to enforce not only the derogation but also the proprogation element of the arbitration agreement: Courts not only refrain from exercising jurisdiction over the subject matter, they also actively force the parties to arbitrate in good faith. This positive enforcement is harder to achieve; relevant treaties and the Model Law require courts, somewhat euphemistically, to 'refer' the parties to arbitration.[50] Indeed, courts in many countries hold that 'parties [can] not be compelled to go to arbitration'.[51] The law is different on this issue in the United States, where courts somewhat regularly compel both domestic and international arbitration.[52] Scholarly debate shows the conundrum.[53] Specific performance may at the same time be seen to support and to undermine arbitral autonomy: it makes it possible, and yet threatens to interfere with it.

Seemingly less problematic, at least from the perspective of arbitration, is the anti-suit injunction in favour of arbitration. English courts in particular have always used anti-suit injunctions especially for this purpose.[54] They are more important in favour of arbitration than in favour of court proceedings, because arbitrators, other than courts, have no mechanisms of their own to enforce their own jurisdiction. And yet, they are not unproblematic. Some problems are those of anti-suit injunctions in general: the courts of one state interfere, effectively, with the proceedings in the courts of another state. This has long been the complaint from civil law systems. Others are specific to arbitration. Whereas a court's anti-suit injunction in favour of its own jurisdiction can be justified with the court protecting its own interest, an anti-suit injunction in favour of arbitration is always made in the interest of the parties. It is therefore more vulnerable to the critique of one court arrogating its superiority over another court in view of the enforceability *vel non* of a contractual agreement.

Finally, courts enforce arbitral awards. Enforcing awards is the courts' most important function with regard to arbitration. And yet, even enforcement of arbitral awards is not unproblematic from the perspective of autonomy. First, enforceability is limited: both Conventions and national

50 New York Convention Art. II(3); Geneva Protocol Art. IV(1); Model Law Art. 8(1).

51 Pena Copper Mines Ltd v. Rio Tinto Co. (1911–1913) All Eng. Rep. 209, 214 (C.A).

52 Born (n 10) vol 1, 1265–1267.

53 Born (n 10) vol 1, 1267ff.

54 *E.g.* Ust-Kamenogorsk Hydropower Plant JSC v. AES [2013] UKSC 35.

laws provide (limited) grounds for non-enforcement. Most suspicious among these grounds, from the perspective of arbitral autonomy, is of course public policy, the clearest restriction of arbitral autonomy vis-à-vis the state. Wide agreement exists that the ground should be interpreted narrowly.[55] Proposals have been made to understand public policy in a transnational, not state-based manner.[56] Other grounds for refusal are more in line with the demands of arbitration itself, especially insofar as they concern the proceedings in the arbitration itself. Here, a court rejecting enforcement could be said to be supporting, rather than undermining, the autonomy of arbitration. But these grounds already lead to second, more fundamental, tension between enforcement and autonomy: to the extent that arbitration depends on courts for the enforcement of its awards, it is not fully autonomous.

6.5 The Theory of Autonomy

6.5.1 Tensions

How should we read the results from this brief overview of the practice? There are obviously various tensions between the idea of an autonomous arbitration on the one hand and a role for the state on the other. These tensions, which are not simple, appear in three different forms.

In the first form, the tension between arbitration on the one hand and the state on the other is a mere application of the tension between private and public ordering. In this conflict, proponents of arbitral autonomy present essentially traditional liberal arguments in favour of more arbitration and less state. The argument for stronger autonomy of arbitration and less state intervention is here grounded on the assumption that private parties, especially sophisticated economic, are better able than the state to determine what is good for them. As a consequence, states ought to enforce the parties' agreements as much as possible, and intervene as little as possible. Their role is confined to the enforcement of private rights. In the context of international arbitration, this liberal position comes with a

[55] ILA, Final Report of the Committee on International Commercial Arbitration on Public Policy, TDM (2004) 1.

[56] *Supra* n 10.

special weight that emerges from the international nature of arbitration. Within one state, many liberals concede that the mix between public and private can at least partly be determined through democratic processes, legitimated by a *demos*. Internationally, both a *demos* and a democratic process are lacking, and states with their parochial interests are viewed as particularly illegitimate vis-à-vis private agreements.

The second form of the tension is more complex. After all, the argument for autonomous arbitration goes beyond the traditional liberal idea of the separation of public and private, in which adjudication remains a task of the state. It represents those more extreme ideas of liberalism that are willing to transfer what were once thought of as essential state functions and institutions to private ordering. Here, arbitration is no longer a supplement of the state, but rather a substitute for it. Arbitration is still explained as being grounded in contract, but in order to argue for its autonomy, it is necessary to also defend its institutionalised nature. In this vein, Gary Born proposes bilateral arbitration treaties that would make arbitration the default dispute resolution mechanism even in the absence of an arbitration agreement.[57] Almost necessarily, the argument leads to some necessary inconsistencies. For example, proponents of autonomy are in support of anti-suit injunctions but at the same time opposed to anti-arbitration injunctions. This inconsistency cannot be justified merely with a preference for party agreements, because it goes to the protection of arbitration as an institution, not merely the protection of contractual agreements as such.

A third form of the tension creates the biggest challenge. The problem is a tension within the idea of autonomy itself. Arbitration, in order to be

[57] Gary Born, 'BITs, BATs and Buts: Reflections on International Dispute Resolution' (2014) 4 *Young Arbitration Review* 6; Bruno Guandalini, 'Bilateral Arbitration Treaties and Efficiency: A New Proposal on and an Old Challenge to International Commercial Arbitration' (2013) 10 *Revista Brasileira de Arbitragem* 16; Petra Butler and Campbell Herbert, 'Access to Justice vs Access to Justice for Small and Medium-Sized Enterprises: The Case for a Bilateral Arbitration Treaty' (2014) 26 *New Zealand U. L. Rev.* 186; Gary Born and Petra Butler, 'Bilateral Arbitration Treaties: An Improved Means of International Dispute Resolution' in UNCITRAL, Modernizing International Trade Law to Support Innovation and Sustainable Development Proceedings of the Congress of the United Nations Commission on International Trade Law. Vienna, 4–6 July 2017, Volume 4: Papers presented at the Congress (2017) 314–326, available at www.uncitral.org/pdf/english/congress/17-06783_ebook.pdf. *See* already Gilles Cuniberti, 'Beyond Contract – The Case for Default Arbitration in International Commercial Disputes' (2008) 32 *Fordham International Law Journal* 417.

truly autonomous, needs the courts to do two things that are incompatible. On the one hand, courts should stay outside of the business of arbitration altogether. On the other hand, they are expected to support arbitration along the way and enforce ensuing awards. These two functions would not be incompatible if they could be neatly distinguished from each other, but that is not the case. Take the problem of competence-competence. Under this doctrine (which is a crucial element of autonomy) it is up to the arbitrator, not the court, to determine whether jurisdiction exists. Courts are therefore required to refer parties to arbitration if an arbitration clause exists, even if that arbitration clause might be invalid. The problem is that even for this limited step, courts must necessarily assess the arbitration clause. They must assess whether what the parties agree upon is arbitration or something else. Or, take enforcement. Arbitrators must determine whether the arbitrator was biased, whether the parties were granted due process and so on. In order to enforce the autonomy of arbitration, courts must therefore necessarily interfere with it, take a position on it. This is of course possible. But it cannot be done on the ground of an abstract idea of autonomy. The enforcement, or the non-enforcement, of arbitral agreements and arbitral awards, is at the same time a recognition of the autonomy of arbitration and an intervention in it.

6.5.2 Public/Private

This last argument is well known in scholarship since legal realism, though it is rarely discussed, as far as I can see, in arbitration scholarship and case law.[58] Scholars in the early twentieth century demonstrated that the distinction between private and public law, private and public ordering, which had been a cornerstone of legal theory and practice, was brittle.

[58] An important exception is A. Claire Cutler, *Private Power and Global Authority: Transnational Merchant Law in the Global Political Economy* (Cambridge: Cambridge University Press, 2003), 32ff; *see also* Amr A. Shalakany, 'Arbitration and the Third World: A Plea for Reassessing Bias under the Specter of Neoliberalism' (2000) 41 *Harvard International Law Journal* 419, 466–468; Ralf Michaels, 'Public and Private Law in the Global Adjudication System: Three Questions to the Panelists' (2008) 18 *Duke Journal of Comparative & International Law* 253, at 254; Peer Zumbansen, 'Debating Autonomy and Procedural Justice: The Lex Mercatoria in the Context of Global Governance Debates – A Reply to Thomas Schultz' (2011) 2 *Journal of International Dispute Settlement* 427, at 430–431. More generally, see, Katharina Pistor, The Code of Capital (2019).

Property and contract, the core institutions of private law, were actually, arguably, institutions of public law. Morris R. Cohen showed how a property right is not a private right but an instance of sovereignty.[59] The seemingly private right of the property owner is actually a right to force others to commit or refrain from certain activities. The same Morris R. Cohen made a similar demonstration for contract:[60] The law of contract, in enabling contract parties to have courts enforce the contracts, grants limited sovereignty to them. It is, in essence, therefore, a public institution. The consequence of these realisations is that the enforcement *vel non* of property rights and contractual promises is not a mere, quasi-automatic, enforcement of private rights. It is, instead, a political decision. Similarly, then, the decision to enforce arbitration agreements and arbitral awards is not a somehow necessary consequence of an aprioristic public/private distinction. It is, instead, a deliberate policy choice and in this sense a public matter. Arbitration is not autonomous of its own doing; the autonomy and its limits are ultimately matters of public determination.

But is not the enforcement of agreements a natural (if not necessary) consequence of respect for individual autonomy? This is a frequent argument in favour of enforcing arbitration agreements and thus, by extension, of arbitral awards resulting from such agreements. Unfortunately, enforcing agreements is not as straightforward as it is made to seem. The arbitration agreement itself, often consisting of no more than a few words, can hardly bear the weight of the entire system of arbitration. One may well say that parties who opted into a system can therefore not complain against possible negative results from that system. But one cannot say that the parties have actively chosen these results or even the precise processes that led to the results. Rather, in the long passage between signing the agreement and the enforcement of an award, a huge number of policy decisions must be made that do not derive directly from the agreement.

The ultimate goal of the legal realist argument against a natural public/private distinction was a political and reformist one: to demonstrate that the state has options in the enforcement of private rights and agreements, that it is not bound by a naturalist idea of a public/private distinction. But these political goals are only possible consequences from the analytical argument that predates them and makes them possible, namely that

59 Morris R. Cohen, 'Property and Sovereignty' (1927) 13 *Cornell Law Review* 8

60 Morris R. Cohen, 'The Basis of Contract' (1933) 46 *Harvard Law Review* 553, at 588.

public and private are necessarily intertwined, that an autonomous private sphere, isolated against intervention by the state, is an internally inconsistent position. That analytical argument applies to arbitration as well. There is no natural state of autonomy, and there is no natural duty for states to respect such autonomy. Rather, what is called autonomy of arbitration, and respect thereof by states and their institutions, are in fact the results of important policy choices. Those policy choices may well be defensible – in fact, many legal realists themselves were in favour of alternative dispute resolution mechanisms. But the defence must derive, ultimately, from concrete policy arguments, not from abstract concepts like autonomy.

6.5.3 Globalisation Shift?

The realist argument just presented has long been well known in the domestic context. Some scholars have expressed puzzlement as to why it has not similarly taken ground in the international realm.[61] One main reason is that the frameworks are different. The realist argument was developed in and for situations within one state. There, it was one state (with its institutions) that was called upon to enforce, or not, private rights and agreements. That is not the situation of international arbitration, which exists in relation to multiple states. Before we can ask whether the state should enforce agreements and awards or not, we must ask: which state? There are many.

This difference is important. The multitude of states is an important independent argument in favour of autonomous arbitration in the international realm, regardless of the domestic realm.[62] Within one state, arguments from democracy suggest that it should be up to the state, legitimised through elections and institutions, to lay out binding policies with regard to the discretions of private parties. Internationally, analogous arguments counsel against allocating these policy decisions with one state that does not represent both parties. Here, all of a sudden, it is the state that represents particular interests, while arbitration on the other hand can

[61] Joel Paul, 'The Isolation of Private International Law' (1988) 7 *Wisconsin International Law Journal* 149.

[62] *E.g.* Paulsson (n 25) 174ff.

claim neutrality – at least as between the parties that have selected it. The stronger argument for arbitration autonomy emerges not from respect for individual choice but instead from the contingency of state courts and institutions in the international realm. It is in and for this realm that Fouchard and Goldman developed their theories of an autonomous legal order. And it is in this realm that Gaillard now defends a concept of arbitration as based on all national laws in the world at the same time, and thus able to transcend them.

And yet, ultimately the argument from multitude is incomplete, too. In the international realm, the tension between private and public that is familiar from the domestic context does not go away. Instead, it gets translated into what Robert Wai has called 'transnational liftoff and juridical touchdown'.[63] Arbitration – the private – can indeed become transnational (and arguably always has been). However, as long as it depends on state courts for its enforcement, it needs to touch down back within the law of states. The fact that this touchdown can take place in many different states has a number of implications: it enables forum shopping and regulatory competition; it may require arbitrators to consider enforceability of their awards in all relevant states instead of just one; it may create difficult problems of choice of law. However, as long as the touchdown is necessary for arbitration, its autonomy is no longer complete.

6.6 Conclusion

The argument in this chapter has ultimately been simple. If autonomy is meant to be isolation from states, it is implausible: in a world governed by states, a realm wholly outside of states does not exist.[64] What proponents of autonomous arbitration really want is not actually autonomy but a set of particular policy choices, made both within arbitration and within state institutions, that enhance the power of arbitration and require states to support that power. I say nothing here about whether those policy choices are desirable or not. That answer has a lot to do with

[63] Robert S Wai, 'Transnational Liftoff and Juridical Touchdown: The Regulatory Function of Private International Law in an Era of Globalization' (2002) 40 *Columbia Journal of Transnational Law* 209.

[64] Ralf Michaels, 'The Mirage of Non-State Governance' (2010) *Utah Law Review* 31.

the relative attractiveness of states and their institutions on the one hand, arbitration and its institutions on the other. It requires detailed and fact-specific analysis – of the concrete state and the concrete arbitral issue at stake, and of the concrete policy decision that is needed. What is impossible is to derive answers to these policy questions from an abstract concept like autonomy.

The situation of arbitration does not fit with a binary scheme of autonomy (where it can rule itself) and heteronomy (where it is ruled by the state). Our world is not one of autonomous isolated realms, nor is it one in which states are the institutions that ultimately determine matters from a hierarchically superior position. Rather than autonomy or heteronomy, our world is characterised by interdependence – not only between different states, but also between states and the arbitral system. The traditional distinctions between public and private, domestic and international, have become problematic, but they are not going to be replaced by new neat concept like privatisation or autonomy. Instead, the transnational law of dispute resolution combines both state courts and arbitration – sometimes in mutual support and coordination, sometimes in conflict and competition (or, in Lady Gloster's words, sometimes as symbiosis and sometimes as sadism and masochism).[65] Talk of autonomous arbitration conceals more than it reveals.

[65] Elizabeth Gloster, 'Symbiosis or Sadomasochism? The Relationship between the Courts and Arbitration' (2018) 34 *Arbitration International* 321.

7 The Future of International Commercial Arbitration

George A. Bermann

7.1 Introduction

Although international commercial arbitration is not subject to as much criticism as investor-State arbitration, it is nonetheless facing challenges going forward. These challenges are several, and only some can be addressed in this chapter. Some relate to concerns that have been with international arbitration for a long time. These include costs, delay and excessive formality, as well as arbitrator neutrality. Others – arbitration ethics, diversity, and transparency – are not new, but are taking on greater urgency. Still others simply represent new developments more or less extrinsic to international arbitration but with which international arbitration must cope. Among these changes to the broader international arbitration landscape are the data protection movement and the rise of both settlement agreements and international commercial courts.

These are by no means the only ways in which the future of international commercial arbitration may look somewhat different from what we have come to know. At the very least, they suggest the wide range of developments to which international commercial arbitration will be called upon to respond.

This chapter does not enter into the question of the impact of remote hearings on international arbitration going forward in a post-pandemic world. That matter is the subject of countless articles and other writings and communications.

7.2 Cost, Delay, and Excessive Formality

Within international commercial arbitration circles, there is increasing concern that the arbitration process is becoming "judicialized,"[1] through complex procedural rules and greater legal intricacies, with an attendant

[1] *See, e.g.*, Leon Trakman and Hugh Montgomery, "The 'Judicialization' of International Commercial Arbitration: Pitfall or Virtue?" (2017) 30 *LJIL* 405.

increase in costs and delays in a field of dispute resolution originally envisioned to be "quick, efficient, and universal."[2] The 2018 International Arbitration Survey by White & Case LLP and the Queen Mary School of International Arbitration found that, while 97 percent of respondents stated that international arbitration was their preferred method of dispute resolution, "costs" continued to be seen as its greatest weakness, followed by "lack of effective sanctions during the arbitral process," "lack of power in relation to third parties," and "lack of speed."[3]

The problem of excessive formality is widely attributed to the following factors:[4]

1. the increased complexity of the procedural rules prescribed by various arbitral institutions;
2. the reluctance of arbitral tribunals to depart from strictly applying these rules, for fear of endangering the validity and enforceability of an award;
3. the greater involvement of lawyers, who tend toward being predisposed to formalized proceedings; and
4. the lack of an appeal process, which may, arguably, place additional stress on both counsel and arbitrators to ensure that the "right" result is achieved even if this costs disproportionate time and money.

On point 3, in particular, it merits specific mention that a total of 85 percent of costs associated with arbitration are estimated as being party costs, chiefly in the form of counsel and expert fees.[5]

The international arbitration community, urged in part by users, has taken steps to increase the efficiency of the arbitral process.

7.2.1 Arbitral Mechanisms Designed to Expedite Proceedings

Arbitral mechanisms designed to expedite proceedings have recently emerged in various forms. These include (1) institutional rules to "fast

[2] *Id.*, 406.

[3] Queen Mary University of London, 2018 International Arbitration Survey: The Evolution of International Arbitration (2018), www.arbitration.qmul.ac.uk/media/arbitration/docs/2018-International-Arbitration-Survey–The-Evolution-of-International-Arbitration-(2).PDF.

[4] *See, e.g.*, V. K. Rajah, "W(h)ither Adversarial Commercial Dispute Resolution?" (2017) 33 *Arb Int'l* 17, 25.

[5] Louis Flannery and Benjamin Garel, "Arbitration Costs Compared: The Sequel" (2013) 8(1) *GAR* 4.

track" or expedited proceedings, (2) the Prague Rules, as guidelines to simplify dealing with evidence, and (3) summary dispositions.

7.2.1.1 Institutional Rules for "Fast Track" or Expedited Proceedings

First, institutional rules providing for "fast track" or expedited proceedings have gained widespread acceptance. These procedures entail early case management conferences, tight timeframes accompanying each step in the process, and the possibility of dispensing with an oral hearing, that is, streamlining.

For example, the ICC's Expedited Procedure Provisions apply where the parties expressly consent (or do not opt out, if the arbitration agreement was concluded after March 1, 2017, and the dispute is valued at US$2 million or less). Unlike the normal ICC procedure, there are no terms of reference. The process requires an early case management conference and issuance of a final award within six months of that date. Both the HKIAC and SIAC have similar provisions, albeit with a higher monetary threshold (at HK$25 million and US$6 million, respectively). However, the expedited procedure must be requested by a party; it does not apply by default. The award must be rendered within six months from the time the tribunal receives its file (HKIAC) or is constituted (SIAC).

There is in principle no reason why an award resulting from "fast track" or expedited proceedings should be any less regarded than any other, as confirmed by the Singapore High Court case of *AQZ v. ARA*.[6]

7.2.1.2 The Prague Rules

A more radical solution is embodied in the Prague Rules on the Efficient Conduct of Proceedings in International Arbitration (the "Prague Rules") adopted in December 2018. Drafted by a Working Group consisting mainly of legal professionals from Central Europe with a continental civil law background,[7] the Prague Rules seek to promote procedural efficiency through procedures more akin to a civil law inquisitorial style of taking evidence.[8] They are designed to offer an alternative to the IBA Rules on the Taking of Evidence in International Arbitration (the "IBA Rules"), which

[6] [2015] 2 SLR 972 (Singapore).

[7] Prague Rules, Working Group Note, Appendix I.

[8] *See* Gonzalo Stampa, "The Prague rules" (2019) 35(2) *Arb Int'l* 221 for a more detailed discussion.

some commentators perceive as being biased in favor of promoting an Anglo-American "adversarial approach" widely thought to heighten cost and delays.[9]

The key features of the Prague Rules include the following. The arbitral tribunal may give an indication at the case management conference of its preliminary views on the issues in dispute, the relief sought, and the evidence submitted. The arbitral tribunal is entitled and encouraged to take a proactive role in establishing the facts of the case which it considers relevant for the resolution of the dispute. The Rules take narrow and restrictive approach to document production, with the tribunal and parties encouraged to avoid any form of document production, including e-discovery. As for experts, the preferred approach is direct appointment by the arbitral tribunal, with input and submissions from the parties. The arbitral tribunal and the parties are encouraged to seek to resolve disputes on a documents-only basis in appropriate cases. Although a party may request a hearing, it is unclear whether the tribunal retains discretion to disallow a hearing. The tribunal may assist the parties in reaching an amicable settlement of the dispute at any stage of the proceedings, unless one of the parties objects. Upon the prior written consent of all parties, any arbitrator may act as a mediator to assist in the amicable settlement of the dispute. If a settlement is not achieved, the arbitrator who acted as a mediator will need the written consent of all parties to continue to act as arbitrator in the proceedings.

7.2.1.3 Rise of Summary Dispositions

Traditionally, arbitral tribunals have been more reluctant to adopt summary procedures than some courts, perhaps in part due to the lack of an appeals mechanism. However, institutions are coming around to viewing dispositive motions as an efficiency device. Thus, the SIAC rules allow for early dismissal of claims or defenses that are either "manifestly without legal merit" or "manifestly outside the jurisdiction of the Tribunal."

[9] *See, e.g.*, Kluwer Arbitration Blog, Prague Rules v. IBA Rules and the Taking of Evidence in International Arbitration: Tilting at Windmills – Part I (July 5, 2018), http://arbitrationblog.kluwerarbitration.com/2018/07/05/prague-rules-v-iba-rules-taking-evidence-international-arbitration-tilting-windmills-part/; DLA Piper, The Prague Rules: "Civil" War on The Evidence In International Arbitration (January 24, 2019), www.dlapiper.com/en/czech/insights/publications/2019/01/the-prague-rules/.

In the United States, neither the FAA nor the Uniform Arbitration Act expressly provides for dispositive motions. However, arbitrators have long had the implicit authority to grant such motions. The AAA made that authority explicit for its arbitrators when it amended its rules in 2013. Rule 33 of the AAA Commercial Rules states, "The arbitrator may allow the filing of and make rulings upon a dispositive motion only if the arbitrator determines that the moving party shows that the motion is likely to succeed and dispose of or narrow the issues in the case." JAMS, FINRA, and CPR rules also allow for summary judgment. Even before Rule 33, courts assumed arbitrators' summary disposition authority, and have upheld such awards.[10]

7.2.2 Emergency Interim Relief

Although the availability of emergency relief does not render arbitral proceedings shorter and less expensive, it does tend to make arbitration more efficient by helping ensure that an eventual award is effective, much as ordinary interim relief by arbitrators does. Many arbitration rules now provide for the appointment of an "emergency arbitrator" to consider any application for interim relief on an expedited basis, before an arbitral tribunal has been constituted. See, for instance, Rule 38 of the AAA Rules and Art. 6 of the ICDR Rules. Requests for emergency relief are increasingly common and not infrequently granted.

7.2.3 Specialized International Arbitration Institutes and Tribunals

In 2012, the Panel of Recognized International Market Experts in Finance (PRIME Finance) was launched in the Hague, to create a leading panel of experts with specialist knowledge to arbitrate resolve complex financial transactions (CFTs),[11] in the belief that few national judges are familiar with or confident in their ability to decide CFT disputes.[12]

[10] *See* British Ins. Co. v. Water St. Ins. Co., 93 F. Supp. 2d 506, 517 (S.D.N.Y. 2000) (US); TIG Ins. Co. v. Global Int'l Reinsur. Co., 640 F. Supp. 2d 519 (S.D.N.Y. 2009); Campbell v. American Family Life Assur. Co. of Columbus, 613 F. Supp. 2d 1114 (D. Minn. 2009).

[11] *See* Jonathan Ross, "The case for P.R.I.M.E. Finance: P.R.I.M.E. Finance cases" (2012) 7(3) *CMLJ* 221.

[12] *See id.*

This panel has developed its own arbitration and mediation rules, based closely on the UNCITRAL Arbitration Rules, with some important procedural differences to enable PRIME Finance to act as an administering institution.[13] For instance, it intends to publish awards and advisory opinions (where appropriate, when agreed with the relevant parties, and if necessary on an anonymized basis), to create a corpus of case law governing CFTs. The premise is that the more expert an arbitral body, the more efficient the procedure.

This is only one illustration of what may become a trend. There exist other specialist arbitration bodies in various fields, including intellectual property (WIPO Arbitration and Mediation Centre), marine and salvage (LMAA, GMAA, and TMAC), commodities (NGFA Arbitration System), and insurance (ARIAS).

7.2.4 Hybrid Dispute Resolution Mechanisms

Mediation has palpably emerged as a nonadversarial alternative to international commercial arbitration, often surpassing it in terms of time and cost efficacy. In the US, over 66 percent of AAA commercial cases settle.[14] FINRA's statistics exceed this, with an 83 percent settlement rate (57 percent by direct negotiations of the parties and an additional 12 percent settled with the assistance of a mediator).[15] In other institutions, settlement rates are equally high. In the United Kingdom, the current size of the civil and commercial mediation market is estimated at in the order of 12,000 cases per annum, that is, 20 percent more than the 10,000 cases estimated in 2016.[16] In Singapore, of the more than 1,700 disputants who took part in the mediations held at SMC's offices at the Supreme Court, more than 84 percent reported saving costs while more than 88 percent said they saved time.[17]

[13] *See id.*

[14] American Arbitration Association (AAA), Arbitration Myths (undated), http://info.adr.org/arbitration-myths/.

[15] FINRA, Dispute Resolution Statistics (2019), www.finra.org/arbitration-mediation/dispute-resolution-statistics.

[16] Centre for Effective Dispute Resolution (CEDR), The Eighth Mediation Audit (July 10, 2018), www.cedr.com/docslib/The_Eighth_Mediation_Audit_2018.pdf.

[17] Singapore Mediation Centre (SMC), About Us (2019), http://mediation.com.sg/about-us/.

However, it is not always easy to bring parties to the mediation table. This may explain the proliferation of multitier dispute resolution mechanism in today's commercial market. Notwithstanding initial skepticism as to the enforceability of "good faith" requirements to negotiate or mediate, such obligations have been held to bind parties across multiple jurisdictions.[18]

With the signing of the Singapore Mediation Convention to enforce the settlement agreements resulting from mediation, hybrid dispute resolution mechanisms will be on the rise. The most popular of these is Mediation-Arbitration (or "Med-Arb"), in which the same neutral person acts first, as mediator, and then as arbitrator, if mediation fails. There are other variations, like Arbitration-Mediation-Arbitration (or "Arb-Med-Arb"), starting with arbitration before moving on to mediation, and eventually returning to arbitration, if need be. In Singapore, the latter gained recognition with the announcement of the SIAC-SIMC Arb-Med-Arb Protocol on November 5, 2014.[19] While the SIMC generally encourages appointing different individuals as mediator and arbitrator to maintain the integrity and confidentiality of both processes and comply with natural justice rules,[20] the Protocol allows parties to agree otherwise. The Protocol also proposes fixed time lines, to avoid abuse of the process by delays.

7.2.5 Technology Assisted Review

At the same time, software programs may help to reduce time and costs in arbitration through such mechanisms as e-filing[21] or streamlining document review through "predictive coding," which entails using software to

[18] *See, e.g.*, SIGA Techs., Inc. v. PharmAthene Inc. (SIGA II), 132 A.3d 1108 (Del. 2015) (US); HSBC Institutional Trust Services (Singapore) Ltd v. Toshin Development Singapore Pte Ltd [2012] 4 SLR 738 (Singapore); Emirates Trading Agency LLC v. Prime Mineral Exports Private Limited [2014] EWHC 2104 (Comm) (UK); United Group Rail Services v. Rail Corporation New South Wales (2009) 127 Con LR 202. (Aust).

[19] *See* Aziah Hussin, Claudia Kuck and Nadja Alexander, "SIAC-SIMC's Arb-Med-Arb Protocol" (2018) 11(2) *New York Dispute Resolution Lawyer* 85.

[20] Singapore International Mediation Centre (SIMC), Arb-Med-Arb (undated), http://simc.com.sg/arb-med-arb/; Nadja Alexander, "Global Trends in Mediation" *Mediation und Konflikt management* 16 (2017).

[21] *See* Opus 2 Magnum, which is "an online platform that facilitates communication and procedural understanding between parties in arbitration."

determine whether documents are relevant or privileged.[22] In the case of *Rio Tinto v. Vale*,[23] the US District Court for the Southern District of New York gave parties approval to use predictive coding. It is estimated that parties' costs may be reduced by up to 86 percent.[24]

Procedural hearings of various kinds may also be conducted virtually via video-conference. With the quality of video facilities rapidly improving, it is likely that physical hearings, with all parties at the same premises, will diminish, resulting in faster and less costly hearings.

Other tools may also help to establish forecasts or probabilities of success or failure based on an analysis of case law and findings by individual arbitrators.[25] Artificial intelligence (AI) could potentially predict costs and duration, and, perhaps more controversially, at the express request of the parties, propose settlement ranges based on arbitrations of similar size and complexity, thus nudging parties toward settlement.[26]

Given the sensitivity of information exchanged between parties, institutions and arbitrators, cybersecurity is increasingly becoming an issue in international arbitration. The ICC Commission on Arbitration's 2017 Report on the Use of Information Technology in International Arbitration urges counsel and arbitrators to comply with strict information security requirements and adopt guidelines for the secure transmission of matter-related information. Under the 2018 HKIAC Rules, governing arbitrations commenced on or after November 1, 2018, technology is to be utilized more effectively, with document delivery via a secure online platform.

There is no reason why these emerging trends should not take hold, as have previous innovations. They can only help raising confidence in the system among users.

[22] *See* Nicholas M. Pace and Laura Zakaras, "Where the Money Goes Understanding Litigant Expenditures for Producing Electronic Discovery" (RAND Institute for Civil Justice 2012) ("RAND Report") 59.

[23] No 14 Civ 3042 (SDNY, March 2, 2015).

[24] *See* RAND Report, *supra* note 22, 68.

[25] *See* Arbitrator Intelligence, which aims to "to increase transparency, accountability, and diversity in arbitrator selection by making key information about arbitrators' past decision-making more generally available through publication of AI Reports."

[26] Kluwer Arbitration Blog, International Arbitration and Artificial Intelligence: Time to Tango? (February 23, 2018) http://arbitrationblog.kluwerarbitration.com/2018/02/23/international-arbitration-artificial-intelligence-time-tango/.

7.3 Arbitration Ethics

Consciousness of ethics in international arbitration has been constantly on the rise, made all the more salient with the dramatic widening of the pool of arbitrators. In a 2011 survey, 68 percent of respondents reported experiencing ethical misconduct, including the deployment of so-called guerrilla tactics, in international arbitration.[27]

Even with the best of good faith, practitioners face serious uncertainty over the ethical norms to which they are subject. The situation is exacerbated by the disparities in cultural norms and assumptions across jurisdictions.

7.3.1 Illustrative Issues

There are a large number of practices, the following among them, that illustrate the problem.

7.3.1.1 Communicating Directly with Adverse Parties

Different rules govern the interviewing of employees of an adverse corporate party known to be represented. While this is permissible in the United Kingdom,[28] it is strictly forbidden in the United States,[29] as it is in Germany.[30] An incidental result is the potential inequality in the abilities of lawyers across different jurisdictions to access evidence or information.

7.3.1.2 Preparing Witnesses for Testimony

In the United States, it is common practice for counsel to rehearse or "coach" witnesses in anticipation of direct and cross-examination in detail, although the witness is not to be influenced to adopt testimony he or she would not otherwise give.[31] In stark contrast, civil law systems

[27] Edna Sussman and Solomon Ebere, "All's Fair in Love and War – Or Is It? Reflections on Ethical Standards for Counsel in International Arbitration" (2011) 22 *Am. Rev. Int'l. Arb.* 611, 612.

[28] Cyrus Benson, "Can Professional Ethics Wait? The Need for Transparency in International Arbitration" (2009) 3(1) *Disp. Res. Int'l* 78, 83.

[29] *See id.*

[30] *See id.*

[31] *See id*; Steven Lubet, "Expert Witnesses: Ethics and Professionalism" (1999) 12 *Geo. J. Legal Ethics* 465, 471.

traditionally permit little if any contact with witnesses prior to trial,[32] and the same may be said of the United Kingdom.[33]

7.3.1.3 Counsel's Duty to Disclose Damaging Precedents

In the United States, the United Kingdom, and other common law jurisdictions, advocates owe independent duties to the tribunal and must, accordingly, disclose any relevant such authorities they come across, however damaging to their case they may be.[34] In a large number of jurisdictions, including in Germany and elsewhere in the civil law world, no obligation exists.[35]

7.3.1.4 Rules Applicable to Discovery

Lawyers from the United States are accustomed to the practice of discovery whereby counsel for one side may ask opposing counsel to produce any and all documents meeting a particular description that are claimed to be relevant and material.[36] However, civil law practice is different. Counsel are required to produce all documents on which they intend to rely as well as any documents whose production the tribunal may require.[37] Civil law practitioners commonly view extensive discovery requests as a costly *"fishing expedition"* or abuse of process.[38]

These ethical inconsistencies, which riddle international commercial arbitration, have provoked deep concern among leading judicial figures and practitioners.[39] If left unchecked, they may, among other things,

32 *See* Benson, *supra* note 28, 84; Hans Van Houtte, "Counsel-Witness Relations and Professional Misconduct in Civil Law Systems" (2003) 19 *Arb. Int' l* 457, 461.

33 *See id*; The Bar Standards Board, "Section C: The Conduct Rules" in *Handbook*, Rule C9.4 (4th ed. 2019) (UK).

34 *See* Benson, *supra* note 28; Handbook, *supra* note 33, Rule C25.3 (UK).

35 *See* Benson, *supra* note 28.

36 *See* Civil Procedure Rules (CPR), Rule 31 (UK); Practice Directions 31A and 31B (UK).

37 *See* Benson, *supra* note 28, 84.

38 Stefan-M. Tiessen, R. P. Brown and D. R. Grantham, "International Construction Arbitration: When Cultures Collide" (May 2, 2003), www.martindale.com/international-law/article_Smith-Gambrell-Russell_2421.htm.

39 *See, e.g.*, Sundaresh Menon CJ, "International Arbitration: The Coming of a New Age for Asia (and Elsewhere)" (2012),www.arbitrationicca.org/media/0/13398435632250/ags_opening_speech_icca_congress_2012.pdf; Bernard Hanotiau, "International Arbitration in a Global Economy: The Challenges of the Future" (2011) 28(2) *J. Int'l Arb.* 89; David Rivkin, "Ethics in International Arbitration" (2014), www.debevoise.com/ ~/media/files/insights/news/2014/davidrivkinseoularbitrationlecture.pdf.

imperil the finality of awards, and there has in fact been a palpable increase in the number of challenges in recent years.[40]

7.3.2 Recent Movements in Arbitration Ethics

To address these issues, while at the same time maintaining a system of self-regulation, the international arbitration community has begun taking action.[41] The easiest place to start is with individual arbitral institutions, but broader strategies are under consideration.

7.3.2.1 Recent Institution-Specific Ethical Regulations

In the United States, the AAA has, in conjunction with the ABA, produced a Code of Ethics for Arbitrators in Commercial Disputes, the most recent version of which sets out 10 canons to formalize the standards of arbitrators' conduct, including special duties on party-nominated arbitrators.[42] This led the way to the AAA's devising "due process protocols" for different types of arbitration, intended in part to control overreaching by parties who hold superior bargaining power over their counterparts.[43] While Jan Paulsson acknowledges that this requirement "may be valuable in the course of parties' due diligence," he suggests that this remains insufficient.[44]

The latest LCIA Rules introduce ethical norms, such as barring the making of false statements, relying on false evidence, or concealing documents.[45] They also prohibit counsel from engaging in so-guerrilla tactics, enjoining them to "not engage in activities intended unfairly to obstruct

[40] David Hacking, "Challenges: Theirs Is to Reason Why" (2006) 1(6) *GAR*.

[41] *See* Toby Landau QC at the 2012 ICCA Conference, as quoted in GAR, observing that we may be "regulating ourselves out of existence." Regulation debate continues in Singapore (June 13, 2012), http://globalarbitrationreview.com/news/article/30608/regulation-debate-continues-singapore. *See* V. K. Rajah SC, *supra* note 4.

[42] American Arbitration Association (AAA), The Code of Ethics for Arbitrators in Commercial Disputes (March 1, 2014), www.adr.org/sites/default/files/document_repository/Commercial_Code_of_Ethics_for_Arbitrators_2010_10_14.pdf

[43] *See* Jan Paulsson, Universal Arbitration What We Gain, What We Lose, Chartered Institute of Arbitrators (CIArb) Alexander Lecture (November 29, 2012).

[44] *Id.*

[45] *See* LCIA Rules, Annex at paras. 3–5.

the arbitration or to jeopardize the finality of any award."[46] The LCIA Rules, as amended, now empower tribunals to impose sanctions on non-compliant counsel.[47]

In 2008, the Singapore Institute of Arbitrators (SIArb) published "Guidelines on Party-Representative Ethics," which are nonbinding and comprise only three very broad guidelines,[48] namely, that

1. a party representative should respect the integrity of international proceedings, including the independence of the tribunal, the tribunal's members, and any potential arbitrators;
2. a party representative should act honestly and with integrity in all of his or her dealings with the tribunal and parties involved in the arbitration proceedings; and
3. a party representative should treat the tribunal and other parties with respect and act with the highest degree of professionalism.

7.3.2.2 IBA Guidelines on Party Representation

In May 2013, the IBA launched its Guidelines on Party Representation in International Arbitration, "inspired by the principle that party representatives should act with integrity and honesty and should not engage in activities designed to produce unnecessary delay or expense, including tactics aimed at obstructing the arbitration proceedings."[49] Subject to applicable national laws, the IBA Guidelines provide guidance on some of the matters discussed above. Thus, the IBA Guidelines provide that, before seeking any information from a potential witness or expert, lawyers

[46] *Id.* para. 2 provides that: "A legal representative should not engage in activities intended unfairly to obstruct the arbitration or to jeopardise the finality of any award, including repeated challenges to an arbitrator's appointment or to the jurisdiction or authority of the Arbitral Tribunal known to be unfounded by that legal representative."

[47] *Id.* Annex at para. 7 read with Arts. 18.5 and 18.6.

[48] Singapore Institute of Arbitrators (SIArb), SIArb Guidelines on Party-Representative Ethics (April 26, 2018), www.siarb.org.sg/images/SIARB_Party-Rep-Ethics_Guidelines_Aprl18.pdf

[49] IBA Guidelines on Party Representation in Intl. Arbitration ("IBA Guidelines"), pmbl. at 2: "The Guidelines are not intended to displace otherwise applicable mandatory laws, professional or disciplinary rules, or agreed arbitration rules, in matters of Party representation. The Guidelines are also not intended to derogate from the arbitration agreement or to undermine either a Party representative's primary duty of loyalty to the party whom he or she represents or a Party representative's paramount obligation to present such Party's case to the Arbitral Tribunal."

should identify themselves, their clients, and the reason for which the information is sought.[50] They should also inform such persons of their rights to inform their own counsel about the contact and, if they so wish, discontinue their communications.[51]

The IBA Guidelines permits the interviewing of witnesses for the purpose of preparing witness statements or giving oral testimony, subject to such mandatory rules as may be applicable.[52] In regard to document production, the Guidelines require party representatives to inform their clients of the necessity to preserve potentially relevant documents, not to use discovery to "harass or cause unnecessary delay," to conduct a reasonable search to produce relevant documents, and not to conceal such documents.

Though the IBA Guidelines only apply to the extent that parties or tribunals elect to adopt them,[53] solely focus on counsel, rather than arbitrator, conduct, and favor brevity over depth, they are a good starting point for a genuine transnational code of ethics.

7.3.2.3 Toward a Universally Accepted Transnational Code of Ethics

In recent years, the idea of a universally accepted transnational code of ethics for arbitration has become increasingly popular.[54] As Singapore's Chief Justice has put it, "with signs of the emergence of a global international law of arbitration despite national differences, why shouldn't the same apply in relation to arbitrator standards?"[55] To be

[50] *See* IBA Guidelines, Guideline 18.

[51] *See id.*, Guideline 19.

[52] *See id.*, Guidelines 20 to 25; LCIA Rules, Art. 20.5.

[53] *See* IBA Guidelines, Guideline 1.

[54] *See, e.g.*, Menon, *supra* note 39; Rajah, *supra* note 4; Charles N. Brower and Stephan W. Schill, "Regulating Counsel before International Tribunals" in Pieter H. F. Bekker, Rudolf Dolzer and Michael Waibel (eds.), *Making Transnational Law Work in a Global Economy: Essays in Honour of Detlev Vagts* (NY: Cambridge University Press, 2010), 488, 489; Doak Bishop, "Ethics in International Arbitration, Speech at the International Council for Commercial Arbitration Conference in South America" (May 26, 2010), www.arbitration-icca.org/conferences-and-congresses/ICCA_RIO_2010/ICCA_ RIO_2010_ Doak_Bishop.html; Robert W. Wachter, "Ethical Standards in International Arbitration: Considering Solutions to Level the Playing Field" (2011) 24 *Geo. J. Legal Ethics* 1143; John M. Townsend, "Clash and Convergence on Ethical Issues in International Arbitration" (2004) 36 *U. Miami Inter-Am. L. Rev.* 1. There are, however, others who argue against this: *see, e.g.*, Kristen Weisenberger, "Peace Is Not the Absence of Conflict: A Response to Professor Rogers's Article 'Fit and Function in Legal Ethics'" (2007) 25 *Wisc. Int'l L.J.* 89.

[55] *See* Menon, *supra* note 39.

truly effective in standardizing the ethical behavior of counsel and arbitrators across the board, such a code must deal with the contentious ethical issues subject to cultural divergences across multiple jurisdictions on matters such as those discussed earlier. At the same time, the code should also have enough flexibility to meet the ever evolving demands of international commercial arbitration, while aligning well with such institutional or ad hoc rules as exist.

These initiatives should produce a code of ethics that will, eventually if not immediately, come to be recognized as "universally accepted" practice, to be applied irrespective of the particular jurisdiction or arbitral institution before which a particular matter arises. To ensure consistency in ad hoc international commercial arbitrations, one possibility would be to incorporate the code directly into the governing rules on arbitration (such as, for instance, the UNCITRAL Arbitration Rules), to hold the key players in such proceedings to the same ethical standards.[56] Arbitral institutions could coordinate their efforts with a view to producing an international system of accreditation, imposing sanctions from an internationally approved list, as set out within the code, and even performing a supervisory role in reviewing cost awards.[57]To the same end, the Swiss Arbitration Association has recently floated the idea of a "Global Arbitration Ethics Council."[58]

Once adopted, a transnational code of ethics of the sort envisaged must be enforced. The annulment of awards is obviously not the answer, given that arbitral awards are only set aside in the most egregious of circumstances and that its deterrent effect may be minimal.[59]

Arbitral institutions can regulate the profession, in a manner akin to bar associations, by implementing an international system of accreditation, by which arbitrators are recognized, imposing sanctions from an internationally approved list, as set out within the code, and, possibly, performing a supervisory role in reviewing costs award.[60]

[56] *See* Menon, *supra* note 39.

[57] *See* Menon, *supra* note 39.

[58] Swiss Arbitration Association (ASA), Statement on the Global Arbitration Ethics Council Discussions (November 27, 2015), www.arbitration-ch.org/en/asa/asa-news/details/983.statement-on-the-global-arbitration-ethics-council-discussions.html.

[59] *See* Menon, *supra* note 39.

[60] *See* Menon, *supra* note 39.

7.4 Data Protection and Arbitration

Data protection is one of the major challenges that international commercial arbitration is facing. The European Union's General Data Protection Regulation (GDPR),[61] which came into force on May 25, 2018, imposes serious obligations on persons or entities processing personal data and provides rights to individuals about whom data are being processed. Although data protection regulation in the EU context is anything but new,[62] its vast reach and high sanctions[63] have given data protection a whole new significance with which international arbitration must cope.

The GDPR applies to the processing of personal data of persons within the EU by a "controller" or "processor," whether or not it is located in the EU or the processing takes place in the EU. "Controller" means any natural or legal person, public authority, agency or other body which, alone or jointly with others, determines the purposes and means of the processing of personal data,[64] whereas "processor" means a natural or legal person, public authority, agency or other body, which processes personal data on behalf of the controller.[65] In the context of arbitration, this implies that basically every participant in an arbitral proceeding – the parties, counsel, experts, arbitral institutions and arbitrators – are likely to be considered data controllers both because such control is inherent in their function and because, as a matter of fact, they determine the purpose and means by which personal data are processed in order to perform their functions.[66] Counsel, institutions, and tribunals are also very likely to be also considered as processor when they are transmitting files or evidence to one another on behalf of a controller.[67] As a matter of fact, even if only one of

[61] Regulation (EU) 2016/679 of the European Parliament and the Council of April 27, 2016, on the Protection of Natural Persons with Regard to the Processing of Personal Data and on the Free Movement of Such Data, and Repealing Directive 95/46/EC (General Data Protection Regulation), 2016 O.J. L 119/1.

[62] *Among others see generally* Directive 95/46/EC of the European Parliament and of the Council of October 24, 1995, on the Protection of Individuals with Regard to the Processing of Personal Data and on the Free Movement of Such Data, 1995 O.J. L 281/31.

[63] The GDPR permits maximum fines up to €20 million, or 4 percent of annual worldwide turnover, whichever is greater, *see* Art. 83 of the GDPR.

[64] *See* Art. 4 (7) of the GDPR.

[65] *See* Art. 4 (8) of the GDPR.

[66] Kathleen Paisley, "It's All about the Data: The Impact of the EU General Data Protection Regulation on International Arbitration" (2018) 41 *Fordham Int. L. J* 841, 870.

[67] *Id.*, 864–865.

the arbitrators or one of the parties is to be bound by the GDPR, it is more than likely that the whole proceeding will somehow be affected by the rules and the application of the GDPR.[68]

7.4.1 Material Scope of the GDPR

The GDPR encompasses the processing of personal data wholly or partly by automated means and to the processing, other than by automated means, of personal data that form part of a filing system or is intended to form part of a filing system.[69] The term *personal data* signifies any information relating to an identified or identifiable natural person (data subject). In this regard, an "identifiable natural person" is one who can be identified, directly or indirectly, in particular by reference to an identifier, such as a name, an identification number, location data, an online identifier or to one or more factors specific to the physical, physiological, genetic, mental, economic, cultural or social identity of that natural person.[70] Processing refers to any operation on personal data, such as collecting, recording, organizing, storing, adapting, retrieving, consulting, indexing, combining, blocking, disseminating and deleting personal data.[71] Each controller and processor incurs legal liability for failure to comply with their duties as outlined in the GDPR.[72]

The material scope of the GDPR, on the other hand, encompasses the *processing* of *personal data* wholly or partly by automated means and to the processing, other than by automated means, of personal data that form part of a filing system or is intended to form part of a filing system.[73] Due to the apparently broad definition of personal data, all business-related information exchanged during a typical arbitral proceeding that contains information by which an individual is, or can be, identified will be considered personal data as defined by the GDPR.[74] These include

[68] *See also* Emily Hay, "The Invisible Arm of GDPR in International Treaty Arbitration: Can't We Make It Go Away?" http://arbitrationblog.kluwerarbitration.com/2019/08/29/the-invisible-arm-of-gdpr-in-international-treaty-arbitration-cant-we-make-it-go-away.

[69] *See* Art. 2 (1) of the GDPR.

[70] *See* Art. 4 (1) of the GDPR.

[71] *See* Art. 4 (2) of the GDPR.

[72] *See* Paisley, *supra* note 66, 864–865.

[73] *See* Art. 2 (1) of the GDPR.

[74] *See id.*

memorials, witness statements, expert reports, and the award itself.[75] Processing covers a wide range of activities, including document retention, document review, document transfer, disclosure of materials during the arbitral process, tribunal-ordered disclosure of materials, exchange and issuance of an award, taking notes at a hearing and document destruction.[76] Additionally, since it is irrelevant to application of the GDPR whether personal information is contained in a business-related document or not,[77] the playing field of the GDPR is practically without boundaries.

7.4.2 Lawfulness of Processing Personal Data

The question then arises of when and to what extent the processing of personal data is lawful under the GDPR. According to Article 6(1) of the GDPR, processing personal data is, inter alia, lawful if and to the extent that at least one of the following exceptions applies: (1) the data subject has given consent to the processing of his or her personal data for one or more specific purposes; (2) processing is necessary for compliance with a legal obligation to which the controller is subject; and (3) processing is necessary for the purposes of the legitimate interests pursued by the controller or by a third party, except where such interests are overridden by the interests or fundamental rights and freedoms of the data subject which require protection of personal data.[78]

The problem with relying on Article 6 (1) (a) ("consent") is that obtaining consent may be cumbersome and consent can be revoked at any time.[79] Relying on Article 6(1)(c) ("necessity for compliance with legal obligation") comes along with the problem that the need to comply with a legal obligation only legalizes data processing where the legal obligation is created under Member State law, not third country law.[80] This would not cover a tribunal order to produce documents.[81] The processing of personal data will most likely be lawful under Article 6(1)(f) GDPR ("legitimate

[75] *See id.*
[76] *See* Paisley, *supra* note 66, 864–865.
[77] Paisley, *supra* note 66, 847.
[78] *See* Art. 6 (1) of the GDPR.
[79] *See* Art. 7 (3) of the GDPR.
[80] Paisley, *supra* note 66, 875.
[81] *Id.*

interest"), although this exception requires a careful weighing of interests in each individual case, by considering what type of data are being processed (e.g., if they are especially sensitive), the volume involved, and possible safeguards that can be adopted, such as redacting the relevant documents.[82] This will require carefully limiting document production to the extent necessary.[83]

The GDPR also provides that the transfer of data to a third country must be lawful under EU law. A distinction is drawn between secure and unsecure third countries, the former representing those that the European Commission has determined through an "adequacy decision" to have a suitable level of data protection, that is, comparable to those of EU law.[84] That there is no adequacy decision for a country does not necessarily foreclose the transfer of data to that country. Rather, the controller must ensure in some other way that the personal data will be sufficiently protected by the recipient.[85] On the other hand, Article 46 of the GDPR expressly allows transfers that are necessary for the establishment, exercise, or defense of a legal claim, which would likely also apply to certain aspects of arbitration.[86] The standard of necessity is however high, and adequate steps must be taken to ensure that only relevant documents are transferred.[87] Since engaging external counsel as well as correspondence with the tribunal will require a transfer of personal data possibly across EU borders,[88] it might be wise to raise data protection issues in a data protection protocol early in the proceedings.[89]

[82] Markus Borianski, "Data Privacy in International Arbitration" (October 19, 2018), www.whitecase.com/publications/alert/data-privacy-international-arbitration.

[83] *See id*; Paisley, *supra* note 66, 876.

[84] *See generally* chapter V of the GDPR. At the time that the General Data Protection Regulation became applicable, the third countries which ensure an adequate level of protection were: Andorra, Argentina, Canada (only commercial organizations), Faroe Islands, Guernsey, Israel, Isle of Man, Jersey, New Zealand, Switzerland, Uruguay, Japan and USA (if the recipient belongs to the Privacy Shield), *see* https://gdpr-info.eu/issues/third-countries.

[85] *See* https://gdpr-info.eu/issues/third-countries.

[86] *See* Paisley, *supra* note 66, 881.

[87] Borianski, *supra* note 83.

[88] *See id.*

[89] *See id.*

7.4.3 Obligations in the Processing of Personal Data

Under the GDPR, personal data must be (1) processed lawfully, fairly and in a transparent manner in relation to the data subject; (2) collected for specified, explicit, and legitimate purposes and not further processed in a manner that is incompatible with those purposes; (3) relevant and limited to what is necessary in relation to the purposes for which data are processed; (4) kept up to date with every reasonable step taken to ensure that any inaccurate personal data are erased or corrected without delay; (5) kept in a form that permits the identification of data subjects for no longer than is necessary for the purposes for which the data are processed; and (6) processed in a manner that ensures appropriate security of the personal data, including protection against unauthorized or unlawful processing and against accidental loss, destruction or damage, using appropriate administrative and technical means.[90]

In the context of arbitration, the GDPR thus mandates that parties, counsel, tribunals, and arbitral institutions implement Cyber Security measures regarding personal data,[91] make efforts to minimize the risks of retaining personal data, which may include data scrubbing and eliminating sensitive data, even before the data are processed for use in an arbitration, and anonymizing of the relevant data where feasible.[92]

At the time data are collected from a data subject, the latter must be provided with detailed information on the manner and means by which the data will be processed.[93] In a complex arbitration, this could mean that data controllers are required to send multiple data privacy notices to potentially hundreds of individual data subjects named in the evidence.[94] Similar rights attach when the controller did not collect the data in the first place, which often is the case in international arbitration.[95] For example, the law firms and arbitrators may not have

[90] *See* Art. 5 (1) of the GDPR.

[91] This probably led to arbitral institutions starting to take their first steps toward regulating cyber security in arbitral proceedings. For instance, *see* the ICCA/NY Bar/CPR *Draft Cybersecurity Protocol for International Arbitration* was subsequently released for consultation in 2018, www.arbitrationicca.org/media/10/43322709923070/draft_cybersecurity_protocol_final_10_april.pdf.

[92] *See* Paisley, *supra* note 66, 903.

[93] *Id.*

[94] *Id.*

[95] *Id.*

originally collected the data that it controls after a party transfers data to it for use in arbitration.[96]

Another burden imposed by the GDPR is the so-called right to be forgotten. Article 17 of the GDPR provides that under certain circumstances, the data subject has the right to request erasure of his or her personal data at any time. However, the right to be forgotten, which would be problematic to apply in the context of international arbitration, contains an exemption for processing that is "necessary for the establishment, exercise or defense of legal claims."[97] Just as above in context with the third country restrictions, the question will be what is deemed "necessary."

All data controllers and processors must demonstrate that they are compliant with the law at all times.[98] Such measures include, among others, adequate documentation on what personal data are being processed, as well as how, to what purpose, and how long.[99] For this purpose, Article 37 of the GDPR mandates that controllers and processors designate a data protection officer responsible for compliance.

In short, data protection regulation may have wide-ranging effects on basically every stage and nearly every activity in the arbitral lifecycle, starting from the arbitration agreement up until a long time after the arbitral award has been rendered. Data protection issues should therefore be discussed as early as the drafting of the arbitration clause, especially when they are subject to different data protection laws. Compliance is not only a challenge from a process management point of view, but also from a cost point of view, always an issue in contemplating international commercial arbitration's future.

7.5 Neutrality of Arbitrators

Unlike other issues traced in this chapter, arbitrator neutrality has been with us for a long while. This is because one of the main reasons for choosing arbitration over litigation is that parties to an international

[96] *Id.*

[97] *See* Paisley, *supra* note 66, 906.

[98] *See* Art. 39 of the GDPR.

[99] *See* https://edps.europa.eu/data-protection/our-work/subjects/accountability_en.

contract wish to avoid resolving disputes through the local courts of the other party, for fear of favoritism. Arbitration promises a neutral dispute resolution system. One of the primary sources of legitimacy for international arbitration is actual and perceived independence and impartiality.[100]

There are data to support the view that party-appointed arbitrators are less than perfectly neutral. The ICC's 2018 statistics showed in 41 of the 296 awards rendered were accompanied by dissenting opinions,[101] of which 36 were written by the party that had appointed him or her.[102]

Real or perceived lack of neutrality can of course result from personal relations and financial stakes. But there is always the reality that familiarity with a discipline often comes at the expense of complete impartiality or neutrality. An arbitrator may have formed strong views on certain topics and published on them. The international arbitration world is quite small, so that key members know each other and work with one another in different capacities,[103] and yet such expertise and familiarity is one of the reasons that parties choose arbitration over litigation. The challenge is to strike the proper balance between having the most qualified arbitrators and ensuring that arbitrators are and appear to be neutral.

Before the issue of arbitrator neutrality is further tackled, it should first be clarified what can be understood by neutrality and to what extent it is actually legally required.

7.5.1 General Definition of Neutrality

Neutrality relates to the arbitrator's potential predisposition toward a party personally or a party's position.[104] An international arbitrator should be

[100] *See* Ronán Feehiyl, "Neutrality, Independence and Impartiality in International Commercial Arbitration, a Fine Balance in the Quest for Arbitral Justice" (2019) 7 *Penn St. J.L. & Int'l Aff.* 88, 110.

[101] *See* ICC Dispute Resolution Bulletin, 2018, Issue 2, 61.

[102] *See id.*

[103] Morelite Construction v. New York City District Council Carpenters, 748 F.2d 79, 83 (2d Cir. 1984).

[104] *See* Nigel Blackaby and Constantine Partasides, *Redfern and Hunter on International Arbitration*, 6th ed. (Oxford: Oxford University Press, 2015), 254.

neutral not only as between the parties specifically, but also as to nationality and political and legal systems, thus possessing a high degree of "international-mindedness."[105] That a sole arbitrator must be neutral is self-evident. However, according to the prevailing view, party-*appointed arbitrators* should be as well, unless the parties' agreement, the *arbitration* rules agreed to by the parties or applicable law provides otherwise.[106]

7.5.2 Legislative Approaches to Neutrality

Most modern arbitration laws require independence and impartiality on the part of arbitrators. The UNCITRAL Model Law[107] does not use the term *neutrality* but provides that if circumstances exist that gives rise to justifiable doubts regarding the independence or impartiality of an arbitrator, he or she may be challenged on that basis.[108] The justifiable doubts standard is objective and does not require evidence of certainty or likelihood of partiality or dependence.[109]

While the Federal Arbitration Act provides that "evident partiality" by the arbitrator is a basis upon which an arbitral award may be vacated,[110] it does not directly address the standards of neutrality and impartiality required of arbitrators.[111] Unfortunately, US courts have not yet agreed on a common definition of "evident partiality". The leading case in the United States remains *Commonwealth Coatings Corporation v. Continental Casualty Company*,[112] in which the Supreme Court set aside an award based on the principle of "evident partiality" as the presiding arbitrator failed to disclose a four to five-year consulting relationship with a party to the arbitration.[113] However, the Court failed to provide a clear standard of impartiality and independence. Some courts have followed Justice Black's plurality opinion

105 Feehiyl, *supra* note 101, 92.
106 *See* David J. McLean and Sean-Patrick Wilson, "Is Three a Crowd? Neutrality, Partiality and Partisanship in the Context of Tripartite Arbitrations" (2008) 9 *Pepp. Disp. Resol. L.J.* 167, 174–175.
107 UNCITRAL, Model Law on International Commercial Arbitration (1985) (amended 2006).
108 *See* Feehiyl, *supra* note 101, 89 (citing UNCITRAL Model Law Art 12 (2)).
109 *See* Feehiyl, *supra* note 101, 98
110 *See* 9 USC § 10(a)(2).
111 Feehiyl, *supra* note 101, 99.
112 Commonwealth Coatings Corp. v. Continental Casualty Co., 393 US 145 (1968).
113 Feehiyl, *supra* note 101, 101.

according to which arbitrators are held to at least the same standard as judges in order to safeguard their impartiality and arbitration‘s legitimacy. Awards have been vacated based on an appearance of bias or partiality.[114] Other courts have followed Justice White's concurring opinion according to which are not necessarily to be held to the same standards as judges, and have vacated awards only where "a reasonable person … would have to conclude that an arbitrator was partial to one side."[115] The trend in recent years has been a move away from equating standards of impartiality of international arbitrators to those of national court judges.[116]

The English Arbitration Act 1996 also does not use the term *neutrality* but provides in Section 24(1)(a) that an arbitrator may be removed where "circumstances exist that give rise to justifiable doubts as to his impartiality." Furthermore, Section 33(1)(a) relating to the general duty of the arbitral body, imposes the requirement that it "act fairly and impartially as between the parties."[117]

7.5.3 Approaches by Selected Arbitral Institutions

Virtually all arbitral institutions likewise demand independence and neutrality of arbitrators, but likewise are not particularly instructive in this regard.

The AAA Code of Ethics for Arbitrators in Commercial Disputes stipulate that in international disputes all arbitrators including party-appointed arbitrators are to be neutral,[118] providing for disqualification "whenever circumstances exist that give rise to justifiable doubts as to the arbitrator's impartiality or independence."[119] Other institutional rules do as well. Thus, the ICC Rules provide for disqualification on grounds of "lack of

[114] *Id.*, 101–102 (citing Dealer Computer Services Inc. v. Michael Motor Co., 485 F. App'x. 724, 727–728 (5th Cir. 2012).

[115] *Id.*, 101–102 (citing NGXNetnwork Asia v. PAC Pac. Group Intl, Inc., 511 F. App'x 86, 88 (2d Cir. 2013).

[116] Gary B. Born, *International Arbitration: Law and Practice*, 2nd ed., §10.01 (Kluwer Law International, 2015), 1770.

[117] *See* Feehiyl, *supra* note 101, 98.

[118] American Arbitration Association (AAA), International Arbitration Rules, Art. 14 (1) (2014).

[119] American Arbitration Association, Code of Ethics for Arbitrators in Commercial Disputes, Note on Neutrality (2004).

impartiality,"[120] while the LCIA Rules do so when "circumstances exist that give rise to justifiable doubts as to that arbitrator's impartiality or independence."[121] The UNCITRAL Arbitration Rules are to the same effect. As a further precaution, not only the AAA Code of Ethics,[122] but also the International Chamber of Commerce Arbitration Rules,[123] require that the nationality of a sole or presiding arbitrator must be different from that of the parties.

In the future, arbitrators will continue to be guided by the IBA Guidelines on Conflicts of Interest revised as recently as 2014 in the hope of harmonizing the standards of disclosure and setting best practices at the international level.[124] They present not only General Standards but also concrete and practical examples of how those standards are to be applied. They are generally speaking more demanding, and certainly more precise, than most national laws and institutional rules.[125]

7.6 International Commercial Courts

A prominent feature of the landscape facing international commercial arbitration is competition from a new generation of international commercial courts. Specialized commercial courts within a national judiciary are nothing new. They have for a long time been an integral component of court systems in a large number of jurisdictions, notably civil law jurisdictions.[126] However, the phenomenon of *international* commercial courts is a relatively new one. So far, China, several European States,[127] Qatar, Singapore and the

[120] International Chamber of Commerce (ICC), International Arbitration Rules, Art. 14 (1) (2017).

[121] London Court of International Arbitration, Arbitration Rules, Art. 10(3) (2014).

[122] United Nations Commission on International Trade Law (UNCITRAL), UNCITRAL Arbitration Rules (as revised in 2010), Art. 6(7).

[123] International Chamber of Commerce (ICC), International Arbitration Rules, Art. 13 (5) (2017).

[124] Blackaby and Partasides, *supra* note 105, 477.

[125] *See* Born, *supra* note 117, 1857.

[126] *See, e.g.*, the French Code de commerce de 1807 (Commercial Code of 1807) Art. 615 *bis*; in general, *see* The Courts and the Development of Commercial Law (Vito Piergiovanni ed., 1987); as to the history of commercial courts in Germany and Austria, *see* 300 Jahre staatliche Handelsgerichtsbarkeit (Sonja Bydlinski & Maria Wittman-Tiwald eds., 2018).

[127] Among those states are Belgium (Brussels International Business Court), France (Paris Commercial Court and Court of Appeal), Germany (special chambers at regional courts in Frankfurt and Hamburg), the Netherlands (Netherlands Commercial Court), Switzerland

United Arab Emirates have all undertaken efforts to either establish new courts "particularly attuned to the needs and realities of international commerce"[128] or to adapt special procedural rules for international cases in existing commercial courts. No comparable steps have been taken within the United States.

Asian and Middle Eastern initiatives in particular involve using English as the language of the proceedings, foreign-trained judges and elements of the common law tradition on both the substantive and procedural level.[129] Continental European initiatives have been fueled in by the prospect of Brexit, and the possibility that London will become a less attractive forum for resolving international disputes than it has been in the past.[130]

International commercial courts are designed to place adjudicatory authority over international disputes in more expert hands than if they went to the ordinary courts, even the ordinary commercial courts. They are also expected to proceed with their task in a highly cost-efficient manner. Recurring features include, among others, the possibility of party representation by foreign lawyers, expedited proceedings, and dispositive motions.

Future questions concerning international commercial courts include the enforcement of the parties' forum selection clause in favor of an international commercial court and enforcement of the resulting judgments.[131] Neither should be a problem. Forum selection clauses designating international commercial courts should be as widely respected as

(Zurich International Commercial Court), and the United Kingdom (London Commercial Court).

128 This is the description of international commercial courts as employed by Chief Justice of Singapore, Sundaresh Menon, and as relied upon by Andrew Godwin et al., "International Commercial Courts: The Singapore Experience" (2017) 18 *Melbourne J. Int'l L.* 219, 220.

129 Marta Requejo Isidro, "International Commercial Courts in the Litigation Market," 5–6 (Max Planck Institute Luxembourg for Procedural Law Research Paper Series, Working Paper No. 2, 2019), www.mpi.lu/research/working-paper-series/2019/wp-2019-2/.

130 *Id.* 13–14 (relying on data from Portland PR Ltd., Commercial Courts Report 2018, available at https://portland-communications.com/pdf/Portland-commercial-courts-report-2018.pdf

131 Indeed, once the United Kingdom will be a third state from the perspective of the European Union, the recognition and enforcement of judgments obtained in the London Commercial Court could be hampered in the remaining 27 member states as the Brussels I Regulation will no longer command recognition and enforcement. *See* Regulation No. 1215/2012 of December 12, 2012, of the European Parliament and of the Council on jurisdiction and the recognition and enforcement of judgments in civil and commercial matters (recast), arts. 36, 39, 2012 O.J. (L 351) 1, 14 (EU) ("A judgment given in a Member State . . .").

forum selection clauses are generally. Their utility will only increase with future ratifications of the Hague Choice of Court Convention,[132] which entered into force on October 1, 2015.[133] The European Union (acting on behalf of all Member States except Denmark), Mexico, Montenegro, Singapore and the United Kingdom are all parties to the Convention. China, Ukraine and the United States have signed the Convention, but not yet ratified it. Subject to certain narrow exceptions, forum selection clauses will be honored without further question by Contracting States.[134] Perhaps most importantly, judgments by a chosen court must be recognized in all States where the Convention is applicable.[135] This ensures the mobility of judgments in a way similar to the mobility of awards under the New York Convention. Judgments of the new international commercial courts will be able to "travel" across borders more easily, much as international arbitral awards do.

Despite the Hague Convention's limited number of ratifications, its existence, coupled with the rise of international commercial courts, may be viewed as posing something of a threat to international commercial arbitration. Arbitral tribunals and international commercial courts will attract the same kinds of disputes. On the other hand, some have argued that "these two dispute resolution forums will most likely complement one another."[136] Proponents of international commercial courts advance that these constitute but one component of dispute resolution hubs at large.[137] International commercial courts have their own limitations. Issues of accessibility, jurisdictional limitations, applicable law, procedural features, as well as extrinsic factors such as general economic and political stability, might all weigh in parties' choice between international arbitration and international

[132] Convention on Choice of Court Agreements, June 30, 2005, 44 I.L.M. 1294.

[133] For the status with respect to each Contracting State, *see* Hague Conference on Private International Law, Status Table, *Conventions, Protocols and Principles, 37: Convention of 30 June 2005 on Choice of Court Agreements*, www.hcch.net/en/instruments/conventions/status-table/?cid=98.

[134] Convention on Choice of Court Agreements, June 30, 2005, 44 I.L.M. 1294. Art. 6(c).

[135] *Id.* Art. 8.

[136] Michael Hwang, "Commercial Courts and International Arbitration – Competitors or Partners?" (2015) 31 *Arb. Int'l* 193, 193; *see also* Godwin et al., *supra* note 129, 223.

[137] *See, e.g.*, the statement of Singaporean Justice Quentin Loh, *id.*, 200, extracted from Quentin Loh, Opening Address at the 2014 Regional Arbitral Institutes Forum (August 1, 2014), available at www.siarb.org.sg/images/Events/Newsletters/SIArb_Newsletter_Sep2014.pdf.

litigation in international commercial courts.[138] In addition, arbitration will retain a good number of its traditional advantages – confidentiality, neutrality, and potentially costs, among others. Arbitration has also benefited from the frequency with which institutional rules are amended to bring them fully up to date.

The fact remains that international commercial courts will compete with arbitration for the same kind of cases. That competition is likely to encourage international arbitration to make even greater efforts at user-friendliness than it is already making.

7.7 Achieving Diversity

The challenge of achieving and managing diversity in international commercial arbitration and in international dispute resolution overall has of late become an issue throughout the world.[139] There can be no question that international arbitration's preoccupation with diversity will continue well into the future.

While the idea of diversity extends potentially to age, race, nationality, region, disability and religion, among other factors,[140] the lack of gender parity in particular received the greatest attention in recent years. This is not surprising, as statistics show a striking lack of female representation in the pool of international arbitrators. Of all arbitrators at the ICC nominated or appointed by parties, co-arbitrators or the Court in 2017, 16.7 percent were women, while the increase from the year before amounted to only 1.9 percent.[141] At the LCIA, a self-described "leader in gender diversity,"[142] 24 percent of appointees in 2017 were female.[143] Typically, arbitral institutions appoint a significantly

[138] *See*, in more detail, Requejo Isidro, *supra* note 130, 29–32.

[139] *See, e.g.*, Rosabel E. Goodman-Everard, "Cultural Diversity in International Arbitration – a Challenge for Decision-Makers and Decision-Making" (1991) 7 *Arbitration International* 155; K. V. S. K. Nathan, "Well, Why Did You Not Get the Right Arbitrator?" (2000) 15 *Mealey's Int'l Arb. Rep.* 24.

[140] As pointed out by, *e.g.*, Adriana Braghetta, "Diversity and Regionalism in International Arbitration" (2015) 46 *Vic. U. Wellington L. Rev.* 1245, 1246.

[141] ICC, "2017 ICC Dispute Resolution Statistics" ICC Dispute Resolution Bulletin 2018 Issue 2, at 51 *bis*.

[142] LCIA, "LCIA releases 2017 Casework Report" (April 10, 2018), www.lcia.org/News/lcia-releases-2017-casework-report.aspx.

[143] LCIA, Facts and Figures – "2017 Casework Report" 15.

higher percentage of women than parties do, and a much higher percentage than co-arbitrators do, who, in ICC arbitrations in 2017, appointed women in as few as 13.7 percent of cases.[144] On the other hand, parties selected female arbitrators 17 percent of the time in LCIA arbitrations in 2017, which constituted a fourfold increase from the year before. Since 2017 further progress has clearly been made, but a very substantial gender gap remains.

Detailed studies of social scientists have revealed that the median international arbitrator is a 53-year-old male from a developed country who has been appointed in 10 arbitrations, while the median counsel is a 46-year-old male citizen of a developed State having served in 15 arbitrations.[145] An author has gone so far as to speak of an "Invisible College" of international arbitrators.[146]

The lack of female representation on arbitral tribunals is widely perceived as undesirable within the arbitration community, and so is the geographical imbalance in favor of Western Europe and North America.[147] Yet when it comes to finding possible causes and solutions, opinions differ.

Many have advanced the view that the lack of female representation is a corollary of the lack of female visibility among appointing authorities.[148] Limited visibility is often a consequence of an extensive information asymmetry as to the availability of underrepresented groups among decision-makers. At the same time, 92 percent of respondents in Bryan Cave Leighton Paisner's arbitration survey said that they would welcome more information about new and less well-known candidates.[149]

A number of concrete steps have been taken in recent years to accelerate progress. Upon the initiative of members of the international arbitration

[144] ICC, *supra* note 142.

[145] Susan D. Franck et al., "The Diversity Challenge: Exploring the Invisible College of International Arbitration" (2015) 53 *Colum. J. Transnat'l L.* 429, 430.

[146] *Id.*, 432 (with reference to "The Invisible College of International Lawyers" as devised by Oscar Schachter in 1977).

[147] Carol Mulcahy, "International Arbitration Survey: Diversity on Arbitral Tribunals – Are We Getting There?," 6. www.bclplaw.com/images/content/1/5/v1/150194/FINAL-Arbitration_Survey_Report.pdf (in a survey conducted by international law firm Berwin Leighton Paisner, 84 percent of respondents felt too many men were serving as arbitrators).

[148] *E.g.*, Lucy Greenwood, "Tipping the Balance – Diversity and Inclusion in International Arbitration" (2017) 33 *Arb. Int'l* 99, 105–106.

[149] Mulcahy, *supra* note 148, 6.

community, a highly successful pledge has been launched "in recognition of the under-representation of women" and with the "ultimate goal of full parity" in arbitrator appointments.[150] This political process has been advanced in numerous other arenas, and has led to declarations such as Resolution 105 of the ABA Dispute Resolution Section.[151] Second, arbitral institutions have made a concerted effort to start approaching parity in the appointment of women. Third, "arbitrator Intelligence," a global attempt to collect, analyze and publicize data on arbitrators, based on parties' voluntary submission of information,[152] stands to bring greater transparency to the appointment process and introduce new names into the mix. Such steps do not necessarily limit the parties' freedom to select their arbitrators, a prerogative that the parties would retain. They may also lead to fewer repeat appointments of a given arbitrator thereby reducing the number of challenges on that basis, while helping to prevent overcommitment by busy arbitrators.

Surely, attention has been drawn to asymmetries in arbitrator appointments. But greater efforts will be forthcoming in the future, not only in terms of gender balance, but also in terms of the other disparities that have been identified. Contributing to this development will also be an awareness that international arbitration must exploit every opportunity to enhance its legitimacy.

7.8 Transparency

Transparency or the lack thereof has been a long-standing preoccupation in the field of international commercial arbitration,[153] and like diversity, it is unlikely to abate. The apparent dichotomy between confidentiality and transparency implicates due process concerns, the

[150] Equal Representation in Arbitration, www.arbitrationpledge.com.

[151] ABA, Section of Dispute Resolution, "Report to the House of Delegates: Resolution 105," www.americanbar.org/content/dam/aba/images/abanews/2018-AM-Resolutions/105.pdf.

[152] Arbitrator Intelligence, www.arbitratorintelligence.org/.

[153] *See, e.g.*, Michael Collins, "Privacy and Confidentiality in Arbitration Proceedings" (1995) 11 *Arb. Int'l* 321; François Dessemontet, "Arbitration and Confidentiality" (1996) 7 *Am. Rev. Int'l Arb.* 229; Hans Bagner, "Confidentiality – A Fundamental Principle of International Commercial Arbitration?" (2001) 18 *Int'l Arb.* 243; Cindy G. Buys, "The Tensions Between Confidentiality and Transparency in International Arbitration" (2003) 14 *Am. Rev. Int'l Arb.* 121.

legitimate expectations and needs of parties, as well as possible public interests, thus again affecting the perceived legitimacy of arbitration on the whole. The subject achieved unprecedented salience with the advent of investor-State arbitration, with its powerful public interest and public policy dimension.[154]

7.8.1 Institutional Initiatives

Arbitral institutions are among the arenas in which transparency has made its greatest strides. Many institutions have adopted rules allowing for the publication of awards, although most require party consent to publication.[155] However, under the 2018 Vienna Rules, the presumption is somewhat different. The Board and Secretary-General reserve the right to publish anonymized summaries or extracts of awards as long as none of the parties objects within 30 days of issuance of the award.[156] Similarly, starting with awards issued after January 1, 2019, the ICC may also publish any award, except if a party objects or demands anonymization, or if a confidentiality provides otherwise.[157] If the parties consent, proceedings themselves can be fully public, including hearings and all decisions. This policy is announced not in the ICC's Rules, but in a Note on the Conduct of the Arbitration.[158] Needless to say, the parties can override whatever rules exist by way of a confidentiality agreement.[159]

In the future, transparency will probably go well beyond the publication of awards in one form or another. Overall, the ICC seems to have taken the

[154] The demands for a higher level of transparency in investment arbitration and the tremendous amount of criticism from all corners of society, especially in Europe, have mainly been due to the typically extensive involvement of public interests in such proceedings. *See, e.g.*, Nick Dearden, "Think TTIP Is a Threat to Democracy? There's Another Trade Deal That's Already Signed" *The Guardian* (May 30, 2016), www.theguardian.com/commentisfree/2016/may/30/ttip-trade-deal-agreements-ceta-eu-canada.

[155] *See, e.g.*, LCIA Rules. Art. 30 (requiring the parties' consent to be written); SIAC Rules, Art. 32(12) (requiring the tribunal's consent in addition to the parties').

[156] Vienna International Arbitral Centre Arbitration and Mediation Rules 2018, Art. 41. www.viac.eu/en/arbitration/content/vienna-rules-2018-online.

[157] ICC, "Note to Parties and Arbitral Tribunals on the Conduct of the Arbitration under the ICC Rules of Arbitration" (January 1, 2019), https://cdn.iccwbo.org/content/uploads/sites/3/2017/03/icc-note-to-parties-and-arbitral-tribunals-on-the-conduct-of-arbitration.pdf.

[158] ICC, *supra* note 142, paras. 40–46.

[159] *Id.* at paras. 43–44.

lead among institutions in respect to the promotion of transparency. The ICC has also taken steps to heighten organizational transparency. Since June 2016, the ICC has continuously published relevant information as to the composition of tribunals in arbitrations administered by the Court. The information published includes the identity of the arbitrators as well as their nationality, whether the parties or the Court appointed the arbitrator, and the capacity of each arbitrator on the tribunal (e.g., function as President, sole arbitrator or party-appointed arbitrator).[160]

Moreover, requests for the communication of reasons for certain decisions taken by the Court (e.g., appointment[161] and challenges or removal[162]) no longer need to be requested jointly by both parties. A request by any party suffices for the Court to do so under the 2017 Rules. However, a decision whether to comply with a party's request remains at the "full discretion" of the Court.[163] The institutions have also been careful over recent years to report a variety of data as to the demographics of appointed arbitrators overall.[164] These efforts toward greater transparency are linked to concerns over lack of diversity.[165]

[160] *See* Press Release, ICC, "ICC Begins Publishing Arbitrator Information in Drive for Improved Transparency" (June 27, 2016), https://iccwbo.org/media-wall/news-speeches/icc-begins-publishing-arbitrator-information-in-drive-for-improved-transparency/.

[161] Since June 2016, the ICC publishes, among other information, the names of appointed arbitrators and their nationality, as well as if the appointment was made by the court or by the parties, and whether each arbitrator is the president, a sole arbitrator or party-appointed arbitrator. ICC, "ICC Begins Publishing Arbitrator Information in Drive for Improved Transparency" (June 27, 2016) https://iccwbo.org/media-wall/news-speeches/icc-begins-publishing-arbitrator-information-in-drive-for-improved-transparency/ ("The decision to make information available was taken as a direct response to increasing demand for transparency in international arbitration.").

[162] ICC, "Note to Parties and Arbitral Tribunals on the Conduct of the Arbitration under the ICC Rules of Arbitration" (January 1, 2019), paras. 14–17, https://cdn.iccwbo.org/content/uploads/sites/3/2017/03/icc-note-to-parties-and-arbitral-tribunals-on-the-conduct-of-arbitration.pdf.

[163] *Id.* at paras. 14–17.

[164] *See, e.g.,* Arbitration Institute of the Stockholm Chamber of Commerce, "SCC Releases Statistics for 2018" (May 7, 2019), https://sccinstitute.com/about-the-scc/news/2019/scc-releases-statistics-for-2018/.

[165] *See, e.g.,* Susan D. Franck et al., "The Diversity Challenge: Exploring the Invisible College of International Arbitration" (2015) 53 *Colum. J. Transnat'l L.* 429.

7.8.2 Transparency versus Confidentiality

The counterpart of transparency is confidentiality, which Born defines as referring "to the obligation not to disclose information concerning the arbitration to third parties."[166] Absent an express agreement on confidentiality by the parties, arbitral proceedings or at least parts of them may have to be kept confidential on the basis of the rules of international arbitral institutions, national arbitration law, or implied terms in an agreement to arbitrate. Traditionally, confidentiality has been seen as one of the "most compelling" reasons for parties to choose to arbitrate.[167]

Arbitral institutions continue to handle confidentiality in a great variety of ways. The arbitral rules of the Singapore International Arbitration Centre, for instance, include a strong presumption of confidentiality. Parties, arbitrators, experts and virtually all other persons involved in the proceedings are required to "treat all matters relating to the proceedings and the [a]ward as confidential."[168] Disclosure is only permitted in an exclusively enumerated set of circumstances,[169] though parties may always consent to abandon confidentiality by agreement. Similarly, the rules of the Deutsche Institution für Schiedsgerichtsbarkeit (the German Arbitration Institution) permits overcoming the general presumption of confidentiality only to the extent required by law or for purposes of the recognition and enforcement or annulment of an award.[170] The rules of the LCIA as well as the Swiss Rules contain comparable confidentiality regimes,[171] whereas the latter allow the publication of anonymized awards not only by way of the parties' consent, but upon any request for publication addressed to the Secretariat as long as no party objects to the publication within a time limit set by the Secretariat.[172] The rules of the

[166] *See* Born, *supra* note 117. distinguishing between confidentiality and privacy.

[167] Kyriaki Noussia, *Confidentiality in International Commercial Arbitration – A Comparative Analysis of the Position under English, US, German and French Law* (Springer, 2010), 1.

[168] Singapore International Arbitration Centre Rules 2016, Art. 39(1), www.siac.org.sg/our-rules/rules/siac-rules-2016.

[169] *Id.* Art. 39(2).

[170] Deutsche Institution für Schiedsgerichtsbarkeit Arbitration Rules 2018, Art. 44(1–2), www.disarb.org/en/16/rules/-id38.

[171] London Court of International Arbitration Rules 2014, Art. 30, www.lcia.org/Dispute_Resolution_Services/lcia-arbitration-rules-2014.aspx; Swiss Chambers' Arbitration Institution Rules of International Arbitration 2017, Art. 44, www.swissarbitration.org/files/33/Swiss-Rules/SRIA_EN_2017.pdf.

[172] *Id.* Art. 44(3).

Arbitration Institute of the Stockholm Chamber of Commerce also stipulate a presumption of confidentiality.[173]

But there are exceptions. The Vienna Rules contain no presumption of confidentiality. They merely require that the arbitrators keep confidential "all information acquired in the course of their duties."[174] Interestingly, no provision addresses whether the parties are bound by an equivalent duty. Similarly, the rules of the International Centre for Dispute Resolution (ICDR) prohibit only arbitrators and the Administrator from disclosure of the parties' confidential information.[175] Still, unless the parties agree otherwise, an arbitral tribunal may make any orders it deems necessary to protect trade secrets and other confidential information.[176] The ICC Arbitration Rules contain a provision almost identical to the ICDR's allowing for protective orders. UNCITRAL Working Group II produced a set of UNCITRAL Transparency Rules applicable to investment treaties concluded on or after April 1, 2014 and was followed in turn by the Mauritius Convention which extended the treaty's scope of application to all such agreements regardless of the date of their entry into effect.[177]

7.8.3 Recent Criticisms of Confidentiality

The balance between transparency and confidentiality has shifted of late with transparency coming to be valued almost "as an end in itself" in today's arbitration world.[178] Critics have identified a series of drawbacks to confidentiality:

1. the unavailability of arbitral awards which hampers the development of a body of case law and eventual precedent on matters of arbitration and arbitral procedure;[179]

[173] Arbitration Institute of the Stockholm Chamber of Commerce Arbitration Rules 2017, Art. 3, https://sccinstitute.com/media/169838/arbitration_rules_eng_17_web.pdf.

[174] *Supra* note 157, Art. 16(2).

[175] International Centre for Dispute Resolution Arbitration Rules 2014, Art. 37(1), www.adr.org/sites/default/files/ICDR%20Rules_0.pdf.

[176] *Id.* Art. 37(2).

[177] United Nations Convention on Transparency in Treaty-based Investor-State Arbitration (Mauritius Convention), 54 I.L.M. 747 (2015).

[178] Blackaby and Partasides, *supra* note 105, 197.

[179] *See* Paul Comrie-Thomson, "A Statement of Arbitral Jurisprudence: The Case for a National Law Obligation to Publish International Commercial Arbitral Awards" (2017)

2. lack of access by the public even in cases in which the public has a legitimate interest;[180]
3. failure to provide incentives *to* arbitrators and counsel to act properly, and in compliance; and
4. with general moral and ethical/professional expectations good faith.[181]

The latter concern has gained, and will continue to gain, salience with the international arbitration community's increasing concern over corruption and its prevention.[182]

Transparency, along with a corresponding retreat from confidentiality, has become a salient characteristic of investor-State arbitration. There was always a greater impulse toward transparency in investor-State arbitration,"[183] but that tendency has accelerated, with many States undertaking to bring a measurably greater degree of transparency to this genre of arbitration.[184] It has been questioned – and perhaps rightly so – whether the stakes with respect to transparency really so much lesser in commercial arbitration than in investment arbitration.[185]

The future will necessarily bring further thought and initiatives to improve the balance between the values of confidentiality and transparency.

34 *Int'l Arb.* 275; Stefan Pislevik, "Precedent and development of law: Is it time for greater transparency in International Commercial Arbitration?" (2018) 34 *Arb. Int'l* 241; A. S. Sweet and F. Grisel, *The Evolution of International Arbitration: Judicialization, Governance, Legitimacy* (Oxford: Oxford University Press, 2017), 124–125.

180 M. Aden, "Die Nichtöffentlichkeit des Schiedsverfahrens – Verstoß gegen prozessuales Grundrecht?" (2012) 22 *Deutsche Zeitschrift für Wirtschafts- und Insolvenzrecht* 360, 362.

181 *Id.*, 201–202.

182 C. A. Rogers, "Generating Needed Information about Arbitrators, One Arbitration at a Time" Kluwer Arbitration Blog (September 15, 2018), http://arbitrationblog.kluwerarbitration.com/2018/09/15/generating-needed-information-about-arbitrators-one-arbitration-at-a-time/.

183 Born, *supra* note 117, §10.05.

184 *See, e.g.*, UNCITRAL Rules on Transparency in Treaty-based Investor-State Arbitration, G.A. Res. 68/109 (December 18, 2013), G.A.O.R. Supp. (No. 17), annex I (July 26, 2013); United Nations Convention on Transparency in Treaty-based Investor-State Arbitration, Mar. 17, 2015, 54 I.L.M. 747 (2015), U.N. Reg. No. I-54749.

185 Partasides and Maynard, *supra* note 105, 201 ("Already we have seen the outcry against investment arbitration that finds its loudest voice in complaints about a lack of transparency. It would be naïve to presume that such complaints are not affecting the world of commercial arbitration.").

7.9 The Rise of Settlement Agreements

At present, the frequency with which amicable settlements of disputes occur in arbitration is comparable to litigation in courts.[186] According to one estimate, between 20 and 30 percent of the overall arbitration caseload is settled,[187] while one study suggests that about 40 percent of all settlements occur between the initiation of arbitrations and the first hearing.[188] However, the future promises to bring an uptick in settlement and settlement agreements.

The advantages of settlement, especially settlements recorded in awards or settlement agreements, are obvious. To the extent settlement agreements take award form, the future of international commercial arbitration is enhanced. Most institutions are prepared to issue settlement agreements in the form of an award ("consent agreements"), in which case the agreement enjoys all the advantages of an arbitral award, which are considerable, particularly as concerns enforcement.[189] Under Article 30 of the UNCITRAL Model Law on International Commercial Arbitration,[190] parties may obtain a final award that is directly enforceable through the New York Convention,[191] in rendering a consent award, the arbitral tribunal incorporates the settlement reached by the parties

[186] *But see* Alison Ross, "Arbitration Settlements, and Tectonic Shifts, Occupy Other Speakers" *Global Arb. Rev.* (September 23, 2009), https://globalarbitrationreview.com/article/1028630/arbitration-settlements-and-tectonic-shifts-occupy-other-speakers (citing a statement by Tim Taylor, who suggested that parties are more likely to settle in litigation due to the greater influence parties have on the arbitral process and their corresponding greater willingness to engage in arbitrations).

[187] Eugen Salpius, "The Decision to Settle" (2003) 69 *Arb.* 155, 155–158.

[188] Loukas Mistelis and Crina Baltag, "Recognition and Enforcement of Arbitral Awards and Settlement in International Arbitration: Corporate Attitudes and Practices" (2008) 19 *Am. Rev. Int'l Arb.* 319, 334.

[189] *See* Consent award, D. H. Yarn (ed.) *Dictionary of Conflict Resolution* (Wiley, 2002) (distinguishing a consent award from an "agreed award," which "is surreptitious and purports to have been reached by the arbitrator").

[190] UNCITRAL Model Arbitration Law, G.A. Res. 40/72 (December 11, 1985), G.A.O.R. Supp. (No. 17) (June 21, 1985), as revised in 2006, G.A. Res. 61/33 (December 18, 2006), G.A.O.R. Supp. (No. 17) (July 7, 2006).

[191] Convention on the Recognition and Enforcement of Foreign Arbitral Awards, June 10, 1958, 330 U.N.T.S. 3.

into the award it renders. Many national arbitration laws provide for and recognize consent awards.[192]

A settlement agreement not issued in the form of an award presents certain disadvantages. While settlement agreements are clearly final and binding, and can be raised as a defense on the merits in a later proceeding, they do not carry *res iudicata* effect. Also, a party is unable to seek execution of its rights under a settlement agreement without more. Its rights under that agreement may need to be litigated anew. A suit for breach of a settlement agreement may entail difficult determinations of jurisdiction and applicable law. Settlement agreements are less problematic in those States in which they enjoy the status of an enforceable judgment, provided that the settlement has been publicly recorded or meets certain formal requirements. In Germany, for instance, a settlement between parties to an arbitration may be declared enforceable by a notary public usually at the seat of the arbitration.[193]

International arbitration may also benefit from the recent trend toward enforceability of settlement agreements resulting from conciliation and mediation It must be borne in mind that arbitration agreement commonly require, as a precondition to arbitration, that parties engage in conciliation or mediation. Making the agreements that result from these procedures directly enforceable redounds to the benefit of arbitration as well. Under its mandate to further the "progressive harmonization and unification of the law of international trade,"[194] UNCITRAL adopted the first Model Law on International Commercial Conciliation in 2002 ("Model Conciliation Law,"[195] Article 14 of which specifically provides that a settlement agreement arrived at through conciliation is binding and enforceable." However, Article 14 left it to the enacting State to determine the method of enforcement, inviting unlimited variation in approaches.[196] Whether inspired by

[192] This is not surprising against the backdrop that the Model Arbitration Law provides for consent awards in Art. 30. The Model Arbitration Law has been implemented at least partly in 80 states. *See* UNCITRAL, "Status, Model Law on International Commercial Arbitration" (1985), with amendments as adopted in 2006, www.uncitral.org/uncitral/en/uncitral_texts/arbitration/1985Model_arbitration_status.html.

[193] Zivilprozessordnung [ZPO] [Civil Procedure Code], December 5, 2005, BGBl. I at 3202, § 1052(4) (Ger.).

[194] G.A. Res. 2205 (XXI), at 99, 100 (para. 8) (December 17, 1966).

[195] UNCITRAL Model Conciliation Law, G.A. Res. 57/18, annex (January 24, 2003).

[196] For an overview as to the diversity of legislative approaches, *see* A/CN.9/WG.II/WP.110, paras. 106–111.

the Model Law or not, numerous States have enacted legislation facilitating the enforcement of settlement agreements. Some went so far as to put settlement agreements on an equal footing with arbitral awards in terms of their status and effect.[197] In 2014, the United States proposed to Working Group II that it develop a multilateral convention on the enforceability of international commercial settlement agreements reached through conciliation. This US initiative aimed at creating a treaty parallel to the New York Convention, which would ideally find equal acceptance thanks to a brief and simple structure.[198]

Shortly thereafter, UNCITRAL Working Group II commenced work on the enforceability of settlement agreements resulting from international commercial mediation,[199] hopefully resulting in a new Model Law.[200] Only three years later, the UN General Assembly endorsed amendments to the 2002 Model Conciliation Law in the form of an UNCITRAL Model Law on International Commercial Mediation and International Settlement Agreements Resulting From Mediation ("Model Mediation Law") as well as a United Nations Convention on International Settlement Agreements Resulting from Mediation, signed in Singapore ("Singapore Convention")[201] and open for signature starting on August 7, 2019.[202] It will enter into force six months after deposit of the ratification instruments by at least three Contracting States.[203]

The new Convention and the 2018 Model Law are designed to work in tandem to ensure the "stand-alone" enforceability of international settlement agreements resulting from mediation in commercial disputes, similar to the

[197] Pieter Sanders, "UNCITRAL's Model Law on International Commercial Conciliation" (2007) 23 *Arb. Int'l* 105, 137–139 (*see, e.g.*, Section 74 of India's Arbitration and Conciliation Act 1996: "The settlement agreement shall have the same status and effect as if it is an award on agreed terms on the substance of the dispute rendered by an arbitral tribunal").

[198] UNCITRAL, "Planned and possible future work – Part III: Proposal by the Government of the United States of America: future work for Working Group II, Note by the Secretariat" U.N. Doc. A/CN.9/822 (June 2, 2014).

[199] UNCITRAL, "Rep. of Working Group II (Arbitration and Conciliation) on the Work of Its Sixty-Second Session" paras. 13–59, U.N. Doc. A/CN.9/832 (February 11, 2015).

[200] UNCITRAL, Rep. of Working Group II (Arbitration and Conciliation) on the Work of Its Sixty-Third Session, para. 3, U.N. Doc. A/CN.9/861 (September 17, 2015).

[201] G.A. Res. 73/199 (December 20, 2018), G.A.O.R. Supp. (No. 17) (July 13, 2018); G.A. Res. 73/198 (December 20, 2018), G.A.O.R. Supp. (No. 17) (July 13, 2018); for the full text of the Model Mediation Law, *see* Rep. of the UNCITRAL on Its Fifty-First Session, annex II, U.N. Doc. A/73/17 (July 13, 2018); for the full text of the Singapore Convention, *see id.*, annex I.

[202] G.A. Res. 73/198, *supra* note 185, Art. 11(1).

[203] *Id.* Art. 14(1).

enforcement of arbitral awards under the New York Convention.[204] This is achieved in two ways: enforcement of the agreement may be had without the need to file a suit for breach of contract[205] and any qualifying agreement enjoys *res iudicata* effect, much as awards do.[206] In States that will implement both the Singapore Convention and the Model Law, parties to a mediation will thus be able to directly invoke international settlement agreements as either a "sword" or a "shield."[207] The defenses to the enforcement of agreements under the Singapore Convention closely track the defenses to enforcement of awards under the New York Convention).[208] As stated in the *travaux préparatoires*, these grounds are exhaustive.[209] In order to benefit from the Model Law or Convention, the settlement agreement must result from mediation, be in writing, and settle a commercial dispute that is international in character.[210] Satisfactions of these conditions should not ordinarily be difficult. It would come as no surprise if the Singapore Convention was to be adopted by a vast number of States, especially in light of almost universal acceptance of the New York Convention.[211]

[204] Note the similarity, or, rather, partial identity, between the New York Convention and the Singapore Convention in terms of wording and structure, especially as regards the main substantive provisions in Arts. 3–6.

[205] G.A. Res. 73/198, *supra* note 185, Arts. 3(1), 5.

[206] *Id.* Art. 3(2).

[207] Jan O'Neill, "The new Singapore Convention: will it be the New York Convention for mediation?" Dispute Resolution Blog (November 18, 2018), http://disputeresolutionblog.practicallaw.com/the-new-singapore-convention-will-it-be-the-new-york-convention-for-mediation/.

[208] G.A. Res. 73/198, *supra* note 185, Art. 5.

[209] UNCITRAL, "Settlement of commercial disputes – International commercial conciliation: preparation of an instrument on enforcement of international commercial settlement agreements resulting from conciliation, Note by the Secretariat," para. 93, U.N. Doc. A/CN.9/WG.II/WP.198 (September 23, 2016); UNCITRAL, Rep. of Working Group II (Arbitration and Conciliation) on the Work of Its Sixty-Third Session, *supra* note 201, para. 93.

[210] G.A. Res. 73/198, *supra* note 185, Art. 1(1).

[211] To date, 159 states have ratified the New York Convention. *See* U.N. Treaty Collection, Status of Treaties, Convention on the Recognition and Enforcement of Foreign Arbitral Awards, https://treaties.un.org/pages/ViewDetails.aspx?src=TREATY&mtdsg_no=XXII-1&chapter=22&clang=_en.

Part III

Investor-State Arbitration

8 Rise of a Discipline

Jan Paulsson

8.1 Introduction

The expression "international arbitration" encompasses everything from historic State-to-State border disputes to routine business transactions having an international dimension (such as contracts for the transportation of goods). International commercial arbitration frequently involves State-controlled entities, and indeed a lesser but still significant number of arbitrations have been brought by foreign investors having a direct contractual relationship with a State, such as the famous *Aramco* case[1] involving the effectiveness against Aramco of a 30-year preference granted to Aristotle Onassis by Saudi Arabia to transport oil produced in the Kingdom and *AMINOIL v. Kuwait*,[2] which dealt with the international lawfulness of the expropriation of an important oil concession.

Here, however, we are talking about a kind of investor-State arbitration which had not materialized as a possibility before April 14, 1988: cases involving claimants having no necessary contractual relationship with the respondent State and possibly even being unknown to the latter before they raised their complaint. For that day, with the appearance of a decision on jurisdiction in what is known as the *SPP v. Egypt* case,[3] was established

[1] Award of August 23, 1958, Arabian American Oil Company v. Kingdom of Saudi Arabia, 27 *International Law Reports* 117–229.

[2] American Independent oil Company v. Kuwait, March 24, 1982; 21 *International Legal Materials* 976.

[3] Southern Pacific Properties (Middle East) Limited v. Arab Republic of Egypt, ICSID Case No ARB/84/3, Decision on Jurisdiction (April 14, 1988) (Jiménez de Aréchaga, Pietrowski, Jr., El Mahdi) [hereinafter SPP v. Egypt]. The dispute lasted 14 years and gave rise to a number of arbitral decisions (by an ICC tribunal as well as the ICSID tribunal which is center stage in this account) and several national court judgments. The most convenient source of the principal documents is Vol. 3 of ICSID Reports (Cambridge University Press), where the April 14, 1988, ICSID Decision is reproduced at page 131. The commentary on this case is vast. As

the principle that a State could be held to an offer of arbitration extended to an indeterminate class of potential investors, any of whom might raise an international claim that the State had failed to live up to substantive promises. This opened the door to arbitrations founded on either investment treaties or investment laws that give foreign investors access to international arbitration, or what I long ago referred to, somewhat imprecisely, as "arbitration without privity."[4]

The first part of this contribution considers a matter of technique. How does this process function? The second part is far more important, namely, to consider the objectives of its inventors – who were after all States looking at ways to serve their national interests.

8.2 How It Works

Students of ICSID arbitration had already known that this outcome was a conceptual possibility. It had been expressly mentioned in paragraph 24 of the foundational Report of March 18, 1965, to the Executive Directors of the World Bank which accompanied the text of the ICSID Convention when it was first presented to them:

> Consent of the parties must exist when the Centre is seized ... but the Convention does not otherwise specify the time at which consent should be given. Consent may be given, for example, in a clause included in an investment agreement, providing for the submission to the Centre of future disputes arising out of that agreement, or ... a host State might in its investment promotion legislation offer to submit disputes arising out of certain classes of investments to the jurisdiction of the Centre, and the investor might give his consent by accepting the offer in writing.

That may have been the intention, but would it work? Would international tribunals accept it? It merits mention that *SPP v. Egypt* was decided by a

it happened, I represented SPP in this case; by the mid-1980s, I was also acting for the respondent States in Klöckner Industrie-Anlagen BmbH et al. v. United Republic of Cameroon and Société Camerounaise des Engrais, ICSID Case No. ARB/81/2 (Jiménez de Aréchega, Schmidt, Rogers) and Atlantic Triton Company Limited v. People's Revolutionary Republic of Guinea, ICSID Case No. ARB/84/1 (Sanders, Prat, van den Berg). In 2012, I was invited to give an informal personal account of SPP v. Egypt as the 2012 Berthold Goldman Lecture on Historic Arbitration Stories at the Paris International Academy for Arbitration Law, available at www.arbitrationacademy.org/wp-content/uploads/2014/01/Arbitration-Academy-Jan-Paulsson.pdf.

4 Jan Paulsson, *Arbitration without Privity*, 10 ICSID Rev. F.I.L.J. 232 (1995).

Tribunal that was presided by Judge Eduardo Jiménez de Aréchaga of Uruguay, who, after serving for nine years on the United Nation's International Law Commission, had been elected to a seat on the International Court of Justice, and for the last three years of his tenure there served as its President (1976–1979). It may thus be said that in the end the principle of this path to arbitral jurisdiction was upheld under the authority of someone who had not only reached a pinnacle of achievement in the field of public international law, but was also a scholar and former government minister of a country (Uruguay) in a region known for its historical distrust of arbitrations imposed by European and North American powers.

This was a vote of confidence in the mechanism created by the ICSID Convention as a manifestation of the rule of law, intended to depoliticize investor-State disputes in a context of equality of arms. It opened the doors to a new age for ICSID. Given his stature, one may well suppose that if Jiménez de Aréchaga had reached the opposite conclusion, the idea of arbitration without privity would have been still-born, and ICSID would today have remained a tiny institution with only 86 registered cases in its half-century of existence (namely, those based on contractual arbitration clauses alone) rather than 507 (which includes 56 cases in which the claimant relied on a mixture of jurisdictional bases) – more than five times as many. (The latest statistics available from reveal that 16 percent of ICSID arbitrations were based on contractual arbitration clauses.[5])

Shortly after coming to power, President Sadat of Egypt reversed the pro-Soviet tilt of the Nasser years and announced a new open-door policy in relation to foreign investment. It took the legislative form of Law No. 43 of 1974 Concerning the Investment of Arab and Foreign Funds and the Free Zones.

The two crucial features of Law No. 43 for present purposes were Article 7, which prohibited the "confiscation"[6] of covered investment projects, and Article 8:

Investment disputes in respect of the implementation of the provisions of this Law shall be settled in a manner to be agreed upon by the investor, or within the

[5] *The ICSID Caseload – Statistics* (2019–1).

[6] Understood by the ICSID Tribunal as "expropriation . . . if not accompanied by fair compensation." *See* Southern Pacific Properties (Middle East) Limited v. Arab Republic of Egypt, ICSID Case No. ARB/84/3, Decision on Jurisdiction (November 27, 1985) 3 ICSID Rep. 125, 69 (1995).

framework [of BITs] or within the framework of [the ICSID Convention] to which Egypt has adhered . . ., where such Convention applies.

The first foreign investment project to be approved under Law No. 43 was proposed by Southern Pacific Properties, a hotel company led by two prominent Canadian businessmen, Peter Munk and David Gilmour, and incorporated in Hong Kong. Munk and Gilmour negotiated directly with Sadat and a number of Ministers of the Egyptian Government, notably the Minister of Housing and Reconstruction and the Minister of Tourism. It was agreed that the project, contemplating two large destination resorts, one in the region of the Giza Pyramids and the other on a site on the Mediterranean coast, would take the form of a joint venture between SPP and the Egyptian General Organization for Tourism and Hotels (EGOTH), a public sector entity under the Ministry of Tourism.

In September 1974, tripartite "Heads of Agreement" were signed by SPP, the Minister of Tourism, and EGOTH. The document was expressly entered into in accordance with Law No. 43. In December of the same year, a more detailed Agreement was signed by SPP and EGOTH. It too was expressly concluded in accordance with Law No. 43. It contained an arbitration clause by which the parties agreed to ICC arbitration in Paris. On its last page, these words appeared, below the signatures of the representatives of SPP and EGOTH: "Approved, agreed and ratified by the Minister of Tourism," followed by the signature of the Minister and an official stamp. In April 1975, the venture was approved by the Board of the Investment Authority which had supervisory power under Law No. 43.

Construction works began in July 1977. By the end of that year, political opposition emerged. In early 1978, a parliamentary inquiry began and heated debate in the media gained momentum. Opponents of the project claimed that it was a threat to undiscovered antiquities. Supporters viewed this as a pretext devised by local business interests, whose numerous illegal installations near the Pyramids were not part of the plan. In late April, Sadat expressed public support for the project. But one month later, in May 1977, after an unfavorable Parliamentary Report, the government reversed tracks and took a series of measures which made pursuit of the venture impossible. It notably declared the allocated land in Giza to be public property; the Investment Authority withdrew its approval; and EGOTH instructed the venture to cease construction activities and began a court action to sequester its assets and declare judicial receivership.

SPP asked the government for compensation for its losses, but to no avail. It thereafter initiated an ICC arbitration in Paris, against both the government and EGOTH.[7] That process lasted nearly five years. It included extensive hearings and a site visit in Egypt. In the end, the three-member tribunal presided by the Italian Professor Giorgio Bernini rendered its award in March 1983. On the basis of their contextual reading of the relevant documents and in the light of their assessment of testimonial evidence, the arbitrators upheld arbitral jurisdiction over the government, declared that it had breached its undertakings, and ordered it to pay compensation in the amount of US$12.5 million. On the other hand, they dismissed the claim against EGOTH, finding in paragraph 61 that "the events of May/June 1978 were beyond EGOTH's reasonable powers to control," and that EGOTH had agreed only to deploy "its best efforts to obtain the necessary action from the Government."

Egypt sought annulment of the award. On July 12, 1984, the Paris Court of Appeals overturned the award for lack of arbitral jurisdiction, holding that the Ministerial endorsement of the December 1974 agreement ("[a]greed, approved and ratified") was not sufficient to bind the government to the ICC arbitration clause contained therein. Concluding that all enforcement actions of the ICC award were doomed by its annulment in France – although, not wishing to forego any chances, it was also pursuing an ultimate appeal to the Court of Cassation there – SPP reverted to the text of Law No. 43 and the possibility of ICSID arbitration mentioned in Article 8. On August 15, 1984, SPP notified the Minister of Tourism that it added its own consent to ICSID arbitration to that expressed by Egypt in Law No. 43. On August 24, it filed its claim with ICSID. In due course, the tribunal was constituted.[8]

There were two separate decisions on jurisdiction. The first, handed down on November 27, 1985, dealt with three of Egypt's four jurisdictional objections which are not of present interest.[9]

[7] Herein "SPP" will for the sake of simplicity be referred to in the singular, and as "the Claimant" although it appeared as one of two joint claimants with its affiliate, Southern Pacific Properties (Middle East) Ltd.

[8] Robert F. Pietrowski, a US national, was SPP's nominee, and Mohamed Amin El Mahdi, an Egyptian national, was Egypt's. SPP waived the objection it could have raised on the grounds of the latter's ineligibility under the ICSID Rules, as a holder of the nationality of one of the Parties.

[9] These (and other details) are accounted for in Jan Paulsson, "The Tipping Point," in Meg Kinnear et al., eds., *Building International Investment Law: The First 50 Years of ICSID* 85 (2016).

Egypt's fourth objection – the all-important one – was to the effect that Article 8 did not constitute self-executing consent to ICSID arbitration, and therefore required "a separate implementing agreement" between Egypt and the foreign investor. The Tribunal, observing that the French Court of Cassation was already seized of the question whether the parties had agreed to "another method of dispute resolution" (namely, ICC arbitration) under the first of the alternatives envisaged by Article 8 of the Law, and that that question necessarily required resolution before considering the specific objection to ICSID jurisdiction, concluded in paragraph 87 of the 1985 decision that it had "inherent powers to stay proceedings when justice so requires," and accordingly held its decision in abeyance until a final resolution by the French courts as to whether the parties had agreed to ICC jurisdiction.

More than two years passed while all concerned awaited the French decision. It was finally handed down on January 6, 1987, affirming the judgment of the Paris Court of Appeal that had annulled the ICC award. The ICSID Tribunal then ordered further written submissions, and heard the parties' oral submissions in September 1987. Thereafter, as stated, the final jurisdictional hurdle was cleared by the Decision of April 14, 1988, which is what most lawyers remember about *SPP v. Egypt*. The reasoning and implications of that decision will be discussed in the next section.

Now the case went on to the merits. They were compendiously briefed. Witnesses were heard, and the parties presented oral arguments. The final Award was rendered in May 1992. Although of lesser import than the essential jurisdictional decision, it was also instructive in the following significant respects. The claim was recognized as one arising from the expropriation of intangible interests in a venture. That venture was a creature of contract between SPP and EGOTH, the Egyptian State entity. The expropriation claim was directed against the State and no one else. The Tribunal held that Egypt's cancellation of the project had the effect of destroying "important rights and interests of the Claimants ... rights and interests of a contractual nature ... the taking of such rights involves an obligation to make compensation therefor" (paragraph 164). This led to an award of some US$27.6 million, much of which unsurprisingly consisted of interest during the 14 years SPP had awaited its entitlement to compensation, as well as some US$5 million on account of costs.

In May 1992 Egypt filed an application with ICSID for the annulment of the Award. The parties subsequently reached a settlement and the proceedings were closed in December of that year, thus ending the *SPP v. Egypt* saga.

The jurisdictional decision rendered in 1988 comprises 257 paragraphs. It was pored over by international lawyers at the time. Today, students of investment arbitration who have read subsequent jurisdictional decisions that deal with further refinements, such as MFN and umbrella clauses, may wonder why all this ink was spent on a question as elementary as the effectiveness of consent expressed in an investment law or an investment treaty. We need to remember that before propositions become commonplace, there is a time when they are unheard of, and therefore emerge as revelatory.

ICSID's published four-volume drafting history of the Convention, edited in three languages, reproduces the evolving drafts and records the interventions of delegates at the meetings that led to the final text of the ICSID Convention (including "Consultative Meetings" with national legal experts in Addis Ababa, Santiago de Chile, Geneva, and Bangkok; as well as the deliberations of a special Legal Committee in Washington).[10] When individual delegates and experts expressed surprise that ICSID jurisdiction could be found in the absence of a joint contractual agreement the response was always clear: the new Convention was designed to have a broader potential reach, at the election of the relevant State (in the case of a law) or States (in that of a treaty).

Opponents of ICSID have on occasion misused these materials to try to demonstrate that there was something improper about the way this matter was handled; they invariably cherry-pick the expressions of hesitation, but ignore the explicit and repeated resolution in favor of the broader possibilities of jurisdictional foundations. (Whether, as a political matter, they would prove to be "bridges too far" and therefore not attractive to States is another matter; there may have been delegates who thought unilateral stipulations in laws and treaties were unlikely to be made, but none of them could have been left in doubt that the Convention provided for that *possibility*.) The important Report to the Executive Directors was crystal clear. Ultimately, of course, nothing proves the point better than the profusion of investment treaties by which the signatory States hold out

[10] *The History of the ICSID Convention: Documents concerning the origin and the formulation of the Convention on the Settlement of Investment Disputes between States and nationals of other States*, vols. I–IV (ICSID, 1970).

the promise of ICSID arbitration in the event of claims of mistreatment of investors or investments.

What remained to be seen was how such stipulations would be received by an international tribunal. What Egypt said, in essence, was that Article 8 did no more than to confirm the availability of ICSID arbitration, but that a specific "implementing" agreement was required nonetheless. To evaluate the argument requires an analysis of the document in question; such an exercise naturally depends on the particular text and is therefore case-specific. For example, 25 years later, attempts to invoke the convoluted Article 22 of the Venezuelan Investment Law of 1999 in the same way have proved unsuccessful, while the more straightforward Article 8(2) of the Albanian Investment Law of 1993 has been held to constitute a sufficiently clear manifestation of consent to ICSID arbitration. There is no inconsistency. The big issue was whether unilaterally expressed consent in national investment laws, or consent expressed in treaties without the reciprocal consent of the potential claimants, should for some reason in principle be deemed an insufficient basis of international jurisdiction.

The answer that emerged is that each of them is sufficient. That was the message of *SPP v. Egypt*, followed ever since – starting with the 1990 award in *A.A.P.L. v. Sri Lanka*,[11] which arose under the United Kingdom–Sri Lanka bilateral investment treaty, where it seems no objection was even raised, and continuing, more interestingly, with *AMT v. Zaire* (1997),[12] which arose under the United States–Zaire BIT, where the issue was debated extensively, and rejected by a tribunal comprising well-known international lawyers from Germany, Senegal, and (in the case of the presiding arbitrator) Thailand.

There seems to be no reason why the broad answer with respect to a law should be any different than with a treaty. Indeed, it may justly be said in regard to a treaty that there is at least a reciprocity of obligations, in that each State signatory to the treaty promises the other that its nationals will have access to arbitration in accordance with the treaty's terms. (Although the *quid pro quo* for the promise of arbitration in a law is surely significant as well: that investments are made, as intended, in reliance on that

[11] Asian Agricultural Products Limited v. Democratic Socialist Republic of Sri Lanka, ICSID Case No. ARB 87/3, Award (June 27, 1990) (El-Kosheri, Goldman, Asante).

[12] American Manufacturing & Trading v. Democratic Republic of the Congo (Zaire), ICSID Case No. ARB/93/1, Award (February 21, 1997) (Sucharitkul, Golsong, Mbaye).

undertaking.) In other words, the arguably stronger start – *SPP v. Egypt* – was with a law; treaties were bound to follow.

In this light, the extensive debates about the words and the syntax of Article 8 of Law No. 43, as well as the consistency and hierarchy of elements of the text enacted by the Egyptian Parliament, as opposed to the English translation provided in an official governmental publication intended for investors, is of little current interest save to note the meticulous care given to that exercise by Jiménez de Aréchaga and his colleagues. A number of elements of the decision, in addition to the essential affirmation of jurisdiction, nevertheless remain of general interest. The following six merit mention:

1. With respect to applicable law, the Tribunal rejected Egypt's argument that the meaning of Article 8 should be ascertained as a matter of Egyptian law. While Law No. 43 was an Egyptian law, that fact did not mean that other Egyptian laws with respect to consent to arbitration would apply. The issue was whether the expressions used in Article 8 created consent for the purposes of the ICSID Convention – an international treaty. At the same time, the Tribunal did not accept SPP's argument that the relevant rules pertained exclusively to treaty interpretation. Law No 43 was of course not a treaty, "but rather the result of a unilateral act by a single State" (paragraph 59). The Decision went on to point out that the PCIJ and the ICJ have established that "a sovereign State's interpretation of its own unilateral consent to the jurisdiction of an international tribunal is not binding on the tribunal or determinative of jurisdictional issues" (paragraph 60). In conclusion, "the Tribunal will apply general principles of statutory interpretation taking into consideration, where appropriate, relevant rules of treaty interpretation and principles of international law applicable to unilateral declarations" (paragraph 61).
2. The following self-explanatory sentence (from paragraph 63) has often been quoted over the years and now forms part of what may safely be considered a bedrock of a *jurisprudence constante*: "Thus, jurisdictional instruments are to be interpreted neither restrictively nor expansively, but rather objectively and in good faith, and jurisdiction will be found to exist if – but only if – the force of the arguments militating in favor of it is preponderant."
3. Rejecting Egypt's argument to the effect that the phrases "within the framework for the Convention" and "where it applies" in Article 8 meant

that a separate agreement must be executed by the parties, the Tribunal expressed its version of the fundamental interpretive principle of *effet utile* (or, to recall its earlier origins, *ut res magis valeat quam pereat*) as follows (in paragraph 94):

> No valid method of legal interpretation would warrant the conclusion that the express reference to the Convention in Article 8 is meaningless or pleonastic. Under general principles of statutory interpretation, a legal text should be interpreted in such a way that a reason and a meaning can be attributed to every word in the text.

4. Egypt noted that its BIT with Sweden envisaged ICSID arbitration provided that there be agreement *by both parties to the dispute* and argued on that basis that "just as Article 8 of Law No. 43 could not override the requirement of agreement by both parties in that treaty, it could not displace the Convention's requirement of consent in writing." This was, it seems, a counterproductive argument, serving as it did – against Egypt's interest – to highlight the absence in Law No. 43 of the qualification found in the Swedish BIT. As the Tribunal said, in paragraphs 97 and 98:

> The question, however, is not whether Article 8 can displace the requirement for a "consent in writing," but whether Article 8 is itself a legally sufficient manifestation of such consent. . . . The fact that Article 8 of Law No. 43 is not the kind of manifestation of consent envisioned by the framework of the Swedish treaty does not mean that it is not consent in writing within the framework of the Convention.

5. Although their nature is intended to be informative rather than normative (paragraph 112), "official investment promotion literature may confirm" certain interpretations (e.g., that under Law No. 43 a separate agreement was not necessary to establish ICSID jurisdiction).
6. Finally, in construing the meaning of Law No. 43, the Tribunal made substantial efforts to make up for the fact that its only native Arabic-speaking member dissented. Expert linguistic testimony was considered, and the arbitrators' engagement is evident in the reproduction of words in Arabic script reflecting verb tenses and modes said to be more or less mandatory. Substantial assistance was provided by a comparison of treaties signed by Egypt in which two languages were acknowledged as equally authentic, thereby giving significant credence

to consistent translations of recurrent Arabic words. In the end, the Tribunal's conclusion (paragraph 82) was the following:

> In view of the expert opinions concerning the Arabic text submitted on behalf of the Claimants, and of the translations into procedural languages that have been submitted by both Parties, the Tribunal is satisfied that the Arabic text of the first paragraph of Article 8 mandates the submission of disputes to the various methods prescribed therein where such methods are applicable.

8.3 Objectives

What were the aims of those who conceived and promoted this form of investor-State arbitration? It cannot be said that their purpose was to advance the interests of international corporations for the simple reason that every negotiator of a BIT (on both sides) was a civil servant of the executive branch of government, and every drafter of an investment law was a legislator charged with promoting the national interests of the host country. Nor is it credible to suggest that these officials were suborned or otherwise influenced by the nefarious interests of foreign commercial interests, foisting concessions in their interest by State representatives who did not understand the import of the instruments they were signing. There is no evidence to that effect. (BITs had been around for two decades before it finally occurred to foreign investors that they might actually be invoked – why were the hypothetical instigators so passive once they had succeeded?) More compellingly, to carry off such a feat – even if conceivable in the case of an isolated text – would be a superhuman challenge given the great similarities of the protections established for foreign investment in thousands of BITs.[13]

For that matter, the Egyptian investment law that featured in *SPP v. Egypt* was promulgated by the Egyptian Parliament, and that Law too contains typical elements of the familiar list of protections: no expropriation except for a public purpose and with compensation; no

[13] BITs between non-Western countries were no exception, as illustrated by the arbitration between an Omani investor and Yemen in the Desert Line case in 2008; ICSID Case No ARB/05/17.

discriminatory treatment; adherence to international law; and access to neutral international arbitration.

It thus seems clear that broad swathes of officials in capital-importing States considered that it was proper to extend these types of protection.

Still, suggesting that the signatories were not dupes does not provide an answer to the question of their objectives. A great number of States were not concerned about attracting investors themselves. (To take an extreme case, Switzerland has no difficulty attracting capital. Even if the return on capital is vanishingly small, the faith in its institutions and their respect for settled law means that many foreigners are happy to place their money against the modest expectation that they will get their money back.) Countries in this category therefore must have been motivated by the objective of protecting their own investors as they venture forth on the world markets. This does not seem dishonorable; they were making it easier for their own nationals to feel comfortable investing abroad, and so in effect supported the host country's quest for needed investment. This point therefore, in the end, turns our focus squarely on the objectives of predominantly *host* countries when enacting foreign investment laws and concluding investment protection treaties.

From their perspective, awakening to the consequences of such laws or treaties may be rude. No State enjoys being on the receiving end of claims that it has violated legal obligations. States are even more irritated when they are required to defend themselves before an international court or tribunal, perceiving it as an affront to their sovereignty.

Let us explore three broad and interrelated questions.[14] First, is a voluntary restriction on sovereignty – on which a foreign party is invited to rely – a violation of sovereignty? Secondly, if restrictions on sovereignty are a matter of sovereign choice, what are the reasons for accepting such limitations? Thirdly, what are good State practices in circumstances when a State has made a commitment of this nature?

[14] This section adapted from "El poder de los Estados para hacer promesas significativas a los extranjeros" (Spring 2009) 6 (21) Revista de Economia y Derecho 79, itself developed from the author's inaugural lecture as honorary professor of the Faculty of Law of the Universidad Peruana de Ciencias Aplicadas on August 29, 2008, and from his contribution to the United Nations Lecture Series on International Law. The author has acted as advocate with roughly equal frequency on behalf of states and investors in disputes under investment treaties.

The word *sovereignty* does not mean "I do what I want." It certainly does not mean "all powerful." Children dream of omnipotence, and long for the day when they no longer have to seek their parents' permission for anything. But adults confront the daily reality of a thousand reasons why they cannot do whatever they want.

A more interesting question is whether sovereignty at least means that no one else can tell us what to do. If all men are equal, then in this sense every person would be sovereign. No one could tell anyone else how to behave. But the fact is that individual human beings *do not really want to be sovereign in this extreme sense*. We are willing to give up some of our freedom, indeed we insist on the opportunity of making a bargain:

- we accept that criminal laws apply to us so that we can be protected by those same laws;
- we accept that we have to pay for our reckless behavior so that we can live in greater tranquility because that rule has the consequence that our fellow citizens will tend to behave less recklessly;
- and we accept that we are held to a bad bargain because if our contracts are not binding we will be stuck in the poverty of a primitive economic system where every transaction is instant – cash and carry – and we are thus left incapable of creating wealth by shared enterprise, by investment in reliance upon long-term commitments, or by the use of capital from willing lenders.

States have similar motives for accepting legal limitations on their future conduct. And just as individuals must accept that it would be calamitous if every individual had the "sovereign" right to decide whether he is guilty of criminal conduct, recklessness or breach of contract, so, too, a State must accept that it cannot be the judge of a controversy as to whether it has transgressed legal limits. No one, even a State, can be a judge in his own cause.

These concepts are simple, but they demand mature reflection. Dictatorships are prone to abuse law, and seek to disguise this abuse by pretentions of sovereignty. This needs to be exposed for what it is. But let us first recall some basic principles, illustrated by a famous example.

On March 21, 1921, a British steamship named the *SS Wimbledon*, operating under charter by a French transporter, was informed by the German authorities that it would not be allowed transit through the Kiel Canal which runs through northern Germany, connecting the Atlantic and the Baltic.

The French government espoused the claim of its national, stating that Germany had violated international law and should be ordered to pay reparations. The ship was carrying munitions loaded in Greece and destined for the Polish naval base at Danzig. As a result of the German refusal of transit, the *Wimbledon* was immobilized for 11 days and then had to seek longer passage north of Denmark. Germany contended that it was in the right, pursuant to its own national Neutrality Orders – concerning Germany's neutrality in the Russo–Polish war – which prohibited the transit of such cargo. France, joined by Britain, Italy and Japan, brought suit before the Permanent Court of International Justice (PCIJ – the predecessor of today's International Court of Justice), asserting that the German refusal breached the Treaty of Versailles, under which the Kiel Canal was to "be maintained free and open to the vessels of commerce and war of all nations at peace with Germany on terms of entire equality." Germany was entitled under the Treaty to impose charges and regulations, but only as long as they did "not unnecessarily impede traffic."

The PCIJ recognized that Germany had "sovereign rights which no one disputes that she possesses over the Kiel Canal." But those rights were subject to a limitation, established as a material condition of the Versailles Treaty. Germany insisted that its right as a neutral power to decide whether munitions destined for a country at war were "an essential part of its sovereignty" which could not be waived by agreement. The PCIJ disagreed, and ordered Germany to pay compensation to France on account of its national, the transport company.

The most famous passage from the Court's judgment, rendered in 1923, reads as follows:

> The court declines to see in the conclusion of any Treaty, by which a State undertakes to perform, or refrain from performing, a particular act, an abandonment of its sovereignty. No doubt any convention creating an obligation of this kind places a restriction upon the exercise of the sovereign rights of the State, in the sense that it requires them to be exercised in a certain way. But the right of entering into international engagements is an attribute of State sovereignty.

This last sentence is portentous. The ability to make a binding commitment is part of what makes a State a State. It is the source of the power to make a meaningful promise. If States did not have that power, they would be handicapped. The act of limiting possible conduct tomorrow is an exercise of authority today. And if that act is to be internationally meaningful, it must first create binding obligations – and secondly be evaluated by an impartial court or tribunal. It is really no different than what we see in relations among ordinary individuals – someone whose promises mean nothing will have great difficulties in life. He will have to work alone, and he will always have to pay cash.

Moving to our second theme: given that the capacity to agree to binding limitations on sovereignty is an *attribute* of that same sovereignty, why should any State adopt that course?

There are many possible reasons. Some reflect a wish to exercise leadership. A State is unlikely to project international influence, and to convince other States to cooperate in certain ways, unless it shows that it abides by its own commitments. The impulse to make international commitments may also be an expression of popular will, as political candidates identify a public desire for the expansion of certain values (such as human rights or environmental protection), are elected on such a platform, and once in office are prepared to join leaders of other countries to pursue a common goal to secure those values.

But perhaps it is easiest for the purposes of analysis to focus on a type of limitation on future government conduct which is accepted predominantly *as a matter of self-interest* – through the mechanism of treaties for the promotion and protection of foreign investment. Thousands of BITs, although not identical in every detail, almost invariably contain four commitments. First, each State promises that it will not expropriate the investments made by national of the other State, or take steps equivalent thereto, without requisite compensation. Second, each State promises that it will not discriminate against the nationals of the other State. Third, each State promises that it will treat investors from the other State in accordance with international law, and therefore notably in accordance with the concept of fair and equitable treatment. Finally, these three broad substantive commitments are given force by a fourth promise, which is that each State accepts that any claim of breach of the substantive promises may be brought by the complaining investor to international arbitration.

There have over the past three decades been hundreds of arbitrations under these BITs. In all of those arbitrations, a State has been the defendant. Sometimes the State has prevailed, sometimes it has lost and sometimes the result was not wholly favorable to either side.

Some of these cases have been politically controversial. It has been pointed out that the arbitrators are private persons, and the question has been asked whether their decisions violate sovereignty. We have already seen that this is a bad question. It is not a violation of sovereignty for a State to be held to its own commitments. The good question is rather whether it is in a State's interest to give the promises contained in these BITs in the first place. Some wonder if it is not against a State's interest to agree to BITs. So let us examine possible objections. Are BITs inherently unfair? Some critics suggest that BITs were the handiwork of powerful investors, who convinced their home States to put pressure on capital-importing States to sign them, or – rather insultingly to the negotiators – that they were signed in ignorance of their consequences.

This is hardly a valid objection. It is easy to test it, by examining the contents of the many BITs which have been entered into by developing States *among themselves*. We might call them "South-South BITs." These are obviously not the handicraft of capital-exporters. And yet as seen they contains the same four broad promises that are prevalent in other BITs.

Is it possible that arbitrators who decide BIT cases render unfair decisions? Many losing parties will say so, and in some instances their complaint may even be seen as well founded in the eyes of impartial observers. Justice is not perfect in every case. Still, advocates who represent States as often as they represent investors are unlikely to say that there is a general bias against respondent States. There are certainly numerous examples of successful defenses against investor claims – and examples of furious protests by investors who considered the rejection of their claims to be miscarriages of justice.[15] Better, from the States' point of view,

[15] When an affiliate of the US corporation Thunderbird Resorts lost its claim under NAFTA against Mexico following closure of its gaming facilities there (and was moreover ordered to pay Mexico US$1,250,000 in legal costs), International Thunderbird Gaming Corporation v. The United Mexican States, January 26, 2006, its Board of Directors issued a press release in which the General Counsel was quoted as saying that "the Company believed that NAFTA would level the playing field in Mexico. . . . Clearly it did not as this same government . . . has given permits for hundreds of new locations." The President and CEO, for his part, was quoted as speculating, "It is not coincidental that the 'permits' were issued to the most powerful interests in the country while [the relevant Minister] was seeking to become the next President of Mexico." Press release dated January 27, 2006, published the same day on the OGEMID mailing list www.transnational-dispute-management.com/ogermid, or ogemid@jiscmail.ac.uk. Subsequently, Thunderbird sought to have the award set aside by the US Federal courts and was not only rebuffed; Mexico's cross-motion for enforcement of the cost award in its favour was upheld – with yet further costs assessed against Thunderbird (an occurrence that merits mention given that US courts do not generally award costs); International Thunderbird Gaming Corp v. United Mexican States, USDC for the District of Columbia, Civil Action No 06-00748; various orders reproduced at italaw.com.

unsuccessful investors have on occasion been ordered to pay significant costs. (A number of States, such as Hungary, Ukraine, Mexico, Pakistan and Turkey, have been beneficiaries of such orders.)

Investment tribunals have, moreover, shown that corruption and other illegality is not tolerated. Kenya, El Salvador and the Philippines have obtained the dismissal of claims without even considering whether they may have been well founded in principle due to the fact that the original investment involved bribery, misrepresentations or other breaches of national law.

And where the investor has prevailed, international tribunals have often reduced lost-profit claims by considerable margins, leaving many investors with the feeling that their recovery was undeservedly reduced.

It is understandable that in notorious cases the public perception tends to be simplistic: any international tribunal is good if we win, bad if we lose. But we are not discussing sporting competitions like the World Cup. Resolving disputes properly is essential to the successful management of relations with investors. A State may be happy to win, but what counts for its long-term reputation is that it confronts the inevitable occasions of disagreements in a loyal, businesslike and efficient way – and that it respects the outcome of international legal proceedings. Mexico has been a good example. When it became a party to the North American Free Trade Agreement (NAFTA), Mexico opened the door to international claims against it by US and Canadian investors. There have been a number of such claims. Mexico has won some of them, and lost others. What the international community has observed is (1) that Mexico defended itself competently, (2) that its losses have been moderate, and (3) that it has paid the amounts ordered. Its reputation has been enhanced. And compared to the vast benefits of NAFTA, in the magnitude of billions,[16] former Mexican observers have pointed out that incidental payments to wrongfully treated investors, in the magnitude of millions, is a small price to pay.[17]

[16] For instance, NAFTA trade in goods in 2009 totaled US$735 billion and regional trade in services during 2008 was US$69.8 billion www.ustr.gov/trade-agreements/free-trade-agreements/north-american-free-trade-agreement-nafta.

[17] Guillermo Aguilar-Alvarez, NAFTA @ 15: *Lessons Learned, Moving Forward*, lecture delivered at the University of Miami School of Law on March 23, 2010. This author, a senior member of Mexico's NAFTA negotiating team, also pointed out that NAFTA has become a remarkable instrument of self-discipline and dispute avoidance.

In highly controversial cases it may indeed be very attractive for States to have the problem resolved once and for all on the international level rather than to fester on the local scene, creating tensions, disruption and adverse reputational consequences for a very long time. A case like *World Duty Free v. Kenya* might have led to disaster if it had not been solved internationally. The claim was for US$500 million, the investor had shown himself willing and able to corrupt national officials at the very highest level, and an official inquiry at the time showed that the Kenyan judiciary itself was severely compromised.[18]

Should we not consider, one might ask, whether acceptance of BITs in fact leads to more foreign investment? This might – just possibly – be an interesting question in particular circumstances. As a general proposition, however, the premise is dubious; it seems most unlikely that the signature of BITs lead directly to an increase in foreign investment. Foreign investments would flow massively into Switzerland even if Switzerland had never signed any BITs. Anyone can understand why. A solvent State with stable good governance attracts investments without BITs. On the other hand, a State with a record of financial crises, repudiation of debts and arbitrary policy changes will not suddenly look attractive just by signing BITs. For a State to demonstrate enduring reliability is a matter of much greater complexity. It requires mature institutions: a tradition of efficient and reliable governance. The rule of law is a part of such an environment, and the network of BITs contributes to the rule of law.

The insight is not complicated: a country governed in accordance with the rule of law has little to fear from BITs, or from international tribunals.

Equally, a failure to accept the concept of investor protection will certainly discourage investors, including *present* investors who should be the first target of capital-importing States: to persuade them to expand their investments in magnitude and duration.

Let us then consider the fundamental purpose of investor protection. It is nonsense to speak of the interests or rights of corporations in the abstract. We have no *a priori* stake in the survival of corporations as a way of doing business. If they did not serve society, they could be abolished without regret. But of course they have proved unsurpassed as levers for the mobilization of capital and the use of technology. So when we protect the "rights"

[18] ICSID Case No. ARB/00/7, October 4, 2004.

of corporations, this of course means the rights of their owners – who may be modest shareholders in public corporations capable of mobilizing capital in a way that cannot be replicated by host States and foreign aid programs. We do so because that is the price of sustaining a valuable system, explicitly embraced by both capitalist and social-democratic theory – and implicitly by the central planners of State capitalism.

When we look at the world in this light, we discover that *the objective of investment protection is to convince investors to invest for the longest time possible and for the lowest possible return.*[19] That is how the capital-importing country maximizes its benefits. In a lawless country, someone will always be prepared to speculate, but only if there is a spectacular rate of return – realized in correspondingly quick order, after which both the investment and the profits vanish. This is not desirable investment.

So let us conclude with respect to this second theme.

The idea that States may be held accountable under international law by arbitral tribunals created by treaty is neither new nor radical. There were hundreds of such cases in the nineteenth century. The defendant States were of all types: rich and powerful, poor and friendless, European or ex-colonial. International tribunals held the United States responsible for actions which its Supreme Court had declared not to be breaches of international law. Those awards were nevertheless respected by the United States.[20] When one of the most illustrious of all awards was handed down against Great Britain in the Alabama Claims (1872), the British arbitrator issued a harsh dissent, calling the award of some US$15 million gold "unjust," but his government – far more powerful at the time than the United States – nevertheless paid the awarded amount.[21]

This tradition of respect for international law as applied by international tribunals should be kept in mind by critics of investment protection. Such critics sometimes imagine that international tribunals can be paralyzed by declarations of municipal courts that the treaties creating international jurisdiction are contrary to national constitutions. But to suggest that the alleged requirements of a nation's own constitution may

[19] I am indebted to insights found in an early contribution to this field by Jürgen Voss, "The Protection and Promotion of Foreign Direct Investment in Developing Countries: Interests, Interdependencies, Intricacies" (1982) 31 *ICLQ* 686.

[20] Jan Paulsson, *Denial of Justice under International Law* (2005) 257.

[21] Jan Paulsson, "The Alabama Claims Arbitration: Statecraft and Stagecraft," in Ulf Franke et al. eds. *Arbitrating for Peace* 7 (Kluwer 2016).

neutralize the international undertakings of its government flies in the face of international law itself. It may happen that such undertakings are an excess of power under national law, or may run afoul of national law in other ways. But they do not (provided of course that the authority to bind the State is sufficient for the purposes of international law) prevent anyone from relying on those undertakings internationally. Whatever their force as a matter of national law, such arguments evaporate on the international plane.

Judge Keba Mbaye (once the Vice-President of the International Court of Justice, and before that the First President of the Supreme Court of Senegal) put it as follows: "A state must not be allowed to cite the provisions of its law in order to escape from an arbitration that it has already accepted."[22] Lord Mustill suggested, "Perhaps it should be classed as a principle of international *ordre public*."[23] This concept was firmly endorsed in a landmark arbitration brought by a German private party against Belgium, in a case called *Benteler v. Belgium* (1984).[24] It has even been incorporated into the *municipal* law of Switzerland, which provides that a State party to an arbitration agreement "cannot rely on its own law to contest the arbitrability of a dispute or its own capacity to be a party to an arbitration."[25]

Criticism of international tribunals on the grounds that they impede democratic policies – whether protection of the environment or the labor market – is misdirected. International tribunals do not establish policy. They give effect to international agreements. To deny the authority of international tribunals is to deprive States of the power to make meaningful promises. The French Professor Pierre Mayer wrote a comprehensive and fundamental article some 30 years ago on "the neutralisation of the normative power of the State with respect to State contracts," in which he queried, "Is it not paradoxical that the exaltation of sovereignty over natural resources implied preventing the sovereign State from entrusting

[22] *60 Years On: A look at the Future* (ICC Publications No 412, a collection of papers from the 60th Anniversary of the International Chamber of Commerce) 296 (1984).

[23] Michael Mustill, "The New *Lex Mercatoria*: The First Twenty-Five Years" in M. Bos and I. Brownlie (eds), *Liber Amicorum for Lord Wilberforce* (1987) 149, at 177, n 91.

[24] Jan Paulsson, "May a State Invoke Its Internal Law to Repudiate Consent to International Arbitration?" (1986) 2 *Arb Int'l* 90.

[25] Federal Act on Private International Law art 177(2).

their temporary exploitation by a foreign corporation possessed of the necessary capital and technology, on the grounds that the State cannot validly accord the guarantees required by the corporation?"[26] He added, "To allow States to undo their commitments means in practice to forbid them from making undertakings in the future."[27]

When France wanted to ensure that the Walt Disney Corporation would build Euro-Disneyland outside Paris and not in Spain, the Parliament passed a special law to authorize the government to accept the jurisdiction of international arbitration (ICSID) in agreements "with foreign corporations for the implementation of operations having a national interest."[28] The US corporation was adamant about a neutral jurisdiction in the event of a dispute with the French government.

Criticism of international tribunals on the grounds that they should operate more efficiently, transparently, coherently and fairly are entirely legitimate. But no human institutions are perfect. International arbitral tribunals have existed for many generations; complaints by those disappointed in their awards have existed for precisely as long. One must be careful to recognize criticism which is only a cover for the disinclination to obey international norms and institutions.

It thus seems that many of those who challenge the legitimacy of international adjudication aim at the wrong target. They criticize the principle of the supremacy of international law when their real complaint has to do with the political choices of their own government in making the bargains reflected in international treaties. The mistake is a dangerous one. For what will happen if they destroy the authority of international law? What then does it matter if they are right about the policy? What will they do once they have prevailed – once they have achieved agreement as to important rules for the protection of the environment, the elimination of child labor, the proper treatment of persons accused of crime, an adjustment of the terms of trade in favor of impoverished producers denied access to markets? What a hollow victory indeed, to stand there empty-handed, deprived of a shattered tool.

[26] Pierre Mayer, "La neutralisation du pouvoir normatif de l'Etat en matière de contrats d'Etat" (1986) *J Droit Int'l* 5.

[27] "[P]ermettre aux Etats de se délier, c'est en pratique leur interdire de se lier dans le futur." *Ibid.*

[28] Article 9, Law No 86972 of August 19, 1986, *Journal official*, August 22, 1986, 10190.

To sum up: in the field of international investments, arbitral tribunals are instruments of the rule of law. Their purpose is not to favor the rich, but to enable States to make reliable promises. To undermine that reliability is to deprive the State of a valuable tool, to generate international transactions on favorable terms. Arbitral tribunals are not to be blamed for the contents of treaties. International tribunals tend to irritate respondent States – whether they are rich or poor – in individual cases; yet their decisions should be respected in order to achieve the long-term benefits of the rule of law. Respect for settled and legitimate expectations is a precondition for healthy international relations.

Now our final question: in very broad terms, what are best practices for a State once it has signed a BIT?

In some countries, international arbitration is viewed in a defeatist and defensive way. There is a failure to perceive that effective use of the arbitral process is an important task in managing international economic relations – indeed, in managing the national debt. Wherever such defeatist views prevail, the attachment of foreign investors to the arbitral process will continue to be viewed as part of a strategy of the rich to take unfair advantage of the poor.

Here are some premises of defensiveness or defeatism that explain negative views of international arbitration:

- States are reluctant to subject themselves to the jurisdiction of tribunals that are not part of their own apparatus. This is generally an especially important consideration with respect to environments in which the weaknesses of the local private sector are such that foreign investors and international banks demand direct contractual commitments by the State itself. As national economies develop, it becomes increasingly rare that ministries act directly as signatories to private law contracts;
- When developing countries find themselves in international arbitration with foreign investors, they often participate with misgivings or even bitterness. Such feelings tend to intensify over time as new officials – or indeed new regimes – look back critically on the work of their predecessors;
- Some parties from developing countries misunderstand the international arbitral process in a number of ways. They assume that it is a mechanism designed for the protection of the investor, when in fact it is a two-way street with significant advantages to the States as

> compared even to its domestic courts. It should be obvious that the failure of foreign investors to fulfill contractual undertakings may give rise to important and justified claims or defenses. International arbitral awards tend to be vastly more enforceable, as a practical matter, than domestic court judgments, which benefit from limited recognition abroad.

Many States still believe that international arbitration intrinsically favors the foreign party, when experience has shown that serious governments – even in less prosperous countries – are able to use the process successfully. Moreover, the leading international arbitral institutions have responded to the vast changes in the identity of their users by making corresponding changes in their governing structure. The challenge to establish and maintain legitimacy is demanding. Institutions must be transparent in their actions, and must avoid the entrenchment of in-groups as well as the danger of capture by frequent users. The selection of arbitrators and the paradoxes of unilaterally appointed arbitrators are equally serious preoccupations. But the leading institutions are well aware of these important issues, and have built sophisticated safeguards – alas too often poorly understood by facile criticisms of the system.

It serves little purpose to tell host States that they should respect the international arbitral process because it is the right and decent thing to do, and that in the long run foreign investors will think better of them for it. To get anywhere, one must rather understand that the arbitral mechanism is something they can use effectively to their concrete benefit.

It is a serious mistake to focus on the opposition between investor and host State. The true dividing line goes within the community of investors; there are good investors and bad investors. Good investors are there for the long haul, and want to make a decent return, as is understood by everyone from the beginning. In order to merit that reward, they expect that they will be held to making a real contribution, which they are happy for anyone to evaluate. Their enemy is not the host State, because they have shared interests, but the bad investor, a dubious operator who wants to make a quick buck, getting vast profits for shoddy goods, procuring signatures on all sorts of opaque documents, contracts, amendments and certificates designed as a legal cover for poor performance – or worse. The bad investor creates a climate of suspicion and despair which also harms good investors.

Those who operate transparently, professionally and rigorously, and create an atmosphere of seriousness and reliability, are on the same side, whether they represent investors or governments. They are united in their desire for an environment in which long-term legitimate expectations may be relied upon. If such an environment is brought about, and if bad investors are discouraged or flushed out, many dubious debts will evaporate and Ministers of Finance will sleep better.

How may such a good environment be created and maintained? It seems clear that good practices include rigor and professionalism in monitoring foreign investment – as it enters the country, as it is implemented, and as returns on investments flow back to the investor. It seems equally clear that it is bad practice to sign a BIT and then forget about it. Unfortunately, as a Swedish saying goes, "Good examples are admired; bad ones followed." But this cycle of negligence can surely be broken. There are many capital-importing countries which develop serious and enduring structures to channel investments in positive ways. This does not happen automatically. If the benefits of foreign investment are to be maximized, the hard work for the capital-importing State begins after the BIT has been signed. It is imperative that officials with adequate knowledge and experience review the regulatory framework critically. Is it clear? Is it effective? Are relevant systems of approvals and licenses comprehensible to foreigners? Is the decision-making process transparent?

In one Latin-American country which has been successful in attracting foreign investment, an important inter-Ministerial Commission ensures oversight, coordination and implementation. It has set up a comprehensive website which contains complete and comprehensible information not only in Spanish and English, but also French, German and Italian – that is to say languages chosen to facilitate relations with major economic partners.

Reducing the obscurity of governance is of benefit not only to the foreign investor, but also to the host State; opaque bureaucratic procedures are breeding grounds for corruption, and corruption obviously leads to pathological decision-making.

BITs should be adjusted to suit the policy desiderata relevant to the particular bilateral relationship. When two countries share a common border, they may wish to achieve substantial integration of their economies, and on that basis provide full investor protection to whatever investment finds its way across the border, even if it has not been specifically approved. Even when the two countries are situated far apart, the attitude may be the same on the reasoning that medium-volume investments should be encouraged as well, and are less likely to be initiated if formal approvals are required from the central government. But some BITs follow the example of Malaysia and Belgium/Luxemburg, who limited the applicability of their BIT to approved projects. In a case called *Gruslin v. Malaysia*,[29] where the claimant was a Belgian national who had done nothing more than to invest in a fund which had made portfolio investments on the Kuala Lumpur Stock Exchange, an ICSID Tribunal refused even to consider the complaint on the basis that it was not covered by the treaty because the investment had not been approved as required under that BIT.

In sum, although the purpose of agreeing to limitations on sovereignty is to gain the power of making meaningful promises, these promises go as far as they go – and no further. This too is an essential element of international law.

[29] ICSID Case No ARB/99/3, November 27, 2000.

9 Consent to Arbitration in Foreign Investment Arbitration

Muthucumaraswamy Sornarajah

9.1 Introduction

As with all arbitration, consent lies at the root of arbitration of foreign investment disputes.[1] It is all the more relevant in such arbitration as a State, a sovereign entity, is involved. Where there is a contract of foreign investment containing an arbitration clause, there can be little doubt that future disputes arising from the contract could be submitted to the tribunal indicated in the arbitration clause as the clause manifests the consent of the parties to such arbitration. The phenomenon that arises in modern foreign investment arbitration which involves a State as one of the parties is the claim that consent to arbitration could be created from a State's unilateral offer of such arbitration. Such a unilateral offer could be made either through its foreign investment legislation or through the dispute resolution provision in an investment treaty. There are few cases where the offer has arisen from foreign investment legislation.[2] The focus of this chapter on settlement of disputes on the basis of dispute settlement provisions in investment treaties. The large majority of the modern awards are based on unilateral offers made by the state contained in the dispute settlement provisions of the investment treaties. From this unilateral offer, consent both of the state and the foreign investor is constructed on the ground that such consent need not be manifested in a single document.

[1] For an earlier exposition, *see* C. Schreuer, 'Consent to Arbitration' in P. Muchlinski et al. (eds.) *Oxford Handbook of International Investment Law* (London: Oxford University Press, 2008). When submitting the draft ICSID Convention to member States, Executive Directors of World Bank explained: 'consent of the parties is the cornerstone of the jurisdiction of the Centre'. *Report of the Executive Directors on the Convention on the Settlement of Investment Disputes between States and Nationals of Other States* 23 (18 March 1965).

[2] SPP v. Egypt (1983) 22 *I.L.M.* 752. Extent of the consent depends on the wording of the statute. It may confine the consent to specific types of disputes like those arising from expropriation. Tradex v. Albania, Award (4 April 1999) 5 *ICSID Reports* 43.

The statement of claim commencing the arbitration is taken as the acceptance of the state's unilateral offer to arbitrate. An arbitration agreement is constructed from such offer and acceptance, the statement of claim initiating the arbitration being taken as consent of the investor.[3]

There are difficulties in explaining the phenomenon. There could be a huge and unusual time gap between the offer contained in the treaty and the acceptance through a statement of claim. The foreign investor may not be in existence or identifiable at the time of the offer. The offeror does not know to whom the offer is being made. It is a standing offer for the time of the duration of the treaty, which taking the sunset clause into account, could exceed more than 30 years in ordinary investment treaties. Whether such an offer of long duration could be made to those probably not in existence at the time of the offer and whose character and qualities are unknowable to the offeror is a teasing issue. Some recent awards have held that the offeree need not be in the territory of the host state to benefit from the offer[4] in which case he will remain entirely unknown to the host state. Besides, the offer is made to a third party to the treaty. These are not issues that have been taken into account in treaty-based investment arbitrations. It is as if a steam-roller had been at work flattening these theoretical difficulties and making them irrelevant. Many of the problems in the area arise because the pro-investor exuberance has clouded out consideration of the fact that the enterprise of constructing consent is one that is based on insecure foundations. It has now become conventional wisdom that such an offer could be made and that its acceptance creates an obligation on the state to submit to arbitration. But, once this conventional wisdom that the investment treaties contain unilateral offers by host states has reified, states have attempted various ways in which the advanced consent they had given in treaties could be circumscribed even as foreign investors have tried to extend the scope and the circumstances of such consent by the state. The law represents the ongoing tussle that has taken place between these two camps. The pro-investor view seeks expansion of the unilateral offer contained in the dispute settlement clause of the investment treaty as to arbitration to a wider category of persons who could

[3] There cannot be 'arbitration without privity'. The phrase originates from an article published by Jan Paulsson. *See* Jan Paulsson, 'Arbitration without Privity' (1995) 10 *ICSID Rev. F.I.L.J.* 235.

[4] Abaclat v. Argentina, ICSID Case No. ARB/07/5, Award (4 August 2011).

consent to the offer and create arbitral jurisdiction. The contrary view seeks to circumscribe the nature of the offer by finding limitations in the language of the treaty and its purpose. Arbitral awards have oscillated between these competing positions. Some arbitrators, those in the majority, have shown a tendency towards an expansionary view seeing the offer as made to a wider class than originally contemplated by the states making the treaties. Others, fearing that such expansive views would cause a backlash against investment arbitration, have been restrained from taking expansionist views. The fact that arbitrators have responded differently to the same or similar situation relating to jurisdiction adds to the legitimacy crisis that afflicts investment arbitration at present. It makes the law on consent in arbitration, a fundamental issue, mired in controversy.

This chapter explores the basis of such construction of offer and consent to arbitration in treaty-based investment arbitration. It begins with the statement of the origins of the idea of constructing an agreement to arbitrate by finding an offer of the host State in the investment treaty and its acceptance by the statement of claim the investor makes in initiating the arbitration. It explores the circumstances of such construction. It examines the situations in which such construction has been thwarted as a result of circumstances that eschew the possibility of such consent. Equally, it looks at the efforts to expand the class of persons who could accept the unilateral offer by the state. It then deals with the efforts of states to narrow the instances of such construction of consent by imposing additional requirements that must be satisfied before consensual agreement of the parties can be constructed. It looks at the newer treaties that may make the creation of a consensual base for arbitration more difficult.

9.2 The Origin and Basis of Construction of Consent in Investment Treaty Arbitration

Investment treaties have been in existence from 1957.[5] *AAPL v. Sri Lanka*,[6] decided in 1992 was the first case in which the notion of construction of consent through a dispute resolution clause in an investment treaty

[5] The first such treaty is the one between Pakistan and Germany concluded in 1957.

[6] AAPL v. Sri Lanka, Award (27 June 1990), 4 *ICSID Reports* 250; American Manufacturing & Trading v. Democratic Republic of the Congo (Zaire), Award (21 February 1997), 5 *ICSID Reports* 11.

was accepted. In the intervening period, there were several treaties, containing dispute settlement provisions of various types. Not all of them contained language capable of constituting unilateral offers. The type of British treaty like the UK–Ceylon treaty had been in existence for some time. It was made on the then existing British model treaty which was the basis of other contemporary British treaties like the one with the Philippines, Singapore or Malaysia. No commentator, including commentators known to have negotiated the British treaties, indicated that the dispute settlement provision of the British investment treaties created a unilateral offer that could be converted into an agreement to arbitrate through a memorandum of arbitration submitted to the state. Percipient commentators would have picked up such a monumental change. None did.[7] It could well be that the notion of constructing of consent through the unilateral offer of the state in the treaty and its later acceptance by the foreign investor to whom it was not directly made is an original sin that has afflicted the whole basis of consent in investment arbitration.[8]

That is not to say that the view taken in *AAPL v. Sri Lanka,* the basis of which was not explained in the award is not a possible conclusion or that the words of the treaty did not lend themselves to such a construction. The enormity of the change was staggering. The justification for such a step is said to be the now spurious suggestion that there would be greater investment flows into the developing state if there were secure means of dispute settlement.[9] The extent of the loss of sovereignty that this method of constructing consent

[7] One of the commentaries was by Frederick Mann, a highly respected figure in the field. He was commenting on the United Kingdom–Philippines Treaty. Frederick Mann examined the Philippines–United Kingdom treaty in an article in the British Yearbook of International Law without picking up such a technique of arbitration. Eileen Denza and Shelagh Brooks, 'Investment Protection Treaties: The British Experience' (1987) *I.C.L.Q.* 908. The authors of the article, two British diplomats who wrote with experience of negotiating British Treaties do not mention the possibility of such construction of an arbitration agreement.

[8] In terms of contract, the making of benefit to a third party through contract was always problematic, more so in English law which required privity of contract. Roman systems did not recognise an *ius alteri,* the right in a third party through contract. The law has since changed but it took a while to do so. English law was changed by legislation Contracts (Rights of Third Parties) Act. States were having recourse to a type of contract that would be unusual in their own domestic systems. Though human rights conventions, particularly the European Convention on Human Rights, give a specially created court jurisdiction to individuals to bring actions against their own home states, this procedure is different from investor-state arbitration.

[9] The view that investment treaties lead to greater investment flows has been subjected to doubt in recent times. *See* Lauge Poulsen, *Bounded Rationality and Economic Diplomacy:*

was not discussed in the awards or in the contemporary literature. It has become a matter of concern only in recent times. It is too late in the day to make theoretical objections to the situation of construction of contracts. It could well be that such criticisms have resulted in more careful scrutinising of the basis on which such consent is constructed and states are carefully circumscribing the extent of their consent by requiring conditions for the use of the protection mechanism in the treaty

9.3 Arbitral Scrutiny of the Capacity to Consent

Despite the fact that the treaty has been interpreted as permitting the construction of an arbitration agreement, arbitrators must find that the capacity of the foreign investor to accept the State's offer is not tainted either by the fact that the original entry is not illegal or that he as a foreign investor or the foreign investment he made does not qualify for protection under the terms of the treaty. It is an exercise that the arbitral tribunal must perform with care as it is the very basis of its existence. The consent must be inferred not only from the words of the investment treaty but all circumstances relevant to the formation of such consent. As the tribunal in *Inceysa Vallisoletana v. El Salvador* said:[10]

> Analysis of the content and scope of the consent of the parties who sign an [investment treaty] cannot be considered as an imposition of limitations on such consent. On the contrary, it is a mandatory exercise that must be undertaken by any Arbitral Tribunal in order to decide whether or not the dispute brought before it is subject to its competence, according to the real content of the consent manifested by the parties.

The circumstances vitiating consent of the foreign investor occur where the original contract on the basis of which entry was made was illegal and where the foreign investment does not fall within the qualifications set out by the treaty for protection.

The Politics of Investment Treaties in Developing Countries (London: Cambridge University Press, 2015).

[10] Inceysa Vallisoletana v. El Salvador, ICSID Case No. ARB/03/26 (2 August 2006).

9.3.1 Consent and the Taint of Illegality

As in the case of commercial arbitration, the legality of the original transaction, which was the basis of the entry of the foreign investment, is always an issue. Consent cannot be found if the original contract was tainted by illegality. There has emerged a body of arbitral awards, founded on sound theory, which deny jurisdiction to arbitration tribunals based on investment treaties on the ground that the contract on the basis of which the entry made was not legal either because it was not made in accordance with prescribed procedure or because it was tainted with substantive illegality. The way to explain the situation would be to say that despite the existence of a unilateral offer by the state provided in the dispute resolution provision of the treaty, the investor lacked the capacity to make acceptance of it as he had made entry on the basis of an illegal or tainted contract or had not acted in accordance with the host state's law in making entry. The alternative explanation that the investment made through an illegal contract and such contract is not a protected investment under the treaty is a possibility but lacks cogency. It is the capacity of the investor which is affected as it is the offer that is made to him that cannot be completed into an arbitration agreement as he had made entry on the basis of a substantive or procedural illegality. The taint is not in the subject matter of the investment. It arises from the misconduct of the investor. The lack of capacity in the investor to consent to the unilateral offers as a result of his own misconduct is the better explanation as to why no agreement to arbitrate could arise and jurisdiction is consequently refused.

9.3.2 Procedural Illegality

The contract may be invalid if formal procedure required by domestic law had not been followed. The circumstances of such illegality which impedes the construction of a consensual base for arbitration can be identified in case law. They fall into two categories. The first is where there is procedural fault in the making of the contract as when the designated procedure for making a foreign investment in the domestic law of the host state had not been followed. This could occur where, for example, the designated authority had not signed the contract[11] or where the contract is ultra vires the authority effecting it. Some efforts have been made to argue that these procedural requirements of domestic law do not apply to international contracts which are subject to an international regime which require objective conditions being satisfied and not peculiar domestic requirements. This argument is a relic of the internationalisation theory whose traction in modern times is low.[12] Likewise, an old argument that the domestic law of the host state should not be set up as an excuse is no longer valid. These were techniques of the old law which are no longer relevant. There is no reason why a foreign investor who enters a country should not be aware of the procedural or substantive law of the host state. In domestic legal systems, there is a presumption that the alien has knowledge of the local laws with which he deals.

Besides the requirements of administrative law of the host state for the making of state contracts, protection may also be denied where special procedures for entry in the foreign investment law or the treaty itself have not been followed. In these circumstances too, the foreign investor who did not comply with procedure lacks capacity to make an arbitration agreement. He cannot give a valid consent to arbitration.

Investment treaties may prescribe additional requirements such as that there must be an 'approved' investment[13] or that the investment must have been made 'according to the laws and regulations of the host state' and in addition be approved in writing.[14] Though these constitute formal requirements, they can be explained as forbidding construction of consent in the absence of a satisfaction of the requirement. The neat explanation would be that the foreign investor lacks capacity to consent because he had bypassed the procedural method of entry prescribed by the law of the host State.

One award raised the question as to whether such qualifications of the investment that their entry must be made in accordance with the law are

[11] Mozambique Channel Discovery Ltd v. Government of Comoros, ICC Case No. 19040/AGF/Zf (20 October 2015).

[12] Recently, a Mauritius Court set aside an award on the ground that the state contract on which it was based violated the procurement laws of Mauritius. State Trading Corporation v. Betamax Ltd [2019] SCJ 139.

[13] Grueslin v. Malaysia, Award (28 November 2000), 5 *ICSID Reports* 483.

[14] The ASEAN Investment Agreement interpreted in Aung Chi Oo Ltd v. Myanmar requires that in addition to licenses from the admitting investment authority, there must be specific approval of the investment for the purposes of protection under the treaty.

necessary in an investment treaty. It expresses the view that it must be understood that a foreign investment can only make a valid entry necessary for the purpose of treaty protection only in accordance with the law of the host state.[15] If it makes entry otherwise than in accordance with the law, there is no reason why the investment should be protected. This view is based on sound reasoning. It is beginning to be accepted.[16] States admit in accordance with their economic plans. Their laws ensure that only such investments as further these plans are admitted. Their administrative screening mechanisms have the purpose of ensuring that only investments that comply with their developmental objectives are allowed entry. The objective of the treaty being the furtherance of economic development of the parties, it must follow that investments which do not accord with host state's law should be denied protection and the investors are deemed unable to provide consent for arbitration under the treaty when they make initial entry in violation of the law even where the investment treaty itself does not contain a legality requirement. This view as to legality has received increasing support in recent awards.[17]

There is a general good faith requirement that has been recognised so that a foreign investor who had broken entry laws or had been fraudulent in making the investment would not be able to give a valid consent under the treaty. There is an implicit legality requirement in investment treaties Where there is no compliance with the host state's entry laws, the investment will lack legality. The tribunal in *Alvarez y Marin v. Panama* observed it was reasonable to assume that states have only consented to the curtailment of their sovereignty, under the condition that this protection mechanism is limited to investments made in accordance with their own legal systems. This is all the more so where there is a licensing system involved as a precondition to entry as the licence always has to be lawfully obtained to be valid.[18]

15 Inceysa Vallisoletana v. El Salvador, ICSID Case No. ARB/03/26 (2 August 2006).

16 In Hamester v. Ghana, ICSID Case No. ARB/07/24, Award (18 June 2010), the tribunal stated the position widely: 'An investment will not be protected if it has been created in violation of national or international principles of good faith; by way of corruption, fraud, or deceitful conduct; or if its creation itself constitutes a misuse of the system of international investment protection under the ICSID Convention. It will also not be protected if it is made in violation of the host State's law'.

17 Cortec Mining Ltd v. Kenya, ICSID Case No. ARB/15/25 (22 October 2018).

18 Cortec Mining Ltd v. Kenya, ICSID Case No. ARB/15/25 (22 October 2018). SAUR International v. Argentina ICSID Case No. ARB 04/4 (22 May 2014).

The view has been stated that the legality requirement could be ignored where the host state has habitually ignored prior breaches.[19] The soundness of this view is to be questioned. Whether a breach should be condoned or not is not for a tribunal but the state to judge. In *Al-Warraq v. Indonesia*, the tribunal took the view that illegality subsequent to entry is relevant in showing that the claimant did not have 'clean hands'. This could be ground for refusal of jurisdiction. This qualification would mean that jurisdiction would be defeated in situations like environmental misconduct, human rights violations and violation of corporate responsibility standards all of which are stated as defences in the new balanced treaties. The 'clean hands' requirement short circuits the defences in the balanced treaties.[20] It would take some time for such views to be commonplace.

9.3.3 Substantive Illegality

Substantive illegality is firmly established in certain obvious circumstances. Bribery has been the certain candidate. Though vigorous efforts have been made to locate the rule regarding illegality of contracts secured through bribery in transnational law, the more secure foundation for it is the domestic law legislation making corruption criminal.[21] This is where inquiry must begin and end. Clearly, bribery will constitute procedural illegality as well as the officer signing the contract would be acting ultra vires making his exercise of discretion based on the bribery than on the merits of the situation. Consent secured through bribery cannot be regarded as valid consent.

As with ordinary contracts, fraud, duress and misrepresentation as to fundamental terms nullify the contract.[22] It is not the illegality of the contract that affects jurisdiction but the fact that the misconduct involved affects the capacity of the foreign investor to give consent to the State's offer to arbitrate.

[19] David Aven et al. v. Costa Rica, ICSID Case No. UNCT/15/3 (18 September 2018); Railroad Development Corporation v. Republic of Guatemala, ICSID Case No. ARB/07/23 (29 June 2012) refused to consider illegality on the ground that the state had knowingly overlooked it.

[20] The clean hands doctrine was rejected in Yukos v. Russia PCA Case A 227 (18 July 2014).

[21] World Duty Free Company Limited v. Republic of Kenya, ICSID Case No. ARB/00/7 (4 October 2004); Siemens A.G. v. Argentine Republic, ICSID Case No. ARB/02/8 (6 February 2007).

[22] Feldman v. Mexico (2002) 42 ILM 625.

9.3.4 Qualifications of the Investment for Consent

All treaties require that the foreign investor who claims his statement of arbitration amounts to a consent must have made an investment which falls within the definition of an investment protected by the treaty. The types of investment are mentioned in the treaty but apart from this, there is read into the treaty a requirement that it should satisfy an additional test that depends on the identification of the criteria of a protected investment. A transaction which is predominantly a sales transaction cannot qualify as an investment.[23] This is a large subject which has been addressed in the literature. The *Salini* test[24] is generally accepted but there is debate as to whether economic development induced by the investment is a necessary part of the definition.[25] Since the treaty itself states that development is the objective of the treaty, it is to be inferred that the investment to qualify for protection must promote economic development and it is an investor who makes such an investment who can give a relevant consent under the treaty. The ICSID Convention itself is premised on economic development so that only investments that promote economic development come under its purview.

The discussion as to consent above reveals that some arbitrators have interpreted investment treaties by limiting the circumstances of consent in a manner that favours the state. Thus, the view taken that the legality requirement, that the foreign investment entry must have complied with the laws of the host state should be read into the treaty even if it is not stated expressly, favours the host State. So too, the definition of a protected investment in *Salini*, adds requirements that are not present in the investment treaty. Its requirement that the ability to promote economic development must be a characteristic of a protected foreign investment is a controversial addition to the definition of such investment.[26] Such

[23] Nova Scotia Power v. Venezuela ICSID Case No. ARB/11/1 (30 April 2014).

[24] Salini Construttori SpA v. Morocco ICSID Case No. ARB/00/4 (23 July 2001).

[25] Caratube International Oil Company LLP v. Republic of Kazakhstan, ICSID Case No. ARB/08/12 (5 June 2012).

[26] Malaysian Historical Salvors v. Malaysia, ICSID Case No. ARB/05/10 (16 April 2009) (Annulment Award) where the majority award held that economic development is not a necessary feature; Caratube International Oil Company LLP v. Republic of Kazakhstan, ICSID Case No. ARB/08/12 (5 June 2012); Electrabel v. Hungary and Deutsche Bank v. Sri Lanka, ICSID Case No. ARB/09/2 (31 August 2012) are awards which did not require economic development as an aspect of investment.

interpretations may seem expansive as they constrain the ability of the foreign investor to consent to arbitration. But, they fit in logically with the scheme of investment treaties. There are expansive interpretations which enable the investor to consent to arbitration though they do not appear to have been thought of by the parties to the treaties.

9.4 Expansive Interpretations Favouring the Foreign Investor

There are a number of expansive interpretations that favour the foreign investor. They involve creative interpretations justified on the basis that they are indicated by a strict interpretation of the treaties or are in accordance with the objective of economic development stated in the preamble to the treaties. They expand the capacity of the claimant to consent. They seem to be more at variance with the intention of the parties than the extensions made through interpretation which support the host states. These could now be looked at.

9.4.1 National Securing a Right to Consent through Round Tripping

Investment treaties as well as the ICSID Convention is generally premised on the view that their protection does not extend to nationals of the states making the treaty. In *Tokio Tokeles v. Ukraine*, the issue arose as to whether nationals of a state could go into the other state with which their state had a treaty, incorporate a company which secures the nationality of that state and then route their investment through that company into their own state so that they could secure the protection of the treaty. The majority in *Tokio Tokeles* answered this was possible against a strong dissent by the chairman of the tribunal. Since then, arbitrators have sought to extend this notion of corporate nationality, essentially holding that a corporation, being a foreign investor, could simply by incorporating in a state which has a better standard of protection use the arbitration mechanism in the treaty.[27]

Many of the older treaties which make incorporation the sole test for nationality enable this technique to be adopted. Consequently in disputes

[27] For a recent award, *see* Mera Investments v. Serbia, ICSID Case No. ARB/17/2 (20 November 2018). In Aguas del Tunari v. Bolivia, ICSID Case No. ARB/02/3 (21 October 2005) the tribunal said that corporations could migrate to better climes even as people do.

brought to arbitration under these treaties tribunals follow the *Tokios Tokeles*[28] rule on the basis of strict interpretation.[29] Newer treaties qualify the incorporation test by requiring effective management of the company in the state of incorporation or a denial of benefits provision.[30] Until the older treaties are terminated or lapse, the problem will continue. enabling the national of a state to obtain a right to consent to arbitration through round tripping.

9.4.2 Migration of Companies and Consent

Another controversial issue in the area is whether an investor who 'migrates' to another state having better treaty terms could secure a right to consent to the treaty of the state to which he had migrated. The expansionary view is that, like persons, companies could migrate as well.[31] It then becomes possible for a company to 'migrate' to a state which uses incorporation as the sole test of nationality and thereby acquire the nationality of that state. Thereafter, the claim is that the company can use the treaties of its new home state to bring claims against other states with which the home state has treaties. Some states favoured such 'migration' by keeping the protection standards in their investment treaties high so as to promote such 'migration' into their states. This would attract large companies into the state. But, since a 'post box' company would do to engage this technique of acquiring the benefits of the more advantageous treaty, the state desiring such influx of companies seldom stands to benefit.

The view that protection of more advanced treaties could be secured through 'migration' runs against the purpose of investment treaties

[28] Tokios Tokelės v. Ukraine, ICSID Case No. ARB/02/18 (29 April 2004); Banro American Resources, Inc. and Société Aurifère du Kivu et du Maniema S.A.R.L. v. Democratic Republic of the Congo (2002) ICSID Rev. 380.

[29] *See* Mera Investments v. Serbia, ICSID Case No. ARB/17/2(2018); A11Y LTD. v. Czech Republic, ICSID Case No. UNCT/15/1 (29 June 2018). Indirect ownership of investments such as shares also are given treaty protection unless excluded. South American Silver v. Bolivia tribunals have inferred that such indirect investments are to be protected as their protection is consistent with the treaty objective of promoting investment flows.

[30] On denial of benefits, *see* Masdar Solar and Wind Cooperatief v. Spain, ICSID Case No. ARB/14/1 (16 May 2018).

[31] Aguas del Tunari v. Bolivia, ICSID Case No. ARB/02/3 (21 October 2005).

which is said to be to promote 'reciprocal' flows of funds. No flow takes place from the country to which the company 'migrates' except to enable it to take advantage of the better provisions of the treaty. This expansionary view also adds to the legitimacy crisis in arbitration for it promotes misuse of the system to the advantage of foreign investors. No host state could possibly have contemplated that such a technique would be adopted or that an offer is made to a company that seeks to 'migrate' to another state purely for the sake of obtaining arbitral advantages despite the fact that no benefits had flowed through the new home state to the host State Since Holland maintains a treaty system that contained the best standards of protection, such 'migration' is largely to Holland. The technique of 'migration' for purposes of jurisdiction came to be known as the 'Dutch sandwich'. The newer Dutch treaties do not favour such migration and cannot be seen as advantageous to foreign investors as it contains several defences to liability.

Newer treaties prevent the possibility of such migration. Some treaties make it impossible by making departures from the test of incorporation by imposing additional requirements such as that management must take place in the state of incorporation for nationality of that state to be claimed. It is unlikely that after the adverse criticisms of this technique and the harsh reaction of states to its adoption, there is likelihood of the technique being adopted in the future.

Corporate nationality has become a technique for forum shopping. This was never intended by states. It is clearly an expansionary interpretation effected by arbitrators. It is an example of the inclination of some arbitrators to expand the category of persons and entities that could give consent to arbitration. States have reacted by plugging this possibility through the inclusion of denial of benefits clauses which give the discretion whether to treat such corporations as nationals of the other state party. However, these clauses appear in the newer treaties. The conflict will go on as many old treaties that make incorporation the only test of corporate nationality are still extant.

9.4.3 The Umbrella Clause

Umbrella clauses again provide an example of the classic clash between the expansionist view that stresses protection of investment and seeks to expansively interpret treaty provisions to achieve such protection and the narrower view that going beyond the revealed intention of the parties in the treaty provisions will add to the legitimacy crisis as it takes the law further away from the intention of the parties. Umbrella clauses fortunately do not appear in all investment treaties. In treaties where they are found, the clause would simply state that contractual commitments entered into by the state would be protected by the treaty. It does give rise to the impression that the whole of the contract, which is essentially founded in domestic law, is made subject to treaty protection and thereby elevated into the sphere of international protection. The controversy is not acute now as before as states have indicated in a sense what their intention was by leaving out the umbrella clause in their newer treaties, so indicating that they never thought that the umbrella clause would be put to such expansive use.[32]

The impression of protection so given has been avidly embraced in some awards. It has been rejected in other awards on the ground that such an effort at internationalisation.[33] Since the two cases involving virtually similar facts though different treaty formulations divided on the scope of the umbrella clauses, two lines of authorities have arisen on the basis of the two awards.[34] If the more extreme of the expansive views is taken, then, the arbitral consent would exist to elevate contractual violations into the treaty sphere. The scope of consent comes to be considerably expanded on this view. This is an area on which there is much literature. Having stated the position, it is best to move out of this rather complex debate, made complex by the different views that have been expressed in the literature.[35]

[32] Tellingly, the US Model BIT (2012) does not contain the umbrella clause though earlier models did include it.

[33] Pointedly, the initial cases were brought by the same Claimant on similar facts against different states.

[34] SGS v. Pakistan tribunal had rejected the purported umbrella clause in the Switzerland–Pakistan BIT, while the SGS v. Philippines tribunal subsequently upheld the umbrella clause. Later cases have divided behind these awards. Those which accept the expansionary view giving effect to the umbrella clause rely on the plain meaning of the clause and the purpose of the investment treaty being the protection of the investor. Noble Ventures; Eureko v. Poland. The other strand relies largely on the illogicality of such an interpretation (Noble Ventures, Eureko v. Poland), stressing the fact that the contract itself is of a commercial nature and that the treaty is concerned with sovereign acts, the mere violation of a contract not being always a sovereign act but induced by commercial considerations.

[35] I adhere to my view that a domestic contract cannot be internationalised unless there is a specific treaty which contemplates the particular treaty that is selected for affecting such a

9.4.4 Most Favoured Nation Clause and Consent

The extent to which an offer could be constructed through the use of a most favoured nation clause in a treaty that does not contain liberal provisions on dispute settlement first arose in *Maffezini v. Spain.* In *Maffezini*, the treaty invoked was the Argentine-Spain BIT. It required a waiting period of 18 months during which a negotiated settlement was to be attempted. The BIT contained a most favoured nation clause which stated that 'in all matters' the treatment given to an investor will not be 'less favourable than that extended to the investments made by investors of a third country'. This was a classic MFN clause that is found in investment treaties of a certain period. Relying on the MFN clause, the Argentinian investor argued that he could make use of the dispute settlement provision in the Chile–Spain treaty which did not contain any waiting period. The tribunal held that this was possible. It stated,

> In light of the above considerations, the Tribunal is satisfied that the Claimant has convincingly demonstrated that the most favored nation clause included in the Argentine-Spain BIT embraces the dispute settlement provisions of this treaty. Therefore, relying on the more favourable arrangements contained in the Chile–Spain BIT and the legal policy adopted by Spain with regard to the treatment of its own investors abroad, the Tribunal concludes that Claimant had the right to submit the instant dispute to arbitration without first accessing the Spanish courts.

So, another Pandora's box was opened permitting the expansion of jurisdiction by enabling the construction of an offer and acceptance through the mechanism of an MFN clause and the existence of a more favourable treaty containing unrestricted terms of dispute settlement. The awards immediately following *Maffezini* supported the invocation of the MFN

process. The umbrella clause has no effect of internationalising the original investment contract rooted in domestic law. Investment contracts are based on domestic law. It becomes final once concluded as representing the meeting of the wills of the parties as to the specific transaction. That it could be added to by some external act which does not specifically contemplate the terms carefully negotiated by the parties for the contract and that this process of internationalisation applies even to future contracts defies logic. Also, as a matter of logic, states need not go through the process of negotiating an investment treaty and its provisions as a simple statement that all commitments made to the foreign investor are protected by the arbitral mechanism would suffice is the expansionist view is accepted. But, for the powerful, the life of the law is not logic. It is the repetition ad nauseam of illogicalities until they are accepted as law.

clause to secure better forms of dispute settlement.[36] But, contrary views emerged. In *Plama v. Bulgaria,*[37] the treaty that was invoked did not contain a provision on investor-State arbitration. It did contain an MFN clause on the basis of which the investor argued that it is possible to import into the treaty provisions in other treaties the Respondent State had made which contained reference to arbitration as the method of resolving disputes. The tribunal rejected this contention holding that the MFN clause did not have the effect of incorporating other dispute settlement provisions in other treaties the host state had made.

There is again an essential illogicality in the argument that an MFN clause enables the investor to skirt around the treaties of the Respondent state to find the better dispute settlement provisions among them. The aim of an MFN clause as the tribunal in *Telenor v. Hungary* pointed out was to put the foreign investor on par with investors from third-party states in matters relating to substantive rights even as the national treatment clause provision puts him on par with nationals as far as substantive rights are concerned.

States which negotiated the terms of the treaties did not intend to produce the results such as those contemplated in the *Maffezini* line of cases. There is little logic in the reasoning in this line of cases. Jurisdiction must first be established before a tribunal can decide on any matter. The view is possible only on assuming jurisdiction without consent and then pronouncing that the MFN clause can be used to find jurisdiction on the basis of other treaties.[38] This use of the MFN clause will drive states away from investment arbitration or seek to restrict its scope. Thus, India was a victim of the adoption of this view in *White Industries v. India*[39] It resulted in India terminating its treaties and making a new model treaty without an MFN clause. As in India's case, and as in the case of umbrella clauses, the tendency in the newer treaties is to leave the MFN clause out. Though there will be recourse to the use of MFN clauses in future arbitrations, these will be restricted to a fewer number of treaties and it could well be that

[36] *See* Gas Natural v. Argentina, ICSID Case No. ARB/03/10 (17 June 2005); Teinver v. Argentina, ICSID Case No. ARB/09/1 (21 December 2012).

[37] Palma Consortium Ltd v. Bulgaria, ICSID Case No. ARB/03/24 (27 August 2008).

[38] The contrary view was taken in ICS Inspection Services Ltd v. Argentina PCA Case No. 20109 (21 December 2012) where the important of state consent is stressed. Using the MFN clause requires construction of consent where no direct consent is available.

[39] UNCITRAL Award (30 November 2011).

arbitration tribunals may desist from exorbitant uses of the MFN clause in the future as the displeasure of the states with the use of MFN clauses are being made evident through their absence or restriction in the newer investment treaties.[40]

There are procedural requirements on consent that are to be found in treaties. These relate to the time at which the protection of the treaty commences so that investments made before the time cannot qualify for protection. But, the more common issue relates to waiting periods that require a cooling off time so that parties may rethink the dispute, voluntarily withdraw from contentious means of its resolution or attempt negotiation or mediation. Such clauses are often couched in mandatory language. Despite such language, tribunals have sought to create exceptions where it may not be necessary to follow the requirement of a waiting period.

9.4.5 Waiting Periods

Many treaties require a waiting period during which parties will have an opportunity of negotiating settlement. The waiting period could be from 6 to 18 months. The waiting period must be seen as a qualification on the state's consent agreeing to arbitration only with an investor who had waited for the period and tried out some form of alternative dispute settlement.[41] The efforts made to avoid the requirement through use of the MFN clause have been differently treated in the awards. Taking a cue from the local remedies rule, it has been suggested that it is not necessary to satisfy this requirement if waiting for the period would not produce any result. This is not a sound view. It is not for a later tribunal to pronounce on this issue. The waiting period is mandatory. The fact that the courts of a state are not effective does not mean that there are other means of settlement that could not be attempted during the waiting period.[42]

[40] *E.g.* the recent Australian treaties with Uruguay (2018) and Hong Kong (2018) specifically exclude dispute resolution from the scope of MFN clauses and exclude importation of third party rights. It may have been better to simply leave out the MFN clause.

[41] Giovanni Alemanni v. Argentina, ICSID Case No. ARB/07/8 (17 November 2014).

[42] The futility argument was used in *Alemanni v. Argentina* on the grounds that Argentinian courts were not effective. Courts are not the only means through which a settlement could be effected.

9.4.6 Fork in the Road

The fork in the road provision, found in some treaty provisions on dispute settlement, forbids a party, who has the option of proceeding by way of arbitration under the treaty or bringing an action before the local courts, to resort to arbitration after he had embarked on domestic court proceedings relating to the dispute. He must travel the course he had chosen and not attempt the other course after his choice. The pro-investor view is to require that the cases brought before arbitration and the local courts in respect of the dispute are exactly similar. This was the course accepted in but later awards have said that if there was a fundamental similarity in the two cases, arbitration should be denied. Later tribunals have taken the view that the fork in the road clause would debar treaty arbitration where the fundamental basis of the claim submitted to the domestic court was the same as the one submitted to the domestic courts. Here again one can see a difference that can be explained on the basis of attitudes of differently constituted tribunals.

9.4.7 Exhaustion of Local Remedies

Consequent on the legitimacy crisis, some modern treaties have asserted the requirement that proceedings must first be brought before the local courts. Since these treaties also emphasise denial of justice as the principal cause of action, it is implicit that the court must have refused justice in an egregious manner before a successful claim can be made. Exhaustion of local remedies then becomes a condition precedent to the expression of consent by the foreign investor. His claim to arbitration must follow the exhaustion of local remedies and denial of justice. If this formula is adopted, then, there is a blow to the roots of investment arbitration. What effectively happens is the restoration of the old customary international law, as claimed by the United States, being revived. The conventional wisdom in customary international law as explained in *ELSI v. US* is that there must be an inference of the requirement of exhaustion of local remedies. This requirement has been dispensed with in investment arbitration, though there are no express worlds of such exclusion. There is a link between the exhaustion of local remedies and denial of justice. The local remedies that are exhausted must indicate a denial of justice for a wrong to arise. The local remedies rule is not a procedural rule but leads to the establishment of an actionable remedy.

The new Indian model treaty attempts to introduce exhaustion of local remedies though in a tenuous manner. It requires local remedies to be attempted for five years before arbitration is attempted. Given the slowness of the Indian courts, this is too short a period for any result unless special procedure is devised. But, coupled with the emphasis on denial of remedies, the result is to truncate investment arbitration considerably. One view would then be that it is only an investor who has exhausted local remedies who can relevantly consent to arbitration. A further constriction may be that he must also be able to show after this exhaustion that he had been denied a remedy.

9.4.8 Preclusionary Defences and Consent

Treaties are undergoing changes in response to the legitimacy crisis in investment arbitration. One trend is to make treaties which are 'balanced' in the sense that while the traditional part relating to protection remains intact, there is a new part introduced which deals with the recalcitrant foreign investor who had misconducted while carrying out the investment or had caused damage to the host state and its people through environmental mismanagement, human rights violations and corporate irresponsibility. The effort is to balance the need for investment protection with the regulatory power of the state to act in the public interest. The new treaties open up vistas that, if the intransigent pattern of investment arbitrators can be removed, will open up new vistas.

Some of these defences are preclusionary in the sense that they indicate circumstances when established provide justification for the state's conduct and do not indicate a preliminary liability on the part of the state requiring the proof of a defence to avoid liability. Necessity has been identified as such a plea in the Argentinian cases. There is good authority for it being so considered in general international law. National security is another preclusionary plea. This could also be so where the subject matter of the contract, e.g. the mining of land, affects indigenous rights. Indigenous rights are prior rights which displace the rights of the foreign investor. In such situations, the theoretical explanation is that there can be no valid consent to arbitration either by the state or by the foreign investor who loses the right to arbitration in situations where preclusionary circumstances exist. If a hierarchy of rights are created, then, the scope for preclusion would increase. Thus, if international law develops to give precedence to climate change, then, state measures which reduce climate change must be regarded as rights which displace investment protection in priority, thereby destroying the ability of the investor to consent to arbitration.

Clearly then, there can be no consent when external circumstances indicate a preclusionary plea. Would the situation be different where there are the defences mentioned in the treaty are present, such as measures taken to protect the environment, human rights, labour standards and standards of corporate responsibility? Should the investor have the right to invoke arbitration where, for example, he had engaged in corporate misconduct harmful to the state? *In Al-Warraq v. Indonesia*, the tempting suggestion was made that illegality is relevant for consent not only at the time of making the investment contract but at the subsequence stages of operating the contract.[43] The view was that if accordant behaviour with host state's law are relevant at time of entry, it continues to be relevant at every stage of the investment process. After all, expansionary arbitrators have justified their expansion by stating that good investment benefits the host state. Bad investment does not do so. It would be logical to take the view that if there is subsequent misconduct, the capacity of the arbitrator to consent is affected. These are possibilities that are opened up in the new trends in investment treaties. Whether arbitrators, schooled in stressing investment protection, would be amenable to such arguments remains to be seen.

9.4.9 Consent and Counterclaims

In the more recent arbitrations, the issue has arisen whether the investor's conduct that was harmful to the host state could be pleaded as counterclaims. The treaties are silent on this. But, there is a trend in recent awards which permit counterclaims on the ground that the broad nature of the investor's consent to arbitration must be taken as his consent to counterclaims.[44] Though this is not a settled point, the law would be expected to move towards this position.

[43] The OIC-Indonesia treaty contains specific wording which permits this. But, without such wording, the logic of the argument is unassailable.

[44] Antoine Goetz & Others and SA Affinage des Metaux v. Republic of Burundi, ICSID Case No. ARB/01/2 (21 June 2012).

9.5 Conclusion

This is a short survey of situations in which the construction of consent which forms the basis of investment arbitration has arisen. The fact that there has to be construction of such consent and there is no direct consent in the form of a definite expression by both parties of their consent is the root cause of the problems that have arisen in this area. Construction has to depend on arbitral tribunals and the methods of construction employed has been at the caprice of each tribunal. This has resulted in a clash of interests between those who have emphasised and broadened the scope of circumstances in which consent, particularly of the foreign investor can be found and the interests of other tribunals which have not been able to engage in such expansionary techniques as they feel constrained by the exorbitance of the views adopted by the first group of tribunals, conscious of the fact that reaction of states would be provoked by such exuberance. The clash has furthered the legitimacy crisis in investment arbitration. The response of the states has varied but the new ideas that are being opened will ensure that investment protection will not be the aim of investment treaties and consequently, the situations in which consent of the foreign investor could be implied will become heavily circumscribed in the future.

10 Applicable Law in International Investment Arbitration

Andrea K. Bjorklund and Lukas Vanhonnaeker

10.1 Introduction

The issue of applicable law is something that all investment tribunals must inevitably address. Yet it is one of the most misunderstood and misaddressed (or ignored) topics in the field. The basics of applicable law are relatively straightforward – the law applicable to the dispute is that which arbitrators use to come to a decision about whether or not there has been a breach of that law. Thus, whether they are adjudicating a contractual or treaty-based dispute, investment arbitrators must first *identify* the law applicable to the dispute and then *use* it to assess the liability of the defending party or parties. These statements are deceptively simple, since the selection of applicable law, its application, and its intersection with other laws, whether international or domestic, continue to be contentious and difficult questions.

In the choice of applicable law arbitrators are assisted by specific provisions in the applicable arbitration rules. The most important in the realm of investment arbitration is Article 42 of the ICSID Convention,[1] which directs the choice-of-law exercise, in much the same way that the choice-of-law rules of the forum do in the private international law context. The ICSID Convention recognizes party autonomy in the first instance, and then sets out the laws that are applicable in the absence of party choice. Other frequently used arbitration rules, such as the UNCITRAL Arbitration Rules, also give deference to party autonomy, but in the absence of party direction leave the question up to the arbitrators.[2]

[1] Convention on the Settlement of Investment Disputes Between States and Nationals of Other States, signed March 18, 1965, entered into force October 14, 1966 (ICSID Convention), Art. 42.

[2] UNCITRAL Arbitration Rules (2010), Art. 35: "The arbitral tribunal shall apply the rules of law designated by the parties as applicable to the substance of the dispute. Failing such designation by the parties, the arbitral tribunal shall apply the law which it determines to be appropriate."

Whether or not one has a choice-of-law directive such as Article 42 of the ICSID Convention, in individual cases difficult questions can arise that the rule does not itself answer. In the case of investment law, which is embedded in the public international law order, laws other than those chosen by the parties might very well have a role, sometimes in an incidental manner, and often as a matter of interpretive direction rather than as a rule of decision. Their influence, regardless of the precise manner in which they play a role, can alter the outcome of a case.

As if identifying and applying the proper applicable law were not complex enough for adjudicators, their decision is also subject to intense scrutiny once the award has been rendered. Applying the wrong law can have far-reaching consequences for the parties and for the work of the arbitral tribunal. First, applying the wrong law can lead to different – if not diametrically opposed – conclusions on almost every aspect of an investment case – jurisdiction, liability, quantum, and available interest. Second, the choice of the wrong applicable law (i.e., the law which is not dictated by the applicable choice-of-law rules) can expose the arbitral award to annulment under Article 52(1)(b) of the ICSID Convention or Article V(c) of the New York Convention.

This chapter starts by offering some general observations about applicable law in investment arbitration. It then outlines the approach to applicable law taken by the ICSID Convention. Finally it discusses the consequences ensuing from a tribunal's failure to apply the appropriate law.

10.2 General Observations about Applicable Law in Investment Arbitration

Investment arbitrations can be based on a treaty, on a contract, or can involve both. The defining feature of an investment treaty dispute is that public international law will be involved, at least insofar as interpretation and application of the treaty itself is concerned, but likely for other reasons as well. An investment contract, on the other hand, will more likely be governed by municipal law, though if the dispute is one arising under the ICSID Convention especially international law could also play a role.

International investment agreements (IIAs) and the applicable arbitration rules identify three main sources of substantive law relevant for the adjudication of investor-State dispute settlement cases: the applicable investment treaty itself (in a treaty case); the domestic law of the host State; and applicable international law. It is likely that all three sources of law will play some role in an investment treaty dispute regardless of the applicable law clause contained in the treaty or in the relevant arbitration rules. Most treaties that do contain applicable law clauses recognize these sources; even if they do not conflict-of-laws rules will tend to direct their application.

There is no consistent approach in treaties to the question of applicable law. Most treaties contain no directive as to applicable law.[3] If the treaty does not contain a directive about applicable law, the applicable arbitration rules will, though often in relatively rudimentary form.

In those treaties with applicable law clauses, it is quite common to find compound choice-of-law clauses which refer to multiple sources of law.[4] For example, the Energy Charter Treaty provides that a tribunal "shall decide the issues in dispute in accordance with this Treaty and applicable rules and principles of international law."[5] Some treaties explicitly refer to host State law as well as international law. For example, Article 13(5) of the Azerbaijan-Croatia BIT provides:

> Dispute[s] shall be resolved in accordance with law, applying the terms of this Agreement, the national legislation of the Contracting Party to the dispute, and principles of public international law.[6]

Party autonomy to choose the applicable law is accepted in both treaty and contract disputes.[7] The selection by the parties can be explicit or implicit.[8]

[3] Yas Banifatemi, "The Law Applicable in Investment Treaty Arbitration" in Katia Yannaca-Small (ed.), *Arbitration under International Investment Agreements: An Analysis of the Key Jurisdictional, Substantive & Procedural Issues* (Oxford: Oxford University Press, 2010), 191; Christopher F. Dugan, Noah Rubins, Don Wallace, Jr., & Borzu Sabahi, *Investor-State Arbitration* (Oxford: Oxford University Press, 2008), 202.

[4] For several examples, *see* Taida Begic, *Applicable Law in International Investment Disputes* (The Hague: Eleven International Publishing, 2005), 27–29.

[5] Energy Charter Treaty, concluded December 27, 1994, entered into force March 16, 1998, 2080 UNTS 95, Art. 26(6).

[6] Agreement between the Government of the Republic of Croatia and the Government of the Republic of Azerbaijan on the Promotion and Reciprocal Protection of Investments, October 2, 2007, entered into force May 30, 2008, Art. 13(5).

[7] Andrea K. Bjorklund, "Mandatory Rules of Law and Investment Treaty Arbitration" (2007) 18 *American Review of International Arbitration* 175.

[8] If it is implicit, the choice should be clear. Banifatemi (note 3) pp. 198–200; Begic (note 4) pp. 57–59.

In an investment treaty arbitration the treaty is the first place to seek party agreement on the applicable law. The classic formulation is that the State offers to arbitrate according to the terms contained in the treaty and the investor accepts that offer by commencing arbitration.[9] The treaty provisions thus represent the parties' choice as to the applicable law.[10] In the case of a concession contract, the parties are quite likely to have identified the applicable law in the contract itself.

Even if the parties have agreed to the applicable law, arbitral tribunals have a great deal of discretion to determine the law applicable to matters that are not governed directly by the parties' choice of law or that are not clearly encompassed by that choice. This discretion is often seen as desirable as it is difficult to foresee in advance the appropriate law applicable to all situations.[11] Aside from the law forming the basis for the claims brought before the tribunal, municipal law (most often the law of the host State) and other international law may be relevant insofar as they guide the interpretation of the treaty or fill *lacunae* in treaties. For example, there is no international law of property; to the extent that "shares" are an investment, domestic law defines what shares are and how they can be legally transferred.[12] If there are questions of attribution, the international rules on State responsibility contain principles relevant to determining whether challenged acts are attributable to the State.[13] Some investment treaties contain an "umbrella" clause, by which a State promises to honour any obligations it has undertaken with respect to the foreign investor or its investment. These obligations have been interpreted at times as permitting claims based on a concession contract or other undertaking that a State might have made toward an investor to be elevated to the level of treaty

[9] Jan Paulsson, "Arbitration Without Privity" (1995) 10 *ICSID Review – Foreign Investment Law Journal* 232, 232–234.

[10] Antoine Goetz et al. v. Burundi, ICSID Case No. ARB/95/3, Award, para. 94 (February 10, 1999); Banifatemi (note 3) pp. 194–195.

[11] For an attempt to distill principles relating to applicable law in different situations, *see* Zachary Douglas, *The International Law of Investment Claims* (Cambridge: Cambridge University Press, 2009), 39–133.

[12] *See generally* Monique Sasson, *Substantive Law in Investment Treaty Arbitration: The Unsettled Relationship between International and Municipal Law*, 2nd ed. (Alphen aan den Rijn: Wolters Kluwer, 2017).

[13] Draft Articles on Responsibility of States for Internationally Wrongful Acts, with Commentaries, (2001) Yearbook of the International Law Commission, Vol. II Part II, Arts. 4–11.

claims.[14] If a tribunal is deciding a dispute under an umbrella clause it would ordinarily then be applying international law because the tribunal's authority would derive from a breach of the investment treaty and not of the contract.[15]

Applicable law is argued most vociferously when it matters – when there is a potentially strong impact on the outcome of a dispute. When two potentially applicable laws would lead to the same result, parties more easily agree, either explicitly or implicitly, on which law to apply.

10.2.1 Applicable Law as the Rules of Decision

The foundation of any case are the rules of decision that will be used by a tribunal to determine the outcome of the dispute – the causes of action that will form the basis of the decision and any award of reparations. Other laws might have an effect on the outcome of the case, but the crux of the parties' arguments and of the tribunal's decision will rest on the rules of decision.

Many investment treaties limit investors' claims to arguments that a State has failed to abide by the substantive protections it promised in the treaty. Even if the treaty scope is broader than that and permits the submission to arbitration of, for example, "any dispute relating to an investment," allegations of violations of the treaty obligations typically form the bulk of the investor's claim against the host State.[16]

[14] Katia Yannaca-Small, "What about This 'Umbrella Clause'?" in Katia Yannaca-Small (ed.) *Arbitration Under International Investment Agreements: A Guide to the Key Issues* (Oxford: Oxford University Press, 2010), 479, 487–493.

[15] In *Vivendi v. Argentina*, the committee stated, "[W]hether there has been a breach of the BIT and whether there has been a breach of contract are different questions. Each of these claims will be determined by reference to its own proper or applicable law – in the case of the BIT, by international law; in the case of the Concession Contract, by the proper law of the contract, in other words, the law of Tucumán. For example, in the case of a claim based on a treaty, international law rules of attribution apply, with the result that the state of Argentina is internationally responsible for the acts of its provisional authorities. By contrast, the state of Argentina is not liable for the performance of contracts entered into by Tucumán, which possesses separate legal personality under its own law and is responsible for the performance of its own contracts." Compañia de Aguas del Aconquija S.A. and Vivendi Universal S.A. v. Argentine Republic, ICSID Case No. ARB/97/3, Decision on Annulment, para. 96 (July 3, 2002) [footnote omitted].

[16] *See, e.g.*, Giorgio Sacerdoti, "Arbitration of Investment Disputes" in Steven Charnovitz et al. (eds.) *Law in the Service of Human Dignity: Essays in Honour of Florentino Feliciano* (Cambridge: Cambridge University Press, 2005), 276, 288.

Cases in which investors allege breaches of a treaty provision require a tribunal to assess the respondent State's conduct against the treaty requirements. Has a State violated the fair and equitable treatment obligation? Has a State expropriated the investor's property, and if it has was the act lawful or unlawful? The treaty's provisions on fair and equitable treatment and on expropriation provide the rules of decision that will be employed by the tribunal as it attempts to answer those questions. Because some treaties differ with respect to their formulations of these obligations, parties must take care in arguing their case. The fair and equitable treatment provision, in particular, might have different content depending on the applicable treaty.[17]

Those rules of decision do not exist in isolation. Other laws might also contribute to, or even form an essential part of, a tribunal's decision, even if they are not the basis on which relief can be granted. For example, an investor might argue that it has property rights in the form of a license to mine for gold in a particular State. The status of that license under municipal law might well affect the outcome of the case – it could determine the extent to which the investor can claim a property interest which might then be expropriated, or whether the investor's legitimate expectations were ignored in a fair and equitable treatment case. The determination of the extent to which any right has vested in the investor will dictate the outcome of the dispute, but the tribunal will not grant relief directly on the basis of municipal law. These and similar issues can usefully be conceptualized as "incidental;" they are essential to determining the outcome of a dispute, but are not the basis for the principal cause of action.[18]

[17] Dugan et al. (note 3) pp. 207–209. For example, the United States and Canada have specified that their treaties protect only against violations of the international minimum standard of treatment and do not accord any free-standing "fair and equitable" treatment obligation to the investments of investors. Agreement between Canada and ––– for the Promotion and Protection of Investments, 2003 (published in 2004), Art. 5, available at http://italaw.com/documents/Canadian2004-FIPA-model-en.pdf; 2012 US Model Bilateral Investment Treaty, Art. 5 & Annex A, available at www.ustr.gov/sites/default/files/BIT%20text%20for%20ACIEP%20Meeting.pdf.

[18] Yuliya Chernykh, *Contract Interpretation in Investment Treaty Arbitration* (2021) (unpublished manuscript on file with the author); Douglas (note 11).

10.2.2 Otherwise Applicable Law – Interpretative Principles and Factual Determinations

The rules of decision employed by a tribunal are likely to be quite limited, yet many other laws will apply to greater or lesser degrees in the decision of a case. Though they do not form the basis for relief, they might apply in such a way that the outcome of the case is affected.[19]

The line between using law as a rule of decision and as an interpretive principle is often not clear-cut. International law, as well as municipal law, is almost certain to play a role in the outcome of any investment treaty case. Importantly, the customary international rules on treaty interpretation, codified in the Vienna Convention on the Law of Treaties, serve as a guide to interpreting the provisions of the applicable IIA.[20] Relevant international law can involve more than the Vienna Convention; general principles of international law and customary international law might also be relevant.[21] Topics that can affect investment treaty case outcomes include various issues such as attribution of conduct to a State, denial of justice, the minimum standard of treatment of aliens, remedies, circumstances precluding wrongfulness of State conduct, and so forth. Customary international law might also be used to elaborate on the meaning of a treaty provision or to fill *lacunae* in the treaty,[22] assuming the latter is not *lex specialis* intended to displace custom.[23]

[19] *See, e.g.*, Joost Pauwelyn, "The Role of Public International Law in the WTO: How Far Can We Go?" (2001) 95 *American Journal of International Law* 535, 560–561.

[20] Christoph H. Schreuer et al., *The ICSID Convention: A Commentary*, 2nd ed. (Cambridge: Cambridge University Press, 2009), 605; W. Michael Reisman and Mahnoush H. Arsanjani, "Applicable Law under the ICSID Convention: The Tortured History of the Interpretation of Article 42" in Meg Kinnear et al. (eds.) *Building International Investment Law: The First 50 Years of ICSID* (Alphen aan den Rijn: Kluwer Law International, 2015), 10.

[21] Banifatemi (note 3) pp. 204–205.

[22] For example, in *ADC v. Hungary*, the Tribunal concluded that Hungary had engaged in an unlawful expropriation of ADC's investment. The treaty set forth the standard of compensation for a lawful expropriation, but did not address the standard for an unlawful expropriation; to fill the gap, the Tribunal turned to customary international law and in particular to the principles announced in the *Chorzów Factory* case. ADC Affiliate Limited v. Hungary, ICSID Case No. ARB/03/16, Award of the Tribunal, paras. 483–494 (October 2, 2006).

[23] *See, e.g.*, AAPL v. Sri Lanka, ICSID Case No. ARB/87/3, Final Award, para. 54 (June 27, 1990) ("[T]he tribunal is convinced that, in the absence of a specific rule provided for in the Treaty itself as *lex specialis*, the general international law rules have to assume their role as *lex generalis*."); Amoco International Finance Corp. v. Iran, Partial Award, para. 112 (July 14, 1987), available in 27 ILM 1314 (1988) ("As lex specialis in the relations between the

One should not underestimate the potentially significant impact of these other relevant laws. Interpreting a State's obligation under a treaty provision by reference to another law might limit the liability of a State in a particular case. To offer a simple example, a State might be charged with violating the fair and equitable treatment provision of a treaty because it revoked the operating permit of a power plant. The State might offer in its defense the argument that it revoked the permit on the grounds that the investor had failed to comply with municipal environmental law. If that argument is accepted, the investor's claim might well fail. A State might argue that its actions were compelled by a different *international* law obligation; that claim, too, might succeed. These laws are treated more as a matter of fact than as applicable law, but their significance for the outcome of a case is unquestioned.

10.3 The Choice-of-Law Regime in the ICSID Convention

Given that a majority of investment treaty arbitrations are held under the auspices of the ICSID Convention, examining applicable law questions that arise under the Convention provides a strong basis to understand the types of issues that arise when applicable law questions are at issue in almost any investment arbitration.

The core of the ICSID's rules on the choice of the applicable law are located in the first paragraph of Article 42, pursuant to which:

> (1) The Tribunal shall decide a dispute in accordance with such rules of law as may be agreed by the parties. In the absence of such agreement, the Tribunal shall apply the law of the Contracting State party to the dispute (including its rules on the conflict of laws) and such rules of international law as may be applicable.

This provision establishes a two-step process which entails first the identification of the agreement of the parties on the applicable law and, in the absence of that agreement, a turn to the municipal law of the host State and to "such rules of international law as may be applicable."

two countries, the Treaty supersedes the lex generalis, namely customary international law. This does not mean, however, that the latter is irrelevant in the instant Case. On the contrary, the rules of customary law may be useful in order to fill in possible lacunae of the Treaty to ascertain the meaning of undefined terms in its text or, more generally, to aid interpretation and implementation of its provisions.").

This two-step process is, however, much more intricate than it appears to be on the surface.

10.3.1 The Sacrosanct Principle of Party Autonomy: Article 42(1), First Sentence

The principle of party autonomy is a golden thread running through the ICSID Convention,[24] including through Article 42: the parties are free to choose the law applicable to the substance of a claim in case of a dispute. The exercise of their right to choose the applicable law can arise from the desire to increase legal certainty, to ensure familiarity with the legal regime that will be applicable to a dispute, or to guarantee that the most (or least) protective legal regime will be applicable. Consistent with the critical importance of the principle of party autonomy, tribunals have generally[25] been inclined to determine the existence of an agreement of the parties on the applicable law in the presence of an indirect (by reference to an instrument containing a clause on applicable law) or implicit choice of law.[26]

Article 42 does not require that the agreement of the parties on applicable law be found in any particular type of instrument. Especially with the advent of investment treaty arbitration, the agreement of the parties to arbitrate is based in an international investment treaty. However, most investment treaties do not have a specific applicable law clause that

[24] ICSID, *History of the ICSID Convention: Documents Concerning the Origin and the Formulation of the Convention on the Settlement of Investment Disputes between States and Nationals of Other States* (ICSID, 1968) Vol. II, pp. 266–267, 330, 514, and 569–570.

[25] Some tribunals have, however, required a clear and unequivocal agreement of the parties on choice of law. *See, e.g.*, Compania del Desarrollo de Santa Elena, S.A. v. The Republic of Costa Rica, ICSID Case No. ARB/96/1, Final Award, paras. 60–68 (February 17, 2000).

[26] *See, e.g.*, Ceskoslovenska Obchodni Banka, A.S. v. The Slovak Republic, ICSID Case No. ARB/97/4, Award, para. 63 (December 29, 2004); ADC Affiliate Limited and ADC & ADMC Management Limited v. The Republic of Hungary, ICSID Case No. ARB/03/16, Award of the Tribunal, para. 290 (October 2, 2006); UAB E Energjia v. Republic of Latvia, ICSID Case No. ARB/12/33, Award, para. 792 (December 22, 2017): "In the Tribunal's view, acceptance of the offer to arbitrate in Article 7 of the BIT establishes an implicit agreement that the applicable law consists primarily of the standards of protection contained in the BIT, but that recourse may be had to general international law as well as to the domestic law of Latvia." *Cf.* LG&E Energy Corp., LG&E Capital Corp. and LG&E International Inc. v. Argentine Republic, ICSID Case No. ARB/02/1, Decision on Liability, para. 85 (October 3, 2006); *see also* Schreuer et al. (note 20) pp. 570–580.

explicitly sets out the parties' agreement on applicable law.[27] In the IIAs that do contain an applicable law clause, variations are apparent: while some treaties refer in a circular fashion to the law agreed upon by the parties;[28] others opt for the treaty itself and applicable international law;[29] or for the treaty, applicable international law, and host State law.[30]

Many investment agreements contain what might be viewed as indirect choice-of-law provisions. They specify that investors are permitted to submit claims for treaty breaches, thus implying the selection of the treaty itself as governing law.[31]

In contract-based disputes, applicable law is often provided in the contract or in the host State's laws on foreign investment.[32] The range of laws which can be chosen is vast and can include the law of a third State or the laws of the investor's home State[33] as well as the law of the contract.[34]

[27] Andrea K. Bjorklund, "Applicable Law in International Investment Disputes" in Chiara Giorgetti (ed.) *Litigating Investment Disputes* (Leiden: Brill, 2014), 261, 271; *see also* Andrea K. Bjorklund and Lukas Vanhonnaeker, "Article 42" in Julian Fouret et al. (eds.) *The ICSID Convention, Regulations and Rules: A Practical Commentary* (London: Edward Elgar, 2019).

[28] *See, e.g.*, Agreement on Encouragement and Reciprocal Protection of Investments between the Government of the People's Republic of China and the Government of the Kingdom of the Netherlands, signed November 26, 2001, entered into force August 1, 2004, Art. 10(4): "The ad hoc tribunal shall decide a dispute in accordance with such rules of law as may be agreed by the parties. In absence of such agreement the tribunal shall apply the law of the Contracting Party to the dispute (including its rules on the conflict of laws), the provisions of this Agreement and such rules of international law as may be applicable."

[29] *See, e.g.*, Energy Charter Treaty (note 5) Art. 26(6); North American Free Trade Agreement, concluded December 17, 1992, entered into force January 1, 1994, 32 ILM 289, 605 (1993), Art. 1131.

[30] *See, e.g.*, Azerbaijan-Croatia BIT (note 6) Art. 13(5): "Dispute [sic] shall be resolved in accordance with law, applying the terms of this Agreement, the national legislation of the Contracting Party to the dispute, and principles of public international law."

[31] The oft-found references in IIAs to "all investment disputes" or to "disputes arising from an investment" create some legal uncertainties as such broad terminology can involve a wider range of applicable laws.

[32] Bjorklund (note 27) p. 272: "states and state entities frequently enter into contracts with private entities involving investment. ... Those contracts frequently select international arbitration as the parties' chosen forum should any dispute arise, and often specify the governing law."

[33] *See, e.g.*, Southern Pacific Properties (Middle East) Limited v. Arab Republic of Egypt, ICSID Case No. ARB/84/3, Award on the Merits, para. 225 (May 10, 1992); CDC Group PLC v. Republic of the Seychelles, ICSID Case No. ARB/02/14, Award, para. 43 (December 17, 2003); World Duty Free Company Limited v. The Republic of Kenya, ICSID Case No. ARB/00/7, Award, paras. 158–159 (October 4, 2006).

[34] Opting for this last option is, however, riskier as a consequence of the prohibition in Art. 42 (2) of a *non liquet*. In particular, the tribunal could be compelled to resort to another law,

How do these variations intersect with Article 42 of the ICSID Convention, which was drafted primarily with a view to a tribunal's consideration of contractual disputes? There is some disagreement about where disputes brought under investment treaties fit into the scheme of Article 42. Some argue that they belong in Article 42(1) second sentence, both because of the explicit reference to international law in Article 42(1) second sentence,[35] and because an investment treaty dispute cannot be resolved exclusively by reference to international law, thus requiring the application of both domestic and international law, as foreseen by the second sentence of Article 42(1).[36]

We submit that this approach fails to take into account the fact that by submitting a dispute under an investment treaty, the disputing parties have made a choice of applicable law, which is in the first instance the treaty itself and any relevant international law principles. According to Michael Reisman and Mahnoush Arsanjani,

> a BIT, even if it does not contain an explicit provision on the applicable law, constitutes the *eo ipso* applicable law to claims for the breaches of the protections contained therein. Because the parties have agreed on the applicable law, it is the first sentence of Article 42(1) and not its second sentence that settles the question. A BIT, being a treaty, would have to be interpreted in accordance with international law. Any ambiguity in the provisions of the BIT would call for the application of the Vienna Convention on the Law of Treaties.[37]

The fact that the rules of decision in a dispute are those of international law does not preclude all application of municipal law, but any such resort to municipal law is part of the structure of the investment treaty itself. Thus, depending on the IIA, other laws might be applicable to different

whether domestic or international, for issues not contemplated and answered by the set of contractual rules chosen by the parties. *See* Schreuer et al. (note 20) pp. 562–563.

[35] *See, e.g.*, Ole Spiermann, "Applicable Law" in Peter Muchlinski et al. (eds.) *The Oxford Handbook of International Investment Law* (Oxford: Oxford University Press, 2008), at 107 *et seq.* and Asian Agricultural Products Ltd. (AAPL) v. Republic of Sri Lanka, ICSID Case No. ARB/87/3, Final Award, paras. 18–19 (June 27, 1990). Jan Asmus Bischoff makes a more complex argument distinguishing between those treaties that have a choice-of-law clause (which he believes fall under Art. 42(1), first sentence, and those without, which he would place under Art. 42(1), second sentence). Jan Asmus Bischoff, "Conflict of Laws and International Investment Arbitration" (2018) 7(1) *European International Arbitration Review*.

[36] Sasson (note 12) p. 69.

[37] Reisman and Arsanjani (note 20) p. 10.

parts of the dispute, including the laws of the host State if the IIA contains a complex choice-of-law clause.[38] We believe it is more accurate to regard the choice to bring a claim under the treaty as itself a choice of the applicable law.

Particularly when the case is based on a contract, the parties can decide on the scope of their choice of the applicable law.[39] They can decide to refer to only some rules of a system of law instead of selecting the entire system or to exclude specific laws of a domestic legal regime.[40] Similarly, parties can refer to the "whole law" of a legal system, which includes that system's choice-of-law rules, which would then be applied to ascertain the applicable law. They do not usually do so, however, and if they fail to specify whether the substantive law clause includes conflict-of-laws rules, the latter are usually excluded on the grounds that, if the parties chose an applicable law, it was arguably to avoid the uncertainties inherent in the application of any choice-of-law rules, including the doctrine of *renvoi.*

If a tribunal concludes that the parties have not agreed on the applicable law, it turns to the second sentence of of Article 42(1), which directs the application of the the law of the host State – including its conflict-of-laws rules – and such principles of international law as "may be applicable."

[38] For example, the applicable law clause at issue in *Achmea v. Slovak Republic* provided that: "The arbitral tribunal shall decide on the basis of the law, taking into account in particular though not exclusively: the law in force of the Contracting Party concerned; the provisions of this Agreement, and other relevant Agreements between the Contracting Parties; the provisions of special agreements relating to the investment; the general principles of international law." Achmea B.V. v. The Slovak Republic, PCA Case No. 2008–13, Final Award, para. 272 (December 7, 2012).

[39] *See* Bjorklund (note 27) pp. 268–272. The treaty itself might constrain such choices in treaty-based claims.

[40] *See, e.g.,* Autopista concesionada de Venezuela, C.A. v. Bolivarian Republic of Venezuela, ICSID Case No. ARB/00/5, Award, paras. 96–97 (September 23, 2003): "The Tribunal observes that the first sentence of Art. 42(1) refers to 'rules of law' rather than to systems of law. It is generally accepted that this wording allows the parties to agree on a partial choice of law, and in particular to select specific rules from a system of law. Accordingly, the Tribunal finds that clause 5 of the Agreement represent a valid choice of law agreement providing for the application of Decree Law 138 and Executive Decree Nr. 502. The Tribunal further notes that the reference to specific texts of Venezuelan law, i.e., Decree Law 138 and Executive Decree Nr. 502, does not necessarily amount to a general choice of Venezuelan law."

10.3.2 Host State Law

The ICSID Convention was drafted on the assumption that most disputes would be contract-based. In the absence of party agreement on choice of law, the drafters of the Convention ultimately chose the law of the host State as governing law. This selection accords with the law that would likely be chosen by default under most choice-of-law rules – the law of the place of performance of a contract.

The reference is to the "whole law" of the host State – in other words, to host State law, including its choice-of-law rules. This specification ensures that host State law will be applied to the dispute if that State's law would itself direct a decision-making body to another applicable law. Accordingly, a tribunal should consider the conflict-of-laws rules of the host State to see where they point the tribunal.

10.3.3 Such Rules of International Law tribunal "As May Be Applicable"

The second sentence of Article 42(1) is not limited to municipal law, but also directs the application of "such rules of international law as may be applicable" in the absence of party choice. The reference to international law is taken to refer to traditional sources of international law, such as are found in Article 38(1) of the ICJ Statute.[41] Accordingly, it is not a matter of controversy that ICSID tribunals look at treaties, customary international

[41] Statute of the International Court of Justice, concluded June 26, 1945, entered into force October 24, 1945, 59 Stat. 1031, TS 993, Art. 38(1): "The Court, whose function is to decide in accordance with international law such disputes as are submitted to it, shall apply: a. international conventions, whether general or particular, establishing rules expressly recognized by the contesting states; b. international custom, as evidence of a general practice accepted as law; c. the general principles of law recognized by civilized nations; d. subject to the provisions of Art. 59, judicial decisions and the teachings of the most highly qualified publicists of the various nations, as subsidiary means for the determination of rules of law." This is consistent with the reference made in the Report of the Executive Directors on the treaty's negotiation. International Bank for Reconstruction and Development, "Report of the Executive Directors on the Convention on the Settlement of Investment Disputes Between States and Nationals of Other States," March 18, 1965, para. 40: "The term 'international' law as used in this context should be understood in the sense given to it by Article 38(1) of the Statute of the International Court of Justice, allowance being made for the fact that Article 38 was designed to apply to inter-State disputes." *See also* ICSID, *History of the ICSID Convention* (note 24) p. 802.

law, general principles of law, judicial decisions, and writings when they consider international law under Article 42(1).[42]

The controversy, if it comes, is in determining which rules of international law are applicable. The reference to "such rules of international law as may be applicable" necessarily means that not *all* rules of international law can be applied, but only those that are relevant.

While this provision clearly directs a discretionary selection of applicable international law, it does not direct how that discretion should be exercised or how the applicable international law rules relate to host State law. Some adjudicators have evaded the difficult question of defining the precise relationship between the laws of the host State and international law by looking at both regimes to strengthen their conclusions through mutually supportive findings. Incidentally this approach is not dissimilar to that undertaken by municipal law judges when they are faced with competing applicable laws. Other arbitrators and scholars have addressed this difficult question and reached different conclusions.

Tribunals – and scholarly commentary on tribunal decisions – have identified two primary approaches with respect to the meaning of Article 42(1), second sentence. One approach is to interpret it as limiting international law to a corrective or complementary role. The second position is that the decision as to which law to apply on the basis of Article 42(1), second sentence, is altogether discretionary. There are some variations within these schools of thought, but these are the primary categories.

The corrective or complementary approach is often justified by reference to the *travaux préparatoires* of the ICSID Convention. Although the drafters rejected the idea of textually limiting the role played by international law to a corrective or supplemental function,[43] it appears that this is precisely the role that the drafters intended international law to play.[44] This reading of Article 42(1) is consistent with the "vertical" nature of the relationship between domestic and international law.[45] The international nature of investment cases and the choice of ICSID dispute settlement has consistently been viewed as suggesting that the

[42] Schreuer et al. (note 20) pp. 604–612.
[43] ICSID, *History of the ICSID Convention* (note 24) pp. 802–804.
[44] *Id.*, pp. 570–571.
[45] Spiermann (note 35) pp. 98–99 and 103 *et seq.*

parties expect international law to play some role in the dispute should domestic law prove to be inadequate.[46]

Restricting the role of international law in this manner has the potential effect of eliminating the influence of international law in a given dispute.[47] Moreover, there are different approaches as to what type of inconsistency should trigger international law's corrective function. For instance, Michael Reisman argues that "the test ... is not inconsistency, but whether applying the Contracting State's law would constitute a violation of something fundamental to international law."[48] This view suggests that international law would only exceptionally come into play.

The other primary approach to the interpretation of Article 42(1), second sentence, is that it confers broad discretion upon tribunals to ascertain which law is applicable. Thus, arbitrators can adopt the rules of law, domestic or international, that they regard as appropriate. This approach heavily relies on the use of the word *and* in Article 42(1). It is explained clearly by Emmanuel Gaillard and Yas Banifatemi:

> It is our contention that, under Article 42(1), second sentence, an ICSID tribunal may also apply international law as a body of substantive rules in order to resolve the dispute or a particular issue. The fact that those rules would apply as opposed to the rules of the law of the host State does not mean that the latter, when they simply differ from the former, are set aside, but that the rules of

[46] For example, Art. 27 of the ICSID Convention provides that: "(1) No Contracting State shall give diplomatic protection, or bring an international claim, in respect of a dispute which one of its nationals and another Contracting State shall have consented to submit or shall have submitted to arbitration under this Convention, unless such other Contracting State shall have failed to abide by and comply with the award rendered in such dispute. (2) Diplomatic protection, for the purposes of paragraph (1), shall not include informal diplomatic exchanges for the sole purpose of facilitating a settlement of the dispute."

[47] Indeed, as observed by Monique Sasson, "to confine international law's applicability to *lacunae* in or inconsistencies with municipal law ... is to virtually eliminate an international law role, since *lacunae* in municipal law are very few, and inconsistencies are also infrequent." Sasson (note 12) p. 67. *See also* Emmanuel Gaillard and Yas Banifatemi, "The Meaning of 'and' in Article 42(1), Second Sentence, of the Washington Convention: The Role of International Law in the ICSID Choice of Law Process" (2003) 18(2) *ICSID Review – Foreign Investment Law Journal* 375, 394: "The characteristic feature of a legal order is the framework it provides for general and particular norms. A legal system may not address a particular issue directly, but this by no means implies that it provides no response or legal framework for that issue."

[48] W. Michael Reisman, "The Regime for Lacunae in the ICSID Choice of Law Provision and the Question of Its Threshold" (2000) 15(2) *ICSID Review – Foreign Investment Law Journal* 362, 375. For a critique of Michael Reisman's approach, *see* Sasson (note 12) pp. 68–70.

international law constitute, in the arbitrators' determination, the proper law for the issue under consideration.[49]

Article 42 and the rules on choice of law provided therein are limited to the substance of the claim. By contrast, the procedural aspects of arbitration proceedings are provided in procedural rules[50] and other aspects of arbitration proceedings are regulated – explicitly or implicitly – by the ICSID Convention or by specific rules agreed upon by the parties in their agreement to arbitrate. With respect to procedural aspects, in case of *lacunae*, Article 44 of the ICSID Convention will be applicable. It provides that, instead of turning to the applicable law chosen pursuant to Article 42 to fill any procedural gaps, it is for the tribunal to decide the question.[51]

10.4 The Importance of Choosing the Correct Applicable Law

The question of applicable law in investment arbitration is of critical importance for two primary reasons. First, the goal of the tribunal in any given case should be to come to the best decision possible – to the right decision insofar as that can be ascertained, and to do so within the scope of that tribunal's authority. Second, and from a more utilitarian perspective, applying the wrong law can result in annulment of the award.

10.4.1 Correct Outcomes within the Scope of Tribunal Authority

Although different domestic laws or domestic laws and international standards can align, thus generating no major difference in outcome regardless of which law is applied, legal regimes often diverge. Indeed, within the limits imposed by binding norms of international law, it is within States' sovereign regulatory power to enact legislation tailored to their specific needs. Discrepancies between international norms and domestic rules or, for example, between the laws of an investor's wealthy home State and those of the poorer host State which pursue different

[49] Gaillard and Banifatemi (note 47) p. 399 [footnotes omitted].

[50] ICSID, *History of the ICSID Convention* (note 24) at 418 *et seq.*

[51] *See* Liberian Eastern Timber Corporation v. Republic of Liberia, ICSID Case No. ARB/83/2, Award, March 31, 1986, 2 ICSID Reports 343, 357–358.

economic and social policies are not uncommon. In navigating the plethora of potentially applicable laws in an investment dispute, adjudicators must thus be cautious as the application of a given law can drastically affect conclusions as to liability.

For instance, when both international law and domestic law are potentially applicable, as is generally the case in investment disputes, choosing one or the other can be critical because the State measure at the centre of a given dispute can amount to a violation of international law norms while being consistent with domestic law. In such an instance, "if domestic law applies there is no liability; if international law applies there might be."[52] The same is true in the presence of diverging international laws or of different domestic laws.

Furthermore, erring in identifying the applicable law can also result in inconsistent outcomes even where both potentially applicable laws treat the disputed measure as unlawful. For instance, different laws might impose different rates of interest, thus affecting the amount of recovery.

The possibility that investment tribunals might apply EU law was one of the main grounds for the Court of Justice of the European Union's (CJEU) decision in the *Achmea* case to determine that arbitration under the investment treaty between The Netherlands and the Slovak Republic threatened the autonomy of the EU legal order and the CJEU's exclusive monopoly over the application of EU law.[53] For the European Commission and the EU member States, therefore, it is essential that treaties do not empower investment treaty tribunals to apply EU law, but instead limit their authority to the application of international law. The Comprehensive Economic and Trade Agreement Between Canada and the European Union attempts to do just that, and the CJEU has endorsed its approach.[54]

10.4.2 Applying the Proper Law So as to Withstand Annulment or Vacatur

The question of applicable law is also of critical importance because applying the wrong law ultimately makes the award vulnerable to

[52] Bjorklund (note 27) p. 262.

[53] Slowakische Republic (Slovak Republic) v. Achmea BV, Case C-284/16, ECLI:EU:C:2018:158 (March 6, 2018).

[54] Case No. 1/17, ECLI:EU:C:2019:341 (April 30, 2019).

annulment. In particular, applying the wrong law has been regarded an excess of power under Article 52(1)(b) of the ICSID Convention. Although Article 52 does not expressly refer to the application of the wrong law, this potential ground for annulment was contemplated by the negotiators of the ICSID Convention[55] and has been confirmed by subsequent arbitral case law. Case law on this question generally distinguishes between a mistake in the application of the applicable lawand the application of the wrong law.[56] Only the latter case would amount to a ground for annulment of an ICSID award whereas a mistake in the application of the applicable law does not necessarily do so.

10.5 Conclusion

The choice-of-law provisions in investment treaties and in applicable investment rules give broad authority to tribunals to choose applicable law. In both treaty- and contract-based investment arbitrations the parties' choice of applicable law will be honoured. In a treaty arbitration the applicable law will be the treaty itself (i.e., international law), whereas in a contract-based arbitration it will be the law applicable to the contract, which is very often host State law, perhaps supplemented by international law. Despite this distinction, international law and municipal law are both likely to play some role in every case.

[55] ICSID, *History of the ICSID Convention* (note 24) p. 517. Mr. Broches observed that "the draft Convention did not provide for an appeal against the award and in his opinion a mistake in the application of the law would not be a valid ground for annulment of the award. A mistake of law as well as a mistake of fact constituted an inherent risk in judicial or arbitral decision for which appeal was not provided" (*id.*, at 518). It was later confirmed by Mr. Broches that "failure to apply the right law would constitute an excess of power if the parties had instructed the Tribunal to apply a particular law" (*id.*, at 851).

[56] To this day, the required magnitude for an error in the application of the correct law to amount to the non-application of the proper law remains to be defined. *See, e.g.*, Amco Asia Corporation, Pan American Development Limited and P.T. Amco Indonesia (Amco) v. Republic of Indonesia, ICSID Case No. ARB/81/1 (Resubmitted Case) Decision on Annulment, paras. 7.18–7.29 (December 17, 1992); Wena Hotels LTD v. Arab Republic of Egypt, ICSID Case No. ARB/98/4, Decision on Annulment, paras. 21–55 (January 28, 2002); Daimler Financial Services A.G. v. Argentine Republic, ICSID Case No. ARB/05/1, Decision on Annulment, para. 191 (January 7, 2015); SAUR International S.A. v. Argentine Republic, ICSID Case No. ARB/04/4, Decision on Annulment, paras. 175–177 (December 19, 2016); Venoklim Holding B.V. v. Bolivarian Republic of Venezuela, ICSID Case No. ARB/12/22, Decision on Annulment, para. 204 (February 2, 2018).

To ensure clarity in the application of law and to give guidance to parties, whether they be States or private entities, as to which law or laws govern their behavior, tribunals should clearly set out their approach to applicable law. First one needs to distinguish between the different roles played by various applicable laws. The rule of decision is the law against which a State's conduct is measured and upon whose violation a remedy is given. Other laws might well affect that decision and thus be incidentally applied, but will not themselves form the basis for relief. The second is to recognize that different laws may well apply to different aspects of any particular case. Thus carefully delineating issues and the law applicable to each is essential for a clear and appropriate resolution of a dispute. The third is to pay special attention to the interaction between municipal and international law, ensuring that municipal law applies in its appropriate sphere but that international law performs its protective role where necessary.

11 The Historical Contribution of the World Bank

Olufemi Elias and Siobhán McInerney-Lankford*

11.1 Introduction

The International Bank for Reconstruction and Development ("IBRD" or "World Bank") was established by the United Nations Monetary and Financial Conference held at Bretton Woods in 1944.[1] It was tasked with facilitating the investment of capital in economies destroyed or disrupted by World War II and channeling capital to countries in need of reconstruction and development.

The World Bank's role as a financier is often thought to be its main function.[2] In fact, its primary role was originally conceived as one of facilitator and promoter of private foreign investment, under which the Bank has considerably expanded its activities,[3] turning over time into an economic policy adviser and institution-builder.[4] The Bank's lending activities had originally been intended only to supplement private investment when a loan could not otherwise be obtained on reasonable terms from other sources. According to Ibrahim Shihata, three factors supported by the Bank

* The views expressed in this chapter are those of the author and do not purport to reflect the views of the United Nations or the World Bank. The authors are grateful to Chloe Faucourt, Manuela Corredor Vasquez, Christian Jimenez Tomas and Wendy Melis for invaluable research contributions. Responsibility for any errors remains with the authors.

[1] United Nations Monetary and Financial Conference: Bretton Woods, Final Act and Related Documents (22 July 1944), 11–27 (US Government Printing Office 1944).

[2] *See* I. F. I. Shihata, 'The Settlement of Disputes Regarding Foreign Investments: The Role of the World Bank, with Particular Reference to ICSID and MIGA' (1986) 1 *American University Journal of International Law and Policy* 97.

[3] *See* I. F. I. Shihata, 'The Dynamic Evolution of International Organizations: The Case of the World Bank' (2000) 2 *J Hist Int'l L* 230, 230–231; M. Gavin and D. Rodrik, 'The World Bank in Historical Perspective' (1995) 85 *AEA Papers and Proceedings* 329.

[4] For an overview of the Bank's historical evolution, *see* Gavin and Rodrik (n 4), 329–331. *See also* I. F. I. Shihata, 'Avoidance and Settlement of Disputes – The World Bank's Approach and Experience' (1999) 1 *Int'l LF D Int'l* 90, 93–94; IBRD, *A Guide to the World Bank* (2nd ed., World Bank, 2007), 12–13, http://ida.worldbank.org/about/history.

enhance the foreign direct investment (FDI)[5] climate: (1) the institutional framework, including the political stability of the country, its institutions, its policies (particularly economic) and administrative procedures for initiating and operating investments in the country; (2) infrastructural factors – the availability and efficiency of physical facilities and human resources and (3) legal factors, both in terms of the substantive rules governing foreign investment and the procedures governing the settlement of disputes.[6]

In the 1960s, the Bank turned its focus to the role of the private sector in economic development policies.[7] It actively sponsored the Convention on the Settlement of Investment Disputes between States and Nationals of Other States (ICSID Convention)[8] establishing the International Centre for Settlement of Investment Disputes (ICSID or the Centre) under its auspices. The Centre began operating at the end of the decade. This episode marked the inception of modern investor-State arbitration.

ICSID, and the institutional history that preceded it, will be the focus of this chapter. However, the Centre is but one piece of the institutional architecture sponsored by the Bank to promote private foreign investment. The remaining institutions, the International Finance Corporation (IFC)[9] and the Multilateral Investment Guarantee Agency (MIGA), were similarly conceived by the Bank to promote a healthier investment climate.[10] As Ibrahim Shihata wrote in 1983,

[5] FDI can be defined as 'a category of cross-border investment associated with a resident in one economy having control or a significant degree of influence on the management of an enterprise that is resident in another economy'. *See* https://datahelpdesk.worldbank.org/knowledgebase/articles/114954-what-is-the-difference-between-foreign-direct-inve.

[6] I. F. I. Shihata, 'Factors Influencing the Flow of Foreign Investment and the Relevance of a Multilateral Investment Guarantee Scheme', (1987) 21 *Int'l Lawyer* 671.

[7] Gavin and Rodrik (n 4), 332.

[8] Convention on the Settlement of Investment Disputes between States and Nationals of Other States (adopted 18 March 1965, entered into force 14 October 1966) 575 UNTS 159 (ICSID Convention).

[9] Articles of Agreement of the International Finance Corporation (adopted 25 May 1955, entered into force 20 July 1956) 264 UNTS 117 (IFC). The IFC lends to private investors in developing member countries without governmental guarantees.

[10] Convention Establishing the Multilateral Investment Guarantee Agency (adopted 11 October 1985, entered into force 12 April 1988) 1508 UNTS 99 (MIGA). MIGA provides investors with insurance against non-commercial risks in developing countries. While the IFC, ICSID and MIGA are affiliate organisations of the World Bank, each organisation has its own constituent treaty, membership, assets, and legal personality. Altogether they form the World Bank Group.

in fact, ICSID has been created and attempts to operate as a means for reaching a much greater objective – an objective which explains the close link it maintains with the World Bank and the great number of States which have become members of it. This objective could be broadly stated as the improvement of the investment climate at large and in developing countries in particular. The establishment of ICSID's facilities has been envisaged as 'a major step toward promoting an atmosphere of mutual confidence' between investors and States.[11]

In this way, ICSID would serve the same general purposes of the World Bank Group in securing a stable and increasing flow of resources to developing countries under reasonable conditions. It should therefore be seen as an instrument of international public policy and not just a specialised mechanism of conflict resolution.[12]

Thus, the Bank's assumption[13] was that increased FDI flows would lead to economic development. It explains how the international flow of private capital to developing countries fits squarely within the Bank's mandate.[14] Discussing the various benefits of foreign investment, Ibrahim Shihata opined that 'in spite of the ideological differences over the real benefits of foreign investment, especially direct foreign investment, experience has shown that such investment, operating under appropriate safeguards, can play an important role in accelerating economic growth and development'.[15]

Indeed, in pre-war years, FDI had been more readily associated with imperialism than development assistance.[16] Furthermore, 'the experience of the World Bank has shown that many of the major obstacles to international private investments lie not in the lack of profitable opportunities in the underdeveloped countries, but rather in a lack of mutual confidence between the host government and the foreign

[11] I. F. I. Shihata, ICSID – Overview and Prospects, 18 November 1983.

[12] *Ibid.*

[13] This assumption has since been challenged. *See* A. Kaushal, 'Revisiting History: How the Past Matters for the Present Backlash against the Foreign Investment Regime' (2009) 50 *Harv. Int'l L.J.* 491.

[14] C. Vuylsteke, 'Foreign Investment Protection and ICSID Arbitration' (1974) 4 *Georgia Journal of International and Comparative Law* 343.

[15] Shihata (n 7), 40.

[16] *See* T. St John, *The Rise of Investor-State Arbitration: Politics, Law, and Unintended Consequences* (Oxford: Oxford University Press, 2019), 61–62; *see also generally* K. J. Vandevelde, 'A Brief History of International Investment Agreements' (2005) 12 *U.C. Davis J. Int'l L. & Pol'y* 157.

national'.[17] The shift in perception started in the post-war era, as is evident in the IBRD Articles of Agreement,[18] with the foreign private investor, 'no longer inevitably suspect as the cynical agent of colonial power bent on quick and wasteful exploitation of the natural resources of a subject people' became 'a source of much-needed capital, a purveyor of technical knowledge and skills and even as the essential catalyst needed to assure the growth of a developing economy'.[19]

Interest for arbitration and investment-related disputes was also growing. The International Law Association produced Draft Statutes of the Arbitral Tribunal for Foreign Investment and the Foreign Investment Court in 1948.[20] The work initiated by the International Chamber of Commerce (ICC) in the inter-war period resulted in the adoption of the United Nations Convention on the Recognition and Enforcement of Foreign Arbitral Awards in 1958.[21] The Bank saw an existing gap in international law: there was no forum which functioned effectively to offer suitable means of settling investment disputes directly between a private party and a governmental party.

Therefore, 'ICSID was established in response to the perceived unavailability of adequate machinery for international conciliation and arbitration. This deficiency often frustrated attempts to agree on an appropriate mode for the settlement of investment disputes between sovereign governments and private foreign investors'.[22] As described later in this chapter, the Bank would ultimately take the lead through the creation of an arbitration centre dedicated to the resolution of investor-State disputes.

[17] M. M. Moore, 'International Arbitration between States and Foreign Investors – The World Bank Convention' (1966) 18 *Stan. L. Rev.* 1359.

[18] Articles of Agreement of the International Bank for Reconstruction and Development (adopted 22 July 1944, entered into force 27 December 1945) 2 UNTS 134 (IBRD Articles).

[19] C. W. Pinto, 'Settlement of Investment Disputes: The World Bank's Convention' (1967) 13 *Howard L.J.* 337, 337.

[20] Draft Statutes of the Arbitral Tribunal for Foreign Investment and the Foreign Investments Court, republished in UNCTAD, International investment instruments: A Compendium, Vol. III 259.

[21] United Nations Convention on the Recognition and Enforcement of Foreign Arbitral Awards (adopted 10 June 1958, entered into force 7 June 1969) 330 UNTS 3.

[22] J. Cherian, 'Foreign Investment Arbitration: The Role of the International Center for Settlement of Investment Disputes' 1983 *Third World Legal Studies* 172, 174.

11.2 The World Bank's Early Involvement in the Settlement of Disputes: Setting the Stage for Investor-State Arbitration

The 1950s and the 1960 saw the World Bank and its officials take part in mediation and conciliation efforts to settle disputes arising between Member States and foreign investors. These activities could appear unusual given the Bank's mandate. However, the Bank's officials saw it as a natural corollary to the Bank's purposes established in its Articles of Agreement – promoting private investment and the absence of any international apparatus competent to address such issues.[23] This early practice paved the way for the establishment of ICSID.

11.2.1 The Bank, the President and His Good Offices

Under Article V of the IBRD Articles of Agreement, the management of the Bank is entrusted to the Board of Governors, the Executive Directors and the President. The President is the chief of the operating staff of the Bank and 'shall conduct, under the direction of the Executive Directors, the ordinary business of the Bank'.[24] Moreover, the Articles underscore the international character of the President's role,[25] proscribe the Bank's interference in the political affairs of a member, and require the Bank to base its decisions on economic considerations rather than political ones.[26] In sum, the Bank's Articles of Agreement aim to insulate its decisions and operations as far as possible from the politicisation that often characterises the work of governmental and inter-governmental agencies.

A number of commentators have opined that the credibility and success of the Bank's brokering of the ICSID convention were attributable its non-political mandate. This mandate[27] is seen by some as a characteristic of a

[23] A. Broches, 'Settlement of Disputes between Governments and Private Parties' (28 August 1961), reprinted in History of the ICSID Convention, vol. 2 (ICSID 1968), 1–3. *See also* A. Broches, 'Awards Rendered Pursuant to the ICSID Convention: Binding Force, Finality, Recognition, Enforcement, Execution' (1987) 2 *ICSID Review FILJ* 287.

[24] IBRD Articles, art V(5)(b).

[25] IBRD Articles, art V(5)(c).

[26] IBRD Articles, arts III(5) and IV(10).

[27] Note that the Bank's mandate is non-political as opposed to apolitical. As Cissé clarifies, 'the word "apolitical "is defined as "unconcerned with or detached from politics"; the word *nonpolitical* is defined as "not involved in politics"'. H. Cissé, "Should the Political

functional approach to international organisations, which is reflected in the technical and focused mandate of a number of international organisations created after World War II.[28] Under such a functionalist approach, the Bank is an independent international institution having as its fundamental objective economic development, with development itself conceived of primarily as an economic endeavour concerned with increasing gross domestic product and productivity of economies, all of which could be achieved through technical and non-political solutions.

The exercise of 'good offices' by the World Bank President emerges against the backdrop of these provisions of the Articles.[29] It is also anchored in the functionalist approach historically adopted by the Bank's legal department since a review of the Articles of Agreement reveals that the President's good offices would be based on implied rather than explicit powers.[30] As the then General Counsel asserted, 'the Bank's powers are not limited to those that are granted in express terms. The fact that an operation or transaction is not expressly authorised or contemplated by a specific provision of the Articles, does not mean that the Bank has no power to undertake it. Whether it has or does not have a particular power must be determined in the light of the Bank's purposes, by which all the Bank's decisions must be guided'.[31]

Eugene Robert Black, the thirteenth President of the World Bank, whose tenure lasted from 1949 to 1962,[32] made the most substantial contribution

Prohibition Be Revisited?" in H. Cissé, D. Bradlow and B. Kingsbury (eds.), *International Financial Institutions and Global Legal Governance, vol. 3 of the World Bank Legal Review* (2012), 60.

[28] *Ibid.*, 60, citing P. Sands and P. Klein, *Bowetts Law of International Institutions*, 6th ed. (Sweet & Maxwell 2009), 76.

[29] Shihata (n 5), 95; Paul Szasz, 'Arbitration under the Auspices of the World Bank' (1969) 3 *International Lawyer* (ABA) 312.

[30] This stands in contrast to the exercise of good offices by the UN Secretary-General, which are provided for in the UN Charter under Article 99, under which the Secretary-General may 'bring to the attention of the Security Council any matter that in his opinion may threaten international peace and security'. The term *good offices* is, however, not defined.

[31] A. Broches, 'The Convention on the Settlement of Investment Disputes between States and Nationals of Other States' (1972) 136 *Recueil des Cours de l'Académie de Droit International*, 336.

[32] Black's contribution to the Bank's reputation and success was such that the Bank came to be known as 'Black's Bank'. *See* www.worldbank.org/en/about/archives/history/past-presidents/eugene-robert-black.

to the establishment of the Bank's reputation within the investment community. He took a personal interest in the resolution of investment disputes. One of the first examples of his exercise of 'good offices' emerged in the context of the Anglo-Iranian Oil Company dispute in 1951. The dispute arose from the nationalisation of the oil industry and the termination by Iran of the concession given to a British-owned company. Following protracted company-State and State-State negotiations, the Bank was asked to mediate the dispute. This attempt, however, was not successful.[33] The dispute came to an end in 1954, after the Iranian government was overthrown in the 1953 coup.[34]

Black, who had a certain 'talent for dealing with people' and a 'knack for bargaining and negotiating',[35] also intervened in the resolution of such disputes in a personal capacity.[36] Such was the case in the dispute opposing Japan and French holders of bonds issued in 1912 by the City of Tokyo for the financing of the expansion of the city's tramway and lighting. In 1958, following conflicting court rulings in France and in Japan, Black was formally asked by the parties to act as a conciliator in order to 'draft a concrete and workable plan for settling in a fair and feasible manner the controversy between the parties'.[37] Two years later, Black delivered a plan that provided for the compensation of loss for the bondholders, and the dispute was resolved soon after.[38] After his tenure ended, Black personally acted as a conciliator in 1965 in the dispute between Tunisia and foreign investors over the nationalisation of electric power plants, and in 1968 in the amicable settlement of a dispute arising from nationalisation of foreign mining interests by the Democratic Republic of Congo.[39]

[33] *See* St John (n 17), 65.

[34] *See* A. R. Parra, *The History of ICSID* (Oxford: Oxford University Press, 2017), 21; St John (n 17), 65.

[35] *See* Parra (n 35), 21 and www.worldbank.org/en/about/archives/history/past-presidents/eugene-robert-black.

[36] *See* A. R. Parra, 'Black's Bank' and the Settlement of Investment Disputes' in D. D. Caron, S. W. Schill, A. C. Smutny, and E. E. Triantafilou (eds.), *Practising Virtue: Inside International Arbitration* (Oxford: Oxford University Press, 2015), 152.

[37] *Ibid*., at 153.

[38] *City of Tokyo 5 Per Cent Loan of 1912 – Plan for Resumption of Payment of Principal and Interest on the French Tranche of the Loan*, 1 April 1960, 29 ILR 11. *See* P. F. Sutherland, 'The World Bank Convention on the Settlement of Investment Disputes' (1979) 28 *International and Comparative Law Quarterly* 374, 374; Shihata (n 5), 94.

[39] Shihata (n 5), 94; *see also* Shihata (n 3), 99.

But perhaps one of the greatest successes of the Bank was the settlement of the dispute regarding the compensation of French and British shareholders after the nationalisation of the Suez Canal Company by Egypt in 1956.[40] Here the Bank indirectly compelled the Egyptian government to seek an amicable settlement. Indeed, the Bank was formally requested to mediate the compensation issue only after it had indicated to Egypt that the Bank would not be willing to act as a lender for the country until the dispute had been resolved in an acceptable manner.[41] The Bank 'took a dive into the Suez Canal',[42] and a settlement was reached after Black – who had a close relationship with the Egyptian President Gamal Abdel Nasser[43] – had personally intervened.[44]

In most cases the Bank's member countries sought the Bank's assistance and exercise of the President's 'good offices'.[45] In one instance however, Black directly initiated the Bank's intervention. He approached leaders of India and Pakistan to suggest that the Bank provide technical assistance to resolve a long-standing dispute over the use of water resources in the Indus Basin. Negotiations were conducted under the Bank's supervision, culminating in the signature of the Indus Waters Treaty on 19 September 1960,[46] which Black considered to be his greatest achievement.[47]

Black's commitment to assisting member countries in settling claims arising from financial defaults or nationalisation of foreign assets earned him an international reputation as a 'mediator of wise judgement and absolute integrity', and a 'technocrat standing above the political fray'.[48] The World Bank became known as an impartial and politically neutral mediator and conciliator, equipped with the necessary technical expertise

[40] *See* Parra (n 35), 21; Shihata (n 5), 94.

[41] World Bank Oral History Program, Interview with William Iliff, Vice-President to the World Bank (16 August 1961), 34.

[42] *Ibid.*, at 35; *see also* Parra (n 37), 154–155.

[43] Interview with William Iliff (n 42), 35.

[44] Parra (n 35), 22.

[45] R. W. Edwards, 'The Role of the General Counsel of an International Financial Institution' (2008) XVII:2 *Kansas Journal of Law & Public Policy* 258.

[46] The Indus Waters Treaty 1960 between the Government of India, the Government of Pakistan and the International Bank for Reconstruction and Development (adopted 19 September 1960, entered into force 12 January 1961) 419 UNTS 125.

[47] Shihata (n 5), 95. *See also* www.worldbank.org/en/about/archives/history/past-presidents/eugene-robert-black.

[48] Parra (n 35), 21, quoting D. Kapur, J. P. Lewis and R. C. Webb, *The World Bank: Its First Half Century* (Washington, DC: Brookings Institution Press, 1997), 8.

to resolve complex financial disputes.[49] The intervention of the Bank also appeared to facilitate an efficient and cost-effective resolution of disputes. However, States primarily turned to the Bank in the absence of other adequate alternative to settle investor-States disputes.[50] Despite the successes encountered by the Bank, limitations quickly became evident. Black himself stated the issue:

> You just can't go in and, say, make one side very happy. The other man wouldn't take it. We don't arbitrate, we haven't been asked to arbitrate, just to offer our good offices, services, mediation, but not a compulsory settlement. We haven't been asked to arbitrate. We may be, but we haven't yet.[51]

Neither Black, acting personally, nor the World Bank, acting as a financial institution, attempted to act as arbitrators. Their interventions were limited to mediation and conciliation,[52] two modes of settlement that were considered more appropriate and within the competence of the Bank.[53] While the Bank 'had long realized that its position as a financial intermediary between capital markets and its own borrowers gives it an institutional interest in promoting the avoidance and settlement of investment disputes',[54] it was not equipped to deal with international incidents between foreign investors and host States which had

[49] *See* www.worldbank.org/en/about/archives/history/past-presidents/eugene-robert-black.

[50] Shihata (n 3), 100–101. *See also* Interview with William Iliff (n 42), 43–45: 'The Bank has really been quite concerned about the question of the lack of machinery for resolving disputes between governments and private interests, and we have been called in on several – for example, Suez for one. . . . Now we get into this thing I think as much for this reason as any other, that there isn't any appropriate machinery today, either in the field of conciliation or in the field of arbitration that can settle these disputes'.

[51] World Bank Oral History Program, Interview with Eugene R Black, President of the World Bank (6 August 1961) 51.

[52] Aron Broches, General Counsel of the Bank, made the following distinction between conciliation and arbitration: 'Conciliation is used in the proposals in the sense of any proceeding or method for the adjustment of a dispute, aimed at bringing the parties to an agreed solution with the assistance of one or more persons ('conciliators') empowered to make recommendations. Arbitration is used in the sense of a proceeding contemplating the final decision of a dispute between two or more parties by judges of their own choice or designated by an agreed method'. *See* Note by A. Broches to the Executive Directors on the Settlement of Investment Disputes (19 January 1962) 2, reprinted in *History of the ICSID Convention*, vol. 2 (ICSID 1968) 6.

[53] Parra (n 35), 22.

[54] Shihata (n 5), 96.

multiplied in the late 1950s and the early 1960s,[55] and were becoming major deterrents for FDI.[56]

Black and the World Bank realised that there was a need for apparatus that could 'prevent investment disputes from becoming dangerously political'.[57] Such apparatus, or 'machinery'[58] would need to appear neutral to appeal to both capital-exporting and capital-importing States.[59]

11.2.2 The General Counsel of the World Bank, a Driving Force behind ICSID

Amongst the wide array of functions fulfilled by the General Counsel of the Bank,[60] the drafting of international treaties has been an important task. Here again, the Bank's capacity and credibility in treaty making can be traced to a functionalist approach to its mandate, as well as its non-political character, which allows the Bank to professionally abstract itself from political passions that are present in nationally instigated attempts at treaty making.[61]

The World Bank General Counsel led the drafting that resulted in the creation of the IFC in 1956, ICSID in 1965 and MIGA in 1985. One protagonist, in particular, has been instrumental in the establishment of ICSID: Aron Broches, General Counsel from 1959 to 1979, and Secretary-General of ICSID from 1967 to 1980. Like Black's, Aron Broches' role cannot be overestimated.

55 *See* D. A. Soley, 'ICSID Implementation: An Effective Alternative to International Conflict' (1985) 19 *The International Lawyer* 521.

56 *See* Parra (n 37), 154; Sutherland (n 39), 368.

57 Soley (n 56), 522.

58 The need for some kind of 'international machinery' constituted by an 'impartial body of technical experts' to address investment disputes was identified by the Bank as early as 1947, but would become an imperative for the institution a decade later. *See* Parra (n 35), 19.

59 I. F. I. Shihata, 'Improving the Investment Climate in Developing Countries', *The Nonaligned World* (July–September 1984), 2.

60 For an overview of the duties assumed by the World Bank General Counsel, *see* I. F. I. Shihata, 'Role of the World Bank's General Counsel' (1997) 91 *American Society of International Law Proceedings* 215; and I. F. I. Shihata, 'The Creative Role of the Lawyer – Example: The Office of the World Bank's General Counsel' (1999)48 *Cath. U. L. Rev.* 1041.

61 Thomas Kuchenberg, 'The World Bank: Arbiter Extraordinaire' (1968) 2 *Studies in Law and Economic Development* 259, 283.

A member of the Dutch delegation and the drafting committee for the Articles of Agreement of the International Monetary Fund at the Bretton Woods Conference, Broches joined the Legal Department of the Bank in 1946. As he rose to the position of General Counsel, the size of the Legal Department considerably grew.[62] An 'innovator and institution-builder',[63] he worked alongside Black to lend the 'good offices' of the Bank for the settlement of investment disputes in the 1950s.[64] In sum, Broches was prominently involved in shaping the World Bank Group.[65]

He forcefully defended the Bank's competence to establish an international machinery for the settlement of investment disputes, adopting the following view of the Articles of Agreement: 'everything that's not prohibited is permitted, as long as it serves the purpose of the institution, and as long as it is not inconsistent with anything else in the Articles'.[66] The Bank's power to establish ICSID therefore relied, according to Broches, on a purposive interpretation of the Bank's constituent text[67] and on the established practice of the Bank in the facilitation of settlements between private investors and Member States.[68]

11.3 Brokering the ICSID Convention

Although the 1960s presented favourable historical and geopolitical momentum for initiatives related to the promotion and protection of FDI,

[62] *See* Edwards (n 46), 257.

[63] *Ibid.*, at 258.

[64] World Bank Oral History Program, Interview with Aron Broches, General Counsel of the World Bank (18 April 1984) 29.

[65] *See* Edwards (n 46), 259; Parra (n 37), 156.

[66] Interview with Broches (n 65), 4. *See also* St John (n 17), 65, 125.

[67] IBRD Articles, art I(ii). *See* Parra (n 35), 26 fn 9, citing Broches: 'whether it has or does not have a particular power must be determined in the light of the Bank's purposes, by which all the Bank's decisions must be guided. For a finding that the Bank has such power, the power need not be shown to be necessarily or even reasonably implicit in any power given expressly by the Articles. It is enough that its exercise may further the achievement of the Bank's purposes, and that it is not prohibited by or inconsistent with the Bank's Articles of Agreement'.

[68] W. Liang, 'The World Bank and the Creation of the International Centre for the Settlement of Investment Disputes: Legality and Legitimacy' in P. Quayle, and X. Gao (eds.) *International Organizations and the Promotion of Effective Dispute Resolution – Asian Infrastructure Investment Bank Yearbook of International Law* (Brill/Nijhoff, 2019), 106.

investor-State arbitration did not initially spark widespread interest from investors, capital-importing States and capital-exporting States.

11.3.1 Momentum in the 1960s

The end of the 1950s shook the old world's balance: with the decline of colonialism, 30 newly independent countries joined the United Nations between 1957 and 1962, and joined the Bank's membership.[69] The 'Third World' proclaimed its independence at the Bandung Conference in 1955. For the first time in history, capital-importing States were able to protect their own interests, often at odds with those of capital-exporting States.

At the same time, expressions of interest for alternatives to public development aid intensified.[70] However, investors themselves had doubts about the investment conditions in developing countries. Potential deterrents ranged from expropriation, warfare and currency depreciation, to domestic regulations devised to limit the transfer of capital and income abroad.[71] The World Bank shared those concerns.[72]

In addition to adverse conditions, investors lacked access to effective remedies, were problems to arise. The main challenges were the difference in status between parties and imbalance of power between them.[73] A private investor, devoid of any status or jurisdictional capacity under international law, could not bring an action before an international court or tribunal, or to a commercial arbitration centre.[74] Only a handful of remedies were available: ad hoc arbitration proceedings; action before the domestic courts of the host State; or the exercise of diplomatic protection by the home State. These were unsatisfactory to most investors.[75]

[69] Parra (n 35), 11.

[70] *Ibid.*, at 12.

[71] *See* Soley (n 56), 521–522; Sutherland (n 39), 369.

[72] Note from the President to the Executive Directors Proposing that they Submit a Report to the Board of Governors (31 August 1962), reprinted in *History of the ICSID Convention*, vol. 2 (ICSID 1968), 47.

[73] Sutherland (n 39), 370.

[74] *Ibid.*, at 371–372. *See also* Interview with Broches (n 65), 344.

[75] *See* Sutherland (n 39), 371–373, explaining that foreign investors may not be equipped to negotiate arbitration clauses to their advantage. Domestic courts, on the other hand, may be seen by private investors as prone to support the host State's position.

Therefore, the driving factor behind the establishment of ICSID was the need for an international and impartial arbitral forum that could 'circumvent a traditional area of global hostility'[76] and 'de-politicize' investment disputes.[77] However, ICSID was not the only way to achieve this objective. Indeed, the early 1960s marked a 'critical juncture'[78] in the history of FDI, with a wide array of proposals presented to international actors to promote private foreign investment. The World Bank was involved in all of them, and acted as a catalyst for the realisation of ICSID.

11.3.2 Alternatives to ICSID

Three possible approaches were discussed by the international community to improve the problem of the 'unfavourable investment climate': (1) an international code of conduct, defining international protection standards applicable to FDI; (2) a multilateral insurance system; and (3) an arbitral institution dedicated to the settlement of investment disputes.[79]

The proposal for an international code of conduct was initially conceived by the German banker Hermann J. Abs[80] and his private Society for the Protection of Foreign Investments as an 'international Magna Carta for the protection of private investment abroad'.[81] Another proposal emerged from a group led by the British lawyer Hartley Shawcross, former lead prosecutor at the Nuremberg trial and counsel to the British government in

[76] Soley (n 56), 523.

[77] *Ibid.*, at 543. *See also* I. F. I. Shihata, 'Towards a Greater Depoliticization of Investment Disputes: The Roles of ICSID and MIGA' (1986) 1 *ICSID Review.*

[78] St John defines a 'critical juncture' as a 'brief period in which actors face a "broader than normal range of feasible options" and their choices amongst these options are "likely to have a significant impact on the path-dependent development of an institution"'. *See* St John (n 17), 28.

[79] Paper prepared by the General Counsel and transmitted to the members of the Committee of the Whole, 'Settlement of Investment Disputes – An Analysis of the Bank's Tentative Proposals and of the Principal Issues Raised Thereby' (18 February 1963), reprinted in *History of the ICSID Convention*, vol. 2 (ICSID 1968), 71.

[80] Abs was a central figure of the Deutsche Bank during the World War II and the lead negotiator during the post-war negotiations with Allied powers. Abs was a highly experienced financier recognised for his expertise in expropriation matters – although his participation in Deutsche Bank activities during the war is still controversial. *See* St John (n 17), 75–77.

[81] Parra (n 35), 13.

the Anglo-Persian Oil Company dispute.[82] The idea gained additional momentum with the support expressed by East Asian countries in 1958.[83] Abs and Shawcross joined forces to produce a 'Draft Convention on Investments Abroad',[84] also known as the 'Abs-Shawcross Draft', establishing principles of conduct for the fair and equitable treatment of foreign investors, and just and effective compensation in case of expropriation.[85] An arbitral procedure for the settlement of disputes was annexed to the Abs-Shawcross Draft. The proposal was brought by Germany to the Organisation for European Economic Co-operation (OEEC),[86] and a renamed 'Draft Convention on the Protection of Foreign Property' was circulated by the organisation in 1962 (OECD Draft).[87]

Ultimately, the proposal did not garner as much support as had been expected and was met by indifference,[88] and in some cases outright opposition.[89] The OECD nonetheless requested the World Bank to take over the project, but was met with a refusal. According to Broches, the Bank was unwilling to negotiate the OECD Draft with developing countries, because it felt that

> the code was a one-sided document limited to the protection of foreign property and the obligations of the host countries. If we were to take it over, we would have to look at the other side, namely the obligations of investors. The developing

[82] *Ibid.*, 13. *See also* St John (n 17), 84. Shawcross produced a Draft Convention on Foreign Investments in 1958, which did not include resort to arbitration but to the International Court of Justice (ICJ) for a judicial settlement of investment disputes. *See* 'Draft Convention on Foreign Investments', March 1958, UK T 236/5436.

[83] Parra (n 35), 13.

[84] 'Draft Convention on Investments Abroad' (9 April 1959) (1960)9 *Journal of Public Law* 115, cited in Parra (n 35), 13 fn 26.

[85] Parra (n 35), 14; St John (n 17), 88.

[86] The OEEC was superseded by the Organisation for Economic Co-operation and Development (OECD) in September 1961.

[87] *See* St John (n 17), 87; Parra (n 35), 14, 18.

[88] Developing countries were consulted by the OECD but refused to commit to support or sign the draft convention. *See* St John (n 17), 90.

[89] The United States and the United Kingdom, in particular, did not support the initiative. The United States did not see well the German initiative, perceived as an attempt to gain compensation for expropriated German property during the war. The British, on the other hand, were reluctant to support a convention establishing international standards that they would not be able to uphold, due to balance of payment issues. In general, capital-exporting States could see potential of claims being brought against them on the basis of the projected convention, a risk they were not willing to take. *See* St John (n 34), 77–79, 85–86.

countries would still feel that the Bank presented a proposal cooked up by their adversaries, and the industrialized countries would accuse us of watering down a wonderful document.[90]

The Bank refused to jeopardise its relationship with its client countries for a project that it deemed unlikely to succeed. By the end of the 1960s, the OECD Draft had been supplanted by bilateral investment treaties (BITs), which addressed the substantive concerns contained in the Abs-Shawcross Draft.[91] The proposed convention never passed the draft stage, but was reissued in 1967 as a non-binding resolution of the OECD Council.[92]

The second project, a multilateral insurance system to protect investors against non-commercial risks, was first proposed by the World Bank itself.[93] It received widespread support. Several regional programmes already existed, and were supported by various capital-exporting countries.[94] Once again, the OECD Development Assistance Committee (DAC) asked the World Bank to further study the possibility. In 1962, the Bank delivered a somewhat pessimistic report on the proposal,[95] but the DAC nevertheless convened a group of experts to further consider legal and technical implications of a multilateral insurance scheme. In June 1965, the OECD approached the Bank once more to request its support in the establishment of the international investment insurance agency for what seemed to be a 'surefire success'.[96] While the Legal Department of the Bank prepared a draft charter for discussion with the Executive Directors and Member States, multiple disagreements emerged and the project was abandoned in the early 1970s. Another ten years would elapse before the project would come to fruition with the establishment of MIGA.[97]

[90] Interview with Broches (n 65), 30. *See also* Parra (n 37), 154; P. Kahn, 'The Law Applicable to Foreign Investments: The Contribution of the World Bank Convention on the Settlement of Investment Disputes' (1968) 44 *Indiana Law Journal* 1, 2, noting that the project was unsuccessful due to the draft's inability to take into account the decolonisation context.

[91] *See* St John (n 17), 90, 92–93; Parra (n 35), 19.

[92] OECD Council, 'Resolution on the Draft Convention on the Protection of Foreign Property', 12 October 1967, C(67)102.

[93] *See* Parra (n 35), 12. The Bank issued a first proposal as early as 1948.

[94] *See* Parra (n 35), 13; Kahn (n 91), 3. The Federal Republic of Germany, Japan and the United States had developed such programmes.

[95] *See* Parra (n 35), 17, evoking the 'careful neutrality' of the Bank. *See* IBRD/IDA, Summary Proceedings, 1961 Meetings of the Board of Governors (Annual Address of Eugene R Black) (1961) 8. *See also* St John (n 17), 106.

[96] St John (n 17), 106.

[97] Parra (n 35), 18.

According to St John, the project failed in the 1960s due to the lack of interest on the part of the Bank and its refusal to play the role of broker.[98] Aron Broches, who had been central to the drafting of the 1962 report,[99] was doubtful that a multilateral insurance system would be as effective for a healthy investment climate as a machinery for the arbitration and conciliation of investment disputes between governments and private parties.[100] He also feared that the Bank would be placed in an uncomfortable position:

> the Bank shouldn't be put in a position where it was an insurer and a lender. I mean, an insurer of money invested by others and a lender to that country, which might disturb its relations with both.[101]

Broches' preference for investor-State arbitration would shape the dialogue within the international community and promote ICSID as the ideal solution for 'a favourable climate for attractive and sound investments'.[102]

11.3.3 The Bank's Preference for Investor-State Arbitration

The World Bank had undoubtedly realised that there was greater support for the establishment of an international arbitral body than for the two other initiatives. At the time, the United Nations was supportive of arbitration in all its forms,[103] and endorsed the idea of creating an arbitral machinery, suggesting that it be established under the auspices of its Economic and Social Council (ECOSOC).[104]

98 St John (note 17), 108.

99 *Ibid.*, at 107.

100 A. Broches, 'Awards Rendered Pursuant to the ICSID Convention: Binding Force, Finality, Recognition, Enforcement, Execution' (1987) 2 *ICSID Review FILJ* 287, 290.

101 Interview with Broches (n 65), 30.

102 'Report of the Executive Directors on the Convention on the Settlement of Investment Disputes between States and Nationals of Other States' (18 March 1965), paras. 12–13.

103 The Convention on the recognition and Enforcement of Foreign Arbitral Awards was opened to signature in 1958. *See* Parra (n 35), 16.

104 'The Promotion of the International Flow of Private Capital', Progress Report by the Secretary-General, United Nations Economic and Social Council (26 February 1960) E/3325 79 para. 203 (ECOSOC Report). The ECOSOC deemed preferable to create a separate arbitral body, not identified with a commercial approach, so that it may be more readily acceptable to capital-importing countries, *see* para. 207. *See* also Parra (n 35), 16, for an overview of other initiatives linked to investor-State arbitration in the 1960s.

According to ECOSOC, a treaty on international arbitration was no panacea but rather an intermediate solution that could over time generate the benefits initially expected from a code of conduct and become 'the natural fulcrum for the conclusion of bilateral, and possibly multilateral, agreements between governments on private foreign investment'.[105] President Black relied on the ECOSOC report to promote the idea of ICSID to the Board of Governors in September 1961.[106] In fact, the World Bank, and Broches in particular, had already approached the UN, the United States' State Department and Treasury, as well as British officials behind the scenes, ensuring that support for an arbitral body would be included in the ECOSOC report.[107]

Internally, the initiative was launched by a memorandum of the General Counsel to the Executive Directors in August 1961.[108] Black presented the project to the Bank's Governors during his annual address in September 1961.[109] In his speech, he recalled that the Bank had been called upon its member States to assist in the settlement of disputes involving private parties, but was ill-equipped to handle such matters on a day-to-day basis. Nevertheless the operational contribution of a special forum for the conciliation or arbitration of investor-States disputes was clear.[110]

Black strongly believed that the creation of ICSID would stimulate a greater flow of capital into developing countries, in line with the Bank's purposes.[111] He also supported the idea that allowing investors to bring their claims against a State before an international body, without having

105 ECOSOC Report (n 105), 81.

106 'Excerpt from Address by President Eugene R. Black to the Annual Meeting of the Board of Governors' (19 September 1961) reprinted in *History of the ICSID Convention*, vol. 2 (ICSID 1968), 3.

107 St John (n 17), 131; ECOSOC Report (n 105), para. 206.

108 Note by A. Broches, General Counsel, transmitted to the Executive Directors: 'Settlement of Disputes between Governments and Private Parties' (28 August 1961) reprinted in *History of the ICSID Convention*, vol. 2 (ICSID 1968), 1.

109 'Excerpt from Address by President Eugene R. Black to the Annual Meeting of the Board of Governors' (19 September 1961) reprinted in *History of the ICSID Convention*, vol. 2 (ICSID 1968), 3.

110 *See* Parra (n 37), 155; J. Fouret, 'The World Bank and ICSID: Family or Incestuous Ties' (2007) 4 *International Organizations Law Review* 122. *See also* Soley (n 56), 523.

111 Soley (n 56), 523. *See* 'Note from the President to the Executive Directors Proposing that they Submit a Report to the Board of Governors' (31 August 1962) reprinted in *History of the ICSID Convention*, vol. 2 (ICSID 1968), 47.

to mobilise the support of their home States to embrace their claims, would lead to a depoliticisation of investment disputes,[112] once again building upon the Bank's non-political mandate.

For that reason, the World Bank was eager to take on the project itself rather than support a UN-led initiative, which Broches feared would end up entangled in political opposition.[113] Black explained the Bank's privileged position in a note to the Board of Directors dated 28 December 1961:

> The first question for discussion is whether it would be appropriate and useful for the Bank to take an initiative in furthering the idea of arbitration and conciliation of so-called investment disputes. Improved methods for the settlement of investment disputes would contribute to an improvement in the investment climate and would thereby tend to promote the flow of private foreign capital, an objective of special concern to the Bank. Moreover, this is a field in which the Bank has some competence. We have done quite a lot of work in the way of conciliation and quasi-arbitration; this work not only has done credit to the Bank, but also has given tangible evidence of the potentialities of these procedures. Furthermore, the Bank is regarded as an impartial institution not motivated by political considerations and with an understanding of the problems of capital-exporting and capital-importing countries alike. This means that a recommendation or proposal emanating from the Bank may be expected to receive wide attention and respect.[114]

Despite the Bank's strong emphasis on the promotion of the flow of capital,[115] the effect of the availability of investor-State arbitration to interested parties was not supported by empirical evidence.[116] In fact, some States supported ICSID because they believed it would not stimulate

[112] *See* notably Parra (n 35), 16; Shihata (n 78), 5. St John explains that the depoliticisation language emerged with the drafting of ICSID, first under Broches' tenure, and was later revisited by Shihata (St John (n17), 102. *See also* Interview with Broches (n 65), 343.

[113] Parra (n 35), 17, at fn 58. *See also* Interview with Broches (n 65), 345, explaining that the Bank was also inspired by the IFC and the IDA examples, whose charters were drafted in-house.

[114] 'Note by the President to the Executive Directors' (28 December 1961), reprinted in *History of the ICSID Convention*, vol 2 (ICSID 1968), 4.

[115] *See* Shihata (n 78), 6.

[116] St John (n 17), 3. A survey led by the ICC in 1962 amongst foreign investment firms showed that only 16 per cent of them believed that access to arbitration affected the investment climate. *Ibid.*, at 20–21. St John also argues that the officials of the World Bank themselves were unlikely to believe that investor-State arbitration would significantly affect FDI, but used the argument as a 'useful piece of public rhetoric'. *Ibid.*, at 118, 156.

foreign investment.[117] Indeed some recent studies find that it is unclear whether access to investor-State arbitration has played a major role in bringing about the marked increase in FDI since the 1990s.[118] ICSID was likely successful not because it was the optimal solution, but because it constituted a 'lowest common denominator',[119] a pragmatic proposal focused on procedural rather than substantive rules that would be acceptable for capital-exporting and capital-importing States alike.[120] Speaking in 1967, Aron Broches concluded that based on the Bank's experience, 'the most promising approach would be to attack the problem of the unfavourable investment climate from a procedural angle, by creating an international machinery which would be available on a voluntary basis for the settlement of investment disputes. Accordingly, the Convention does not lay down standard for the treatment of States of property of aliens; nor does it prescribe standards for the conduct of foreign investors in their relations with host states. In other words, the Convention is not concerned with the merits of investment disputes but with the procedure for settling them'.[121]

Another crucial factor was the involvement of the World Bank's officials who carefully brokered[122] the ICSID Convention from its first inception to its final draft.

[117] Such was the case for the United Kingdom, who had no interest in encouraging capital export due to the balance of payments issue they were facing at the time. *See* St John (n 17), 104, 158.

[118] *See* S. D. Franck, 'Foreign Direct Investment, Investment Treaty Arbitration, and the Rule of Law' (2007) 19 *Global Business & Development Law Journal* 339, noting that a variety of actors are involved when it comes to a healthy investment climate, e.g. the stability of investment environment, the availability of human capital, access to enforcement procedures, legal and regulatory framework, and professional and personal relationships. In this context, access to ISDS rather looks like a 'very small piece of the puzzle'. *See ibid.*, at 335. In definitive, 'there is mixed empirical and anecdotal evidence about the impact investment treaties have on FDI, it is not surprising that the evidence with regard to the specific effect of investment treaty arbitration is also unclear'. *Ibid.*, at 373.

[119] *See notably* St John (n 17), 21–22, 118.

[120] Kahn (n 91), 4, Parra (n 35), 24.

[121] A. Broches 'Political, Legal and Economic Aspects of Development Financing' Address of the General Counsel of the World Bank to the Institut Royal des Relations Internationales, Brussels, Belgium, 4 April 1967.

[122] St John defines the term *brokering* as the 'ability to construct coalitions or work skilfully around disagreements and bring actors together'. *See* St John (n 17), 37.

11.4 Drafting the ICSID Convention

Once support for the idea of ICSID had gained momentum with the international community, Broches and the World Bank Legal Department began working on a draft convention. The unorthodox and *sui generis*[123] approach taken by the Bank to produce an agreeable draft as quickly as possible reflects the World Bank's grasp of States' sensibilities and treaty-making challenges at the time.[124]

The first detailed vision for ICSID was presented in a note to the Executive Directors dated 19 January 1962.[125] It was envisioned that the arbitral centre should be 'somewhat removed from, although linked to, the Bank'.[126] The convention would aim at 'institutionalising' the Bank's former dispute settlement activities, but also provide the necessary machinery to encourage the recourse to conciliation and arbitration more broadly.[127] The centre would be a limited apparatus in terms of staff, and have its seat at the Bank's headquarters, making for maximum flexibility and economy in the provision of administrative and clerical services.[128] Interestingly, the establishment of the center was not viewed as preventing the Bank from acting directly in connection with investment disputes, and it was anticipated that the Bank would continue to intervene, but in a more selective manner.[129]

At the request of the Executive Directors, Broches submitted his 'Working Paper in the Form of a Draft Convention for the Resolution of Disputes between States and Nationals of Other States' (Working Paper) modelled after the Articles of Agreement of the IBRD, the IFC and IDA, on 5 June 1962.[130] In September 1962, the Executive Directors were

[123] Liang (n 69), 115. According to Broches, '[t] he method by which the World Bank proceeded to prepare, negotiate and formulate the Convention and to submit it to governments was unorthodox and was characterized by a fair amount of innovation and, sometimes, improvisation'. Broches (n 32).

[124] For an extensive analysis of the successive drafts, *see* Parra (n 35), Chapters 3–5.

[125] 'Note by the General Counsel transmitted to the Executive Directors' (19 January 1962) reprinted in *History of the ICSID Convention*, vol. 2 (ICSID 1968), 6.

[126] *Ibid.*, para. 6.

[127] *Idem.*

[128] *Ibid.*, para. 8.

[129] *Ibid.*, paras. 12–13.

[130] 'Working Paper in the Form of a Draft Convention for the Resolution of Disputes between States and Nationals of Other States' (5 June 1962) reprinted in *History of the ICSID Convention*, vol. 2 (ICSID 1968), 19. *See* Parra, 24–25.

formally asked to consider the desirability and practicability of establishing institutional facilities sponsored by the Bank for the settlement of investment disputes and, as the case may be, to draft an agreement for submission to governments.[131]

The Working Paper formed the basis for discussions between the Executive Directors convened for a Committee of the Whole on the Settlement of Investment Disputes between December 1962 and June 1963.[132] A number of Latin American countries expressed reservations about an international treaty. Broches actively defended the choice of an international convention, without which, he argued, agreements to resort to conciliation or arbitration would not become binding international obligations.[133] Following these discussions, Broches presented the 'First Preliminary Draft of a Convention on the Settlement of Investment Disputes between States and National of Other States' to the Executive Directors on 9 August 1963.[134] In the meantime, the new President of the World Bank, George D. Woods, took up Black's project.[135] The Executive Directors agreed to circulate a slightly amended Preliminary Draft,[136] at four regional consultative meetings in Addis Ababa, Santiago, Geneva and Bangkok taking place between December 1963 and May 1964.[137]

Broches had the idea of a regional 'road show' to present the Preliminary Draft to legal experts from Member States.[138] The objective was twofold: first to receive valuable input on the draft from legal

[131] IBRD Board of Governors, Resolution No. 174 (18 September 1962) reprinted in *History of the ICSID Convention*, vol. 2 (ICSID 1968), 51.

[132] *See* Parra (n 35), 34.

[133] 'Paper Prepared by the General Counsel and Transmitted to the members of the Committee of the Whole' (18 February 1963) reprinted in *History of the ICSID Convention*, vol. 2 (ICSID 1968), 71, para. 19. *See also* Parra (n 35), 34–35.

[134] 'First Preliminary Draft of a Convention on the Settlement of Investment Disputes between States and National of Other States' (9 August 1963) reprinted in *History of the ICSID Convention*, vol. 2 (ICSID 1968), 133.

[135] Woods, then Chairman of the First Boston Corporation, had intervened alongside Black during the Suez Canal negotiations, as a financial consultant. *See* Parra (n 37), 154–155.

[136] 'Preliminary Draft of a Convention on the Settlement of Investment Disputes between States and Nationals of Other States' (15 October 1963) reprinted in *History of the ICSID Convention*, vol. 2 (ICSID 1968), 184.

[137] *See* 'Summary Record of Proceedings' reprinted in *History of the ICSID Convention*, vol 2 (ICSID 1968) 236, 298, 367, 458.

[138] *See* Interview with Broches (n 65), 37. *See also* St John (n 17), 134.

experts,[139] and second to assess the degree to which Member States would welcome the initiative.[140] However, the diplomats, economists and government lawyers who attended the meetings did not act as representatives of their States, but as expert-designates.[141] The meetings were purely consultative in nature and the Bank had the final say on whether or not to incorporate feedback into its draft.[142] In this way, the Bank retained control of the drafting process. In June 1964, Woods requested that the Board of Executive Directors seek the approval of the Board of Governors for the preparation of a convention in its final form, to be submitted to Member States for signature and ratification.[143] Whilst Executive Directors from Latin American countries expressed their opposition, questioning the authority of the Bank to draft such a convention, most others agreed with the President's recommendation.[144]

The Board of Governors officially requested that the Executive Directors formulate a convention on 10 September 1964.[145] Woods immediately convened a Legal Committee tasked with the finalisation of the draft

[139] According to Broches, the Executive Directors alone who reported to Ministries of Finance, did not possess the necessary expertise to provide proper feedback on the Preliminary Draft. *See* St John (n 17), 139.

[140] *See* Sutherland (n 39), 376.

[141] Parra (n 35), 48; St John (n 17), 138; Interview with Broches (n 65), 38.

[142] St John (n 17), 138. In fact, most Latin American participants voiced their opposition at the Santiago meeting, arguing that foreigners and nationals should be treated equally. *See* 'Summary Record of Proceedings, Santiago Consultative Meeting' (3–7 February 1964) reprinted in *History of the ICSID Convention*, vol. 2 (ICSID 1968), 298. *See also* Parra (n 35), 49.

[143] 'Memorandum from the President to the Committee of the Whole' (10 June 1964) reprinted in *History of the ICSID Convention*, vol. 2 (ICSID 1968), 554.

[144] 'Memorandum of the Meeting of the Committee of the Whole' (14 July 1964) reprinted in *History of the ICSID Convention*, vol. 2 (ICSID 1968), 585. As discussed earlier, Broches believed it to be within the implied powers of the Bank. Parra (n 35), 60. *See also* 'Report from the Executive to the Board of Governors' (6 August 1964) reprinted in *History of the ICSID Convention*, vol. 2 (ICSID 1968), 606.

[145] IBRD Board of Governors, Resolution No. 214 (10 September 1964) reprinted in *History of the ICSID Convention*, vol. 2 (ICSID 1968), 608. All Latin American members voted against the proposal. *See* 'Excerpt from the Statement by Felix Ruiz, Governor for Chile' (9 September 1964) reprinted in *History of the ICSID Convention*, vol. 2 (ICSID 1968), 606. This would become known as 'El No de Tokio'. *See also* St John (n 17), 140, indicating that resistance led by Latin American members failed to derail the Bank's initiative in part because the Bank limited possibilities for the opposition to form a unified front by holding regional consultative meetings.

convention.[146] Unlike the regional consultative meetings, the Legal Committee aimed to provide States with the opportunity to be involved in the drafting of the convention. The Legal Committee met between 23 November and 11 December 1964.[147] Nine Committee members were appointed to serve on a Drafting Sub-Committee.[148]

The Executive Directors received a Revised Draft of the Convention dated 11 December 1964.[149] The Committee of the Whole gathered for a last meeting in the following months, and Executive Directors mostly followed the conclusions of the Legal Committee.[150] On 8 March 1965, the Executive Directors adopted a resolution approving the final text of the ICSID Convention and instructing the President to provide a copy of the treaty, accompanied by a report of the Executive Directors, to the World Bank's members for signature and ratification.[151] The text was sent to Member States a few days later,[152] and the ICSID Convention entered into force on 14 October 1966 following the twentieth ratification.

The distinguishing feature of the World Bank's intervention role in the drafting of the ICSID Convention is the fact that no formal negotiations took place – instead a truncated version of the traditional treaty

[146] Parra (n 35), 60. The draft was a revised version of the Preliminary Draft that implemented a number of observations received at the regional meetings. For a detailed overview, *see* Parra (n 35), 61–67. 'Draft Convention on the Settlement of Investment Disputes between States and Nationals of Other States' (11 September 1964) reprinted in *History of the ICSID Convention*, vol. 2 (ICSID 1968), 610.

[147] 'Note from the President to Executive Directors concerning the Legal Committee' (5 August 1964) reprinted in *History of the ICSID Convention*, vol. 2 (ICSID 1968), 604.

[148] *See* Parra (n 35), 68.

[149] 'Revised Draft of Convention on the Settlement of Investment Disputes between States and Nationals of Other States' (11 December 1964) reprinted in *History of the ICSID Convention*, vol. 2 (ICSID 1968), 911. The Revised Draft Convention included changes proposed by the Legal Committee and minor revisions carried out by the Bank's Legal Department. *See* 'Memorandum from the General Counsel and List of Proposed Changes to the Revised Draft Convention transmitted to the Committee of the Whole' (8 January 1965) reprinted in *History of the ICSID Convention*, vol. 2 (ICSID 1968), 943. For a detailed analysis of the draft's contents *see* Parra (n 35), 80–81.

[150] Parra (n 35), 83.

[151] *See* 'Excerpt from the Minutes of the Meeting of the Executive Directors – Approval of Resolution No. 65–14 approving the Text of the Convention and of the Report of the Executive Directors' (30 March 1965) reprinted in *History of the ICSID Convention*, vol. 2 (ICSID 1968), 1039; Parra (n 35), 85.

[152] *See* 'Copy of the Letter sent by the President to all member countries, Governors and Alternate Governors, transmitted to the Executive Directors' (24 March 1965) reprinted in *History of the ICSID Convention*, vol. 2 (ICSID 1968), 1086.

negotiations was undertaken.[153] The Bank succeeded in devising a hybrid law-making model, between a full-fledged international conference and the adoption of an internal resolution. This ensured the broadest representation possible while circumscribing negotiating power and reducing the possibility of delays.[154]

The Bank achieved this in two ways. First, it set aside its weighted voting system, based on members' financial contributions, which would have benefited capital-exporting States.[155] Second, it sought consensus on every decision made by the Legal Committee,[156] through the adoption of specific procedural rules for the conduct of proceedings.[157] Hence the Bank mirrored a diplomatic conference without the burdensome aspects of such gatherings.

The entire process, from Broches' initial Working Paper – June 1962 – to the formulation of an international convention ready to be signed and ratified – March 1965 – took a little less than three years. This was remarkable, given the usual length of negotiations for the making of treaties,[158] and marked a clear success for the Bank.

11.5 Conclusion: Supporting the ICSID Convention

The crucial role played by the World Bank did not stop at the adoption of the ICSID Convention. The Bank's staff remained closely connected with the new

[153] *See* Liang (n 69), 116.

[154] Liang (n 69), 114. *See also* 'Memorandum from the President to the Committee of the Whole' (10 June 1964), reprinted in History of the ICSID Convention, vol 2 (ICSID 1968) 554; and IBRD Board of Governors, Resolution No. 214 (10 September 1964), reprinted in History of the ICSID Convention, vol 2 (ICSID 1968) 608.

[155] *See* Sutherland (n 39), 375; Parra (n 35), 27, 68. Instead, the Executive Directors relied on opinion polls and aimed for consensus. *See* 'Memorandum of the meeting of the Committee of the Whole' (14 July 1964) reprinted in *History of the ICSID Convention*, vol. 2 (ICSID 1968), 589, para. 18. *See also* Liang (n 69), 116.

[156] St John argues that the Legal Committee served only two purpose, consensus-building and representation, and that the Bank could perfectly have formulated the ICSID Convention without its assistance or advice. *See* St John (n 17), 141–142.

[157] 'Legal Committee on Settlement of Investment Disputes: Rules for the Conduct of Proceedings' (17 November 1964) reprinted in *History of the ICSID Convention*, vol. 2 (ICSID 1968), 647. For instance, the Rules of Procedure provided that in case of diverging opinions between experts, they should form a working group to consider the issue, find consensus, and refer it to the Drafting Sub-Committee (para. 4(b), (c) and (d)). In the absence of consensus, the Executive Directors were to give final directions (para. 4(e)).

[158] *See* Sutherland (n 39), 375.

institution for years, and actively lobbied governments to obtain consent to the jurisdiction of ICSID.[159] Broches, in particular, assumed the dual role of General Counsel of the Bank and Secretary-General of ICSID,[160] and made tremendous efforts to increase awareness of the new arbitral body and encourage States to pursue ratification.[161] ICSID published a set of model arbitration clauses – drafted by Broches and the Legal Department of the Bank – to be included in agreements between host States and foreign investors.[162] By the mid 1970s, the inclusion of the model clauses in investment agreements had become commonplace. Reference to ICSID jurisdiction was even included in some domestic laws.[163] Similar model clauses were published in 1969 for insertion into BITs.[164] The Bank's reputation and its special relationship with capital-importing States were critical and pervasive throughout the entire ratification process. The Bank's efforts were particularly efficient as it connected the ratification of ICSID to the broader mandate of the Bank[165] therefore making membership more appealing to States.

The administrative links between ICSID and the Bank,[166] and the unique support provided to the centre by its creator, reflect the close relationship

[159] *See* Parra (n 35), 88–89. St John (n 17), 173–174.

[160] Pursuant to art 10(1) of the ICSID Convention, Broches was nominated for the position by Woods, President of the World Bank and Chairman of the ICSID Administrative Council. Broches was deemed the best candidate for the position, as least for a temporary period, due to his unique expertise and familiarity with the ICSID Convention. From then on, the General Counsel of the Bank traditionally assumed the role of Secretary-General, until the practice ceased in 2009. *See* ICSID Doc A/67/14, 'Election of the Secretary-General, Report and Recommendations of the Chairman' (6 January 1967) paras. 2, 30. *See also* Parra (n 35), 91.

[161] *See* St John (n 17), 173–174 for a description of the initiatives undertaken by the Bank to follow-up on States until ratification was achieved. By the early 1970s, the main capital-exporting States had ratified, as well as former British colonies. Amongst capital-importing States, the Latin American countries remained strongly opposed to ICSID.

[162] ICSID, 'Model Clauses recording Consent to the Jurisdiction of the International Centre for Settlement of Investment Disputes' (1968) Doc. ICSID/5. *See* Parra (n 35), 121. St John notes that Broches' staff heavily promoted the model clauses, meeting with governments to discuss implementation under domestic law or in contracts and treaties. St John (n 17), 14.

[163] *E.g.* Afghanistan and Egypt. *See* Parra (n 35), 121.

[164] ICSID 'Model Clauses Relating to the Convention on the Settlement of Investment Disputes Designed for Bilateral Investment Treaties' (1969) Doc. ICSID/16. *See* Parra (n 35), 121–122.

[165] St John (n 17), 155.

[166] *See* ICSID Administrative Council Resolution, 'Approval of Administrative Arrangements with the International Bank for Reconstruction and Development' (2 February 1967) AC (IM)/RES/3.

between the two institutions. Woods was fully aware of the need for ICSID to achieve more independence when he 'reaffirmed his hope and intention that the Centre would finally emerge as a wholly independent entity, with a completely independent staff under the leadership of a full-time Secretary-General'.[167] The appropriate relationship between the Bank and ICSID had been one of the fundamental issues discussed by the Executive Directors at the drafting stage. Finding the right balance is key: on the one hand, the centre had to remain sufficiently independent to protect its credibility in relation to the settlement of disputes,[168] and on the other, ICSID could benefit being associated with the Bank's international standing .[169] A compromise was reflected in various provisions of the ICSID Convention,[170] such that the sponsorship offered by the mother organisation would decrease over time, once ICSID's activities had grown sufficiently for it to become a self-standing organisation.

ICSID's independence evolved progressively – though at a slower rate than originally contemplated by President Woods. The General Counsel of the Bank customarily occupied the position of Secretary-General of ICSID until Robert B. Zoellick was selected as President of the World Bank in 2007.[171] Citing the increasing incompatibility of the two positions and

[167] Administrative Council Proceedings, 'Inaugural Meeting' (2 February 1967), Doc AC/67/7 para. 19. The Legal Committee had also emphasised the role of ICSID as an independent tribunal: 'notwithstanding the link between the Bank and the Centre, which to some extent is easy to understand, in organizing the Centre we should not lose sight of the fact that it is a tribunal; that is, an organ having as one of the basic reason for its existence the security and independence of its members'. *See* 'Comments by Mr. Da Cunha (Brazil) to Legal Committee' (25 November 1964) reprinted in *History of the ICSID Convention*, vol. 2 (ICSID 1968), 690.

[168] 'Memorandum of the meeting of the Committee of the Whole' (28 May 1963) reprinted in *History of the ICSID Convention*, vol. 2 (ICSID 1968), 86, paras. 14, 21–24. Some Executive Directors feared that the Bank may be placed in situations of conflict of interest and try to influence the proceedings concerning projects financed by the institution. *See* 'Memorandum of the meeting of the Committee of the Whole' (6 June 1963) reprinted in *History of the ICSID Convention*, vol. 2 (ICSID 1968), 106, paras. 38, 50. *See* Parra (n 35), 36. *See* Fouret (n 111), 123–124, referring to criticism received by ICSID as to its 'incestuous ties' with the World Bank.

[169] *See* 'Memorandum of the meeting of the Committee of the Whole' (4 June 1963) reprinted in *History of the ICSID Convention*, vol. 2 (ICSID 1968), 99.

[170] *See* Fouret (n 111), 128; Parra (n 35), 50. For an overview of the Legal Committee discussions on the topic, *see* Parra (n 35), 71.

[171] Broches occupied the position until 1980. He was notably succeeded by Shihata, who left the Secretariat of ICSID in 2000. Three successive General Counsel acted as Secretary-General of ICSID from 2000 to 2009.

their respective workloads, he proposed that an independent Secretary-General be nominated to head ICSID.[172] Meg Kinnear, former Senior General Counsel of the Trade Law Bureau of Canada, was elected in 2009 and still holds the position.[173]

Until the mid 1980s, ICSID's expenditures were covered by annual contributions from the Bank's overall budget for the Legal Department,[174] but ICSID's budget is now separate. Between 2000 and 2010, the caseload of ICSID increased significantly, like its membership.[175] The expenditures, which had been covered by the Bank for 40 years, escalated quickly, and ICSID increased its fees in order to reduce the budgetary support received from the Bank.[176] Today, while ICSID is still part of the World Bank Group, it has essentially achieved the institutional autonomy originally envisaged by its founders.

The broader involvement of the Bank in the promotion of FDI should also be recognised.[177] A sound investment climate hinges on a range of qualitative and quantitative factors, the actual impacts of which are difficult to assess.[178] Access to investor-State arbitration is one piece of a larger picture. In that regard, the World Bank has led a number of other initiatives designed to 'encourag[e] international investment for the development of the productive resources of members'.[179] The Bank has broadened the scope of its activities and now provides technical and legal expertise to Member States in order to 'improv[e] the policies, laws, and regulations that affect domestic and foreign investors and influence their decisions to invest'.[180]

172 Parra (n 35), 217.
173 *Ibid.*, at 218.
174 *Ibid.*, at 117.
175 For an overview of ICSID's first two decades, *see* Parra (n 35), Chapter 7. As of 1 September 2019, the ICSID Convention counts 154 contracting States.
176 *See* Parra (n 35), 219. In 2015, the Bank was still contributing to 35 per cent of ICSID's budget. *See* Parra (n 35), 271.
177 *See generally* I. F. I. Shihata, 'Promotion of Foreign Direct Investment – A General Account, with Particular Reference to the Role of the World Bank Group' (1991)n4 *ICSID Review FILJ* 484, including an analysis of this in the context of the Bank's purposes which include to 'promote private foreign investment'.
178 *See* J. Gladstone and A. Kirkpatrick, 'The Contribution of International Organizations to Investment Arbitration: Responding in Times of Crisis?' (2016) 13 *Manchester Journal of International Economic Law* 296.
179 IBRD Articles, art I(iii).
180 IBRD, 'The World Bank Group A to Z' (2016) 88, https://openknowledge.worldbank.org/handle/10986/20192.

Today the World Bank's activities are less centred on the mediation and conciliation roles once played by Black's Bank. Yet, they still reflect the vision shared by Black, Broches and Woods of an institution that could bridge the gap between capital-importing and capital-exporting States – the same vision that gave birth to ICSID.

12 ICSID Today

Meg Kinnear and Daniela Argüello

12.1 Introduction

The International Centre for Settlement of Investment Disputes ("ICSID" or "the Centre") is the world's leading institution devoted to international investment dispute settlement. It was established in 1966 by the Convention on the Settlement of Investment Disputes between States and Nationals of Other States (the "ICSID Convention"),[1] a multilateral treaty proposed by the Executive Directors of the International Bank for Reconstruction and Development (the "World Bank"). ICSID provides a unique treaty framework, procedural rules and independent facilities for the settlement of disputes between foreign investors and host States.

The ICSID of today owes much to the vision of its founders, who designed a mechanism that "would offer international methods of settlement designed to take account of the special characteristics of the disputes covered, as well as of the parties to whom it would apply."[2] In proposing the ICSID Convention, the Executive Directors were motivated by the desire to strengthen the partnership between countries in the cause of economic development. As stated in their report, the creation of ICSID was intended to "facilitate the settlement of disputes between States and foreign investors," by "promoting an atmosphere of mutual confidence, and thus stimulating a larger flow of private international capital into

[1] Convention on the Settlement of Investment Disputes between States and Nationals of Other States (opened for signature March 18, 1965, entered into force October 14, 1966) (ICSID Convention).

[2] *Report of the Executive Directors of the International Bank for Reconstruction and Development on the Convention on the Settlement of Investment Disputes between States and Nationals of Other States* (March 18, 1965) para 11. *See* I. F. I. Shihata, "Promotion of Foreign Direct Investment – A General Account, with Particular Reference to the Role of the World Bank Group (1991) 6 *ICSID Rev-FILJ* 484.

those countries which wish to attract it,"[3] "while maintaining a careful balance between the interests of investors and those of the host States."[4] In particular, the mechanisms in the ICSID Convention and Rules served to depoliticize and de-escalate conflict between States by providing an effective mechanism to redress breaches of obligation by host States with respect to foreign nationals. These goals remain at the core of ICSID's activities today.

While the goals of ICSID dispute settlement have remained constant, the founders of ICSID might have been surprised by the trajectory and nature of ICSID's growth in the past 50 years. As of June 2020, 163 States had signed the ICSID Convention, and 155 States had ratified it.[5] Today, ICSID is the premier institution for international investment dispute settlement. It has administered approximately 70 percent of all known cases[6] initiated under various international treaties, contracts and laws, and it is offered in more than 95 percent of all investment treaties.[7] Having administered more than 800 cases overall, ICSID is the undisputed global leader in investor-state dispute settlement (ISDS). As such, it has significantly contributed to the development of international investment law jurisprudence, treaty practice and the promotion of international investment and the rule of law across the globe.[8]

The ICSID of tomorrow will continue to evolve to best serve States and investors. The current ICSID Rules amendment project is addressing new areas, demonstrating ongoing leadership in the field. This includes proposals with respect to disclosure of third-party funding, transparency of proceedings and security for costs. The proposals also offer new forms of dispute resolution such as mediation and fact-finding, and they expand the availability of the Additional Facility. At the same time, ICSID is offering new services that supplement its traditional role as an arbitration facility under the ICSID Convention and Additional Facility. For example, ICSID is increasingly administering cases under the UNCITRAL Arbitration

[3] *Ibid.*, para 9.

[4] *Ibid.*, para 13.

[5] ICSID, "List of Contracting States and Other Signatories of the Convention," Doc ICSID/3 https://icsid.worldbank.org/en/Documents/icsiddocs/List%20of%20Contracting%20States%20and%20Other%20Signatories%20of%20the%20Convention%20-%20Latest.pdf.

[6] UNCTAD, IIA Note, Issue 2 (May 2019), "Figure 1, Trends in known treaty-based ISDS cases, 1987–2018" (May 2019).

[7] ICSID, "Database of Bilateral Investment Treaties," https://icsid.worldbank.org/en/Pages/resources/Bilateral-Investment-Treaties-Database.aspx.

[8] International Centre for Settlement of Investment Disputes, *ICSID Annual Report* (2016).

Rules and ad hoc rules. It is also expanding its role as an administering institution, by acting as the Administrative Registry under recent investment treaties such as the European Union agreements with Canada, Mexico, Singapore, and Viet Nam.[9]

12.2 Historic Roots

In March 1965, the Executive Directors of the World Bank submitted the ICSID Convention to the member governments for their consideration.[10]

Numerous efforts to negotiate multilateral rules governing cross-border investment were initiated prior to the ICSID Convention, however, consensus proved elusive, especially with respect to elaboration of substantive investment obligations. These included efforts to create an International Trade Organization in 1947–1948 (ITO),[11] an International Code of Fair Treatment for Foreign Investment (ICC Code) in 1949, and the International Law Association Draft Statutes of the Arbitral Tribunal for Foreign Investment and the Foreign Investment Court (ILA Statute)[12] in 1948. The Draft Convention on Investments Abroad (the Abs-Shawcross Draft Convention) was the first international instrument to pair the basic

[9] Comprehensive Economic and Trade Agreement between the European Union and Canada (signed October 30, 2016, provisionally entered into force September 21, 2017) (CETA) Art. 8.23.2; Free Trade Agreement between the European Union and the United Mexican States (agreement in principle as of April 2018) (EU-Mexico FTA) Art. 7.2; Free Trade Agreement and Investment Protection Agreement between the European Union and Singapore (signed October 19, 2018, not yet entered into force) (EU-Singapore FTA) Art. 3.6; Free Trade Agreement between the European Union and the Socialist Republic of Vietnam (signed August 2018, not yet entered into force) (EU-Vietnam FTA) Art. 3.33.

[10] Report of the Executive Directors (note 2). The Convention entered into force 30 days after the date of the deposit of the twentieth instrument of ratification, acceptance and approval: Benin, Burkina Faso, Central African Republic, Chad, Republic of Congo, Côte d'Ivoire, Gabon, Ghana, Iceland, Jamaica, Madagascar, Malawi, Malaysia, Mauritania, the Netherlands, Nigeria, Sierra Leone, Tunisia, Uganda, and the United States.

[11] United Nations Conference on Trade and Employment, "Havana Charter for an International Trade Organization" (Havana, Cuba, from November 21, 1947 to March 24, 1948) UN Doc. E/Conf.2/78. The conditions for the entry into force of the Havana Charter were not fulfilled within the prescribed time-limit in Article 103, https://treaties.un.org/doc/Publication/MTDSG/Volume%20I/Chapter%20X/X-1-b.en.pdf.

[12] International Law Association, Draft Statutes of the Arbitral Tribunal for Foreign Investment and of the Foreign Investments Court (1948), Reprinted in UNCTAD, International Investment Instruments: A Compendium, vol. 3 (United Nations 1996) 259.

substantive obligations of host States (the minimum standard of treatment, protection against unreasonable or discriminatory measures, observance of undertakings, and "just and effective" compensation against expropriation) with a proposal for direct investor-State arbitration.[13] In 1961, Louis Sohn and Richard Baxter prepared the Draft Convention on the International Responsibility of States for Injuries to Aliens (1961 Harvard Convention)[14] which sought to codify international law on State responsibility. However, none of these efforts were able to garner the necessary international support.

Observing this, the management of the World Bank and in particular its General Counsel, Aron Broches, recognized that the Bank "could make a contribution to an improvement in the investment climate, by reducing the likelihood of unresolved conflicts between host countries and investors, and in particular by doing so in a manner which would eliminate the risk of a confrontation of the host country and the national State of the investor."[15] The Bank therefore proposed to explore the creation of "facilities for the voluntary settlement of investment disputes through conciliation and arbitration proceedings to which a host country and the foreign investors would be parties on an equal procedural footing, without requiring or permitting the intervention of the investor's national State."[16] As Broches remarked, "at first, it may seem strange that a financing institution ... would sponsor an international agreement concerned with investment disputes between States and private foreign investors."[17] However, while the World Bank's principal mandate is to provide finance, it does so as a development institution;[18] "as such, the Bank was vitally concerned with capital flows from developed to the developing

[13] Draft Convention on Foreign Investment (1959 Abs-Shawcross Draft Convention) (April 1959) 9 JPL 116 (1960). The Draft Convention, which was under consideration by the Organisation for European Economic Co-operation (OEEC), was not adopted, www.international-arbitration-attorney.com/wp-content/uploads/137-volume-5.pdf.

[14] Other recent efforts such as the unsuccessful Multilateral Agreement on Investment (MAI) from 1995 to 1998 and the failure to embrace investment in the Singapore Round of negotiations of the World Trade Organization (WTO) in 1996 demonstrate the continuing difficulty of concluding a single set of substantive international investment rules.

[15] Aron Broches, "The Convention on the Settlement of Investment Disputes between States and Nationals of Other States" (1972) 136 *Recueil des Cours d l'Académie de Droit International*, p. 343.

[16] *Ibid.*, p. 344.

[17] *Ibid.*, p. 342.

[18] *Ibid.*

countries."[19] This objective is consistent with the Articles of Agreement of the World Bank, specifically its role in promoting investment by private investors.[20] Thus, the creation of ICSID was a way to implement the World Bank mission, by addressing the effects of political risk on investment of private capital.[21]

The World Bank was also a logical home for ICSID given its experience in offering its "good offices" in several high-profile cross-border investment cases. For example, in 1951 the World Bank President, Eugene R. Black, offered to act as a trustee between Iran and the Anglo-Iranian Oil Company, after Iran had nationalized its oil industry and terminated its concessions.[22] Five years later, the World Bank and President Black were asked to help French and British shareholders' settle their claims for compensation after Egypt nationalized the Suez Canal Company.[23] In 1958, the President of the World Bank was asked to conciliate differences over the payment of the principal and interest on City of Tokyo and French bonds.[24] This experience reinforced the perception that there was a need for a standing, impartial, international facility to resolve investment disputes.

Not only was the World Bank an apt institution to host ICSID, but political and legal developments in the 1960s made the timing of ICSID opportune. Politically, "disputes over the treatment of foreign investment increased and intensified after World War II as the process of decolonization resulted in colonial territories becoming states."[25] Many of these disputes arose in newly independent States that had nationalized key sectors of their economies.[26] At the same time, developing States "sought

[19] *Ibid.*

[20] International Bank for Reconstruction and Development (IBRD) Articles of Agreement (As amended effective February 16, 1989, and subsequently June 27, 2012).

[21] Shihata (note 2).

[22] Antonio R. Parra, *History of the ICSID Convention* (Oxford University Press 2012), p. 23. Taylor St. John, *The Rise of Investor-State Arbitration: Politics, Law, and Unintended Consequences* (Oxford University Press 2018) p. 152.

[23] *Ibid.*, p. 24.

[24] *Ibid.*, fn. 92.

[25] Andrew Newcombe and Lluís Paradell, *Law and Practice of Investment Treaties* (Kluwer Law International 2009) p. 18.

[26] *Ibid.*, p. 19, fn. 103: "In the period from 1960 to 1977, there were on average ninety-eight cases of expropriation of foreign property a year." Andreas F. Lowenfeld, *International Economic Law* (Oxford University Press 2002) p. 405; F. N. Burton and Hisashi Inoue, "Expropriation of Foreign-Owned Firms in Developing Countries: A Cross National Analysis" (1984) 18 *JWTL* 396, 397.

to reconstruct the legal framework for international economic relations,"[27] by asserting national sovereignty. For example, in 1974, developing States concluded the Declaration on the Establishment of New International Economic Order (NIEO Declaration) and the Charter of Economic Rights and Duties of States,[28] which included specific measures concerning foreign investment in accordance with national laws.

From a legal perspective, the shortcomings of existing domestic and international dispute settlement mechanisms for cross-border disputes had become increasingly evident. In terms of domestic remedies, foreign investors and their investments were subject to the jurisdiction of the host State, and the primary recourse for a foreign investor was to initiate a claim in domestic courts. However, such claims frequently were not recognized by domestic courts, and even if they were, sovereign immunity often provided a complete defense to the claim. Investors also found that courts in their home States were often reluctant to take jurisdiction over a claim where the relevant facts took place abroad and the respondent was a foreign State. Indeed, the investor's State might be concerned that this would be perceived as an "unfriendly act by the host government and interfere with bilateral relations on other matters."[29]

At the same time, international law remedies were also limited. State-to-State dispute settlement and diplomatic protection might be invoked to address a dispute between an investor and a host State. However, State-to-State dispute resolution was only available if there was an agreement between the two States in question, which was not always the case. In some instances, ad hoc commissions and arbitral tribunals were established to adjudicate specific claims or classes of claims, but this required States to establish a special mechanism to resolve the dispute.[30] Diplomatic protection also had its shortcomings: home States were often reluctant to espouse their investor's claims because of broader concerns about political relations with the host State.[31] Furthermore, the decision to espouse a claim by the home State was discretionary, and investors had to clear

[27] Newcombe and Paradell (note 25) p. 31.

[28] *Ibid.*

[29] Broches (note 15) p. 344.

[30] Newcombe and Paradell (note 25) p. 7.

[31] *Ibid.*, p. 5. Even though the exercise of diplomatic protection had been recognized by the Permanent Court of International Justice (PCIJ) in 1924, as an "elementary principle of international law."

procedural hurdles including demonstrating a strong claim, exhausting local remedies, convincing the home State to espouse the claim, and giving up control over the claim.

In addition to procedural barriers, there were substantive gaps in customary international law. These included uncertainty over the standard of compensation for expropriation and the threshold for breach of the minimum standard of treatment as well as an absence of protection in areas such as national treatment, transfer of funds, performance requirements and convertibility of currency obligations. In response, States began to incorporate relevant substantive protections in treaties at the bilateral and regional level. In particular, the Friendship, Commerce and Navigation (FCNs) treaties focused on developing trade and provided basic protection for the property of foreign nationals.[32] FCNs were the precursors of modern bilateral investment treaties (BITs) and their coverage usually included guarantees of "equitable treatment," "most constant protection and security," "most-favored nation" treatment and "just compensation for expropriation."[33]

Finally, the increased use of arbitration to settle commercial and investment disputes between private entities "exposed the practical difficulties involved in enforcing international arbitral awards."[34] A major development in addressing this difficulty was the adoption of the Convention on the Recognition and Enforcement of Foreign Arbitral Awards, signed on June 10, 1958 (the "New York Convention").[35] The need for effective enforcement was especially clear in the international context and with respect to awards involving States, and this became one of the key features of the ICSID Convention. Articles 53 and 54 of the ICSID Convention make an ICSID award binding and directly enforceable in every ICSID Contracting State, as if it were a final judgment of the State court. These provisions remain unique in international arbitration

[32] *Ibid.*, p. 41.

[33] FCNs were no longer concluded after the 1960s when their main function was addressed through the implementation of the General Agreement on Tariffs and Trade (GATT), *Ibid.*, p. 23; General Agreement on Tariffs and Trade (October 30, 1947) 55 UNTS 814 (applied provisionally as from January 1, 1948, pursuant to the Protocol of Provisional Application). Agreement on Trade Related Investment Measures (April 15, 1994) Marrakesh Agreement Establishing the World Trade Organization, Annex 1A, 1867 UNTS 187.

[34] Newcombe and Paradell (note 25) p. 25.

[35] Convention on the Recognition and Enforcement of Foreign Arbitral Awards (June 10, 1958) 21 UST 2517; 330 UNTS 38 (New York Convention).

and provide ICSID award holders with an expedited and simplified option to realize an Award.[36]

Against this background, the World Bank concluded that the solution was to conclude "arrangements, embodied in a treaty, which would ensure that arbitration agreements voluntarily entered would be implemented."[37] The ICSID Convention was that treaty.

12.3 ICSID as an International Organization

12.3.1 Governance

The ICSID Convention entered into force on October 14, 1966, one month after the twentieth State deposited its instrument of ratification.[38] It created an international institution to facilitate ISDS, accompanied by procedural rules for arbitration and conciliation.

The Convention established a light governance structure, consisting of an Administrative Council and a Secretariat. The ICSID Administrative Council is the governing body of ICSID. Its composition, functions and decision-making procedure are set out in Articles 4–8 of the ICSID Convention. Pursuant to Article 4 of the ICSID Convention,[39] the ICSID Administrative Council is composed of one representative of each Contracting State. Each Contracting State has one vote on the Administrative Council.[40]

The President of the World Bank Group is the Chairman of the Administrative Council (Article 5 of the ICSID Convention[41]). The Chairman has no vote on matters before the Administrative Council but convenes and presides over its meetings. The Administrative Council plays no role in the administration of individual cases. Rather, its mandate is to address organizational matters related to ICSID's institutional framework. This separation of functions reinforces the operation of an impartial and independent global dispute resolution facility.

36 Albert Jan van den Berg, "Some Recent Problems in the Practice of Enforcement under the New York and ICSID Conventions" 1987 2(2) *ICSID Rev-FILJ*, 440.
37 Broches (note 15) p. 345.
38 ICSID 3 (note 5).
39 ICSID Convention (note 1) Art. 4.
40 ICSID 3 (note 5).
41 ICSID Convention (note 1) Art. 5.

The ICSID Secretariat carries out the day-to-day operations of the Centre, including the administration of arbitration and conciliation cases and supporting other ICSID activities. Its composition and principal functions are set out in Articles 9–11 of the ICSID Convention and in the Administrative and Financial Regulations. The ICSID Secretariat is led by the Secretary-General, who is assisted by two Deputy Secretaries-General. Currently ICSID staff are organized into, five case management teams, a general administration and financial management team, a general administration and financial management team, and a front office. The Secretariat consists of approximately 70 staff of diverse backgrounds and nationalities.[42] It assists the parties and the tribunals throughout the process and provides expert support in the administration of cases. It also maintains an active outreach and publications program in foreign investment law and international investment dispute settlement.

12.3.2 Membership in ICSID

Membership in the ICSID Convention is available to all Member States of the World Bank. There is no cost or fee to join ICSID. Currently 163 countries have signed the ICSID Convention, of which 155 are Contracting States.[43] On April 12, 2019, the Republic of Djibouti signed the ICSID Convention and on June 9, 2020,[44] became the most recent State to deposit its instrument of ratification.[45]

All Contracting States are equally represented on the ICSID Administrative Council. As ICSID's governing body, the Administrative Council adopts the Centre's annual budget, elects the Secretary-General and Deputy Secretaries-General, and approves the annual report. Contracting States also vote on amendments to the ICSID Convention and Rules. In addition, ICSID Contracting States designate individuals to the ICSID Panels of Arbitrators and Conciliators, from which adjudicators may be selected to act in ICSID cases.[46]

[42] ICSID, "Secretariat," https://icsid.worldbank.org/en/Pages/about/Secretariat.aspx.

[43] The World Bank Group, "Member Countries of the International Bank of Reconstruction and Development," www.worldbank.org/en/about/leadership/members#1.

[44] ICSID News Release, "Djibouti Signs the ICSID Convention" (April 12, 2019).

[45] ICSID News Release, "Djibouti Ratifies the ICSID Convention" (June 9, 2020).

[46] *See* ICSID, "Members of the Panels of Arbitrators and of Conciliators," Doc. ICSID/10 https://icsid.worldbank.org/en/Documents/icsiddocs/ICSID%2010%20-%20Latest.pdf.

ICSID Contracting States can make designations and notifications under the ICSID Convention for the purposes of implementing the Convention.[47] For example, under Article 25(4) of the ICSID Convention, a Contracting State may notify ICSID of any class of disputes that it would exclude from ICSID jurisdiction. To date, only seven States have made such notifications.[48] An ICSID Contracting State may also exclude certain territories whose international relations they are responsible for from the application of the Convention pursuant to Article 70 of the ICSID Convention. To date, only five States have notified ICSID of this type of exclusion.[49] One of the most important functions of ICSID States is the creation of a world-wide network of courts for enforcement of ICSID Convention awards through designations pursuant to Article 54 of the Convention. To date, 93 States have made such designations.[50] This unique aspect of the Convention ensures a high level of compliance with ICSID awards, giving States and investors' confidence in the system.

12.3.3 Unique Features

Unlike other arbitral rules, ICSID is not merely a set of procedural rules. Rather, the design of the ICSID Convention reflects the role and vision of States to create an impartial, effective and delocalized facility that would promote foreign investment by improving the investment climate for investors and host States alike.[51] It features a number of provisions to reflect the unique characteristics of international investment disputes, with a view to maintaining a careful balance between the interests of investors and host States.

[47] *See* ICSID, "Measures taken by Member States," Doc ICSID/8 https://icsid.worldbank.org/en/Documents/icsiddocs/ICSID%208-Contracting%20States%20and%20Measures%20Taken%20by%20Them%20for%20the%20Purpose%20of%20the%20Convention.pdf.

[48] China (1993), Guatemala (2003), Indonesia (2012), Jamaica (1974), Papua New Guinea (1978), Saudi Arabia (1980), and Turkey (1989).

[49] Moldova (2011); New Zealand (1980); United Kingdom (1973). Denmark excluded the application of the Convention to the Faroe Islands in 1968, however, it withdrew this exclusion in 1969; in 1966 the Netherlands restricted the application of the Convention to Suriname and the Netherlands Antilles, however, in 1970 it withdrew that restriction.

[50] *See* ICSID 8 (note 47).

[51] Broches (note 15) p. 348.

The Convention creates a self-contained dispute resolution system, meaning that proceedings are delocalized (or separate) from domestic procedures and local courts cannot intervene in the ICSID process. This takes disputes from a national plane to an international level, putting parties on a level playing field and insulating them from the appearance or reality of domestic biases.[52] States give their specific consent to submit to dispute settlement by concluding an international investment agreement, contract or law. Once given, no party can unilaterally withdraw its consent. Another feature which ensures the efficacy of the ICSID system is that the Convention expressly prohibits a Contracting State from giving diplomatic protection or bringing an international claim in respect of a dispute which one of its nationals and another Contracting State have consented to submit to ICSID arbitration.[53] Furthermore, participants in cases under the ICSID Convention enjoy immunity from legal process in the conduct of the proceedings.[54]

Perhaps the most important feature is the unique enforcement mechanism in the Convention. Pursuant to Article 53(1) of the ICSID Convention,[55] an award rendered under the Convention is binding on the parties and not subject to any remedy outside the Convention. Each State must recognize the award as binding and enforce the pecuniary obligations in the award as if it were a final judgment of a court in that State. As a result, an ICSID award may not be appealed or challenged before national courts.[56] Challenges of ICSID awards must be brought within the framework of the Convention, which offers limited remedies that "reflect the deliberate election by the drafters of the Convention to ensure the finality of the awards."[57] These remedies include: rectification (Article 49 of the Convention), supplementary decision (Article 49 of the Convention), interpretation (Article 50 of the Convention), revision (Article 51 of the Convention) and annulment (Article 52 of the Convention). Annulment

[52] Shihata (note 2).

[53] ICSID Convention (note 1) Art. 27.

[54] Para (note 22) p. 23.

[55] ICSID Convention, Art. 53(1). *See also* Report of the Executive Directors (note 2): "Article 53 declares that the parties are bound by the award and that it shall not be subject to appeal or to any other remedy except those provided for in the Convention."

[56] ICSID Convention (note 1), Art. 53.

[57] ICSID Secretariat, "Updated Background Paper on Annulment for the Administrative Council" (May 5, 2016).

can only be brought on the basis of the five limited grounds in Article 52 and is intended to be an extraordinary remedy.[58]

ICSID awards are enforceable as a final judgment of the courts in every ICSID Member State, without the requirement of recognition and enforcement in the State where enforcement is sought. Awards issued under other rules, including under the UNCITRAL Arbitration Rules,[59] are subject to the recognition and enforcement provisions in the New York Convention,[60] which envisages a review or set aside process in local courts. This invariably adds cost and time to the overall proceeding which are avoided in the ICSID system.

12.4 Early Experience

After its entry into force, the Centre's first task was to familiarize potential parties with the availability and principal characteristics of the new institution."[61] The Centre's activities were focused on promoting ICSID's readiness to administer conciliation and arbitration of investment disputes between governments and foreign investors.[62]

In 1967, a year after the ICSID Convention entered into force, the OECD concluded the Draft Convention on the Protection of Foreign Policy. The OECD Convention "reaffirmed the adherence of member countries "to the principles of international law embodied in the Draft Convention" and commended it "as a basis for further extending and making more effective the application of these principles."[63] In the late 1960s, the first BITs with

[58] *Ibid.*, p. 2. "An ad hoc Committee may fully or partially annul an award on the basis of one or more of the following grounds: (1) the Tribunal was not properly constituted; (2) the Tribunal manifestly exceeded its powers; (3) there was corruption on the part of a Tribunal member; (4) there was a serious departure from a fundamental rule of procedure; or (5) the award failed to state the reasons on which it is based." The rate of annulment in ICSID cases remains low. The annulment rate for the years 1971–2000 is 13 percent, the rate for the decade 2001–2010 is 8 percent, and the rate of annulment for the decade 2011-2020 is 3 percent. Since January 2011, 225 Convention awards were rendered, 116 annulment proceedings were instituted, and seven awards were annulled in part or in full.

[59] Arbitration Rules of the United Nations Commission on International Trade Law (UNCITRAL Arbitration Rules) (1976 and 2014) (UNCITRAL Rules).

[60] New York Convention (note 35).

[61] ICSID Annual Report (1967).

[62] *Ibid.*

[63] Antonio Parra, "The Convention and Centre for Settlement of Investment Disputes," Lectures at the Hague Academy of International Law (July 11–15, 2005) p. 18.

ISDS began to be negotiated incorporating the principles contained in the Abs-Shawcross and OECD Conventions.[64] In 1968 the first BIT allowing investors to commence arbitration was concluded between the Netherlands and Indonesia.[65]

In 1969 ICSID published Model Clauses[66] which explained how States and investors could incorporate an ICSID clause in its treaties or contracts.[67] The Centre also concluded its first facilities cooperation agreement in 1968, allowing it to make arrangements with appropriate institutions to host ICSID conciliation and arbitration proceedings.[68]

In 1968, the Centre also began a collection of national legislation and international treaties related to foreign investment.[69] This has matured into a comprehensive publications program. ICSID publishes many specialized texts relating to international investment law and investment dispute settlement, including the ICSID Review-Foreign Investment Law Journal, and two multivolume loose-leaf collections of Investment Treaties and Laws of the World. In 2016 ICSID published "Building International Investment Law: The First 50 Years of ICSID," which analyzed 50 landmark cases decided its auspices.

In 1978 the Administrative Council approved the ICSID Additional Facility Rules.[70] These rules authorized the Secretariat to administer certain types of disputes between States and nationals of other States which fell outside the scope of the ICSID Convention because one of the parties was not an ICSID Contracting State or a national of an ICSID Contracting State.

64 The first bilateral investment treaty (BIT) was concluded in 1959 between the Republic of Pakistan and the Federal Republic of Germany, offering State-State dispute settlement only.

65 Agreement on economic cooperation between Netherlands and Indonesia, signed July 7, 1968, entered into force July 17, 1971.

66 The ICSID Convention requires that the parties' consent to ICSID jurisdiction be in writing. The ICSID Model Clauses were written to suggest how model clauses could be recorded. ICSID Model Clauses, https://icsid.worldbank.org/en/Pages/resources/ICSID-Model-Clauses.aspx.

67 *ICSID Annual Report* (1969).

68 To date the Centre has 25 of these agreements.

69 ICSID, Investment Promotion and Protection Treaties and Investment Laws of the World looseleaf collections.

70 The Administrative Council adopted the Additional Facility Rules on September 27, 1978. They offer (1) conciliation or arbitration proceedings for the settlement of investment disputes arising between parties one of which is not a Contracting State or a national of a Contracting State; (2) conciliation or arbitration proceedings between parties at least one of which is a Contracting State or a national of a Contracting State for the settlement of disputes that do not directly arise out of an investment; and (3) fact-finding proceedings. To date, these Rules have been used in 66 cases.

ICSID registered its first case in January 1972, based on consent in a contract.[71] The case concerned a dispute arising out of an agreement between the Government of Morocco and two private companies, Holiday Inns and Occidental Petroleum Inc. The first investment treaty case was registered in 1987, *Asian Agricultural Products Limited v. Democratic Republic of Sri Lanka*.[72] The government of Sri Lanka was ultimately found liable in that case for the destruction of the investor's shrimp farm during a military operation by Sri Lankan security forces, and it was ordered to pay damages under the United Kingdom–Sri Lanka BIT.

Despite these early cases, it wasn't until the mid-1990s and early 2000s that ICSID started to see a real increase in the Centre's caseload.[73] This was primarily attributable to the increase in the number of BITs concluded between States offering ISDS. By the late 1990s and 2000s, foreign direct investment had become increasingly important as a source of finance for developing countries.[74] The number of BITs increased from 265 in the late 1980s to over 400 in early 1990s, rising to 1857 in 2000[75] and estimated at 3284 today.[76] The United States, Canada and Mexico signed the North American Free Trade Agreement in 1992,[77] and 49 States signed the Energy Charter Treaty in 1994. Both of these treaties ultimately became the basis for numerous cases, with more than 67 cases filed under the North Free Trade Agreement (NAFTA) Chapter 11 to date and more than 128 cases based on the ECT.[78] At the same time, ICSID membership began to increase, rising from 90 Contracting States by early 1990 to 134 Contracting States by 2001,[79] 144 Contracting States by 2010[80] and currently at 155 Contracting States.[81]

[71] Holiday Inns S.A. and others v. Morocco (ICSID Case No. ARB/72/1). *See also* ICSID Annual Report 1972.

[72] Asian Agricultural Products Limited v. Democratic Socialist Republic of Sri Lanka (ICSID Case No. ARB/87/3).

[73] ICSID, "The ICSID Caseload-Statistics (Issue 2021-1)."

[74] Para (note 63) p. 19.

[75] UNCTAD, "Bilateral Investment Treaties 1959–1999" (United Nations 2000) https://unctad.org/en/Docs/poiteiiad2.en.pdf, figure 1.

[76] UNCTAD, World Investment Report 2020, figure III.6.

[77] North American Free Trade Agreement (signed December 17, 1992, entered into force January 1, 1994) (NAFTA).

[78] UNCTAD, "IIA Issue Note: International investment Agreements – Fact Sheet on Investor-State Dispute Settlement Cases in 2018" (Issue 2, July 2020) p. 4.

[79] *ICSID Annual Report* (2001) p. 4.

[80] *ICSID Annual Report* (2010) p. 9.

[81] *See ICSID Annual Reports* 1990 and 2000.

12.5 ICSID Today

The expansion in ICSID's membership is evidence of continued confidence in the Centre and in ISDS.

The growth in cases has been accompanied by several new trends in the discipline. Many States have begun to incorporate investment obligations into free trade agreements (FTAs), making them part of comprehensive regulation of economic relations between the Contracting States. Some States have concluded plurilateral or regional investment treaties, for example the North American Free Trade Agreement (NAFTA) or Comprehensive and Progressive Agreement for Trans-Pacific Partnership (CPTPP), and the Regional Comprehensive Economic Partnership (RCEP).[82] An even more recent trend has been the negotiation of investment obligations by Regional Economic Integration Organizations (REIOs), notably the European Union.

Investment treaties have also evolved in terms of their substantive and procedural obligations. A number of States have adopted or are drafting Model BITs which serve as their template in negotiations. Among the new provisions found in such treaties are sustainable development obligations,[83] clauses addressing corporate social responsibility,[84] and reciprocal obligations imposed on investors.[85] The wording of substantive obligations in many treaties has become more specific, frequently based on case experience. In particular, many new treaties have updated their fair and equitable treatment[86] and expropriation[87] clauses, the two most frequently

[82] *Ibid.*, p. 88: "In 2017, 18 new IIAs were concluded, from which 9 were BITs and the other 9 were treaties with investment protections (TIPs)."

[83] For example, India Model BIT (2015); Netherlands Model BIT (2018).

[84] For example: Morocco-Nigeria BIT (signed December 3, 2016, not yet entered into force); Chile-Hong Kong-China BIT (signed November 6, 2016, not yet entered into force); CETA (note 9) preamble; Brazil-Peru ETA (signed April 29, 2016, not yet entered into force) Art. 2.3; CPTPP Article 9.17; Colombia-France BIT (signed October 7, 2014, not yet entered into force) Art. 11; Canada-Chile FTA (2017).

[85] For example: Argentina–Japan BIT (2018); Armenia–Japan (2018); Australia–Peru FTA (2018); CPTPP (note 101), USMCA (note 101); Mauritania–Turkey BIT; EU–Singapore IPA (note 9), CETA (note 9). *See also* UNCTAD, "IIA Issue Note – International Investment Agreements: Taking Stock of IIA Reform: Recent Developments (Issue 3, June 2019) https://unctad.org/en/PublicationsLibrary/diaepcbinf2019d5_en.pdf.

[86] Bilateral investment treaty between Bangladesh and India (October 2017); CETA (note 9), CPTPP (note 101).

[87] Bilateral investment treaty between Bangladesh and India (October 2017).

invoked obligations in ISDS. Some treaties have also updated their definitions of "investor" and "investment,"[88] and added denial of benefit provisions to ensure the benefits of the treaties accrue to the users intended by the treaty negotiators. Another feature of new investment treaties has been an expansion of procedural conditions in the treaty, which supersede ordinary procedural rules. Examples of this include clauses addressing transparency requirements,[89] enabling *amicus curiae* participation,[90] imposing preconditions to filing a claim such as exhaustion of local remedies or cooling-off periods,[91] adding prescription periods and the like.

The increase in the number of treaties with investment obligations and in their complexity has quadrupled the number of cases at ICSID.[92] ICSID has administered 843 cases since its first case was registered in 1972. In the last five years ICSID registered an average of 50 cases per year, with a record 58 cases registered in 2020. The majority of these cases have been instituted under the ICSID Convention Arbitration Rules (721 cases), followed by the Additional Facility Arbitration Rules (69 cases)[93], the ICSID Convention Conciliation Rules (11 cases) and the ICSID Additional Facility Conciliation Cases (2 cases).[94] Notably, in recent years ICSID has also administered cases under other sets of rules, such as the United Nations Commission on International Trade Law (UNCITRAL) Arbitration Rules.

The basis of the parties' consent to ICSID jurisdiction has been found in a variety of sources, including investment laws, contracts concluded between a foreign investor and the host State of the investment, and

[88] *Ibid.* For example, (1) conditioning treaty coverage on the economic contribution of the investment to the host State economy, by including this requirement in the definition of investment Argentina-United Arab Emirates BIT, Belarus-India BIT (2018), Belarus-Turkey BIT (2018), Lithuania-Turkey BIT (2018), State of Palestine-Turkey BIT (2018); (2) excluding intangible rights from the definition of investment. Noting that rights such as goodwill, brand value and market share are excluded from the definition of investment (*e.g.*, Belarus-India BIT (2018)).

[89] Armenia-EU Comprehensive and Enhanced Partnership Agreement (limiting investment provisions, such as national treatment and most favored nation.

[90] CPTPP; CETA; USMCA (note 101); Lithuania-Turkey BIT (2018); Japan-UAE BIT (2018); EU-Singapore IPA (note 9); Canada-Mongolia BIT (2019), Australia-China FTA (2015).

[91] USMCA (note 101), Morocco-Nigeria BIT (2016); Netherlands-UAE BIT (2016); Malta-Serbia BIT (2010).

[92] ICSID *Annual Report* 2002 and 2003. In early 2000s, ICSID was administering a record for the time of 100–129 cases.

[93] ICSID *Annual Report* (1997).

[94] ICSID Caseload-Statistics 2021-1 (note 73).

bilateral or multilateral treaties. By the end of 2020, bilateral investment treaties were the primary instrument invoked in ICSID cases (60 percent), followed by investment contracts between the investor and the host State (15 percent), the Energy Charter Treaty (10 percent), and the investment law of the host State (8 percent). Recent cases have involved a broad range of economic sectors, including the oil, gas and mining sector (24 percent), followed by electric power and other energy sources at 17 percent and construction at 9 percent.

Outcomes in ICSID cases are balanced as between States and investors – a trend that has been consistent for the past several decades. By the end of 2020, 35 percent of the concluded cases were settled or otherwise discontinued, and the remaining 65 percent were decided by a Tribunal. Of the cases resulting in an Award, slightly more than half were decided in favor of the respondent (the tribunal dismissed all claims in 18 percent of cases, declined jurisdiction in 15 percent of cases, and decided that the claims were manifestly without legal merit in 1 percent of the cases). In the other half of the cases (31 percent) the tribunal upheld the claims in part or fully.[95]

Parties to ICSID cases are turning to an increasingly diverse set of arbitrators, conciliators and ad hoc committee members. For example, in 2020, 181 appointments were made from all geographic regions, with 44 nationalities represented.[96] Gender diversity has also increased. Twenty-three percent of the appointments in 2020 were women, up from 19 percent in 2019.[97] More than half of female appointments were made either by the parties or by the party-appointed arbitrators (61 percent), and the remaining female appointments (39 percent) were made by ICSID, based on an agreement of the parties or the applicable default provisions. Where the Centre has acted as appointing authority, about 32 percent of the appointments involved nationals of low-or middle-income economies, and 27 percent of ICSID appointees were women.[98]

With a growing caseload, it has become increasingly important for States to make designations to the ICSID Panels. ICSID encourages Member States to designate their full complement of four arbitrators and

95 ICSID Caseload-Statistics 2021–1 (note 73) pp. 29.

96 *Ibid.* p. 30 Cf. The ICSID Caseload -Statistics (Issue 2020–1), p. 30.

97 ICSID Caseload-Statistics (Issue 2021-1) (note 73), p. 30.

98 *Ibid.*

four conciliators and to fill vacancies with expert arbitrators specialized in public international law, international investment law, and arbitration or ADR techniques. By the end of 2018, the number of individuals on the ICSID Panel of Arbitrators and of Conciliators had increased from 496 in early 2000s to 690.[99]

Another aspect of ICSID's global services is its ability to hold hearings in any location. ICSID has modernized and improved its facilities in its primary hearing locations, Washington, DC, and Paris, France. These facilities offer first-class technology and hearing rooms, with full-time technical support. To increase its ability to offer hearings in all regions of the world, ICSID continuously develops partnerships with arbitration institutions. Since the 1990s ICSID has developed 25 agreements with institutions in Australia, British Virgin Islands, Egypt, Colombia, China, Ireland, Germany, Bahrain, Hong Kong, Rwanda, Malaysia, Netherlands, Singapore, Spain, Nigeria, Korea, Morocco, France, United States, Qatar, and most recently in Belgium.[100] ICSID also holds hearings in other locations around the world, having access to more than 130 World Bank country offices.

The demand for the Centre's services continues to increase, demonstrating the importance of its role. ICSID offers a wide range of services in relation to investment disputes, including acting as appointing authority, naming consolidation tribunals under certain treaties, deciding party challenges of arbitrators or conciliators, administering State-State disputes, and acting as the registry for dispute settlement under investment treaties and free trade agreements. Recent European Union Free Trade Agreements (EU FTAs) and other megaregional treaties (namely, the Comprehensive and Progressive Agreement for Trans-Pacific Partnership (CPTPP) and the United States, Canada and Mexico Agreement (USCMA)) offer investment arbitration under the ICSID Convention, the ICSID Additional Facility Rules, and the UNCITRAL Arbitration Rules.[101] Some of these agreements have also named ICSID as the appointing authority for the selection of arbitrators where an appointment is missing,[102] and as the consolidating

[99] ICSID Annual Report 2001. *See also* ICSID News Release, "New Designations to the ICSID Panels 2020" (January 14, 2021).

[100] ICSID, "Other Facilities," https://icsid.worldbank.org/en/Pages/services/Other-Facilities.aspx.

[101] *See* (note 90) CETA Art. 8.23.2; EU-Mexico FTA Art. 7.2; EU-Singapore FTA Art. 3.6; EU-Vietnam FTA Art. 3.33; CPTPP Art. 9.19.4; USCMA Art. 14.D.3.3.

[102] CETA Art. 8.27.17 ; CPTPP Art. 9.22 ; USCMA Art. 14.D.6.2.

authority for consolidation of claims.[103] In addition, ICSID has been selected as the Secretariat for ISDS mechanism under the Comprehensive Economic and Trade Agreement between Canada and the European Union (CETA) as well as the European Union (EU) Free Trade Agreements (FTAs) with Singapore, Vietnam and Mexico.[104] In performing this role, ICSID will administer investment disputes initiated under these agreements and provide support for the Investment Tribunal and the Appellate Body that is envisioned under each of these FTAs.[105]

Another aspect of ICSID's increasing service is to promote greater awareness of international law on foreign investment and the ICSID process. In the past decade, ICSID has provided extensive technical assistance in ISDS and investment law matters, reflecting its established expertise and involvement in this field. In 2020, ICSID gave over 140 presentations in more than 30 different countries around the word. These presentations include advice on prevention and preparation for claims, mediation of ISDS, and how to navigate the ICSID Rules for arbitration and conciliation.

12.6 ICSID Rule Amendment Process

As the preeminent center in ISDS, ICSID has also been a leader in modernizing the rules and practice of ISDS over the years. The ICSID Rules have been modified three times since 1966 and it is currently undertaking its fourth, and most comprehensive, rules revision process.

The current rules were approved in 2006 and came into effect on April 10, 2006. These amendments followed an extensive 2-year period of public consultation.[106] This resulted in several key proposals that have been groundbreaking for investment arbitration. In particular, these rules changed prevailing practice related to transparency of arbitral proceedings, participation of *amicus curiae*, and expedited preliminary objections.

103 CPTPP Art. 9.28 ; USCMA Art. 14.D.12.2.

104 CETA Art. 8.27.16; EU-Mexico FTA Arts. 11.17 and 12.15; EU-Singapore FTA Arts. 3.9.16 and 3.10.14; EU-Vietnam FTA Arts. 3.38.18 and 3.39.18.

105 CETA Art. 8.27.16; EU-Mexico FTA Arts. 11.17 and 12.15; EU-Singapore FTA Arts. 3.9.16 and 3.10.14; EU-Vietnam FTA Arts. 3.38.18 and 3.39.18.

106 ICSID News Release, "Suggested Changes to the ICSID Rules and Regulations, 'Working Paper of the ICSID Secretariat'" (May 12, 2005), https://icsid.worldbank.org/en/Documents/resources/Suggested%20Changes%20to%20the%20ICSID%20Rules%20and%20Regulations.pdf

ICSID commenced its fourth amendment process in October 2016. The overarching goals of this amendment are to modernize, simplify, and streamline the rules. It draws on the lessons learned from hundreds of ICSID cases, and encompasses changes to the existing rules for arbitration, conciliation and fact-finding, and the introduction of a new set of mediation rules.

The proposals for amendment are available in a series of Working Papers published on the ICSID website.[107] They address a range of topics that have been raised by Member States, private sector and other stakeholders, including transparency in the conduct and outcome of proceedings, disclosure requirements for third-party funders, security for costs, reducing the time and cost of proceedings and expanded declarations of independence and impartiality for arbitrators.[108]

The adoption of these rules will continue ICSID's tradition of innovative leadership in ISDS and service to investors and States.

[107] ICSID, "Working Paper #1 – Proposals for Amendments of the ICSID Rules" (August 2018); ICSID, "Working Paper #2 – Proposals for Amendment of the ICSID Rules" (March 2019); "Working Paper #3 – Proposals for Amendment of the ICSID Rules" (August 2019); "Working Paper #4 – Proposals for Amendment of the ICSID Rules" (February 2020).

[108] See ICSID News Release "ICSID Proposes Updates to Investment Dispute Settlement Rules" (August 3, 2018); ICSID News Release "Updated Proposals for Amendment of the ICSID Rules" (March, 2019); ICSID News Release "ICSID Publishes Third Working Paper on Rule Amendments" (August 16, 2019); ICSID News Release "ICSID Publishes Fourth Working Paper on Rule Amendments" (February 29, 2020).

13 The Future for International Investment Arbitration

Michael Reisman*

13.1 Introduction

The architecture of the world order that was constructed from the ruins of the World War II has preserved a precarious peace, while allowing historically unprecedented economic growth. In his Nobel Peace Prize speech, Barack Obama warned that "[a] decade into a new century, this old architecture is buckling under the weight of new threats." It is dispiriting to reflect on how prescient Obama's words, delivered in 2009, were. Even allowing for the fact that at any moment there will be contrary trends toward and away from goals, key pillars of that world order do seem wobbly and in danger of buckling. Consider just two foundational arrangements. First, the prohibition of conquest and acquisition of territory by force continues to be flouted in an increasing number of cases – Crimea, Nagorno Karabakh, Abkhazia, South Ossetia, Abyei, the West Bank, East Jerusalem, the Golan Heights, Western Sahara, South China Sea, Tibet, the list goes on. Second, judgments of the International Court of Justice are effectively ignored, not by States ordinarily thought to be international renegades but also by sister judiciaries with long-standing claims to championing the rule of law: the US Supreme Court and the Italian Constitutional Court. China and Russia, designers of the Charter of the United Nations (UN) and principal custodians of world order by virtue of their permanent membership in the UN Security Council, simply ignore inter-State awards of the Permanent Court of Arbitration.[1]

Now, one of the girders of the economic system that has allowed for the unprecedented production and wider distribution of wealth – the

* This chapter was previously published as "The Past and Future of the Great Compact" (Lamm Lecture, University of Miami School of Law, February 9, 2017), (2018) 33 ICSID Review 56.

[1] Charter of the United Nations (opened for signature June 26, 1945, entered into force October 24, 1945).

international trade and investment system – seems to be wobbling. Whether it is actually buckling or is only adjusting, as part of the ongoing dialectic of all law, requires us to identify and trace the origins of what I will call "the Great Compact," the foundational normative arrangement that undergirds the contemporary international investment system.

13.2 From the Drago Letter to the Porter Convention

From the rise of European imperialism, in particular, direct foreign investment acquired, in many quarters, the image, not entirely undeserved, of an exploitative instrument of mercantilism and foreign domination. Later, the staggered distribution of the fruits of the industrial revolution enabled European transportation and communication companies to carry their technologies to comparatively less developed countries. Key parts of direct foreign investment were henceforth dedicated to, and often controlled, the exploration and exploitation of natural resources and infrastructural development and its management in other national economies. To many citizens of those States, it seemed that the great corporations and mighty banks and financial institutions of a distant metropolitan "owned" their natural resources, their electrical grids, their water supply, their railroads and their countries.

Customary international law, the product of the practice and *opinio juris* of the major powers of the time, had established minimum standards for the protection of aliens and their property, but, in the absence of institutional methods for applying those standards, their modes of implementation were left to the discretion of the investors' States. Euphemistically called "diplomatic protection of nationals," these methods of protection could be as coercive as the investor's State wanted.

This functioned as an effective system for protecting foreign investments from political interference by the governments of States where the investments had been made. But "diplomatic protection," like all unilateral exercises, was susceptible to abuse for the State exercising it was judge, jury and executioner. Predictably, it generated discontent among – and efforts to push back by – the weaker States who found themselves on the receiving end. Many were in Latin America.

Luis M. Drago, then Minister of Foreign Relations of Argentina, gave voice to this discontent in a letter to the USA, the country that President James Monroe had summarily appointed as the regional gendarme.

Drago protested the British, German and Italian naval blockade of the principal ports of Venezuela in 1902 in a debt collection exercise[2] and proposed that "the public debt cannot occasion armed intervention nor even the actual occupation of the territory of American nations by a European power."

Drago's proposal provoked heated discussion at the third Pan-American Conference (Rio Conference) in 1906. It did not produce a draft treaty thanks largely to Theodore Roosevelt's ostensible concern that a meeting attended mostly by debtor States was not the forum to resolve the matter.[3] Without American support, the conference only recommended that the matter be referred to the Second Peace Conference at the Hague.[4]

One year later, this conference adopted the Porter Convention.[5] Its Article 1 endorsed the limitation on the use of force sought by Drago but, in return for a mandatory *quid pro quo*, international arbitration:

> The Contracting Powers agree not to have recourse to armed force for the recovery of contract debts claimed from the Government of one country by the Government of another country as being due to its nationals.

[2] Reprinted in the Supplement to (1907) 1 *AJIL* 1.

[3] Amos S Hershey, "The Calvo and Drago Doctrines" (1907) 1 *AJIL* 26, 40; Theodore Roosevelt, "Sixth Annual Message to the Senate and House of Representatives" (December 3, 1906), www.presidency.ucsb.edu/ws/?pid=29547, "Such action ... would have the appearance of a meeting of debtors resolving how their creditors should act, and this would not Inspire respect. The true course is indicated by the terms of the program, which proposes to request the Second Hague Conference, where both creditors and debtors will be assembled, to consider the subject." As President Theodore Roosevelt, in Message to Congress, explained: "It is doubtless true that the non-payment of public debts may be accompanied by such circumstances of fraud and wrongdoing or violation of treaties as to justify the use of force. This Government would be glad to see an international consideration of the subject which shall discriminate between such cases and the simple nonperformance of a contract with a private person, and a resolution in favor of reliance upon peaceful means in cases of the latter class. It is not felt, however, that the conference at Rio should undertake to make such a discrimination or to resolve upon such a rule. Most of the American countries are still debtor nations, while the countries of Europe are the creditors. If the Rio conference, therefore, were to take such action it would have the appearance of a meeting of debtors resolving how their creditors should act, and this would not inspire respect. The true course is indicated by the terms of the program, which proposes to request the Second Hague Conference, where both creditors and debtors will be assembled, to consider the subject."

[4] Roosevelt (note 3).

[5] Hague Convention on the Limitation of Employment of Force for Recovery of Contract Debts (opened for signature October 18, 1907, entered into force January 26, 1910) (Porter Convention).

This undertaking is, however, not applicable when the debtor State refuses or neglects to reply to an offer of arbitration, or, after accepting the offer, prevents any *compromis* from being agreed on, or, after the arbitration, fails to submit to the award.

It is further agreed that the arbitration mentioned in paragraph 2 of the foregoing Article shall be subject to the procedure laid down in Part IV, Chapter 3, of the Hague Convention for the Pacific Settlement of International Disputes. The award shall determine, except where otherwise agreed between the parties, the validity of the claim, the amount of the debt, and the time and mode of payment.[6]

The Porter Convention, coinciding with the Permanent Court of Arbitration, laid the groundwork for a later Great Compact in international investment law: investors' States waiving the deployment of their superior power to protect their investors in return for host States' agreeing to submit the disputes with those investors to international arbitration by independent third-party determination.

13.3 The Washington Convention and ICSID

After the World War II, as the great European empires were dismantled, many of the new States that emerged from them adopted the command economy model and, along with it, an image of foreign investment and its international modalities of protection as an equally sinister, but more subtle, neocolonialist instrument. The most explicit normativization of this view of foreign investment was to be found in the UN General Assembly's Declaration on the Establishment of a New International Economic Order (NIEO)[7] and its Charter of Economic Rights and Duties of States (CERDS).[8] In excluding the application of international law by a tribunal independent of the State, the lawfulness of whose actions is in issue, NIEO and CERDS purported to reject an integral part of the package that comprised the Great Compact.

Ironically, this burst of economic nationalism in many of the newer States coincided with a demand for national economic development. The political imperative for elites in many of these States was to grow their

[6] *Ibid.*, 2251–2252.

[7] GA Resolution A/RES/S-6/3201 (May 1, 1974).

[8] GA Resolution A/RES/40/182 (December 17, 1985).

national economies, increase the national wealth and, through some form of distribution, whether by provision of opportunity, entitlement or some mix of both, to expand the economic and other life opportunities of their citizens. For nondemocratic elites, the promise and delivery of economic development became a substitute basis for political legitimacy. No surprise then that in 1986 the UN General Assembly that had earlier decreed a "new international economic order" resolved not only that "the right of development is an inalienable human right" but also that "states have the duty to take steps individually and collectively to formulate international development policies with a view to facilitating the full realization of the right to development."[9]

The International Bank for Reconstruction and Development (IBRD), which was the original name of the World Bank, had been established as a UN specialized agency with the task of assembling and then lending the public international funds necessary for reconstructing a Europe that had been devastated by the World War II. The IBRD project succeeded. By the late 1950s, Europe's economies had rebounded. But, by then, more and more of Europe's former colonial territories, now independent, desperately needed to develop.

Development cannot simply be secured by legislative fiat. The new States turned for assistance to the international organizations that had midwifed them. Because the demand for development capital exceeded the supply of public international funds available to meet that demand, the only available source that could realistically address the shortfall was private direct foreign investment. Recall, however, that foreign investment was then being vilified as a neocolonial tool rather than as a potential adjunct tool for national development.

The real significance of the 1965 Washington Convention, by which developed and developing States established the World Bank's International Centre for Settlement of Investment Disputes (ICSID),[10] was the consensus decision that underlay it. As a result of the indispensability of private investment to national economic development, an international seal of approval was accorded to private direct foreign investment as an indispensable means

[9] Declaration on the Right to Development, GA Resolution A/RES/41/128 (December 4, 1986).

[10] Convention on the Settlement of Investment Disputes between States and Nationals of Other States (opened for signature March 18, 1965, entered into force October 14, 1966) (ICSID Convention).

for assisting in national development. According to a central plank of the consensus, the capital-exporting States bound themselves to abjure the espousing of "diplomatic protection" on behalf of their investors, while capital-importing States bound themselves to submit to the arbitration of disputes with foreign investors.

So far, this tracked the Porter Convention. But a critical addition was that the initiative to establish a tribunal, theretofore through the agreement of both State parties, was henceforth to be at the instance of the foreign investors themselves. Powerful governments of capital-exporting States, which were already removed from the process of forcefully implementing customary international law's standards of protection of aliens, were also excluded from any role in establishing and managing the arbitral process. Now the responsibility for their application was assigned to international tribunals, constituted on the initiative of the private foreign investor.

The package that comprised the Great Compact, in its 2.0 version, had something for everyone. From the perspective of the capital-importing State, the Compact exorcised the specter of coercive collection. From the perspective of the Foreign Office of the capital-exporting State, the Compact depoliticized investment disputes by transferring the politically expensive burden of espousing national claims to a reliable external applier. From the perspective of the foreign investor, it dispelled uncertainty about whether its own government would be willing, when needed, to bear the political cost of bringing a claim against another State. And from the perspective of the arbitrators to whom the exclusive responsibility for resolving the dispute was being assigned, it cleared the way for deciding solely on legal grounds. This was, in sum, the Great Compact on which the modern system of international investment law was built. And I might say that all States – developed, developing, liberal, socialist and communist – participated on an equal footing in fashioning it.

13.4 Refinement of the International Standard

In short order, a network of bilateral and plurilateral international agreements and their dispute resolution mechanisms assumed a role in two dimensions: first, in confirming, as the *lex specialis* agreed to by both State parties, what will constitute the standards for the governance of foreign investment by the host State and, second, and equally important, in designating the default modalities with the exclusive competence for supervising and implementing them. Bilateral investment treaties (BITs) are the handiwork of State officials. Although there are variations between them, their common assumptions are striking. Each BIT validates and endorses the value of international investment and, moreover, undertakes to establish an orderly framework for it by creating, in the language of the trilateral investment treaty between South Korea, China, and Japan (I intentionally choose three non-Western States, each with its own distinct political economy), "stable, favorable and transparent conditions for investment by investors of one Contracting Party in the territory of the other Contracting Parties."[11] This Treaty, thus acknowledges, as do thousands of BITs using similar language, that "stable, favorable and transparent conditions" comprise more than natural phenomena, such as climate, ecology, geography and natural and human resources. Critically, "favourable conditions" encompass appropriate internal legal, administrative and regulatory arrangements, conducted through procedures designed to ensure that the arrangements are applied as they are supposed to be applied. This, in turn, requires an effective system of implementation, composed of impartial courts, an efficient and legally restrained bureaucracy and transparency in decision-making.

This international standard of governance is a prescriptive component of international law's control mechanism over governments, whether dealing, through its human rights law "window," with their own nationals or, through its investment law "window," with foreign investors. Thus, parallel to international human rights institutions extending into the erstwhile reserved domain of domestic jurisdiction, the institutions of contemporary international investment law were being called upon to play a more particularized and increasingly intrusive and assertive role in supervising governance arrangements within State parties. In investment law, the Compact assigned this role to compulsory international arbitration – at the initiative of the investor. BITs, in the aggregate, were being applied in ways that raised international law's bar for the way States conducted their internal affairs.

[11] Investment Promotion and Protection Agreement between Japan, Republic of Korea and China (signed May 13, 2012, entered into force May 17, 2014). An unofficial English translation of the treaty was published by the Japanese Ministry of Trade.

13.5 Reaction from a Surprising Quarter

As far as capital-exporting States were concerned, this part of the Great Compact was fine as long as it was confined to appraising the actions of developing countries in disputes with foreign investors. But, to paraphrase the poet Robert Southey,[12] the chickens were coming home to roost, for, in the meanwhile, the once rather clear delineation between capital-importing or developing States and capital-exporting or developed States had become blurred, as the developed States became magnets for foreign investment, and it became critical to the growth of their own national economies. One of the consequences of this role reversal has been the increasing number of treaty-based investment disputes launched against developed countries – with more in the wings. Now developed countries were facing the prospect of their own regulatory actions being subjected to review by international tribunals in terms, *inter alia*, of a fair and equitable treatment (FET) standard.[13] Now it was the turn of constituencies in developed countries to complain that their sovereign right to regulate was being arrogated by international investment law.

It was only a matter of time until developed States, theretofore the proponents and champions of international legal protection of their foreign investors, would begin to think more like prospective respondents and use their considerable influence to push back against their own creation.[14] This pushback has given rise to a number of changes that they, until then, had stoutly resisted:

- The content of the substantive obligations of FET and expropriation, compared to earlier formulations, has been defined and confined in the newer generations of investment agreements; henceforth the effort has been to anchor FET in the customary international law of the minimum

[12] R. Southey, *The Curse of Kehama* (London: Longman, Hurst, Rees, Orme, and Brown, Paternoster-Row, 1810).

[13] G. Aguilar Alvarez and W. W. Park, "The New Face of Investment Arbitration: NAFTA Chapter 11" (2003) 28 *Yale J Intl L* 365.

[14] *See, e.g.*, M. Waibel and others, "The Backlash against Investment Arbitration: Perception and Reality" (Kluwer Law International, 2010); E. Warren, "The Trans-Pacific Partnership Clause Everyone Should Oppose" *Washington Post* (February 25, 2015), www.washingtonpost.com/opinions/kill-the-dispute-settlement-language-in-thetrans-pacific-partnership/2015/02/25/ec7705a2-bd1e-11e4-b274 e5209a3bc9a9_story.html.

standard of treatment.[15] A State's nondiscriminatory and, perhaps, nonconfiscatory regulatory actions adopted for public purposes generally will not constitute indirect expropriations. For reasons I explored in "Canute Confronts the Tide," this effort at pushback promises limited and only short-term success.[16]

- The generative force and intergenerational equalizing effect of a most-favored-nation clause has been defined restrictively and, in particular, will not be applied to international dispute resolution procedures.[17]
- A new model of an independent investment court system, consisting of a permanent tribunal and an appeal tribunal, has been introduced in the recently signed European Union–Canada Comprehensive Economic and Trade Agreement, replacing the traditional investor-State arbitration mechanism.[18] At least in investment disputes between the large economies of the European Union and Canada, only the State parties will be selecting the judges; claimant investors will henceforth have no role in constituting the tribunals.

Finally, the Trans-Pacific Partnership is gone,[19] and the Transatlantic Trade and Investment Partnership is in the balance.[20]

None of these changes, to date, goes to the heart of the Great Compact. But, with the surge of antiglobalization and nationalist sentiment in many economically important States, the future of international investment law could be at a critical crossroads. Many of the features of this complex reaction to the Great Compact prove, on close examination, to be counterintuitive. First, the reaction is not being led by the governments of developing and

[15] Whether the contents of the fair and equitable treatment and the minimum standard of treatment are different is another question. *See* W. Michael Reisman, "Canute Confronts the Tide: States vs Tribunals and the Evolution of the Minimum Standard in Customary International Law" (2015) 30(3) *ICSID Rev – FILJ* 616.

[16] W. Michael Reisman, "Negotiating Investment Treaties: Mechanisms for Anticipating and Controlling Textual Drift" (2016) *Yale Law Economic and Research Paper no 546*, 17–19, https://ssrn.com/abstract=2789796.

[17] *See, e.g.*, art 9.5(3) of the now defunct Trans-Pacific Partnership (TPP) (signed February 4, 2016, not entered into force), http://tpp.mfat.govt.nz.

[18] European Commission, "CETA: Summary of the Final Negotiating Results" (February 2016) 11. European Commission–Canada Comprehensive Economic and Trade Agreement (CETA) (final draft of February 29, 2016).

[19] Peter Baker, "Trump Abandons Trans-Pacific Partnership, Obama's Signature Trade Deal" *New York Times* (January 23, 2017), www.nytimes.com/2017/01/23/us/politics/tpp-trump-trade-nafta.html.

[20] Transatlantic Trade and Investment Partnership (TTIP) (draft dated November 12, 2015).

capital-importing countries, from whom antipathy to foreign investment law's increasing application of high international standards to domestic governmental actions would usually have been expected. Although a few mineral-rich States have denounced some of their investment treaties, the vast majority of the developing countries continue to subscribe to arrangements that were forged to encourage cross-border direct foreign investment.[21] Indeed, many of the developing countries that had formerly led the chorus denouncing as "neocolonial" the international legal arrangements fostering foreign investments have adjusted, or are now adjusting, their own policies and laws to accommodate them. Rather, the current reaction is impelled by the governments of developed countries, who were the original leaders, shapers and champions of the Great Compact and international law's investment system.

Second, the reaction is not elite led or "top-down," as is the usual pattern with the initiation of complex economic programs but, to a significant extent, is "bottom-up" or rank-and-file driven. This participation is enhanced by the fact that many of the States that are leading the reaction are still vibrantly democratic.

I submit that the reasons for these reactions have less to do with the failings of the Great Compact, which I submit is a remarkable achievement that has accomplished its mission, and more to do with the convergence of momentous social changes.

13.6 The Costs of Globalization

In an increasing number of sectors, the transnationalization of civic activity is rendering the corresponding parts of the State's governmental apparatus,

[21] One notable example is Argentina, which had been the respondent in many investment disputes at the end of the twentieth and the beginning of the twenty-first centuries. This bitter experience notwithstanding, on November 6, 2016, it signed its first bilateral investment treaty in 15 years with Qatar. Nevertheless, some provisions have reflected lessons learned from previous disputes – *e.g.*, (1) art 1(2) on the definition of "investment" does not include express reference to bonds and other financial instruments; (2) the definition of "investor" under art 1(1) has been much more narrowly crafted; (3) art 4(4) states that the most-favored-nation clause will not be applied to the dispute settlements procedure; and (4) art 13 can be viewed as an express self-judging essential security clause as it provides that "nothing in this Treaty shall be construed to preclude a Contracting Party from applying measures that it *considers* necessary." Agreement for Reciprocal Promotion and Protection of Investments between the Argentine Republic and the State of Qatar (signed November 6, 2016, not entered into force) (Argentina-Qatar BIT).

with the resources at its disposal, insufficient for the protection of national public order. Whether one looks at efforts to maintain viable national economies, to control health, crime, market monopolization, immigration or the protection of intellectual and material property and, of course, protection of the environment, a single State's government, whether of a micro-State or a superpower, can no longer accomplish what is expected of it without locking itself into increasingly complex and durable intergovernmental arrangements – each of which promises some palpable gains while requiring a coordinate surrendering of some erstwhile exclusively national competence. There are no exceptions to this phenomenon.

The growing networks of intergovernmental arrangements that all of these changes have necessitated may enhance the political and economic security of those who participate in them, but they also lead to deep ambivalences and insecurities in the strata of the populations of these States. Robert A. Dahl has written:

> A country's economic life, physical environment, national security, and survival are highly, and probably increasingly, dependent on actors and actions that are outside the country's boundaries and not directly subject to its government. Thus the members of the demos cannot employ their national government, and much less their local governments, to exercise direct control over external actors whose decisions bear critically on their lives.[22]

In Europe, one regional laboratory, centralized transnational bureaucracies are making more and more decisions that penetrate deeply into the fabric of national and local life. Not surprisingly, this trend has already generated powerful counterforces: the broad spectrum of anti-Maastricht reaction in Europe, the increased influence of far-right political parties on many continents, Brexit and beyond, and the recrudescence and, surprisingly, legitimization of isolationism in the politics of a superpower. In Europe, even the center's promise of deference to local decision – the so-called subsidiarity principle – has not stemmed the reaction.

Yet, in a further paradoxical twist, rational responses to this increasingly "global" condition always seem to require and involve the creation of alternative alliances and more transnational governmental structures, which in turn further minimize opportunities for individual agency in the policy decisions that affect one's life.

[22] R. A. Dahl, *Democracy and Its Critics* (Yale University Press, 1989), 319.

The point is that globalization, for all of its manifest and promised benefits, has a darker underside that exacerbates at many levels a sense of personal insecurity or even inessentiality. These experiences compel some to throw themselves into desperate searches for security, thereby providing fertile soil for proponents of authoritarian systems and celebrations of nativism.

Incomplete and disruptive transnational integration is coinciding with, and being exacerbated by, a second aggravating factor: a radical transition in the production process. Dramatic technological advances, especially in artificial intelligence, automation and robotics, are opening up production possibilities that are rendering obsolete manufacturing as it has been understood since the beginning of the industrial revolution. Of course, each new technique – from Johannes Gutenberg's movable type to the present – has had profound and often transforming effects on politics, economics, sociology, military strategy and practice and possibly on the individual neurological organization. But, compared to devices like the telegraph and the telephone, the cybernetic revolution promises to have more far-reaching consequences in many spheres. Their potentially radical character and implications for world order are not entirely understood.

One consequence, with special relevance to international investment law, is that opportunities for certain types of employment have been substantially reduced. Work is more than a source of individual income; it is also a status, affording its bearer self-respect and functioning as a central part of the organization of the individual self-system. Sigmund Freud, *pace* Erik Erikson, said that "love and work are the cornerstones of our humanness."[23] While the loss of work opportunities for critical strata is part of what Joseph Schumpeter called capitalism's "creative destruction," the destructive component of the dyad is supposed to be succeeded by capitalism's creative counterpart. This has not yet occurred on a sufficient scale, and it may not. Here again, national programs to address this have proved inadequate.

[23] S. Freud, *Civilization and Its Discontents*, translated by James Strachey (W. W Norton, 1961), 48. In this work, Freud wrote, "The communal life of human beings had, therefore, a two-fold foundation: the compulsion to work, which was created by external necessity, and the power of love." Freud's writing was paraphrased into "love and work are the cornerstones of our humanness" by Erik Erikson. Erik H. Erikson, *Childhood and Society* (W. W Norton, 1986).

Even where employment opportunities have not suffered, the profit from the new technologies has favored capital more than labor, for many of the labor-saving innovations permit the producer to operate more economically while reducing the pool of work opportunities and increasing the competition for them among laborers. This has also skewed the calculus of economic equity that had existed until then and has aggravated class conflicts. Once again, there is resentment of international investment law as if it were the *causa causans* of these developments.

All of these effects have been exacerbated by the coinciding phase of the business cycles in many States. Still another coinciding factor is the aggregating effects of climate change. One would have expected this to provoke governmental programs, which would have been an economic stimulus, but this has not occurred.

Another factor is the "too-big-to-lose" syndrome: the political willingness to dismantle the Great Compact, which has proven itself an efficient and fair program of dispute resolution supporting transnational productive economic activity, simply because your State might lose a case. This simply boggles the mind!

At the center of this perfect storm of uncertainties about the future of the international legal arrangements for the protection of cross-border investment is the new administration in the United States.

13.7 The Future of the Great Compact?

The stresses that investment law-making and law applying have experienced in the recent past are part of a dialectical process characteristic of all robust systems of law. Every legal arrangement is the product of the identification of some common interest shared by those who have shaped it. No sooner than any such arrangement is installed, however, it begins to be tested and challenged – not only by those who do not share in that specific common interest but even by actors within the entities and communities that established and participated in the arrangement but who have since come to believe that their interests are either being insufficiently served or have changed. Thus, every legal arrangement, whether substantive or procedural, is always under some pressure for change. The net result is that law, for all of its pretensions to being stable and unchanging, is actually a continuously dynamic process of agreement, challenge, adjustment, accommodation, new agreement, new challenges and so on *ad infinitum*. The struggles through which this process operates are not indicative of a weak system but, rather, of a robust one.

A coalition of States, which I have referred to figuratively as "the Empire," is striking back at some current trends and tendencies. Until now and for the most part, the agitation for adjustments has taken place within the Great Compact and has not shaken its foundational arrangements, but every moment of a constantly eroding present contains a wide range of embryonic futures. We cannot assume a straight-line projection from the past or an organic extension of the current situation into the future. Especially in view of the political and economic vicissitudes that the world is now experiencing, there is no assurance that the Great Compact will survive intact. If it does not, the Empire will have struck back at its own interests.

Most proponents of international investment law, no matter where they stand on particular issues, seek a future that promises enhanced production and the efficient use of the resources of our planet in ways that sustain the environment, a future in which everyone is net better off and in which there are efficient and timely procedures for the adjustment of arrangements that benefit all yet have downsides for some and in which there are internationally supervised modes of dispute resolution. The resulting interdependence, one hopes, will also act as a restraint on the unilateral use of violence, one of the objectives of the Great Compact and, in my view, an ancillary objective of all economic integration.

At the moment, however, it seems to have become fashionable in some quarters to see everything in zero-sum terms. President Theodore Roosevelt, certainly no "softie" on international politics, in his sixth annual message to Congress, in which he laid the diplomatic groundwork for the Porter Convention and, through it, the Great Compact, said:

> It is a mistake, and it betrays a spirit of foolish cynicism, to maintain that all international governmental action is, and must ever be, based upon mere selfishness, and that to advance ethical reasons for such action is always a sign of hypocrisy. ... It is neither wise nor right for a nation to disregard its own needs, and it is foolish – and may be wicked – to think that other nations will disregard

theirs. But it is wicked for a nation only to regard its own interest, and foolish to believe that such is the sole motive that actuates any other nation. It should be our steady aim to raise the ethical standard of national action just as we strive to raise the ethical standard of individual action.[24]

Let us hope that our leaders, the current custodians of the Great Compact, will have the wisdom to act – internationally, nationally and individually – as Roosevelt counseled.

[24] Roosevelt (note 3).

Part IV

Inter-State Arbitration and the Pursuit of Peace

14 Arbitration and World Peace

Christopher Greenwood

14.1 Introduction

It is a truth universally acknowledged – or at least it should be[1] – that the importance of arbitration between States extends beyond the subject matter of the arbitrations themselves and has wider implications for the peace of the world. The idea that wars can be avoided if States have access to peaceful means of settling the disputes which might lead to war has played an important part in international relations for at least 150 years. Yet it is an idea which has waxed and waned in popularity. Its apogee was in the last decades of the nineteenth century and the first years of the twentieth. At that time there were many – by no means all of them international lawyers – who saw international arbitration as one of the principal instruments for preserving the peace.[2] That idealism waned after the World War I. More hard-headed views about the behaviour of States and the creation of the Permanent Court of International Justice in 1922 and the International Court of Justice after the World War II have led most observers to take a more modest view of the contribution to world peace which might be expected from arbitration.

Yet recourse to arbitration featured in the Covenant of the League of Nations[3] and continues to feature in the Charter of the United Nations[4] in connection with the maintenance of international peace. Moreover, while the number of inter-State arbitrations since the World War II is small compared with the number of cases submitted to the International Court of Justice,[5] it is by no

[1] With apologies to Jane Austen, *Pride and Prejudice* (London, 1813), 1.

[2] That ideal played a major part in the 1899 and 1907 Hague Peace Conferences; *see* F. Kalshoven, *The Centennial of the First International Peace Conference* (The Hague: 2000).

[3] *See*, in particular, Articles 12 and 13.

[4] Article 33.

[5] *See* Chapter 15 of this volume. Sadly, the combined total of cases before the Court and arbitrations still represents a minority of inter-State disputes, particularly of those likely to threaten international peace and security.

means negligible and some of these cases have involved important issues of international peace.

The present chapter will, therefore, attempt an examination of how arbitration came to be seen as an instrument for the preservation or restoration of the peace and whether it deserves to be seen as such today. The focus will be on inter-State arbitration although mention will be made of one case which was not strictly one between two States but had sufficiently similar features.[6]

14.2 Arbitration as an Alternative to War: The Alabama Case

The arbitration between the United States of America and Great Britain regarding the *Alabama* claims,[7] which was held in Geneva in 1871–1872, was certainly not the first arbitration between two States,[8] but it can make a good claim to be the first arbitration to adopt what has become the model in respect of several aspects of contemporary inter-State arbitrations. The Tribunal consisted of five members: only one appointed by each party (Charles Adams appointed by the United States and Sir Alexander Cockburn by Great Britain) and three from other States,[9]

[6] *Abyei Arbitration* (2009) 144 ILR 348 between the Government of Sudan and the Sudan People's Liberation Movement/Army. The Republic of South Sudan became an independent State only after the award was given.

[7] J. B. Moore, *International Arbitrations* (Washington, 1898), vol. I, Chapter XIV. Fascinating analyses of different aspects of the *Alabama* arbitration are given by Lord Bingham, 'The *Alabama* Claims Arbitration', 54 *I.C.L.Q.* (2005) 1, and V. V. Veeder, 'The Historical Keynote to International Arbitration' in D. Caron, S. Schill, A. Cohen Smutny and E. Triantafilou, *Practising Virtue: Inside International Arbitration* (Oxford: Oxford University Press, 2015), 132–149.

[8] That accolade probably belongs, at least in respect of cases from the modern era of international law, to the Jay Treaty Commissioners' decisions (Moore, *op. cit.* n. 7, Chapters IX and X).

[9] Count Sclopis (Italy), who chaired the Tribunal; Mr Staempfli (Switzerland) and Baron d'Itajuba (Brazil). All three were distinguished jurists and Staempfli had once been President of the Swiss Confederation. Adams was an inspired choice by the United States, although today he would certainly be regarded as conflicted given that he had been the United States Ambassador in London during the Civil War. Cockburn was a less sensible choice. Clever and a good linguist (an important consideration since none of the three neutral arbitrators spoke good English), he was notoriously bad tempered. A bachelor but definitely not celibate, he was the only Lord Chief Justice not to have been granted a peerage, reportedly because of Queen Victoria's objection to his notorious moral character.

whereas party-nominated arbitrators had dominated previous cases.[10] It was also the arbitration which brought to the fore the relationship between arbitration and international peace.

The case had its origins in the American Civil War.[11] In an attempt to break the Union's dominance at sea, the Confederacy arranged to have a number of warships built in Great Britain for the purpose of attacking Union shipping. The *Alabama* was the most prominent of these commerce raiders. The construction of the ships was discovered by representatives of the Government of Washington and Charles Adams, then the United States Ambassador in London, demanded that the British Government, which had declared itself neutral at the start of the War, prevent them from sailing. Due to a series of misfortunes,[12] the British Government failed to do so in the case of the *Alabama* and a number of other raiders, which caused considerable damage to Union shipping before the *Alabama* was sunk in June 1864 and the other vessels captured. After the Civil War ended, the United States, which had always considered that Great Britain had violated the international law of neutrality by its failure to prevent the ships from sailing, demanded an apology and compensation for the losses caused by the *Alabama* and the other raiders.

The damage directly attributable to the *Alabama* and the other raiders was considerable – the *Alabama* alone had destroyed or captured 65 US ships – so any claim for compensation would be substantial. Moreover, the United States also sought an admission by the British Government that it had violated the law of neutrality and an apology, which the British Government was unwilling to give. Raising the stakes still further, a powerful lobby in the United States maintained that Great Britain should be required to pay not only for the direct damage but also for 'indirect damages', by which they meant the entire cost of the last 20 months of the Civil War on the basis that it was only the acts of the raiders which had allowed the South to continue fighting. This argument was put in a characteristically belligerent way by Senator Charles Sumner in a speech

[10] Members of the Jay Treaty commissions had all been party appointees.

[11] A. Foreman, *A World on Fire: An Epic History of Two Nations Divided* (London: Penguin Books Ltd., 2010), 223–224, 579–581, 627–631 and 804–814.

[12] These included the fact that the Law Officer originally consulted by the Foreign Office had become insane. In addition, the relevant legislation was, to say the least, unsatisfactory; Bingham, loc. cit. n. 7, 5–11.

in the Senate in 1869, in which he proposed a figure of US$2 billion[13] for the indirect damages and suggested that the United States might take Canada and British possessions in the West Indies.[14] At this point, there was serious talk of war in both countries and it was to avert that threat and try to restore good relations that the two governments concluded the Washington Convention in 1871 referring the dispute to arbitration.

Unfortunately, the two governments had very different ideas about what they had agreed to arbitrate. The United States Government believed that the arbitration tribunal was to deal with both the direct and the indirect damages. While the claim for indirect damages was, at least in most respects, as far-fetched a claim as might be imagined, feelings in the United States ran so high that it could not be abandoned. The British Government, however, was convinced that the claim – which would have bankrupted any country[15] – was not included. When the United States counsel presented a claim for the indirect damages in their written pleadings, therefore, the British Government, Parliament and public opinion were horrified and the future of the arbitration was cast into doubt. Talk of war resumed in both countries.

What saved the day was a compromise brokered by Adams and, to some extent, by Cockburn during five days in June 1872.[16] After extensive consultation with the other members of the Tribunal and with their respective governments what emerged was a 'declaration' by the Tribunal regarding the indirect claims. After referring to the difference between the parties regarding jurisdiction over the indirect claims, the Tribunal continued,

> The Arbitrators think it right to state that, after the most careful perusal of all that has been urged on the part of the Government of the United States in respect of these claims, they have arrived, individually and collectively, at the conclusion that these claims do not constitute, upon the principles of international law

[13] In the money of the day.

[14] Bingham, loc. cit. n. 7, 12–13. Sumner had a penchant for making belligerent speeches whatever offence he might cause. One of his early speeches before the Civil War had so outraged a Congressman from the South that he had beaten Sumner over the head with his walking stick until it broke. The criminal assault was rightly condemned but the Congressman was sent dozens of replacement sticks by admirers; J. McPherson, *Battle Cry of Freedom: The Civil War Era* (New York: Oxford University Press, 1988), 150–151.

[15] The Prime Minister, Gladstone, told the House of Commons that it would be 'insane to accede to demands which no nation with a spark of honour or spirit left could submit to even at the point of death' (Foreman, *op. cit.* n. 11, 812).

[16] There is a graphic description in Veeder, loc. cit. n. 7, 141–147.

applicable to such cases, good foundation for an award of compensation or computation of damages between nations, and should, upon such principles, be wholly excluded from the consideration of the Tribunal in making its award, even if there were no disagreement between the two Governments as to the competency of the Tribunal.[17]

The statement was made with the agreement of the two governments but without either side having fully presented its arguments on jurisdiction over, or the merits of, the indirect claims. It is not part of the award, nor is it described as a preliminary ruling. But it resolved the difficulties. The United States withdrew the indirect claims in light of the Tribunal's statement, the case proceeded and eventually the Tribunal awarded the United States US$15.5 million in respect of the direct claims. Cockburn wrote a vigorous dissenting opinion (though not on the part of the award which dealt with the *Alabama* herself), which was highly critical of his fellow arbitrators and of the drafting of the Washington Convention which he considered lacked clarity.[18] The British Government paid the damages within the time required.[19]

The significance of the *Alabama* arbitration lies less in what was actually decided than in the wider effects of the award. First, it had a dramatic effect on relations between the United States and Great Britain. These had never been particularly cordial in the years since American independence. The *Alabama* award, accepted by both governments, put an end to the talk of war between the two countries and removed what could easily have been a running sore in their relations. Its success paved

[17] Bingham, loc. cit. n. 7, 21.

[18] Cockburn was less than fair either to the rest of the Tribunal or the draftsmen of the Convention. As to the former, commentators then and now have generally been supportive, while readers of Lord Bingham's article might think the Convention had been drafted with a great deal more clarity than the English legislation on un-neutral acts.

[19] As Roy Jenkins, a former Chancellor of the Exchequer, points out (R. Jenkins, *Gladstone: A Biography* (London: Macmillan, 1995), 359), the damages were equivalent to over £160 million today and added approximately 5 per cent to the Government's budget. In fact, Britain paid only just over half the amount awarded, because it was able to set off amounts owed by the United States to British nationals and to Canada for access to fishing waters (Foreman, *op. cit.* n. 11, 813), although of course that did not reduce the burden on the British Government since the set off payments still had to be made to the individual claimants and to Canada. Cockburn was probably right that the amount awarded was unduly generous, since the United States was left with a considerable surplus after it had satisfied the claims made by shipowners and other US nationals who had suffered direct losses (Veeder, loc. cit. n. 7, 133).

the way for the settlement of other differences between them and ushered in a long period of amicable relations. Secondly, its success encouraged other States to look at arbitration as a means of resolving differences, especially with their neighbours, and gave considerable impetus to the various observers and campaigners for better international governance who were looking for ways of reducing the risk of war. Arbitration it seemed, in light of what had happened over the *Alabama,* really could be an alternative to war.

This spirit of optimism lasted for a good four decades. The volumes of the United Nations *Reports of International Arbitral Awards* bear testimony to the popularity of arbitration between 1872 and 1914.[20] The influence of the *Alabama* can also be seen in the Hague Peace Conferences of 1899 and 1907. These were the first conferences to include not only States from outside the circle of European 'Powers' (and the United States) but also participation from what would today be called 'civil society'. For many of the civil society representatives, such as W. T. Stead and Bertha von Suttner, the promotion of arbitration was an important element in their attempts to create a more peaceful world. That view was shared by a good number of the government representatives, especially from the smaller countries, and was responsible for arbitration and the peaceful settlement of disputes constituting one of the three strands in the negotiations.[21] The fruit of these negotiations included the adoption in 1899, and then in a revised form in 1907, of the Hague Convention on the Pacific Settlement of Disputes, Part IV of which provided for arbitration,[22] and the establishment of the Permanent Court of Arbitration.[23] Expectations ran high.

[20] 57 awards in inter-State cases are reported from this period. In addition, there are 220 awards in cases between an individual and a State. Many of these were presented by the State of nationality of the claimant in the exercise of the right of diplomatic protection. In addition, some were the product of international agreements closely connected with inter-State disputes. The Washington Convention, 1871, under which the *Alabama* claims were heard also provided for arbitration of various claims by British nationals against the United States; *see e.g. Smith,* XXIX *RIAA* 138.

[21] The others were disarmament and a strengthening of the laws of war. *See* F. Kalshoven (ed.), *The Centennial of the First Hague Peace Conference* (The Hague: Nijhoff, 2000).

[22] *See* A. Pearce Higgins, *The Hague Peace Conferences and Other International Conferences Concerning the Laws and Usages of War: Texts of Conventions with Commentaries* (Cambridge: Cambridge University Press, 1909), 95–179.

[23] *See* Chapter 11 of this volume.

14.3 Disappointment and Perceptions of Decline

Those expectations were not to be realised. None of the participants in the disputes which led to the World War I seemed interested in resorting to arbitration. After the War, much of the steam seemed to go out of the idea that arbitration could and should be used as an alternative to war. Although the Covenant of the League of Nations, as has been seen, made provision for arbitration, much more attention was paid in the inter-war years to the Permanent Court of International Justice, which was established in 1922 and offered what seemed a very different means of settlement from arbitrations like the *Alabama*. There were, of course, numerous important inter-State arbitrations during this period. Indeed, the number of arbitrations each year was greater than that in the pre-war period. Moreover, many of them were directly concerned with matters of war and peace, like those concerning the sinking of the *Lusitania*[24] or the German invasion of Portuguese territories in Africa.[25] But these dealt with the aftermath of a war which had already been fought to a conclusion; they were not the means of averting war, as the *Alabama* was considered to have been, and did not play a prominent part in the conclusion of the peace. Those cases which involved not the aftermath of terrible events that had passed but future relations between States often seemed to involve relatively minor disputes. The arbitration awards in the *Clipperton Island*[26] and *Island of Palmas*[27] cases were important contributions to the jurisprudence and scholarship of international law (something which could not really be said of the award in the *Alabama*) but the first concerned an uninhabited island and the second an island which, though populated, seems to have been largely unknown to the governments of the Parties. It is impossible to conceive of the disputes in those cases leading to war, or even causing serious long-term damage to relations between the parties.

The same is even more true of the period after the World War II. During the 75 years since the end of the War, arbitrations between States were markedly less numerous,[28] the focus of third-party

[24] VII *R.I.A.A.* 32.

[25] *Naulilaa*, II *R.I.A.A.* 1011.

[26] Netherlands/United States of America, II *R.I.A.A.* 1105.

[27] France/Mexico, II *R.I.A.A.* 829.

[28] *See* Chapter 15 of this volume.

settlement again being a court (the International Court of Justice) and political means of settlement. By the 1970s there was also a growing sense that the likelihood of arbitration contributing to international peace was in decline. For example, boundary disputes between Argentina and Chile, which had escalated tension between the two States, were most effectively settled by two arbitrations in 1902[29] and 1966.[30] Yet when the two States again had recourse to arbitration over a boundary dispute in the 1970s, the award[31] (though undoubtedly a fine piece of legal reasoning) so far from settling the dispute led the two States to the brink of war. In the event, it was Papal mediation, not the arbitration, which prevented outright hostilities.[32]

When the number of inter-State arbitrations did pick up again, towards the end of the twentieth century, a major driving force was the United Nations Convention on the Law of the Sea. Although the dispute settlement provisions in Part XV of the Convention offer a choice of recourse to the International Court of Justice, the International Tribunal for the Law of the sea or arbitration under Annex VII of the Convention, arbitration is the default option.[33] These arbitrations have undoubtedly been of great importance in the development of the law of the sea and the settlement of disputes but they are not widely discussed in the context of preservation of world peace.

14.4 Decline Reconsidered

Developments since the Hague Peace Conferences have thus engendered a widespread sense of disappointment. Important as inter-State arbitration may be in other respects, in relation to world peace it is perceived as never having fulfilled the potential suggested by the *Alabama* case. That perception – however widely shared – is misleading for several reasons. First, it is based upon a misreading of the *Alabama* proceedings and all that they

[29] *Cordillera of the Andes Boundary Case* (1902) 1X *R.I.A.A.* 24.

[30] *Frontier Case* (1966) 38 ILR 10.

[31] *Beagle Channel Case* (1977) 52 ILR 93.

[32] 82 ILR 671. *See also* L. de Lafayette 'Beagle Channel Dispute' in *I Max Planck Encyclopaedia of Public International Law* (Oxford: Oxford University Press, 2012), 863.

[33] Article 287. For some types of dispute there is also the possibility of a special arbitration tribunal constituted under Annex VIII.

entailed. Secondly, it overlooks the ways in which variations upon the traditional model of inter-State arbitration have been used – often, if not always, to good effect – in matters directly bearing on war and peace. Lastly, it underestimates the importance of the contribution to international peace made by arbitrations which have no apparent connection with matters of peace and security. Each of these considerations will be explored in turn.

14.4.1 The Alabama Reassessed

For many commentators, the *Alabama* case is the paradigm of recourse to impartial arbitration avoiding an imminent war between two great Powers. The reality is not quite so clear. In the first place, the risk of war between Great Britain and the United States was perhaps not as great as has often been suggested. Although there was no shortage of belligerent rhetoric, such as Sumner's Senate speech and editorials in newspapers on both sides of the Atlantic, there were also powerful forces working for a peaceful solution. As United States Ambassador to the United Kingdom, Adams told the British Government as early as 1863 that 'there is no fair and equitable form of conventional arbitrament or reference to which [the United States] will not be willing to submit'.[34] While that approach was initially rebuffed by Earl Russell (then the Foreign Secretary in Lord Palmerston's Liberal Government), later governments, both Liberal and Conservative, worked hard to find a peaceful solution. Similarly, Sumner's bellicose intransigence was far from representing the views of the administrations of Presidents Johnson and Grant in the United States. There were also economic factors at work; Sumner's speech had been followed by a sharp drop in the price of US government bonds on the London market,[35] access to which was important to the US government in raising funds for reconstruction. Cultural ties between the two countries were strong and there was a long history of them finding peaceful settlements to disputes which had threatened war.[36]

[34] Moore, *op. cit.* n. 7, 496.

[35] Foreman, *op. cit.* n. 11, 809.

[36] Although the two countries had gone to war in 1812, since then they had always managed to find negotiated settlements in spite of their rhetoric; for example, the *Caroline* dispute of 1837–1842 was settled by the Webster-Ashburton Treaty of 1842, while the 'Oregon

Secondly, the *Alabama* proceedings were far from a model of what we now regard as arbitration. Both Adams and Cockburn kept in close touch with the governments which had appointed them[37] and it was Adams' skilful negotiation with the two government legal teams and his fellow arbitrators that produced the compromise which resolved the potentially disastrous dispute over the indirect claims.[38] Moreover, the manner in which that resolution was achieved would be inconceivable today. The Tribunal set aside the differences between the Parties over jurisdiction, proceeded direct to the merits of the indirect claims and dealt with them by means of a 'statement' which had been cleared with the Parties' representatives beforehand and formed no part of the award which was subsequently rendered. The *Alabama* proceedings are better seen as a mixture of diplomacy and third-party adjudication than as an example of what we now regard as arbitration.

Thirdly, if the Tribunal had proceeded in what we would now regard as the proper manner, it would first have given a ruling on jurisdiction with regard to the indirect claims. Had it done so, then the arbitration might well be remembered today as one which had exacerbated an inter-State dispute and made war more, rather than less, likely. A ruling that the Tribunal possessed jurisdiction would almost certainly have led Great Britain to withdraw from the proceedings as no British Government could have taken the risk of losing the indirect claims on the merits and suffering an award which would have bankrupted the country. On the other hand a ruling that the Tribunal lacked jurisdiction over the indirect claims would have led to a political crisis in the United States since many senators had voted to approve the 1871 Treaty only on the basis that it did include the indirect claims.

The sense that inter-State arbitration in the twentieth and early twenty-first centuries has failed to live up to the legacy of the *Alabama* is thus due in part to the fact that international lawyers tend to read more into the

dispute' over the border between Canada and the United States was settled by treaty in 1846 establishing a border along the 49th parallel but leaving the whole of Vancouver to Canada, notwithstanding a campaign in the United States for a border far to the north ('Fifty-four forty or fight').

[37] Something which would be wholly unacceptable today; *see* the 2016 Partial Award in *Slovenia/Croatia*, 179 ILR 1.

[38] *See* above, text accompanying notes 16 and 17, and the very detailed account in Veeder, n. 7.

Alabama case than they should. It was certainly a very important arbitration and its effect in reducing tension between the United States and Great Britain is beyond doubt. Even if the risk of war over the *Alabama* claims has been exaggerated, it cannot be denied that such a risk existed. Moreover, the arbitration removed from the relations between the two States a dispute which, even had it not led to war, would probably have poisoned those relations for decades. The arbitration was, therefore, a significant contribution to international peace. Yet it was able to make that contribution precisely because it was not a classic arbitration in which the arbitrators were impartial and independent adjudicators detached from the Parties but part and parcel of a diplomatic and political process.[39] Above all, the arbitration succeeded because there was the political will in both countries to implement it – and to regard it as ending the dispute – even though neither side was entirely satisfied with the outcome.[40]

14.4.2 Inter-State Arbitrations and the Restoration of Peace

The second reason for doubting the perception that arbitration no longer makes such an important contribution to world peace is that it underestimates the different ways in which different arbitrations can contribute – and have contributed – to that cause. Admittedly there have been few cases since the *Alabama* in which two States have threatened war and then decided to arbitrate instead. Yet it would be a mistake to imagine that it is only in such cases that arbitration between States makes a positive contribution to international peace.

Such an approach overlooks the fact that it is not just the prevention of war but also the restoration of peace to which arbitrations can and do contribute. That has been a particularly important feature of arbitral work

[39] It is noticeable that when the British and American governments drew up a Permanent Treaty of Arbitration at the end of the nineteenth century, the United States Senate refused to give the advice and consent necessary for ratification; Moore, *op. cit.* n. 7, 965–989.

[40] Cockburn appended to the Award a vigorous dissent which was criticised by Robert Lowe – who, as Chancellor of the Exchequer, had to find the money to pay the substantial damages awarded – on the ground that its intemperate language made the task of persuading Parliament to accept the Award more difficult (Veeder, loc. cit. n. 7, 147). There is a lesson there for party-appointed arbitrators and for Judges ad hoc at the International Court of Justice. However, even Cockburn also made an eloquent plea to both States to accept the Award (Veeder, 133).

in the twentieth century and into the early years of the twenty-first. There has long been, for example, extensive use of claims commissions to determine, in the aftermath of war, questions of liability and compensation. In addition, more traditional inter-State arbitration has been employed to resolve disputes as part of a peace settlement. Since space does not permit a full examination, three instances must suffice.

The first example, the *Taba* arbitration[41] between Egypt and Israel, is an example of the arbitration of a boundary dispute between two States in the aftermath of a peace treaty. The 1979 Peace Treaty between Egypt and Israel,[42] which put an end to the state of war between the two countries, provided for the forces of both Parties to return to the international border, which was defined as the boundary between Egypt and the former mandated territory of Palestine. The precise location of that boundary was, however, unclear in a number of places, including the Taba enclave on the coast of the Gulf of Aqaba. Negotiations between the two States failed to produce agreement. In those circumstances, Article VII of the Peace Treaty provided that the dispute should be resolved by conciliation or arbitration. The Parties chose arbitration and concluded a *compromis* in 1986, referring the case to a five-member arbitration tribunal,[43] which rendered an award (more favourable to Egypt, though also finding for Israel on certain matters) in 1988. Both States implemented the award. The boundary dispute had nothing to with the causes of the war between Egypt and Israel and its resolution might be dismissed as the settlement of a minor side-show with no relevance for international peace. That would be a mistake. The 1979 Peace Treaty was far from easy to conclude; the provision for arbitration helped to ensure that it was not derailed by disputes over its interpretation or application and thus made the conclusion of the Treaty and the establishment of peace easier. The negotiations and subsequent arbitration over Taba were also helpful in maintaining peaceful relations between the two States at a time of considerable tension in the region.

[41] 80 ILR 225; R. Lapidoth, 'Taba Arbitration' in *IX Max Planck Encyclopaedia of Public International Law* (Oxford: Oxford University Press, 2012), 722.

[42] 18 ILM (1979) 362.

[43] One of the legacies of the *Alabama* is that a tribunal of five members, only two of whom are directly appointed by the Parties, has become the norm in inter-State arbitration, although it is not always adopted.

Very different from *Taba* in several ways is the second example, the *Abyei* arbitration.[44] *Abyei* is not strictly an inter-State arbitration at all, although it has many of the same characteristics.[45] Following a lengthy civil war in Sudan, a Comprehensive Peace Agreement (the CPA) was concluded between the Government of Sudan and the Sudan People's Liberation Movement/Army (the SPLM/A). The CPA provided for the recognition of a separate southern region which, in time, became the separate State of South Sudan. Abyei, which lies to the north of the southern region, was the subject of a separate protocol, which provided for delimitation of the boundaries of the Abyei Area by an expert panel. The outcome of the panel's work was, however, sharply debated with allegations by the Government of Sudan that the panel had exceeded its mandate.[46] The Government and the SPLM/A agreed to refer to arbitration the question whether the panel had exceeded its mandate.[47] In approaching this question, the Tribunal held that it was not a court of appeal and that its task was similar to that of deciding whether or not to annul an arbitration award. It concluded that the panel had exceeded its mandate in part but upheld some of the most important parts of the report. Despite the fact that the issue concerned an internal boundary in the context of a civil war, the arbitration is very similar to an inter-State case in the way in which it was established and the manner of its proceeding. It played an important role in defusing tension at the time but, two years after the award, the dispute flared into violence again and, at the time of writing cannot be regarded as ended.

The third example is of the arbitrations which followed the 1998–2000 armed conflict between Eritrea and Ethiopia. That conflict had its origins in a border dispute between the two countries but by the time it was brought to an end by a treaty of peace in 2000, relations between the two countries were further poisoned by a series of accusations which each State levied

[44] 144 ILR 348; B. Daly and G. Schofield 'Abyei Arbitration' in *I Max Planck Encyclopaedia of Public International Law* (Oxford: Oxford University Press, 2012), 26.

[45] In addition, the United Nations Security Council had characterised the conflict in Sudan as a threat to international peace and security.

[46] D. H. Johnson, 'Why Abyei Matters: The Breaking Point of Sudan's Comprehensive Peace Agreement ?' (2008) 108 *African Affairs* 1.

[47] The Tribunal consisted of five members but this time two were appointed by the Government and two by the SPLM/A with a president appointed by the Secretary-General of the PCA. All were distinguished international lawyers unconnected with either Party.

against the other regarding alleged violations of humanitarian law in the conduct of the conflict. The peace treaty thus established two arbitral bodies. The Eritrea–Ethiopia Boundary Commission was charged with delimiting and demarcating the boundary between the two States,[48] while the Eritrea–Ethiopia Claims Commission had responsibility for deciding claims between the two States (including claims made by a State on behalf of its nationals) arising out of the conflict.[49] The Boundary Commission issued its decision on delimitation with remarkable speed[50] and clarity but agreement between the Parties with regard to the implementation of the award and of the later statement on demarcation[51] proved elusive. The Claims Commission issued a total of 15 awards on liability[52] and 2 on damages.[53] The work of the Claims Commission is particularly interesting, because traditional arbitrations of this kind leading to carefully reasoned awards have been rare in the aftermath of conflicts in recent decades.[54] Both commissions show what role arbitration is capable of playing as part of a process of restoring peace, although they are also a useful reminder of the limits of that role if the States concerned lack the political will to implement their decisions.

[48] *See* V. Wiener, 'Eritrea' in *III Max Planck Encyclopaedia of Public International Law* (Oxford: Oxford University Press, 2012), 642, paras. 39–42.

[49] N. Klein 'Eritrea-Ethiopia Claims Commission' in *III Max Planck Encyclopaedia of Public International Law* (Oxford: Oxford University Press, 2012) 651.

[50] 130 ILR 1.

[51] 130 ILR 147.

[52] 135 ILR 197–670.

[53] 140 ILR 235 and 376. For analysis of the jurisprudence of the Commission, *see* S. Murphy, W. Kidane and T. Snider, *Litigating War: Mass Civil Injury and the Eritrea-Ethiopia Claims Commission* (Oxford, New York: Oxford University Press, 2013).

[54] The 1990–1991 Kuwait conflict was followed by the establishment, by the United Nations Security Council, of the United Nations Compensation Commission. That body, however, was not a classic arbitration tribunal; it derived its jurisdiction from a decision of the Security Council (resolution 687 (1991)), not the agreement of the States concerned, and its approach was one of mass claims processing; *see* R. Lillich (ed.) *The United Nations Compensation Commission* (Irvington: Nijhoff, 1995). A closer analogy to the Eritrea-Ethiopia Claims Commission is the Iran-United States Claims Tribunal, which was set up by the two States in the aftermath of the 1979–1981 hostage crisis to hear claims by nationals of one State against the other and between the two States; *see* G. Aldrich, *The Jurisprudence of the Iran-United States Claims Tribunal* (Oxford: Oxford University Press, 1996) and C. Brower and J. Brueschke, *The Iran-United States Claims Tribunal* (The Hague: Nijhoff, 1998).

14.4.3 Arbitration and the Removal of Potential Causes of War

The third consideration is perhaps the most important of all. The core function of any arbitration tribunal is to settle the dispute submitted to it by the parties. Even if that dispute is not itself one which is perceived as likely to lead to war, it may yet pose a danger to peace. That is particularly true of boundary disputes (both land and maritime) as each State deploys its police and armed forces to enforce its law in what it regards as its territory. While the resultant action may be relatively minor, there is always the chance of it leading to violence.[55] The arbitration proceedings between Guyana and Suriname in 2004–2007 over their maritime boundary also involved complaints about enforcement activities in a disputed area by the Suriname coastguard. That action was condemned by the tribunal as a threat to use force contrary to the United Nations Charter.[56]

The rapid expansion of maritime areas subject to the sovereignty or sovereign rights of coastal States, which came about as a result of developments in the 1970s and culminated in the adoption of the United Nations Convention on the Law of the Sea in 1982,[57] gave rise to numerous disputes between States with overlapping maritime claims. The complexity of these disputes and the resultant risk of confrontations by rival naval forces was exacerbated by the relatively vague standards laid down in the Convention (and now recognised as part of customary international law) regarding how boundaries were to be determined.[58] Yet, with one or two exceptions,[59] disputes which could not be settled by negotiation have been peacefully resolved by judgments of the International Court of Justice or of the International Tribunal for the law of the Sea, or by international arbitration.[60]

[55] The 'cod wars' between Iceland and the United Kingdom involved confrontations between Icelandic fisheries protection gunboats and British warships sent to protect British fishing vessels.

[56] *Guyana/Suriname* (2007) 139 ILR 566. The author was one of the counsel for Suriname in these proceedings.

[57] *See* C. Sanger, *Ordering the Oceans* (London: Zed Books Ltd., 1986).

[58] *See* Article 74 (exclusive economic zone) and Article 83 (continental shelf).

[59] *See*, in particular, the *South China Sea Arbitration* between the Philippines and the People's Republic of China, (2016) 170 ILR 1, which was boycotted by China.

[60] While it has been the International Court of Justice which has dealt with the largest number of such cases, there have been several important arbitrations: in addition to the *Guyana/Suriname* case, n. 56, mention should be made of the *Barbados/Trinidad and Tobago* arbitration (2006) 139 ILR 449, and the *Bay of Bengal* case between Bangladesh and India, (2014) 167 ILR 1.

Moreover, even if there is no clash between border units or patrol boats and thus no direct threat to the peace (however small), a dispute which is left unresolved over a long period of time can fester and poison relations between the parties in a way which can ultimately undermine peaceful relations. The capacity of arbitration to resolve such disputes may, therefore, have an impact upon relations between the parties which goes beyond the immediate dispute itself.

14.5 Conclusions

While the importance of arbitration for international peace may, therefore, have fallen short of what was hoped for in the aftermath of the *Alabama* arbitration, it remains the case that arbitration has had a significance which should not be underestimated. Arbitration, of course, requires the consent of the Parties as that is the basis for a tribunal's jurisdiction. That consent may be given in advance of a dispute arising,[61] although that occurs less frequently than is the case with the International Court of Justice where jurisdiction also depends upon consent[62] but an extensive network of bilateral and multilateral treaties furnish that consent in advance of a dispute arising. The fact that arbitration more often requires the States party to an existing dispute to agree upon recourse to arbitration, and upon the form and terms of reference of that arbitration, is one of the factors which has contributed to the greater role which the International Court has played in cases where tensions have run high enough to give rise to a risk of force being used.[63] Yet arbitration still

[61] As is the case with the Law of the Sea Convention.

[62] Statute of the Court, Article 36.

[63] Another factor is the power of the International Court of Justice to indicate provisional measures of protection which can have a significant effect in bringing about a ceasefire in a case where a dispute has already led to violence; *see e.g.* the proceedings involving the *Request for Interpretation of the Judgment of 15 June 1962 in the case Concerning the* Temple of Preah Vihear (Cambodia v. Thailand), *I.C.J. Reports, 2011*, p. 537 (Provisional Measures) and *2013*, p. 281 (Merits), concerning a border dispute which had led to fighting. It is sometimes possible to employ the power of a standing court or tribunal to indicate provisional measures in support of arbitration proceedings; *see e.g.* the proceedings between the Netherlands and the Russian Federation concerning the *Arctic Sunrise*, a vessel belonging to the organisation Greenpeace which had been seized by Russian security forces. In 2013 the International Tribunal for the Law of the Sea indicated provisional measures (159 ILR 68) in support of an arbitration which took place in 2014–2015 (171 ILR 1).

has many attractions for States and the very fact that it generally requires agreement may make it easier to secure the political will to abide by the result even if that result is unwelcome. In terms of maintenance and restoration of international peace, that is by far the most important condition for determining the effectiveness of any method of peaceful settlement.

15 Inter-State Arbitration

Current Issues and Contemporary Challenges

Maurice Mendelson*

15.1 Introduction

'There is nothing new under the sun', said Ecclesiastes; and this is broadly true of inter-State arbitration (ISA), though some recent developments have perhaps thrown certain issues into greater prominence. So I shall here provide a fairly standard account of the factors which lead States to choose or refuse to arbitrate with other States. In the course of doing so, I shall allude to some issues that have recently arisen. I will consider: whether ISA is even available in a given situation; the need for consent; and the many pros and cons of this form of dispute settlement.

I shall consider these issues primarily from the perspective of the States parties or potential parties, leaving an analysis of the history of this type of procedure and its benefits for international society as a whole to other contributors.

Because of the relative paucity of ISAs, I shall have recourse to the law and practice of the International Court of Justice to illustrate some of the principles which apply also to its arbitral equivalent.

15.2 Is ISA Even Available to the Parties?

Before a State starts to consider whether it wishes to institute or consent to ISA, it is necessary to consider whether it is even available. There are a variety of circumstances in which it is not available.

One such circumstance is where the relevant treaty mandates a different type of dispute settlement. A well-known example is European Union law. The treaties confer exclusive jurisdiction on the European Court of Justice

* I gratefully acknowledge the research assistance of Ms Xiao Mao, LLB, LLM, MSc, doctoral student at Brasenose College, University of Oxford. This essay was written in 2019.

to deal with disputes between member States on matters of EU law, thereby ousting other remedies, such as ISA. Moreover, since there is no presumption that States have consented to any form, let alone any particular form, of third-party dispute settlement, even a mere failure to make provision for ISA in a treaty can preclude its deployment – unless the parties subsequently agree ad hoc.[1] Furthermore, if proceedings regarding essentially the same dispute have already been instituted, the principles of *lis alibi pendens* and/or *forum non conveniens* may preclude ISA (or a new iteration of it) in a particular case.[2]

15.3 The Need for Consent

In modern municipal legal systems, whilst arbitration depends on the consent of both parties, adjudication at least is compulsory, in the sense that the consent of the defendant is not normally needed for proceedings to be instituted and maintained against him, her or it. But when it comes to disputes between States, all third-party dispute settlement mechanisms are dependent on the consent of both parties.

So far as concerns the claimant, by instituting proceedings it has obviously consented to the jurisdiction.[3] The real issues therefore normally relate to the consent of the respondent.

15.3.1 Consent ad hoc

Consent can be given ad hoc, as it has been in a not inconsiderable proportion of the cases before the International Court of Justice, and in an even greater proportion of ISAs. Between 22 May 1947 and 1 July 2019, 177 cases were entered in the Court's General List, including 150 contentious cases and 27 advisory opinions; 18 contentious cases were submitted to the Court by means of special agreement. So the proportion is 18/150,

[1] *See e.g.* the Italy–Chad BIT of 1969, Article 7, which provided for ICSID arbitration in investor-State disputes but, in the case of inter-State disputes, envisaged only that they should be resolved through diplomacy.

[2] *See e.g.* Order No. 3 of the Tribunal constituted pursuant to Article 297 (1) and Annex VII of the Law of the Sea Convention 1982 in the *Mox Plant case*, 42 ILM 1187 (2003), para. 28.

[3] How far this extends to counterclaimsneeds not be considered here.

i.e. 12 per cent.[4] The proportion is even greater when it comes to ISA. Of the 38 inter-State cases available on the website of the Permanent Court of Arbitration, 20 were submitted on the basis of a special (i.e. ad hoc) agreement; this comes to some 52.6 per cent.[5]

15.3.2 Consent post hoc

In principle, consent can also be given post hoc, by means of what is called *forum prorogatum*. Essentially, this is a process by which, when proceedings are instituted, the court or tribunal has no jurisdiction but the respondent nevertheless submits to the jurisdiction either expressly or by joining issue on the merits.

Acceptance of jurisdiction over the entire dispute by *forum prorogatum* is exceedingly rare. An often-cited example in the ICJ is the *Corfu Channel case,* but there the submission to the jurisdiction was accidental, in the sense that Albania seems to have been under the misapprehension that it was obliged to submit.[6] But, as can be imagined, in matters of importance governments rarely make this sort of mistake – if anything, they tend to object to the jurisdiction on all grounds possible, and some that are impossible. It has also occasionally happened that States have instituted proceedings in the ICJ, knowing that there is no basis of jurisdiction, but hoping thereby to shame the respondent into accepting the competence of the Court. But governments are too thick-skinned for this stratagem to work. At any rate, I am unaware of any ISA in recent decades where consent has been given post hoc in a case where there was no jurisdictional basis to begin with.

Alternatively it is theoretically possible that there may be a jurisdictional basis in respect of at any rate *some* issues, but the claimant[7] frames its claim more widely, to include further issues which the respondent has not, or arguably has not, consented to have decided. The respondent may

[4] *See* International Court of Justice, Basis of the Court Jurisdiction, www.icj-cij.org/en/basis-of-jurisdiction.

[5] Not all inter-State arbitrations are reported, and not all are conducted under the auspices of the PCA. Nevertheless, these figures are a useful guide. The MOX Plant arbitration (Ireland v. UK), PCA Case No. 2002–01, did not really get off the ground, and is listed on the PCA website as 'other proceedings' rather than as an ISA.

[6] *Judgment on Preliminary Objection, ICJ Rep.* 1948, p. 15.

[7] For present purposes, 'the claimant' can include a counterclaimant.

then consent to those additional issues also being decided –deliberately or even carelessly.

It seems that the only case in recent times where *forum prorogatum* has occurred was in the ICJ case relating to the *Arbitral Award of the King of Spain on 23 December 1906* between Honduras and Nicaragua. One of the points in dispute was whether the Gámez-Bonilla Treaty, which granted the arbitrator jurisdiction over the dispute, was in force when he was designated. There was no express provision in the Treaty about when it came into force, so the ICJ interpreted the intent of the parties regarding this issue by reference to the fact that Nicaragua agreed the designation of the King of Spain as the arbitrator, and fully participated in the arbitral proceedings. Thus the Court concluded that the Treaty was in force when the arbitrator was designated, and Nicaragua was not allowed to rely on this issue as a ground for the nullity of the arbitral award.[8]

15.3.3 Consent ante hoc

Finally, and most importantly, consent can also be given ante hoc – that is, in advance of any particular dispute arising. This can arise, broadly, in two ways. First, a treaty can provide for States to consent to the jurisdiction over a potentially unlimited, or at any rate very broad, range of subjects. Secondly, a treaty on a particular substantive area may contain what is called a 'compromissory clause' providing for adjudication and/or arbitration of disputes arising in relation to the interpretation or application of that particular treaty:

1. A well-known example of the first type of ante hoc consent to jurisdiction is the so-called optional clause set out in Article 36 (2) to (5) of the Statute of the ICJ. This enables, but does not require, States to make unilateral declarations accepting in advance the jurisdiction of the Court, either over all legal disputes or over a more restricted class defined by the State making the declaration. If another State makes another declaration which, it later turns out, also covers the subject matter of a dispute, the Court will have jurisdiction over it.[9] There is no exact equivalent of the 'optional clause' in respect of

[8] *Judgment of 18 November 1960, ICJ Rep.* 1960, pp. 192, 207–209.

[9] There also needs to be an overlap *ratione temporis* and *personae*, but there is no need to elaborate on this here.

ISA. However, there are a small number of multilateral treaties on the peaceful settlement of disputes which provide that, in certain circumstances, parties to them can unilaterally institute arbitral (or judicial) proceedings against other parties to those same treaties.[10] Examples are the 1949 Revised General Act for the Pacific Settlement of International Disputes[11] and the European Convention for the Peaceful Settlement of Disputes 1957.[12] But arbitrations based on such treaties are very rare. This is partly because these treaties have not received many ratifications; partly because they often offer or require the prior employment of other dispute settlement techniques, such as conciliation and adjudication; and partly because in some of them, such as the European Convention, significant numbers of parties have opted out of the arbitration provisions.

2. The other form of consent ante hoc is in treaties dealing with particular subjects, where consent is given in advance to a court or arbitral tribunal, as the case may be, having jurisdiction over disputes concerning (typically) the application or interpretation of that treaty. Examples are the International Convention for the Suppression of the Financing of Terrorism 1999, Article 24;[13] the Convention for the Protection of the Marine Environment of the North-East Atlantic 1992, Article 32;[14] and the Convention on the Protection of the Rhine against Pollution by Chlorides 1976, Article 13.[15] Part XV of the Law of the Sea Convention

[10] In the early part of the twentieth century, a number of bilateral treaties for the pacific settlement of disputes were also concluded. *See* the General Treaty of Arbitration between Chile and the Argentine Republic (28 May 1902); Bolivia-Peru Treaty of General Arbitration (21 November 1901); General Arbitration Treaty between Great Britain and the United States (3 August 1911); General Arbitration Treaty between the United States of America and the French Republic (3 August 1911); General Arbitration Treaty between Great Britain and the United States (4 April 1908). These treaties, enabling future disputes to be brought to arbitration, did not generally enable arbitral jurisdiction to be established by a mere unilateral application. Usually a special agreement had to be concluded. *See e.g. Beagle Channel (Argentina/Chile)* (1977) 21 IRAA 53, 64; *Argentine-Chile Frontier Case* (1966) 16 RIAA 111; *The Boundary Case between Bolivia and Peru* (1909) 11 IRAA 133; *The North Atlantic Coast Fisheries* Case (Great Britain, United States) (1910) 11 IRAA 167.

[11] Revised General Act for the Pacific Settlement of International Disputes. New York, 28 April 1949. https://treaties.un.org/doc/Treaties/1950/09/19500920%2010-17%20PM/Ch_II_1p.pdf; *see especially* Article 17.

[12] European Treaty Series, number 23; *see especially* Article 19.

[13] 2178 UNTS 197.

[14] 2354 UNTS 67.

[15] 1840 UNTS 372.

1982 sets out a rather elaborate menu of dispute settlement mechanisms, including conciliation; the ICJ; the International Tribunal for the Law of the Sea; ad hoc arbitration in accordance with Annex VII; and arbitration under Annex VIII by technical experts over disputes concerning the interpretation or application of the articles of the Convention relating to (1) fisheries, (2) protection and preservation of the marine environment, (3) marine scientific research or (4) navigation, including pollution from vessels and by dumping.

There was a period after World War II when there was considerable resistance on the part of many States to making it compulsory to resort to the ICJ under the dispute settlement mechanisms of new multilateral treaties. This was partly due to the Cold War, and partly due to mistrust on the part of many newly independent States. In such circumstances, arbitration was sometimes regarded as preferable. With the thawing of the Cold War and increasing confidence in the ICJ on the part of third world States, there emerged a slightly greater readiness to confer this competence on the Court. See, for example, Article 66 (a) of the Vienna Convention on the Law of Treaties 1969, which gives the ICJ ultimate jurisdiction over disputes involving *ius cogens* if the parties do not agree to arbitration. However, the honeymoon period following the end of the Cold War did not last very long, and it would be unwise to expect recourse to the International Court to become the norm in the foreseeable future.[16] Hence, there will continue to be a place for ISA.

Turning to bilateral treaties, they do not always contain any sort of dispute settlement mechanism. If a dispute does arise, and it cannot be settled by negotiation, conciliation or mediation, then it is usually up to the parties to agree to ad hoc arbitration or reference to the ICJ, but there is no obligation on them to do so, apart from the generalised obligation in Article 33 of the UN Charter to seek to resolve disputes peacefully.

[16] The Appellate Body of the World Trade Organization is more akin to a court then an arbitral tribunal, not least because it is not constituted ad hoc, as most arbitral tribunals are. (Though *see* the Iran-US Claims Tribunal.) At the time of writing, however, the Appellate Body is in serious danger of grinding to a halt, because the United States is blocking the appointment of new judges to replace those whose terms have expired. Moves are therefore afoot to have recourse to binding appellate arbitration under Article 25 of the Dispute Settlement Understanding as an alternative; and in July 2019 the European Union and Canada agreed to have interim recourse to such a system if necessary. *See* Interim Appeal Arbitration Pursuant to Article 25 of the DSU, 25 July 2019, https://trade.ec.europa.eu/doclib/docs/2019/july/tradoc_158273.pdf.

An exception to this pattern is to be found in the over 3000 bilateral treaties for the promotion and protection of investments (BITs).[17] As well as provisions for investor-State arbitration (which are beyond the scope of this essay), they typically also provide for ad hoc arbitration between the States parties,[18] if they have a dispute concerning the treaty's interpretation or application which they cannot otherwise settle.[19]

One institution that is quite popular with States that wish to engage in ISA is the Permanent Court of Arbitration.[20] Its website lists 38 ISAs, including 3 pending ones.[21] 18 of them were instituted by unilateral application, approximately 47.4 per cent. However, it is important to note that this list stretches back as far as 1902. If we confine ourselves to cases after World War II – and there is a big gap there until 1996 – the total of ISAs is reduced to 23, with the same 18 cases having been introduced by unilateral application, i.e. approximately 78.2 per cent. 12 of these 18 cases

[17] There are also a few multilateral ones containing broadly similar provisions. *See e.g.* Energy Charter Treaty, Article 27: https://energycharter.org/fileadmin/DocumentsMedia/Legal/ECT-Positive_Annex_W.pdf

[18] Some of the previous US friendship, commerce, and navigation treaties provided for the settlement of inter-State disputes by the International Court of Justice. *E.g.* Article XXVI of the Treaty of Friendship, Commerce and Navigation between the United States of America and the Italian Republic (26 July 1949) provides: 'Any dispute between the High Contracting Parties as to the interpretation or the application of this Treaty, which the High Contracting Parties shall not satisfactorily adjust by diplomacy, shall be submitted to the International Court of Justice, unless the High Contracting Parties shall agree to settlement by some other pacific means'. Under this treaty, a dispute between the United States and Italy concerning an alleged expropriation gave rise to the ICJ *Case Concerning Elettronica Sicula SPA (ELSI) (US v. Italy)* (*Judgment*) *ICJ Rep.* 1989, p. 15.

[19] 2012 US Model Bilateral Investment Treaty (2012) arts. 24, 37, https://ustr.gov/sites/default/files/BIT%20text%20for%20ACIEP%20Meeting.pdf; German Model Treaty Concerning the Encouragement and Reciprocal Protection of Investments (2008) arts. 9, 10, www.italaw.com/sites/default/files/archive/ita1025.pdf; Canada Model Agreement for the Promotion and Protection of Investments (2004) arts. 24, 48, http://italaw.com/documents/Canadian2004-FIPA-model-en.pdf; France Draft Agreement on the Reciprocal Promotion and Protection of Investments (2006) arts. 7, 10, http://italaw.com/documents/ModelTreatyFrance2006.pdf; Colombian Model Bilateral Agreement for the Promotion and Protection of Investments (2007) arts. 9, 10, http://italaw.com/documents/inv_model_bit_colombia.pdf; Indian Model Agreement for the Promotion and Protection of Investments (2003) arts. 9, 10, www.italaw.com/sites/default/files/archive/ita1026.pdf.

[20] Though *see* the caveat at fn. 5.

[21] https://pca-cpa.org/en/cases/.

were based on a single multilateral treaty: the Law of the Sea Convention of 1982. Two were based on another multilateral convention;[22] the remainder were based on bilateral agreements. Overall, a tally of 23 ISAs in nearly three-quarters of a century is not impressive.

Though the phrase is commonly used in the context of adjudication, it is a little misleading to describe the susceptibility of a State to be brought before an arbitral tribunal by the unilateral application of another State as 'compulsory jurisdiction': it depends on consent, even if this consent has been given well in advance in a treaty. But even so, the phrase does reveal something about the process, and not necessarily in a positive sense. Although we lawyers tend to assume that the more jurisdiction there is, the better, it has to be acknowledged that compulsory jurisdiction can give rise to difficulties in compliance. If two States go 'hand in hand' (to use the picturesque phrase of Lord McNair) to a court or arbitral tribunal, they have made up their minds to have the case heard, and there is a high likelihood – though no certainty – that they will participate fully in the procedure and accept the outcome. But if they have simply signed up – perhaps at some distant date in the past – to the arbitration of some as yet unknown disputes with some as yet unknown opponents, their consent is somewhat attenuated in practical, if not in legal, terms. A recent illustration of this is the *South China Sea arbitration* in the PCA.[23] The Philippines objected to China's jurisdictional claims in the South China Sea and, relying on Part XV of the Law of the Sea Convention, unilaterally instituted arbitral proceedings. China, however, refused to appear or to appoint an arbitrator and disputed the jurisdiction of the tribunal on a number of grounds. In the past, the failure of a party to appoint an arbitrator or to participate in the proceedings has been fatal to the arbitration: see the *ICJ Advisory Opinion on the Interpretation of Peace Treaties with Bulgaria, Hungary and Romania (Second Phase)*.[24] However, those drafting compromissory clauses have learned to avoid these difficulties by expressly stipulating that, if a party fails to appoint an arbitrator or arbitrators, a pre-ordained person or institution shall make the appointment for it.

[22] The Rhine Chlorides Arbitration concerning the Auditing of Accounts (The Netherlands/France), PCA Case No. 2000–02); Ireland v. United Kingdom (OSPAR Arbitration), PCA Case No. 2001–03.

[23] PCA Case No. 2013–19.

[24] *ICJ Rep.* 1950, p. 221.

And such clauses also usually provide that, if one of the parties does not appear, this does not constitute a bar to the proceedings though, before making an award, the tribunal must satisfy itself, not only that it has jurisdiction over the dispute, but also that the claim is well founded in fact and in law. In the present case, this is what Articles 3 and 9 of Annex VII to the Law of the Sea Convention provided, and so the case proceeded even in the absence of the respondent. Even though the five-man tribunal unanimously dismissed China's objections and held that it had jurisdiction over the merits in 2015,[25] China continued its refusal to participate; and when, in the following year, the tribunal handed down a final award on remaining issues of jurisdiction and admissibility and on the merits, largely in favour of the claimant,[26] China refused to accept it, declaring it a nullity.

It is not necessary here to make an assessment of the contesting parties' relative positions or of the tribunal's decisions to appreciate that this kind of problem is much less likely to arise where the parties have agreed to go 'hand in hand' to an arbitral tribunal by means of an ad hoc agreement.

15.4 Advantages and Disadvantages of ISAs from the Point of View of the Parties

If, then, it is normally the choice of the States parties to a dispute whether or not they institute or submit to ISA, it is necessary to consider various advantages and disadvantages of doing so. In conducting this analysis, it is customary and helpful to bear in mind the alternative of adjudication before the ICJ; but it should be borne in mind that the latter is not the only possible comparator. Other possibilities, depending on the circumstances, include such bodies as the Law of the Sea Tribunal and various international courts or similar tribunals for human rights.

Before considering various factors which claimants and respondents will consider in deciding whether they wish their dispute to be settled by arbitration, there is one important general consideration to be mentioned – which also applies to adjudication. States normally consider litigation (in the broad sense) to be a zero-sum game. That is to say, they are not

[25] https://pcacases.com/web/sendAttach/2579.

[26] https://pcacases.com/web/sendAttach/2086.

concerned with the benefits to the international system (in which they themselves have a stake) of having legal disputes settled by impartial third parties; they just see the particular case as one where somebody must win and somebody must lose,[27] and they do not want to be on the losing side. Thus a potential claimant State will in general not wish to run the risk of losing and hence will not tend to bring a case unless it is rather confident of success. But for its part the respondent, knowing that the claimant has sufficient confidence in its case to bring proceedings, may be very chary about submitting to arbitration unless it thinks that the claimant is very mistaken in its estimation. Of course, there are exceptions. First, there are cases where it is particularly important that the dispute be settled. One example is seabed boundary disputes. It is widely thought – though not invariably with justification – that international mining companies are unwilling to explore or exploit minerals under the bed of a disputed offshore area until the respective entitlements are settled by agreement, award or judgment. Again, a small land boundary dispute may create tensions out of all proportion to their importance, and the parties may wisely choose third-party settlement in order to lance the boil. Sometimes, also, a government which would be willing in principle to make some concessions to the other side may find the necessary political 'cover' if some authoritative third party imposes the decision on it.[28] Furthermore, there are cases where the disputing parties are, perhaps for geopolitical reasons, pressured by more powerful States into going to arbitration. But where States do have a freedom of choice, as I have indicated they tend to be very chary of the risk of losing. What may be at risk is a valuable national resource, prestige and costs, which in international arbitration can be significant.

Aside from these rather fundamental obstacles to ISA, States must also consider the advantages and disadvantages of this particular procedure as compared to (in particular) adjudication. The factors – positive or negative – that I shall consider here are speed; the ability to choose the

[27] I am of course conscious of the fact that there can be cases where party A wins some points, whereas party B wins others; but this does not seriously detract from the point being made here.

[28] One should not, however, under-estimate the pressure of nationalist sentiment, which will tend to accuse the losing government of treachery, betrayal of the motherland and so on, even for submitting its claims to a third-party, let alone being willing to comply with an unfavourable decision.

arbitrators; flexibility of procedure; confidentiality; finality or lack of it; legal binding force; political binding force; and costs. The relative importance to be attached to each of these factors will of course depend on the circumstances of each case and the views of the particular parties.

15.4.1 Speed

Proceedings in the ICJ can be extremely slow in reaching a conclusion. Much of the blame for this lies with the disputing parties, who request, and are often accorded, lengthy periods to prepare their written submissions and oral arguments, not to mention further prolongations. But the fact remains that proceedings can be very slow, even though the Court's docket is rather small. Of the 133 contentious cases decided between 1945 to 2018, the judgments in 8 cases were rendered more than 10 years after the filing of the application, with the longest being 16 years,[29] and the average being about 3 years.[30] Conclusion of a case can also be delayed by a third State's intervention. *Land and Maritime Boundary between Cameroon and Nigeria* was delayed by Equatorial Guinea's request for permission to intervene and lasted for 8 years.[31] Admittedly, cases in the ICJ might be decided relatively more speedily through a Chamber. Of the six cases decided by this procedure, the longest lasted 6 years even with third-party intervention: *Land, Island and Maritime Frontier Dispute (El Savador/Honduras: Nicaragua Intervening) (Judgment)*.[32] In ISA, third-party intervention is not normally possible.[33]

Normally, ISAs can be concluded more expeditiously. For PCA-administered inter-State cases since 1996, the average duration of a case was two and a half years, although individual cases have deviated

[29] *Application of the Convention on the Prevention and Punishment of the Crime of Genocide (Croatia v. Serbia)* (Merits), *ICJ Rep.* 2015, p. 3.

[30] www.icj-cij.org/en/contentious-cases.

[31] *Land and Maritime Boundary between Cameroon and Nigeria (Cameroon v. Nigeria: Equatorial Guinea intervening) (Judgment)* [2002] *ICJ Rep.* 2002, p. 303.

[32] *ICJ Rep.* 1992, p. 351.

[33] There are exceptions, however. For instance, the 1991 Environmental Protection Protocol to the Antarctic Treaty does provide for intervention before the Arbitral Tribunal. Article 7 of the Schedule on Arbitration States: 'Any Party which believes it has a legal interest, whether general or individual, which may be substantially affected by the award of the Arbitral Tribunal, may, unless the Arbitral Tribunal decides otherwise, intervene in proceedings'.

significantly from this average. The longest case took eight years and eight months to be resolved, resulting in 17 separate awards – the *Eritrea-Ethiopia Claims Commission* (PCA Case No. 2001–02) – while the shortest cases were decided in only two months, though they were not ISAs in the normal sense.[34] As with all arbitration, sometimes one party – usually the claimant – is interested in a speedy resolution, whilst the other is not. But if the parties are in agreement, it is possible for them to arrange speedy proceedings. For example, the *compromis* between Eritrea and Ethiopia provided a 3-year limit for the Boundary Commission to complete its work,[35] and the total amount of time for this arbitration was 16 months from the establishment of the Commission to the final award.[36] The fixing of time limits by parties in arbitral agreements can also be found in *Eritrea/Yemen – Sovereignty and Maritime Delimitation in the Red Sea*;[37] *Guinea-Bissau/Senegal Case*;[38] and the *Taba Arbitration* (1988).[39] See also *Kingdom of Belgium/Kingdom of the Netherlands (Iron Rhine Arbitration)*, where the States parties agreed to dispense with a hearing.[40]

15.4.2 The Ability to Choose the Arbitrators

Another perceived advantage of arbitration is the ability to choose the arbitrators. One aspect of this is the ability to limit the size of the tribunal. In the ICJ, the full court (which is the norm) comprises 15 Judges plus possibly one or two ad hoc judges; in the International Tribunal for the Law of the Sea this could be as many as 21, plus ad hoc judges. By contrast, in ISA the tribunal is normally limited to 3 or 5 members, and there have also been cases where the parties have been content with a sole arbitrator.[41]

34 *Review Panel established under the Convention on the Conservation and Management of High Seas Fishery Resources in the South Pacific Ocean*, PCA Case No. 2013–14; *Review Panel established under the Convention on the Conservation and Management of High Seas Fishery Resources in the South Pacific Ocean*, PCA Case No. 2018–13.

35 Agreement between the Government of the Federal Democratic of Ethiopia and the Government of the State of Eritrea, art. 5(12), https://pcacases.com/web/sendAttach/786

36 *Eritrea-Ethiopia Boundary Commission* (PCA Case No. 2001–01).

37 PCA Case No. 1996–04.

38 (1989) 20 RIAA 119.

39 20 RIAA 1.

40 PCA Case No. 2003–02.

41 *See Island of Palmas* (Netherland/USA), (1928) 2 RIAA 829 (arbitrated by Max Huber).

Another aspect is that the parties have some control over the identity of the members of the tribunal, in contrast to a court whose members have already been appointed by an outside body, such as the UN Security Council and General Assembly in the case of the ICJ. Although, according to Article 2 of the Statute of the ICJ, its members are meant to be 'persons of high moral character, who possess the qualifications required in their respective countries for appointment to the highest judicial offices, or are jurisconsults of recognised competence in international law', the reality is that they vary to some degree in ability, impartiality, diligence and expertise in the particular subject matter. In arbitration, the parties have the chance to select people who they think are best suited to hear and decide the case, and who will do so with reasonable expedition.

This is not to say, however, that this freedom is completely unfettered or that it is necessarily invariably benign. First, where there are to be three arbitrators, it is common for each party to nominate one arbitrator, and for the presiding arbitrator to be selected either by agreement between the parties or between the party-appointed arbitrators or, in the absence of agreement, by some outside body, such as the President of the ICJ. If the three arbitrators cannot achieve unanimity, in effect the case will be decided by the presiding arbitrator and one other. *Mutatis mutandis* where there are 5 (or, exceptionally, 7) arbitrators. Moreover, whilst it would be very improper for parties to select arbitrators who agree to uphold their position, it is a well-known fact that parties research very carefully the 'track record' of potential candidates for appointment, and are only likely to nominate those whose previously expressed views, in publications or judicial or arbitral decisions, are sympathetic (or at least not antipathetic) to the type of argument that that party intends to put forward. Whether this is a good thing or not, States tend to find it comforting that they can influence the composition of the tribunal, and the existence of ad hoc judges in the ICJ is a hangover from this.

It would be wrong, however, to draw too sharp a contrast between the freedom to choose arbitrators and the lack of such freedom when it comes to, for instance the ICJ. In the *Gulf of Maine* case, Canada and the United States not only requested the Court to appoint a 5-man Chamber to hear the case, but specified exactly who they wanted those members to be. They also made it clear that their submission of the case to the Court was conditional on its complying with these requests.

Despite misgivings on the part of some Judges, the request was complied with. So, in effect, the parties were able to choose the members of their tribunal, just as in ISA.[42]

15.4.3 Flexibility of Procedure

It is widely believed that international arbitration is more flexible than adjudication, and there is some basis of truth in that belief. States intending to go to arbitration with each other can, if they choose, draw up a unique set of procedural rules – as happened in the early days of ISA. These days, States parties tend to find it helpful to take as the starting point the Arbitration Rules of the UN Commission on International Trade Law,[43] though they are free to vary these rules by agreement. Furthermore, Article 17 of the UNCITRAL Rules gives the tribunal itself great flexibility in adapting the rules and devising new solutions to meet the circumstances. By contrast, the Statute of the ICJ, the principal constitutive instrument of the Court, is an integral part of the Charter of the United Nations and so is, in practical terms, unalterable and embodies relatively little flexibility. It is, true that some flexibility is to be found in the more detailed Rules of Court,[44] but only subject to the overriding constraints of the Statute. For example, Article 43 of the latter specifically ordains in paragraph 1 that 'the procedure shall consist of two parts: written and oral'; paragraphs 2–4 set out some detailed rules about the written proceedings; and paragraph 5 does likewise for the oral proceedings. These parameters cannot be changed, even though the Rules may provide a degree of flexibility within them.[45]

There is also a very specific, and potentially important, difference between proceedings in the ICJ and those before an international arbitration tribunal. Article 102 (1) of the UN Charter provides that every treaty

[42] *ICJ Rep.* 1984, p. 246.

[43] www.uncitral.org/pdf/english/texts/arbitration/arb-rules-revised/arb-rules-revised-2010-e.pdf. These rules were originally designed for use in the context of international commercial relations, but have been found useful in a variety of different contexts, such as ISA.

[44] www.icj-cij.org/en/rules.

[45] *See*, in particular, Article 101 of the Rules.

and every international agreement entered into by any member of the UN shall be registered as soon as possible with the UN Secretariat and published by it. However, States are not always scrupulous in complying with this obligation. Paragraph 2 of Article 102 goes on to say that 'no party to any such treaty or international agreement which has not been registered in accordance with the provisions of paragraph 1 of this Article may invoke that treaty or agreement before any organ of the United Nations'. The ICJ is an organ – indeed, the principal judicial organ – of the ICJ. The Judgment in *Fisheries Jurisdiction (United Kingdom v. Iceland), Jurisdiction of the Court,* highlights the importance of complying with this obligation. It records that the UK government was very insistent that an exchange of notes with Iceland should contain a provision for its registration with the UN Secretariat, for fear that it could not otherwise be relied upon before the Court, and that Iceland eventually acquiesced in this.[46] Arbitral tribunals, on the other hand, are not organs of the UN. Hence, in the *Guinea-Bissau Senegal* arbitration, the tribunal held that the fact that the 1960 Franco-Portuguese Agreement was not registered with the UN Secretariat did not prevent the tribunal from using it, since it was not a UN organ and thus Article 102(2) was not applicable.[47]

15.4.4 Confidentiality

In commercial arbitration, the parties normally set very great store by the confidentiality of the proceedings and the outcome, and in general – at least in developed countries – this is not thought to be contrary to the public interest. In international adjudication, on the other hand, because public (international) law is involved, and the issues are often of considerable public importance, the proceedings in, and the decisions of, the ICJ and comparable bodies are open to public scrutiny. ISA carries with it some of the heritage of private arbitration, and in principle the proceedings and decisions of the tribunals are confidential, unless the parties otherwise agree. The *compromis* usually specifies

[46] *ICJ Rep.* 1973, pp. 3, 12–13. *See also Appeal Relating to the Jurisdiction of the ICAO Council (India v. Pakistan)* (Judgment), *ICJ Rep.* 1972 pp. 46, 51.

[47] *Guinea-Bissau Senegal arbitration* (1989), 20 RIAA 119, para. 78.

this, or the tribunal so orders.[48] In some cases, this confidentiality is regarded as a definite advantage.[49]

It is very difficult in practice for confidentiality to be maintained, though. If I may be permitted a personal anecdote, in 1976 Dubai and Sharjah signed a *compromis* setting up a Court of Arbitration to determine their land and maritime boundary. Not only was the award, which was handed down in 1981, meant to be confidential; even the existence of the arbitration was supposed to be secret. One of the arbitrators – now deceased – let me see a copy of the award for my personal interest, but on the strict condition that I was not to cite or divulge to anyone either the content of the award or even the very existence of the arbitration. I personally respected this prohibition to the full; but evidently not everyone did so, because in *Maritime Delimitation and Territorial Questions between Qatar and Bahrain (Qatar v. Bahrain),* which commenced in 1991, the case was freely cited to the ICJ by the parties before it.[50]

In the *Channel arbitration*[51] between France and the United Kingdom, the parties were willing for the award to be published, but not the pleadings. This may have been because they did not want confidential information about submarine geology or mineral resources to be divulged. It may also have been because a naval facility of considerable strategic importance was located in the area subject to the delimitation. Or it may have been because they did not want arguments that they had deployed in these particular proceedings to be used against them in subsequent negotiations or proceedings with different parties. Or of course, it may have been a combination of these considerations.

[48] *E.g.* Republic of Ecuador v. United States of America , PCA Case No. 2012-5, Award, para. 11, which records that Procedural Order No. 1 required the pleading and submissions to remain confidential with some exceptions); Arbitration between Barbados and the Republic of Trinidad and Tobago (2006) 27 RIAA 147, para. 39: 'All written and oral pleadings, documents, and evidence submitted in the arbitration, verbatim transcripts of meetings and hearings, and the deliberations of the Arbitral Tribunal, shall remain confidential unless otherwise agreed by the Parties'.

[49] For instance, the award of the tribunal in the *Timor Sea* arbitration (Timor-Leste v. Australia) has not been officially published: *see* https://pca-cpa.org/en/cases/141; and the *Heathrow* arbitration between the United Kingdom and the United States was conducted discreetly in The Hague.

[50] The award was eventually published in *International Law Reports* in 1993: 91 ILR 543.

[51] 1977–1978, 18 RIAA 3.

15.4.5 Finality (or Its Absence)

Judgments of the ICJ are final, and so, generally, are the awards of inter-State arbitral tribunals.[52] However, in the latter case this can be subject to exceptions.

It is always possible for the jurisdictional instrument to make provision for an appeal to, or review – for example, for lack of jurisdiction – by, some other body, such as the ICJ. Thus, the *Appeal Relating to the Jurisdiction of the ICAO Council* concerned a provision in Article 84 of the Convention on International Civil Aviation of 1944, and the same provision in the International Air Services Transit Agreement of the same year.[53]

Furthermore, notwithstanding the apparent finality of an arbitral award, it may be possible to challenge it on the grounds that it was not validly given, because the tribunal lacked jurisdiction or exceeded it due to corruption, and so on. In the *Case concerning the Arbi.tral Award made by the King of Spain on 23 December 1906 (Honduras v. Nicaragua)*, Nicaragua unsuccessfully challenged the award on various grounds, such as lack of jurisdiction, absence of reasons and the 'inexecutability' of the award.[54] However, the ICJ clearly considered that it had jurisdiction to deal with these issues; and likewise in *Arbitral Award of 31 July 1989.*[55]

Although, in general, the parties to ISAs prefer a (relatively) quick and final resolution, not subject to appeal or a more limited review, occasionally, if they are dissatisfied with the outcome, they may seek to overturn the award by means of revision prceedings or challenge it in the ICJ on the grounds of nullity and so forth.

15.4.6 Legally Binding Force

Like judgments of the ICJ, awards of inter-State arbitral tribunals are, by the terms of their *compromis,* legally binding – subject to the points made

[52] I am not dealing here with the question of the interpretation or revision of judgments or arbitral awards, or the correction of clerical errors.

[53] Judgment, *ICJ Rep.* 1972, pp. 46, 48 (para. 1) and 54–55 (para. 17).

[54] *ICJ Rep.* 1960, p. 192 (Honduras/Nicaragua).

[55] Though there, too, the Court dismissed the claims by Guinea-Bissau that the award was 'inexistent' due to the absence of a majority and that it was a nullity because the tribunal had not drawn a map provided for by the *compromis: Guinea-Bissau v. Senegal, Judgment, ICJ Rep.* 1991, p. 53.

in the immediately preceding section. However, in the case of ICJ judgments not only is the obligation to comply embedded in Article 94 (1) of the Charter of the United Nations – the supreme legal instrument of the international community – but the following paragraph goes on to say, 'If any party to a case fails to perform the obligations incumbent upon it under a judgment rendered by the Court, the other party may have recourse to the Security Council, which may, if it deems necessary, make recommendations or decide upon measures to be taken to give effect to the judgment'. There is nothing comparable in the case of inter-State arbitral awards.

Sadly, however, Article 94 (2) of the Charter is not, in practice, as fearsome as it appears on paper. Resolutions of the Security Council to impose sanctions on States who do not comply with judgments are subject to the veto of each of the five permanent members, and they do not hesitate to wield it to protect themselves or their friends.[56] Consequently, the Security Council has never so far applied sanctions to compel compliance with a judgment, and it seems unlikely to do so in the foreseeable future. So in this sense, there may not be much practical difference between judgments and awards.

15.4.7 Politically Binding Force

Even though inter-State awards are normally equally as legally binding as ICJ judgments, from a political and diplomatic viewpoint there can be a difference. The ICJ, as the 'principal judicial organ' of the UN, stands at the top of the international hierarchy, and it is a serious matter for a party to ignore a judgment from this body. Even if failures to comply do occur from time to time, they are usually temporary. Inter-State arbitral tribunals come somewhat lower in the hierarchy. This may at first sight seem nothing but a disadvantage, but that is not necessarily so. States may want their disputes to be settled in a rather more low-key way; and governments may consider that if they lose, the lower the profile the better. And here, the greater confidentiality of arbitral, as opposed to judicial, proceedings can assist in keeping the outcome low-key.

[56] Or those who, with the veto in mind, at least temporarily seek their protection.

15.4.8 Costs

There are two elements of costs to consider – the amount, and the allocation:

1. In the ICJ, the cost of running the Court (stipends, pensions, maintenance of premises, administrative costs etc.) is met by the parties to the Statute, in effect all of the members of the UN, and no separate fee is charged to the States who engage in litigation there. The position is different in ISA, where the contesting parties have between them to foot the bill for the fees of the arbitrators and other administrative costs, such as the fees of any administrating institution. These can amount to several hundreds of thousands of dollars. So in this respect there is a definite saving in going to the ICJ rather than to arbitration.

   The other expense of litigation and arbitration is the fees of counsel, experts and so on. Given the length of proceedings and the size of the teams which are thought necessary to deal with what are often quite important issues for the contesting States, these fees can amount to millions of dollars. Whatever may be the position with regard to investor-State arbitration, in ISA there does not seem to be an enormous difference in the size and cost of the teams deployed, compared to those in ICJ proceedings. Perhaps in at least some ISAs they are a little more modest, but not greatly so.
2. The difference between adjudication and arbitration can be far more serious when it comes to the apportionment of the costs (both court/tribunal costs and counsel/expert costs) between the parties. In the ICJ, as I have already indicated, the apportionment of Court costs between the contesting parties does not arise. So far as concerns the apportionment of the other costs, the Court seems very disinclined to apportion them, even where there is a clear winner and a clear loser. Although such an apportionment is very common in the case of domestic litigation and in all sorts of international arbitration, the ICJ's hesitancy may perhaps be understandable in some cases. For example, if there is a straightforward dispute about title to territory, it is at any rate arguable that resolving territorial disputes with neighbours is a normal part of the process and expense of government, and there is no need to penalise one side in costs just because it has lost the case. But what if the case involves allegations of wrongdoing by one party – possibly even the illegal use of force – and the accused party loses the case? It is not the

wronged State's fault that it had to seek redress from the Court; and so the case seems stronger that it should be entitled to its costs. It is, I suggest, no answer to respond that the ICJ's role is not to punish States. As opposed to 'exemplary' damages, an award of costs to the victim is simply putting it back (so far as the legal expenses are concerned) in the position it would have been in had the illegal act not occurred. It is true that not all domestic legal systems follow the British model that 'costs follow the event'; in some systems 'costs lie where they fall'. But I do not think that it is due to an unreasoning attachment to my native system if I declare my preference for the British approach: the victim of a wrongful act has had to undertake the considerable expense of bringing proceedings to put matters right, and it ought to have that made good. A fortiori, if one party has caused unnecessary additional expense to the other party by means of indefensible procedural ploys, the proffering of demonstrably false testimony, forged documents and so on, there is a good case to be made that the innocent party should be compensated for its additional costs. But be that as it may, this is not an approach that has so far found favour in the Court.

The position could *in theory* be rather different when it comes to ISA. Although inter-State arbitration has many similarities to inter-State adjudication, it also shares many characteristics and attitudes with other types of international arbitration: international commercial, and investor-State. In these other types of arbitration, tribunals are often quite robust in the apportionment of costs. Frequently they favour – at least to some degree – the 'costs follow the event' approach; and they feel quite free to make parties who act inappropriately in the proceedings compensate their opponents for costs unnecessarily incurred.

But because the arbitrators in inter-State cases tend to be people who are or have been, or could be, international judges, they tend to be somewhat more diplomatic and more attuned to political sensitivities than, say, most commercial arbitrators. So there is no evidence that they are more open than the ICJ to requests to apportion costs. In the few cases where the awards make reference to costs, they provide that they shall be borne equally.[57] And perhaps the relative rarity of ISAs means

[57] In the *Bay of Bengal Maritime Boundary Arbitration between Bangladesh and India* PCA Case No. 2010–16, the Tribunal took note of the Parties' agreement that 'all costs incurred

that even tribunals who are not fettered by the *compromis* are unlikely to become more proactive about the apportionment of the costs in the foreseeable future.[58]

15.5 Conclusion

Prior to the establishment in 1922 of the Permanent Court of International Justice,[59] if States with legal disputes wanted them to be determined on legal grounds by independent third parties with binding effect, the only possibility was ISA.[60] Now that there exists not only the ICJ (the successor of the PCIJ) but a variety of other inter-State courts, States parties have a choice between adjudication and arbitration. As we have seen, consent – either in advance or ad hoc, is needed in either event. As this essay has attempted to show, there are circumstances where one or both contesting States might find it more advantageous to have recourse to arbitration than to adjudication. Nevertheless, in the period following the World War II – almost 75 years – only 23 ISAs have been administered in some way by the Permanent Court of Arbitration; and even including secret ones and others conducted outside the PCA's aegis, I doubt whether the total significantly exceeds 40. Why so few?

Partly, this is due to the existence of the ICJ and other international courts. The ICJ went through a fairly bad patch in the first three decades or so of its existence. Some groups of States were distrustful of what they considered to be too much Western influence in the Court's membership

in connection with activities conducted exclusively in the territory of one of the Parties shall be borne by that Party' (Procedural Order 1), https://pcacases.com/web/sendAttach/376.

[58] In preparing this essay, I also considered a number of what might broadly be called procedural issues, such as disclosure of documents, the possibility of corruption of one or more arbitrators, and conflicts of interest of arbitrators. I have not discussed them here, however, because the available material is rather thin. Broadly speaking, the approach in ISA seems similar, *mutatis mutandis*, to what obtains in investor-State arbitration.

[59] Despite the similarity of names, the Permanent Court of Arbitration, which pre-dates the PCIJ, is not a court, but a body of rules for the conduct of arbitrations and a roster of potential arbitrators.

[60] Other forms of peaceful settlement, such as negotiation, conciliation and mediation, do not satisfy these three criteria. Either they do not involve third-parties, the decision is not binding, or it is not based on legal grounds but on considerations like expediency or acceptability.

and in the body of law that it was to apply. However, there is greater trust now, and with its increasing docket the Court is also somewhat more self-confident. Depending on the subject, there are also other courts available to decide inter-State disputes.

Another reason for the under-use of ISA is probably the greater availability and sophistication of other third-party dispute settlement mechanisms. For one thing, there is now a great variety of international organisations – not just the United Nations – to which States can bring their disputes, even if those fora will not be applying strictly legal criteria. Again, mediation is extensively carried out by the Secretary-General of the UN, and also by or under the auspices of other institutions such as the European Union, the Organisation of American States and so on. The institution of conciliation, which entails third parties making binding or non-binding recommendations to the parties, not mainly based on legal considerations, has also become more sophisticated and more available.

Furthermore, as we have seen in Section 15.4, as well as the advantages of ISA there can also be disadvantages, or what one or both of the parties consider to be disadvantages, compared with adjudication or indeed with other peaceful means of settlement.

Nevertheless, even despite all of these explanations, the low number of ISAs is rather surprising. The remaining explanation is perhaps the most important one. It has to be remembered that, although under the UN Charter States are supposed not to resolve their disputes by force or the threat of force, but peacefully, in reality there is not normally any compulsion to resort to any particular means of dispute settlement, including ISA. And governments are rather reluctant to engage in binding procedures for resolving their disputes, either because they think they have a better chance of success through military, diplomatic or economic pressure or because they are afraid of the possible consequences of losing. Governments who are dubious about their chances of success in a lawsuit will be hesitant about either launching one or submitting to it. And even governments who think that they have a strong case will be aware of the many possible risks of going to law, which makes it dangerous to predict the outcome with confidence. Politicians are worried about the political risks of losing a case, and in general they would rather forgo the chance of winning for the sake of avoiding the perceived catastrophe of losing. Similarly with officials. A And legal disputes with other States are not necessarily a matter of urgency; so those who have to decide whether to go to court or arbitration may prefer to leave the problem for their successors.

These are the sorts of considerations which have kept the numbers of ISAs down, and in general are probably likely to do so for the foreseeable future.[61] Nevertheless, ISA remains a useful, if underused, item in the toolbox of international diplomacy.

[61] A possible exception to this sceptical prognosis concerns some very recent developments in the field of international trade and investment. For a variety of reasons, many states – including those playing a leading role in international trade and investment - are beginning to regret allowing investors and other affected parties the right to bring proceedings in their own right. There is hence a distinct trend in some important recent treaties in this area to confine dispute-settlement wholly or partially to ISA.

The Permanent Court of Arbitration 16

From 1899 to the Present

Garth Schofield*

16.1 Introduction

The Permanent Court of Arbitration (PCA) is an international organisation with 122 Contracting Parties, established to facilitate arbitration and other forms of dispute resolution. The PCA is a creation of the first Hague Peace Conference of 1899, and at the same time, a modern centre for the resolution of disputes involving States. It is a pre-cursor to creation of permanently constituted international courts and historically important in the development of international dispute resolution, yet is also more active in its own right today than at any point in its history.

Today, the PCA stands at the centre of efforts to resolve disputes involving States, but the path to reach this point has not been a straight one. This chapter is an effort to tell the story of the PCA and its development in the context of more than a century of change in the practice of international arbitration and in the preferences of States with respect to the resolution of disputes. During that time, other international organisations have come and gone, international courts have emerged as an alternative to arbitration, and the role of the individual in international law has dramatically changed. Through this, the PCA is not only relevant, but flourishing.

The PCA's development follows the long arc of the twentieth century, yet its resilience and success is, in no small part, a reflection of wise choices taken in 1899 to create an organisation with the capacity to adapt and prove useful over time. The organisation today constitutes an essential complement to permanently constituted courts in the resolution of inter-State disputes and a hub that brings together inter-State dispute resolution, mixed arbitration between States and private parties, proceedings involving international organisations, and non-binding forms of dispute resolution, including conciliation, mediation and enquiry.

* Opinions expressed in this chapter are the personal views of the author.

16.2 The PCA in History

16.2.1 The Establishment of the PCA

The genesis of the PCA lies in the particular circumstances of a meeting between great power diplomacy and the international peace movement.

At the close of the nineteenth century, the world was in the midst of a period of unprecedented technological change and innovation. For the governments of Europe, this took the form first and foremost of an arms race, as innovations in weaponry rapidly rendered even newly acquired armaments obsolete and demanded continuous expenditure.[1] Concerned that Russia was falling behind, and facing the costs of matching a new generation of artillery about to be introduced by Austria-Hungary, the new Czar, Nicholas II, sought to pause a process that seemed without end.[2] On 24 August 1898, the diplomatic representatives accredited to St. Petersburg were presented with a circular, inviting the participation of their governments in a diplomatic conference intended to 'check[] these increasing armaments and ... seek[] the means of averting the calamities which threaten the entire world'.[3] The Czar's actual aim was limited – a mere moratorium of a few years, sufficient to enable Russia to catch its breath – yet his proposal caught the attention of a public opinion eager for an alternative to militarism and was lauded globally as a call for disarmament.

As Russia sought to refine the programme for the conference, however, it rapidly became apparent that significant progress on the limitation of armaments was unlikely. Accordingly, the Czar's second circular note, transmitted in December 1898, introduced the possibility of discussing 'the use of good offices, mediation and voluntary arbitration ... with the purpose of preventing armed conflicts between nations' and of

[1] *See generally* M. Pearton, *Diplomacy, War, and Technology Since 1830* (Kansas: University Press of Kansas, 1982), 95–154; D. Stevenson, 'Land Armaments in Europe, 1866–1914' *in* T. Mahnken, J. Maiolo and D. Stevenson (eds.) *Arms Races in International Politics* (Oxford: Oxford University Press, 2015).

[2] D. L. Morrill, 'Nicholas II and the Call for the First Hague Conference' (1974) 46 *The Journal of Modern History* 296.

[3] M. N. Mouravieff, 'Russian Circular Note Proposing the First Peace Conference' *reproduced in* J. B. Scott, *Instructions to the American Delegates at the Peace Conference and Their Official Reports* (New York: Oxford University Press, 1916), 1–2.

establishing 'a uniform practice in employing them',[4] as well as six topics concerning the extension of the laws of war. Following the success of the *Alabama* arbitration in 1872,[5] the last decades of the nineteenth century had seen a boom in inter-State arbitration, with more than 80 proceedings initiated.[6] In the process, arbitration also became a favourite objective of the international peace movement, as it sought to substitute legal proceedings for war.[7] Arbitration societies flourished with a progressive optimism about the perfectibility of international relations that seems almost hopelessly naive to modern eyes.

The Peace Conference convened in The Hague in May 1899, and – as anticipated – agreement on any disarmament, or even limits on new purchases of weaponry, proved elusive. Expectations, however, had been raised, and it was all but unthinkable that the Conference could conclude without a significant agreement. Hopes for a successful outcome rapidly shifted to the conference's Third Commission, concerned with arbitration.[8] Here too, however, the powers came to The Hague with differing agendas. The United States arrived with a proposal for the establishment of a

[4] M. N. Mouravieff, 'Russian Circular Note Proposing the Program of the First Conference' *reproduced in* J. B. Scott, *Instructions to the American Delegates at the Peace Conference and Their Official Reports* (New York: Oxford University Press, 1916), 3–5.

[5] *See* T. W. Balch, *The Alabama Arbitration* (Philadelphia: Allen Lane & Scott, 1900).

[6] A. M. Stuyt, *Survey of International Arbitrations, 1794–1989*, Third Survey (Dordrecht; Boston: M. Nijhoff Publishers, 1990); *see also* W. E. Darby, *International Tribunals: A Collection of the Various Schemes Which Have Been Propounded; and of Instances in the Nineteenth Century* (London: J. M. Dent and Co., 1904).

[7] *See generally* D. D. Caron, 'War and International Adjudication: Reflections on the 1899 Peace Conferences' (2000) 94 *American Journal of International Law* 4.

[8] For a concise overview of the politics of the Hague Conference, *see* B. Tuchman, *The Proud Tower* (New York: The Macmillan Company, 1966), 229–288. For first-hand and contemporary accounts, *see* F. W. Holls, *The Peace Conference at The Hague: and Its Bearings on International Law and Policy* (New York: The Macmillan Company; London, Macmillan & Co., Ltd., 1900); F. De Martens, *La Conférence de la Paix à la Haye: Étude d'histoire contemporaine* (Paris: A. Rousseau, 1900); J. W. Foster, *Arbitration and The Hague Court* (Boston and New York: Houghton Mifflin, 1904); W. I. Hull, *The Two Hague Conferences and Their Contributions to International Law* (Boston: Ginn & Company, 1908); M. L. Renault, *L'Œuvre de la Haye: 1899 et 1907* (Paris: Félix Alcan, 1908); L. Bourgeois, *Pour La Société des Nations* (Paris: Bibliothèque-Charpentier, 1910); A. D. White, *The First Hague Conference* (Boston: World Peace Foundation, 1912); J. H. Choate, *The Two Hague Conferences* (Princeton: Princeton University Press, 1913).

permanent international tribunal.[9] Britain envisaged a tribunal of arbitrators from which individual panels would be formed.[10] And Russia sought to define a list of potential subjects of dispute sufficiently removed from politics and the vital interests of States such that their resolution through arbitration could be made obligatory.[11] Germany, in contrast, was opposed to anything that might potentially constrain its freedom of action and was brought to a compromise only by the prospect of being blamed if the conference were to conclude without result.

The structure of the PCA that thus emerged reflects the circumstances of its creation. The American idea of a permanently constituted court was never seriously considered. The British formula of a standing body of arbitrators, from which individual tribunals would be formed, was selected as the basis for discussion, in preference to the Russian and American drafts. That body became the PCA's Members of the Court (from which individual tribunals were intended to be formed) in the Convention ultimately adopted, with four individuals from each Contracting Party appointed to six-year terms.[12] The Convention also established the PCA's International Bureau, to serve as the registry of the Court, and its Administrative Council, to provide a diplomatic forum for oversight by the Contracting Parties. Any hint of making recourse to arbitration obligatory, even for decidedly minor disputes, was rigorously excised as the price for securing German participation.

In establishing the PCA, its founders sought to secure as much permanency and consistency in the composition of arbitral tribunals as could be

[9] *See* 'Plan for an International Tribunal: Proposal of the Commission of the United States of America' *reproduced in* J. B. Scott (ed.), *The Proceedings of the Hague Peace Conferences: The Conference of 1899* (New York: Oxford University Press, 1920), 833.

[10] *See* 'Proposition of Sir Julian Pauncefote' *reproduced in* J. B. Scott (ed.), *The Proceedings of the Hague Peace Conferences: The Conference of 1899* (New York: Oxford University Press, 1920), 813.

[11] *See* 'Outlines for the Preparation of a Draft Convention to be Concluded between the Powers Taking Part in the Hague Conference: Russian Draft' *reproduced in* J. B. Scott (ed.), *The Proceedings of the Hague Peace Conferences: The Conference of 1899* (New York: Oxford University Press, 1920), 797; 'Explanatory Note Concerning Article 10 of the Russian Draft' *reproduced in* J. B. Scott (ed.), *The Proceedings of the Hague Peace Conferences: The Conference of 1899* (New York: Oxford University Press, 1920), 808.

[12] The PCA continues to maintain the list of Members of the Court, with four individuals nominated by each Contracting Party. For arbitrations not initiated pursuant to the Hague Conventions, however, there is no requirement that arbitrators be selected from the list of Members of the Court.

achieved within the political constraints of the conference. The British proposal had originally envisaged the appointment of only two Members of the Court by each Contracting Party, and this was increased to four only at Germany's insistence and over a number of concerns that this would dilute the coherence of the Court and diminish its prestige. The Hague delegates certainly anticipated that the PCA would become the principal form of inter-State arbitration. Yet they were above all pragmatic, and the Hague Convention can be understood to stand for the principle that achieving effective dispute resolution is more important than the promotion of any particular procedure. Mediation, good offices and commissions of enquiry are given equal weight to arbitration within the Convention. An article that would have codified a preference for arbitration by tribunals drawn from the PCA Members of the Court over other forms of inter-State arbitration was considered and expressly rejected.[13] Instead, Article 21 of the Convention provides, in even-handed terms, that 'the Permanent Court shall be competent for all arbitration cases, unless the parties agree to institute a special Tribunal'. Moreover, the Convention empowered the PCA's International Bureau to make its facilities and staff available to support any such special Tribunal, on the same terms as one constituted pursuant to the Convention. This pragmatic flexibility has since proved enormously important in the development of the PCA as an institution, and many of the PCA's early arbitrations were formally special Tribunals, involving one or more arbitrators not among the PCA's Members of the Court.

Away from the political spotlight, the delegates from The Hague also made significant strides in codifying arbitral procedure, both for the tribunals of the newly created PCA and generally, as default rules for any arbitration between the Contracting Parties not specifying another procedure.[14] Through this codification, the drafters succeeded in

[13] Third Commission, 'Report to the Conference', *reproduced in* J. B. Scott (ed.), *The Proceedings of the Hague Peace Conferences: The Conference of 1899* (New York: Oxford University Press, 1920), 130–131; Third Commission, Fifth Meeting, 17 July 1899, *reproduced in* J. B. Scott (ed.), *The Proceedings of the Hague Peace Conferences: The Conference of 1899* (New York: Oxford University Press, 1920), 605.

[14] The drafting history of the 1899 Hague Convention indicates that the procedural rules of the Convention were intended to 'fill up the gaps' in any later *compromis* or agreement to arbitrate concluded between the Parties where the States concerned 'have not otherwise provided'. Third Commission, 'Report to the Conference', *reproduced in* J. B. Scott (ed.), *The Proceedings of the Hague Peace Conferences: Translation of the Official Texts: The Conference of 1899* (New York: Oxford University Press, 1920), 139–140.

capturing the key elements of arbitral procedure in terms that remain recognisable to arbitration practitioners today. The Hague Convention procedures were subsequently to prove highly influential in the formulation of the statute of the Permanent Court of International Justice (and its successor, the International Court of Justice) and in the International Law Commission's work on arbitral procedure in the 1950s.[15]

16.2.2 Seeking a Permanently Constituted Court

The PCA was established in September 1900, and by 1907 had convened four arbitral tribunals.[16]

This, however, represented only a small fraction of the more than 40 inter-State arbitrations commenced during this period, many of which involved the Central and South American States that had not been present at The Hague in 1899 and remained excluded from the Convention.[17] Perhaps more significantly, the 1899 Hague Conference precipitated the widespread conclusion of general arbitration treaties among the European powers. While the conclusion of such general treaties for the resolution of disputes had been common among the American States in the nineteenth century, it was a practice largely confined to the New World. Following the Conference, the adoption of the Anglo-French Arbitration Treaty in 1903

[15] *See generally* International Law Commission, 'Model Rules on Arbitral Procedure with a General Commentary', *Yearbook of the International Law Commission*, vol. II (New York: United Nations, 1958), 83.

[16] *The Pious Fund of the Californias* (The United States of America v. The United Mexican States); *Japanese House Tax* (Germany, France and Great Britain/Japan); *Preferential Treatment of Claims of Blockading Powers against Venezuela* (Germany, Great Britain and Italy v. Venezuela); *Muscat Dhows* (France/Great Britain). A fifth agreement was reached between the Netherlands and Portugal in 1904 to submit a dispute over the boundary between them on the island of Timor to the PCA, but proceedings were only actively commenced in 1913. The International Bureau also provided administrative support during this period to the sole Arbitrator in the *Bering Fur Seal Arbitration*, Tobias Asser, although the parties' agreement to arbitrate preceded the establishment of the PCA.

[17] Eleven of these proceedings concerned private claims arising out of Venezuela's civil war, brought before a series of mixed commissions between Venezuela and other States. In contrast to many modern treaties, the 1899 Hague Convention was a closed treaty, with accession limited to the Powers participating in the Hague Conference (subject to a subsequent agreement on the accession of other Powers); participation in the 1899 Hague Conference, in turn, was limited to those Powers with diplomatic representation in St. Petersburg, a criteria that excluded most of Latin America.

(referring disputes to the PCA) sparked the conclusion of more than 50 such treaties, most between various combinations of European States.[18] Although the excision of obligatory arbitration from the 1899 Hague Convention had removed the ability of that instrument to direct cases to the PCA, the new bilateral treaties offered a promising source of activity.

Despite these steps, it was with a feeling of dissatisfaction with their creation that the Powers reconvened in The Hague for the second peace conference of 1907. The United States, in particular, was determined to improve upon the PCA. Having floated, but not seriously pursued, the idea of a permanently constituted court in 1899, the United States returned to The Hague in 1907 intent on creating such a body.[19] This mission was principally driven by the US Secretary of State, Elihu Root, who concluded that the lack of greater recourse to arbitration was a direct result of the ad hoc composition of arbitral tribunals and distrust in the identity of the arbitrators.[20] In his instructions to the US delegation, Root diagnosed the difficulties with inter-State arbitration in the following terms:

> There can be no doubt that the principal objection to arbitration rests not upon the unwillingness of nations to submit their controversies to impartial arbitration, but upon an apprehension that the arbitrations to which they submit may not be impartial. It has been a very general practice for arbitrators to act, not as judges deciding questions of fact and law upon the record before them under a sense of judicial responsibility, but as negotiators effecting settlements of the questions brought before them in accordance with the traditions and usages and subject to all the considerations and influences which affect diplomatic agents. The two methods are radically different, proceed upon different standards of honorable obligation, and frequently lead to widely differing results. It very frequently happens that a nation which would be very willing to submit its differences to an impartial judicial determination is unwilling to subject them to this kind of diplomatic process. If there could be a tribunal which would pass upon questions between nations with the same impartial and impersonal judgment that the Supreme Court of the United States gives to questions arising

[18] *See* D. P. Myers, *Arbitration Engagement Now Existing in Treaties, Treaty Provisions and National Constitutions* (Boston: World Peace Foundation, 1915).

[19] *See generally* B. A. Coates, *Legalist Empire: International Law and American Foreign Relations in the Early Twentieth Century* (Oxford: Oxford University Press, 2016), 88–95.

[20] On the historical role of party-appointed arbitrators *see* V. V. Veeder, 'The Historical Keystone to International Arbitration: The Party-Appointed Arbitrator – From Miami to Geneva', *Proceedings of the ASIL Annual Meeting*, vol. 107 (Cambridge: Cambridge University Press, 2013), 387–405.

between citizens of the different States, or between foreign citizens and the citizens of the United States, there can be no doubt that nations would be much more ready to submit their controversies to its decision than they are now to take the chances of arbitration.[21]

Subsequent developments (discussed below) call the accuracy of this diagnosis into question, but it was accepted as true by many of the delegates in 1907.

Although initially an American concern, the quest for a permanently constituted court was quickly adopted by a number of the other powers. Tobias Asser and Friedrich Martens were the foremost individuals responsible for the establishment of the PCA in 1899, yet neither hesitated in 1907 to heap criticism on their creation: Martens dismissed the PCA as 'an idea which occasionally assumes shape and then again disappears',[22] while Asser memorably observed that 'the Convention of 1899 gave but the phantom of a court, an impalpable specter, or to be more precise yet, it gave us a recorder with a list'.[23] Years later, in considering this period, Sir Hersch Lauterpacht correctly noted a 'tendency to deny the judicial character of arbitration, as it then existed, in order to strengthen the argument for the establishment of a true international court able to develop International Law by the continuity of its pronouncements and the permanency of its personnel'.[24]

The US proposal envisaged a permanently established court operating alongside – but not replacing – the PCA. Indeed, freedom of choice and the equal treatment of the two mechanisms are recurring themes in the discussions of 1907.[25] Ultimately, the American effort foundered on the

[21] J. B. Scott (ed.), *Instruction to the American Delegates to the Hague Peace Conference and Their Official Reports* (New York: Oxford University Press, 1916), 79–80.

[22] F. Martens, 'Speech delivered on 1 August 1907', *reproduced in* J. B. Scott (ed.), *The Proceedings of the Hague Peace Conferences: Translation of the Official Texts*, vol. II (New York: Oxford University Press, 1921), 327.

[23] T. M. C. Asser, 'Speech delivered on 16 July 1907', *reproduced in* J. B. Scott (ed.), *The Proceedings of the Hague Peace Conferences: Translation of the Official Texts*, vol. II (New York: Oxford University Press, 1921), 234.

[24] H. Lauterpacht, *Oppenheim's International Law*, 7th ed., vol. II (London: Longmans, 7th ed., 1952), 23, n. 1

[25] The Draft Convention Relative to the Creation of a Court of Arbitral Justice expressly envisages the parallel existence of the two institutions and provides that judges for the new court should be selected 'as far as possible from the members of the Permanent Court of Arbitration'. *See* J. B. Scott (ed.), *The Proceedings of the Hague Peace Conferences: The Conference of 1907*, vol. I (New York: Oxford University Press, 1920), 690. During the

critical question of the method of selecting judges. Unlike in 1899, the Latin American States were fully represented in the Conference of 1907 and were entirely unwilling to compromise their sovereign equality when it came to the appointment of a permanently constituted court. The principal European States were equally unwilling to countenance the creation of a court in which their influence would be diluted by the appointment of a large number of judges from the 'lesser' powers. No solution to this deadlock was apparent, and the Conference settled on approving, in principle, the statute of a 'Court of Arbitral Justice' and recommending its adoption 'as soon as an agreement has been reached respecting the selection of the judges and the constitution of the Court'.[26] It would only be with the establishment of the League of Nations that a compromise could be reached through a system of parallel elections in the Assembly (where the small States predominated) and the Council (controlled by the Great Powers).[27]

While agreement on a permanently constituted court proved elusive, the 1907 Conference succeeded on a number of efforts intended to reinforce the work of the PCA. Agreement was reached on the procedure for

discussion on the need for a *compromis*, it was emphasised that any steps to remove the need for a *compromis*, or remove obstacles to its preparation, would need to be applicable both to the Court of Arbitral Justice and to the code of arbitral procedure, it having 'always been understood that the two institutions, the Permanent Court and the tribunal which is to be created – should be put on the same footing, and that the parties might address themselves impartially either to one or the other'. First Commission, 'Committee of Examination C, Tenth Meeting', 14 September 1907, *reproduced in* J. B. Scott, (ed.), *The Proceedings of the Hague Peace Conferences: The Conference of 1907*, vol. II (New York: Oxford University Press, 1921), 763.

26 *See* Hague Peace Conference, 'Final Act of the Second International Peace Conference', 15 June 1907, *reproduced in* J. B. Scott (ed.), *The Proceedings of the Hague Peace Conferences: The Conference of 1907*, vol. I (New York: Oxford University Press, 1920), 679, at 689; *see also* Draft Convention Relative to the Creation of a Court of Arbitral Justice, *reproduced in* J. B. Scott (ed.), *The Proceedings of the Hague Peace Conferences: The Conference of 1907*, vol. I (New York: Oxford University Press, 1920), 690.

27 Under the structure of the League, all members formed part of the Assembly, while the Council was composed of fthe our permanent members (France, Italy, Japan, and the United Kingdom) and four (later nine) rotating members. The election of judges by both bodies served to reconcile the principle of sovereign equality with the particular interests of the larger powers, laying the groundwork for acceptance of a court composed of a small number of judges. The same compromise (now with the General Assembly and Security Council) remains for the election of judges to the International Court of Justice. On the history of the PCIJ generally, *see* M. O. Hudson, *The Permanent Court of International Justice, 1920–1942* (New York: The Macmillan Company, 1943).

international fact-finding commissions of enquiry, something that had been left largely undeveloped in 1899. Agreement was also reached to revise the code of arbitration procedure to include a summary arbitration procedure to expedite the resolution of small disputes and a mechanism that could, with agreement, be invoked to fix the *compromis* (i.e. the special agreement between the parties to define the subject matter of the dispute and the terms of the arbitration, then considered necessary even where the general obligation to arbitrate had already been accepted) in the event that the disputing parties had been unable to do so themselves.

The 1907 Conference also came tantalisingly close to agreement on a general multilateral treaty for the obligatory resolution of disputes through arbitration. Again based on a proposal from the United States, and described by Theodore Roosevelt as the 'most important' matter being advanced at the Conference,[28] the proposed treaty envisaged acceptance of arbitration through the PCA for all 'differences of a legal nature or relating to the interpretation of treaties'. This acceptance would be subject, as in many of the bilateral arbitration treaties concluded previously, to a self-judging reservation excluding differences involving 'the vital interests or independence or honor of any of the said parties'.[29] The American proposal was joined by a British initiative that would have gone still further, appending a list of subjects and treaties for which obligatory arbitration would be accepted without reservation.[30]

Much of the time of the First Commission of the 1907 Conference was ultimately devoted to this proposal and to the question of obligatory arbitration, with intense debates on the subjects for which obligatory arbitration could be accepted without reservation, the legal effect of bilateral arbitral awards on existing multilateral treaties (which governed many of the subjects considered potentially appropriate for obligatory arbitration), and

[28] 'Letter from Theodore Roosevelt to the National Arbitration and Peace Congress', *reproduced in* R. E. Ely (ed.), *Proceedings of the National Arbitration and Peace Congress* (New York: American Peace Congress, 1907), 30–34.

[29] 'Proposition of the Delegation of the United States of America: Plan for obligatory arbitration', *reproduced in* J. B. Scott (ed.), *The Proceedings of the Hague Peace Conferences: Translation of the Official Texts*, vol. II (New York: Oxford University Press, 1921), 876–877.

[30] 'Proposition of The British Delegation: New articles to be added to the Convention of July 29, 1899', *reproduced in* J. B. Scott (ed.), *The Proceedings of the Hague Peace Conferences: Translation of the Official Texts*, vol. II (New York: Oxford University Press, 1921), 886–887.

whether arbitration could be considered truly obligatory when subject to a self-judging reservation. The Anglo-American proposal was approved by a vote of 32 to 9 in the First Commission, over vociferous German opposition, but was never advanced to the plenary session.[31] Recalling this decision, the head of the US delegation, Joseph Choate, observed,

> We thought that this gave us a right to carry it before the Conference in plenary session for final decision, but it was intimated that one great nation, if this were done, would break up the Conference by its withdrawal.
>
> We thought that it ought to be presented to the world in the Final Act as a doctrine favoured by the votes of four nations to one, carried to an advanced position which had never been dreamed of. But, on the whole, it was deemed wiser that a somewhat colorless resolution should be adopted, to the effect that the Conference approved of the general principal [*sic*] of arbitration, and that there were subjects that ought always to be referred to arbitration, and leaving it so to the future consideration of the nations.[32]

States would have to wait another 20 years before agreement would be reached on a general multilateral treaty providing for the obligatory resolution of disputes.[33] And then it would take a very different form.

While the two most far-reaching innovations failed to secure agreement in 1907, greater success was had with a third US initiative, in the form of a convention (known by the name of its proponents, Luis Drago and Horace Porter) precluding the use of force in the recovery of contract debts owed to a State's nationals, provided that the allegedly liable State accepted an offer of arbitration.[34] Disputes concerning the rights and actions of nationals abroad already formed a significant portion of the disputes submitted

[31] First Commission, 'Seventh Meeting, 7 October 1907', *reproduced in* J. B. Scott (ed.), *The Proceedings of the Hague Peace Conferences: Translation of the Official Texts*, vol. II (New York: Oxford University Press, 1921), 119.

[32] J. H. Choate, *The Two Hague Conferences* (Princeton: Princeton University Press, 1913), 81.

[33] The Pan-American General Obligatory Arbitration Treaty, providing for the obligatory reference of disputes among American States to the PCA had been concluded among Argentina, Bolivia, the Dominican Republic, Guatemala, Mexico, Paraguay, Peru, Salvador, and Uruguay on 29 January 1902. The text is reproduced in W. R. Manning (ed.), *Arbitration Treaties among the American Nations: To the Close of the Year 1910* (New York: Oxford University Press, 1924), 307.

[34] Hague Convention No. II of 18 October 1907, Respecting the Limitation of the Employment of Force for the Recovery of Contract Debts, U.S.T.S. No. 537. The current status of the Drago-Porter Convention can be found on the website of the depository, the Netherlands Ministry of Foreign Affairs: http://treatydatabase.overheid.nl/nl/Verdrag/Details/003317.html.

to inter-State arbitration, and the acceptance of the Drago-Porter Convention was a significant step in efforts to de-politicise such disputes. This effort continued throughout the twentieth century, ultimately culminating in the widespread adoption of modern bilateral investment treaties.

16.2.3 Inter-State Arbitration across the Twentieth Century

Following the Second Hague Conference, the PCA administered a further 11 arbitrations (out of 33 inter-State proceedings commenced during this period) before the outbreak of the World War I brought such activity to a pause.[35] When peace returned to Europe, the landscape for inter-State dispute settlement quickly shifted. In the immediate aftermath of the war, a significant number of issues were referred to arbitration pursuant to the various peace treaties. Thirteen inter-State arbitrations were initiated pursuant to the treaties of Versailles, Saint-Germain-en-Laye, Neuilly, Trianon, Sèvres and Lausanne; none of these disputes, however, were referred to the PCA.[36] And by 1922, a new alternative became available with the establishment of the Permanent Court of International Justice (PCIJ).[37]

With the establishment of the PCIJ, the place of arbitration in the pacific settlement of international disputes came under challenge from a strong sentiment that the newly created court should be preferred in the resolution of international disputes. Throughout the inter-war years, States continued to conclude bilateral treaties for the resolution of disputes.

[35] *The Grisbådarna Case* (Sweden/Norway); *Deserters of Casablanca* (France/Germany); *The North Atlantic Coast Fisheries Case* (Great Britain/United States of America); *The Orinoco Steamship Company case* (United States of America/Venezuela); *Canevaro claim* (Italy/Peru); *Russian Claim for Interest on Indemnities* (Russia/Turkey); *Arrest and Return of Savarkar* (France/Great Britain); *French Postal Vessel 'Manouba'* (France/Italy); *The Carthage* (France/Italy); *The 'Tavignano', 'Camouna' and 'Gaulois' Incident* (France/Italy); *Boundaries in the Island of Timor* (The Netherlands v. Portugal).

[36] *See* A. M. Stuyt, *Survey of International Arbitrations, 1794–1989*, 3rd ed. (Dordrecht; Boston: M. Nijhoff Publishers, 1990).

[37] For the discussions in the Advisory Commission of Jurists preceding the adoption of the PCIJ Statute, *see* Advisory Committee of Jurists, *Procès-Verbaux of the Proceedings of the Committee, 16 June to 24 July 1920, with Annexes* (The Hague: Van Langenhuysen, 1920). For an analysis of the relationship between compulsory arbitration and the establishment of the PCIJ, *see* B. C. J. Loder, 'La Difference Entre l'Arbitage International et la Justice Internationale', (1923)9 *Bulletin de l'Institut Intermédiaire International* 257.

Many of these treaties provided for both judicial settlement and arbitration, often along with procedures for diplomatic settlement through conciliation.[38] A number of bilateral treaties, however, sought to establish a difference between the disputes appropriate for judicial settlement and those suitable for arbitration. Convinced that the proper place for disputes of a legal character was with the newly created PCIJ, these treaties envisaged arbitration as a dispute settlement method principally for 'non-legal' disputes, or expressly for 'political' disputes.[39] Whereas the Hague Conventions had seen arbitration as a strictly legal process,[40] it was now being proposed as most suited for an entirely different category of dispute.

The same transformation can be seen in the efforts to advance the pacific settlement of disputes within the League of Nations. Here, however, the objective of favouring the referral of cases to the PCIJ was joined with an interest in somehow using arbitration to close the remaining loopholes and ensure that all disputes would necessarily be resolved through some peaceful means, obviating any possibility of war. In 1924, agreement was nearly reached on a Protocol for the Pacific Settlement of Disputes that envisaged a radically new and coercive role for arbitration.[41] Under the Protocol, all States were required to accept the compulsory jurisdiction of the PCIJ. Disputes not submitted to the PCIJ would be submitted to the Council of the League, which would be given the power to compel arbitration at the request of either party,

[38] *See* M. Habicht, *Post-War Treaties for the Pacific Settlement of International Disputes* (Cambridge: Harvard University Press, 1931), 974–1058; League of Nations, Arbitration and Security Committee, *Systematic Survey of the Arbitration Conventions and Treaties of Mutual Security Deposited with the League of Nations* (Geneva: League of Nations, 1927); N. H. Field, *Banishing War through Arbitration: A Brief Sketch of Post-War Arbitration Treaties* (Washington, DC: National Capital Press, Inc., 1926).

[39] For a theoretical examination of the role of obligatory arbitration alongside the League system and the distinction between judicial and arbitral settlement, *see* D. Schindler, 'Les progrès de l'arbitrage obligatoire depuis la création de la Société des Nations' (1928)25 *Recueil des cours* 233; *see also* L. B. Sohn, 'The Function of International Arbitration Today' (1963)108 *Recueil des cours* 1; J. H. W. Verzijl, *International Law in Historical Perspective*, Part VIII (Leiden: A. W. Sijthoff, 1976), 86–108, 140–160; L. B. Sohn, 'International Arbitration in Historical Perspective: Past and Present' *in* A. H. A. Soons (ed.), *International Arbitration: Past and Prospects* (Dordrecht; Boston: M. Nijhoff, 1990).

[40] Convention for the Pacific Settlement of International Disputes, art. 15, 29 July 1899, [1901] U.K.T.S. No. 9, U.S.T.S. 392; Convention for the Pacific Settlement of International Disputes, art. 37, 18 October 1907, [1971] U.K.T.S. No. 6, U.S.T.S. 536.

[41] Protocol for the Pacific Settlement of Disputes, 2 October 1924, http://dl.wdl.org/11582/service/11582.pdf.

appointing arbitrators and dictating the terms of the proceedings as necessary. Moreover, if the efforts of the Council to conciliate the resolution of a dispute were unsuccessful, it would be empowered to compel arbitration over the wishes of both parties. Such arbitration, however, would not be a legal process, and indeed arbitral tribunals would be required to refer legal questions to the PCIJ for an advisory opinion. In effect, the 1924 Protocol envisaged arbitration as a mechanism for imposing political outcomes within the structure of the League.

The 1924 Protocol was ultimately doomed when it was rejected by the United Kingdom (largely due to concerns regarding the effect on Imperial interests)[42] and efforts turned instead to securing peace through specific arrangements with Germany, in the form of the Locarno treaties.[43] The distinction between legal and non-legal disputes was maintained in the dispute resolution provisions of these treaties, with legal disputes to be referred to the PCIJ and other disputes to conciliation; arbitration was omitted entirely.[44] The use of arbitration for political disputes returned, however, with the adoption of the 1928 General Act on the Pacific Settlement of International Disputes.[45] Under the system of the General Act, all disputes could be submitted to conciliation; disputes 'with regard to which the parties are in conflict as to their respective rights' – i.e. legal disputes – would be submitted to the PCIJ. All disputes *not* concerning a conflict over respective rights would be submitted to arbitration, where the tribunal would apply 'the rules in regard to the substance of the dispute enumerated in Article 38 of the Statute of the Permanent Court of International Justice' – i.e. international law; a potential contradiction, given the nature of the disputes envisaged for arbitration – and otherwise decide the dispute *ex aequo et bono*. In effect, the General Act anticipated an extraordinarily far-reaching role for arbitration in which tribunals would be accorded a compulsory role in taking binding decisions on non-legal disputes, and on a basis other than that of international law.

[42] Committee of Imperial Defence, *Report of the Sub-Committee on the Geneva Protocol*, January 1925.

[43] *See* F. P. Walters, *A History of the League of Nations* (London: Oxford University Press, 1952), 283–294.

[44] *See* C. C. Hyde, 'Commissions of Conciliation and the Locarno Treaties' (1926)20 *American Journal of International Law* 103.

[45] General Act (Pacific Settlement of International Disputes), 26 September 1928, L.N.T.S. Vol. XCII, p. 343.

The scheme of the General Act was cautiously welcomed by some as creating a new procedure of political arbitration[46] and sharply criticised by others as being, at best, unclear and, at worst, pathological.[47] The entire distinction between legal and non-legal, or justiciable and non-justiciable disputes, was likewise strongly criticised on conceptual grounds.[48] Despite this, the system of the General Act was accepted by 22 States, including the United Kingdom, France and Italy. Perhaps unsurprisingly, however, the arbitration provisions of the General Act went entirely unused.

A notable feature of the steps taken in the League with respect to arbitration is the complete absence of any reference to the PCA (except indirectly, through the acceptance of the code of procedure contained in the 1907 Hague Convention). Arbitration, as conceived in the 1924 Protocol and the 1928 General Act, appeared to be entirely distinct from the institution created only a few years earlier at The Hague. This reimagining of arbitration was also a distinctly European affair. None of the American States accepted the structure of the General Act, and the General Treaty of Inter-American Arbitration, signed in January 1929, continued to envisage arbitration as a legal process operating through the PCA. That instrument was ultimately accepted by 16 States in the Americas.[49] Throughout this period, the PCA also remained reasonably active with 7 arbitrations.[50]

Arbitration continued to be marginalised in the major treaties concluded after the World War II. The 1928 General Act was revised under the auspices of the United Nations and adopted in a new form in 1949,

46 *See* M. Gonsiorowski, 'Political Arbitration under the General Act for the Pacific Settlement of International Disputes' (1933)27 *American Journal of International Law* 469.

47 *See* J. L. Brierly, 'The General Act of Geneva, 1928' (1930) 11 *British Yearbook of International Law* 119.

48 *See generally* H. Lauterpacht, *The Function of Law in the International Community* (Oxford: Clarendon Press, 1933).

49 General Treaty of Inter-American Arbitration, 5 January 1929, OAS Treaty Series No. 16.

50 *Expropriated Religious Properties* (Spain, France and United Kingdom/Portugal); *French Claims against Peru* (France/Peru); *Norwegian Claims* (United States/Norway); *Island of Palmas* (United States/Netherlands); *Chevreau Claims* (United Kingdom/France); *Claims of the Nordstjernan Company* (Sweden/United States of America); *Radio Orient* (States of Levant under French Mandate/Egypt). For the history of the PCA to this point, *see* J. P. A. François, 'La Cour permanente d'arbitrage, son origine, sa jurisprudence, son avenir' (1955) 87 *Recueil des cours* 461.

maintaining the earlier vision of the role of arbitration.[51] This time, however, the treaty failed to attract significant support, with only eight States (almost exclusively in Europe) adhering thereto. The same structure was used as the basis for the 1957 European Convention for the Peaceful Settlement of Disputes, but with an important distinction in that a decision *ex aequo et bono* was made the principal – rather than the subsidiary – basis for decision by the envisaged arbitral tribunal. The European Convention attracted slightly more support with 14 parties.[52] In a testament to the reception of the General Act's vision of arbitration, however, fully half the signatories of the European Convention appended reservations excluding acceptance of the provisions on arbitration, which have correspondingly gone entirely unused.[53] The experiment with the General Act formula can be summarised thus: there is simply no evidence that States are interested in using international arbitration for the resolution of non-legal disputes. Instead, a review of the instances of inter-State arbitration taking place since 1945 reveals, if anything, an increase in the legal character of arbitration.[54]

The chimera of political arbitration did not make its way to the Americas, but arbitration was nonetheless marginalised in the 1948 American Treaty on Pacific Settlement (the 'Pact of Bogota').[55] While recourse to the International Court of Justice is automatic under Articles XXXI and XXXII of that instrument, arbitration is available only subject to agreement and further requires the conclusion of a *compromis*. Unsurprisingly, the judicial provisions of this treaty have been invoked repeatedly, while the arbitration provisions have gone unused.

Arbitration was likewise marginalised in the compromissary clauses incorporated into major multilateral treaties concluded in the aftermath

[51] Revised General Act for the Pacific Settlement of International Disputes, 28 April 1949, 71 U.N.T.S. 101.

[52] European Convention for the Peaceful Settlement of Disputes, 29 April 1957, 320 U.N.T.S. 243.

[53] For a contemporary account concluding that the European Convention had gone too far with respect to the obligatory arbitration of political disputes, *see* H. Rolin, 'L'arbitrage obligatoire: une panacée illusoire' in *Liber Amicorum J.P.A. François* (Leiden: Sijthoff, 1959), 254.

[54] C. Grey and B. Kingsbury, 'Developments in Dispute Settlement: Inter-State Arbitration since 1945', (1992) 63 *British Yearbook of International Law* 97, at 105.

[55] American Treaty on Pacific Settlement, arts. XXXI–XXXII, art. XXXVIII, 30 April 1948, 30 U.N.T.S. 55.

of the World War II. The first generation of these treaties sought to provide exclusively for the jurisdiction of the International Court of Justice, but were subjected by participating States to widespread reservations in respect of these provisions.[56] Such reservations were, indeed, the subject of an early advisory opinion by the Court itself, which – although it refrained from considering any particular reservation – accepted generally the permissibility of reservations not bearing on the object and purpose of the treaty, unless the treaty itself were to preclude reservations.[57] A second generation of treaties sought to address the issue of reservations by providing for dispute settlement – again with provisions for arbitration absent, or given secondary importance – through optional protocols, but found far fewer States willing to accede to the protocols than to the conventions themselves.[58] A third generation of treaties forewent binding dispute settlement entirely, in favour of other mechanisms such as compulsory conciliation.[59]

None of this is to suggest that inter-State arbitration was not occurring in the decades after 1945. On the contrary, at least 40 inter-State arbitrations took place between 1945 and 1990, including a number of significant disputes such as the *Beagle Channel Arbitration*, the *Lac Lanoux Arbitration*, the *Anglo-French Continental Shelf Arbitration*, and the various proceedings concerning the boundaries between India and Pakistan. The International Law Commission also took significant steps to modernise the practice of inter-State arbitration through its Model Rules of Arbitration Procedure. While the Model Rules do not dispense with the notion that an agreement to arbitrate requires a subsequent agreement on the terms of a *compromis*, they do limit the scope of the *compromis* (instead leaving many items for the determination of the tribunal) and

[56] *See e.g.* Convention on the Prevention and Punishment of the Crime of Genocide, art. IX, 9 December 1948, 78 U.N.T.S. 277; International Convention on the Elimination of All Forms of Racial Discrimination, art. 22, 7 March 1966, 660 U.N.T.S. 195.

[57] *Reservations to the Convention on Genocide*, Advisory Opinion, I.C.J. Reports 1951, p. 15.

[58] *See e.g.* Optional Protocol of Signature concerning the Compulsory Settlement of Disputes [to the 1958 Geneva Conventions on the Law of the Sea], arts. 1–2, 29 April 1958, 450 U.N.T.S. 169; Optional Protocol to the Vienna Convention on Diplomatic Relations, concerning the Compulsory Settlement of Disputes, arts. 1–2, 18 April 1961, 500 U.N.T.S. 241.

[59] *See e.g.* Vienna Convention on the Law of Treaties, art. 66, 23 May 1969, 1155 U.N.T.S. 331.

provide for an arbitration to proceed if a tribunal can be constituted, even if the parties otherwise fail to agree on a *compromis*. The need for a *compromis* in all cases had been essentially dispensed with for judicial proceedings through the possibility of accepting the compulsory jurisdiction of the PCIJ through the optional clause, and in this respect, arbitration procedure had heretofore lagged behind. The Model Rules can thus be seen as a step in the direction of ready recourse to compulsory arbitration, as accepted in modern treaties.

Many States also continued to include arbitration provisions in their bilateral treaties, in particular in respect of treaties relating to technical, scientific or commercial matters. What was absent after 1945 was rather any multilateral effort to promote the resolution of inter-State disputes by arbitration or any effort to gather such arbitrations at the PCA. Those proceedings that did take place were largely one-off affairs, and – following the *Lighthouses Arbitration* in 1956[60] – it was not until the 1980s that inter-State arbitration was seen again at the PCA.[61]

16.3 The PCA Today

The revival of the PCA from the nadir reached at the beginning of the 1980s is remarkable. In the first two decades of the twenty-first century, the PCA has seen more inter-State disputes submitted to arbitration than at any point in the history of the organisation, including during the peak of activity that preceded the World War I.[62] The PCA's overall docket, including mixed arbitrations between States and other parties, has likewise

[60] *Administration of Lighthouses* (France/Greece).

[61] Beginning in the early 1980s, the PCA supported the establishment of the Iran-United States Claims Tribunal, a standing mechanism that is both an inter-State and a mixed arbitral tribunal. The Claims Tribunal has since established its own registry, but the PCA continues to serve as the secretariat to the Tribunal's appointing authority. In 1988, the PCA also served as the registry in the *Heathrow Airport User Charges Arbitration* (United States/United Kingdom).

[62] For statistics on inter-State arbitration prior to 1990, *see* A. M. Stuyt, *Survey of International Arbitrations, 1794–1989*, 3rd ed. (Dordrecht; Boston: M. Nijhoff Publishers, 1990). For an update of Stuyt's work to the present date and identifying evidence of an increase in recourse to arbitration for dispute settlement between States, *see* B. Daly, 'The Renaissance of Inter-State Arbitration', *Recueil des cours* (course delivered in 2014, publication forthcoming).

expanded beyond all recognition.[63] This resurgence is a product of contemporary trends, but is also directly attributable to a series of developments with their roots in decisions taken in 1899 and 1907 and to the vision of dispute resolution enshrined in the Hague Conventions by the PCA's founders.

First, with the adoption of the UN Convention on the Law of the Sea, the international community has, at last, moved away from efforts to favour a particular procedure for the resolution of international disputes and, in so doing, reversed the marginalisation of arbitration prevalent in earlier multilateral instruments. Instead, the Convention unequivocally favours the resolutions of disputes, but remains open-minded with respect to the means of doing so, an approach more in keeping with the philosophy of the Hague Conferences. The Convention has provided the basis for a large number of inter-State arbitrations at the PCA, a development that has also corresponded with an increase in the use of inter-State arbitration under other instruments.

Second, the long-standing effort to depoliticise questions about the treatment of foreign nationals through the use of legal procedures (the concern at the root of the Drago-Porter Convention of 1907) has borne fruit. Such disputes historically constituted a regular subject of inter-State arbitration, and were the basis of many of the PCA's early cases, but are now routinely submitted to arbitration in a different form, through mixed arbitration between States and private parties. In 1976, the PCA was incorporated into the highly successful Arbitration Rules of the UN Commission on International Trade Law (UNCITRAL) to facilitate tribunal constitution. Originally prepared with commercial disputes in mind, the UNCITRAL Rules have been widely adopted in the context of State contracts and treaties and have brought mixed arbitrations and disputes involving international organisations to the PCA in large numbers.

Third, the open structure with which the PCA was created in 1899 has proven its value. While the PCA is now busier than ever, arbitration by the PCA's Members of the Court has not revived. Had the institution been created only for that procedure, it would likely remain moribund today. The Hague Conventions, however, empowered the International Bureau

[63] For an earlier account of the (then nascent) revival of the PCA, *see* H. Jonkman, 'The Role of the Permanent Court of Arbitration in International Dispute Resolution' (1999) 279 *Recueil des cours* 12.

more broadly, putting special Tribunals on an equal footing with those composed from the Members of the Court and providing an open door for the conduct of mediation, conciliation and fact-finding procedures. As a result, the PCA is not limited to offering a single procedure, but can support States in the conduct of whatever dispute resolution appears most appropriate, whether in the form of standing tribunals, claims commissions, customised arbitral procedures or non-binding methods. Such bespoke dispute settlement arrangements form an important element of the PCA's workload.

16.3.1 The Law of the Sea and Inter-State Arbitration

The law of the sea constituted an active forum for post-war international law making, with three major diplomatic conferences over a 27-year period. The First UN Conference on the Law of the Sea led to the adoption in 1958 of four conventions, which in terms of dispute resolution were fairly typical of multilateral treaties of that period: compulsory dispute settlement was confined to an optional protocol, accepted by significantly fewer States than the substantive treaties themselves, and explicitly favoured the judicial resolution of disputes, permitting arbitration only by agreement, with no effort to enable or facilitate its use. The Second UN Conference concluded without result. The Third Conference, however, was far more ambitious, and sought to forge a consensus on a new regime for all issues relating to the law of the sea, leading ultimately to the adoption of a treaty known informally as the 'constitution for the oceans'.[64]

In light of the scope of the proposed treaty, there was substantial support among the conference participants for the inclusion of effective compulsory dispute settlement and a bar on reservations, lest the consensus forged in the text dissolve into a mass of conflicting interpretations and individual understandings. A number of States, however, remained deeply apprehensive regarding compulsory settlement, in particular with respect to such matters as the delimitation of maritime boundaries. Both the scope of the disputes subject to compulsory

[64] T. T. B. Koh, 'A Constitution for the Oceans', www.un.org/depts/los/convention_agreements/texts/koh_english.pdf.

settlement and the applicable procedures were heavily negotiated before a consensus was finally achieved.[65]

In the course of these negotiations, it became apparent that no consensus would be reached on any single procedure for the compulsory settlement of disputes. One faction strongly favoured the creation of a new international court of the law of the sea that would have jurisdiction also over the private entities then expected to play a major role in the exploitation of the deep seabed. Another was adamantly against unnecessarily duplicating the jurisdiction of the International Court of Justice with a new institution. And a third group of States was opposed, for various reasons, to accepting the jurisdiction of any international court. Resolution of this deadlock came in the form of the 'Riphagen compromise': acceptance of compulsory jurisdiction would be mandatory, but parties to the Convention would be able to choose from a menu of potential procedures and fora.[66] Moreover, the dispute resolution provisions of the Convention would be subsidiary to any other procedure for the compulsory settlement of disputes accepted by the States in question, for instance under a general treaty for the resolution of disputes or a regional agreement.

The creation of a menu of procedures, of course, required some method to determine the procedure applicable for the resolution of a dispute between two States having selected different fora. Originally, it was proposed that such disputes be submitted to the forum chosen by the respondent State.[67] Ultimately, however, another approach prevailed.[68] The French delegation was strongly opposed to accepting, in the new convention, the compulsory jurisdiction of any permanently constituted court, arguing

[65] *See* S. Rosenne and L. Sohn (eds.), *United Nations Convention on the Law of the Sea 1982: A Commentary*, vol. V, (Dordrecht: M. Nijhoff, 1989) 1–15.

[66] S. Rosenne, 'UNCLOS III: The Montreaux (Riphagen) Compromise' *in* A. Bos and H. Siblesz (eds.), *Realism in Law-Making: Essays on International Law in Honour of Willem Riphagen* (Dordrecht; Boston: M. Nijhoff, 1986), 170; Comments by W. Riphagen, Summary Record of the 60th Plenary Meeting, 6 April 1976, UN Doc. A/CONF.62/SR.60 in *Official Records of the Third United Nations Conference on the Law of the Sea, Volume V (Summary Records, Plenary, General Committee, First, Second and Third Committees, as well as Documents of the Conference, Fourth Session)*, 21.

[67] L. B. Sohn, 'Settlement of Law of the Sea Disputes' (1995)10(2) *The International Journal of Marine and Coastal Law* 205.

[68] For an analysis of the UNCLOS negotiations and identifying in particular the positions espoused by France for the ultimate form of the dispute resolution provisions of the Convention, *see* B. Daly, 'The Renaissance of Inter-State Arbitration', *Recueil des cours* (course delivered in 2014, publication forthcoming).

that 'a tribunal constituted beforehand, however well chosen it might appear in the abstract, bore the strong risk, in the case of a concrete difference, of being badly constituted, perhaps open to challenge or at all events without moral prestige'.[69] Insofar as a default procedure would necessarily be imposed on some parties in respect of disputes among States with different preferences, France argued – successfully – that it should be the least intrusive and most flexible procedure: arbitration.[70]

As adopted, the Convention permits certain limited exceptions to compulsory settlement, notably for disputes relating to the exercise of coastal State jurisdiction in the exclusive economic zone[71] and, by declaration, for disputes involving maritime boundary delimitation or historic title, disputes concerning military activities or disputes with which the United Nations Security Council is engaged.[72] Other reservations to compulsory dispute settlement, however, are not permitted. For the compulsory resolution of disputes, States may elect the jurisdiction of the International Tribunal for the Law of the Sea (ITLOS, established by the Convention), the International Court of Justice, an arbitral tribunal (pursuant to Annex VII to the Convention), or a special arbitral tribunal (an alternative procedure pursuant to Annex VIII to the Convention, intended for scientific or technical disputes). In the absence of a common choice, however, a dispute may be submitted only to Annex VII arbitration.[73] As of the time of this

[69] Comments by G. de Lacharrière, Summary Record of the 59th Plenary Meeting, 5 April 1976, UN Doc. A/CONF.62/SR.59, in *Official Records of the Third United Nations Conference on the Law of the Sea, Volume V (Summary Records, Plenary, General Committee, First, Second and Third Committees, as well as Documents of the Conference, Fourth Session)*, 13.

[70] Considering the French position a return to the view of arbitration as the 'most effective, and at the same time the most equitable, means of settling disputes which diplomacy has failed to settle' (Convention for the Pacific Settlement of International Disputes, art. 16, 29 July 1899, [1901] U.K.T.S. No. 9, U.S.T.S. 392), *see* B. Daly, 'The Renaissance of Inter-State Arbitration', *Recueil des cours* (course delivered in 2014, publication forthcoming). For an internal account of the French position by the head of the French delegation to the conference, *see* G. de Lacharrière, 'La réforme du droit de la mer et le role de la conférence des Nations Unies' *in* M. Virally and D. Bardonnet (eds.), *Le nouveau droit international de la mer* (Paris: A. Pedone, 1983), 236.

[71] United Nations Convention on the Law of the Sea, art. 297, 10 December 1982, 1833 U.N.T.S. 3.

[72] United Nations Convention on the Law of the Sea, art. 298, 10 December 1982, 1833 U.N.T.S. 3.

[73] United Nations Convention on the Law of the Sea, art. 287, 10 December 1982, 1833 U.N.T.S. 3.

writing, 37 States have expressed a preference for ITLOS and 21 have expressed a preference for the ICJ; the remaining 127 parties to the Convention have either expressed a preference for arbitration or made no declaration, such that they are deemed to have accepted arbitration pursuant to Annex VII.[74] The majority of the disputes referred to compulsory settlement under the Convention, accordingly, have been initiated as Annex VII arbitrations.[75]

The Convention marks a philosophical shift in the approach to the settlement of disputes in a major multilateral treaty. Rather than prescribing a particular method of dispute resolution, the Convention favours the resolution of disputes itself, permitting disputing parties the greatest degree of leeway in the procedure to be applied but requiring the acceptance of some form of compulsory settlement. Where the Convention imposes a procedure – through the default rule, where disputing parties' preferred procedure differs – it does so as lightly as possible, and in favour of arbitration rather than a permanently constituted court. Even this procedure is made subordinate to any other procedure leading to a binding result that may be applicable between the disputing parties. In terms of approach, this flexible menu of potential procedures recalls the flexibility of the Hague Conventions, albeit underpinned with a foundation of compulsory procedure that was unobtainable in 1899 and 1907. Perhaps for that reason, the Convention formula has secured the adherence to

[74] United Nations Convention on the Law of the Sea, art. 287(3), 10 December 1982, 1833 U.N.T.S. 3. Parties that have expressed a preference for multiple fora are counted in respect of each in the above statistics. An up-to-date list of the declarations made pursuant to Article 287, as well as the order for those States that have provided a ranking of preference, is maintained by the Treaty Section of the Office of Legal Affairs of the United Nations. *See* http://treaties.un.org/doc/Publication/MTDSG/Volume%20II/Chapter%20XXI/XXI-6.en.pdf.

[75] As of the time of this writing, 23 disputes have been referred to Annex VII arbitration, although seven were subsequently transferred to ITLOS by agreement of the Parties. Two proceedings were initiated directly with ITLOS, which has also handled a number of applications for the prompt release of vessels, an area over which it has automatic jurisdiction. ITLOS has also been called on to indicate provisional measures in nine Annex VII arbitrations prior to the constitution of the tribunals and has issued two advisory opinions. No dispute has yet been referred to the ICJ pursuant to the dispute resolution provisions of the Convention, although the ICJ has handled a large number of cases involving the law of the sea initiated pursuant to special agreements or other instruments, such as the American Treaty on Pacific Settlement (the Pact of Bogotá) or optional clause declarations pursuant to the ICJ's own statute. No dispute has yet been referred to special arbitration pursuant to Annex VIII of the Convention.

compulsory dispute settlement of a larger number of States – and in respect of a much wider scope of application and possible disputes – than nearly any other multilateral treaty.[76]

The Convention has, to date, led to 14 inter-State arbitrations at the PCA.[77] It would be a mistake, however, to ascribe the revival of inter-State arbitration to the law of the sea alone. Instead, the choices made during the negotiation of the Law of the Sea Convention are better seen as an early herald of a broader trend, holding true likewise in other areas of treaty making.[78] Since 2000, the PCA has administered an even larger number of inter-State arbitrations initiated pursuant to other treaties or special agreements, including a number of exceptionally high-profile matters.[79] What this revival indicates is that Elihu Root's 1907 diagnosis of the ills of inter-State arbitration was wrong (or, at least, is no longer true). Inter-State arbitration is not an inferior alternative that States will abandon as soon as a permanently constituted court is made available; the preferences of States with respect to dispute resolution are considerably more nuanced. Recent cases and a number of prominent commentators have demolished the myth that arbitral tribunals are more likely than a permanent court to stray from the law in search of a compromise

[76] Those universal treaties that have included compulsory dispute settlement, such as the International Convention on the Elimination of All Forms of Racial Discrimination and the Convention on the Elimination of all Forms of Discrimination against Women, have been subject to extensive reservations in respect of those provisions. Only the founding instruments of some international organisations, such as the Constitution of the World Health Organization, have included more widespread acceptance of compulsory dispute settlement, but with significantly narrower scope.

[77] With the exception of the *Southern Bluefin Tuna Cases*, initiated by Australia and New Zealand against Japan in 1999, and several matters that were initiated as arbitrations but thereafter submitted to ITLOS by agreement, all arbitrations conducted pursuant to Annex VII have been administered by the PCA. For a discussion of recent law of the sea cases at the PCA, *see* J. Levine and G. Schofield, 'Navigating Uncharted Procedural Waters in a Rising Sea of Cases at the Permanent Court of Arbitration' *in* S. Minas and H. J. Diamond (eds.), *Stress Testing the Law of the Sea: Dispute Resolution, Disasters & Emerging Challenges* (Leiden; Boston: Brill Nijhoff, 2018), 95.

[78] L. B. Sohn, 'The Role of Arbitration in Recent International Multilateral Treaties' *in* T. E. Carbonneau (ed.), *Resolving Transnational Disputes through International Arbitration* (Charlottesville: University Press of Virginia, 1984), 21, at 37.

[79] For a detailed discussion of why particular cases appear to have been referred to arbitration and of how the practice of arbitration has responded to historic criticism, *see* B. Daly, 'The Renaissance of Inter-State Arbitration', *Recueil des cours* (course delivered in 2014, publication forthcoming).

solution (if anything, the opposite is true)[80] or that arbitration is somehow suited for non-legal disputes. And for many disputes, the small format of an arbitral tribunal, the flexibility of procedure, and the possibility of selecting arbitrators with particular expertise and enjoying the confidence of the parties may be preferable.

The continued availability of the PCA also serves to negate many of the potential drawbacks of an entirely ad hoc proceeding.[81] As the registry, the PCA offers the convenience of a permanently established institution, providing a neutral channel for communications, maintaining an archive of documents, offering access to the hearing facilities of the Peace Palace, arranging venues for proceedings worldwide, managing the deposit for fees and expenses, and providing support throughout the proceedings to members of the tribunal, experts, parties and their representatives. The effect of this support is both to streamline the proceedings and to reduce the parties' costs by significantly lightening the tribunal's administrative load.

Ultimately, inter-State arbitration remains an essential complement to judicial settlement, with each reinforcing the other. The growth in the PCA's caseload has not come at the expense of the International Court of Justice, which is also busier than ever. Rather, the activity at both institutions reflects the extent to which inter-State arbitral and judicial settlement have come of age. One hundred years ago, it was common to debate the implications of 'gaps' in international law and the limits on dispute resolution in relation to subjects on which international law had nothing to say.[82] Today, that concern is hardly recognisable. Similarly, there is now a substantial body of international jurisprudence, providing ready parallels for many issues of treaty interpretation and questions of

80 R. Jennings, 'The Differences between Conducting a Case in the ICJ and in an ad hoc Arbitration Tribunal – An Inside View' *in* N. Ando et al. (eds.), *Liber Amicorum Judge Shigeru Oda* (The Hague; New York; London: Kluwer Law International, 2002), 893 at 894; P. Sands, *The Permanent Court of Arbitration: Remarks on the occasion of a Celebration of the Centenary of the PCA*, 18 October 2007, http://pca-cpa.org/wp-content/uploads/sites/6/2016/01/Reflections-on-the-Current-Relevance-of-the-PCA-Presentation-by-Professor-Philippe-Sands-QC.pdf.

81 When not specified in the underlying treaty or agreement to arbitrate, PCA administration of inter-State proceedings is generally agreed on early in the proceedings, either directly between the States concerned or at the instance of the tribunal in its first communications with the parties.

82 For an early argument against this position, *see* H. Lauterpacht, *The Function of Law in the International Community* (Oxford: Clarendon Press, 1933).

procedure. While international law has no formal system of precedent, courts and arbitral tribunals routinely look to past cases to inform their consideration of the matter before them. This body of established practice is such that recourse to dispute settlement is substantially less uncertain than in the past, and States more able to predict the potential course and outcome of any litigation.

16.3.2 Mixed Arbitration

Another major force behind the revitalisation of the PCA has been the rapid growth in mixed arbitration between States and private parties. Since 2000, the PCA has administered more than 260 mixed arbitrations under bilateral and multilateral investment treaties and national investment laws, alongside more than 200 arbitrations pursuant to contracts between States and State entities and private parties. The PCA has also seen a large number of mixed arbitrations between international organisations and private parties, with more than 35 cases over the same period. While the explosive growth in mixed arbitration is a comparatively recent trend, the practice itself has deep roots, leading back to the Hague Conferences and the very founding of the PCA. It should not be seen as a change in the purpose of the organisation, but as a reflection of the flexibility of the PCA in the face of the changing dispute resolution needs of the international community.

Historically, much of international dispute resolution has concerned disputes arising from private activity, in particular the difficulties encountered by private parties engaged in activity abroad. Traditionally, however, such disputes were resolved through inter-State proceedings, either through inter-State arbitration or through the various bilateral mixed claims commissions that were established among different combinations of States in the late nineteenth and early twentieth centuries to resolve large numbers of private claims.[83] Indeed, private claims were considered one of the most promising avenues for the development of obligatory arbitration insofar as they typically did not involve the vital interests or independence of the States concerned. Thus, the Russian proposal at the

[83] *See* R. Dolzer, 'Mixed Claims Commissions', *Max Planck Encyclopedia of Public International Law* (Oxford; New York: Oxford University Press, 2012).

1899 Hague Conference called for the obligatory arbitration first and foremost of 'differences or disputes relating to pecuniary damages suffered by a State, or its nationals, as a consequence of illegal actions or negligence on the part of another State or its nationals'.[84] While even this proved unacceptable in 1899 (and again in 1907), the obligatory arbitration of the pecuniary claims of private parties enjoyed the broadest support among the potential subjects for obligatory arbitration within the discussions at The Hague. The conclusion in 1907 of the Drago-Porter Convention (discussed above) further sought to advance this goal through a general renunciation of the use of force on behalf of private parties against States that had accepted to arbitrate such claims.

In this historical form, disputes concerning the damages suffered by private parties were considered as an inter-State matter. Although affording the injured private party an additional avenue for redress through diplomatic protection, such claims were generally understood to be State claims, presented by agents of the State (with a greater or lesser degree of coordination with the private parties involved) in proceedings under the control of the two governments.[85] Compensation was resolved between the States concerned, and its distribution to the injured party remained an internal matter. States were also at liberty to settle such international claims without the consent of the private party concerned. Many of the PCA's early arbitrations thus involved disputes that were, fundamentally, in respect of private claims.[86] The same is true of many of the early cases of the PCIJ and International Court of Justice.[87] Far from

[84] 'Outlines for the Preparation of a Draft Convention to be concluded between the Powers taking part in the Hague Conference, Russian Draft', Art. 10, *reproduced in* J. B. Scott (ed.), *The Proceedings of the Hague Peace Conferences: The Conference of 1899* (New York: Oxford University Press, 1920), 797.

[85] *See* E. Borchard, *Diplomatic Protection of Citizens Abroad* (New York: Banks Law Pub. Co., 1927), 349–380.

[86] *See e.g. The Orinoco Steamship Company* (United States of America/Venezuela); *Canevaro Claim* (Italy/Peru); *Expropriated Religious Properties* (Spain, France, and United Kingdom/Portugal); *French Claims against Peru* (France/Peru); *Norwegian Claims* (United States/Norway); *Chevreau Claims* (United Kingdom/France); *Claims of the Nordstjernan Company* (Sweden/United States of America).

[87] *See e.g. Factory at Chorzów* (Germany v. Poland); *Serbian Loans* (France v. Serbia); *Brazilian Loans* (France v. Brazil); *Oscar Chinn* (United Kingdom v. Belgium); *Pajzs, Csaky and Esterhazy* (Hungary v. Yugoslavia); *Losinger & Co.* (Switzerland v. Yugoslavia); *Panevezys-Saldutiskis Railway* (Estonia v. Lithuania); *Electricity Company of Sofia and Bulgaria* (Belgium v. Bulgaria); *Société Commerciale de Belgique*

being an ancillary element, such claims were historically at the heart of inter-State dispute settlement.

Arbitration directly between a State and private party was not unknown, but was comparatively rare and limited to cases of significant national importance.[88] The first such case brought to the PCA concerned an arbitration between the Radio Corporation of America and the Republic of China regarding the exclusivity of a contract for the operation of a radio-telegraph link between China and the United States. In 1934, the arbitral tribunal approached the PCA seeking the administration of the proceedings. This was put to the Administrative Council, which in early 1935 endorsed the view that, while arbitration pursuant to the Hague Conventions (i.e. by a tribunal formed from the PCA Members of the Court) was limited to States, the provisions empowering the International Bureau to support the work of special Tribunals were not so limited.[89] Subsequently, the Administrative Council charged the Secretary-General to explore the means by which the PCA could more effectively facilitate the conduct of mixed arbitrations,[90] culminating in the adoption in 1962 of the PCA's first *Rules of Arbitration and Conciliation for Settlement of International Disputes between Two Parties of which only one is a State.*[91]

The expansion of mixed arbitration at the PCA drew further impetus from two broad developments in the resolution of international disputes: first, the evolution of commercial treaties into modern bilateral investment treaties, providing for arbitration, and second, the development in the

(Belgium v. Greece); *Ambatielos* (Greece v. United Kingdom); *Electricité de Beyrouth Company* (France v. Lebanon); *Certain Norwegian Loans* (France v. Norway); *Interhandel* (Switzerland v. United States of America); *Barcelona Traction, Light and Power Company, Limited* (Belgium v. Spain).

[88] *See e.g.* Egypt v. Suez Canal Co., Award of 6 July 1864, *reproduced in* G. Lapradelle, *Recueil des arbitrages internationaux, Vol. II: 1856–1872* (Paris: A. Pedone, 1923), 362; U.S.S.R. v. Lena Goldfields Co. Ltd, Award of 2 September 1930, *reproduced in* A. Nussbaum, 'Arbitration between the Lena Goldfields Ltd. and the Soviet Government' (1950) 36 *Cornell Law Quarterly* 31.

[89] *See* Report of the Administrative Council of the Permanent Court of Arbitration, 1934, 7.

[90] *See* Report of the Administrative Council of the Permanent Court of Arbitration, 1960, 6–7.

[91] Rules of Arbitration and Conciliation for Settlement of International Disputes between Two Parties of Which Only One Is a State, February 1962, *reproduced in* (1963) 57(2) *The American Journal of International Law* 500. These rules have since been superseded by an updated version adopted on 6 July 1993 and by the PCA Arbitration Rules 2012.

1970s and widespread adoption of the of arbitration rules by the UN Commission on International Trade Law (UNCITRAL).

States had long sought to regulate the treatment of their nationals abroad through the conclusion of commercial treaties, often touching also on other subjects under the general rubric of 'amity, commerce, and navigation'. With some exceptions, nineteenth-century commercial treaties typically did not include provisions specifically in respect of the resolution of disputes, which were left to be resolved on an ad hoc basis or under the terms of any general treaty on the resolution of disputes that might be applicable between the States concerned. Beginning in the early twentieth century, commercial treaties increasingly incorporated provisions for the resolution of disputes, most often through inter-State arbitration, either at the PCA or before a special Tribunal.[92] Following the World War II, the extensive US network of friendship, commerce and navigation treaties, in particular, began to include provisions referring disputes for inter-State resolution at the International Court of Justice.[93] Over the same period, commercial treaties increasingly began to incorporate provisions relating specifically to long-term international investment. Then, as issues of international trade came from 1947 onward to be largely addressed on a multilateral basis through the General Agreement on Trade and Tariffs process, bilateral treaty development turned to agreements focused specifically on investment, initially also with provisions for inter-State dispute resolution.

While the early twentieth century largely saw the removal of armed force from disputes over the treatment of foreign nationals and investments, the resolution of such matters through diplomatic protection and inter-State proceedings remained highly political and potentially unsatisfactory for all parties concerned. Whether to espouse a claim was a discretionary matter, and an investor had no assurances that a claim would be taken up at the inter-State level (or that, once taken up, it would not be settled on unfavourable terms).[94] The investor's government,

[92] *See* League of Nations, *Memorandum Relating to the Pacific Settlement of International Disputes concerning Economic Questions in General and Commercial and Customs Questions in Particular* (Geneva: League of Nations, 1931).

[93] *See generally* K. J. Vandevelde, *The First Bilateral Investment Treaties: U.S. Postwar Friendship, Commerce, and Navigation Treaties* (New York: Oxford University Press, 2017).

[94] *See Barcelona Traction, Light and Power Co. Ltd. (Belgium v. Spain), 1970 ICJ Rep.* 4, p. 44, paras. 78–79.

meanwhile, was burdened with the resolution of a dispute not of its making, potentially infringing on other priorities and complicating a broader diplomatic relationship. And the host State faced the prospect of having an investment matter fully politicised if a powerful government standing behind an investor brought its full weight to bear. Precisely to address this concern, agreement was reached in 1965 on the establishment of the International Centre for the Settlement of Investment Disputes (ICSID)[95] as a forum for mixed arbitration directly between investors and the government of the host State, with the investor's own government foreswearing the possibility of diplomatic protection.[96] Although it was originally envisaged that ICSID jurisdiction would be founded principally on contracts between governments and foreign investors, the Centre published in 1969 a set of model clauses intended for incorporation in a bilateral investment treaty.[97] The first investment treaty providing for investor-State arbitration was concluded the same year, and investment treaties rapidly became the principal basis for ICSID jurisdiction.[98] A further step would be required, however, for investment arbitration to assume a role within the work of the PCA.

In parallel with the changes taking place in the resolution of investment disputes, the groundwork for the PCA's modern involvement with mixed

[95] For an in-depth discussion on investment arbitration, *see* the relevant chapters earlier in this volume.

[96] *See* A. von Walter, 'Le contentieux lié à l'investissement: entre dépolitisation et repolitisation', http://convention-s.fr/wp-content/uploads/2015/07/CNV_journ%C3%A9e04032011_-arbitrage_dossier.pdf; I. F. I. Shihata, 'Towards a Greater Depoliticization of Investment Disputes: the Roles of ICSID and MIGA' (1986)1 *ICSID Review* 1; A. Broches, 'The Convention on the Settlement of Investment Disputes between States and Nationals of Other States' (1972)136 *Recueil des cours* 331, at 342–348.

[97] A. Parra, *The History of ICSID* (Oxford: Oxford University Press, 2012), 132–135. In formulating the arbitration rules for the new Centre, the drafters of the ICSID Convention drew heavily on the work of the International Law Commission in the preparation of the model rules for inter-State arbitration and on the PCA's *Rules of Arbitration and Conciliation for Settlement of International Disputes between Two Parties of which only one is a State. See ibid.*, 17, 52.

[98] On the historical development of bilateral investment treaties, *see* A. Newcombe and L. Paradell, *Law and Practice of Investment Treaties: Standards of Treatment* (Alphen aan den Rijn: Kluwer Law International, 2009), 1–57; K. J. Vandevelde, *Bilateral Investment Treaties: History, Policy and Interpretation* (Oxford; New York: Oxford University Press, 2010), 19–74. On the juridical nature of investor claims within a treaty system, *see* Z. Douglas, *The International Law of Investment Claims* (Cambridge: Cambridge University Press, 2009), 1–38.

arbitration was laid in the efforts by UNCITRAL to develop a set of arbitration rules intended specifically for the international conduct of ad hoc commercial arbitration. Early in its work, UNCITRAL identified the harmonisation and unification of laws in respect of international commercial arbitration as a potentially fruitful area of work and, in 1969, appointed a special rapporteur to study the question. Following two reports on the subject,[99] UNCITRAL undertook to develop a set of arbitration rules, which were adopted in 1976.[100] The UNCITRAL Rules are unique in that they are intended for worldwide application, and the UNCITRAL negotiating process was heavily concerned with ensuring the compatibility of the rules with different national legal systems and approaches to arbitration.

The UNCITRAL Rules were intended to be suitable for un-administered, ad hoc arbitration and independent, to the greatest extent possible, from any particular institution. Certain aspects of arbitration, however, cannot readily be divorced entirely from outside authority. This is particularly true with respect to the constitution of the tribunal and the resolution of arbitrator challenges, where some entity in needed to facilitate the proceedings in default of action or agreement by the parties and on issues which the tribunal cannot (or should not) itself be empowered. For these essential functions, the drafters of the UNCITRAL Rules turned to the Secretary-General of the PCA, who is authorized under the Rules to designate an appointing authority and who may also himself act as the appointing authority with the agreement of the parties. This role has involved the PCA in a large number – more than 700 to date – of arbitrations under the UNCITRAL Rules in which the designation of an appointing authority, the appointment of an arbitrator, or the resolution of a challenge to the independence or impartiality of an arbitrator was required.[101]

Although the UNCITRAL Rules were prepared with international commercial arbitration in mind, they succeeded in capturing the essence of

[99] *See* United Nations Commission on International Trade Law, *International Commercial Arbitration: Preliminary Report by Ian Nestor, Special Rapporteur*, UN Doc. A/CN.9/42 (18 February 1970); United Nations Commission on International Trade Law, *Problems Concerning the Application and Interpretation of Existing Multilateral Conventions on International Commercial Arbitration and Related Matters: Report by Mr. Ion Nestor, Special Rapporteur*, UN Doc. A/CN.9/64 (1 March 1972).

[100] United Nations General Assembly, Resolution 31/98 (15 December 1976).

[101] The PCA is also accorded additional functions with respect to the review of arbitrator fees under the 2010 and later revisions of the UNCITRAL Rules.

arbitral procedure generally, and their use has never been confined to the commercial sphere. Not long after their adoption, the Rules were accepted, with light modifications, as the procedural rules for the Iran–United States Claims Tribunal, a hybrid entity competent for both inter-State and mixed arbitration. The PCA served as the initial secretariat to the Tribunal, until the establishment of an independent registry, and remains to this day the secretariat to the Tribunal's appointing authority.[102] The Rules have also never been limited to ad hoc arbitration. The experience of the Iran–United States Claims Tribunal quickly proved their suitability for administered proceedings and the Rules are regularly used in an administered context (a development already anticipated during their drafting). Many arbitral institutions, including the PCA, have also based their own institutional rules on a modified version of the UNCITRAL Rules.

From the beginning, the UNCITRAL Rules were heavily promoted by the Asian-African Legal Consultative Organization (AALCO), which saw them as preferable to existing arbitration centres for disputes involving parties in the developing world. The UNCITRAL Rules were used as the basis for the institutional rules of a number of regional arbitration centres established at AALCO's instance and, in 1985, were incorporated into AALCO's model bilateral investment treaty (BIT).[103] The first use of the Rules in an investment treaty appears to have been in the China-Kuwait BIT concluded that same year,[104] and the Rules were quickly incorporated into the investment treaty practice of Italy and Bulgaria.[105] In 1987, the UNCITRAL Rules

[102] *See* C. N. Brower and J. D. Brueschke, *The Iran–United States Claims Tribunal* (The Hague: M. Nijhoff, 1998), 14.

[103] Asian-African Legal Consultative Committee Model Agreements (1985). The UNCITRAL Rules were also incorporated into the 1984 Caribbean Community Secretariat's *Guidelines for use in the Negotiation of Bilateral Treaties* on the grounds that the Rules 'are favoured by developing countries'.

[104] Agreement between the Government of the People's Republic of China and the Government of the State of Kuwait for the Promotion and Protection of Investments, 23 November 1985.

[105] *See* Treaty between the Federal Republic of Germany and the People's Republic of Bulgaria concerning the Reciprocal Encouragement and Protection of Investments, 12 April 1986; Accordo fra il Governo della Repubblica Popolare Ungherese e il Governo della Repubblica Italiana sulla Promozione e Protezione degli Investimenti, 17 February 1987; Agreement between the Government of the People's Republic of Bulgaria and the Government of the Republic of Cyprus on Mutual Encouragement and Protection of Investments, 12 November 1987; Agreement between the Government of the People's Republic of China and the Government of Malaysia Concerning the Reciprocal Encouragement and Protection of Investments, 21 November 1988; Accordo fra la

replaced the International Law Commission's Model Rules as the procedure for inter-State dispute settlement in the US model BIT,[106] and from 1990 onward have been widely incorporated into the investment treaties of many States, both for inter-State dispute resolution and for investor-State disputes, either in the case of States not party to the ICSID system or as an option for investors who may prefer an alternative to ICSID. Procedurally, the UNCITRAL Rules differ from those of ICSID in several significant respects, most notably in relation to the procedure for the review and possible set aside of awards and the standard for challenges to the independence and impartiality of an arbitrator.[107] To date, approximately one-third of known investment arbitrations, or more than 390 cases, have been commenced under the UNCITRAL Rules. Of these, approximately two-thirds, or more than 250 arbitrations, have been administered by the PCA.[108] While PCA administration is optional under most investment treaties,[109] it is commonly agreed between the parties at

Repubblica Italiana e la Repubblica Popolare di Bulgaria Relativo alla Reciproca Promozione e Protezione degli Investimenti, 5 December 1988; Agreement for the Promotion and Protection of Investments between the Republic of Italy and the Arab Republic of Egypt, 2 March 1989; Agreement between the Government of the People's Republic of Bulgaria and the Government of the People's Republic of China Concerning the Reciprocal Encouragement and Protection of Investments, 27 June 1989; Agreement between the Government of the People's Republic of Bulgaria and the Government of the Republic of Ghana concerning the Mutual Promotion and Protection of Investments, 20 October 1989.

106 *See* K. J. Vandevelde, *U.S. International Investment Agreements* (New York: Oxford University Press, 2009), 711.

107 For an in-depth comparison of UNCITRAL and ICSID investment arbitration, *see* J. Levine, 'Navigating the parallel universe of investor-State arbitrations under the UNCITRAL Rules' *in* C. Brown and K. Miles (eds.), *Evolution in Investment Treaty Law and Arbitration*, (Cambridge: Cambridge University Press, 2015), 369.

108 The PCA's role has also expanded over time. Over the past ten years, the PCA has administered more than three quarters of the known investment arbitrations under the UNCITRAL Rules.

109 The growth in UNCITRAL Rules arbitration at the PCA is, however, now being reflected in treaties. The Netherlands 2018 Model BIT, for instance, provides for arbitration pursuant to 'the arbitration rules of the United Nations Commission on International Trade Law (UNCITRAL Arbitration Rules), with the understanding that the Permanent Court of Arbitration (PCA) shall administer the proceedings'. Certain investment treaties also provide directly for the application of the PCA's own Optional Rules. *See e.g.* Agreement between the Government of the United Kingdom of Great Britain and Northern Ireland and the Government of the United Mexican States for the Promotion and Reciprocal Protection of Investments, art. 11(4)(d), 12 May 2006.

the outset of the proceedings or decided upon by the tribunal after an initial consultation with the parties.

The UNCITRAL Rules have also been widely adopted in the context of State contracts, where States may be reluctant to submit disputes for resolution under the auspices of a private arbitral institution. Such contracts cover a very wide variety of potential subjects, but are particularly common with respect to infrastructure and natural resources. Here again, PCA administration is most often agreed upon only once proceedings are commenced, but the PCA has seen a growing number of such cases, with 15–20 new arbitrations initiated each year. Increasingly, PCA administration has been incorporated into States' model contracts, in particular for contracts involving natural resources.[110]

Finally, the availability of the PCA for mixed arbitration is not limited to disputes between States and international organisations and private parties, but extends also to disputes involving political entities within a State (or whose status as a State may be disputed). In the *Abyei Arbitration* in 2008 and 2009, the PCA was called on to administer arbitral proceedings between the Government of Sudan and the Sudanese People's Liberation Movement/Army over the boundaries of the Abyei area, a region adjacent to the border of what is now Sudan and South Sudan. Under the terms of the Comprehensive Peace Agreement of January 2005 that brought Sudan's long-running civil war to a close, the Abyei area was accorded special status and the right to a referendum on whether to become part of South Sudan. The Peace Agreement also provided for a boundary commission to define the historical boundaries of the Abyei area.[111] When a dispute arose over the manner in which the boundary commission had interpreted and executed its mandate, the parties agreed to establish an arbitral tribunal at the PCA to review the work of the

[110] *See e.g.* República Federativa do Brasil, Ministério de Minas e Energia, 'Minuta de Contrato de Concessão para Exploração e Produção de Petróleo e Gás Natural' (2017), art. 34.5, http://rodadas.anp.gov.br/arquivos/Round15/Edital/modelo_contrato_R15.pdf; Gobierno de México, Comisión Nacional de Hidrocarburos, 'Contrato para la Exploración y Extracción de Hidrocarburos bajo la Modalidad de Producción Compartida en Aguas Someras' (2018), art. 27.5, www.rondasmexico.gob.mx/media/3007/05-mar-2018.pdf. Argentina, Ecuador, Mozambique and the Seychelles have also recently adopted model contracts with similar provisions.

[111] Comprehensive Peace Agreement, Abyei Protocol, 26 May 2004 http://peacemaker.un.org/sites/peacemaker.un.org/files/SD_060000_The%20Comprehensive%20Peace%20Agreement.pdf.

commission and, as necessary, to fix the boundaries of the Abyei area. Following expedited proceedings, the tribunal issued an award defining the boundaries of the Abyei area in July 2009.[112] While tensions remain in the Abyei area and the Peace Agreement has not been fully implemented, both sides have, in subsequent agreements, re-affirmed their acceptance of the boundaries for the area established at the PCA.[113]

Although the *Abyei Arbitration* remains a singular example to date, it represents a potentially promising precedent for employing the procedures of international dispute settlement as part of peacebuilding within a civil conflict. As armed conflict has become predominantly an intra-State affair, this may be a useful model for situations in which some neutral authority is required to interpret and safeguard the terms of a peace agreement, but where a permanent international structure is neither feasible nor desirable.

16.3.3 Standing Tribunals, Bespoke Procedures and Conciliation

A third element of the PCA's resurgence stems directly from the flexibility built into the organisation and its mandate by its founders. Empowered by the Hague Conventions to support the work of any 'special Tribunal', the PCA is available to administer bespoke dispute resolution procedures envisaged for a particular dispute. While international arbitral procedure is well developed, no single approach to dispute resolution will ever be appropriate in all circumstances and there are many disputes for which States may prefer another procedure. The PCA is available both to administer and to assist in the development of such bespoke procedures, which constitute an important element of the PCA's caseload. A few prominent examples bear noting.

First, the PCA is available to support the work of permanently constituted, standing tribunals. While arbitration will most often involve the formation of a tribunal in connection with a particular dispute, this is not an essential element and the line between judicial and arbitral procedure is a fluid one. A prominent example of a standing tribunal operating under

[112] *Abyei Arbitration* (Government of Sudan/Sudan People's Liberation Movement/Army), Final Award, 21 July 2009.

[113] Agreement between the Government of the Republic of Sudan and the Sudan People's Liberation Movement on Temporary Arrangements for the Administration and Security of the Abyei Area, art. 2 (Addis Ababa, Ethiopia), 20 June 2011.

the auspices of the PCA is the tribunal of the Bank for International Settlements. Originally established to facilitate reparation payments by Germany during the inter-war years, the Bank for International Settlements now functions as a central bank for central banks and is mandated to 'promote the co-operation of central banks and to provide additional facilities for international financial operations'.[114] Both the Convention concerning the Bank for International Settlements[115] and the Statutes of the Bank itself provide that disputes will be resolved through recourse to the tribunal established as part of the Hague Agreement of January 1930 concerning German reparations (BIS Tribunal).[116] Under the terms of the Hague Agreement, the BIS Tribunal is composed of five arbitrators appointed to five-year terms by the governments concerned.[117] The BIS Tribunal applies the arbitral procedure of the 1907 Hague Convention as modified by the 1930 Hague Agreement,[118] and the PCA serves as the tribunal registry. The BIS Tribunal was called on in 2000 when a dispute arose over the Bank's decision to buy out its private shareholders (prior to which, ownership of the bank was divided between national central banks and private parties) and rendered two awards in 2002 and 2003.[119] In effect, this structure enables the Bank to maintain a permanent, independent tribunal without the cost or administrative burden of a separate institution. Whenever the BIS Tribunal is called on to act, the staff and resources of the PCA can be made available, as necessary. The PCA performed a similar role for the Iran–United States Claims Tribunal during its initial operations

[114] Statutes of the Bank for International Settlements, art. 3, 20 January 1930.

[115] Convention respecting the Bank for International Settlements, 27 February 1930, 104 L.N.T.S. 441.

[116] Agreement regarding the Complete and Final Settlement of the Question of Reparations from Germany, art. XV, 20 January 1930.

[117] Under the Hague Agreement, the five seats are apportioned between Germany, its reparation creditors from the 1930s, and States that were neutral during the World War I. In effect, a tribunal originally established for another purpose now functions as the dispute resolution mechanism for the Bank.

[118] In 2001, the Tribunal also adopted *Rules of Procedure for Disputes between the Bank and Private Parties.*

[119] *Bank for International Settlements Arbitration*, Partial Award on the Lawfulness of the Recall of the Privately Held Shares on 8 January 2001 and the Applicable Standards for Valuation of Those Shares, 22 November 2002; *Bank for International Settlements Arbitration*, Final Award on the Claims for Compensation for the Shares Formerly Held by the Claimants, Interest Due Thereon and Costs of the Arbitration and on the Counterclaim of the Bank Against First Eagle Sogen Funds, Inc., 19 September 2003.

(although ultimately a separate registry was established), and this approach could readily be contemplated for any circumstances in which States consider it appropriate to establish a standing court or tribunal, but wish to avoid the complexity of creating a separate institution.

Second, the PCA is available to support the work of mass claims commissions. While mixed claims commissions are no longer a fixture of international organisation, claims commissions have been frequently established in the wake of armed conflict or international crises, in order to address the particular circumstances of a large number of individual claimants and often challenging questions of evidence. The Iran–United States Claims Tribunal was one such process; others have included the United Nations Compensation Commission (established in respect of Iraq's invasion and occupation of Kuwait) and the Commission for Real Property Claims of Displaced Persons and Refugees in Bosnia and Herzegovina (established by the Dayton Peace Accords).[120] While the latter bodies were created as independent organisations, a claims process can also be established under the auspices of the PCA, as was the case for the Eritrea–Ethiopia Claims Commission. Established in December 2000 as part of the Algiers Peace Agreement that ended fighting between Eritrea and Ethiopia, the Claims Commission operated for nearly a decade, issuing 15 distinct awards before concluding its operations in August 2009.[121] Like the BIS Tribunal, the Claims Commission drew on the staff and resources of the PCA to support its operations.

Third, the PCA is available to support appellate or review mechanisms to consider disputes over the decisions of other tribunals or organisations. In a recent example, the PCA has twice been called on to support review panels established by the South Pacific Regional Fisheries Management Organisation (SPRFMO).[122] Under the Convention on the Conservation and

[120] On mass claims generally, *see* Permanent Court of Arbitration, *Redressing Injustices through Mass Claims Processes: Innovative Responses to Unique Challenges* (New York: Oxford University Press, 2006); H. M. Holtzmann and E. Kristjánsdóttir (eds.), *International Mass Claims Processes: Legal and Practical Perspectives* (New York: Oxford University Press, 2007).

[121] For an overview of the Claims Commission's work, *see* S. D. Murphy, W. Kidane, and T. R. Snider, *Litigating War: Mass Civil Injury and the Eritrea-Ethiopia Claims Commission* (New York: Oxford University Press, 2013).

[122] SPRFMO Review Panel, *Objection by the Russian Federation to a Decision of the Commission*, Findings and Recommendations of the Review Panel, 5 July 2013; SPRFMO Review Panel, *Objection by the Republic of Ecuador to a Decision of the Commission*, Findings and Recommendations of the Review Panel, 5 June 2018.

Management of High Seas Fishery Resources in the South Pacific Ocean (SPRFMO Convention), any member may raise an objection to the decisions of the Organization's executive body, the Commission, in which case a review panel will be established to consider whether the Commission's decision is discriminatory or otherwise inconsistent with the SPRFMO Convention, the Law of the Sea Convention, or the 1995 Fish Stocks Agreement.[123] The findings and recommendations of a review panel are only partially binding (depending on the outcome) and the procedure is envisaged as a precursor to binding dispute settlement under the Law of the Sea Convention and has a correspondingly light procedural footprint and rapid timetable. Both PCA-administered SPRFMO review panels issued their findings and recommendations within three months of the objection being lodged, and the procedure is considered a best practice among regional fisheries management organisations.[124]

In addition to innovations in binding inter-State dispute settlement, the PCA has seen renewed interest in non-binding procedures, in particular conciliation. Under the 1899 and 1907 Hague Conventions, the PCA was empowered to support the work of international fact-finding commissions of enquiry. Conciliation as a distinct procedure developed subsequently, building on the approach of the commission of enquiry in the *Dogger Bank* case, which with the agreement of the parties went beyond fact-finding to make a finding of responsibility in the interest of resolving the dispute.[125] A few years later, the Covenant of the League of Nations envisaged a conciliation-like procedure through which States involved in a dispute that they were unwilling to submit to judicial or arbitral settlement could request an enquiry by the Council of the League, which would attempt to broker a settlement of the dispute and, if unsuccessful, would publish a report on the facts of the dispute and such recommendations as it considered appropriate.[126] Concerned that the Council of the League was

[123] Convention on the Conservation and Management of High Seas Fishery Resources in the South Pacific Ocean, art. 17 and annex II, 14 November 2009, 2899 U.N.T.S. 211.

[124] *Report of the South Pacific Regional Fisheries Management Organisation Performance Review Panel*, x–xi, 68–71, 1 December 2018, www.sprfmo.int/assets/Basic-Documents/Convention-and-Final-Act/2018-SPRFMO-Performance-Review/2018-12-01-REPORT-SPRFMO-PERFORMANCE-REVIEW-FINAL.pdf.

[125] *The Dogger Bank Case (Great Britain/Russia)*, Report of 26 February 1905, reproduced in 2 *American Journal of International Law* 931 (1908).

[126] *See* C. de Visscher, 'La procédure de conciliation devant la Société des Nations' (1923)4(1) *Revue de Droit International et de Legislation Comparée* 21.

dominated by the Great Powers, a number of smaller States, including Sweden and Norway, began to develop bilateral conciliation commissions as an alternative to the League's procedure. Switzerland then began to routinely include conciliation in its bilateral treaties on the resolution of disputes. Other States copied this and, in short order, conciliation provisions came to be found in many of the dozens of bilateral conventions concluded among various States in the 1920s and 1930s.[127]

Although conciliation is not referenced in the Hague Conventions, which predated its development, the Contracting Parties to the PCA determined in 1937 that the competence of the PCA should be understood as extending to the administration of conciliation proceedings.[128] In the following years, the PCA provided support to three conciliation commissions involving the governments of Denmark and Lithuania, France and Switzerland, and Greece and Italy.[129] Subsequently, conciliation was introduced into the Vienna Convention on the Law of Treaties – after a consensus in favour of a binding procedure could not be found[130] – for the resolution of most disputes concerning the invalidity, termination, withdrawal from, or suspension of a treaty, and into the Law of the Sea Convention for certain disputes excluded from compulsory settlement, in particular disputes over maritime boundaries.[131] While conciliation under the Vienna Convention has gone unused, the conciliation provisions of Annex V to the Law of the Sea Convention recently produced a successful resolution in the PCA-administered *Timor Sea Conciliation* concerning the

[127] *See generally* M. Habicht, *Post-War Treaties for the Pacific Settlement of International Disputes* (Cambridge: Harvard University Press, 1931). On the history of conciliation generally, *see* S. M. G. Koopmans, *Diplomatic Dispute Settlement: The Use of Inter-State Conciliation* (The Hague: T.M.C. Asser, 2008); J. P. Cot, *La Conciliation Internationale* (Paris: A. Pedone, 1968).

[128] *See* Circular Letter from the President of the Administrative Council to the Contracting Parties, 3 May 1937; J. P. A. François, 'La Cour permanente d'arbitrage, son origine, sa jurisprudence, son avenir', (1955)87 *Recueil des cours* 535.

[129] *See* P. Hamilton, et al. (eds.), *The Permanent Court of Arbitration: International Arbitration and Dispute Resolution – Summaries of Awards, Settlement Agreements and Reports* (The Hague: Kluwer Law International, 1999), 285–293.

[130] *See* I. Sinclair, *The Vienna Convention on the Law of Treaties*, 2nd ed. (Manchester: Manchester University Press, 1984), 226–244; S. Rosenne, 'The Settlement of Treaty Disputes under the Vienna Convention of 1969' (1971)31 *Heidelberg Journal of International Law* 1.

[131] Compulsory conciliation provisions have also been included in a number of other prominent treaties where a consensus on binding settlement could not be reached, including in the UN Framework Convention on Climate Change.

maritime boundary between Timor-Leste and Australia.[132] After a year and a half of intensive meetings between the two governments and the conciliation commission, agreement was reached on a new maritime boundary treaty that was signed in March 2018 and ratified in August 2019.

16.4 Conclusion

The landscape of international law and organisation is littered with the detritus of past initiatives: draft conventions that sought to reach beyond what States could accept and failed therefore to win significant adherence; organisations that failed to achieve the high ambitions of their founders; and other instruments and bodies that, however suitable they may once have been, proved inapt in the face of the great changes of the twentieth century. That the PCA remains not merely active, but flourishing, 120 years after its establishment is a remarkable testament to the wisdom of its founders.

This volume examines international arbitration in a wide variety of forms and contexts. What unites it is the extent to which certain core values are common to arbitration in all of its forms and are of enduring merit: flexibility, the autonomy of the parties in the resolution of *their* dispute, procedural innovation and core aspects of due process.[133] The same values underpin the present success of the PCA. The delegates to the Hague Conferences of 1899 and 1907 had no foresight, of course, on the dramatic changes to come in international law and politics. Instead, what they managed to identify and capture in the creation of the PCA were the enduring elements of dispute settlement that remain as relevant as ever today.

[132] *Timor Sea* conciliation (Timor-Leste v. Australia), Report and Recommendations of the Compulsory Conciliation Commission, 9 May 2018.

[133] *See generally* M. C. W. Pinto, 'Structure, Process, Outcome: Thoughts on the "Essence" of International Arbitration', (1993)6(2) *Leiden Journal of International Law* 241.

Part V

Systemic, Trans-Substantive and New Issues

17 Regulating Arbitrators and Rules on Professional Responsibility

Christopher K. Tahbaz and Natalie L. Reid*

17.1 Introduction

As international arbitration has become increasingly popular over the years as a mechanism for resolving substantial cross-border disputes, stakeholders in the process – parties, counsel, and arbitrators themselves – have devoted significant and increasing attention to how principles of professional ethics should apply in the context of these proceedings.

Much of the discussion that has occurred can be loosely divided into two broad categories. *First*, there has been substantial discussion and debate about the types of conduct in arbitration that should be subject to regulation. Relatively early on, this discussion focused on how arbitrators could assure parties and courts that they were free of conflict, with something of a consensus emerging that arbitrator disclosure standards could have a useful role to play. More recently, focus has shifted to the ethical standards that should apply to the conduct of counsel and other participants in international arbitration, including third-party funders. The *second* area of attention has focused on the sources that should supply the ethical standards applicable in arbitration. Although many in the field resort almost instinctively to influential, international soft law sources – such as the now widely used IBA Guidelines on Conflict of Interest in Arbitration – others argue that national law and regulations cannot be ignored, especially when it comes to matters of counsel conduct in arbitration. And of course many arbitral institutions have their own rules and guidelines governing various aspects of professional ethics in arbitration.

This brief chapter provides an overview of current sources and principles of ethical regulation applicable to various aspects of international

* The authors are grateful to Julia Wang Chang, Jonathan Florez, and Samantha Singh, associates at Debevoise & Plimpton LLP, for their invaluable assistance with this chapter. Any errors are ours alone.

arbitration. Particularly given the extent of writing that has been done in the field, this chapter could not pretend to be exhaustive. Rather, the authors hope to provide a useful introduction to the topic of professional ethics in arbitration, as well as a survey of some of the important sources of hard and soft law in the field. Further discussion of the topic is also included in a separate chapter in this volume.[1]

17.2 Sources of Applicable Rules and Principles

As a transnational field of legal practice, questions of "what law governs" arise frequently in international arbitration. In the area of professional ethics, no single law – national or otherwise – provides a universal or comprehensive set of obligations for arbitrators, counsel, or other participants in the international arbitral process. The lack of clear, consistent, and mandatory rules that apply across the board has led some to term international arbitration an ethical "no-man's land."[2]

In practice, of course, the stakeholders who rely on international arbitration to resolve disputes and facilitate cross-border commerce, trade, and investment require some assurance of the integrity of that process. In the absence of binding uniform standards created and imposed by a legislature or bar association, as in domestic jurisdictions, what has developed is essentially a self-governing regime, created by the international arbitration community, and characterized by a combination of influential soft law instruments, rules promulgated and enforced by international arbitral institutions for the proceedings they administer, and the persuasive authority of decisions by institutions or tribunals resolving procedural disputes regarding alleged ethical misconduct.

Chief among these sources are:

- the Guidelines on Conflicts of Interest in International Arbitration, first issued by the International Bar Association (IBA) in 2004 and updated in 2014 ("IBA Conflict Guidelines"), concerning disclosure of conflicts

[1] *See* George A. Bermann, "The Future of International Commercial Arbitration," Section II (discussing arbitration ethics).

[2] Catherine Rogers, *Ethics in International Arbitration* (Oxford: Oxford University Press, 2013), 18.

of interest by arbitrators, and distinguishing circumstances which may or may not be grounds for disqualification;[3]

- the Guidelines on Party Representation in International Arbitration, issued by the IBA in 2013 ("IBA Party Representation Guidelines"), concerning a range of critical – though sometimes controversial – topics, including permissible communications with arbitrators; candor in submissions to tribunals; obligations regarding preservation, collection, and production of information; contact with fact and expert witnesses, including preparation of testimony; and remedies for misconduct;[4]
- the rules and practices of the leading arbitral institutions, which have long included provisions mandating and enforcing the independence and impartiality of arbitrators,[5] and which in some cases have been amended in recent years either to impose more explicit ethical obligations or to offer greater clarity and predictability, especially for challenges to arbitrators;[6] and

[3] *See* IBA Conflict Guidelines, p. i ("[The IBA Conflict Guidelines] have gained wide acceptance within the international arbitration community. Arbitrators commonly use the Guidelines when making decisions about prospective appointments and disclosures. Likewise, parties and their counsel frequently consider the Guidelines in assessing the impartiality and independence of arbitrators, and arbitral institutions and courts also often consult the Guidelines in considering challenges to arbitrators."); *see also id.*, 2 ("[T]o promote greater consistency and to avoid unnecessary challenges and arbitrator withdrawals and removals, the Guidelines list specific situations indicating whether they warrant disclosure or disqualification of an arbitrator.").

[4] *See* IBA Party Representation Guidelines, Contents & pp. 1–2 (explaining that Guidelines "are inspired by the principle that party representatives should act with integrity and honesty and should not engage in activities designed to produce unnecessary delay or expense, including tactics aimed at obstructing the arbitration proceedings").

[5] *See, e.g.*, Arbitration Rules of the International Court of Arbitration of the International Chamber of Commerce, effective as of 2017 ("ICC Rules"); London Court of International Arbitration Rules, effective as of 2014 ("LCIA Rules"); International Arbitration Rules of the International Centre for Dispute Resolution, effective as of 2014 ("ICDR Rules"); Administered Arbitration Rules of the Hong Kong International Arbitration Centre, effective as of 2018 ("HKIAC Rules"); Arbitration Rules of the Singapore International Arbitration Centre, effective as of 2016 ("SIAC Rules"); Arbitration Rules of the Arbitration Institute of the Stockholm Chamber of Commerce, effective as of 2017 ("SCC Rules"); International Centre for Settlement of Investment Disputes, Rules of Procedure for Arbitration Proceedings, effective as of 2006 ("ICSID Rules"). As of the date of this writing, some of these institutions were considering or had largely completed revisions to their rules, but had not yet promulgated them.

[6] *See, e.g.*, LCIA Rules, Annex (a set of "General Guidelines for the Parties' Legal Representatives" "intended to promote the good and equal conduct of the parties' legal representatives"); International Chamber of Commerce ("ICC"), *ICC Court to communicate*

- any publicly available reasoned decisions by institutions or tribunals – a relatively limited set, given the confidentiality attaching to many aspects of international arbitration proceedings.[7]

As some of these instruments take pains to note, they do not displace any agreement of the parties or otherwise applicable mandatory laws or professional codes imposed by domestic law.[8] Instead, like arbitration itself, they are largely contractual in nature. Whether parties select them by choice of arbitral rules or expressly opt in after a case has started, the guidelines and rules are intended to provide ethical guard-rails that take account of the differing legal cultures and practices of the participants in international arbitral proceedings, while seeking to preserve the integrity of the process and encourage trust in its results.

To illustrate how these guidelines and rules are applied in practice, the sections below briefly summarize certain key issues in professional ethics for arbitrators, counsel and other party representatives, and other participants such as third-party funders and experts.

17.3 Arbitrators

Broadly speaking, an international arbitrator must be impartial and independent.[9] Although definitions of the scope and content of these

reasons as a new service to users, October 8, 2015, https://iccwbo.org/media-wall/news-speeches/icc-court-to-communicate-reasons-as-a-new-service-to-users/ ("In response to growing user demand, the [ICC] has announced that it will communicate reasons for many of the administrative decisions it is called on to take under the ICC Rules of Arbitration," including "(i) a decision made on the challenge of an arbitrator and (ii) a decision to initiate replacement proceedings and subsequently to replace an arbitrator on the Court's own motion").

[7] *See, e.g.*, London Court of International Arbitration ("LCIA"), LCIA Challenge Decision Database, *available at* https://lcia.org/challenge-decision-database.aspx (providing digests of decisions from 2010 onward; noting that "[w]ritten challenge decisions are an invaluable resource" as "guidance in relation to acceptable standards of conduct, and provide a greater understanding of the reasoning applied by the Court"); A. Carlevaris & R. Digón, "Arbitrator Challenges under the ICC Rules and Practice" (2016), ICC Dispute Resolution Bulletin 2016 No. 1 (synthesizing practice of the ICC Court).

[8] *See, e.g.*, IBA Party Representation Guidelines, p. 2; LCIA Rules, Annex para. 1.

[9] *See, e.g.*, A. Gomez-Acebo, "The Standard of Impartiality and Independence" *Party-Appointed Arbitrators in International Commercial Arbitration* (2016), 69–96; G. B. Born, "Rights and Duties of International Arbitrators" *International Commercial Arbitration*

obligations may vary, it is generally accepted that arbitrators must fulfill their duties without bias for or against any party, and are obliged – at a minimum – to disclose connections to the parties or the dispute which could call into question their ability to serve without favor or antipathy. These fundamental expectations are reflected in the model arbitration law developed by the UN Commission on International Trade Law ("UNCITRAL Model Law") and appear as standard provisions in the leading international arbitration rules.[10]

These instruments are largely silent, however, on exactly which facts and circumstances must be disclosed – or at the extreme, might require refusal of an appointment or disqualification of a sitting arbitrator.[11] That lack of clarity, which fostered uncertainty and concerns about potential disparity in outcomes, was compounded by the reticence of most arbitral institutions to disclose the precise reasons for their challenge decisions.[12] The IBA Conflict Guidelines were specifically designed to fill that gap, and are frequently expressly adopted by parties, tribunals, and institutions as guidance in disputes regarding alleged arbitrator conflicts of interest.

The Conflict Guidelines are divided into two sections: (1) General Standards setting out fundamental principles, with explanatory notes,

(2014), 2nd ed. ("Born, Rights & Duties"), § 13.04; J. M. Waincymer, "Part I: Policy and Principles, Chapter 2: Powers, Rights and Duties of Arbitrators," *Procedure and Evidence in International Arbitration* (2012), § 2.7; E. Schwartz and Y. Derains, "The Arbitral Tribunal (Article 7–12)" *Guide to the ICC Rules of Arbitration* (2005) ("Schwartz & Derains"), 120–123.

10 *See, e.g.*, UNCITRAL Model Law, Rule 12(1) (arbitrator must "disclose any circumstances likely to give rise to justifiable doubts as to his impartiality and independence"); ICSID Rule 6(2) (requiring arbitrators to disclose any circumstances "that might cause [their] reliability for independent judgment to be questioned by a party"); ICC Rules, Art. 11(2) (arbitrator must disclose circumstances "which might be of such nature as to call into question the arbitrator's independence in the eyes of the parties as well as any circumstances that could give rise to reasonable doubts as to the arbitrator's impartiality"); ICDR Rules, Art. 13(2) (requiring disclosure of circumstances that "may give rise to justifiable doubts"; SCC Rules, Art. 18(2) (same); SIAC Rules, Art. 10(4) (same); LCIA Rules, Art. 5(4) (requiring disclosure of circumstances "likely to give rise ... to justifiable doubts"); HKIAC Rules, Art. 11(4) (same).

11 One recent (and limited) exception is the ICC's January 2019 note to parties and arbitral tribunals, which provides a list of illustrative situations that could trigger the obligation to disclose. *See* International Chamber of Commerce, Note to Parties and Arbitral Tribunals on the Conduct of the Arbitration under the ICC Rules of Arbitration (January 1, 2019), para. 23, https://iccwbo.org/content/uploads/sites/3/2017/03/icc-note-to-parties-and-arbitral-tribunals-on-the-conduct-of-arbitration.pdf.

12 *See, e.g.*, Born, Rights & Duties § 13.01; Schwartz & Derains, 115–207.

and (2) for practical application of the General Standards, illustrative lists of situations likely to occur in practice, intended to "provide specific guidance … as to which situations do or do not constitute conflicts of interest, or should or should not be disclosed."[13]

In broad strokes, the General Standards provide that an arbitrator must refuse or withdraw from an appointment if he or she has doubts – or if a reasonable, informed third party would have justifiable doubts – about the arbitrator's impartiality and independence.[14] Arbitrators are also obliged to make reasonable inquiries to ascertain any relationship to the dispute or the parties and their representatives, and to disclose facts or circumstances that may give rise to doubts about independence or impartiality.[15] Parties also have a duty to inform other participants in the proceeding about their relationships or related parties' relationships with the arbitrator.[16]

The second section of the Guidelines sets out three lists illustrating practical application of the Standards. For ease of reference, these non-exhaustive lists adopt a traffic-light color-coding system:[17] (1) the Red List addresses examples of situations in which "an objective conflict of interest exists,"[18] and thus would be a basis to decline appointment or disqualify a sitting arbitrator, if the conflict is not or cannot be waived; (2) the Orange List identifies situations where an arbitrator has a duty to disclose, because the circumstances may give rise to doubts in the eyes of the parties; and (3) the Green List contains situations that do not require disclosure, because from an objective point of view, no actual or apparent conflict exists.

The Red List is further divided into nonwaivable and waivable conflicts. Nonwaivable conflicts are those which would contravene the principle that "no person can be his or her own judge," and include instances where the arbitrator is a legal representative, employee, or board member of a party in the arbitration; the arbitrator has a controlling or significant financial relationship with a party;[19] or where the arbitrator or his or her firm "regularly advises the party" or "derives significant financial income

[13] IBA Conflict Guidelines, 17.
[14] IBA Conflict Guidelines, General Standard 2.
[15] IBA Conflict Guidelines, General Standard 3, 7(d).
[16] IBA Conflict Guidelines, General Standard 7.
[17] IBA Conflict Guidelines, Part II, 17–19.
[18] IBA Conflict Guidelines, 17.
[19] IBA Conflict Guidelines, Non-Waivable Red List, 1.1–1.3.

therefrom."[20] Examples of waivable conflicts include where the arbitrator or a close family member holds shares in one of the parties; the arbitrator is a lawyer in the same law firm as the counsel to one of the parties; or the arbitrator's law firm currently has a significant commercial relationship with one of the parties.[21]

Circumstances requiring disclosure under the Orange List generally concern services performed for a party, or a relationship to a participant in the arbitration. Examples include acting as counsel for or against one of the parties within the past three years; repeat appointments by a party or counsel within the past three years; working in the same law firm as another member of the tribunal; and association with a party in a professional capacity.[22] For situations on the Orange List, if no timely objection is made by the parties after disclosure, the parties are considered to have accepted the arbitrator.[23] Consistent with the cautionary color assigned to this list, the Guidelines emphasize that conclusions should not be lightly drawn: disclosure does not automatically imply a conflict of interest; nondisclosure should not necessarily result in disqualification; and determination of a potentially disqualifying conflict of interest should be based on an assessment of the facts that were not disclosed.[24]

Situations outlined in the Green List include more attenuated relationships with the parties or other arbitrators, such as having served together as arbitrators with counsel for one of the parties, having previously expressed a legal opinion concerning an issue that also arises in the arbitration, or having connections on social media platforms.[25]

17.3.1 Challenges to Arbitrators

The rules of all of the leading arbitral institutions – and the most frequently used rules for ad hoc or nonadministered arbitration, developed

[20] *Id.* 1.4.

[21] IBA Conflict Guidelines, Waivable Red List, 2.2.1, 2.2.2, 2.3.3., 2.3.6.

[22] IBA Conflict Guidelines, Orange List, 3.1.1, 3.1.2, 3.1.3., 3.2.1., 3.4.2.

[23] IBA Conflict Guidelines, 18.

[24] IBA Conflict Guidelines, 18.

[25] IBA Conflict Guidelines, Green List, 4.3.2, 4.1.1., 4.4.4.

and periodically updated by UNCITRAL[26] – all allow the parties to seek the removal of an arbitrator for lack of independence and impartiality.

The different rules use similar language, but what may appear to be small variations in terminology have given rise to some divergence and debate in practice. Most of the rules provide that parties may challenge an arbitrator whenever there are circumstances that "give rise to *justifiable doubts* as to the arbitrator's impartiality or independence."[27] Under the ICC Rules an arbitrator can be challenged "for an *alleged lack* of impartiality or independence,"[28] while in ICSID arbitration, an arbitrator may be disqualified if the facts evidence "a *manifest lack*" of independence.[29] Most of the rules designate the relevant arbitral institution as the authority to decide the challenge, but the ICSID Rules allow unchallenged co-arbitrators to decide such applications,[30] and the UNCITRAL Rules call for decisions to be made by the authority designated to appoint arbitrators for the case, in practice often selected by the Secretary-General of the Permanent Court of Arbitration.[31]

Given the common requirements of independence and impartiality, and the significant harmonizing influence of the IBA Conflict Guidelines, there is broad agreement regarding many of the circumstances that fall clearly within or outside of the disclosure obligations of arbitrators. Subtle differences remain, however, in the interpretation and application of these standards by different institutions, especially in complicated or nuanced cases.[32]

17.3.1.1 Repeat Appointments

One area in which such divergence has arisen concerns challenges based on repeated appointments of the same arbitrator by the same party or

[26] United Nations Commission on International Trade Law, Arbitration Rules, as most recently amended in 2013 ("UNCITRAL Rules").

[27] ICDR Rules, Art. 14(1); SCC Rules, Art. 19; SIAC Rules, Art. 11(1); LCIA Rules, Art. 10(1); HKIAC Rule, Art. 11(6); UNCITRAL Rules, Art. 12(1) (emphasis added).

[28] ICSID Convention, Art. 57; ICC Rule, Art. 14(1). (Emphasis added).

[29] ICSID Rule 57 (emphasis added).

[30] ICSID Rule 9(4). Challenges to more than one arbitrator, or cases where the two unchallenged arbitrators are unable to resolve the application, are decided by the Chairman of the ICSID Administrative Council, a position held by the President of the World Bank. *See* ICSID Rules 9(4), 9(5).

[31] UNCITRAL Rules, Arts. 6, 7, 12(1).

[32] *See, e.g.*, A. Carlevaris & R. Digón, "Arbitrator Challenges under the ICC Rules and Practice" (2016) ICC Dispute Resolution Bulletin 2016 No.1, 26–28 (discussing the role of IBA Guidelines on in the Court's decisions on challenges); Born, Rights & Duties § 13.02 F (discussing ethical codes and guidelines for international arbitrators).

counsel. As noted above, the IBA Conflict Guidelines indicate that disclosure is generally required where "[t]he arbitrator has, within the past three years, been appointed as arbitrator on two or more occasions by one of the parties, or an affiliate of one of the parties,"[33] or "been appointed on more than three occasions by the same counsel, or the same law firm."[34]

ICSID tribunals considering challenges on this and other grounds have placed particular emphasis on the language of the ICSID Rules, and have held that to prove that an arbitrator "manifest[ly] lack[s]" independence, a claimant must "establish facts that make it *obvious and highly probable*, not just possible, that [the arbitrator] is a person who may not be relied upon to exercise independent and impartial judgment."[35] Applying this standard, the tribunal in *Tidewater v. Venezuela* dismissed a challenge arising from the repeat appointments of the arbitrator in question on four different occasions by the same party and three different times by counsel.[36] Noting that the IBA Guidelines were "no more than a rule of thumb,"[37] the tribunal concluded that the requirements under the ICSID Rules were not breached merely by virtue of multiple appointments by the same party.[38]

In contrast, in at least one case concerning multiple appointments, the SCC Board reportedly reached a different result.[39] In light of the "justifiable

[33] IBA Conflict Guidelines, Orange List, 3.1.3.

[34] *Id.* 3.3.8.

[35] Suez and Vivendi v. Argentina (II), ICSID Case No. ARB/03/19, Decision on Disqualification dated May 12, 2008, para. 29 (emphasis added); Elitech B.V. and Razvoj Golf D.O.O. v. Republic of Croatia, ICSID Case No. ARB/17/32, Decision on the Proposal to Disqualify Professor Brigitte Stern dated April 23, 2018 ("*Elitech* Decision"), para. 40 (Administrative Council Chairman, confirming that "a number of decisions have concluded that the word *manifest* in Article 57 of the Convention means "evident" or "obvious," and that it relates to the ease with which the alleged lack of the required qualities can be perceived"); *see also* Will Sheng Wilson Koh, *Think Quality not Quantity: Repeat Appointments and Arbitration Challenges* 6 (2019) (concluding that the threshold for a successful challenge to an arbitrator in ICSID proceedings is more demanding in practice than that applied by other institutions).

[36] Tidewater Inc. v. Venezuela, Case No. ARB 10/5, Decision on Disqualification dated December 23, 2010, para. 64.

[37] *Id.* para. 59 (noting that "the question of whether multiple appointments to arbitral tribunals may impugn the independence or impartiality of an arbitrator is a matter of substance, not of mere mathematical calculation").

[38] *Id.* para. 64; *see also Elitech* Decision paras. 48–51 (citing *Tidewater*, and rejecting challenge to arbitrator appointed by same party in four simultaneously pending cases).

[39] SCC Board Case No. 14/2004 (unpublished), as reported in Will Sheng Wilson Koh, *Think Quality Not Quantity: Repeat Appointments and Arbitrator Challenges* 2 (2017).

doubts" standard used in its Rules, the SCC Board has focused its attention on the *risks* or *possibilities* of bias rather than evident or probable partiality of the arbitrator.[40] Under this standard, the Board found in Case No. 14/2004 that multiple appointments of an arbitrator by the same party – on eight separate occasions in five years – did raise justifiable doubts about his independence and impartiality, and concluded that removal was warranted.[41]

In ICC proceedings, where the rules permit challenges "for an alleged lack of impartiality or independence,"[42] the ICC Court is called upon to decide challenges raised both at the outset of an arbitration – when confirmation of an appointment is sought – and later in the proceedings.[43] While the Court's determinations are focused on the specific facts of each case, its practice confirms that it will decline to confirm the appointment of an arbitrator based on the number of prior repeat appointments by a party.[44]

To be sure, the impact of these terminology differences in the Rules should not be overstated. Decisions on challenges are highly fact-dependent, and even ICSID decisions have underscored that the Convention "do[es] not require proof of actual dependence or bias; rather, it is sufficient to establish the appearance of dependence or bias."[45] Different approaches to repeat appointments may also arise, not from the terms of the applicable rules, but from the custom in a particular specialized form of arbitration.[46]

40 F. M. Tellez, *Arbitrators' Independence and Impartiality: A Review of SCC Board Decisions on Challenges to Arbitrators (2010–2012)*, p. 1. (Emphasis added).

41 SCC Board Case No. 14/2004 (unpublished), as reported in Will Sheng Wilson Koh, *Think Quality Not Quantity: Repeat Appointments and Arbitrator Challenges* 2 (2017).

42 ICC Rules, Art. 14(1).

43 *See* C. Giorgetti, *Challenges and Recusal of Judges and Arbitrators in International Courts and Tribunals* (Leiden: Brill, 2015), 142. (arguing that the ICC Court applies a stricter standard to challenges brought later in the proceedings).

44 *See id.* p. 154 (discussing decision upholding challenge where arbitrator had previously served in five different tribunals in which the claimant had been a party, three as co-arbitrator and two as chair); K. Daele, *Challenge and Disqualification of Arbitrators in International Arbitration* (Wolters Kluwer, 2012), 387 (discussing decision refusing to nominate an arbitrator who had served in a related arbitration, involving the same nominating party but different respondents). *But see* Giorgetti, p. 154 (discussing decision rejecting challenge, brought later in proceedings, where arbitrator had been previously appointed by the claimant to two related cases between the same parties).

45 *Elitech* Decision para. 45; *id.* note 51 (collecting prior decisions).

46 *See, e.g.*, IBA Conflict Guidelines, Orange List, 3.1.3 & note 5 (explaining that in certain specialized areas, such as maritime, sports, or commodities arbitration, no disclosure of repeat appointment is required "if in such fields it is the custom and practice for parties to

17.3.1.2 Relationship between the Arbitrator and a Party

Given the importance of arbitrator independence, concerns about relationships between tribunal members and parties often give rise to challenges, with widely varying degrees of success. In the LCIA, for example, there is evidence that few such challenges have been accepted. Of the nearly three dozen decisions available in the LCIA's challenge database, only seven were partially or fully upheld, and of those, only two decided removal was warranted due to an arbitrator's relationship with a party.[47]

In a recent case, for example, the LCIA Court rejected the respondent's claim that the arbitrator's prior connections to the claimant and its counsel were grounds for removal. Noting that the alleged connections had taken place more than a decade before, the Court concluded that the arbitrator's prior representation of the claimant and working relationship with claimant's counsel did not raise "justifiable doubts" or "suggest that [the arbitrator] [was] conflicted and potentially biased."[48]

17.3.1.3 Prior Procedural Rulings

Parties to arbitrations – and especially their counsel – often complain that some arbitrators are too concerned with ensuring that each side has a more than ample opportunity to prepare and present its case, out of an apparent fear that the award could otherwise be set aside on due process grounds.[49] Well before an award is issued, however, parties may decide to challenge

frequently appoint the same arbitrator in different cases ... where all parties in the arbitration should be familiar with such custom and practice"). As of the time of this writing, the Supreme Court of England and Wales is seized of an appeal in *Halliburton Company v. Chubb Bermuda Insurance Limited*, UKSC 2018/0100, a case concerning repeat appointments in multiple insurance arbitrations arising from the Deepwater Horizon disaster in which such arguments of custom have been asserted. The judgment is expected to be a landmark decision regarding disclosure obligations under English law.

[47] *See generally* LCIA Challenge Decision Database, *supra* note 8 (Case No. 111947, decision of September 4, 2012, upholding challenge due to increased "danger" that impartiality and independence are jeopardized when arbitrator's law firm is "instructed" by party, even in an unrelated matter; Case No. 142862, decision of June 2, 2015, upholding challenge where respondent's chairman sat on Board of Trustees of state university where co-arbitrator was professor, because Board's reach and responsibilities raise "justifiable doubts as to the appearance of the Co-arbitrator's independence").

[48] LCIA Court Case No. 173566, decision of July 21, 2017, paras. 32, 34.

[49] *See, e.g.*, A. Bates Jr. & R. Z. Torres-Fowler, "Abuse of Due Process in International Arbitration: Is Due Process Paranoia Irrational?" (2017) 1 *American Journal of Construction Arbitration & ADR* 245.

an arbitrator for apparent bias on the basis of decisions allegedly causing prejudice to their procedural rights. Such challenges are often rejected.

In one ICSID decision, for example, the Chairman of the Administrative Council underscored that the test for disqualification of an arbitrator is an "objective standard based on a reasonable evaluation of the evidence by a third party."[50] The Chairman rejected the challenge to a majority of the tribunal, finding that the granting of a procedural order ostensibly granting the claimant more time to prepare its reply than the respondent had to prepare its rejoinder did not meet that standard. The decision quoted with approval the majority's decision pointing to a number of factors undermining the respondent's claim of unequal treatment, including its agreement to the time interval for preparation of its submission, and that "it would be inappropriate to assume" claimants in fact "enjoyed" the full period between submission deadlines to prepare their filing, since "both Parties ha[d] been occupied with various aspects of these proceedings" during the same period.[51]

The LCIA Court has framed the test in similar terms, namely, "whether a fair-minded and informed observer, having considered the facts, would conclude that there was a real possibility that the tribunal was biased."[52] Applying that standard, the LCIA Court rejected a challenge where the arbitrator limited the claimant to short submissions at a hearing, stating that nothing in these situations "give[s] rise to justifiable doubts as to the impartiality or independence of the arbitrator."[53]

17.3.1.4 Prejudgment of the Merits

Recent years have seen a rise in challenges alleging that arbitrators have in some manner prejudged the merits of issues pending before them. The topic that has attracted the most attention is the so-called issue conflict, which is perhaps best described as involving "an issue likely to be relevant to the dispute on which the parties have a reasonable expectation of an open mind," but where the concern is "that an arbitrator will not approach [the] issue impartially, but rather with a desire to conform to his or her own

[50] Abaclat and Others v. Argentina, Case No. ARB 07/5, Decision on Disqualification dated February 4, 2014, para. 77.

[51] *See id.* para. 43.

[52] LCIA Court Case No. 152906 (May 25, 2016) para. 29.

[53] LCIA Court Case No. 142778 (March 31, 2017) para. 36.

view," as expressed in a previous decision or prior speech or publication.[54] This ground for challenge is highly controversial, and has been the subject of heated debate, divergent decisions, and substantial analysis.[55] Given the limited scope of this chapter, it suffices to note that this kind of challenge arises most frequently in investment arbitration, where the higher incidence of published decisions and awards provides greater opportunity for scrutiny of the opinions of arbitrators.

Nevertheless, there are instances in commercial arbitration where parties challenge arbitrators for prejudgment on the basis of decisions in the course of the same proceedings. In one such case, for example, the LCIA Court removed an arbitrator on the basis of a dissenting opinion issued at the jurisdictional phase of the arbitration. The Court held that by expressing his views on the merits in definite terms at that preliminary stage of the proceeding, the arbitrator "conveyed the impression to an objective and informed observer that he had prejudged the merits . . . creating thereby an appearance of bias."[56]

* * *

In practice, there are widely differing – and strongly held – views on whether challenges are an effective way of ensuring independence and impartiality in international arbitration. Some stakeholders call for more disclosure, transparency, and party involvement in the decision-making process,[57] while others caution against the liberal use of challenges, and raise concerns about potential abuse by unscrupulous parties as a tactical disruption of the proceedings.[58] Some of the proposals for reform have

[54] CC/Devas (Mauritius) Ltd., Devas Employees Mauritius Private Limited, and Telcom Devas Mauritius Limited v. Republic of India, UNCITRAL, Decision on the Respondent's Challenge to the Hon. Mark Lalonde as Presiding Arbitrator and Prof. Francisco Orrego Vicuña as Co-Arbitrator dated September 30, 2013, para. 58, *quoted with approval in* Report of the ASIL-ICCA Joint Task Force on Issue Conflicts in Investor-State Arbitration, ICCA Reports No. 3, March 17, 2016 ("ASIL-ICCA Issue Conflicts Task Force Report"), para. 14.

[55] *See generally* ASIL-ICCA Issue Conflicts Task Force Report.

[56] LCIA Court Case No. 132498 (December 24, 2014), para. 50.

[57] *See, e.g.*, The Hague Rules on Business and Human Rights, www.cilc.nl/cms/wp-content/uploads/2019/12/The-Hague-Rules-on-Business-and-Human-Rights-Arbitration_CILC-digital-version.pdf ("Hague Rules"), 34.

[58] *See, e.g.*, G. J. Hovarth *et al.*, "Chapter 1, § 1.02: Categories of Guerilla Tactics," *Guerilla Tactics in International Arbitration*, International Arbitrational Law Library Vol. 28. (stating that, while an indispensable right, challenges are often used to "derail" the proceedings and to "reverse undesirable decisions").

gained traction, with leading institutions providing greater access to anonymized decisions on challenges, while other proposals like oral hearings on challenge applications appear to have less institutional support.

17.4 Party Representatives

While arbitrator conflicts and other ethics-related aspects of arbitrator conduct have long been a subject of discussion by practitioners and institutions, more recently attention has shifted to efforts to articulate standards for professional conduct by parties and their counsel in international arbitration. The most prominent of these is the IBA Party Representation Guidelines, issued in 2013. As the Preamble to those Guidelines notes, this topic can be especially complicated and fraught in the cross-cultural context of international arbitral proceedings:

> Unlike in domestic judicial settings, in which counsel are familiar with, and subject to, a single set of professional conduct rules, party representatives in international arbitration may be subject to diverse and potentially conflicting bodies of domestic rules and norms. The range of rules and norms applicable to the representation of parties in international arbitration may include those of the party representative's home jurisdiction, the arbitral seat, and the place where hearings physically take place.[59]

The potential for conflict or confusion is especially high where norms or practices from different jurisdictions suggest, or even require, divergent approaches on matters that are critical to the orderly conduct of the arbitration, such as disclosure, contact with witnesses, or alternative funding arrangements.[60] Those challenges are further compounded if differences between domestic professional codes impose greater restrictions on one party's counsel than the other, potentially creating tactical advantages.

It is perhaps unsurprising, therefore, that efforts to develop influential transnational soft law standards in this area have proved to be challenging. The IBA Party Representation Guidelines met with varying reactions

[59] IBA Party Representation Guidelines, 1.

[60] *See, e.g.*, Rogers, *supra* note 3, 107 (giving example of German attorney fined for not making a disclosure required under English law, but which would have given rise to professional sanctions in Germany, as illustrative of difficulties of representing clients in international arbitral proceedings).

when they were first issued, and in the face of strong criticism by some civil law practitioners,[61] "have not been taken up by the international arbitration community to the same extent as the other IBA Rules and Guidelines."[62] These Guidelines are of more recent vintage than other IBA soft law instruments, however, so additional time (and any amendments that may be made) may yet change the impact they have on any shared views of best practices.[63]

Whatever the views of the specific provisions in the IBA Party Representation Guidelines – which sought to cover a wide range of topics, including communications with arbitrators,[64] information exchange and disclosure,[65] contact with and preparation of witnesses,[66] and remedies for alleged misconduct[67] – it appears uncontroversial and widely accepted that the fundamental principles of integrity, honesty, and good faith which underlie the Guidelines do apply to parties and their counsel.[68]

The same principles animate a parallel effort by at least one leading arbitral institution to introduce ethical standards and guidelines that address counsel

[61] *See, e.g.*, F. Dasser, "A Critical Analysis of the IBA Guidelines on Party Representation" in *The Sense and Non-Sense of Guidelines, Rules and other Para-regulatory Texts in International Arbitration*, ASA Special Series No. 37 (2015).

[62] IBA Arbitration Guidelines and Rules Subcommittee, *Report on the Reception of the IBA Arbitration Soft Law Products*, September 2016 ("IBA Reception Report"), para. 247. *See also id.* para. 201 ("The Party Representation Guidelines were the least frequently used . . ., with references to [them] being made in less than 20 percent of arbitrations involving issues of counsel conduct. That being said, the Party Representation Guidelines appeared to be more frequently used in common law jurisdictions than civil law jurisdictions."); Dasser, *supra* note 62, at 33–34 (noting that an earlier effort to articulate a set of common standards, termed the Rio Code, did not gain traction).

[63] *See* IBA Reception Report paras. 248–250 (noting that the Guidelines' relative lack of application may be explained by their relative newness, but also by perceptions that they do not fill a gap to the same extent as other IBA instruments, or "that issues of counsel conduct arise far less frequently than issues of evidence or conflicts of interest, and may be regulated by other legal or ethical norms").

[64] IBA Party Representation Guidelines, Guidelines 7 & 8.

[65] IBA Party Representation Guidelines, Guidelines 12–17.

[66] IBA Party Representation Guidelines, Guidelines 18–25.

[67] IBA Party Representation Guidelines, Guidelines 26–27.

[68] *See, e.g.*, IBA Party Representation Guidelines, p. 2; Dasser, *supra* note 62, 37; Singapore Institute of Arbitrators, *Guidelines on Party-Representative Ethics*, April 2018, Introduction, para. 6 (leading Asia-Pacific arbitration association proposing its own set of standards, developed after research, consultation, and review of existing soft law instruments; noting that its text "is based on the overarching principle that Party Representatives, in advising and representing their client, should at all times act with honesty, integrity and professionalism, both with respect to their client and the Tribunal.").

conduct. The 2014 amendments to the LCIA Rules introduced both a set of guidelines regarding the conduct of party representatives and an express obligation imposed on each party to "ensure that all its legal representatives appearing by name before the Arbitral Tribunal have agreed to comply with the general guidelines ... as a condition of such representation."[69]

The LCIA General Guidelines, which are set out in an annex to the 2014 Rules, list five straightforward standards, stating that a party's "legal representative should not" (1) "engage in activities intended unfairly to obstruct the arbitration or to jeopardise the finality of any award," including meritless repeated challenges to arbitrators or jurisdiction; (2) "knowingly make any false statement to the Arbitral Tribunal or the LCIA Court"; (3) "knowingly procure or assist in the preparation of or rely upon any false evidence presented to the Arbitral Tribunal or the LCIA Court"; (4) "knowingly conceal or assist in the concealment of any document (or any part thereof) which is ordered to be produced by the Arbitral Tribunal"; and (5) engage in "unilateral contact" with a member of the tribunal or of the LCIA Court, except in narrow, specified circumstances.[70] Sanctions for a breach of these standards may go beyond the imposition of a costs order – the typical remedy available to international arbitral tribunals – and include "(*i*) a written reprimand; (*ii*) a written caution as to future conduct in the arbitration; and (*iii*) any other measure necessary to fulfill within the arbitration the general duties required of the Arbitral Tribunal."[71]

17.5 Other Participants in Arbitral Proceedings

Attention has also increasingly been paid to ethical considerations related to other stakeholders, including third-party funders and expert witnesses. We touch on these issues briefly below.

17.5.1 Third-Party Funding

As the use of third-party funding has continued to grow in international arbitration, questions about disclosure of such arrangements have arisen

[69] LCIA Rules, Art. 18.5 (referring to General Guidelines set forth in Annex).
[70] LCIA Rules, Annex, paras. 2–6.
[71] LCIA Rules, Art. 18(6).

with greater frequency. Until relatively recently, the consensus appeared to be that there was no general obligation for a party to disclose that a third party is providing financial assistance for the case, unless it is relevant to arbitrators' independence and impartiality.[72] Some reports on challenges, however, suggest that potential connections between arbitrators and third-party funders remain a source of concern for parties.[73] Increasingly, however, parties are pressing for even greater disclosure of third-party funding arrangements – not just the existence of such funding, or the identity of the funder, but also the terms of the funding agreement.[74] Such applications have met with mixed success.[75]

17.5.2 Experts

Experts retained for international arbitration proceedings should provide their own independent professional assessments to the tribunal.[76] Unlike

[72] J. von Goeler, *Third-Party Funding in International Arbitration and its Impact on Procedure* (Wolters Kluwer, 2016), 125; IBA Conflict Guidelines, General Standard 7(a) (parties must disclose any relationship "between the arbitrator and any person or entity with a direct economic interest in, or a duty to indemnify a party for, the award to be rendered in the arbitration").

[73] *See, e.g.*, Muhammet Çap Sehil Inşaat Endustrive v. Turkmenistan, ICSID Case No. ARB/12/6, Procedural Order No. 3, dated June 12, 2015, paras. 9–10 (ordering disclosure of existence and identity of funder, as well as funding terms, given "the importance of ensuring the integrity of the proceedings and to determine whether any of the arbitrators are affected by the existence of a third-party funder").

[74] *See* I. C. Popova & K. R. Seifert, "Gatekeeping, Lawmaking, and Rulemaking: Lessons from Third-Party Funding in Investment Arbitration" in *Private Actors In International Investment Law* (2020), Section III.2 (discussing survey results and decisions regarding disclosure of third-party funding).

[75] *Compare, e.g.*, South American Silver Ltd. (Bermuda) v. Plurinational State of Bolivia, UNCITRAL, PCA Case No. 2013-15, Procedural Order No. 10 dated January 11, 2016, paras. 79–81 (concluding that funding agreement terms irrelevant to issues for decision; rejecting request to disclose agreement itself), *with* Interocean Oil Development Company and Interocean Oil Exploration Company v. Federal Republic of Nigeria, ICSID Case No. ARB/13/20, Procedural Order No. 5 dated October 15, 2016, paras. 87–89 (ordering respondent to reveal identity of any third party funder and the terms of any agreement).

[76] *See, e.g.*, IBA Rules on the Taking of Evidence in International Arbitration (2010), Art. 5(2)(c) (specifying that an expert retained by a party must submit "a statement of his or her independence from the Parties, their legal advisor and the Arbitral Tribunal"); *id.* Art. 5(2)(g) (same for experts engaged by the tribunal); ICC International Court of Arbitration Bulletin Vol. 20 No. 1, *Issues for Experts Acting Under the ICC Rules for Expertise or the ICC Rules of Arbitration* (2009) ("You should be impartial and disinterested in the outcome of the proceeding or the conclusions to be drawn from your work product.").

concerns about professional standards for arbitrators or counsel, however, this expectation for experts remains largely uncodified.[77] The leading institutional rules tend to focus on provisions for tribunal-appointed experts, with little or no attention paid to party appointees,[78] though of course any witness appearing before the tribunal will typically make an oath or affirmation to testify honestly[79] – or in the specific case of an expert, in accord with "his or her genuine belief."[80]

Different proposals have periodically been offered in an attempt to address the concern about whether an expert selected and retained by a party could in fact provide truly independent evidence to the tribunal. These include a code of conduct developed by the Chartered Institute of Arbitrators,[81] and a proposed mechanism for experts suggested by the parties to be retained by the tribunal and paid out of common funds.[82]

17.6 Conclusion

Calls for greater regulation of professional conduct in international arbitration are not new. The increasing scrutiny to which international arbitration has been subject in recent years has attracted critical review from new and different stakeholders – including national governments – and ensured further debates and proposals in this arena. Among other developments, ongoing discussions of the UNCITRAL Working Group on investor-state dispute settlement reform have included substantial discussion of States' concerns about arbitrator independence and

[77] *See, e.g.*, M. Kantor, "A Code of Conduct for Party-Appointed Experts in International Arbitration – Can One Be Found?" (2010) 26 *Arbitration International* 323, 324 ("Arbitration laws and arbitration rules generally say nothing about the ethics duties of party-appointed experts" but this silence "stands in contrast with judicial practice," where "[c]ourts, and their codes of civil procedures, do impose a code of conduct on party-appointed experts").

[78] *See, e.g.*, LCIA Rules Art. 21; SCC Rules Art. 34; HKIAC Rules Art. 25; ICDR Rules Art. 25; ICC Rules Art. 25; SIAC Rules 23; ICSID Rules 35, 36; Kantor, *supra* note 78, 327.

[79] *See, e.g.*, Kantor, *supra* note 78, 328 (discussing ICSID witness affirmations); LCIA Rules Art. 20.

[80] Kantor, *supra* note 78, 330.

[81] Chartered Institute of Arbitrators Protocol for the Use of Party-Appointed Expert Witnesses in International Arbitration (September 2007).

[82] Kantor, *supra* note 78, 336–339 (discussing proposal made by Dr. Klaus Sachs at 2010 ICCA annual conference, generally referred to as "Sachs Protocol").

impartiality;[83] the recently issued Hague Rules on Business and Human Rights Arbitration includes a separate code of conduct for arbitrators;[84] and discussions about harmonization and the adoption of transnational ethics codes continue, including contemplation of an international system of accreditation.[85] If nothing else, these efforts demonstrate an enduring desire on the part of at least some stakeholders to account for and incorporate ethical considerations in the further development of international arbitration.

[83] Report of Working Group III (Investor-State Dispute Settlement Reform) on the work of its thirty-sixth session (Vienna, October 29–November 2, 2018), UNCITRAL fifty-second session, https://undocs.org/en/A/CN.9/964.

[84] Hague Rules, 95–99.

[85] George A. Bermann, *The Future of International Commercial Arbitration*, 10.

18 Dealing with Corruption

Florian Haugeneder

18.1 Introduction

The issue of corruption is exemplary for the role of public policy in arbitration. Corruption is a "bilateral" criminal act involving the briber and the taker of the bribe, with varying nuances of solicitation on both sides.[1] Both sides have an interest in keeping corrupt activities secret. Yet, regardless of the intentions of the parties, there is a universal consensus that corruption cannot be tolerated in international business relations. When international business transactions tainted by corruption are submitted to international arbitration, the notion of party autonomy finds its limits in the transnational public policy against bribery and corruption. No award can be allowed to take effect if it is seen to condone corruption. International arbitration derives its legitimacy from applying the law, including public policy rules prohibiting corruption.

If proven, corruption is virtually always outcome-determinative.[2] Under most laws, a contract providing for, or masking, corruption is void, and a contract obtained through corruption may be voided by the victim.[3] In investment arbitration, the investor who procured the investment through bribing officials of the host State will generally lose protection under investment protection treaties.

The condemnation of corruption in the arbitral practice is uniform and usually accompanied by moral undertones. Corruption was described as

[1] A. P. Llamzon and A. C. Sinclair, "Investor Wrongdoing in Investment Arbitration: Standards Governing Issues of Corruption, Fraud, Misrepresentation and Other Investor Misconduct" in A. J. van den Berg (ed.), *Legitimacy: Myths, Realities, Challenges* (Alphen aan den Rijn: Kluwer Law International, 2015), 460–463.

[2] D. Baizeau and T. Hayes, "The Arbitral Tribunal's Duty and Power to Address Corruption Sua Sponte" in A. Menaker (ed.), *International Arbitration and the Rule of Law: Contribution and Conformity* (Alphen aan den Rijn: Kluwer Law International, 2017), 227.

[3] There is no victim in the relationship between the briber and the taker of the bribe. However, the entity (state or private body) whose representative abused his or her position for private gain is an often forgotten victim of corrupt relationships.

"internationally abhorred,"[4] "more odious than theft,"[5] "vile," and "repugnant."[6] This attitude is, however, relatively new and coincides with the adoption of international law instruments aiming at combating cross-border corruption.[7] Until shortly before the turn of the millennium, corruption was considered a displeasing but necessary part of foreign business relations.[8] Bribes paid to foreign officials were until recently tax-deductible in a number of countries.[9]

The condemnation of corruption contrasts with the actual practice of tribunals when corruption emerges from the parties' pleadings or the evidence. Arbitral tribunals tended to avoid making determinations on the issue of corruption even in the presence of strong indications that corruption played a role in the relationship between the parties.[10] Despite

[4] M. Hwang and K. Lim, "Corruption in Arbitration – Law and Reality" (2012) 8 *Asian International Arbitration Journal* 1.

[5] World Duty Free Company v. Republic of Kenya, ICSID Case No. ARB/00/7, Award, October 4, 2006, para. 173.

[6] V. Pavic, "Bribery and International Commercial Arbitration – The Role of Mandatory Rules and Public Policy" (2012) 43 *Victoria University of Wellington Law Review* 661; A. Sayed, "La question de la corruption dans l'arbitrage commercial international: Inventaire des solutions" (2001) 19 *ASA Bulletin* 653; H. Raeschke-Kessler and D. Gottwald, "Corruption" in P. Muchlinski, F. Ortino and C. Schreuer (eds.), *The Oxford Handbook of International Investment Law* (Oxford: Oxford University Press, 2008) 609; Himpurna California Energy Ltd. v. PT. (Persero) Perusahaan Listruik Negara, Final Award, May 4, 1999, (1999) 25 *Yearbook Commercial Arbitration* 13.

[7] *See* Section 18.2.3.

[8] J. Drude, "*Fiat iustitia, ne pereat mundus*: A Novel Approach to Corruption and Investment Arbitration" (2018) 35 *Journal of International Arbitration* 665; for a discussion of the Siemens corruption affair, *see* J. W. Yackee, "Investment Treaties and Investor Corruption: An Emerging Defense for Host States?" (2012) 52 *Virginia Journal of International Law* 723; L. E. Peterson, "Siemens pleads guilty to breach of Foreign Corrupt-Practices Act; Evidence of arbitration over illicit payments," *Investment Arbitration Reporter*, December 17, 2018, www.iareporter.com/articles/siemens-pleads-guilty-to-breach-of-foreign-corrupt-practices-act-evidence-of-arbitration-over-illicit-payments/.

[9] R. H. Kreindler, *Competence-Competence in the Face of Illegality in Contracts and Arbitration Agreements* (Leiden: Brill Nijhoff, 2013), 179–180.

[10] C. Rose, "Questioning the Role of International Arbitration in the Fight against Corruption" (2014) 31 *Journal of International Arbitration* 183; International Systems & Controls Corp. v. Industrial Development & Renovation Organization of Iran, Iran Wood & Paper Industries, Mazandaran Wood & Paper Industries & Islamic Republic of Iran, Award 256–439–2 (1986) 12 Iran-USCTR 239; Empresas Lucchetti, S.A. & Lucchetti Peru, S.A. v. Republic of Peru, ICSID Case No. ARB/03/4, Award, February 7, 2005, para. 57; Bayindir InsaatTurizm TicaretVe Sanayi A.S. v. Islamic Republic of Pakistan, ICSID Case No. ARB/03/29, Decision on Jurisdiction, November 14, 2005, paras. 150–151; TSA Spectrum de Argentina S.A. v. Argentine Republic, ICSID Case No. ARB/05/5, Award, December 19, 2008, paras. 175–176.

the empiric pervasiveness of corruption in foreign business relations, only relatively fee tribunals have made a positive finding that there was corruption. Corruption is "notoriously difficult to prove," as a prominent tribunal held.[11] Parties face the difficulty of having to decide if they wish to rely on corruption at all, and if they decide in the affirmative, of gathering sufficient evidence. The proof of corruption is therefore central to any discussion of corruption in international arbitration.

This contribution will start with a short introduction of corruption as a legal and economic phenomenon. In line with the dichotomy between the theoretical clarity of the legal consequences of corruption and the actual difficulty of successfully pleading corruption in arbitration, the contribution will then discuss the legal consequences of corruption in arbitral proceedings and the proof of corruption in the arbitral practice.

18.2 Corruption as an Economic and Legal Phenomenon

18.2.1 Defining Corruption

There is no universally accepted definition of corruption. Transparency International defines corruption as "the abuse of entrusted power for private gain."[12] At the core of notion of corruption is the bribery of public officials. The United Nations Convention Against Corruption adopted in 2003 (UN Convention against Corruption), the most important international instrument against corruption, defines bribery of public officials as "the promise, offering or giving, to a public official, directly or indirectly, of an undue advantage, for the official himself or herself or another person or entity, in order that the official act or refrain from acting in the exercise of his or her official duties."

While there is little doubt about the prohibition of "public bribery," there is less certainty at the margins of the notion of corruption. The UN Convention against Corruption covers corruption in the private sector, but only asks States to "consider" adopting measures against private bribery, while States are under an obligation to criminalize the bribery of public

[11] EDF (Services) Limited v. Romania, ICSID Case No. ARB/05/13, Award, October 8, 2009, para. 221.

[12] Transparency International, "How Do You Define Corruption?," www.transparency.org/what-is-corruption.

officials.[13] "Trading in influence" or "influence peddling" is the payment of persons who have real or supposed influence with public authorities with a view to an undue advantage.[14] No monetary advantage is passed directly to the official. The UN Convention against Corruption contains no binding obligation of States to criminalize influence peddling but, again, provides that States should "consider" establishing a criminal offense. Low-level corruption to obtain legitimate government services is sometimes referred to as "facilitation" or "grease" payments. It is considered less reprehensible because the payment is usually the response to extortion from government officials to perform routine governmental services.[15]

Outside the core area of bribery of public officials, the exact limitations of corruption depend on the applicable domestic law. In the arbitral practice, these limitations are important as the picture emerging from the evidence is often gray rather than clear. While outright bribery may be impossible to prove, the facts that are possible to establish possibly fall under one of the other iterations of corruption under the applicable law.[16] Future legislation may further modify the delineations between permitted inducements, such as lobbying, donations, and campaign financing, and illegal practices.

18.2.2 The Economics of Corruption

There is, obviously, no hard data on the exact share of corrupt payments of the economy. According to Word Bank estimates, about US$1.5 trillion, or about 3 percent of the global GDP, is paid in bribes.[17] Corruption in

[13] United Nations Convention Against Corruption (adopted October 31, 2003, entered into force December 14, 2005) 2349 UNTS 41 (UNCAC) Art. 21.

[14] United Nations Convention Against Corruption (adopted October 31, 2003, entered into force December 14, 2005) 2349 UNTS 41 (UNCAC) Art. 18.

[15] The US Foreign Corrupt Practices Act exempts facilitation payments from its scope of application. *See* 15 USC § 78dd-1 (*b*), § 78dd-2 (*b*) and § 78dd-3 (*b*); Kreindler, *Competence-Competence, op. cit.*, 422.

[16] Hilmarton (Agent) v. Omnium/Algeria, ICC Case No. 5622, Final Award, 1988, (1994) 19 *Yearbook Commercial Arbitration* 105; Omnium de Traitement et de Valorisation – OTV (France) v. Hilmarton (UK), Court of Appeal of the Canton of Geneva, November 17, 1989 and Federal Supreme Court of Switzerland, April 17, 1990, (1994) 19 *Yearbook Commercial Arbitration* 214; Hilmarton Ltd. v. Omnium de traitement et de valorisation – OTV, Cour de Cassation of France, March 23, 1994, (1995) 20 *Yearbook Commercial Arbitration* 663.

[17] A. P. Llamzon, *Corruption in International Investment Arbitration* (Oxford: Oxford University Press, 2014), 4.

developing countries is often compared to a 20 percent tax on foreign investment.[18] Under any measure, corruption is endemic in foreign business relations.

There would not be corruption in foreign business relations if it were not profitable. Investors will try to recover the costs of bribes in addition to a markup for profit. Ultimately, the costs of corruption are borne by the public in multiple ways, as corruption distorts the competition, weakens the attraction to foreign investment and reduces the available government funds.[19] The political costs are probably even higher: corruption undermines the trust in government and fuels inequalities, leading to conflict and extremism.

Some decades ago, there were still views regarding corruption as a by-product of human development, with a number of positive aspects.[20] These views of corruption as "grease" to foreign business relations and investment, are no longer prevalent in social sciences. In the prevailing public discourse, corruption is viewed as exclusively negative.[21]

18.2.3 The Condemnation of Corruption as a Rule of Transnational Public Policy

The tribunal in the landmark case of *World Duty Free v. Kenya* held in 2006, "In light of domestic laws and international conventions relating to corruption, and in light of the decisions taken in this matter by courts and arbitral tribunals, this Tribunal is convinced that bribery is contrary to the international public policy of most, if not all, States or, to use another formula, to transnational public policy."[22]

[18] *Id.*

[19] World Bank, *Anticorruption in Transition: A Contribution to the Policy Debate* (2000) 18–19; European Bank for Reconstruction and Development, "Investigating fraud, corruption and misconduct," www.ebrd.com/who-we-are/our-values/investigating-fraud-and-corruption.html; World Bank, "Combating Corruption," www.worldbank.org/en/topic/governance/brief/anti-corruption; World Bank, *Fraud and Corruption Awareness Handbook* (2010).

[20] A. P. Llamzon, *Corruption in International Investment Arbitration* (Oxford: Oxford University Press, 2014), 23, 25.

[21] K. Annan, "Foreword" in United Nations Office on Drugs and Crime, *United Nations Convention against Corruption* (2004) iii.

[22] World Duty Free Company v. Republic of Kenya, ICSID Case No. ARB/00/7, Award, October 4, 2006, para. 157.

This pronouncement exemplifies the gradual shift from tacit toleration to open condemnation of corruption. A number of States tolerated bribery of foreign officials in foreign business relations (but not in domestic relations) until recently.[23] The turn came in the United States with the realization that corruption in foreign business relations risks influencing domestic political and business practices.[24] In 1977, the United States enacted the Foreign Corrupt Practices Act (FCPA) prohibiting the bribery of foreign officials to obtain or retain business.[25]

The unilateral anticorruption stance of the United States in a global environment that largely tolerated corruption in foreign business relations entailed that US corporations had a competitive disadvantage and foreign investment to certain countries declined.[26] The shift at the international level occurred in 1997 with the OECD Anti-Bribery Convention, which obliged the parties to the Convention to criminalize bribery of foreign officials in the businesses' home country.[27] A number of regional anticorruption instruments followed: the Inter-American Anti-Corruption Convention (1996),[28] the EU Convention against Corruption (1997),[29] the Council of Europe Civil Law Convention on Corruption (1999),[30] the Council of Europe Criminal Law Convention on

[23] A. P. Llamzon, *Corruption in International Investment Arbitration* (Oxford: Oxford University Press, 2014), 45–53; B. M. Cremades and D. J. A. Cairns, "Trans-national Public Policy in International Arbitral Decisionsmaking: The Cases of Bribery, Money Laundering and Fraud" in K. Karsten and A. Berkeley (eds.), *Arbitration: Money Laundering, Corruption and Fraud* (Paris: ICC, 2003) 58 *et seq.*

[24] *See, e.g.*, the investigations in the aftermath of the Watergate affair, R. D. Hershey, "Special Task Force Will Press Charges in Corporate Bribes," *New York Times*, October 14, 1976, 56, www.nytimes.com/1976/10/14/archives/special-task-force-will-press-charges-in-corporate-bribes-sec.html; A. P. Llamzon, *Corruption in International Investment Arbitration* (Oxford: Oxford University Press, 2014), 46.

[25] 15 USC §§ 78dd-1, *et seq.*

[26] A. P. Llamzon, *Corruption in International Investment Arbitration* (Oxford: Oxford University Press, 2014), 50.

[27] Convention on Combating Bribery of Foreign Officials in International Business Transactions (adopted November 21, 1997, entered into force February 15, 1999) (1998) 37 ILM 1.

[28] Inter-American Convention against Corruption (adopted March 29, 1996, entered into force March 6, 1997) (1996) 35 ILM 724.

[29] European Union: Convention on the Fight Against Corruption Involving Officials of the European Communities or Officials of Member States of the European Union (adopted May 26, 1997, entered into force September 28, 2005) (1998) 37 ILM 12.

[30] Council of Europe Civil Law Convention on Corruption (adopted November 4, 1999, entered into force November 1, 2003) ETS No. 174.

Corruption (1999),[31] and the African Union Convention Against Corruption (2003).[32] With the UN Convention against Corruption (2003), which is presently ratified by 186 States, the international policy against corruption reached quasi-universal acceptance. It is therefore apposite to speak of an international consensus prohibiting corruption in the sense of a transnational public policy that applies in all forums.[33]

This should not, however, conceal the fact that the transnational public policy against corruption only extends to the core of the notion of corruption, that is, the bribery of public officials. Practices outlawed only in some countries, such as the prohibition of intermediary contracts for the access to decision takers,[34] need to be analyzed through the prism of the applicable domestic law.

18.3 The Legal Consequences of Corruption

The record of published cases shows that corruption generally appears in two distinct forms in international arbitration: On the one hand, there are actual or perceived contracts of corruption, that is, contracts with the purpose of procuring bribes to decision takers. Typically, these contracts take the form of "intermediary" agreements obliging the intermediary to make use of his or her connections with State officials to obtain business or other favorable decisions, combined with high monetary remuneration and little details about the specific tasks of the intermediary.[35] The second

[31] Council of Europe Criminal Law Convention on Corruption (adopted January 27, 1999, entered into force July 1, 2002) ETS No. 173.

[32] African Union Convention on Preventing and Combatting Corruption (adopted July 11, 2003, entered into force August 5, 2006) 2860 UNTS 50008.

[33] P. Lalive, "Transnational (or Truly International) Public Policy and International Arbitration" in P. Sanders (ed.), *Comparative Arbitration Practice and Public Policy in Arbitration*, ICCA Congress Series, vol. 3 (Alphen aan den Rijn: Kluwer Law International, 1987), 258.

[34] Omnium de Traitement et de Valorisation – OTV (France) v. Hilmarton (UK), Court of Appeal of the Canton of Geneva, November 17, 1989, and Federal Supreme Court of Switzerland, April 17, 1990, (1994) 19 *Yearbook Commercial Arbitration* 214; Hilmarton Ltd. v. Omnium de traitement et de valorisation – OTV, Cour de Cassation of France, March 23, 1994, (1995) 20 *Yearbook Commercial Arbitration* 663.

[35] Hilmarton (Agent) v. Omnium/Algeria, ICC Case No. 5622, Final Award, 1988, (1994) 19 *Yearbook Commercial Arbitration* 105; ICC Case No. 6497, Final Award, 1994, (1999) 24

occurrence of corruption in the arbitral practice typically concerns contracts or other investments that were allegedly procured by corruption.[36]

In the context of commercial arbitration, tribunals facing the issue corruption from the parties' pleadings or the evidence are confronted with a number of typical challenges. First, may claims relating to serious illegality be submitted to arbitration, or is the matter reserved for State courts? Second, is consent to arbitration valid if the agreement of the parties is tainted by corruption? Third, what are the civil law consequences of corruption?

In investor-State arbitration, the challenges to be tackled by arbitrators usually are: First, to what extent are investments tainted by corruption covered by investment protection treaties? Second, is corruption a bar to admissibility of investor claims? Third, may an investor seek damages from a State if representatives of the State sought to extort bribes in exchange to favorable treatment?

18.3.1 Corruption and Private Law Contracts

18.3.1.1 Arbitrability

Arbitrability concerns the question as to whether a subject-matter may be submitted to arbitration.[37] Most arbitration laws define the subject matters

Yearbook Commercial Arbitration 71; ICC Case No. 8891, Award, 1998, (2000) 127 *Journal du droit international (Clunet)* 1076; State-Owned Corporation X v. Corporation Y, ICC Case No. 11307, Final Award, 2003, (2008) 33 *Yearbook Commercial Arbitration* 24; Consultant v. German Company, Higher Regional Court of Hamm, September 7, 2005, (2006) 31 *Yearbook Commercial Arbitration* 685; Thales (formerly Thomson CSF) v. Frontier AG Bern et Brunner, Federal Supreme Court of Switzerland, BGer 4A.596/2008, October 6, 2009, (2010) 28 *ASA Bulletin* 318; V. Pavic, "Bribery and International Commercial Arbitration – The Role of Mandatory Rules and Public Policy" (2012) 43 *Victoria University of Wellington Law Review* 661; Hwang and Lim, *op. cit.*

36 V. Pavic, "Bribery and International Commercial Arbitration – The Role of Mandatory Rules and Public Policy" (2012) 43 *Victoria University of Wellington Law Review* 661; Hwang and Lim, *op. cit.*

37 G. Born, *International Commercial Arbitration*, 2nd ed. (Alphen aan den Rijn: Kluwer Law International, 2014) 943–945, 989–991; E. Gaillard and J. Savage (eds.), *Fouchard, Gaillard, Goldman on International Commercial Arbitration* (The Hague: Kluwer Law International, 1999), para. 1517; B. Hanotiau, "What Law Governs the Issue of Arbitrability?" (1996) 12 *Arbitration International* 391; B. Hanotiau, "The Law Applicable to Arbitrability" in A. J. van den Berg (ed.), *Improving the Efficiency of Arbitration Agreements and Awards: 40 Years of Application of the New York Convention* (Alphen aan den Rijn: Kluwer Law International, 1999) 146.

capable of submission to arbitration broadly, without exceptions for corruption. However, in one of the first published cases dealing with corruption in 1963, the sole arbitrator Judge Lagergren held,

> Both parties affirmed the binding effect of their contractual undertakings and my competence to consider and decide their case in accordance with the terms of reference. However, in the presence of a contract in dispute of the nature set out hereafter, condemned by public decency and morality, I cannot in the interest of due administration of justice avoid examining the question of jurisdiction on my own motion. . . .
>
> . . . The arbitrators are not merely prevented from entertaining cases reserved for the ordinary courts, but they will also, in a general manner, not lend their aid to enforce contracts based on grave offence to bonos moros.[38]

The decision has been understood as providing for the nonarbitrability of the issue of corruption and was highly criticized for this outcome.[39] However, while the term *jurisdiction* may have been used ambiguously by the arbitrator, the central pronouncement of the decision was that arbitrators will not lend their authority to enforce contracts that have the purpose of bribing foreign officials.[40] After a careful evaluation of the evidence, the arbitrator came to the conclusion that a substantial part of commissions to be paid to the Claimant were intended to pay bribes to Argentine officials.[41] The arbitrator's rejection of jurisdiction was, probably, triggered by both parties' insistence that they wished to have a decision on the merits of their dispute.[42]

38 ICC Case No. 1110, Award, 1963, (2013) 10 *Revista Brasileira de Arbitragem* 225, 226.

39 A. S. El Kosheri and P. Leboulanger, "L'arbitrage face à la corruption et aux trafics d'influence" (1984) 3 *Revue de l'Arbitrage* 3; A. Sayed, "La question de la corruption dans l'arbitrage commercial international: Inventaire des solutions" (2001) 19 *ASA Bulletin* 653; C. Albanesi and E. Jolivet, "Dealing with Corruption in Arbitration: A Review of ICC Experience" (2013) 24 *ICC International Court of Arbitration Bulletin, Special Supplement "Tackling Corruption in Arbitration"* 27; B. M. Cremades, "Corruption and Investment Arbitration" in G. Aksen, K.-H. Böckstiegel, M. J. Mustill, P. M. Patocchi and A. M. Whitesell (eds.), *Global Reflections on International Law, Commerce and Dispute Resolution, Liber Amicorum in Honour of Robert Briner* (Paris: ICC, 2005) 203.

40 A. Mourre, "Arbitration and Criminal Law: Reflections on the Duties of the Arbitrator" (2006) 22 *Arbitration International* 95.

41 ICC Case No. 1110, Award, 1963, (2013) 10 *Revista Brasileira de Arbitragem* 228.

42 ICC Case No. 1110, Award, 1963, (2013) 10 *Revista Brasileira de Arbitragem* 225.

All subsequent published awards and court decisions dealing with the alleged bribery nature of contracts have either implicitly[43] or explicitly[44] rejected the notion that corruption issues may not be submitted to arbitration. This is in accordance with the widely recognized principle that issues of public policy and illegality may, and indeed must, be addressed by the arbitrators in their merits decision.[45] The opposite view would have the undesirable consequence that the arbitrators could not address questions of illegality and corruption merely because one of the parties *alleges* bribery and corruption, thus depriving the arbitral tribunal of the opportunity to determine the actual facts.

18.3.1.2 Validity of an Arbitration Agreement Contained in a Contract Tainted by Corruption

According to the principle of the separability of the arbitration agreement from the main contract in which it is contained, the invalidity of the main contract does not ipso facto entail the invalidity of the arbitration clause.[46] The application of the principle to corruption issues has been confirmed in several decisions.[47] The illegal purpose of contracts for corruption does not *per se* affect the validity of the parties' consent to arbitration.

[43] ICC Case No. 3916, Award, 1982 in S. Jarvin and Y. Derains, *Collection of ICC Arbitral Awards: 1974–1985*, vol. 1 (Paris, New York: ICC, 1990) 507; Hilmarton (Agent) v. Omnium/Algeria, ICC Case No. 5622, Final Award, 1988, (1994) 19 *Yearbook Commercial Arbitration* 105; K Ltd. v. M S.A., ICC Award, 1989, (1993) 11 *ASA Bulletin* 216.

[44] ICC Case No. 6248, Final Award, 1990, (1994) 19 *Yearbook Commercial Arbitration* 124; National Power Corporation (Philippines) v. Westinghouse (USA), Federal Supreme Court of Switzerland, September 2, 1993, (1994) 12 *ASA Bulletin* 244.

[45] Kreindler, *Competence-Competence, op. cit.*, 249; Born, *International Commercial Arbitration, op. cit.*, 950–952, 1043–1044.

[46] UNCITRAL Model Law on International Commercial Arbitration (adopted in 1985, amended in 2006), Art. 16(1) provides that "the arbitral tribunal may rule on its own jurisdiction, including any objections with respect to the existence or validity of the arbitration agreement. For that purpose, an arbitration clause which forms part of a contract shall be treated as an agreement independent of the other terms of the contract. A decision by the arbitral tribunal that the contract is null and void shall not entail ipso jure the invalidity of the arbitration clause"; Born, *International Commercial Arbitration, op. cit.*, chapter 3.

[47] Premium Nafta Products Limited v. Fili Shipping Company Limited, House of Lords, October 17, 2007, [2007] UKHL 40, para. 35; Fiona Trust & Holding Corporation and Others v. Yuri Privalov and Others, England and Wales Court of Appeal (Civil Division), January 24, 2007, [2007] EWCA Civ 20, paras. 22–41; National Power Corporation (Philippines) v. Westinghouse (USA), Federal Supreme Court of Switzerland, September 2, 1993, (1994)

However, this does not exclude situations where the arbitration clause is tainted by corruption: the abuse of authority by a bribed representative may, depending on the circumstances, also affect the validity of an arbitration agreement if the representative's defective consent to be bound extends to the arbitration agreement. Likewise, the validity of the arbitration agreement may be fully or partly affected if the parties to a contract of bribery inserted specific provisions to ensure the effectiveness of a contract of bribery.[48]

18.3.1.3 Applicable Law

In accordance with a traditional conflicts of laws analysis, the primary reference for determining claims relating to corruption is the law chosen by the parties.[49] The tribunal may also have to consider the law of the seat of arbitration and the law of the place of performance.[50]

The law of the seat of arbitration is relevant because a violation of the seat's public policy may lead to the setting aside of the award[51] The concept of public policy is, in most jurisdictions, narrow and encompasses only basic notions of morality and justice.[52] The courts of some countries apply the still narrower concept of "international public policy" in cases with a foreign element as opposed to their domestic

12 *ASA Bulletin* 244; Y. Banifatemi, "The Impact of Corruption on 'Gateway Issues' of Arbitrability, Jurisdiction, Admissibility and Procedural Issues" in D. Baizeau and R. H. Kreindler (eds.), *Addressing Issues of Corruption in Commercial and Investment Arbitration* (Paris: ICC, 2015) 20–23.

48 *See, e.g.*, the related decision in *Soleimany*, where the parties to a smuggling "partnership" specifically provided that the illegality of the contract would be irrelevant to the rights and duties in the arbitration; Soleimany v. Soleimany, England and Wales Court of Appeal (Civil Division), January 30, 1998, (1999) 24 *Yearbook Commercial Arbitration* 331.

49 Kreindler, *Competence-Competence, op. cit.*, 169–170; Baizeau and Hayes, "The Arbitral Tribunal's Duty and Power to Address Corruption Sua Sponte" *op. cit.*, 232; Hwang and Lim, *op. cit.*

50 Kreindler, *Competence-Competence, op. cit.*, 169–170; Baizeau and Hayes, "The Arbitral Tribunal's Duty and Power to Address Corruption Sua Sponte," *op. cit.*, 233; Hwang and Lim, *op. cit.*

51 UNCITRAL Model Law on International Commercial Arbitration (adopted in 1985, amended in 2006), Art. 34(2)(b)(ii).

52 Kreindler, *Competence-Competence, op. cit.*, 147–149; V. Pavic, "Bribery and International Commercial Arbitration – The Role of Mandatory Rules and Public Policy" (2012) 43 *Victoria University of Wellington Law Review* 661; Hwang and Lim, *op. cit.*; Parsons & Whittemore Overseas Co Inc v. Société Générale de l'Industrie du Papier (RAKTA) and Bank of America, US Court of Appeals, 2nd Circuit, December 23, 1974, 508 F.2d 969.

public policy.[53] The result is that the public policy of the seat of the arbitration will only rarely overrule the application of the law chosen by the parties.

The law of the place of performance may come into play when a State seeks to enforce its public policy through laws claiming to have universal application ("lois de police").[54] The case *OTV v. Hilmarton* is illustrative of the conflict between the laws of the place of performance and the law chosen by the parties. The arbitral tribunal with the seat in Switzerland applied Algerian law to the question of the validity of a brokerage contract despite the parties' choice of Swiss substantive law because the brokerage services were to be performed by Hilmarton in Algeria: "the law of Algeria lays down a general principle which must be respected by all legal systems wishing to fight corruption."[55] Algerian law contained a mandatory rule which prohibited all trading of influence, even in the absence of proof of bribery. Accordingly, the Arbitral Tribunal held that the contract was void by virtue of Algerian law.

The award was subsequently set aside by the Swiss courts. The Swiss Federal Tribunal held that only Swiss law was relevant to the determination of the validity of the contract: "The contract is not in any case illicit, since it would be illicit only if it violated Swiss law. . . . A contract of mere brokerage/negotiation is in no manner contrary to Swiss law."[56] The position expressed by the Swiss courts is prevailing in many jurisdictions: foreign mandatory law cannot supersede the law chosen by the parties,

[53] P. Lalive, "Transnational (or Truly International) Public Policy and International Arbitration" in P. Sanders (ed.), *Comparative Arbitration Practice and Public Policy in Arbitration*, ICCA Congress Series, vol. 3 (Alphen aan den Rijn: Kluwer Law International, 1987), 258; Kreindler, *Competence-Competence, op. cit.*, 128–132; Hwang and Lim, *op. cit.*; Beverly Overseas SA v. Privnedna Bank Zagreb, Federal Supreme Court of Switzerland, March 28, 2001, (2001) 19 *ASA Bulletin* 807.

[54] Hwang and Lim, *op. cit.*; Baizeau and Hayes, "The Arbitral Tribunal's Duty and Power to Address Corruption Sua Sponte," *op. cit.*, 233; P. Mayer, "Mandatory Rules of Law in International Arbitration" (1986) 2 *Arbitration International* 274; Kreindler, *Competence-Competence, op. cit.*, 170–174, 452.

[55] Hilmarton (Agent) v. Omnium/Algeria, ICC Case No. 5622, Final Award, 1988, (1994) 19 *Yearbook Commercial Arbitration* 115, para. 4.

[56] Omnium de Traitement et de Valorisation – OTV (France) v. Hilmarton (UK), Court of Appeal of the Canton of Geneva, November 17, 1989, and Federal Supreme Court of Switzerland, April 17, 1990, (1994) 19 *Yearbook Commercial Arbitration* 221, para. 23.

except in cases where the rule of foreign law is equivalent to the public policy at the seat of arbitration or transnational public policy.[57]

In addition to the analysis under the law chosen by the parties, tribunals sometimes have applied the prohibition of bribery as a rule of transnational public policy.[58] While this characterization is certainly accurate and commendable, it will have little practical relevance as bribery is likely to be illegal under either the law chosen by the parties, the law of the place of performance and the law of the seat of arbitration.[59] In cases other than proven bribery, the tribunal will normally have to apply the relevant domestic law to determine the qualification and legality of contracts prohibited only by certain jurisdictions (e.g., contracts for influence peddling).

18.3.1.4 Civil Law Consequences of Corruption

The civil law consequences depend primarily on the applicable law. Virtually all laws distinguish between the fate of *contracts of corruption* and contracts procured by corruption.

18.3.1.4.1 Contracts of Corruption The principal wishing to obtain business through bribes is generally not willing to be directly connected to the payment of bribes. Funds are typically channeled to office holders by way of intermediaries appearing as "brokers," "agents," and so on who are paid a percentage of the contract value. If the bribery nature of the contract can be established, it is considered unenforceable: A contract having the purpose of bribing holders of authority is null and void.[60] The principle is affirmed by virtually all domestic laws[61] and international

[57] Kreindler, *Competence-Competence, op. cit.*, 171; Baizeau and Hayes, "The Arbitral Tribunal's Duty and Power to Address Corruption Sua Sponte," *op. cit.*, 233; ICC Case No. 12472, Final Award, 2004, (2013) 24 *ICC International Court of Arbitration Bulletin, Special Supplement "Tackling Corruption in Arbitration"* 46, 49; Mitsubishi Motors Corp. v. Soler Chrysler-Plymouth, Inc., US Supreme Court, July 2, 1985, 473 US 614.

[58] World Duty Free Company v. Republic of Kenya, ICSID Case No. ARB/00/7, Award, October 4, 2006, para. 157.

[59] Kreindler, *Competence-Competence, op. cit.*, 177.

[60] V. Pavic, "Bribery and International Commercial Arbitration – The Role of Mandatory Rules and Public Policy" (2012) 43 *Victoria University of Wellington Law Review* 661.

[61] *See, e.g.*, domestic laws in Austria, Germany, Switzerland, the United Kingdom, and the United States.

conventions[62] and has been confirmed by all published decisions.[63] It has also been identified as a rule of transnational public policy.[64]

The facts in the seminal decision of Judge Lagergren in ICC Case No. 1110 may serve as an illustration of the typical scenario: In that case, the principal had retained "Mr. X," an influential businessman well connected with the Argentine government, to devote "efforts and activity towards influencing the placing of orders for the construction and installation of power stations."[65] The arbitrator held that, while the documents drawn up between the parties "bear the semblance of ordinary commercial documents," they actually contemplated the bribing of Argentine officials.[66]

Many laws provide that no restitution for exchanged performances is due.[67] This means that one of the unconscionable parties may keep the benefit of the other parties' performance (e.g., a paid commission) without providing the due "services" to the principal. While this may appear inequitable, it has been suggested that the potential loss of the intended bribe is a deterrent against corruption.[68]

18.3.1.4.2 Contracts Procured by Corruption If the principal obtains a contract through the payment of bribes, the party whose representative has abused his or her power may generally avoid the contract.[69] However,

[62] Council of Europe Civil Law Convention on Corruption (adopted November 4, 1999, entered into force November 1, 2003) ETS No. 174, Art. 8.

[63] ICC Case No. 1110, Award, 1963, (2013) 10 *Revista Brasileira de Arbitragem* 228–229; Establishment of Middle East country X v. South Asian construction Company, ICC Case No. 4145, Interim Award, 1983, (1987) 12 *Yearbook Commercial Arbitration* 102; Hilmarton (Agent) v. Omnium/Algeria, ICC Case No. 5622, Final Award, 1988, (1994) 19 *Yearbook Commercial Arbitration* 111; ICC Case No. 6497, Final Award, 1994, (1999) 24 *Yearbook Commercial Arbitration* 72; Westacre v. Jugoimport, ICC Case No. 7047, Final Award, 1994, (1996) 21 *Yearbook Commercial Arbitration* 91.

[64] M. Scherer, "Circumstantial Evidence in Corruption before International Tribunals" (2002) 2 *International Arbitration Law Review* 29; World Duty Free Company v. Republic of Kenya, ICSID Case No. ARB/00/7, Award, October 4, 2006, paras. 138–157.

[65] ICC Case No. 1110, Award, 1963, (2013) 10 *Revista Brasileira de Arbitragem* 218.

[66] ICC Case No. 1110, Award, 1963, (2013) 10 *Revista Brasileira de Arbitragem* 228.

[67] *See, e.g.*, Allgemeines bürgerliches Gesetzbuch (Austria), §879; Bürgerliches Gesetzbuch (Germany), §817; Schweizerisches Obligationenrecht (Switzerland), Art. 66.

[68] V. Pavic, "Bribery and International Commercial Arbitration – The Role of Mandatory Rules and Public Policy" (2012) 43 *Victoria University of Wellington Law Review* 661.

[69] J. Fernandez Armesto, "The Effects of a Positive Finding of Corruption" in Baizeau and Kreindler (eds.), *Addressing Issues of Corruption*, *op. cit.*, 171; *see, e.g.*, Bürgerliches Gesetzbuch (Germany), §139.

under most laws, the contract is not void ab initio, as its object as such is not illegal, and the victim may choose to waive his right to rescission.[70] The seminal case of *World Duty Free v. Kenya*, a contract-based case submitted to ICSID arbitration, illustrates this point. The investment agreement for the construction and operation of a duty-free complex in Nairobi was obtained by the investor through the payment of US$2 million to the then President of Kenya, Daniel Arap Moi. Unusually in arbitration proceedings, the claimant openly admitted the payment of the bribe at the time characterized as a culturally accepted "gift" in his witness statement. The tribunal concluded that the investment agreement was voidable under the applicable Kenyan law and that, in view of Kenya's timely avoidance of the agreement, the claims had to be dismissed.[71]

The result of the decision is in line with other decisions that treated contracts procured by corruption as voidable.[72] The avoidance of contracts that have been performed over a longer period of time usually entails difficult questions about how the parties may restitute their respective performances.[73]

18.3.2 Corruption in Investment Arbitration

The typical scenario in investment arbitration is different than the discussed settings in commercial arbitration. The investor is usually the claimant pursuing claims based on the violation of treatment standards contained in a bilateral or multilateral investment treaty.[74] In defense against the investor's claims, the host State typically invokes corruption by the investor as a bar to the arbitral tribunal's jurisdiction or to the admissibility of the investor's claims. Corruption is therefore primarily a defensive plea relied upon by the State. In a few cases, the investor has

70 *See, e.g.*, Council of Europe Civil Law Convention on Corruption (adopted November 4, 1999, entered into force November 1, 2003) ETS No. 174, Art. 8(2).

71 World Duty Free Company v. Republic of Kenya, ICSID Case No. ARB/00/7, Award, October 4, 2006, paras. 164, 183.

72 *See, e.g.*, State-Owned Corporation X v. Corporation Y, ICC Case No. 11307, Final Award, 2003, (2008) 33 *Yearbook Commercial Arbitration* 39.

73 *Ibid.*

74 R. Dolzer and C. Schreuer, *Principles of International Investment Law*, 2nd ed. (Oxford: Oxford University Press, 2012) 235–237.

relied on an alleged attempt of the host State to extort bribes as a violation of treaty standards.

18.3.2.1 Corruption as a Bar to Jurisdiction

In the vast majority of investment cases, the parties' consent to arbitration is based on the State's general offer to arbitrate contained in an investment treaty and the investor's acceptance of that offer through the initiation of proceedings or in another unilateral communication ("arbitration without privity").[75] The treaty sets out the State's conditions of consent to arbitration. Typically, investment treaties set forth conditions for qualifying investments, the investor's nationality and different procedural options for the resolution of disputes (e.g., a choice of the investor between ICSID and UNCITRAL arbitration and the domestic courts). In numerous investment treaties, an investment must be made in accordance with the law of the host State to qualify as protected investment.

In the leading decision *Metal-Tech v. Uzbekistan*, the investor brought claims under the Israel-Uzbekistan Bilateral Investment Treaty (BIT).[76] The BIT required that investments be "implemented in accordance with the laws and regulations of the Contracting Party in whose territory the investment is made."[77] Uzbekistan alleged that the tribunal lacked jurisdiction because the investor engaged in corruption and therefore made the investment in violation of Uzbek law.[78] After an extensive evaluation of the evidence, the arbitral tribunal concluded:

> Corruption is established to an extent sufficient to violate Uzbekistan law in connection with the establishment of the Claimant's investment in Uzbekistan. ... Uzbekistan's consent to ICSID arbitration, as expressed in Article 8(1) of the BIT, is restricted to disputes "concerning an investment." Article 1(1) of the BIT defines investments to mean only investments implemented in compliance with local law. Accordingly, the present dispute does not come within the reach of Article 8(1) and is not covered by Uzbekistan's consent.[79]

[75] *Ibid.*, 254–262; J. Paulsson, "Arbitration without Privity" (1995) 10 *ICSID Review – Foreign Investment Law Journal* 232.

[76] Metal-Tech Ltd. v. Republic of Uzbekistan, ICSID Case No. ARB/10/3, Award, October 4, 2013.

[77] Metal-Tech Ltd. v. Republic of Uzbekistan, ICSID Case No. ARB/10/3, Award, October 4, 2013, para. 164.

[78] *Ibid.*, para. 110.

[79] *Ibid.*, paras. 372–373.

If the investment treaty contains a legality requirement, corruption in the establishment of an investment excludes the investment form the scope of jurisdiction of the treaty.[80] It has been submitted that even in the absence of an explicit legality requirement, arbitral tribunals should deny jurisdiction for illegal investments.[81]

A number of tribunals has held that the legality requirement of investment treaties refers to the time when the investment was initially established, and not to the operation of the investment.[82] This view is often supported by the treaty language but is not uncontested. It has been suggested that the obligation of the investor to comply with domestic law is ongoing.[83] This raises the question as to where to draw the line between relatively minor illegality and illegality that affects the protection of the investment under the treaty. Should the investor be penalized with

[80] *See also* Spentex Netherlands, B.V. v. Republic of Uzbekistan, ICSID Case No. ARB/13/26 (unpublished) reported in V. Djanic, "In Newly Unearthed Uzbekistan Ruling, Exorbitant Fees Promised to Consultants on Eve of Tender Process are Viewed by Tribunal as Evidence of Corruption, Leading to Dismissal of All Claims under Dutch BIT," *Investment Arbitration Reporter*, June 22, 2017; for other illegality in the context of the establishment of the investment, *see, e.g.*, Alasdair Ross Anderson and others v. Republic of Costa Rica, ICSID Case No. ARB(AF)/07/3, Award, May 19, 2010; Inceysa Vallisoletana v. Republic of El Salvador, ICSID Case No. ARB/03/26, Award, August 2, 2006; Fraport AG Frankfurt Airport Services Worldwide v. Republic of the Philippines (II), ICSID Case No. ARB/11/12, Award, December 10, 2014, paras. 469–481.

[81] Kreindler, *Competence-Competence, op. cit.*, 375–380; Phoenix Action Ltd v. Czech Republic, ICSID Case No. ARB/06/5, Award, April 15, 2009, para. 101; SAUR International S.A. v. Argentine Republic, ICSID Case No. ARB/04/4, Decision on Jurisdiction and Liability, June 6, 2012, paras. 307–310; Gustav F. W. Hamester GmbH & Co KG v. Republic of Ghana, ICSID Case No. ARB/07/24, Award, June 18, 2010, para. 123.

[82] Metal-Tech Ltd. v. Republic of Uzbekistan, ICSID Case No. ARB/10/3, Award, October 4, 2013, para. 193; Inceysa Vallisoletana v. Republic of El Salvador, ICSID Case No. ARB/03/26, Award, August 2, 2006, para. 242; Fraport AG Frankfurt Airport Services Worldwide v. Republic of the Philippines (I), ICSID Case No. ARB/03/25, Award, August 16, 2007, para. 345; Gustav F. W. Hamester GmbH & Co KG v. Republic of Ghana, ICSID Case No. ARB/07/24, Award, June 18, 2010, para. 127; Teinver S.A., Transportes de Cercanías S.A. & Autobuses Urbanos del Sur S.A. v. Argentine Republic, ICSID Case No. ARB/09/1, Decision on Jurisdiction, December 21, 2012, para. 318; Vannessa Ventures Ltd. v. Bolivarian Republic of Venezuela, ICSID Case No. ARB(AF)/04/6, Award, January 16, 2013, para. 167; Z. Douglas, "The Plea of Illegality in Investment Treaty Arbitration" (2014) 29 *ICSID Review – Foreign Investment Law Journal* 155; A. P. Llamzon and A. C. Sinclair, "Investor Wrongdoing in Investment Arbitration: Standards Governing Issues of Corruption, Fraud, Misrepresentation and Other Investor Misconduct" in A. J. van den Berg (ed.), *Legitimacy: Myths, Realities, Challenges* (Alphen aan den Rijn: Kluwer Law International, 2015), 500.

[83] Kreindler, *Competence-Competence, op. cit.*, 388–390.

the denial of treaty protection for, for example, a small "facilitation" payment in the course of the operation of the investment if routine and legal services of the State cannot be obtained otherwise? The question is delicate because the State is responsible for the environment it creates for investors, and the investor cannot "escape" once the investment is made. However, bribery of public officials during the operation of the investment in order to obtain an extension of the investment is, it is submitted, equivalent to bribery at the initiation of the investment and should be treated in the same way.

18.3.2.2 Corruption and the Admissibility of Investor Claims

According to numerous decisions, investments tainted by illegality lose the substantive protection under investment treaties if the investment is tainted by illegality.[84] Investments tainted by corruption therefore lose treaty protection even if the treaty contains no explicit legality requirement. The tribunal in *Churchill v. Indonesia* held in relation to the related issue of fraud:

> The Tribunal cannot but hold that all the claims before it are inadmissible. This conclusion derives from the facts analyzed above, which demonstrate that the claims are based on documents forged to implement a fraud aimed at obtaining mining rights. . . . The seriousness, sophistication and scope of the scheme are such that the fraud taints the entirety of the Claimants' investment in the EKCP. As a result, the general principle of good faith and the prohibition of abuse of process entail that the claims before this Tribunal cannot benefit from investment protection under the Treaties.[85]

The exact contours and foundations of the inadmissibility of illegal investments are unclear. A number of tribunals have relied on the principles of good faith and abuse of process as the basis for the denial of protection.[86]

[84] Plama Consortium Limited v. Republic of Bulgaria, ICSID Case No. ARB/03/24, Award, August 27, 2008, paras. 138–146; Churchill Mining and Planet Mining Pty Ltd v. Republic of Indonesia, ICSID Case No. ARB/12/40 and 12/14, Award, December 6, 2016, paras. 488–506, 528; Hesham Talaat M. Al-Warraq v. The Republic of Indonesia, Final Award, December 15, 2014, paras. 645–647; Phoenix Action Ltd v. Czech Republic, ICSID Case No. ARB/06/5, Award, April 15, 2009, para. 101; Gustav F. W. Hamester GmbH & Co KG v. Republic of Ghana, ICSID Case No. ARB/07/24, Award, June 18, 2010, para. 123.

[85] Churchill Mining and Planet Mining Pty Ltd v. Republic of Indonesia, ICSID Case No. ARB/12/40 and 12/14, Award, December 6, 2016, para. 528.

[86] Phoenix Action Ltd v. Czech Republic, ICSID Case No. ARB/06/5, Award, April 15, 2009, paras. 106–113; Plama Consortium Limited v. Republic of Bulgaria, ICSID Case No. ARB/03/24, Award, August 27, 2008, paras. 138–146; Churchill Mining and Planet Mining Pty

Other tribunals relied on the "clean hands doctrine" to justify the denial of treaty claims based on illegal investments.[87]

The tribunal in *Niko v. Bangladesh* expressed doubts as to whether the clean hands doctrine was part of customary international law.[88] In addition, the tribunal held that the application of the clean hands doctrine required a relationship of reciprocity between the relief sought and the violation of host State law.[89] The claimant in this case had admitted bribery in Canadian proceedings, but these actions were unrelated to the joint venture agreement at issue in the arbitration.[90] The tribunal concluded that the admitted bribery was no ground for refusing to examine the merits of the dispute. The tribunal in *Yukos v. Russia* denied the existence of the clean hands doctrine as a general principle of law.[91] Instead, it held that there is an implied condition that investments that were created illegally will not be protected independently of the specific treaty language.[92] According to the tribunal, this condition is limited to the establishment of the investment and does not apply to illegality during the operation of the investment.[93]

18.3.2.3 Investor Claims Based on Corrupt Demands of Host State Officials

While corruption is typically alleged by the respondent State, investors have also invoked corruption in support of treaty claims. In *EDF*

Ltd v. Republic of Indonesia, ICSID Case No. ARB/12/40 and 12/14, Award, December 6, 2016, paras. 488–506.

[87] Hesham Talaat M. Al-Warraq v. The Republic of Indonesia, Final Award, December 15, 2014, paras. 645–648; Fraport AG Frankfurt Airport Services Worldwide v. Republic of the Philippines (II), ICSID Case No. ARB/11/12, Award, December 10, 2014, paras. 328–333.

[88] Niko Resources (Bangladesh) Ltd. v. Bangladesh Petroleum Exploration & Production Company Limited ("Bapex") and Bangladesh Oil Gas and Mineral Corporation ("Petrobangla"), ICSID Case No. ARB/10/18, Decision on Jurisdiction, August 19, 2013, paras. 478–482.

[89] *Ibid.*, para. 483.

[90] Niko Resources (Bangladesh) Ltd. v. Bangladesh Petroleum Exploration & Production Company Limited ("Bapex") and Bangladesh Oil Gas and Mineral Corporation ("Petrobangla"), ICSID Case No. ARB/10/18, Decision on Jurisdiction, August 19, 2013, paras. 484– 485.

[91] Yukos Universal Limited (Isle of Man) v. The Russian Federation, UNCITRAL, PCA Case No. AA 227, Final Award, July 18, 2014, para. 1358.

[92] *Ibid.*, para. 1351.

[93] *Ibid.*, para. 1355.

v. Romania, the investor alleged that Romanian officials solicited bribes from the investor, which the investor refused to pay. According to the investor, its lease contract for the operation of duty-free businesses at the Bucharest airport was not extended for no other reason than the refusal to pay bribes.[94] The corruption claims were ultimately dismissed by the tribunal because the investor had not sufficiently established the demand to pay bribes. However, the tribunal held that, had the investor succeeded in proving its allegations, this would have constituted a violation of the fair and equitable treatment standard:

> The Tribunal shares the Claimant's view that a request for a bribe by a State agency is a violation of the fair and equitable treatment obligation owed to the Claimant pursuant to the BIT, as well as a violation of international public policy, and that "exercising a State's discretion on the basis of corruption is a … fundamental breach of transparency and legitimate expectations."[95]

While so far no investor in investment treaty proceedings has succeeded with corruption claims, the principle that the State is liable for the solicitation of bribes from investors seems well established. The statement in *World Duty Free v. Kenya* that the bribe solicitation of the Kenyan President is not attributable to the State, which was analyzed by the tribunal under Kenyan law, is not applicable in the context of attribution under international law.[96] According to Article 7 of the ILC's Articles on State Responsibility, actions of an organ of a State are attributed also when the organ exceeds its authority or contravenes instructions. The solicitation of a bribe is always connected to the public authority of the organ and not to the person in his or her private capacity, as otherwise there would be no reason to pay a bribe. It is, therefore, submitted that the solicitation of a bribe is attributable to the State and triggers its international responsibility in the absence of exceptional circumstances.[97]

[94] EDF (Services) Limited v. Romania, ICSID Case No. ARB/05/13, Award, October 8, 2009, para. 69.

[95] *Ibid.*, para. 221.

[96] World Duty Free Company v. Republic of Kenya, ICSID Case No. ARB/00/7, Award, October 4, 2006, para. 185.

[97] *See* the criticism of World Duty Free Company v. Republic of Kenya, ICSID Case No. ARB/00/7, Award, October 4, 2006, by Kreindler, *Competence-Competence, op. cit.*, 292–293.

18.4 The Proof of Corruption

Virtually all corruption cases hinge on the proof of corruption. Except in the rare cases where corruption is admitted,[98] parties wishing to rely on corruption allegations face the difficult task of persuading the tribunal of the accuracy of their contention. Their task is not aided by the fact that corrupt schemes are usually given the appearance of legality. Witnesses may not be forthcoming for fear of prosecution by the criminal authorities. Evidentiary issues such as the burden of proof, the standard of proof, the probative value of circumstantial evidence and the arbitral tribunal's power to address corruption on its own motion are of acute relevance in corruption cases.

18.4.1 The Burden of Proof

Most tribunals have applied the well-established rule that each party has the burden of proving the facts relied on to support its claim or defense also in connection with corruption allegations.[99] This means that a party relying on corruption as a claim or defense will normally have the burden of proving this allegation.

Commentators have suggested to shift the burden of proof if there was prima facie evidence of corruption because of the inherent difficulty of prove corruption.[100] In situations where the party opposing corruption

[98] World Duty Free Company v. Republic of Kenya, ICSID Case No. ARB/00/7, Award, October 4, 2006, paras. 110, 111, 121; Azpetrol International Holdings B.V., Azpetrol Group B.V. and Azpetrol Oil Services Group B.V. v. Republic of Azerbaijan, ICSID Case No. ARB/06/15, Award, September 8, 2009, para. 6; J. W. Yackee, "Investment Treaties and Investor Corruption: An Emerging Defense for Host States?" (2012) 52 *Virginia Journal of International Law* 723.

[99] Metal-Tech Ltd. v. Republic of Uzbekistan, ICSID Case No. ARB/10/3, Award, October 4, 2013, para. 237; The Rompetrol Group N.V. v. Romania, ICSID Case No. ARB/06/3, Award, May 6, 2013, para. 178, ICC Case No. 6497, Final Award, 1994, (1999) 24 *Yearbook Commercial Arbitration* 71; Westacre v. Jugoimport, ICC Case No. 7047, Final Award, 1994, (1996) 21 *Yearbook Commercial Arbitration* 93–94; ICC Case No. 13384, Final Award, 2005, (2013) 24 *ICC International Court of Arbitration Bulletin, Special Supplement "Tackling Corruption in Arbitration"* 62; ICC Case No. 14878, Final Award, 2008, (2013) 24 *ICC International Court of Arbitration Bulletin, Special Supplement "Tackling Corruption in Arbitration"* 92 para. 5.

[100] K. Mills, "Corruption and Other Illegality in the Formation and Performance of Contracts and in the Conduct of Arbitration Relating Thereto" in A. J. van den Berg (ed.),

fails to provide adequate explanations for the prima facie appearance of corruption, the tribunal should draw adverse inferences form this failure.[101] This reasoning was followed by some tribunals. In ICC Case 12990, the tribunal held that certain indications of corruption created the "presumption" of illegality.[102] The tribunal in the ICC Case 6497 considered the shifting of the burden of proof appropriate in principle. However, in the circumstances of the case it declined to do so as also the party alleging corruption failed to fully cooperate to establish the facts.[103] ICC Tribunal 18215 held that a shifting of the burden of proof was appropriate exceptionally if the alleging party brought forward relevant but inconclusive evidence.[104]

18.4.2 The Standard of Proof

The authorities on the applicable standard of proof for corruption allegations are divided. A number of tribunals in investment treaty cases have applied the higher standard of "clear and convincing evidence." For instance, the tribunal in *EDF v. Romania* stated, "The seriousness of the accusation of corruption in the present case, considering that it involves officials at the highest level of the Romanian government at the time, demands clear and convincing evidence."[105] The tribunals in *Siag v. Egypt* and *Saba Fakes v. Turkey* also subscribed to the view that the standard of proof for allegations of illegality was high.[106]

International Commercial Arbitration: Important Contemporary Questions (Alphen aan den Rijn: Kluwer Law International, 2003) 295; C. Partasides, "Proving Corruption in International Arbitration: A Balanced Standard for the Real World" (2010) 25 *ICSID Review – Foreign Investment Law Journal* 47 at 60.

101 C. Partasides, "Proving Corruption in International Arbitration: A Balanced Standard for the Real World" (2010) 25 *ICSID Review – Foreign Investment Law Journal* 47 at 60.

102 ICC Case No. 12990, Final Award, 2005, (2013) 24 *ICC International Court of Arbitration Bulletin, Special Supplement "Tackling Corruption in Arbitration"* 52, paras. 251–253.

103 ICC Case No. 6497, Final Award, 1994, (1999) 24 *Yearbook Commercial Arbitration* 74–75.

104 East Mediterranean Gas v. Egyptian General Petroleum, Egyptian Natural Gas Holding and Israel Electric Corporation, ICC Case No. 18215, Final Award, December 4, 2015, para. 568.

105 EDF (Services) Limited v. Romania, ICSID Case No. ARB/05/13, Award, October 8, 2009, para. 221.

106 Waguih Elie George Siag and Clorinda Vecchi v. The Arab Republic of Egypt, ICSID Case No. ARB/05/15, Award, June 1, 2009, paras. 325–326; Saba Fakes v. Republic of Turkey, ICSID Case No. ARB/07/20, Award, July 14, 2010, para. 131.

In many of the older commercial cases, tribunals have equally often requested a heightened standard of proof. In *Himpurna*, the tribunal required "clear and convincing" evidence and suggested that that it would be "contrary to all experience that a State-owned institution whose director is appointed by the head of State engages in activities contrary to the mandatory law of that country."[107] Other tribunals have requested a "high standard of proof,"[108] proof "beyond doubt,"[109] or "with certitude."[110]

A number of tribunals have, however, rejected to apply a higher standard of proof in cases involving illegality. While these cases did not directly deal with corruption allegations, their conclusions are also apposite in the context of corruption. In *Fraport v. Philippines I*, the tribunal rejected the application of a higher standard of proof for illegality because the tribunal's task was not "a determination of crime" but the determination of "whether an economic transaction by a German company was made 'in accordance' with Philippine law."[111] Similar statements were made by the tribunals in *Libananco v. Turkey*[112] and *Rompetrol v. Romania.*[113] In commercial cases, tribunals were equally satisfied with applying the normal standard of proof. In ICC Case 12990, the tribunal concluded from circumstantial evidence, including the agent's excessive remuneration, that the contract at issue was actually a contract of corruption and thus void. It did not apply the requirement of a higher degree of conviction.[114] Likewise, in ICC Case 13515, the tribunal determined form the totality of

[107] Himpurna California Energy Ltd. v. PT. (Persero) Perusahaan Listruik Negara, Final Award, May 4, 1999, (1999) 25 *Yearbook Commercial Arbitration* 42–43, para. 114.

[108] ICC Case No. 13384, Final Award, 2005, (2013) 24 *ICC International Court of Arbitration Bulletin, Special Supplement "Tackling Corruption in Arbitration"* 62, para. 67.

[109] Hilmarton (Agent) v. Omnium/Algeria, ICC Case No. 5622, Final Award, 1988, (1994) 19 *Yearbook Commercial Arbitration* 112.

[110] ICC Case No. 12472, Final Award, 2004, (2013) 24 *ICC International Court of Arbitration Bulletin, Special Supplement "Tackling Corruption in Arbitration"* 51, para. 95 (translation from French language: "avec certitude").

[111] Fraport AG Frankfurt Airport Services Worldwide v. Republic of the Philippines (I), ICSID Case No. ARB/03/25, Award, August 16, 2007, para. 399.

[112] Libananco Holdings Co. Limited v. Republic of Turkey, ICSID Case No. ARB/06/8, Award, September 2, 2011, para. 125.

[113] The Rompetrol Group N.V. v. Romania, ICSID Case No. ARB/06/3, Award, May 6, 2013, paras. 181–182.

[114] ICC Case No. 12990, Final Award, 2005, (2013) 24 *ICC International Court of Arbitration Bulletin, Special Supplement "Tackling Corruption in Arbitration"* 53 *et seq.*

the circumstances that a distribution agreement was in fact a façade for corrupt payments without requiring a higher standard of proof.[115]

There are, in the author's view, powerful arguments for the proposition that arbitral tribunals should apply the same standard of proof for all allegations of fact, including corruption allegations: First, there is no general evidentiary rule according to which "more serious" allegations require a higher standard of proof.[116] Second, both parties have the right to have the facts of the case properly established. Open or implied presumptions when weighing the evidence raise serious issues of equal treatment. Third, implied in the proposition that a serious allegation requires a higher evidentiary standard is that a finding of corruption or illegality has more serious consequences than a finding of breach of contract. While it is true that corruption carries a high stigma, a tribunal's establishment of the facts should not be driven by the legal consequences this may entail, but by an unbiased weighing of the evidence. In arbitration, the consequences are, in any event, civil and not criminal.[117] Fourth, many tribunals openly or impliedly base their decision on the consideration that corruption or illegality is inherently implausible. As a matter of empirical evidence, this is simply not correct.[118]

18.4.3 Evaluation of the Evidence: "Red Flags" and the Practice of Arbitral Tribunals

Most arbitrators were, until recently, reluctant to deal with the issue of corruption. Commentators went as far as suggesting that "corruption has found a safe harbour in arbitration."[119] The conclusions in some of the older cases that no corruption could be established seem, in view of unexplained high commissions and the absence of proof of services

[115] ICC Case No. 13515, Final Award, 2006, (2013) 24 *ICC International* Court *of Arbitration Bulletin, Special Supplement "Tackling Corruption in Arbitration"* 66.

[116] C. Partasides, "Proving Corruption in International Arbitration," *op. cit.*, at 57.

[117] A. Menaker, "Proving Corruption in International Arbitration" in Baizeau and Kreindler (eds.), *Addressing Issues of Corruption, op. cit.*, 90.

[118] *Ibid.*; *see also* Khvalei criticizing the application of a higher standard of proof for corruption allegations: V. Khvalei, "Using Red Flags to Prevent Arbitration from Becoming a Safe Harbour for Contracts that Disguise Corruption" (2013) 24 *ICC International Court of Arbitration Bulletin, Special Supplement "Tackling Corruption in Arbitration"* 15 at 17 *et seq.*

[119] V. Khvalei, "Using Red Flags," *op. cit.*, at 17.

performed by highly paid intermediaries, strained.[120] In more recent cases, extensive and careful discussion of the evidence by arbitral tribunals displays a higher awareness of corruption and the forms it may take.

Arbitrators are increasingly relying by the ICC's publication of "red flags" indicating a risk of corruption.[121] The risk factors identified by the ICC include the following: (1) the agent has been suggested by a public official, (2) the agent's commission is disproportionate in relation to the services to be rendered, (3) the only qualification of the agent is influence over public officials, (4) flawed background or reputation of the agent, and (5) the agent requests the payment of a significant part of the commission before or immediately upon award of the contract.

The tribunal in *Metal-Tech v. Uzbekistan* relied on "red flags" in support of its determination that the investor had engaged in corruption: The Claimant had engaged consultants which received high payments of more than US$4 million as fees, whereas the initial capital investment of the claimant in the project was little more than US$2 million.[122] The consultants had connections with public officials, were not qualified for the tasks for which they were engaged and were unable to provide proof of services performed under their consultancy agreements. Taking into account these circumstances, the tribunal concluded that the facts imposed the conclusion that the consultants were to facilitate the establishment of Metal-Tech's investment in Uzbekistan. Similar risk factors were, for instance, relied upon in the ICC cases 12990 and 13941.[123] The inability of the agent to furnish proof of services rendered has been given special weight in several cases.[124]

[120] *See, e.g.*, Westacre v. Jugoimport, ICC Case No. 7047, Final Award, 1994, (1996) 21 *Yearbook Commercial Arbitration* 91–92, where the tribunal held that an unusually high commission did not imply illicit intentions of the parties.

[121] International Chamber of Commerce, *ICC Guidelines on Agents, Intermediaries and Other Third Parties*, 2010, https://iccwbo.org/publication/icc-guidelines-agents-intermediaries-third-parties-2010/.

[122] Metal-Tech Ltd. v. Republic of Uzbekistan, ICSID Case No. ARB/10/3, Award, October 4, 2013, para. 293.

[123] ICC Case No. 12990, Final Award, 2005, (2013) 24 *ICC International Court of Arbitration Bulletin, Special Supplement "Tackling Corruption in Arbitration"* 52; ICC Case No. 13914, Final Award, 2008, (2013) 24 *ICC International Court of Arbitration Bulletin, Special Supplement "Tackling Corruption in Arbitration"* 77.

[124] Metal-Tech Ltd. v. Republic of Uzbekistan, ICSID Case No. ARB/10/3, Award, October 4, 2013, paras. 204–207; ICC Case No. 12990, Final Award, 2005, (2013) 24 *ICC International Court of Arbitration Bulletin, Special Supplement "Tackling Corruption in Arbitration"* 54.

The evaluation of risk factors in the context of corruption is, however, still far from predictable. In *Kim v. Uzbekistan*, the respondent alleged that a payment of US$8 million to the daughter of the President of Uzbekistan was actually a bribe and invoked a number of so-called red flags in relation to that payment. The tribunal found that respondent had not succeeded in establishing corruption. The tribunal reasoned that, inter alia, the proof of corruption would have required to show that the daughter of the President, was an official of Uzbekistan. It seems curious to require a direct payment to an official despite notoriety of the fact that corrupt officials will seek to avoid traceable direct payments of bribes.

18.4.4 Duties of Arbitrators

The attitude of arbitrators in relation to their investigative duties has considerably evolved over the last decades. In ICC Case 7047 (*Westacre*), the arbitrators still held that "the word 'bribery' is clear and unmistakable. If the defendant does not use it in his presentation of the facts an arbitral tribunal does not have to investigate."[125]

It seems now to be the prevailing view that arbitrators should use their investigative powers ex officio if they have suspicions of corruption even if the issue has not been pleaded by the parties.[126] It has been convincingly argued that "moral and public policy arguments are entirely consistent with – and perhaps even a necessary – corollary of – the arbitral tribunal's basic mandate to evaluate the parties' claims under the applicable law, which includes public policy provisions."[127] Arbitrators failing to address suspicions of corruption risk making themselves accomplices of corruption.[128]

The arbitral practice shows that *sua sponte* investigations by arbitral tribunals can be determinative of the issue of corruption. In *Metal-Tech v. Uzbekistan*, the arbitral tribunal ordered the production of documents and information, asked precise factual statements and ordered the

125 Westacre v. Jugoimport, ICC Case No. 7047, Final Award, 1994, (1996) 21 *Yearbook Commercial Arbitration* 93–94.

126 ICC Case No. 13515, Final Award, 2006, (2013) 24 *ICC International Court of Arbitration Bulletin, Special Supplement "Tackling Corruption in Arbitration"* 71.

127 Baizeau and Hayes, "The Arbitral Tribunal's Duty and Power to Address Corruption Sua Sponte," *op. cit.*, 237.

128 *Ibid.*, 236.

production of additional witness statements.[129] The failure of the claimant to produce adequate documentation of the intermediary retained by it seems to have been decisive for the tribunal's conclusion that the claimants had engaged in bribing officials. In ICC Case No. 1110, the arbitrator's insistence on investigating the parties actual relationship despite the insistence of the parties that their contract was enforceable led to the arbitrator's finding of corruption.[130]

However, subject to the law of the seat of the arbitration, there is no general duty of arbitrators to report suspicions of corruption to the national authorities.[131] Arbitration laws, rules and guidelines contain, to the extent reviewed by the author, no obligation to report corruption to the authorities. Likewise, it seems that most domestic legislations abstain from obliging arbitrators to report suspicions of corruption.

18.5 Conclusion

Given the pervasiveness of corruption in parts of international business, corruption will likely remain an important topic in international arbitration. The issue was the subject of abundant theorization in the legal literature. For some time, this discussion seemed to be disconnected from the practice of arbitral tribunals. Awareness of the toxic effects of corruption and the public policy considerations of the issue seem only very recently to have penetrated the practice of international tribunals. Recent awards like *Metal-Tech v. Uzbekistan* display a careful analysis of evidentiary issues in connection with corruption and of the legal effects of a finding of corruption.

129 N. G. Ziadé, "Addressing Allegations and Findings of Corruption" in Baizeau and Kreindler (eds.), *Addressing Issues of Corruption*, *op. cit.*, 121; C. B. Lamm, B. K. Greenwald and K. M. Young, "From World Duty Free to Metal-Tech: A Review of International Investment Treaty Arbitration Cases Involving Allegations of Corruption" (2014) 29 *ICSID Review – Foreign Investment Law Journal* 328; Metal-Tech Ltd. v. Republic of Uzbekistan, ICSID Case No. ARB/10/3, Award, October 4, 2013, paras. 85–99.

130 ICC Case No. 1110, Award, 1963, (2013) 10 *Revista Brasileira de Arbitragem* 225–226; A. Philip, "Arbitration, Corruption, Money Laundering and Fraud: The Role of the Tribunals" in K. Karsten and A. Berkeley (eds.), *Arbitration: Money Laundering, Corruption and Fraud* (Paris: ICC, 2003), 151.

131 Baizeau and Hayes, "The Arbitral Tribunal's Duty and Power to Address Corruption Sua Sponte," *op. cit.*, 236; A. Mourre, "Arbitration and Criminal Law," *op. cit.*

The practice of international tribunals is, however, far from uniform. In relation to evidentiary issues, the sensorium of arbitrators for "red flags" and plausibility seems to be markedly different in cases that are, in appearance, comparable. An increasingly negative public discourse about international arbitration is fueled by concerns that private arbitrators are incapable of safeguarding public policy objectives. The ability of arbitrators to appropriately address allegations or suspicions of corruption will be key to maintain arbitration as an accepted method of dispute resolution involving the public interest.

19 The 'Problem' of Costs in Arbitration

Controlling, Allocating and Funding Costs

Matthew Hodgson and Jae Hee Suh*

19.1 Introduction

19.1.1 The 'Problem' of Costs

When an international commercial dispute arises, the cost of resolving it may be as important to the parties as the merits of the claims themselves. Indeed, the cost of resolving a dispute may suffice, in some circumstances, to discourage a claim's prosecution in a formal proceeding or to thwart its proper defense.[1]

Despite the wide acceptance of international commercial arbitration as the preferred method for resolving cross-border disputes,[2] it is not without its critics. One key 'problem' is financial in nature – specifically, costs.

Costs topped the list of 'worst' features of international arbitration in the 2018 Queen Mary Survey.[3] Furthermore, other features that go to the efficiency of arbitration as a process (including lack of effective sanctions during the arbitral process, lack of speed, and lack of insight into arbitrators' efficiency) placed highly.[4] Indeed, costs could be seen as a key threat to the success of international commercial arbitration as a transnational justice system.

* The views expressed herein are the authors' and do not represent those of the firm. The authors would like to thank Junianto James Losari for his assistance with the research for this chapter.

1 E. A. Schwartz, 'The ICC Arbitral Process, Part IV: The Costs of ICC Arbitration' (1993) 4 *ICC International Court of Arbitration Bulletin* 8.

2 For example, *see* Queen Mary University of London and White & Case, '2018 International Arbitration Survey: The Evolution of International Arbitration (the 2018 Queen Mary Survey)', 2. 97 per cent of the respondents affirmed that international arbitration is the preferred method of resolving cross-border disputes.

3 This is consistent with the finding in Queen Mary University of London and White & Case, '2015 International Arbitration Survey: Improvements and Innovations in International Arbitration' (the 2015 Queen Mary Survey), 7.

4 *Ibid.*

19.1.2 How Much Does an Arbitration Cost?

With the spotlight on costs, arbitral institutions have started reviewing and publishing data on their 'arbitration costs' or procedural costs (i.e. institutional costs and tribunal fees). The median values[5] of 'arbitration costs' of major arbitral institutions range between approximately US$30,000 and US$100,000.[6]

However, these procedural costs are often only a small part of the overall costs a party incurs. 'Party costs' (including legal fees, costs of experts and witnesses, and other associated costs) make up the bulk (83 per cent on average) of the overall costs of arbitral proceedings, with the tribunal's fees and the ICC administrative fees only representing 15 per cent and 2 per cent (on average) of overall costs, respectively.[7]

Data on 'party costs' are scarce, principally due to the fact that most commercial arbitral awards are confidential. One rare example is the 2011 Chartered Institute of Arbitrators (CIArb) Survey, which considered 254 arbitrations conducted between 1991 and 2010. According to the survey, 'party costs' averaged around £1,348,000 in common law countries, and £1,521,000 in civil law countries.[8]

More data are available regarding investment treaty arbitration. According to a 2017 study conducted by one of the authors, the median of 'party costs' claimed in 324 treaty awards and 52 annulment decisions publicly available as of 31 May 2017 was US$3.375 million for the

[5] Mean figures are not very representative of the overall data set where there are a number of outliers (as were the case in the cost studies). Hence, median figures are presented here.

[6] The London Court of International Arbitration (LCIA): The median arbitration costs of 224 LCIA cases wherein a final award was rendered in the four years between 1 January 2013 and 31 December 2016 was US$97,000. The median for sole-arbitrator cases was US$60,000 and the median for three-member tribunal cases was US$200,000 (*see* LCIA, 'Facts and Figures – Costs and Duration: 2013–2016' (2017)); the Singapore International Arbitration Centre (SIAC): The median arbitration costs of 98 SIAC cases wherein a final award was rendered between 1 April 2013 and 31 July 2016 was US$29,567. The median for sole-arbitrator cases was US$27,941 and the median of three-member tribunal cases was US$80,230 (*see* SIAC, 'SIAC Releases Costs and Duration Study' (2016)); the Hong Kong International Arbitration Centre (HKIAC): The median arbitration costs of 62 HKIAC cases wherein a final award was issued between 1 November 2013 and 31 December 2017 was US$62,537. No further breakdown is available (*see* HKIAC, 'Costs and Duration' (2018)).

[7] ICC Commission Report, 'Decisions on Costs in International Arbitration' (2015) 2 *ICC Dispute Resolution Bulletin* (the 2015 ICC Report), 3.

[8] A difference of nearly 13 per cent. *See* CIArb, 'CIArb Costs of International Arbitration Survey 2011' (the 2011 CIArb Survey), 2.

claimants (investors) and US$2.793 million for the respondents (States).[9] Some caution must be exercised when comparing commercial to investment treaty arbitration (the latter frequently involving complex jurisdictional disputes and large sums). Nonetheless, for high-value commercial arbitrations, anecdotal experience suggests costs may be broadly comparable in commercial and investment treaty arbitrations.

Costs of arbitration are clearly significant, and can even be considered prohibitive in certain cases. Indeed, it is not impossible to imagine a situation where the costs are almost equal to, or exceed the amount in dispute, resulting in a pyrrhic victory for the successful party (subject to any allocation of costs by the tribunal, as discussed later in this chapter).

19.1.3 What Contributes to Costs?

It is not possible to pinpoint a single factor; there are however a few usual suspects. The increasingly complex and multi-jurisdictional nature of the disputes referred to arbitration is no doubt a factor. Other factors include the increasing number of jurisdictional and procedural disputes and the use of dilatory and other tactics by the parties causing inefficiencies.

19.1.4 Responses to the 'Problem' of Costs

Different stakeholders have strived to address the costs of arbitration in various ways. Arbitral institutions have introduced features aimed at cutting costs and increasing efficiency. Many of the recent innovations to the major arbitral institutions' rules have in fact been prompted by this aim. Tribunals are also considering and adopting these features more actively.

There is also a widely accepted power of the tribunal to allocate costs of the arbitration, or a subset thereof (for example, costs of a specific phase or an application). A party may therefore recover some or all of its costs at the tribunal's discretion.

Parties have been looking at external sources to fund all or part of their costs by deploying not only more 'traditional' methods of funding such as

[9] M. Hodgson and A. Campbell, 'Damages and Costs in Investment Treaty Arbitration Revisited' (2017) *Global Arbitration Review*.

insurance, loans and alternative fee arrangements, but also third-party funding (TPF), which has quickly turned from a relatively obscure option only available in a handful of common law jurisdictions to an integral part of the global arbitral landscape.

This chapter addresses the financial aspects of international commercial arbitration by focussing on (1) control on costs (Section 19.2), (2) allocation of costs (Section 19.3) and (3) funding of costs (Section 19.4).

19.2 Part 1: Control on Costs

In the face of increased competition in attracting users, arbitral institutions have introduced features to control costs and increase the efficiency of arbitral proceedings under their arbitral rules. Similarly, the efficiency of an arbitrator is an increasingly important criterion for parties in tribunal selection, with many arbitrators adopting features aimed at controlling parties' costs.

19.2.1 Control on Tribunal Fees

19.2.1.1 *Ad Valorem* System of Remuneration

Many arbitral institutions (including SIAC, ICC, the Arbitration Institute of the Stockholm Chamber of Commerce (SCC), the Korean Commercial Arbitration Board (KCAB) and the Asian International Arbitration Centre (AIAC)) adopt an *ad valorem* system, under which tribunals' remuneration is calculated based on the amount in dispute instead of hourly rates. One exception is LCIA, which calculates tribunals' remuneration using an hourly rate subject to a cap. HKIAC allows parties to choose between an *ad valorem* system and an hourly rate system, with the latter as the default.

An *ad valorem* system in theory removes the potential financial interest an arbitrator may have in prolonging the arbitration. However, it is not necessarily cheaper than the hourly rate system; the relative complexity of the dispute as compared to its size will no doubt have a significant bearing on this comparison, as will any delaying tactics adopted by the parties and the efficiency of the individual arbitrators.

19.2.1.2 Institution's Power to Increase or Decrease Tribunal Fees

Most arbitral institutions' rules using an *ad valorem* system provide that the institution shall fix or ascertain tribunal fees by reference to its schedule of fees. In doing so, institutions may take the efficiency of arbitrators into account, and this is intended to encourage tribunals to conduct the proceedings efficiently.

Indeed, Article 2(2) of Appendix III of the 2021 ICC Rules[10] expressly provides that the ICC Court, in setting the tribunal's fees (either pursuant to the fee schedule or at its discretion where the amount in dispute is not stated) shall consider the following factors: (1) the diligence and efficiency of the arbitrators; (2) the time spent; (3) the speed of the proceedings; (4) the complexity of the dispute and (5) the timeliness of the submission of the draft award.[11] The 2021 ICC Note[12] also states that when the tribunal has conducted the arbitration expeditiously, the ICC Court may increase the tribunal's fees above the amount that it would otherwise consider fixing. On the other hand, if the tribunal submits the draft award after the prescribed time limit, the ICC Court may lower the fees by 5 to more than 20 per cent or more based on the length of the delay, unless it is satisfied that the delay is attributable to factors beyond the tribunal's control or to exceptional circumstances.[13]

Furthermore, some arbitral institutions' rules expressly state that the institution may depart from the applicable range indicated by the fee schedule in certain cases. For example, Article 38(2) of the 2021 ICC Rules provides that the ICC Court may fix the fees of the tribunal at a figure higher or lower than that which would result from the application of the relevant scale 'should this be deemed necessary due to the exceptional circumstances of the case'. Article 44(7) of the 2018 Vienna International Arbitral Centre Rules of Arbitration and Mediation (the 2018 VIAC Rules) goes further and confers on the VIAC Secretary-General the power to increase or decrease the tribunal's fees by up to 40 per cent vis-à-vis the schedule of fees based on, in particular, the tribunal's efficient or inefficient conduct of the proceedings.

The ICC is unique amongst the major institutions in providing for scrutiny of draft awards submitted by tribunals to the ICC Court. The 2021 ICC Note states that, if the Court's scrutiny process is delayed, other

[10] 2021 ICC Arbitration Rules (in force as from 1 January 2021) (the 2021 ICC Rules).

[11] *Ibid.*, Article 2(2) of Appendix III.

[12] ICC, 'Note to Parties and Arbitral Tribunals on the Conduct of the Arbitration under the ICC Rules of Arbitration' (2021) (the 2021 ICC Note).

[13] *Ibid.*, paras. 155 and 161.

than by circumstances that are beyond the ICC Court's control, the ICC Court's administrative expenses may be reduced by up to 20 per cent depending on the length of the delay.[14]

19.2.2 Control on 'Party Costs'

19.2.2.1 Case Management Powers of the Tribunal

All major arbitral institutions' rules expressly link the tribunal's broad case management powers to the need for cost-effectiveness of the process or avoidance of unnecessary delay or expense (or both).[15] However, the goal of efficiency needs to be balanced with the need for due process (or fairness).[16] Major arbitration laws also impose on tribunals the obligation to ensure due process.[17] Currently, there appears to be a widespread perception by arbitration users that tribunals have not sufficiently utilised the case management tools to discourage and address inefficiency.[18] This perceived lack of tribunals' control over the arbitral process has been attributed by some to the so-called due process paranoia, or tribunals' condoning of parties' dilatory tactics or other inefficient behaviour in the fear of potential challenge against their awards based on lack of due process.[19] Although it would be

[14] *Ibid.*, para. 170.

[15] 2016 Arbitration Rules of SIAC (effective 1 August 2016) (the 2016 SIAC Rules), Rule 19; 2021 ICC Rules, *supra* note 11, Article 22; 2018 Administered Arbitration Rules of HKIAC (effective 1 November 2018) (the 2018 HKIAC Rules), Article 13; 2020 LCIA Arbitration Rules (effective 1 October 2020) (the 2020 LCIA Rules), Article 14; 2018 Arbitration Rules of AIAC (effective 9 March 2018) (the AIAC Rules), Article 17(1); 2017 Arbitration Rules of SCC (effective 1 January 2017) (the 2017 SCC Rules), Article 23.

[16] *See* (1) Article 13 of the 2018 HKIAC Rules, which states that 'the arbitral tribunal shall adopt suitable procedures for the conduct of the arbitration in order to avoid unnecessary delay or expense ... provided that such procedures ensure equal treatment of the parties and afford the parties a reasonable opportunity to present their case'; also (2) Article 22 of the 2021 ICC Rules; (3) Article 19 of the 2016 SIAC Rules; (4) Article 14 of the 2020 LCIA Rules; (5) Article 23(2) of the 2017 SCC Rules.

[17] Model Law on International Commercial Arbitration 1985 (United Nations Commission on International Trade Law (UNCITRAL)) UN Doc A/40/17, Annex I, Article 18 states 'the parties shall be treated with equality and each party shall be given a full opportunity of presenting his case'; *see also* Section 33 of the Arbitration Act 1996 (of England) – Chapter 23 (the English Arbitration Act), which provides a 'due process' obligation mirroring that in Article 14 of the 2020 LCIA Rules.

[18] 2018 Queen Mary Survey, *supra* note 2.

[19] *Ibid.*

difficult to justify such concerns in the context of arbitration-friendly jurisdictions where the risk of national courts interfering with even robust case management decisions of the tribunal is low, such concerns may be more legitimate if, for example, enforcement in a more interventionist jurisdiction is contemplated.

The broad case management powers of the tribunal may be supplemented with other guidelines and practice notes that can aid the tribunal in making good case management decisions, without stifling the tribunal's discretion to tailor the conduct of the proceedings to the needs of each case. Such guidelines could also help alleviate the 'due process paranoia' discussed above by providing a formal backing for procedural decisions aimed at promoting efficiency.

The ICC has been particularly proactive in this regard and has published a number of notes.[20] Furthermore, since 2012, the ICC Rules also incorporate, at Appendix IV, the case management techniques that may be adopted by tribunals and parties to control time and costs. The suggested techniques include bifurcation, control on document production, limits on the length of submissions, use of telephone and video conferencing, and use of pre-hearing conference.

19.2.2.2 Expedited Procedure

Most major arbitral institutions' rules now provide for an 'expedited procedure' whereby parties may apply to the institution to have arbitral proceedings conducted on an expedited basis (typically around 6 months, unless the institution grants an extension) and by a sole arbitrator. However, such application may only be made in limited circumstances where (1) the value is below a certain threshold[21] or (2) the parties so agree. Under the 2018 HKIAC Rules and the 2016 SIAC Rules, the additional ground of (3) 'exceptional urgency' is also available. It is worth noting that LCIA has not adopted a form of expedited procedure. Instead, parties can

[20] *E.g.* ICC Commission Report, Techniques for Controlling Time and Costs in Arbitration (ICC, 2012); ICC Commission on Arbitration and ADR, Effective Management of Arbitration: A Guide for In-House Counsel and Other Party Representatives (ICC, 2014).

[21] The applicable threshold under the rules is as follows: SG$6 million under the 2016 SIAC Rules; US$3 million under the 2021 ICC Rules; KRW 500,000,000 under the 2016 International Arbitration Rules of KCAB (effective 1 June 2016) (the 2016 KCAB Rules); HK$25 million under the 2018 HKIAC Rules (as published in the HKIAC website).

apply to LCIA for expedited formation of the tribunal 'in the case of exceptional urgency'.[22]

Based on anecdotal evidence, expedited procedures are not invariably cost-saving, as sometimes the truncated timeline may simply force the parties to complete the requisite work scope and incur the relevant costs over a shorter timeframe, without substantially reducing the overall costs. There is no 'one size fits all' when it comes to arbitration procedure, and the utility of expedited procedure will depend on the circumstances of the individual case.

19.2.2.3 Summary Procedure

The lack of 'summary procedure' was a potentially significant factor militating against the use of arbitration in lieu of courts, but this is no longer the case. In 2016, SIAC became the first major commercial arbitral institution to introduce a form of summary procedure in its Rule 29, which provides that a party may apply to the tribunal for the early dismissal of a claim or defence on the basis that it is (1) manifestly without legal merit or (2) manifestly outside the jurisdiction of the tribunal.[23] The 2018 HKIAC Rules also provides for a similar procedure at Article 43, in respect of points of law and facts that (1) are manifestly without merit; (2) are manifestly outside the arbitral tribunal's jurisdiction or (3) even if assumed to be correct, will not result in an award in favour of the party advancing them.[24]

[22] 2020 LCIA Rules, *supra* note 16, Article 9A. Under this article, if the application is successful, the LCIA Court may abridge any period for constitution of the tribunal in the parties' arbitration agreement.

[23] The tribunal may in its discretion allow the application to proceed. If the application is allowed to proceed, the tribunal must make an order or award on the application within 60 days of the date of the filing of the application unless the SIAC Registrar extends the time in exceptional circumstances. There is no set deadline by which an application for early dismissal should be made, although the reference to 'early' in its title suggests that it is intended to be applied shortly after the relevant claim or defence is raised and timing could be a factor tribunals may consider in deciding whether an application may proceed.

[24] Unlike the SIAC procedure discussed above (which does not have express timelines by which the underlying applications must be made), the HKIAC procedure expressly requires that a request for early determination should be made 'as promptly as possible' after the relevant points of law or fact are submitted, unless the tribunal directs otherwise. Once a request has been made, the tribunal must decide whether it should proceed within 30 days, and if the request is allowed to proceed, the tribunal should make its order or award within 60 days from the decision to proceed. The respective timeframes may be extended by the parties' agreement or by HKIAC.

Whilst the 2021 ICC Rules do not contain a separate procedure for early or summary dismissal of claims, the 2021 ICC Note (discussed above) does clarify that an 'expeditious determination of a manifestly unmeritorious claim or defence' is a procedural tool that is available under the ICC Rules. This Note provides guidance on how the tool may be utilised within the scope of an ICC tribunal's broad case management powers under Article 22 of the 2021 ICC Rules.[25]

There is no formal definition of what *manifest* means in the context of the above procedures. Tribunals may glean guidance from the existing treaty jurisprudence on the early dismissal procedure for claims that are manifestly without legal merit under Article 41(5) of the ICSID Rules,[26] which is often cited as the inspiration for the above procedures. According to the tribunal in *Trans-Global v. Jordan*, 'the ordinary meaning of the word ['manifest'] requires the respondent to establish its objection clearly and obviously, with relative ease and dispatch. The standard is thus set high. Given the nature of investment disputes generally, the Tribunal nonetheless recognises that this exercise may not always be simple. ... The exercise may thus be complicated; but it should never be difficult'.[27] The tribunal in *PNG v. Papua New Guinea* also emphasised the strictness of the test, explaining that the 'manifest' standard was 'intended to capture cases which are clearly and unequivocally unmeritorious' and hence, 'a case is not clearly and unequivocally unmeritorious if the Claimant has a tenable arguable case'.[28]

Article 39 of the 2017 SCC Rules provides a different, widely worded form of summary procedure, whereby a party may request that the tribunal decide 'one or more issues of fact or law by way of summary procedure, without necessarily undertaking every procedural step that might

[25] 2021 ICC Note, *supra* note 13, paras. 109–114.

[26] Rules of Procedure for the Institution of Conciliation and Arbitration Proceedings under the Convention on the Settlement of Investment Disputes between States and Nations of Other States (the ICSID Convention) (effective 10 April 2006) (the ICSID Rules).

[27] Trans-Global Petroleum, Inc. v. Hashemite Kingdom of Jordan, ICSID Case No. ARB/07/25, Decision on the Respondent's Objection Pursuant to Rule 41(5) of the ICSID Arbitration Rules, 12 May 2008, para. 88.

[28] PNG Sustainable Development Program Ltd. v. Independent State of Papua New Guinea, ICSID Case No. ARB/13/33, Decision on the Respondent's Preliminary Objections pursuant to ICSID Arbitration Rule 41(5), 28 October 2014, para. 88. *See more generally* M. Potestà, 'Preliminary Objections to Dismiss Claims That Are Manifestly without Legal Merit under Rule 41(5) of the ICSID Arbitration Rules' in Crina Baltag, *ICSID Convention after 50 Years: Unsettled Issues* (Kluwer Law International, 2016), 249–272.

otherwise be adopted for the arbitration'. The procedure is available throughout the duration of the proceedings and the request may concern issues of jurisdiction, admissibility or merits.

Even where the applicable arbitral rules do not expressly provide for summary procedure, it is generally accepted that use of such procedure should be within the wide procedural discretion of tribunals available under most arbitral rules (explained in Section 19.2.2.1), provided that the requirement for due process (or fairness) can be ensured.[29] However, striking the appropriate balance between the need for a quick, relatively informal disposition of issues and the need to ensure each party's right to be heard can be especially challenging in the context of summary procedure. In this respect, express endorsement of summary procedures by institutions, even non-binding, could provide additional comfort for tribunals that adoption of such procedures would not make their awards susceptible to a challenge based on the lack of 'due process'.

19.2.3 Future Solutions

Arbitral institutions' efforts to control costs are continuing at full speed. Looking forward, some of the following factors are likely to drive the direction of future innovations in the field.

19.2.3.1 Increased Use of Guidelines

The enshrinement of innovations such as expedited procedures and summary procedures in arbitral institutions' rules (and thereby in parties' arbitration agreements) is a welcome development. The flexibility of arbitration as a process is a key driver behind its popularity, and it is crucial that tribunals retain their wide procedural discretion. To control the financial implications of arbitration without stifling this flexibility, the increased use of non-binding guidelines, rather than the imposition of numerous rigid rules, would be preferable.

19.2.3.2 Tribunals' Power to Encourage Cost Efficiency on Parties' Part

The need to control and discourage dilatory tactics has been recognised for some time, and the increased adoption of an express provision allowing

[29] *E.g.* 2020 LCIA Rules, *supra* note 16, Article 14; 2010 UNCITRAL Arbitration Rules, Article 17.

tribunals to take dilatory tactics into account in cost allocation is one way in which institutions have responded to this need. However, some users remain dissatisfied and suggest that tribunals apply monetary sanctions.[30] Whilst such monetary sanctions should arguably be within tribunals' powers under most rules, it remains to be seen whether institutions would expressly endorse such sanctions.

19.2.3.3 Increased Use of Technology

The use of electronic bundles, faster and more accurate translation services and conducting hearings by video conference have already facilitated reduction of costs.[31] There are however more potentially significant developments under way, such as the use of artificial intelligence to conduct legal research or even assist in the decision-making process,[32] although some concerns have been voiced on the latter.[33]

19.3 Part 2: Allocation of Costs

For most users of arbitration, the potential 'price' of an arbitration is not limited to one's own costs. In light of the tribunals' power to allocate costs, the scope and use of such powers are topics of great practical significance to the parties, and have received heightened attention in recent years.

19.3.1 Power to Allocate Costs

It is accepted that the law of the seat and the chosen arbitral rules govern a tribunal's power to allocate costs as between the parties.[34] Subject to any

[30] 2018 Queen Mary Survey, *supra* note 2, p. 8.

[31] *Ibid.*, pp. 31–32; *e.g.* 2018 HKIAC Rules, *supra* note 16, Article 13.1, expressly identifies the effective use of technology as a factor to be considered by a tribunal when determining suitable procedures for the conduct of an arbitration.

[32] *See generally* in T. Snider, S. Dilevka and C. Aknouche, 'Artificial Intelligence and International Arbitration: Going Beyond E-mail' (2018) *Al Tamimi & Co Law Update*.

[33] *E.g.* A. Ross, 'Will Artificial Intelligence Eliminate the Human Factor?' (2018) *Global Arbitration Review*.

[34] The contrary view that the governing law of the contract governs a tribunal's power to allocate costs has been expressed by some commentators, including certain United States state courts, but this now appears to be the minority view (*see e.g.* G. B. Born, *International Commercial Arbitration*, 2nd ed. (Kluwer Law International, 2014), p. 3099; 2015 ICC Report, *supra* note 8, p. 51).

mandatory requirements of the law of the seat,[35] parties may also agree on the allocation of costs. Some jurisdictions are more prescriptive on the question of cost allocation than others:

1. Section 61 of the English Arbitration Act provides that, subject to any agreement of the parties, a tribunal may make an award allocating the costs of the arbitration as between the parties, and sets out the general principle that costs awarded by an arbitral tribunal should follow the event (called the 'costs follow the event' (CFTE) approach) except where this appears inappropriate. Furthermore, section 60 of the Act invalidates a pre-dispute agreement that a party must pay its own costs (in whole or in part) in any event.[36]
2. Section 74 of the Hong Kong Arbitration Ordinance[37] also expressly provides that a tribunal may include an award of costs of arbitral proceedings (including fees and expenses of the tribunal) in its award, and, like the English Act, also specifies that a pre-dispute agreement that the parties, or any of the parties, must pay their own costs in respect of arbitral proceedings is void. Unlike in its English equivalent however, there is no presumption in favour of the CFTE approach in the Ordinance.
3. In Singapore, it is likewise accepted that a tribunal has power to award costs in the absence of the parties' agreement to the contrary. Such power is not expressly identified, but is consistent with various provisions of the Singapore International Arbitration Act (the SIAA).[38]
4. As for the United States, the Federal Arbitration Act[39] is silent on a tribunal's power to award costs. However, the 2000 Uniform Arbitration Act, a model statute for state-level arbitration law that has been adopted with varying levels of modification by a number of states,

[35] *See* the discussion of England and Hong Kong below.

[36] However, an agreement that the losing party will pay the costs would not be invalid as it is not an agreement that a particular party will pay the costs in any event: Roger Shashoua v. Mukesh Sharma [2009] EWHC 957 at [12] and [29].

[37] The Arbitration Ordinance (Cap. 609 of the Laws of Hong Kong) (effective 1 June 2011) (the Hong Kong Arbitration Ordinance).

[38] International Arbitration Act (Cap. 143A, 2002 Rev Ed) (the SIAA), ss. 12, 10(7), 10(8) and 20.

[39] FAA (9 USC). FAA is the main applicable act governing arbitration in the United States, despite that fact that each state may have its own state arbitration legislation. Where there is inconsistency, FAA prevails.

provides at Section 21(b) that there shall be no award of costs where (1) there is no agreement by the parties on costs or (2) the law does not allow such award 'in a civil action involving the same claim'.

Similarly, there is no uniform approach in institutional rules:

1. Some arbitral rules provide for a rebuttable presumption that costs should follow the event (the CFTE approach) or should be allocated based on the degree of success, unless particular circumstances call for a different approach.[40]
2. Other rules provide for a wider discretion for an arbitral tribunal to award costs.[41]

19.3.2 Approaches to Allocation

19.3.2.1 The Apportionment Based on Success, the Pay-Your-Own-Way Approach and the Current Practice

Subject to the relevant provisions in the applicable law and chosen arbitral rules and any agreement by the parties, tribunals have the discretion to allocate costs. Broadly speaking, the two main approaches to allocation of costs in international commercial arbitration are (1) apportionment based on success, such as the traditional CFTE approach whereby the losing party is ordered to bear all of the costs of the arbitration (including the successful party's share) or a more nuanced apportionment based on relative success of the parties and (2) the pay-your-own-way approach, whereby the parties bear their own legal and other costs and share the procedural costs (i.e. the tribunal fees and institutional costs). Traditionally, the former approach has been favoured in England and a number of other common law jurisdictions such as Hong Kong and Singapore, and the latter approach has been adopted primarily in the United States, Japan and China.

[40] 2010 UNCITRAL Arbitration Rules, Article 42; 2020 LCIA Rules, *supra* note 16, Article 28.4; China International Economic and Trade Arbitration Commission (CIETAC) Arbitration Rules (effective 1 January 2015) (the 2014 CIETAC Rules), Article 52(2); AIAC Rules, *supra* note 16, Article 42(1).

[41] 2016 SIAC Rules, *supra* note 16, Rule 35.1; 2021 ICC Rules, *supra* note 11, Article 38(5); 2018 HKIAC Rules, *supra* note 16, Article 34; 2016 KCAB Rules, *supra* note 22, Article 53; 2017 SCC Rules, *supra* note 16, Article 49(6); ICSID Convention, *supra* note 27, Article 61(2).

Arguments of principle are made in support of both approaches. The commonly cited reasons in support of apportionment based on success include indemnification of the winning party at the expense of the losing party (on the basis that, if the claimant is entitled to the remedy at law, the claimant should not have to suffer any expense) and deterrence of frivolous, unmeritorious claims.[42] On the other hand, it has been argued that the pay-your-own-way approach is preferable as (1) given the outcome of any litigation is often uncertain, it would be unfair to punish the losing party for merely defending or prosecuting a lawsuit and (2) if losing parties were forced to bear their opponents' costs and fees, the poor might be unjustly discouraged from instituting actions.[43]

Surveys suggest that a majority of tribunals do apportion costs based on success. For example, the 2012 Queen Mary Survey[44] reports that tribunals allocate costs according to the result in a significant majority of arbitrations (80 per cent).[45] The 2015 ICC Report similarly finds that, despite the fact that a majority of major arbitral institutions' rules contain no presumption in favour of the recovery of costs by the successful party, the majority of arbitral tribunals broadly adopt the CFTE approach as a starting point, thereafter adjusting the allocation of costs as considered appropriate. Costs were allocated based on result in a majority of ICC and the International Centre for Dispute Resolution awards considered by the report, and in 91 per cent of HKIAC awards and 90 per cent of SIAC awards, although these rules do not contain a presumption in favour of the CFTE approach.[46]

19.3.2.2 Definition of 'Success'

Determining the relative success of the parties is not always clear cut, especially in complex disputes involving multiple causes of action,

42 For example, M. Wirth, *Best Practices in International Arbitration* (Association Suisse de l'arbitrage, 2006); M. Savola, 'Awarding Costs in International Commercial Arbitration' (2017) 63 *Scandinavian Studies in Law* 275, at 292.

43 *Ibid.*, Savola, at 216.

44 Queen Mary University of London and White & Case, '2012 International Arbitration Survey: Current and Preferred Practices in the Arbitral Process (the 2012 Queen Mary Survey)'.

45 *Ibid.*, at 40. Furthermore, 85 per cent of the respondents favoured allocation of costs by result. The respondents had a slight preference for apportionment of costs over the CFTE approach (45 per cent vs. 40 per cent).

46 2015 ICC Report, *supra* note 8, para. 13.

counterclaims, set-off claims, multiple contracts and/or multiple parties. Even in relatively 'straightforward' cases with two parties, limited causes of action and no or limited counterclaims, determining who is the 'successful' party may not be easy if, for example, the claimant exaggerated its claim and was awarded only a relatively small portion of the amount it originally claimed, or if the claimant raised numerous arguments of which only a small portion were successful. In these cases, even though there is an award 'in favour of' the claimant, it could be argued that the claimant is not necessarily the 'successful' party when compared to the respondent and the respondent should not be ordered to pay the claimant's costs.

The 2015 ICC Report finds that, in cases of less-than-full recovery by claimants, different approaches have been taken by tribunals. It suggests that tribunals may

1. award all of a party's reasonable costs if a claimant or respondent succeeded in its core or primary claim or outcome;
2. apportion costs on a claim-by-claim or issue-by-issue basis according to relative success and failure; or
3. apportion success against the amount of damages originally claimed or the value of the property in dispute.[47]

The report also notes that whatever approach is used, (1) it is important to consider differences in complexity and importance of different issues and (2) there may be additional assessment based on conduct (see Section 19.3.2.3).

This nuanced approach to ascertaining the relative 'success' of parties is arguably preferable to the simplistic approach of categorising a claimant that is awarded *any* sum as the prevailing party. Although each case should be assessed on its own facts, if, for example, the respondent succeeded in substantially reducing the value of the claim or if the claimant only managed to vindicate a small subset of its numerous arguments, it is difficult to see how the claimant should be awarded all or most of its costs on the basis that there was still an award in its favour. This approach may also accord better with the theoretical underpinnings of apportionment based on success (discussed above).

[47] *Ibid.*, para. 61.

19.3.2.3 Relevance of Parties' (Mis)conduct

There is a broad consensus that parties' conduct should be taken into account in allocating costs, as a factor that is separate and independent from the outcome of the case. Some arbitral institutions' rules have express provisions to this effect:

1. Article 28.4 of the 2020 LCIA Rules allows tribunals to take parties' and their authorised representatives' conduct (including any cooperation in facilitating the proceedings as to time and costs and any non-cooperation resulting in undue delay and unnecessary expense) into account when awarding costs.
2. Similarly, Article 38.5 of the 2021 ICC Rules provides that the tribunal may take into account such circumstances as it considers relevant, including the extent to which each party has conducted the arbitration in an expeditious and cost-effective manner.[48] It is entirely within the tribunal's discretion to find that a party's improper conduct or bad faith is the sole determinative factor in its decisions on costs.[49]

Even where there is no express provision to this effect in the arbitral rules, it is now uncontroversial that parties' conduct is a factor tribunals may consider in exercising their broad discretion to award costs under most major arbitral institutions' rules (e.g. the 2018 HKIAC Rules and the 2016 SIAC Rules).

Tribunals' power to take parties' conduct into consideration in cost allocation is widely considered as a check on dilatory and other tactics that increase costs (see Section 19.2.3.2). The ICC Commission on Arbitration recommends the use of allocation of costs to discourage inefficient behaviour, such as excessive document requests, excessive legal argument, excessive cross-examination, dilatory tactics, failure to comply with procedural orders, unjustified interim applications and so on.[50]

Reported cases and anecdotal evidence consistently suggest that tribunals have embraced this tool. For example, in ICC Case No. 7453 of 1994, the tribunal ordered the first defendant to pay the entire costs of the arbitration, as well as the claimant's entire legal costs and out-of-pocket expenses because the first defendant's conduct was 'dilatory from the

[48] *See also* 2017 SCC Rules, *supra* note 16, Article 49(6).

[49] 2015 ICC Report, *supra* note 8, para. 61.

[50] 2018 ICC Report, *supra* note 21, para. 82.

beginning until the end of the proceedings and the conduct was obstructive, and it was calculated to be obstructive, of the Tribunal in carrying out its task. Much extra and unnecessary work was caused thereby for everyone concerned'.[51]

19.3.3 What Costs Are, and Should Be, Recoverable?

19.3.3.1 Applicable Definitions

National arbitral legislation and arbitral institutions' rules contain broad definitions of what costs fall within the ambit of tribunals' power to award costs. Some have no express definitions at all. Hence, there is much room for interpretation, and potential disagreement. For example, Section 59 of the English Arbitration Act provides that costs of arbitration include (1) the arbitrators' fees and expenses, (2) the fees and expenses of any arbitral institution concerned and (3) the legal or other costs of the parties.[52] Section 74 of the Hong Kong Arbitration Ordinance contains similar language, while the SIAA contains no definition of recoverable costs.

The arbitral institutions' rules exhibit a similar degree of prescription. Articles 28.1 and 28.3 of the 2020 LCIA Rules refer to two types of costs that are subject to the tribunal's power to award costs, namely 'Legal Costs' (legal or other expenses incurred by a party), and 'Arbitration Costs' or procedural costs of the LCIA and the tribunal. Article 38.1 of the 2021 ICC Rules defines 'costs of the arbitration' subject to allocation to include (1) fees and expenses of arbitrators; (2) ICC administrative expenses; (3) experts' fees appointed by the tribunal and (4) 'reasonable legal and other costs incurred by the parties for the arbitration'.[53]

[51] Reported in J. J. Arnaldez, Y. Derains and D. Hascher, *Collection of ICC Arbitral Awards 1996–2000 – Recueil des sentences arbitrals de la CCI* (Kluwer Law International, 2003),111.

[52] D. S. J. Sutton, J. Gill, and M. Gearing, *Russell on Arbitration*, 24th ed. (London: Sweet & Maxwell, 2015), 6–131. *Russell* explains that the third type of costs, also known as the costs of reference, comprises all costs properly and reasonably incurred by either party in preparing and presenting their case in the arbitration, including (1) costs in rebutting the case, (2) costs of legal or lay representation, (3) expenses of fact witnesses, (4) expert witness' fees, (5) costs of negotiating and settling the terms of the submission to arbitration, (6) conditional fee arrangements in relation to arbitration proceedings or (7) appropriate uplift that fulfils the reasonableness test.

[53] Each Rule 35.2 of the 2016 SIAC Rules and Article 34 of the 2018 HKIAC Rules adopt similar definitions of 'recoverable costs' to the ICC Rules.

19.3.3.2 Where Do the Limits Lie?

These broad definitions (e.g. legal and 'other' costs) naturally raise the question of whether some less traditional forms of costs can and should be included in a tribunal's costs award. In practice, the question is resolved at the tribunal's discretion, subject to the overriding requirement of 'reasonableness' (whether express in the applicable rules and law or implied).[54] The recoverability of the following categories of costs has been debated, although there has been some move towards consensus in respect of at least some items.

19.3.3.2.1 Costs Incurred before or after Arbitration Proceedings A number of commentators, including Hanotiau, opine that only expenses that were 'necessary for the preparation of the case' as well as 'directly linked to the filing of the arbitration' are considered costs of arbitration, and costs of 'preliminary mediation or conciliation' will fall outside the scope.[55] Similarly, the future costs of enforcement are not generally recoverable within the arbitral proceedings, although they may be recoverable at the forum of enforcement.

19.3.3.2.2 In-House Costs In-house lawyers' costs are increasingly treated in a similar fashion to those of external lawyers, provided the costs can be proved and were incurred in connection with the arbitration.[56] This seems to reflect the modern reality that many companies devote a significant amount of internal resources to prepare for arbitration both before and after instructing external counsel. In this respect, time sheet or other documentation of the activity of the lawyer may be necessary to establish

[54] Some arbitral institutions' rules (*e.g.* 2018 HKIAC Rules, 2016 SIAC Rules and 2021 ICC Rules) expressly state that 'reasonable' costs shall be recoverable but do not define reasonableness. It has been suggested that a common-sense way of assessing reasonableness is to assess whether the costs are reasonable and proportionate to the amount in dispute or value of any property in dispute and/or the costs have been proportionately and reasonably incurred (2015 ICC Report, *supra* note 8, paras. 63–70). Eventually, the tribunal has discretion to decide on whether or not a party will recover its costs in full.

[55] B. Hanotiau, 'The parties' costs of arbitration' in Y. Derains and R. H. Kreindler (eds.), *Evaluation of Damages in International Arbitration* (Paris: ICC Publication No. 668, 2006), 214.

[56] T. H. Webster and M. W. Bühler, *Handbook of ICC Arbitration*, 3rd ed. (London: Sweet & Maxwell, 2014), 37–47.

the claim.[57] There is also nothing in principle that prohibits recovery of other in-house costs (such as executives' time, and time spent by internal witnesses) incurred for an arbitration. Some tribunals have awarded in-house costs (such as in-house lawyers' costs) insofar as they were necessary, did not unreasonably overlap with external counsel's fees, were substantiated in sufficient detail to be distinguished from ordinary staffing expenses, and were reasonable in amount.[58]

19.3.3.2.3 Costs of Funding Recoverability of the costs of funding has been subject to much debate. The 2018 Queen Mary Survey reports that the participants were almost evenly split as to whether a successful party who is in receipt of external funding should be able to recover any contingency or success fees as party of a costs order in their favour.[59] Despite the controversy, a number of tribunals have awarded such costs. The 2015 ICC Report states that funding costs may be recoverable in certain circumstances.[60] In *Essar Oilfield v. Norscot*,[61] the English High Court refused to set aside an award of costs of TPF, on the basis that such costs can be seen as falling under the category of 'other costs' under the English Arbitration Act and the 1998 version of the ICC Rules. Furthermore, the 2018 HKIAC Rules expressly authorise tribunals to take TPF arrangements into account in determining the costs of the arbitration.[62]

Where an award of such costs is made, the overriding criterion of reasonableness may act as an important check, and prevent or limit the recovery of additional fees if deemed unreasonable in the circumstances.[63]

[57] *Ibid.*, pp. 47–49.

[58] 2015 ICC Report, *supra* note 8, para. 74.

[59] 2018 Queen Mary Survey, *supra* note 2, p. 26. The result was 52 per cent saying yes and 48 per cent saying no.

[60] 2015 ICC Report, *supra* note 8, paras. 92–93.

[61] Essar Oilfield Services Ltd v. Norscot Rig Management Pvt Ltd [2016] EWHC 2361 (Comm) (Essar Oilfield v. Norscot).

[62] 2018 HKIAC Rules, *supra* note 16, Article 34.4. Outside the context of commercial arbitration, Rules 33.1 and 35 of the Investment Arbitration Rules of SIAC (effective 1 January 2017) (the SIAC Investment Arbitration Rules) also allow the tribunal to take TPF arrangements into account in allocating costs.

[63] International Council for Commercial Arbitration (ICCA), *Report of the ICCA-Queen Mary Task Force on Third-Party Funding in International Arbitration* (ICCA, 2018) (the 2018 ICCA Report), 158–159. In its report, ICCA suggests that important factors in assessing reasonableness would be whether (1) the respondent's conduct has caused the impecuniosity of the claimant; (2) the claimant had no other option but to seek funding from a third-party funder in order to pursue its arbitration claim; and (3) the respondent knew that the claimant had funding.

The potential recoverability of TPF has also prompted some commentators to argue that terms regarding the amount payable to the funder should be disclosed to enable the counterparty to ascertain its potential exposure in the event of an adverse costs award (discussed further in Section 19.4.4.1).

19.3.3.2.4 Costs of Ancillary Proceedings and Breach of an Arbitration Agreement It appears that costs of ancillary proceedings are not generally accepted as recoverable costs of arbitration and should instead be claimed and allocated in the relevant local fora.[64] However, in some cases, these costs may be claimed as damages for breach of the arbitration agreement, provided that there is no double recovery (i.e. the amount of costs already recovered from the relevant local fora are taken into account in quantifying the damages claim). For example, costs incurred in respect of local litigation commenced in breach of an arbitration agreement and costs of anti-suit proceedings may be claimed as such damages. The right to damages in such cases is generally governed by the substantive law of the arbitration agreement.

Depending on the applicable law, seeking interim relief (as opposed to substantive, final relief) from a forum other than the court of the seat may amount to a breach of an arbitration agreement. In *Evergreen Marine v. Fast Shipping*, the English High Court opined that, by agreeing to submit disputes to arbitration in England, the parties had impliedly agreed that, as a general proposition, applications for ancillary relief were to be made only to the arbitral tribunal or the English court as the supervisory court[65] but 'a party may exceptionally be entitled to seek interim relief in some court other than that of the seat if for practical reasons the application can only sensibly be made there, provided that the proceedings are not a disguised attempt to outflank the arbitration agreement'.[66] The court noted that such exceptional circumstances include, for example, the fact that assets may be located in another jurisdiction and interim relief may be appropriate to seek to freeze or secure assets in aid of the arbitral proceedings.[67]

64 Hanotiau, *supra* note 56, p. 214.
65 Evergreen Marine v. Fast Shipping [2014] EWHC 4893 (QB), at [8] and [11].
66 *Ibid.*, at [10].
67 *Ibid.*, at [11]. In *Evergreen*, no exceptional circumstances could be made out and the application for interim relief in a foreign court (outside the seat) was deemed to be a breach of the parties' arbitration agreement justifying the grant of anti-suit relief.

Furthermore, where an arbitration agreement expressly incorporates arbitral institutions' rules, the breach of the arbitral rules may be treated as the breach of the arbitration agreement itself. For example, in the English Commercial Court case of *Konkola Copper Mines v. U&M Mining Zambia Ltd*, the failure to pay the deposit due to the LCIA was deemed to be a breach of the arbitration agreement, for which an award of damages could be made.[68]

19.3.3.2.5 Potential Effect of *Essar Oilfield v. Norscot*?

Whilst *Essar Oilfield v. Norscot* (discussed above) concerned the costs of TPF in particular, the court also opined that 'other costs' in the context of arbitration are to be construed to include costs that 'relate to the arbitration and are . . . for the purposes of [the arbitration]' and were 'incurred in order to bring or defend the claim in question'.[69] When the recoverability of a novel or traditionally controversial type of costs is in issue, this dictum may provide support for a broad interpretation of the 'other costs' category based on the function of the relevant costs. However, the overriding requirement of reasonableness may act as an effective check on recoverability. It is not yet clear whether this dictum would have the impact of *broadening* the scope of recoverable costs, particularly given the controversy around the decision.

19.4 Part 3: Funding of Costs

The increased concerns about costs have led to an increased focus on sources of external funding, and a more pronounced presence of the providers of such funding. In recent years, TPF has received particular attention. We use the term TPF to refer to funding provided by a natural or legal person who is not a party to the dispute (or its affiliate or representative), but who enters into an agreement with a party (or its

[68] Konkola Copper Mines v. U&M Mining Zambia Ltd [2014] EWHC 2374 (Comm), at [30]. It would be advisable for such a damages claim to be flagged early on if possible, in order to pre-empt any objection based on lack of sufficient notice of the claim and/or breach of any requirement under the applicable rules for introduction of new claims (*e.g.* the rules relating to introduction of new claims after the signing of the Terms of Reference in the 2021 ICC Rules).

[69] Essar Oilfield v. Norscot, *supra* note 62, para. 58.

affiliate or representative) to finance all or part of all the costs of the proceedings, in exchange for remuneration or reimbursement based on the outcome of the dispute.[70]

Although the proliferation of TPF in the context of international commercial arbitration is a relatively recent phenomenon in most jurisdictions, this type of funding has gained popularity and recognition at a dramatic speed.[71] It is now common for parties to consider TPF when commencing or responding to an arbitration, choosing their counsel or even when negotiating an arbitration agreement. Indeed, sometimes a TPF arrangement may be in place prior to the engagement of external counsel, and, at times, external counsel and third-party funders pitch for cases together as a team. Furthermore, TPF is used not only by impecunious claimants who would otherwise be unable to bring their claims, but also by well-resourced parties as a way of managing financial risk and freeing up corporate capital for other business needs. Anecdotal reports suggest that the global market for dispute funding – for both litigation and arbitration – is currently estimated as exceeding US$10 billion and rapidly growing.[72] Despite the fact that TPF is now an established feature of international commercial arbitration, debates on issues related to TPF are ongoing, and the nature of these discussions continue to evolve.

19.4.1 Different Types of External Funding

There are several types of external funding mechanisms, which are not mutually exclusive. It is not uncommon for parties to utilise multiple

[70] 2018 ICCA Report, *supra* note 64, p. 50. The definition is consistent with the definition adopted in the 2018 ICCA Report, one of the most comprehensive surveys on TPF conducted to date.

[71] 2018 Queen Mary Survey, *supra* note 2, p. 24. According to the 2018 Queen Mary Survey, 97 per cent of the respondents were aware of TPF in the context of international arbitration and the majority of the respondents (particularly those who have actually used TPF) had a generally 'positive' perception of TPF. In comparison, 85 per cent of the respondents were aware of other types of external funding (*e.g.* liability insurance, before the event (BTE) insurance, after the event (ATE) insurance).

[72] 2018 ICCA Report, *supra* note 64, p. 17, fn 30. For example, 'as of Summer 2017, Burford Capital reports that it itself has "over $2 billion invested in and available to invest in the legal market"' and 'Fullbrook management estimated [in 2013] that there is a potential market for claimants in the United States needing financial support in the combined amount of US $ 8–10 billion'.

sources of funding for a single dispute, in which case different stakeholders would normally enter into a 'waterfall' agreement that regulates the order of priority amongst the stakeholders' claims. The common types of external funding other than TPF are as follows.

19.4.1.1 Insurance

Insurance is one of the oldest modes of external funding, and is commonly used as a way to hedge the adverse costs risk and provide security for costs. BTE or ATE insurance is specifically intended to cover the insured's liability for legal fees and costs incurred in relation to litigation or arbitration, but may also cover potential liability for the opponent's legal fees and costs if the claim is unsuccessful.[73]

19.4.1.2 Loan and Corporate Financing

Loans for the purpose of pursuing arbitration can take the form of intergroup financing (e.g. where a parent company makes a loan to its subsidiary to pursue a claim with an expectation that the financial benefit therefrom will flow back to them) or of private equity (e.g. where the funder takes an equity position in the claimant entity, thus gaining control over its investment through traditional corporate governance). The latter option may raise an issue of potential conflict of interest, but at the same time gives the funder greater or total control over the dispute without running afoul of champerty restrictions.[74]

19.4.1.3 External Counsel as Funders

External counsel may effectively act as funders by using amongst others, a conditional fee arrangement or a damages based arrangement whereby the external counsel bears some or all of the costs of the arbitration and assumes the risk of loss. The availability of such arrangement varies significantly across different jurisdictions and a careful consideration of the applicable laws and professional regulations is essential before entering into such setup.[75]

[73] *Ibid.*, pp. 33–35.
[74] *Ibid.*, pp. 35–36 and 40.
[75] *Ibid.*, pp. 36–37 and 78.

19.4.2 Availability and Regulation of TPF

The availability of, and the level of regulation applicable to, TPF in the context of international commercial arbitration vary significantly across different jurisdictions. In common law jurisdictions, the doctrine of maintenance and champerty long operated to prohibit or restrict its availability. The doors for TPF were opened through evolution of case law in England[76] and Australia,[77] and through the enactment of recent legislative measures in Hong Kong[78] and Singapore.[79] In these jurisdictions, TPF is further regulated by codes of conduct, issued by the legislature or by professional bodies.[80] Regulation of TPF through legislation has the advantage of providing certainty, both as to its availability and the extent of its regulation (e.g. as to disclosure, capital requirements). On the other hand, in

[76] *See e.g. Arkin Borchard Lines Ltd and others* [2004] EWCA Civ 2655; Excalibur Ventures LLC v. Texas Keystone Inc and others [2016] EWCA Civ 1144.

[77] *See e.g.* Campbells Cash and Carry Pty Ltd v. Fostif Pty Limited [2006] HCA 41; Minister for Transport for Western Australia v. Civcon Pty Ltd (In Liq), Supreme Court of Western Australia, Full Court, 1 June 2000.

[78] In Hong Kong, TPF has been allowed since 1 February 2019 with the entry into force of Sections 98K–98O of the Hong Kong Arbitration Ordinance. Although the Ordinance ordinarily applies to arbitrations seated in Hong Kong (*see* Section 19.5), Section 98N of the Ordinance extends the application of the TPF provisions (Part 10A) to an arbitration seated outside Hong Kong or an arbitration with no seat, only with respect to funding of the costs and expenses of services provided in Hong Kong in relation to the arbitration.

[79] In Singapore, TPF is allowed pursuant to the Civil Law (Amendment) Act 2017, §5(b)(2) and the Civil Law (Third-Party Funding) Regulations 2017, which make it clear that the use of TPF in 'prescribed dispute resolution proceedings' (defined in Section 3 of the Civil Law (Third-Party Funding) Regulations 2017), including 'international arbitration proceedings' (as defined in the Civil Law (Third-Party Funding) Regulations 2017) and other proceedings related to arbitration, is not prohibited by existing maintenance and champerty laws, nor contrary to public policy.

[80] In England and Wales, TPF is not subject to statutory regulation, but the 2014 Code of Conduct for Litigation Funders (also applicable for arbitration) was published by the Association of Litigation Funders to regulate the members of the Association. In Hong Kong, the Code of Practice for TPF of Arbitration was issued on 7 December 2018 (*see* Section 98S of the Hong Kong Arbitration Ordinance for consequences of non-compliance with the Code of Practice). In Singapore, certain codes of conduct have been introduced to supplement the TPF legislative framework, including (1) SIAC's Practice Note on Arbitrator Conduct in Cases Involving External Funding issued on 31 March 2017, (2) the Law Society of Singapore's Guidance Note 10.1.1 for lawyers on TPF issued on 25 April 2017 and (3) Singapore Institute of Arbitrators' Guidelines for Third-Party Funders issued on 18 May 2017. In Australia, the Australian Securities and Investment Commission issued a regulatory guide detailing how funders may satisfy the obligations to manage conflicts of interest due to divergence of interests between funders, lawyers and parties.

many jurisdictions, particularly civil law jurisdictions where the rule of champerty and maintenance does not exist, it is still unclear whether TPF is allowed given that there is no express prohibition or approval.[81]

19.4.3 Current Trends in TPF

In its simplest form, TPF involves one funder financing the legal fees and other dispute-related costs of one dispute for an individual party, in return for a portion of the award amount or other form of monetary compensation, but without 'owning' or otherwise having a direct stake in the claim. In practice, however, more elaborate and 'non-conventional' arrangements can and do exist.

One major example is portfolio funding. The two main options for portfolio funding are (1) finance structured around a law firm where the claim holders may be various clients of the firm or (2) finance structured around a corporate claim holder that is likely to be involved in multiple legal disputes over a relatively short period of time. Typically, this involves some form of cross-collateralisation – the funder's return is dependent upon the overall net financial performance of the portfolio as opposed to the outcome of each particular claim, and this helps diversify the funder's risk and allows it to offer lower prices to both firms and clients. This type of funding also allows a law firm or a corporate claim holder to draw capital more flexibly than a single case funding scenario.[82]

[81] For example, in South Korea, certain laws may have potential implications for TPF. For instance, Article 6 of the Trust Act provides that 'any trust, the main purpose of which is to have the trustee to proceed with litigation, shall be null and void'. The Trust Act defines 'trust' as requiring 'transfer of [a] specific piece of property' or 'establish[ment] of a right' or any other disposition (Article 2 of the Trust Act) and hence an argument could be made that a standard TPF arrangement, which only involves sharing of some proceeds of the awarded amount as opposed to assignment of any right to pursue the claim, should not fall foul of this provision. The question has never been tested however. Furthermore, it is unclear how various provisions relating to professional ethics in South Korea, including the attorney's obligation under Article 2 of the Attorney-at-Law Act that 'each attorney-at-law shall perform his/her duties independently and freely', would square with a third party funded arbitration (*see* A. Pullen and J. Suh, 'Opening the gates for third party funding – recent developments in Hong Kong and Singapore and lessons for Korea' (2017) *Korean Arbitration Review*, pp. 34–35).

[82] 2018 ICCA Report, *supra* note 64, p. 38.

In certain jurisdictions, assigning or selling a claim to a funder may be possible. From a claim holder's perspective, receiving immediate payment without going through the cumbersome and potentially risky dispute resolution process through this arrangement may be seen as desirable. For a funder, having total and unfettered control of the claim (including control of settlement decisions) may be of great interest. Nevertheless this outright sale or assignment is not possible in a number of jurisdictions, including common law jurisdictions where the rules of champerty may be triggered. Conversely, in some civil law jurisdictions, funders do have the option of purchasing the claim outright, e.g. Germany and the Netherlands.[83]

Assignment or sale of the award (as opposed to the claim) on the other hand is more widely available across different jurisdictions, and offered by some third-party funders as well as other entities that specialise in monetising awards. Furthermore, some funders, subject to the circumstances of the case and their relevant commercial strategy, are willing to offer tailored, non-traditional funding options, e.g. provision of working capital during the proceedings, discharge of existing debts, upfront payment of damages and funding for costs of enforcement.

19.4.4 Current Issues Regarding TPF

TPF raises a number of new issues for international commercial arbitration, many of which are still subject to debate and remain largely unregulated.

19.4.4.1 Conflicts of Interest and Disclosure

One significant issue is the potential conflict of interest, which arises acutely due to the concentrated nature of the international commercial arbitration industry. For instance, a conflict of interest may arise where, as is increasingly common, an arbitrator serves as an adviser to a funder, who may subsequently finance the defence of one of the parties in that arbitrator's case. Or, an arbitrator's law firm may have a significant relationship with a funder involved in the proceedings.[84] Thus, there appears presently

[83] *Ibid.*, pp. 40–41.

[84] N. Darwazeh and A. Leleu, 'Disclosure and Security for Costs or How to Address Imbalances Created by Third-Party Funding' (2016) 33(2) *Journal of International Arbitration* 125, at 132.

to be an increasing consensus that at least certain information, i.e. the existence and identity of the funder, should be disclosed.

As discussed above,[85] the potential recoverability of the costs of funding is seen by many as a justification for allowing disclosure of other terms of the funding agreement that may have a bearing on the counterparty's potential exposure, such as those governing the remuneration of the funder. A party faced with a claim by a funded party may also wish to know whether, for example, the funder has assumed the liability for adverse costs before deciding whether to apply for security for costs.[86] At the same time, terms of the funding agreement may contain confidential and/or privileged information that would make blanket disclosure inappropriate. Parties may also apply to tribunals for such disclosure and tribunals may order such disclosure at their discretion, with appropriate redactions. In fact, a funded party who intends to claim funding costs at the cost allocation stage or faces an actual or potential security for costs application may wish to voluntarily disclose the relevant terms.

The Hong Kong and Singapore statutes on TPF mandate prompt disclosure of the existence and identity of the funder, although they do not govern the disclosure of other terms of the funding arrangement. Notably, the disclosure obligation rests with the funded party in Hong Kong,[87] and with the legal practitioners subject to the local professional

[85] Section 19.3.3.2.3.

[86] In the context of investment treaty arbitration, tribunals have taken differing approaches as regards the significance of TPF in determining whether to grant an order for security for costs. *See e.g.* RSM Production, Inc v. Saint Lucia, ICSID Case No. ARB/12/10, Decision on Saint Lucia's Request for Security for Costs, 12 August 2014, para. 83. In this case, the ICSID tribunal granted the respondent's request for security for costs because, *inter alia*, the TPF arrangement raised a concern that the claimant would not comply with a costs award rendered against it, and in the absence of security or guarantees being offered, it was doubtful that the third party funder would assume responsibility for honouring the award. *Cf.* Guaracachi America, Inc. and Rurelec plc v. Plurinational State of Bolivia, PCA Case No. 2011–17, Procedural Order No. 14, 11 March 2013, paras. 6–7. In this case, the respondent requested for security for costs alleging that the TPF arrangement, together with the balance sheets, evidenced that the second claimant was in a precarious financial situation, and that both the second claimant and its third party funder would not pay the tribunal's costs order. Despite ruling that it had the power to grant an order for security for costs, the tribunal rejected the respondent's request because the respondent, as a factual matter, had not 'shown a sufficient causal link such that the Tribunal can infer from the mere existence of third party funding that the Claimants will not be able to pay an eventual award of costs . . . regardless of whether the funder is liable for costs or not'.

[87] *See* the Hong Kong Arbitration Ordinance, Sections 98U–98V.

conduct rules in Singapore.[88] It remains to be seen whether Singapore's approach in placing the obligation to disclose on counsel, rather than the funded parties, will be more effective.[89]

The issue of disclosure of TPF is also addressed in a number of recently updated arbitral institutions' rules. The 2018 HKIAC Rules require mandatory disclosure of the existence and identity of the third-party funder,[90] and also expressly authorise tribunals to take TPF arrangements into account in determining the costs of the arbitration.[91]

19.4.4.2 Costs

The recoverability of funding costs has been discussed above. Where the funded party is unsuccessful (or otherwise should bear the other side's costs), the question arises as to whether tribunals can render costs orders directly against the third-party funder. Currently, such an order is not possible without a specific undertaking from the funder to that effect, given that (1) the funder is not a party to the arbitration agreement and is therefore not subject to the tribunal's jurisdiction and (2) due to the typically one-off and arm's length commercial relationship between the funder and the funded party, it is difficult to invoke other legal principles, e.g. alter ego, agency or assignee.[92] In contrast, courts in England and the United States may award costs against funders in local litigation if the funders have 'obtained a sufficient degree of economic interest and control in relation to the claim'.[93] It has been argued that cost awards against funders should be made possible, on the basis that a funder who stands to gain a significant profit from a successful claim should also be directly liable where its investment is unsuccessful. Furthermore, some

88 *See* Legal Profession (Professional Conduct) Rules 2015 (Conduct Rules), Rule 49(A).

89 V. K. Rajah, 'The Case for Singapore to Take the Lead in International Arbitration Ethics' (2018) 14(1) *Asian International Arbitration Journal* 37–54.

90 2018 HKIAC Rules, *supra* note 16, Article 44.1.

91 *Ibid.*, Article 34.4; as comparison, *see also* outside the commercial arbitration context, SIAC Investment Arbitration Rules, *supra* note 63, Rules 24, 33.1 and 35. The SIAC Investment Arbitration Rules expressly authorise tribunals to order disclosure of the existence and/or identity of a third party funder and, where appropriate, details of the funder's interest in the outcome of the proceedings, and/or whether or not the third party funder has agreed to assume liability for adverse costs. The rules further allow the tribunal to take TPF into account in allocating costs.

92 2018 ICCA Report, *supra* note 64, p. 161.

93 *Ibid.*, pp. 150–151.

commentators have noted that 'there is no evidence that full liability [of funders] for adverse costs would stifle Third Party Funding or inhibit access to justice',[94] given that if a funder has confidence in the matter it is funding, it should not be concerned with adverse costs liability. It remains to be seen whether national laws or arbitral institutions' rules would directly regulate this issue.

19.4.4.3 Funders' Control

The degree of control funders exercise over the conduct of the arbitration is a matter of contract and may vary significantly. Some funders may take an active role in the due diligence of the claim, as well as give their input on the issues such as the choice of counsel, the appointment of the tribunal, and case strategies.[95] Indeed, some parties may view such input from funders as desirable, particularly if the funders are operated by experienced ex-practitioners. Whilst the interests of the funders and the funded parties would mostly align, it is not impossible for them to diverge, e.g. due to disagreements about strategy or allocation of resources or due to the specific methods by which the funders' remuneration is calculated. Issues arising from such situations may be mitigated, or at least managed, through an appropriately worded conflict resolution clause in the TPF agreement, and sufficient safeguards in the relevant professional conduct rules to allow counsel to act in the best interest of the funded parties as their clients in all circumstances.

19.5 Conclusion

Consideration of costs is not a minor afterthought for the users of international commercial arbitration. Rather, costs are often at the forefront of users' minds from the very early stages of a dispute, and significantly influence their strategy, including the decision of whether to pursue arbitration in the first place.

[94] The Law Reform Commission of Hong Kong, 'Consultation Paper: Third Party Funding for Arbitration' (2015), para. 4.70, quoting Lord Justice Jackson.

[95] K. H. Shahdadpuri, 'Third-Party Funding in International Arbitration: Regulating the Treacherous Trajectory' (2016) 12(2) *Asian International Arbitration Journal* 77, at 84.

Whilst the negative reputation of international commercial arbitration as being costly is not wholly unjustified, it is also important to recognise that the costs involved in resolving what can be complex and high-value disputes across multiple jurisdictions, will sometimes necessarily be high. A more realistic solution to the 'problem' of costs would be to seek to prevent unnecessary costs where possible and to make costs more manageable through a principled and active approach to controlling, allocating and funding costs.

It is hoped that a combination of the efforts discussed in this chapter – features introduced by arbitral institutions and adopted by tribunals to promote efficiency and to control costs, development of sensible, nuanced approaches to allocating costs, and increased availability and clear and appropriate regulation of funding options – will assist in this process.

20 Regression, a Conclusion

C. L. Lim

20.1 Arbitration as Regression

An older narrative may be re-asserting itself. The view that international arbitration is an imperfect realisation of international judicial settlement now lingers. Similarly, there is the sense in some quarters that greater judicial supervision is desirable, not just by national courts but also at the international level. Such views may be expressed in various ways.

The discussion on the EU's proposal for a Multilateral Investment Court is currently ongoing in UNCITRAL Working Group III.[1] The EU proposal currently is to replace international investment arbitration with a multilateral court, or alternatively to have the appellate component of such a court serve as an avenue for the appeal of arbitration awards. The former seeks to substitute arbitration with judicialisation whereas the latter is about increased curial supervision at the international level. The last also mirrors calls to re-assert judicial supervision of arbitration in England, for example, where presently the procedure for appeals to the courts on the legal merits is seen as being too restrictive.[2] Elsewhere, there are mutterings that non-implementation of international arbitration awards, such as the award in the *South China Sea* arbitration,[3] only shows that non-compliance would likely not have given trouble had the award been an ICJ judgment.[4] In Geneva, the

[1] *See* Chapters 8, 9 and 13 of this volume.

[2] *See* Section 20.6.

[3] *See e.g.* Ted L. McDorman, 'The South China Sea Arbitration' (2016) 17 *ASIL Insights*, 18.

[4] Although one cannot read too much into the following, the difference between a judgment of the Court and the award of the tribunal in the South China Sea arbitration did become the subject of Chinese news coverage, *see e.g.* 'UN: Arbitral Tribunal Is Not a UN Organ', 13 July 2016 (Beijing); 'Ex-ICJ Judge: PCA and ICJ Are Different' CCTV News, 14 July 2016 (Beijing) (quoting Abdul Koroma). The People's Republic of China is also likely to take the view that the tribunal's awards on both jurisdiction and the merits have been in some of its aspects inconsistent with the jurisprudence of the International Court of Justice. For such possible inconsistencies, *see e.g.* Chris Whomersley, 'The South China Sea: The Award of the

World Trade Organisation's dispute settlement system, which for many years was seen as a great advance for introducing a verisimilitude of compulsory adjudication, has stalled.[5] This has now led to the Multi-Party Interim Appeal Arbitration Arrangement.[6] It may seem a positive development for international arbitration. Yet the idea that arbitration could fill the gap in the settlement of global trade disputes is unsatisfying because the model for WTO dispute settlement was never arbitration. Arbitration was always second best.[7]

Thus, we have again – although in so many different ways – the reassertion of an older view. The view that international arbitration is but an imperfect realisation of the quest for inter-State judicial settlement or even a global judicial system.[8] A similar notion is, as I have mentioned with the example of the supervision of the courts of England and Wales above, to be found in international commercial arbitration too. At the same time, international commercial courts have proliferated especially in recent years. The former Lord Chief Justice of England and Wales, Lord Thomas has proposed a standing forum which might foster a closer cooperation between commercial courts worldwide. For after all – as the English experience teaches – it was the Commercial Court in England and Wales and the intimate relationship between Bench and arbitration Bar

Tribunal in the Case Brought by Philippines against China – A Critique' (2016) *Chinese JIL* 239; Bing Bing Jia, 'Have Chinese Historic Rights in the South China Sea Been Superseded by UNCLOS?' May 2017, forthcoming in a volume by Jacques de Lisle and William Burke-White, conference paper for 'The United States, China and International Law', Penn-Wharton Centre, Beijing, 5–6 May 2017.

[5] For now at least, with the Trump Administration's prevention of the renewal of Appellate Body members. Thus, any appeal from a panel report will – unless the situation is corrected – now fall into a procedural void. *See e.g.* Steve Charnovitz, 'The WTO Appellate Body Crisis', Int'l Economic Law & Policy Blog, 2 June 2019, available at: https://ielp.worldtradelaw.net.

[6] Council of the EU, Press Release, 15 April 2020.

[7] *Cf.* Dispute Settlement Understanding, article 25.

[8] For the latest example of this long-standing utopian vision, *see* Antonio Cassese, 'The International Court of Justice: It Is High Time to Restyle the Respected Old Lady' in Antonio Cassese (ed.), *Realizing Utopia: The Future of International Law* (Oxford: Oxford University Press, 2012), 239. One might imagine too a global commercial court where judges from diverse legal systems and traditions form a 'true world court'; *see* Sundaresh Menon, 'International Commercial Courts: Towards a Transnational System of Dispute Resolution' DIFC Courts Lecture Series 2015, para. 16. The use of the term *world court* in reference to the International Court of Justice is of course a very informal and misleading shorthand. No appeals from national courts lie there.

which led to the worldwide influence and prestige of English commercial law.[9] Elsewhere, there is even the undignified suggestion that commercial courts should 'compete' with arbitration for primacy.[10] This would be ironic. It was the perceived inadequacy of the courts and of common law procedure which originally gave birth to the Law Merchant.[11]

We might characterise such sentiments today as embracing a view of 'arbitration as regression'.[12]

20.2 The Transnational View

Against this there is another view, one explored in this volume, and which considers international arbitration as a transnational justice system.[13]

[9] Yves Dezalay and Bryan Garth, *Dealing in Virtue* (Chicago: University of Chicago, 1996), 130–150. Other factors include the common law of contracts which it might be thought makes no room for the unpredictable operation of a good faith doctrine.

[10] The candidacy of some as 'international' commercial courts may be questioned. For example, the Dubai International Financial Centre's Courts offer in the words of its Chief Justice, Justice Hwang CJ 'a common law island in a civil law ocean', ensconced as it is in civilian Dubai within a civilian Union and the civilian Gulf States. As with the Commercial Court in England and Wales, it is a common law court with common law judges. In contrast the Singapore International Commercial Court has a mix of common lawyers and civilians on its bench. In the case of the Chinese International Commercial Court, Chinese law prevents foreign judges from sitting on the Mainland Chinese bench. Thus one of these is not necessarily like the other, and the common law singularity of the English Commercial Court does not stop it from being arguably the world's pre-eminent commercial court.

[11] For T. E. Scrutton's revival of seventeenth-century arguments that the Law Merchant had Roman foundations, *see* Mary Elizabeth Basile et al., *Lex Mercatoria and Legal Pluralism: A Late Thirteenth Century Treatise and Its Afterlife* (Cambridge, MA: Ames Foundation, 1998), 164–165. Scrutton's argument that the Law Merchant was a part of the Laws of England for it sprang from the agreement of States resonates in Gaillard's views today; Gaillard, 'Transnational System of Justice', in Albert Jan van den Berg (ed.), *Arbitration – The Next Fifty Years* (Alphen aan den Rijn: Kluwer, 2012), 66–73. In the context of arbitration, *see* Chapter 6 in this volume for a discussion of where the sources of autonomy lie (*i.e.* in contract, in State law or because international arbitration is an international institution).

[12] It is not by any means the only critical view. There is also the critical, post-colonial literature. *See e.g.* M. Sornarajah, *The International Law on Foreign Investment*, 3d. ed. (Cambridge: Cambridge University Press, 2010), 302 *et seq* (on the *lex mercatoria* and State contracts).

[13] *See* Emmanuel Gaillard, *Legal Theory of International Arbitration* (Boston: Nijhoff, 2010), 39. *See further* Emmanuel Gaillard, 'Transnational System of Justice', *op. cit.*, 66.

In Gaillard's view as we saw in Chapter 1, delocalisation is not to be portrayed in terms of a tension between party autonomy and State authority at all. Rather, Gaillard accepts that transnational justice is also the product of national authority, not least through the exercise of sovereign treaty-making powers.[14] On this view, ultimately, international arbitration has its conceptual basis in sovereign will in one way or another. It is an elegant viewpoint for at least Gaillard's view presents the prospect of a unified basis for the principal forms of international arbitration, a unified basis for the 'arbitral legal order'. Not, as Dupuy had once said in *Texaco v. Libya*,[15] one whose ultimate basis is the order of the international law of contracts but rather one in which State will and collective international lawmaking – the New York Convention, bilateral investment treaties, as well as inter-State consent to arbitration – play a crucial role.

The French school and in the United States those such as Philip Jessup[16] deserve credit for having conceptualised transnational law during the course of the twentieth century. In France, the French School took this idea far in the field of international arbitration. The point which that school of thought has sought to test is whether each arbitration and tribunal need be under the supervision of some single, national court – in other words, is there a role still for the supervisory authority of the courts of the seat? What the French School does not necessarily deny however is some role for State authority.[17] In comparison, the North American transnational law movement which began in the 1950s questioned the bold distinctions drawn between public and private law and between domestic and international law. Here lies Jessup's contribution.[18] Contracts which typically are viewed as creatures of domestic law may be governed by public international law. Not only because the contractual parties have so agreed expressly.[19] Public international instruments such as treaties prescribe international laws which in turn prescribe private law

[14] Gaillard, 'Transnational System of Justice', *op. cit.*, 66–73.

[15] Texaco v. Libya, 19 January 1977, 17 I.L.M. 1, para. 44.

[16] Philip C. Jessup, *Transnational Law* (New Haven: Yale, 1956), 2.

[17] Gaillard, 'Transnational System of Justice', *op. cit.*, 66–73.

[18] *Ibid. See further* the writers discussed in C. L. Lim, 'The Function of the Transnational Chinese Contract' (2019) 20 *JWIT* 313, 314 (Katz, Brewster, Steiner, Vagts, Koh).

[19] C. L. Lim, Jean Ho and Martins Paparinskis, *International Investment Law and Arbitration: Commentary, Awards and Other Materials* (Cambridge: Cambridge University Press, 2018), 22–24, 37–55.

solutions to private law disputes. The CISG is a good example. In the arbitration sphere, such devices and instruments feature especially strongly. In international investment arbitration the protection given by international law to contracts grew out of disputes over natural resource contracts.[20] In international commercial arbitration, the New York Convention limits the authority of domestic courts in what is seen as the sphere purely of private law. The question becomes, inevitably, how far these instruments can go to free international arbitration from the supervision of any judicial authority.

20.3 Autonomy

Today, debate on how foreign courts should treat an award that has been set aside by the courts of the place where the award was given illustrates those old problems anew. Seen in the most rudimentary manner, if two contractual parties have chosen arbitration what role is there left for the courts? The answer usually is this – if party autonomy demands it, but no more.[21] Even in England, the elevation of party autonomy was, historically, seen to have been sanctioned by the consent or agreement of nations.[22] It is at once the same explanation as that given of the sovereign's autonomy to enter into an agreement to arbitrate with another sovereign.[23] There is something Austinian about it all.[24] Asked why States should then obey an arbitral award, the classical writer Vattel had responded by saying that the faith of treaties must be preserved.[25]

Today, the supposed justification at least in international commercial arbitration for restricting national authority, and to prevent undermining

[20] *Ibid.*

[21] The two parties could be States – in the case of a commercial dispute we fall back on autonomy as an explanation, while if the dispute is of a public international law nature we might embellish the explanation by calling it 'sovereign' autonomy.

[22] Basile, *op. cit.*, 164–165, citing T. E. Scrutton.

[23] Brierly states the orthodox view that ultimately even the International Court of Justice has no jurisdiction other than based upon sovereign consent; J. L. Brierly, *The Law of Nations* (Oxford: Clarendon, 1963), 355.

[24] John Austin, *The Province of Jurisprudence Determined*, Wilfrid E. Rumble ed. (Cambridge: Cambridge University Press, 2009).

[25] Translated in John Bassett Moore, *International Adjudications: Ancient and Modern* (Oxford: Oxford University Press, 1929), xlv.

party autonomy, appears four-fold: (1) the obligation of treaties, notably the New York Convention, requires it (2) the interest of harmonisation, not least in the form of the UNCITRAL Model Law, (3) respect for general international law by national courts, such as where respect for foreign State immunity prevents setting aside an award resulting from inter-State, or even intra-State arbitration and (4) where the parties themselves chose to preclude national judicial supervision (i.e. true party autonomy).

20.4 The Latest Delocalisation Debate

Imagine two commercial parties. They choose arbitration; specifically that seated in an UNCITRAL Model Law jurisdiction. It is also the jurisdiction of a New York Convention Contracting State. Have they chosen to preclude national judicial supervision? One argument today is that they have not. By choosing a specific seat they have chosen one national authority over others, one whose courts will have curial supervision over the arbitration even if, at the same time, they might well expect the courts to be restrained, perhaps very restrained, in interfering with the tribunal's jurisdiction. Yet however restrained such curial supervision may be that party choice remains a choice of a national authority whose arbitration regime and courts are in fact not only chosen but preferred. This is the type of situation envisaged when it is said today that the exercise of national authority may itself be justified by party choice – i.e. by the party autonomy doctrine itself.

The Singaporean Chief Justice, writing extra-judicially, has come to support this view publicly.[26] Citing Lord Mance, Chief Justice Menon considers that an award which has been set aside by the courts of the place of the seat ought *not* to be enforced therefore by any other national authority anywhere.[27] This viewpoint revives the old double exequatur or

[26] Sundaresh Menon, 'Patron's Address', CIArb London Centenary Conference, 2 July 2015. *See further* Sae Youn Kim and Marieke Minkkinen, 'An Asian Perspective on the Enforcement of Annulled Awards' in Andrea Menaker (ed.), *International Arbitration and the Rule of Law: Contribution and Conformity*, ICCA Congress Series, Vol. 19 (Hague: Kluwer, 2017), 382, discussing PT First Media TBK v. Astro Nusantara International and Others [2013] SGCA 57 (Court of Appeal, Singapore).

[27] *See* the UNCITRAL Model Law (hereinafter ML), art. 34.

double control problem.[28] It is perhaps the latest example of a challenge to Gaillard's and the French School's argument that it is precisely because an award is made enforceable across New York Convention Contracting States that international arbitration is delocalised.

Notice, however, that Gaillard's argument is based not on the elevation of party autonomy to an international law doctrine but on the will or consent of New York Convention Contracting States:[29]

> [T]he transnational vision, goes one step further than the Westphalian approach to contemplate the states collectively, rather than individually. This representation recognizes the source of legitimacy of arbitration as rooted in the views developed collectively by the community of nations through instruments such as the 1958 New York Convention, the UNCITRAL Model Law and numerous guidelines. . . . In other words, in this vision, the source of validity and legitimacy of the arbitral process is found in the collective normative activity of states. This representation also corresponds to international arbitrators' strong perception that they do not administer justice on behalf of any particular state, but that they play a judicial role for the benefit of the international community.

Thus while one argument calls for international judicial cooperation in preventing the circulation of annulled awards on the basis of party autonomy, the other cites international law – the New York Convention – in suggesting that awards which have been annulled should remain, in principle, enforceable. The debate is at one level doctrinal but on the other theoretical for it reaches to questions about the basis of obligation in international arbitration – i.e. sovereign consent versus party autonomy. At the doctrinal level all that can be said is that the Convention neither requires refusal of enforcement of the award nor obligates its enforcement.[30] What is beyond doubt is that a great number of States have

[28] *See* Section 1.2.3 in Chapter 1 of this volume.

[29] Emmanuel Gaillard, 'International Arbitration as a Transnational System of Justice', *op. cit.*, 66, 68.

[30] Emmanuel Gaillard and George A. Bermann (eds.), *Guide on the Convention on the Recognition and Enforcement of Foreign Arbitral Awards* (Leiden: Brill, 2017), 235 *et seq. See also* ML, art. 36, one difference being that ML art. 36 also applies to domestic awards whereas the NY Convention applies to international awards. However, ML art. 36 is modelled on the NY Convention, in particular it states that recognition and enforcement of an award 'may' be refused. *See further* Howard M. Holtzmann and Joseph E. Neuhaus, *A Guide to the UNCITRAL Model Law on International Commercial Arbitration: Legislative History and Commentary* (Deventer: Kluwer, 1989), 1054, 1062–1063.

consented to the New York Convention regime. The trouble is that interpretations of that regime will vary, depending upon the kinds of doctrinal and theoretical arguments raised.

Similar questions have been raised in the sphere of foreign investor-State arbitration. As discussed albeit only in passing before[31] the arbitrator in *BP v. Libya* had considered the law of the seat the *lex arbitri*,[32] whereas the *Aramco* tribunal reasoned that since one of the parties was a State international law should be the procedural law.[33] According to Judge Lagergren in *BP*:[34]

> By providing for arbitration as an exclusive mechanism for resolving contractual disputes, the parties to an agreement; even if one of them is a State, must, however, be presumed to have intended to create an effective remedy. The effectiveness of an arbitral award that lacks nationality – which it may if the law of the arbitration is international law – generally is smaller than that of an award founded on the procedural law of a specific legal system and partaking of its nationality.

Today, one might say that if parties truly had preferred delocalised arbitration, then ICSID arbitration would have presented that choice.

Why do parties choose arbitration? In foreign investment disputes it is precisely because private law protection of contract and property were once seen to be paramount considerations that arbitration was preferred to judicial settlement by host State courts or any other court. International investment arbitration offers an instructive example precisely because such disputes involve the exercise of public power over private rights. From this viewpoint, the new wave of judicialisation involves a shift in sensibilities towards public law concerns. The concerns today relate to the development of the law itself, as Lord Thomas has explained, and what – in the foreign investor-to-State disputes sphere – is a repackaging of an idea long held by Third Worlders; that arbitration is institutionally biased and international law doctrines developed by tribunals are too.[35]

Are matters different in international commercial arbitration?

[31] In Chapter 1 of this volume.

[32] BP v. Libya (1997) 53 I.L.R. 297, Part III of the Award.

[33] Aramco Arbitration, 27 I.L.R. (1963), 117, at 155–156.

[34] BP v. Libya, *op. cit.*, Part III.

[35] *See* Amr Shalakany, 'Arbitration in the Third World: A Plea for Reassessing Bias under the Spectre of Neoliberalism' (2000) *Harvard ILJ*. 419; and C. L. Lim (ed.), *Alternative Visions of the International Law on Foreign Investment* (Cambridge: Cambridge University Press, 2016), generally.

20.5 Is Judicialisation Adverse to Arbitration?

Let us look first to foreign investor-State arbitration. There is a host of new treaty initiatives. The European Union has entered into various treaty commitments in which (1) foreign investor-State arbitration is modified to the extent that the freedom of the parties to select arbitrators is removed and (2) a two-tier structure is adopted which imposes an appellate mechanism which, in time, is hoped might lead to a Multilateral Investment Court.[36] Albeit to a lesser extent, there is a parallel development in respect of international commercial arbitration.

The wide enforceability, at least in theory, of commercial arbitration awards under the New York Convention is said to tilt the balance too much in favour of arbitration to the detriment of international litigation. Hence the new Hague Convention on Choice of Court Agreements aims to curb arbitromania by ensuring a similar wide circulation for national court judgments.[37] In the inter-Statal sphere, there has for long been the ICJ's ad hoc chambers procedure. It was at least hoped that this might bring some of the advantages of international inter-State arbitration into international judicial settlement.[38]

Such developments assume a competitive relationship. Whereas the truth may well be that there is a more complex interdependent ecosystem. Courts, arbitration and also mediation as well as the other techniques and devices of alternative dispute resolution interact, often to useful effect. Some people now speak of a plurality of forms of international dispute settlement. Others however insist upon having a system of logically

[36] Lim, Ho and Paparinskis, *op. cit.*, 504–512.

[37] 30 June 2005.

[38] *See e.g.* Eduardo Jiménez de Aréchaga, 'The Amendments to the Rules of Procedure of the International Court of Justice' (1973) 67 *AJIL* 1; Stephen M. Schwebel, 'Ad Hoc Chambers of the International Court of Justice', (1987) 81 *AJIL* 831; Shigeru Oda, 'Further Thoughts on the Chambers Procedure of the International Court of Justice', (1988) 82 *AJIL* 556; Rudolf Ostrihansky, 'Chambers of the International Court of Justice', (1988) 37 *ICLQ* 30, noting (at 36) the initial preference of States during the 1970s following the amendments to the ICJ's rules of procedure for ad hoc arbitration, often by ICJ judges; Eduardo Valencia-Ospina, 'The Use of Chambers of the International Court of Justice' in Vaughan Lowe and Malgosia Fitzmaurice (eds.), *Fifty Years of the International Court of Justice* (Cambridge: Cambridge University Press, 1996), 503.

inter-related courts and norms,[39] and mention has already been made of Chief Justice Menon's views.[40]

We exaggerate perhaps the competitive aspects. Delocalisation itself is a kind of exaggeration. We are, as Ralf Michaels has reminded us, speaking only about competing visions,[41] about different dreams.[42] The judges and national courts may well say in reply, as did J. S. Ewart of the Law Merchant:[43]

> Judge-made law (not merchant-made), with Lord Mansfield as the chief builder, is what we have here.

The French School may have elevated party autonomy to a transnational principle. But as Adrian Briggs in this volume argues, as does Menon CJ, whether an arbitration is subject to national supervision is also – potentially – a matter of choice. If it seems as if there is no national judicial supervision, then perhaps it only seems so.

20.6 Calls to End Arbitromania

But there is discontent brewing. Still, it might be asked whether the transnational justice system – in the absence of any immediate prospect of a global judicial system, one which addresses public and private law disputes between and amongst private and sovereign parties – will be improved if one or another method were to be superseded or abolished.

[39] Gaillard, 'Transnational Law', *op. cit.*, 66–68.

[40] Yet others have viewed transnational law in a less systemic manner – against positivism they articulate realist and functionalist views which envisage transnational lawyering as an evolving social process. *See e.g.* Harold Hongju Koh, 'Transnational Legal Process' (1996) 75 *Nebraska L Rev* 181; Harold Hongju Koh, 'Why Transnational Law Matters' (2006) 24 *Penn State Int'l L Rev* 745; Andrea Bianchi, *International Law Theories* (Oxford: Oxford University Press, 2016), 101–109.

[41] Ralf Michaels, 'Dreaming Denationalised Law – Scholarship on Autonomous International Arbitration as Utopian Literature', (2013) 1 *London Int'l L Rev* 35.

[42] Julian Lew, 'Achieving the Dream: Autonomous Arbitration' (2006) 22 *Arb Int'l* 179, 179, quoting F. A. Mann, 'Lex Facit Arbitrum' (1986) 2 *Arb Int'l* 241, 244, and quoted again in Michaels.

[43] J. S. Ewart, *An Exposition of the Principles of Estoppel by Misrepresentation* (Chicago: Callaghan & co, 1900), 373–374, 375. *Contra* T. E. Scrutton, *Elements of Mercantile Law* (London: William Clowes & co, 1891), 6 showing that Mansfield believed the Law Merchant to be the 'law of all nations'. Thus, on this view, the internationalised contract is hardly a twentieth-century invention.

The idea of a World Court had begun as a rallying cry of international pacifists. Pacifism itself[44] has subsided,[45] although – as we saw in Professor Garth's chapter – not before European pacifist international lawyers were co-opted by commercial men. International commercial arbitration, and in turn international investment arbitration, have on some accounts reached their apogee with twentieth-century economic globalisation. The current period of de-globalisation, witnessing a resurgent interest in the idea of international judicial settlement, is potentially at least symptomatic of larger economic changes.[46] It is not that arbitration is regressive. Rather, neo-liberalism has become unpopular.[47]

The deceleration of globalisation, rising economic nationalism and the risk even of dis-globalisation could see a reassertion of national sovereignty and national judicial authority. In the wider international economic law field both international commercial arbitration and investment arbitration have flourished during a previous, unprecedented era of global trade and investment. But as the time of the arbitrologists and the age of dreams – what in future we might yet look back and view as a Golden Age – threatens to draw to a close, three sorts of question emerge.

First, what becomes now of our 'dream',[48] or 'representation' of denationalised or delocalised arbitration?[49] What happens to that

[44] John Bassett Moore, *International Adjudications: Ancient and Modern* (Oxford: Oxford University Press, 1929), xxxvi–xci.

[45] Martti Koskenniemi, *The Gentle Civilizer of Nations* (Cambridge: Cambridge University Press. 2002), 209 *et seq*, esp. 214, 450 *et seq*., 510–517; however, *contra* Mónica Garcia-Salmones, 'Walther Schücking and the Pacifist Traditions of International Law' (2011) 21 *EJIL* 755.

[46] *See also* Ralf Michaels, who shares this view, in Chapter 6 in this volume. He calls it a 'backlash to the idea of autonomy'.

[47] In the sphere of investor-State arbitration, *see generally* M. Sornarajah, *Resistance and Change in the International Law on Foreign Investment* (Cambridge: Cambridge University Press, 2015); C. L. Lim (ed.), *Alternative Visions of the International Law on Foreign Investment: Essays in Honour of Muthucumaraswamy Sornarajah* (Cambridge: Cambridge University Press, 2017). The pressures which seek to rebalance international litigation and international commercial arbitration lie elsewhere, *see e.g.* Lord Thomas, 'Developing Commercial Law through the Courts: Rebalancing the Relationship between the Courts and Arbitration', Bailii Lecture, 9 March 2016, and the territorial approach advocated by Menon CJ of Singapore; Menon, 'International Commercial Courts', *op. cit.*; and Menon, 'Patron's Address', *op. cit.*

[48] Julian Lew; Lew, *op. cit.*

[49] Emmanuel Gaillard; Gaillard, 'Transnational System of Justice', *op. cit.*, 66–73.

'disciplinary sensibility'?[50] One answer is that our views are adaptable. We have seen that Gaillard does not consider even delocalisation as – to Ralf Michaels' language – 'arbitration and law outside the State'. Even if that has become a commonplace view.[51] Following Gaillard, if we view international arbitration as being 'outside the State' then enforcing courts need pay no heed to annulment by the courts of the place of the Seat. But if we view it as being embedded within an international treaty framework established by States we will instead ask what the New York Convention means. Likewise, viewed 'outside the State' we might ignore local conflicts rules. We might choose freely between equally valid choice of law approaches. But if we view international arbitration as Gaillard would as part of a transnational justice system, we should ask what an internationally acceptable approach towards conflicts rules, rooted in the approach of State courts all over the world, might suggest.[52]

Secondly, is the rise of the new international commercial courts likely to diminish the importance of international global commercial arbitration?[53] Will commercial arbitration – as had been the case of inter-State arbitration – risk losing out in the face of an increased effectiveness of courts?[54] With the proliferation of these new global commercial courts – and new instruments, such as the Hague Choice of Court Convention – will international commercial arbitration fail to keep up?[55] Lord Thomas has answered in practical terms:[56]

> The debate is a false one. Whether to litigate, arbitrate, or for that matter mediate, a dispute will rest on many factors. What is good for one dispute may not be for another.

[50] Amr Shalakany, *op. cit.*, 452–465.

[51] W. Michael Reisman and Brian Richardson, 'Tribunals and Courts: An Interpretation of the Architecture or International Commercial Arbitration', in Van den Berg, *op. cit.*, 17–18.

[52] Emmanuel Gaillard; Gaillard, 'Transnational System of Justice', *op. cit.*, 69–70.

[53] As some have asserted in the case of foreign investor-State arbitration; Sornarajah, *Resistance and Change*, *op. cit.*

[54] *See* Chapter 15 of this volume.

[55] *See e.g.* Gary F. Bell, 'The New International Commercial Courts: Competing with Arbitration? The Example of the Singapore International Commercial Court', (2018) 11 *Contemp Asia Arb. J* 193; Janet Walker, 'Specialised International Courts: Keeping Arbitration on Top of Its Game', (2019) 85 *Arb* 2.

[56] Lord Thomas, 'Developing Commercial Law', *op. cit.*

This answer falls within Michaels' 'realist' philosophy.[57] Lord Thomas' other – famous – view that England goes now too far in restricting appeals from tribunal decisions on the merits,[58] is not unrelated to this practical view; that the rise of courts need not mean the demise of arbitration. Such a view may be said too to flow naturally from an almost uniquely English sensibility – that what is good for forum London is good for London arbitration. That, is because English arbitration's success is often seen to depend upon the relevance and appeal of English Law. English Law as practised by a specialist London commercial bar.[59] The position of English arbitration might best be maintained by increasing rather than restricting the role and influence of the English courts. Thus, arbitration's constraint on the development of judge-made law is bad for arbitration itself. It is to be noticed that elsewhere, not only in the latest developments in Europe, such as with the establishment of the Netherlands Commercial Court and the Brussels International Business Court, but also in the case of the more established variants in the Far East and in the Middle East, all these are intended not as competitors but alternatives to the London Commercial Court. They were not designed to replace international arbitration as such. Indeed, the true question may be how they could mimic arbitration so as to better compete and to cooperate amongst themselves as courts.[60]

Thirdly, should courts – going back to Lord Thomas' views – have closer supervision of arbitration? As we know this is often posed as a theoretical question. What is the relationship of international arbitration to the State?[61] As we have seen, the debate presently, in the case of international commercial arbitration, may tend to lean in favour of a more moderate form of rebalancing of the division of labour between arbitration and national courts. This in turn is viewed in the knowledge that parties will seek what is in their own commercial interests. In foreign investor-State

[57] Chapter 6 in this volume.

[58] Lord Thomas despairs of the 'Nema Principles' – *The Nema* [1982] AC 724 – as codified subsequently in Section 69 of the Arbitration Act 1996 – and which applies in England and Wales for imposing overly restrictive conditions on permission to appeal a tribunal's determination on a point of law; *op. cit.*

[59] Dezalay and Garth, *op. cit.*, 130–150.

[60] Even leading to the suggestion that judgments may be turned into more readily enforceable awards; *see* Giles Cuniberti, 'Signalling the Enforceability of the Forum's Judgments Abroad', *RDIPP No1/2020*, 33, giving the example of an innovation by the DIFC Courts.

[61] Dezalay and Garth, *op. cit.*, 130–150. *See also* Roger Cottrell, 'What Is Transnational Law?', (2012) 37 *Law & Social Inquiry* 500, 500–502.

arbitration, that debate is altogether rather different. The European Union's attempt is to seek to replace a presently widespread resort to arbitration with international judicial settlement enacted by treaty. It is an interesting proposal.[62] But even if States were to conclude treaties which impose the compulsory jurisdiction of such a Multilateral Investment Court on all foreign investment disputes, parties to investment contracts can simply opt for foreign investor-State arbitration. Such parties could have recourse to the ICSID Convention or the New York Convention,

In contrast, in the case of inter-State arbitration, the emphasis is rightly placed on whether the *compromis* had itself envisaged some form of appeal, or other form of recourse – confined perhaps only to the interpretation of the award–to a further tribunal or to the International Court of Justice.[63] Having said that, where an inter-State or intra-State arbitration were to choose rather than, say, arbitration under the Permanent Court of Arbitration's rules[64] the rules of another arbitral institution which ordinarily deals with commercial cases, there is no reason other than on the ground of immunity or of non-justiciability that curial supervision should be considered to have been excluded. Although an investment contract dispute, the arbitrator in *BP v. Libya*[65] showed us why sovereign States may themselves choose curial supervision by the courts of the seat.[66] There is no reason too why States could not choose by treaty to arbitrate under national judicial supervision by the courts of a third State. They can do as they wish.

It would seem then that international arbitration will continue to play a very significant role where States, State entities and private parties find themselves facing each other in transnational and cross-border investment and commercial disputes. So long as arbitromania makes commercial sense. Questions about how international arbitration is represented, dreamt

[62] *See further* Lim, Ho and Paparinskis, *op, cit.*, 504–512.

[63] Assuming the all-important matter of first establishing the court's jurisdiction. J. G. Merrills, *International Dispute Settlement*, 5th ed (Cambridge, Cambridge University Press, 2011), 100–106.

[64] *See further* Daly, *op. cit.*, 807–808, where, in discussing the PCA's State-to-State rules, he explains: 'When adapting the UNCITRAL Rules, which were designed with commercial disputes between private parties in mind, to inter-state disputes, the drafters deleted the provisions that appeared to indicate the supervisory jurisdiction of a national court'.

[65] BP v. Libya (1997) 53 I.L.R. 297, Part III of the Award.

[66] Touching then upon the question whether any immunity has been waived.

of, imagined, framed or sensed by the arbitrologists, and how international arbitration compares to litigation before national or even new international courts, or how much scope there should be for curial supervision, are likely to continue to shape the practice of international arbitration. Not to seal international arbitration's fate.

Index

For EU product safety concerns, contact us at Calle de José Abascal, 56–1°, 28003 Madrid, Spain or eugpsr@cambridge.org.

www.ingramcontent.com/pod-product-compliance
Lightning Source LLC
LaVergne TN
LVHW011533200926
848484LV00001B/251

* 9 7 8 1 1 0 8 4 8 0 5 9 8 *